NEW PERSPECTIVES IN AMERICAN JEWISH HISTORY

NEW PERSPECTIVES IN American Jewish HISTORY

A DOCUMENTARY TRIBUTE TO
Jonathan D. Sarna

EDITED BY Mark A. Raider and Gary Phillip Zola

Brandeis University Press ◇ Waltham, Massachusetts

Brandeis University Press
© 2021 by Mark A. Raider and Gary Phillip Zola
All rights reserved
Manufactured in the United States of America
Designed by Eric M. Brooks
Typeset in Quadraat by Tseng Information Systems, Inc.

For permission to reproduce any of the material in this book, contact Brandeis University
Press, 415 South Street, Waltham MA 02453, or visit brandeisuniversitypress.com

Library of Congress Cataloging-in-publishing Data

Names: Raider, Mark A., editor. | Zola, Gary Phillip, editor. | Sarna, Jonathan D. honoree
Title: New perspectives in American Jewish history : a documentary tribute
    to Jonathan D. Sarna / edited by Mark A. Raider, and Gary Phillip Zola.
Other titles: Documentary tribute to Jonathan D. Sarna
Description: Waltham, Massachusetts : Brandeis University Press, 2021. | Series: Brandeis
    series in American Jewish history, culture, and life | Includes bibliographical references
    and index. | Summary: " "New Perspectives in American Jewish History: A Documentary
    Tribute to Jonathan D. Sarna," compiled by Sarna's former students, presents heretofore
    unpublished, neglected, and rarely seen historical records, documents, and images that
    illuminate the heterogeneity, breadth, diversity, and colorful dynamism of the American
    Jewish experience"—Provided by publisher.
Identifiers: LCCN 2021029019 (print) | LCCN 2021029020 (ebook) | ISBN 9781684580521
    (cloth) | ISBN 9781684580538 (paperback) | ISBN 9781684580545 (ebook)
Subjects: LCSH: Jews—United States—History—Sources. | Judaism—United
    States—History.
Classification: LCC E184.32 .N49 2021 (print) | LCC E184.32 (ebook) |
    DDC 973/.04924—dc23
LC record available at https://lccn.loc.gov/2021029019
LC ebook record available at https://lccn.loc.gov/2021029020

5 4 3 2 1

Cover art: Jewish chaplain insignia of the U.S. military superimposed upon an American flag,
Alumni Service Window (1948), S. H. and Helen R. Scheuer Chapel, Hebrew Union College–
Jewish Institute of Religion, Cincinnati, OH. The window inscription reads: "In honor of our
colleagues, students, and alumni of the Hebrew Union College who served their country in
two World Wars, 1917–18 and 1941–45." Photo credit: Ady Manory.

The publication of this documentary tribute to Jonathan D. Sarna

has been made possible by the generosity of

the Posen Foundation, Robert S. Rifkind, the Charles and

Lynn Schusterman Family Foundation, Lance J. Sussman, and

Justin and Genevieve (z"l) Wyner.

Valuable support was also provided by

Michael Jesselson, Sidney R. Lapidus, and

Jehuda and Shulamit Reinharz,

as well as

the Jacob Rader Marcus Center of the American Jewish Archives,

the Charles Phelps Taft Research Center, and the University of

Cincinnati's Department of History.

CONTENTS

NOTE TO READERS

This anthology is organized chronologically and reflects the course of historical events that shaped the American Jewish experience from the colonial era to the present. The entries are accompanied by headnotes and annotations that seek to situate and explain each document in its specific cultural, political, and historical context. While not intended as a comprehensive treatment, the volume has been designed to complement scholarly works that survey American history, American religious history, modern Jewish history, and American Jewish history. Though the book might have included many more items, our aim from the outset has been to produce a collection that broadly represents the history of the Jews in the United States and presents hitherto unpublished and rarely seen primary sources. Interspersed throughout the volume are thirteen images that highlight the vast and rich genre of visual materials available to enhance the study of the historical record.

A brief explanation is in order concerning the volume's organization. In general, the contributors have attempted to make each document as accessible and useful as possible to students, researchers, and interested lay readers alike. While each entry is relatively self-contained, thus enabling readers to gain a full understanding of its content, the framework of the volume as a whole is designed to be an overarching treatment and includes cross-referenced annotations and citations of key historical works. In cases where the documents refer to well-known people (for example, Aristotle and President Theodore Roosevelt) and major historical events (such as the American Civil War and World War II), the notes tend to be brief. Where a more detailed explanation seems warranted owing to a discussion of particular people, issues, or developments, the contributors have included pertinent discursive material. While cross-referenced notes generally appear in chronological and sequential order, readers will notice some overlap and variation in this regard owing to the authorship of specific annotations. In a handful of instances, the documents refer to seemingly obscure names and/or events, and it has not been possible to provide detailed or precise information with certainty; this, too, is duly noted. A glossary is included to assist readers unfamiliar with Hebrew and Yiddish terms and other information used frequently in the documents. Information that appears infrequently has been inserted directly into the main body of the text.

Throughout the volume, we have endeavored to refer readers to English-language materials and contemporary scholarship concerning specific texts, themes, and concepts rather than routinely citing original sources (for example, the Hebrew Bible, premodern rabbinic texts, European literary works, and Yiddish and Hebrew texts). Our purpose is to help guide students to materials that will support further study and independent investigation. That said, we have also determined that in some instances the elucidation of given components of a text are best served by identifying and explicating the references in question.

Lastly, we have retained most of the specific locutions found in the primary sources because of their cultural and historic value. Accordingly, in various documents readers will note the use of anachronistic and capitalized terms, phraseology, and idiomatic expressions. In many instances, common English spellings have been retained and/or inserted for the sake of ease of understanding and readability (examples include haggadah, Hanukkah, and kibbutz). In general, we have used a simplified orthography and transliteration of Hebrew, Aramaic, and Yiddish terms to give English-speaking readers as clear and consistent a phonetic equivalent as possible without introducing complex diacritical marks and special linguistic values. The volume also uses standard abbreviations for classical and premodern Jewish sources, such as "Gen." (Genesis), "Exod." (Exodus), "1 Kgs." (First Kings). Citations for the Babylonian Talmud are indicated by the letters "BT," followed by the names of specific tractates and folio numbers. All emphases in the documents have been retained from the original texts. Wherever necessary, minor emendations and stylistic adjustments were made to the documents (for example, transcripts of sermons or selections from historic newspapers) to unify and enhance the volume overall. Square brackets within quotations indicate additions intended to clarify the meaning of the original text.

ACKNOWLEDGMENTS

Provide yourself with a teacher, get yourself a companion,
and judge each human being favorably.
◇ Ethics of the Sages 1:6

The gestation of this volume can be traced to a conversation at the 2016 Biennial Scholars' Conference on American Jewish History in New York City, when a handful of Professor Jonathan D. Sarna's former doctoral students, including us, were reflecting on his towering impact on the field. We realized that the time had come to produce a Festschrift celebrating Dr. Sarna's many achievements and honoring his unique scholarly contribution to the academy. A few months later, we consulted with Professor Ruth Langer, Dr. Sarna's wife, about the idea of creating a tribute volume. "Rather than a collection of essays," she suggested, "I think he would be most pleased if the project was truly useful in the classroom. How about a collection of new archival documents?"

Recognizing the value and considerable potential of such a volume, we turned to the three dozen (and counting) of Dr. Sarna's former doctoral students with a bold proposition—namely, to identify one or more hitherto unpublished or rarely seen documents that open up possibilities for rethinking the field of American Jewish history. Such a strategy, we explained, whether centered on archival research, excerpts from historic newspapers, evocative visual images, or other generative texts, would honor Dr. Sarna's trailblazing work with primary source materials, enhance the scholarly arena, and enliven the range of options for teaching about the American Jewish experience. Not surprisingly, our colleagues responded with enthusiasm, and the process of collecting, preparing, and editing the array of fascinating materials assembled here began in earnest. Happily, Sylvia Fuks Fried, editorial director of Brandeis University Press, embraced the project's two-year journey from concept to realization, bringing to the effort sage guidance and a deep personal commitment. The net result is a robust and expansive (albeit by its very nature somewhat eclectic) multifaceted volume that traces the arc of the American Jewish experience from the colonial era to the present.

In addition to our esteemed colleagues, who invested countless hours in their contributions to the volume, numerous scholars, archivists, librarians, and other friends of this project helped solve research queries, locate obscure materials, identify the provenance of archival documents, provide copies of various texts and images, assist with permissions inquiries, and much more. Here at last we are able to publicly acknowledge their expertise and thank them for their generous assistance: Marlene Adler, Aaron Amit, Diana Bachman, Siona Benjamin, Shulamith Z. Berger, Aaron B. Bisno, Kaela Bleho, Charlotte R. Bonelli, Kathy Cohen, Tony Dudek, Leo Ferguson, Christopher Giorgione, Didi Goldenhar, Geir Gunderson, Todd Herzog, Kenneth Hoffman, Maurice L. Kamins, Peter Kupersmith, Vitoria Lee, Jane Rachel Litman, David L. Locketz, Michael A. Meyer, Melanie Meyers, Miranda Mims, Devin Naar, Maura O'Connor, Joshua Parshall, Randall L. Patton, Josh Perelman, Alice B. Perkins, Sean Pitts, Annie Polland, Joe Rooks Rapport, Haim O. Rechnitzer, Paul and Sheri Robbins, Gail Rubin, Tilly Shemer, Tami Siesel, Ann K. Sindelar, Mary Anne Stets, Irvin Ungar, T. Adams Upchurch, Melissa Wertheimer, Laurel S. Wolfson, and Jessica Zimmerman Graf.

Special thanks are due to Sue Ramin, director, and Lillian Dunaj, coordinator, of Brandeis University Press, as well as Doug Tifft and Ann Brash of Redwing Book Services and the designer, Eric Brooks. We are also deeply grateful to our colleagues at the Jacob Rader Marcus Center of the American Jewish Archives. Lisa B. Frankel, Dana Herman, Elisa Ho, and Joe Weber were always at the ready with cheerful and expert assistance. Ady Manory's talent as a graphic designer was critical to the project's overall success.

Several people have played essential roles behind the scenes. Our respective wives, Miriam B. Raider-Roth and Stefi Zola, have been a source of unflagging support and encouragement. Our deep thanks go to Ruth Langer for her counsel and to the Sarna family for helping keep the book project under wraps until the "big reveal." *Aharon aharon haviv* (Hebrew for "in a special place of honor"), on behalf of all the volume's contributors, we offer our profound and heartfelt gratitude to our dedicated teacher Dr. Jonathan D. Sarna—a scholar's scholar, an extraordinary mentor, and a consummate mensch. Your imprint on the field of American Jewish history is incalculable, and we are proud to call ourselves your students.

MARK A. RAIDER AND GARY PHILLIP ZOLA
Cincinnati, Ohio
October 2020

NEW PERSPECTIVES IN AMERICAN JEWISH HISTORY

"THE DYNAMIC WORLD OF THE AMERICAN JEW"

Jonathan D. Sarna and the Varieties of Jewish Experience

◇◇◇

MARK A. RAIDER AND GARY PHILLIP ZOLA

I

In 1899, the Jewish Publication Society of America, directed by a handful of elite figures of central European ancestry, launched the *American Jewish Year Book* to disseminate "literary, scientific, and religious works, giving instruction in the principles of the Jewish religion."[1] The founding editor Cyrus Adler (1863–1940), a prominent semitics scholar and librarian of the Smithsonian Institution, explained that "everything must have a beginning" and that "the spread of Jews all over our vast country," including the mass immigration to the United States of Yiddish-speaking Jews from southern and eastern Europe, warranted documentation and scientific study.[2] "Jewish ideals have a strong hold upon the Jews of the United States," Adler opined, and the yearbook aimed to provide reliable and "authentic" data concerning the country's Jewish population.[3]

The task of compiling a record of American Jewry fell to Abram S. Isaacs (1851–1920), the well-known editor of New York's weekly *Jewish Messenger*. Isaacs was also a rabbi and a professor of Hebrew, German, and semitics at New York University. A longtime observer and voice of American Jewish affairs, Isaacs celebrated American society as a "peculiarly happy atmosphere . . . so genial for all religions."[4] The United States, he asserted, differed fundamentally from many European countries and Islamic lands where "the medieval spirit still prevails, making the Jew a wanderer and an outcast."[5] Jewish life on "American soil," by contrast, betokened "a distinctly new era . . . composed of represen-

---

1. "The Jewish Publication Society of America," *American Jewish Year Book* 1 (1899), 57.
2. Cyrus Adler, preface to *American Jewish Year Book* 1 (1899), ix.
3. Ibid., x.
4. Abram S. Isaacs, "The Jews of the United States," *American Jewish Year Book* 1 (1899), 14.
5. Ibid.

tatives of every clime and nationality."[6] Thereupon, Isaacs surveyed an array of developments and challenges shaping the American Jewish landscape: the acculturation of Yiddish-speaking immigrants ("new immigrants are building communities throughout the Union"; "they are proving themselves capable American citizens, yielding to no class in patriotism and public spirit"), anti-semitism ("properly condemned"), educational activity ("the distinct impulse towards the improvement of religious school methods"), debates concerning the Jewish people's future ("Mr. [Israel] Zangwill's . . . scintillating lectures . . . awakened vigorous and generally good-natured criticism"), challenges in the religious sphere ("the Sunday Sabbath . . . has not made the headway anticipated . . . [and] keenly suggests the difficulties that beset Jewish observance"), the role of women ("the growth of the Council of Jewish Women . . . whose branches extend throughout the country is a happy augury"), the rough-and-tumble of Jewish politics ("the flag of Zionism continued to be unfurled") as understood by proponents of the status quo ("the movement has failed to influence American Jewish sentiment") and a hint of immigrant radicalism ("the body of [Zionist] adherents is made up from among our Russian brethren" who subscribe to "the fantasy of a *Judenstaat*"),[7] and the status of fraternal groups ("the condition of various Jewish orders has not changed for the better").[8]

Before concluding with a necrology of American Jewish notables, Isaacs elaborated on the "marked increase in new institutions and enlargement of old ones."[9] He noted several examples of American Jewry's "growth both in numbers and benefactions":

- *Atlanta*: [Hebrew] Orphan Asylum
- *Chicago*: Hebrew Orphans' Home
- *Cincinnati*: Meeting of Jewish charities to create a "national society"
- *Newark, NJ*: [Hebrew] Orphan Asylum
- *New Orleans*: Touro Infirmary
- *New York*: Baron de Hirsch Trade School, Clara de Hirsch Working Girls' Home, Emanu-El Sisterhood Home, Mt. Sinai Hospital, Beth Israel Hospital, Young Men's Hebrew Association, United Hebrew Charities, and Hebrew Infant Asylum

6. Ibid.

7. A reference to *Der Judenstaat* (The Jews' state: An attempt at a modern solution of the Jewish question), a polemical treatise published in 1896 by Theodor Herzl (1860–1904), father of modern political Zionism and founder of the World Zionist Organization.

8. Isaacs, "The Jews of the United States," 15–17.

9. Ibid., 18.

- *Philadelphia*: Young Women's Union, Lucien Moses Home for Incurables, and National Farm School (Doylestown)
- *San Francisco*: Mt. Zion Hospital
- New synagogues "were dedicated in Denver, Brooklyn, Chicago, Philadelphia, New York, Cleveland, [and] Atlantic City."[10]

Notwithstanding its eclectic nature, Isaacs's overview surfaced a variety of important data and provided a basic categorization of the key elements of American Jewish life—such as communal infrastructure, religious observance, cultural institutions, immigrant absorption, Jewish politics, political engagement, philanthropic activity, and so forth. Together with the work of the fledgling American Jewish Historical Society, Isaacs's 1899 treatment marked the beginning of a serious data-driven effort to document and assess "noteworthy" developments in American Jewry's size, composition, and organization.[11] At the same time, he omitted much that would be open to question or might reflect poorly on American Jewry, including incriminating issues such as intracommunal strife, poverty and disease, political radicalism, labor unrest and exploitation, criminal behavior and conflict with non-Jewish groups, and so forth. Such elisions betray a tinge of Victorian-era propriety and a general wariness of gentile misperceptions of Jews. In addition, the absence of confounding information enabled Isaacs to unapologetically assert the "genius of the Jew"— in particular, American Jewry's "adaptiveness, energy, and persistency."[12] The encounter between America and the Jews, he insisted, represented an unprecedented and exceptional amalgam—a fusion of modernity, emancipation, democratic liberalism, and Judaism. "No such phenomena have ever been ex-

10. Ibid.

11. Addressing the American Jewish Historical Society's first scientific meeting in 1892, Oscar S. Straus (1850–1926), the former (and future) U.S. minister to the Ottoman empire, proclaimed the group's aims to be "not sectarian, but American" and to "throw an additional ray of light upon the discovery, colonization, and history of our country." He asserted that "substantial reasons exist why the relation of the Jews with the discovery of this continent, and their participation in the early settlement of the colonies, have not been fully disclosed. First, because the early chronicles relating to America have been imbued with a strong religious bias; secondly, the spirit of intolerance was such that the Jews ... [themselves] concealed their race and religion in many instances. . . . The uses of a society such as this, with a special line of inquiry, are in the contributions it can make to the general history of our country, and to that extent broaden our field of vision by disclosing actors and forces that have been overlooked, or for other reasons, have escaped the searching eye of the historian" ("Address of the President," *Publications of the American Jewish Historical Society* 1, 2nd ed. [1905] 1, 3, and 4).

12. Isaacs, "The Jews of the United States," 14.

perienced by the Jew in all the lands and ages of his dispersion as are here presented," Isaacs stated.[13] "American Israel," he bullishly proclaimed, "meets with full confidence the currents of the time."[14]

II

Nearly a century later, the venerable Jewish Publication Society (JPS), preparing to mark its centennial, turned to Jonathan D. Sarna to tell its story. Sarna, then a thirty-two-year-old scholar, Hebrew Union College–Jewish Institute of Religion faculty member, and rising star in American Jewish history, seized the opportunity. At first blush, Sarna's decision to navigate the minefield that became JPS: The Americanization of Jewish Culture (1989) may seem curious. Why would a serious historian agree to undertake a project fueled, in part, by public relations considerations? How might he avoid the pitfalls of other institutional chronicles saddled by top-down narrative models, dull minutiae, and insularity? Could he successfully negotiate the potentially fraught relationship of researcher and patron while maintaining intellectual independence and integrity?

The JPS "galaxy of Jewish writers," Sarna reasoned, was the engine that powered the publishing house and made it, in the words of the historian Moses Rischin, the "semiofficial voice of American Jewish literary and artistic culture" in the nineteenth and twentieth centuries.[15] Drawing on a rich background in American history, American religious history, and Jewish history, Sarna envisioned JPS not as a "benevolent educational undertaking" but as a living metaphor, and he approached his assignment "not as a 'back-slapping in-house chronology'" but as a scholarly "microcosm" of American Jewry's communal history.[16] The society's hitherto unexplored voluminous archive—"an embarrassment of riches" containing hundreds of published and unpublished manuscripts, as well as hundreds of thousands of "yellowing pages" of correspondence, reports, minutes, and business records—contained the DNA of the

13. Ibid.

14. Ibid.

15. Jonathan D. Sarna, "My Life in American Jewish History," in *Conversations with Colleagues: On Becoming an American Jewish Historian*, ed. Jeffrey S. Gurock (Boston: Academic Studies Press, 2018), 167; Moses Rischin, review of Jonathan D. Sarna, JPS: The Americanization of Jewish Culture, 1888–1988 (Philadelphia: Jewish Publication Society, 1989), *Journal of American History* 77, no. 2 (September 1990), 687.

16. "The Jewish Publication Society of America," 57; Jonathan D. Sarna, JPS: *The Americanization of Jewish Culture, 1888–1988* (Philadelphia: Jewish Publication Society, 1989), ix.

phenomenon that Abram S. Isaacs called "American Israel."[17] When Sarna's JPS: The Americanization of Jewish Culture appeared, the volume broke new ground as the first full-length analytic study of its kind. Praised as a "model" of ethnic cultural history, it demonstrated the extent to which American Jewry, conscious of its distinctiveness and place in the American tapestry, coalesced around "a common vision, the quest to be fully a Jew and fully an American, both at the same time."[18] It also became a touchstone for historians of American publishing.

Against the backdrop of Sarna's other books on Jews in the colonial and early national periods, the American synagogue, and communal histories of the Jews of New Haven and Cincinnati, the JPS volume cemented his reputation as one of the most creative, innovative, and productive figures of his generation.[19] It is also worth noting the extent to which his scholarly articles leavened the fields of Judaica (in publications such as the American Jewish Archives Journal, American Jewish History, Commentary, Jewish Social Studies, and Modern Judaism) and Americana (the Journal of American History, Journal of American Ethnic History, and Journal of Ecumenical Studies), entwining American Jewish history with cognate disciplines in ways for which there was strikingly little precedent. The Jews of the United States, Sarna demonstrated, evolved from a diaspora outpost in the colonial era to become a distinctive, creatively interactive, and vital component of the "American kaleidoscope."[20] "Perpetuated generation after generation" by a diverse array of individuals and groups, Sarna observed, the American Jewish experience at its most elemental level centered on "reconciling Judaism and modernity" while contending "with the tensions and paradoxes inherent in American Jewish life."[21]

To fully probe this core problematic, Sarna embedded his investigations in the broad historical context of the United States and North America. Punctuated by memorable titles and aphorisms, his body of work introduced a lexicon that

17. Sarna, JPS, ix.

18. Pamela S. Nadell, review of Jonathan D. Sarna, JPS: The Americanization of Jewish Culture, 1888–1988 (Philadelphia: Jewish Publication Society, 1989), Pennsylvania Magazine of History and Biography 114, no. 4 (October 1990), 583; Jonathan D. Sarna, introduction to The American Jewish Experience, ed. Jonathan D. Sarna (New York: Holmes and Meier, 1986), xiii.

19. Rischin, review of Sarna, JPS, 687–88.

20. "No metaphor can capture completely the complexity of ethnic dynamics" in American history, Lawrence H. Fuchs asserts, because American society is "kaleidoscopic, i.e., 'complex and varied, changing form, pattern, color . . . continually shifting from one set of relations to another; rapidly changing'" (The American Kaleidoscope: Race, Ethnicity, and the Civic Culture [Hanover, NH: Wesleyan University Press, 1990], 276).

21. Sarna, introduction to The American Jewish Experience, xiii; Sarna, JPS, 247.

swiftly entered the bloodstream of the academy—""Jacksonian Jew" (on the rise of a new Jewish consciousness in early America), "the myth of no-return" (on Jewish return migration to Europe), "the Great American Jewish Awakening" (akin to the Protestant Great Awakening in the late nineteenth century), "the 'mythical Jew' and the 'Jew next door'" (on Jewish-Christian relations and anti-semitism), "the democratization of American Judaism" (on American Jewry's affinity for American republican values), "the Israel of American Jews" (on American Jewry's lofty vision of the Zionist project and the Jewish state), "from synagogue community to community of synagogues" (on voluntary pluralism in American Judaism), "a projection of America as it ought to be" (on American Jewry and social justice), and more.

A cornerstone of Sarna's innovative historiographic parlance, "the cult of synthesis," first crystallized in his biographical study of Mordecai M. Noah (1785–1851).[22] "Overall," he noted, "the American Jewish search has always been a search for synthesis."[23] He argued that Noah—a well-known figure in his day who was a journalist, playwright, diplomat, and utopian adventurer—was "a highly significant figure on the American scene, a leader of the American Jewish community, and most important, the first man in history to confront and grapple boldly with the tensions between these two roles."[24] He further explained:

> The tensions which he sought to resolve are tensions which are rooted in American Jewish history. More broadly, they are the tensions faced by all minority groups which seek to preserve a measure of their identity while integrating into a larger, and at times hostile, mass society.... [His life] is part of a larger story, one which might be titled, "The Making of the American Jew." Somehow, in their 325 years in America, American Jews have become a unique community—different from other Americans, different from other Jews. The forces that shaped these American Jews were, I think, many of the same forces that shaped Mordecai Noah. To understand Noah is to begin to understand the process which transformed radically dissimilar Jews, from very different backgrounds, into the vibrant American Jewish community of today.[25]

22. Jonathan D. Sarna, "The Cult of Synthesis in American Jewish Culture," *Jewish Social Studies* 5, nos. 1–2 (Fall 1998–Winter 1999), 52–53.

23. Jonathan D. Sarna, *Jacksonian Jew: The Two Worlds of Mordecai Noah* (New York: Holmes and Meier, 1981), 160.

24. Ibid., ix.

25. Ibid.

The forces of acclimatization and adaptation that, Sarna points out, transformed all ethnic-religious minorities in the predominantly Protestant American setting have since the colonial era prompted American Jews "to interweave their 'Judaism' with their 'Americanism'" and to "fashion for themselves some unified synthetic whole."[26] On an ideational level, the American Jewish embrace in this regard draws on the traditional Jewish value of *dinah demalkhutah dinah* (Aramaic for "the law of the land is the law") and the philosemitic strain of New World thought dating to the colonial era—namely, the dual vision of Jewish and American election, chosen peoples "destined for an errand in sacred history."[27] The notion of chosenness fueled the theological and philosophical matrix honed by, among others, John Winthrop (1587–1649) of the Massachusetts Bay Colony ("we shall be as a city upon a hill. The eyes of all people are upon us");[28] the liberal Congregational minister Jonathan Mayhew (1720–1766) of Boston ("That being brought out of the house of bondage, they might be conducted into a good land, flowing with milk and honey; that they might there possess property, enjoy the blessing of equal laws, and be happy");[29] and the founders of the American republic—including Benjamin Franklin (1706–1790) and Thomas Jefferson (1743–1826), the two most radical Deists among the framers, who envisioned the biblical story of Exodus emblazoned on the Great Seal of the United States.[30]

In structural terms, as Sarna explains, the decidedly hegemonic theme of election, so central to American religious and political culture, is fundamental to understanding the self-perception of Jews in American society and their intercourse with American society at large. Propelled across time and space by tenacity, educational aspirations, professional success, and upward mobility, American Jewry developed from numerical inconsequence and, at best, modest influence in the colonial and early national periods into a robust national community of considerable importance at the turn of the nineteenth and twentieth centuries. Possessed of a growing sense of attachment, belonging, and authority, American Jews from across the social, religious, and political spectrum became increasingly interwoven with the tapestry of American society. Though

26. Sarna, "The Cult of Synthesis in American Jewish Culture," 52–53.

27. Sacvan Bercovitch, *The American Jeremiad* (Madison: University of Wisconsin Press, 2012), 69.

28. John Winthrop, "A Model of Christian Charity," 1630, https://teachingamericanhistory .org/library/document/a-model-of-christian-charity-2/.

29. Quoted in Deborah L. Madsen, *American Exceptionalism* (Jackson: University of Mississippi Press, 1995), 35.

30. Jon Meacham, *American Gospel: God, the Founding Fathers, and the Making of a Nation* (New York: Random House, 2006), 83.

fear of dissolution weighed heavily on American Jewish minds in every generation—post-emancipationist America always held out the possibility of leaving
the Jewish fold and converting to Christianity—generations of American Jews,
on the whole, yearned for a synthesis of their identity. The search for a "golden
mean," Sarna states, is a hallmark of American Jewry's quest for "a tension-
resolving unity" and "longing for utopia."[31]

What Sarna artfully describes as the "cult of synthesis" in American Jewish life, an elegant term for delineating the complex relationship between Jews
and American society, serves as the cornerstone of his scholarly oeuvre.[32] The
exquisite plasticity of this multivalent and mediatory concept is evident in the
nearly two dozen anthologies Sarna has produced since his arrival at Brandeis
University in 1990. To name just a few, *The Jews of Boston* (1995), coedited with
Ellen Smith; *Religion and State in the American Jewish Experience* (1997), coedited with
David G. Dalin; and *Jews and the American Public Square* (2002), coedited with Alan
Mittleman and Robert Licht, each underscore the "double bond" at the heart of
American Jewish culture while emphasizing critical dimensions of the historical landscape (ethnic diversity; civic identity; minority faiths and the Protestant
mainstream; religion and state; the American Civil War; the publishing industry
and the press; the relationship of regional and communal history to national
and global history; formal and informal religious education; secularism and traditionalism; liturgical, theological, and denominational changes in American
Judaism; entrepreneurialism and capitalism; women and gender; and Zionism
and Israel).[33] The notion of synthesis also informs Sarna's *The History of the Jewish People: A Story of Tradition and Change* (2006–7), a two-volume Jewish history
textbook for young people coauthored with Jonathan B. Krasner, and *A Time to
Every Purpose: Letters to a Young Jew* (2008), a series of discussions exploring "central issues in American Jewish life" organized around the Jewish calendar.[34]
Inarguably, Sarna's greatest scholarly impact to date stems from three highly
acclaimed monographs: *American Judaism: A History* (2004), *When General Grant Expelled the Jews* (2012), and *Lincoln and the Jews: A History* (coauthored with Benjamin
Shapell, 2015).

American Judaism, the most important and influential study of its kind to appear in a generation, showcases Sarna's vast knowledge and unrivaled exper-

31. Sarna, *Jacksonian Jew*, 160.

32. Sarna, "The Cult of Synthesis in American Jewish Culture," 52. See also Jonathan D.
Sarna, *American Judaism: A History* (New Haven, CT: Yale University Press, 2004), 371.

33. See Daniel J. Elazar, Jonathan D. Sarna, and Rela Geffen Monson, eds., *A Double Bond:
The Constitutional Documents of American Jewry* (Lanham, MD: University Press of America, 1992).

34. Sarna, "My Life in American Jewish History," 176.

tise. Exhibiting an extraordinary grasp of the subject matter and prodigious research, the book analyzes American Jewry's development from the colonial era to the present in six chronological and thematic chapters. Sarna's investigation introduces new periodization schema based on American history instead of (as traditional in American Jewish historiography) waves of Jewish immigration to the United States and emphasizes the long-term growth and trajectory of American Jewry's institutional culture, communal infrastructure, religious and cultural composition, and leadership structures. Starting with the arrival in 1654 in New Amsterdam of a small group of "bedraggled Jewish refugees from Recife, Brazil," Sarna explores the social, cultural, and political interaction of the Jews and American society from the era of North America's European colonization through the American Revolution, the early republic's formation, the nation's westward expansion, the Civil War, Reconstruction, and the rise of Jim Crow, World Wars I and II, the Holocaust, the establishment of Israel, the Cold War, and the civil rights movement and counterculture upheavals of the mid- to late twentieth century.[35] Despite the "sheer amount of material" involved in such an effort, the historian David Biale remarks, Sarna's treatment "deftly cuts to the essential," "weaves a seamless story," and is "scrupulously fair."[36] In a similar vein, David Brion Davis made note of Sarna's "great sensitivity and open-mindedness" to "the effects of Judaism on the larger society" and "the revolutionary transformations within Judaism itself, on spiritual as well as worldly levels."[37] Paying close attention to the dynamic and pluralistic nature of the American Jewish experience, American Judaism emphasizes the paradigm of self-conscious revitalization as the axis of American Jewry's collective response to assimilatory and declensionist pressures. In each generation, Sarna contends, those who lamented American Jewry's imminent demise were repeatedly proven wrong by individuals and groups, often arising from the margins, seeking to rebuild and renew Jewish communal life.

Sarna's American Judaism concludes on a note of optimism tempered, in characteristic fashion, by a word of caution. American Jewish life, he observes, stands at a "crossroads." At the turn of the twentieth and twenty-first centuries, he states, American Jewry "seems to be experiencing both revitalization and assimilation, it radiates optimism concerning the future . . . as well as bleak pessimism."[38] He explains that no group in the United States is "more number-

35. Sarna, American Judaism, 1.

36. David Biale, review of Jonathan D. Sarna's American Judaism: A History (New Haven, CT: Yale University Press, 2004) in Jewish History 19, nos. 3–4 (2005), 389.

37. The quote by David Brion Davis appears on the jacket of Sarna's American Judaism.

38. Sarna, American Judaism, 1 and 365–66.

conscious" or more preoccupied with the notion of "continuity" than the Jews, and he points to an array of "questions and issues and tensions" challenging American Jewry.[39] Quoting the twentieth-century Jewish philosopher Simon Rawidowicz (1897–1957), who famously described the Jews as an "ever-dying people," Sarna suggests American Jewry's obsession with "incessant dying means uninterrupted living, rising, standing up, beginning anew."[40] Indeed, "today, as so often before," he professes, American Jews are seeking "creative ways to maintain and revitalize" their community.[41] "With the help of visionary leaders, committed followers, and generous philanthropists," he suggests, "it may still be possible for the current 'vanishing' generation of American Jews to be succeeded by another 'vanishing' generation, and then still another."[42]

If Sarna's *American Judaism* demonstrated the study of American Jewish history had "unquestionably reached maturity," his ensuing exploration of Civil War–era themes reinvigorated both American Jewish history and the broader arena of American history.[43] In two exceptional books, he thoroughly reconceptualizes relations between America's Jews and, respectively, Ulysses S. Grant (1822–1885) and Abraham Lincoln (1809–1865). *When General Grant Expelled the Jews* revisits Grant's antisemitic General Orders No. 11, published on December 17, 1862, in which the Union commander characterized the Jews "as a class violating every regulation of trade" established by the U.S. Treasury Department and "hereby expelled" the Jewish communities from the wartime theater in the Military Department of Tennessee, which included parts of Tennessee, Kentucky, Alabama, and Mississippi.[44] Casting aside timeworn assumptions, Sarna investigates the order's provenance, its limited wartime impact, its immediate rescission by Lincoln, and the event's long-range implications. Sarna also scrutinizes the event's repercussions for the 1868 presidential election, when Grant was the Republican party's standard-bearer. The campaign season sparked renewed interest in Grant's wartime mistreatment of the Jews and the question of the so-called Jewish vote now came into full public view. "Never before," asserts Sarna, "had a Jewish issue played so prominent a role in any presidential campaign."[45] Though Grant never fully recanted—neither his *Personal Memoirs*

39. Ibid., 357 and 360.
40. Ibid., 374.
41. Ibid.
42. Ibid.
43. Biale, review of Sarna's, *American Judaism*, 393.
44. Quoted in Jonathan D. Sarna, *When General Grant Expelled the Jews* (New York: Schocken Books, 2012), 7.
45. Ibid., xi.

(1885) nor his other published writings offer any commentary on the subject—
he did mention, in a private letter written during his presidential campaign,
that the order "would never have been issued if it had not been telegraphed the
moment it was penned, and without reflection."[46] This historical episode, Sarna
argues, is important because of what it reveals about the relatively unknown
"'Jewish' chapter" in Grant's biography.[47] It is also critical to understanding
"one of the most tumultuous eras in American history, the era of the Civil War
and Reconstruction ... [when] the definition of what America is and the determination of who 'we the people' should include convulsed the country."[48]

The lavishly illustrated Lincoln and the Jews: A History appeared in the 150th anniversary year of Abraham Lincoln's assassination. Lauded by the historian Harold
Holzer as "nothing less than the definitive study of a long-neglected aspect of
Civil War history and Lincoln biography," the volume opens with the twin observations that Lincoln's "life coincided with the emergence of Jews on national
scene" and that his "interactions with Jews" are "in microcosm, the story of how
America as a whole began to come to terms with its growing Jewish population
and how Americans and Jews were both changed by that encounter."[49] Moreover, as Sarna contends, Lincoln was "personally broadened by his encounters
with Jews and also worked to broaden America so that Jews might gain greater
acceptance as equals nationwide."[50] Following from these key insights, Sarna
and Shapell's volume assembles and analyzes hundreds of letters, diary entries,
maps, ledgers, photographs, paintings, lithographs, handbills, advertisements,
newspaper reports, poll books, calling cards, rare books and booklets, broad-
sides, business records, financial instruments, event admission tickets, government proclamations, telegraph cables, published debate records, handwritten
manuscripts, fragments of notes, and other artifacts, including a sizable quotient of material in Lincoln's hand.

In the 1860s, the 150,000–200,000 Jews living in the United States accounted for barely 0.5 percent of the total American population of thirty-one
million.[51] Even so, Sarna points out, Lincoln's "connections to Jews went fur-

46. Quoted in Joseph Lebowich, "General Ulysses S. Grant and the Jews," Publications of the
American Jewish Historical Society 17 (1909), 76.

47. Sarna, When General Grant Expelled the Jews, xii.

48. Ibid.

49. The quote from Harold Holzer appears on the jacket of Sarna and Shapell's Lincoln and the
Jews. The other quotes are from Jonathan D. Sarna, introduction to Jonathan D. Sarna and Benjamin Shapell, Lincoln and the Jews: A History (New York: Thomas Dunne Books, 2015), xii.

50. Sarna, introduction to Lincoln and the Jews, xii.

51. Sarna, American Judaism, 375.

ther and deeper than those of any previous American president."[52] Moreover, despite the fact that a majority of American Jews did not initially support Lincoln's presidential ambitions, nor did all American Jews oppose slavery before the Civil War (many had extensive kinship ties and commercial interests in the South), Lincoln displayed a consistently generous and sympathetic attitude to Jews and Judaism during his "tragically foreshortened life."[53] Probing Lincoln's variegated personal and professional encounters with American Jews, Sarna and Shapell present detailed accounts of Lincoln's direct involvement in the appointment of Jews to government offices and military positions (including the first Jewish chaplains in the U.S. military) and pardons of Jews wrongfully convicted of illegal activity, as well as his famous revocation of Grant's wartime "Jew order."[54] The authors note that whether a majority of "Israelites" voted in 1864 for Lincoln's reelection "cannot be known," but certainly by this stage, the tide in relations between Lincoln and the Jews had turned.[55]

Within the space of a few months, the actor and Confederate sympathizer John Wilkes Booth (1838–1865) assassinated Lincoln as the president and his wife watched a performance of *Our American Cousin* at Ford's Theatre in Washington, D.C. The next day, Saturday, April 15, 1865, American Jewry grieved Lincoln's loss in Sabbath services across the country as if it had lost a favorite son. Rabbi Isaac Mayer Wise (1819–1900) of Cincinnati, the architect of Reform Judaism in America, who had once disdained Lincoln as "a country squire who would look queer in the White House with his primitive manner," now described the slain statesman as "the greatest man ever sprung from mortal loins."[56] He further insisted that Lincoln was "fully a Jew, 'bone from our bone and flesh from our flesh. He supposed himself to be a descendant of Hebrew parentage. He said so in my presence.'"[57] Wise's unproven claims were no doubt a product of rhapsodic hyperbole. What is significant, as Sarna and Shapell point out, is the way "the Jewish love affair with all things Lincoln" throws light on Lincoln's "own remarkable regard for the Jews."[58] In his lifetime, Lincoln "interacted with Jews, represented Jews, befriended Jews, admired Jews, commissioned Jews, trusted Jews, defended Jews, pardoned Jews, took advice from Jews, gave jobs

52. Sarna and Shapell, *Lincoln and the Jews*, 226.
53. Ibid.
54. Quoted in Sarna and Shapell, *Lincoln and the Jews*, 121.
55. Ibid., 182.
56. Quoted in Isaac Markens, "Lincoln and the Jews," *Publications of the American Jewish Historical Society* 17 (1909), 109.
57. Quoted in Sarna and Shapell, *Lincoln and the Jews*, 218.
58. Ibid., 226.

to Jews, extended rights to Jews, revoked an expulsion of Jews, and even chose a Jew as his confidential agent."[59] That he did so as countless Americans, including members of his "own inner circle, displayed overt [anti-Jewish] prejudice" speaks volumes about Lincoln's singular stamp on the civic and legal treatment of America's Jews, the prosecution of the Civil War, and American society's struggle to create a "more perfect union."[60]

III

"Publishing something new about Abraham Lincoln," Sarna later confessed, "the subject of more books than anyone in the whole history of the United States, [was] no easy task."[61] Yet, as repeatedly demonstrated over the course of his career, the insatiable curiosity that drove him to "writ[e] about subjects that nobody has previously explored" was undiminished by the challenge.[62] Moreover, he brought to the project a seasoned scholar's keen insight, an enormous reservoir of finely tuned talent, and the cumulative wealth of decades of intellectual and archival spadework. *Lincoln and the Jews* also illustrates a foundational truth of Sarna's oeuvre—namely, his steadfast commitment to empirical research and reliance upon newly discovered primary sources to generate historical knowledge. Thus, even amid the well-trodden arena of Lincolnalia, Sarna's unrelenting interrogation of published and unpublished archival records, historic newspapers, ephemera, artifacts, and the vast corpus of secondary literature on the history of the Civil War yielded significant new findings.

Sarna's zeal for exploring the uncharted "highways and byways" of American Jewish history is evident in other data-sleuthing missions.[63] Consider, for example, the fascinating manuscripts he unearthed by two all-but-forgotten figures: Cora Wilburn's *Cosella Wayne, Or, Will and Destiny* (1860),[64] the first English-language novel written by an American Jewish woman; and Moses Weinberger's Hebrew-language polemic *Jews and Judaism in New York* (1887), an invaluable source for understanding the transformation on "American soil" of eastern European immigrant Orthodox Judaism.[65] Sarna's substantial and extensive im-

59. Ibid.
60. Ibid.
61. Sarna, "My Life in American Jewish History," 179.
62. Ibid., 162.
63. Ibid.
64. Cora Wilburn, *Cosella Wayne, Or, Will and Destiny*, ed. Jonathan D. Sarna (Tuscaloosa: University of Alabama Press, 2019).
65. *People Walk on Their Heads: Moses Weinberger's Jews and Judaism in New York*, trans. and ed. Jonathan D. Sarna (New York: Holmes and Meier, 1982), 6.

print is likewise apparent in hundreds of articles and dozens of edited volumes, as well as his instrumental leadership of the American Jewish Historical Society, Jacob Rader Marcus Center of the American Jewish Archives, National Museum of American Jewish History, national "Celebrate 350: Jewish Life in America, 1654–2004" commission, and many other academic venues.

Widely regarded as today's foremost American Jewish historian, Sarna ranks alongside his mentor Jacob Rader Marcus (1896–1995), the founding dean of the field, as an exceptional personality of unmatched capacity and brilliance. Where Marcus single-handedly put American Jewish history on the map of the academy—from the 1940s to the 1970s he was the driving force in this emerging subfield—his star protégé Sarna has hewn a pathway as its most innovative, productive, and influential exponent in the post-Marcus era. Of the hundreds of researchers whose work Sarna has helped shape and guide, nowhere is his influence more apparent than among his former doctoral students—a veritable "Sarna diaspora" of over three dozen active scholars in North America, Europe, Asia, South Africa, and Israel, many of whom hold positions in colleges and universities, research libraries, or Jewish communal institutions.

The present volume, a collaborative undertaking by Sarna's students, follows in his footsteps. The perceptive reader will no doubt recognize that ours, while not a comprehensive treatment, draws upon and in many ways expands the orbit of Sarna's repertoire. Animated by the challenge of excavating new data, this anthology presents heretofore unpublished, neglected, and rarely seen historical records, documents, and images that demonstrate the breadth, heterogeneity, diversity, and dynamism of the American Jewish experience.[66] Anchored by Sarna's masterful analysis of George Washington's 1790 correspondence with the Hebrew congregation of Newport, Rhode Island, the collection offers a chronological and thematic road map of American Jewry's evolving self-understanding and encounter with American society over the course of four centuries. Each document is introduced by a brief comment that sets up its specific analytic context and helps unpack and explore its cultural and historical

66. Fully appreciative of the excellent documentary histories available to students and researchers, we seek to complement the existing body of published source material that upholds the fields of modern Jewish history, American ethnic history, American religious history, and American history in general. See, for example, Paul Mendes-Flohr and Jehuda Reinharz, eds., *The Jew in the Modern World: A Documentary History*, 3d ed. (New York: Oxford University Press, 2011); Gary P. Zola and Marc Dollinger, eds., *American Jewish History: A Primary Source Reader* (Waltham, MA: Brandeis University Press, 2014); and Michael Marmur and David Ellenson, eds., *American Jewish Thought since 1934: Writings on Identity, Engagement, and Belief* (Waltham, MA: Brandeis University Press, 2020).

significance. The fact that the materials are cross-referenced indicates the inter-relationship of key themes, including ritual observance, Jewish-Christian relations, education, liturgical innovations, civil rights, the evolution of the synagogue, gentile perceptions of American Jews, philanthropy and fund-raising, Jewish politics, Zionism and Israel, women in Jewish communal life, Jewish leadership, Sephardic Jewry, immigration, the plight of Soviet Jewry, LGBTQ Jews, regional Jewish history, and more. The net result is an anthology of materials that uncovers generative texts and opens up new pathways for exploring American Judaism and American Jewry's multivalent engagement with American society from the colonial era to the present.

Beginning with the earliest known Jewish divorce on the North American continent, a series of entries illustrates the evolution of changing attitudes to Jewish rituals, customs, and liturgical practices across time and space. Discourses concerning the tension between tradition and praxis—including the use of head coverings, observance of dietary restrictions, marriage and divorce customs, and Sabbath and holiday observance, as well as externalities such as conversion to and from Judaism, proselytism, and interfaith relations—are intermingled with discussions of Sephardic, Ashkenazic, and transcultural Jewish acclimatization to the American setting. Other entries explore the nature of Jewish political engagement with American society. Not surprisingly, moments of national and international crisis (the American Revolution, the Civil War, World Wars I and II, and the Vietnam War) and conflict in the Middle East (Israel's War of Independence, the War of Attrition, the Six-Day War, the Yom Kippur War) bring the distinctive and complex dimensions of American Jewish political behavior to the fore. The theme of civil and humanitarian rights underpins the volume as a whole. From Washington's famous dictum ("the Government of the United States . . . gives to bigotry no sanction, to persecution no assistance")[67] to the appointment of Jewish chaplains in the Union forces during the Civil War, from the 1916 election of Democratic party activist Simon Bamberger as governor of Utah to the civil rights movement of the mid-twentieth century, from the struggle to free Soviet Jewry to the Black Lives Matter movement, the collection demonstrates the manifold ways in which American Jewish history is inextricably bound up with the struggle to realize America's vision of "a more perfect union" and the promise of "liberty and justice for all."[68] The omnipresent yet elusive nature of American Jewry's cultural profile and American Jewry's impact on broader American culture—in letters, music, visual arts, theater, film, and

67. See chapter 2.
68. The preamble to the U.S. Constitution; the Pledge of Allegiance.

science—surfaces again and again throughout the volume. Many of the texts reproduced here throw light on specific moments that illuminate the relationship between Jews and middle- and high-brow American cultural phenomena. The Hollywood icon Marlon Brando (1924–2004), as the historian Stephen J. Whitfield relates, once claimed that "per capita ... Jews have contributed more to American—the best of American—culture than any other single group."[69] We do not purport to test Brando's proposition. However, the disparate findings included here (from the American press, Broadway, commerical advertising, the world of comic book superheroes, and more) certainly warrant serious consideration. Finally, it is worth noting the collection includes materials that situate black-Jewish relations; lesbian, gay, bisexual, transgender, and queer rights; Jews of color; and tattoos and body art as critical dimensions of American Jewish life and culture.

The capacious and multifaceted quality of the American Jewish experience is further amplified here by a sample of artistic texts—photographs, sketches, posters, advertisements, paintings, cartoons, periodical cover art, and more. The fact that such materials ought to be considered seriously has long been recognized by scholars of popular culture who stress that "textual shifts [are frequently] signs of cultural shifts" and possess "symbolic significance reaching far beyond the explicit content of the particular text, melody, or artifact."[70] Jewish arts scholars, as the historian Carol Zemel notes, view "cultural production and interaction [as] a hallmark of diasporic vigor."[71] The "cultural space of a minority population," Zemel argues, can be "fluid and irregular," defying "a fixed geography," and should be considered "interactively, as cultural life in relationship to—and with—a neighbor, a contiguous but different society."[72] The salience of such insights for American Jewish history ought not to be underestimated.

Of course, any assessment of the visual images included in this volume will naturally lead to questions concerning what, specifically, constitutes the items' "American" and "Jewish" dimensions. That is as it should be. We do not seek to impose a uniform standard for identifying the "Americaness" and "Jewishness"

69. Quoted in Stephen J. Whitfield, *In Search of American Jewish Culture* (Waltham, MA: Brandeis University Press, 1999), xi.

70. Janet L. Langlois, "Folklore and Semiotics: An Introduction," *Journal of Folklore Research* 22, nos. 2–3 (May–December 1985), 79; Dan Ben-Amos, "Toward a Definition of Folklore in Context," *Journal of American Folklore* 84, no. 331 (1971), 11.

71. Carol Zemel, *Looking Jewish: Visual Culture and Modern Diaspora* (Bloomington: Indiana University Press, 2015), 11.

72. Ibid., 1.

of the artists, their art, or the impact of their work on American Jews and American society. Instead, taking our cue from the historians Barbara Kirshenblatt-Gimblett and Jonathan Karp, we acknowledge that while "no single definition of 'Jewish art' can suffice," what matters most is their "contingent and contextual" dimensions and their inherent "relational and transactional terms."[73] Adopting a semiotic approach, the models of textual analysis included here propose interpretations, invite explication, and seek to engender discussion about themes and issues that might otherwise be overlooked.

IV

In his magnum opus, *American Judaism: A History*, Sarna relates that when he first became interested in American Jewish history, a senior rabbinic scholar sneered at the idea. "'American Jewish history,' he growled, 'I'll tell you all that you need to know about American Jewish history: the Jews came to America, they abandoned their faith, they began to live like *goyim* [gentiles], and after a generation or two they intermarried and disappeared.' 'That,' he said, 'is American Jewish history; all the rest is commentary. Don't waste your time. Go and study Talmud.'"[74] Undaunted, Sarna pursued his intellectual passion and never looked back. In the course of his many investigations, though cognizant of the "long-standing fear that Jews in America are doomed to assimilate," he demonstrates the manifold ways in which each generation of American Jews "wrestles anew with the question of whether its own children and grandchildren would remain Jewish."[75] American Jewry's vitality, he explains, has always been bolstered by the community's ability to creatively adapt to the American arena and advance a pluralistic agenda.

It is hoped that students, researchers, and lay readers alike will find the trove of documentation presented here in honor of Jonathan D. Sarna helpful to uncovering and exploring the varieties of experience that constitute the "dynamic world of the American Jew."[76] To be sure, the rich assortment of data, in the words of Abram S. Isaacs from over a century ago, illustrates American Israel's distinctive capacity to meet "with full confidence the currents of the time."[77]

73. Barbara Kirshenblatt-Gimblett and Jonathan Karp, preface to *The Art of Being Jewish in Modern Times*, ed. Barbara Kirshenblatt-Gimblett and Jonathan Karp (Philadelphia: University of Pennsylvania Press, 2008), 3.

74. Sarna, *American Judaism*, xiii.

75. Ibid.

76. Sarna, introduction to *The American Jewish Experience*, xiii.

77. Isaacs, "The Jews of the United States," 14.

1

"CONCERNING A *GATE* HE SEND TO OUR *KAKAM*"

A Circum-Atlantic Divorce in the Eighteenth Century (1774)

◇◇

HOLLY SNYDER

Divorce is hardly novel in Jewish history. It has long been an acknowledged part of Jewish law and is discussed in a number of surviving rabbinical responsa from the period prior to 1900. Yet it is rarely the subject of discussion by Jewish historians of the premodern era. This may be because while divorce was available to Jewish couples, it was rarely used as a legal remedy except in the most exigent circumstances.[1] Thus, when Hannah Minis (1744–1812) and David Leion (1749–1842) "parted from each other under writings" at Savannah, Georgia, in August 1799, after just sixteen months of marriage, Levi Sheftall (1739–1809) noted in his communal record that "No instance of the kinde ever happend here before amongst people of our [Jewish] profesion."[2]

The letters presented here refer to a document for a Jewish ritual divorce (in Hebrew *get*, transliterated here as *Gate*) sent to Jamaica in 1774. This is the earliest Jewish divorce yet documented in British America; the two other eighteenth-century Jewish divorces for which we have records date from the postrevolutionary period on mainland North America.[3]

---

1. A remarkable responsum from thirteenth-century Spain discusses the case of a married woman who took a lover and then (likely due to her husband's continued refusal to initiate divorce proceedings because she had provided just cause by means of adultery) converted to Christianity to force her husband's hand in granting her a divorce. After obtaining the divorce, she and her lover moved to another city and resumed their lives as Jews, presenting themselves as a married couple even though as an adultress she could not marry again under Jewish law. See Sarah Ifft Decker, "Conversion, Marriage, and Creative Manipulation of Law in Thirteenth-Century Responsa Literature," *Journal of Medieval Iberian Studies* 6, no. 1 (March 2014), 42–53.

2. Quoted in Malcolm H. Stern, "The Sheftall Diaries: Vital Records of Savannah Jewry, 1733–1808," *American Jewish Historical Quarterly* 54, no. 3 (March 1965), 268–69. See also Kaye Kole, *The Minis Family of Georgia* (Savannah: Georgia Historical Society, 1992), 33–35.

3. The earliest known Jewish divorce on the North American mainland took place in Charleston in 1788, when Mordecai Lyon (1735–1818) divorced his wife, Elizabeth (Binche) Chapman (fl. 1782–1788) before a *beit din* (Jewish religious court). The case is discussed in some detail in

In this case, we do not have particulars—or even names—of the divorcing couple. What we have, instead, is a record of the other participants in this drama: the synagogue official who married them, the rabbi in Jamaica who inherited the responsibility to ensure that the *get* was delivered to the wife, and the other parties called upon by the rabbi for assistance in completing that task.

The initiator of the letters was Joshua Hezekiah DeCordova (1720–1797). Born and raised in Amsterdam, DeCordova was one of the few New World congregational leaders of the time who had had a rabbinical education, and as such he was something of an anomaly in early American Jewish history. During the eighteenth century, most New World congregations were led by *hazanim*, lay leaders who could chant the prayers, lead services, and officiate at religious ceremonies but whose understanding of Judaism was practical rather than intellectual.[4] While rabbis occasionally visited New World communities, many congregations were too small to support a full-time rabbi. So visiting *hahamim* (Hebrew for sages or scholars) generally did not stay long. It was a mark of the size and sophistication of the Sephardic community in Jamaica that it was able to engage *Haham* DeCordova in 1755, who left a subordinate post at K. K. Mikve Israel in Curaçao. DeCordova led the Princess Street synagogue in Kingston for forty-two years, a term in office that ended only with his death.[5]

The second figure in this piece, whose absence was the direct cause of the complications surrounding delivery of the *get* to the divorced wife, was Abraham Mimenton (fl. 1750–1774). Mimenton did not leave many clues behind, but some facts can be surmised from snippets of information within the letters: In 1774, Mimenton lived in Surinam, but he had previously lived in Kingston and,

---

James W. Hagy, "Her 'Scandalous Behaviour': A Jewish Divorce in Charleston, South Carolina, 1788," *American Jewish Archives* 41, no. 2 (Fall–Winter 1989), 193–95. Though the documents do not define the nature of the wife's behavior, Hagy suggests that it was probably adulterous conduct. The second, as described above, was the divorce of Hannah and David Leion, who "disagree[d] for a length of time before they parted" (Stern, "The Sheftall Diaries," 268–69).

4. One such example would be Gershom Mendes Seixas (1745–1816), who served as *hazan* at New York's K. K. Shearith Israel. See Jacob Rader Marcus, "The Handsome Young Priest in the Black Gown: The Personal World of Gershom Seixas," *Hebrew Union College Annual* 40–41 (1969–70), 409–67. As Marcus points out, there are no documented instances of ordained rabbis officiating over North American mainland congregations in the manner that Seixas did prior to 1840 (ibid., 410–11).

5. [Isaac Dias Fernandes], "Some account of the life of the Late Revd Chief Rabbi Joshua Hezekiah De Cordova of this town," *Columbian Magazine; or, Monthly Miscellany* (Kingston, Jamaica), October 1, 1797, 267–71, accessed through American Antiquarian Society Historical Periodicals Collection, Series 1; Bertram W. Korn, "The Haham DeCordova of Jamaica," *American Jewish Archives* 18, no. 2 (November 1966), 141–54.

while there, had officiated in some capacity at the Princess Street synagogue—most likely as *hazan*. It was during this sojourn that he apparently performed the marriage ceremony for the divorcing couple.[6]

The remaining figures were three Jewish merchants: Jacob Alvarenga (fl. 1750–1780) in Jamaica and Abraham Pereira Mendes (fl. 1766–1774) and Aaron Lopez (1731–1782) in Newport, Rhode Island. Lopez, an émigré from Portugal to British America, was by 1774 one of the wealthiest and most successful of Newport's mercantile class. Alvarenga and Pereira Mendes were cousins who had grown up together in Jamaica, but in 1767 Pereira Mendes left the island to marry Lopez's daughter, Sarah (called Sally).

Rabbi DeCordova began with what would seem to us to be a simple problem: how to get a letter from Kingston to Surinam. Without the right language skills and access to an international postal system (which did not yet exist), there was no easy means for an ordinary person to achieve this end.[7] One had to ask for help from someone else with the right connections. So DeCordova asked Alvarenga, a local merchant known to him, for assistance in achieving the delivery of a letter to Mimenton. In the two letters, we see how Alvarenga combined his strong language and writing skills with his connection to Pereira Mendes to create a polite request for a mercantile favor from Lopez, a man he had never met.

6. Surviving records in Surinam suggest that the family name was actually Mementon: an Abraham Mementon, who died in 1735, was a landholder and founding member of the Jewish settlement at Jodensavanne, on the Surinam River. See Richard Gottheil, "Contributions to the History of the Jews of Surinam," *Publications of the American Jewish Historical Society* 9 (1901), 128–44; P. A. Hilfman, "Notes on the History of the Jews in Surinam," *Publications of the American Jewish Historical Society* 18 (1909), 179–208. Tombstones for Abraham Mementon and two other members of the Mementon family are still extant in the Jodensavanne Cemetery. See Aviva Ben-Ur and Rachel Frankel, *Remnant Stones: The Jewish Cemeteries of Suriname: Epitaphs* (Cincinnati: Hebrew Union College Press, 2009), 250. Hilfman provides a list of rabbis in the synagogue at Paramaribo, but our Abraham Mimenton is not among them, and there is no other record that he or anyone named Mementon served as an officiant there.

7. In the preface to the single text he published during his lifetime, titled *Reason and Faith* (first published at Kingston in 1788), DeCordova begged to be excused for "improprieties" in language that he claimed were due to his being "a foreigner who learned the English language, without a master, in his old age" (*Emet vEmunah: Reason and Faith, or, Philosophical Absurdities, and the Need for Revelation, intended to Promote Faith among Infidels, and the Unbounded Exercise of Humanity among all Religious Men. By one of the Sons of Abraham to his Brethren* [Kingston: Strupar and Preston, 1788], iii–iv; rev.ed. [Philadelphia: F. Bailey, 1791], vi). Isaac Dias Fernandes would later point to DeCordova's program of devoted individualized study as having produced a fluent comprehension of written English, without commenting on DeCordova's capacity to speak or write in English ("Some account of the life of the Late Revd Chief Rabbi Joshua Hezekiah De Cordova of this town," 269).

Though each letter is brief and simple on its face, what is remarkable about these two short letters is the web of transatlantic connections they reveal with just a little teasing. To resolve DeCordova's problem required enlisting a Jewish merchant on the mainland to facilitate communications between two religious figures, previously unknown to him, in Jamaica and Surinam, for the goal of delivering the *get*. Remarkably, these places were more proximate to one another across the Caribbean than either was to Rhode Island, where Lopez resided. These letters thus underscore not only the long-distance performance of Jewish ritual around the Atlantic colonies but also the key role that Jewish merchants frequently played as intermediaries in matters of eighteenth-century religious practice.

◇◇◇

Letter from Jacob Alvarenga in Kingston, Jamaica, to Aaron Lopez in Newport, Rhode Island, November 10, 1774

> Source: Letter from Jacob Alvarenga to Aaron Lopez (November 10, 1774), Aaron Lopez Papers, 1773–78, Manuscript Collection VFM 734, G. W. Blunt White Library, Mystic Seaport Museum, Mystic, CT.

Kingston in Jamaica Novr 10th 1774

Dear Sir

Inclosed a Letter for Mr Abraham Mimenton in / Surinam, which Our Kakam[8] the Rev^d M^r De Cordova / and my Self beg you as a particular favour, youl / forward to him as Soon as possible, its Concerning / a Gate[9] he Send [*sic*] to Our Kakam, my best Complem^ts / to you and famely, as Also to my Cousin Abm / your Son in Law & his Wife, your Comply^ce / will Greatly Oblige

D^r S^r

Your most Obed^t Humble Servant,

/s/ Jacob Alvarenga

VERSO: "November 10th 1774 — / from Jacob Alvarenga / Jamaica"

---

8. *Haham* (transliterated here as *Kakam*) is the traditional Hebrew term used to denote a sage or scholar.

9. *Get* (transliterated here as *Gate*) is a ritual Jewish divorce. See also chapter 10, note 4.

Letter from Jacob Alvarenga in Kingston, Jamaica, to Aaron Lopez in Newport, Rhode Island, December 18, 1774

Source: Letter from Jacob Alvarenga to Aaron Lopez (December 18, 1774), Aaron Lopez Papers, box 164A, folder 16, Newport Historical Society, Newport, RI.

Kingston Jamaica Decem^br 18th 1774

Dr Sir

Tho I have not the pleasure of your Good acquaintance at / the same time I have taken the Liberty of Inclosing a / Letter directed to mr Ab^m Mimenton in Surinam, / which Our Kakam mr DeCordova & my self will take / it as a particular favour, you will be so Kind as to forward / to him as soon as possible, its an Answer to a Letter he / wrote to Our Kakam & Self. Concerning a Gate he sent us / for a woman he Gave Kidusim[10] in this Island, which / he was in Sinna [synagogue]. & Since he went to Surinam, the / Mahamad[11] as also the Kakam there, obliged him to send / to her, hoping you Enjoy perfect helth in company / of all your Good family, as also my Cousin Ab^m your / son in Law. & his Spouse, in the Intereem I Remain / very Respectfully

D^r S^r

Your most Obliged humble Servant

/s/ Jacob Alvarenga

---

10. *Kidushin* (transliterated here as *Kidusim*) is Hebrew for "betrothal."

11. *Maamad* (transliterated here as *Mahamad*) is the Hebrew term used to describe the board of directors of a Spanish-Portuguese congregation.

2

"TO BIGOTRY NO SANCTION"

George Washington, America's Jews, and Religious Freedom[1]
(1790)

◇◇

JONATHAN D. SARNA

George Washington was inaugurated as president of the United States of America on April 30, 1789. The federal Constitution, by then, had been ratified by the requisite nine states and was in effect. Two other states soon signed on, and the twelfth state, North Carolina, ratified the Constitution in November 1789. Only Rhode Island, fearful that as a small state its rights would be trampled upon by others, held back. It refused to ratify the Constitution, although it was already bound by it.

The new Constitution did not contain any clause guaranteeing religious liberty; that would only appear in the Bill of Rights in 1791. Article Six of the Constitution did outlaw religious tests "as a qualification to any public office or public trust under the United States." That, for Jews and other non-Christians, marked a huge step forward as it guaranteed them the right to hold public offices in the federal government. The United States, unlike most countries with Christian majorities, promised non-Christians that they could, at least in theory, hold the highest governmental office in the land.

Washington wanted the new Constitution to be unanimously approved. He believed that would make all Americans feel a part of the great experiment that the United States represented; it would signify consensus. When Rhode Island held out against ratification, Washington publicly demonstrated his unhappiness by refusing to visit the state when he toured New England in the autumn of 1789. Only after Rhode Island finally ratified the Constitution on May 29, 1790, did he agree to travel there.

---

1. Reprinted with permission from the National Museum of American Jewish History, Philadelphia. This item previously appeared in a publication accompanying a 2012 exhibition in the museum (Jonathan D. Sarna, "George Washington's Correspondence with the Jews of Newport," in *To Bigotry No Sanction: George Washington and Religious Freedom*, ed. Josh Perelman, [Philadephia: National Museum of American Jewish History, 2012], 17–24). A digitized and interactive version of the document is available online at religiousfreedom.nmajh.org.

Three days after Congress adjourned, on August 15, he and a large entourage, including Secretary of State Thomas Jefferson, set out for Newport.

On August 18 four addresses (written, in keeping with the literary style of the day, in the form of open letters) were read out to the president at a prearranged ceremony; it was customary to greet visiting dignitaries in this way. There was an address from the town, a joint statement of welcome from all of the Christian clergy, and a greeting from the Masonic order—whose president was also the warden of the city's synagogue, Moses Seixas (1745–1816). The final and most historically important address came from the "Hebrew Congregation"— the community's Jews.

The fact that the Jews were included at all is noteworthy. They formed a small but significant merchant community in Newport, and had built a beautiful synagogue, Yeshuat Israel (Salvation of Israel), now known as the Touro Synagogue, in 1763. So, at the very end of Washington's visit to Newport, their representative stepped up to read an address to him. This was not the first Jewish address to Washington. That had come from the Jews of Savannah months earlier. And it was also not the last Jewish communication he received that year. Jews of New York, Philadelphia, Charleston, and Richmond sent him a joint letter several months later. But the Newport letter was, by general consensus, the most important of the lot, partly because of its content, and mostly because of its celebrated reply, sent a few days later from New York City.

Both letters were carefully written documents that reward close reading and minute study. To facilitate this, the letters are reprinted here with commentary.

George Washington's correspondence with the Hebrew Congregation of Newport was published in newspapers across the country in 1790 and was frequently reprinted thereafter. A search on Google Books yields thousands of volumes that quote or reprint the letters, spanning the entire history of the United States. Though Washington directed his address to a small community of Newport Jews, it was understood, from the beginning, that his words carried far wider significance. In defining religious liberty as an "inherent natural right" and promising that "the Government of the United States ... gives to bigotry no sanction, to persecution no assistance," George Washington set a high bar, not only for his successors, but for Americans of every faith and creed.

◇◇

Address of the Hebrew Congregation of Newport, Rhode Island, to President George Washington, August 17, 1790

To the President of the United States of America,

Sir:

Permit the children of the stock of Abraham[2] to approach you with the most cordial affection and esteem for your person and merits—and to join with our fellow citizens[3] in welcoming you to New Port.

With pleasure we reflect on those days—those days of difficulty, and danger—when the God of Israel, who delivered David from the peril of the sword[4] shielded Your head in the day of battle. And we rejoice to think, that the same Spirit, who rested in the Bosom of the greatly beloved Daniel[5] enabling him to preside over the Provinces of the Babylonish Empire, rests and ever will rest upon you, enabling you to discharge the arduous duties of Chief Magistrate[6] in these States.

Deprived as we heretofore have been of the invaluable rights of free Citizens,[7] we now with a deep sense of gratitude to the Almighty disposer[8] of all events, behold a Government, erected by the Majesty of the People, a Government,

---

2. In colonial America, the word "Jew" carried negative associations in some Christian circles. Therefore, in writing to George Washington, Newport's Jews used a more positive term which, ironically, they found in the King James version of the Book of Acts (13:26) which describes Paul's address to "Men and brethren, children of the stock of Abraham."

3. In 1790, Jews could speak of themselves as "fellow citizens" almost nowhere else in the world. Newport's Jews emphasized this point in the opening sentence of their address. Later in the text, they again underscored how much citizenship meant to them: "Deprived as we heretofore have been of the invaluable rights of free Citizens . . ."

4. From Psalms 144:10, this verse is also included in the traditional Jewish prayer for the government (*hanoten teshuah*), regularly recited in early American synagogues.

5. Dan. 5–6. Note that Babylon, where Daniel resided, was, like America, a diaspora land. The various references to Daniel, an apocalyptic book of the Bible, also hint at an apocalyptic interpretation of the American Revolution. Some Jews viewed the colonists' miraculous victory as a harbinger of the messiah.

6. The term "president" had not yet come into common usage.

7. In 1762, Aaron Lopez (1731–1782) and Isaac Elizer (c. 1720–1807) had petitioned to obtain naturalization in Newport, and were denied. The court ruled that the 1740 Naturalization Act only applied to under-populated settlements and that local law limited citizenship to believing Christians. This may well have been what Newport's Jews had in mind when writing to the President.

8. On March 20, 1779, the Continental Congress employed a similar term: "WHEREAS, in just Punishment of our manifold Transgressions it hath pleased the Supreme Disposer of all Events to visit these United States with a calamitous War . . ."

which to bigotry gives no sanction, to persecution no assistance, but generously affording to all Liberty of conscience, and immunities of Citizenship,[9] deeming every one, of whatever Nation, tongue, or language equal parts of the great governmental Machine. This so ample and extensive Federal Union whose basis is Philanthropy, Mutual confidence and Public Virtue, we cannot but acknowledge to be the work of the Great God, who ruleth in the Armies of Heaven and among the Inhabitants of the Earth,[10] doing whatever seemeth him good.

For all these Blessings of civil and religious liberty which we enjoy under an equal and benign administration, we desire to send up our thanks to the Ancient of Days,[11] the great preserver of Men,[12] beseeching him, that the Angel who conducted our forefathers through the wilderness[13] into the Promised Land, may graciously conduct you through all the difficulties and dangers of this mortal life. And, when, like Joshua,[14] full of days and full of honour, you are gathered to your Fathers, may you be admitted into the Heavenly Paradise to partake of the water of life, and the tree of immortality.[15]

Done and Signed by order of the Hebrew Congregation[16] in New Port, Rhode Island, August 17, 1790

Moses Seixas, Warden[17]

9. Washington understood that the Jewish community sought his personal guarantee that Jews would be included in the word "all." He therefore sent the congregation's words back to them as if they were his own: "All possess alike liberty of conscience and immunities of citizenship." His slight modification of language is nevertheless noteworthy. The Jewish community viewed its liberty as an act of American generosity ("generously affording"). George Washington let Jews know that they possessed these liberties and immunities as a matter of right ("all possess alike").

10. Dan. 4:32 (4:35 in King James Version).

11. Dan. 7:9.

12. Job 7:20.

13. Exod. 23:20.

14. The comparison to the biblical Joshua was apt for he both entered the Promised Land and, like Washington, was a military leader.

15. Judaism does not hold that heaven is restricted only to Jews. Here Washington is considered to be among "the righteous among the nations" who will find their repose in paradise.

16. Once again, the congregation deliberately avoided using the term "Jewish" (see note above). The official name of the "Hebrew Congregation" was Yeshuat Israel (Salvation of Israel), and it became known as the Touro Synagogue in the nineteenth century.

17. Moses Mendes Seixas (1744–1809) of Newport signed the letter to Washington in the name of the city's entire Jewish community. Seixas was a banker, an organizer of the Bank of Rhode Island, the grand master of Rhode Island's Masons, and a Jewish communal leader. He was also a community leader and served as parnas (president or, as he was sometimes called,

A Reply from President George Washington to the Hebrew Congregation of Newport, Rhode Island, c. August 17, 1790

To the Hebrew Congregation in Newport, Rhode Island

Gentlemen:

While I receive, with much satisfaction, your Address replete with expressions of affection and esteem; I rejoice in the opportunity of assuring you, that I shall always retain a grateful remembrance of the cordial welcome I experienced in my visit to Newport,[18] from all classes of Citizens.[19]

The reflection on the days of difficulty and danger which are past is rendered the more sweet, from a consciousness that they are succeeded by days of uncommon prosperity and security. If we have wisdom to make the best use of the advantages with which we are now favored, we cannot fail, under the just administration of a good Government, to become a great and a happy people.[20]

The Citizens of the United States of America have a right to applaud themselves for having given to mankind examples of an enlarged and liberal policy: a policy worthy of imitation.[21]

All possess alike liberty of conscience and immunities of citizenship. It is now no more that toleration is spoken of,[22] as if it was by the indulgence of

------

"warden") of Newport's Jewish congregation. His brother was Gershom Seixas (1745–1816), famed *hazan* (reader) of Congregation Shearith Israel in New York.

18. The use of the past tense confirms that Washington did not send his letter from Newport, but after he had departed. The letter to the Jews of Newport is undated, but since the handwriting is that of Tobias Lear (1762–1816), who did not accompany Washington to Newport, there can be no doubt that it was sent from New York.

19. Just as the Jews referred to themselves as "citizens" in the first sentence of their letter, so Washington underscored in his first sentence that they form a "class of citizens."

20. Washington wrote in a similar vein to other groups. See, for example, his letter to Roman Catholics in America (March 1790): "The prospect of national prosperity now before us is truly animating, and ought to excite the exertions of all good men to establish and secure the happiness of their Country, in the permanent duration of its Freedom and Independence. America, under the smiles of a Divine Providence—the protection of a good Government—and the cultivation of manners, morals and piety, cannot fail of attaining an uncommon degree of eminence, in literature, commerce, agriculture, improvements at home and respectability abroad."

21. The idea that America would serve as an example to other countries was commonplace at that time. The bishops of the Methodist Episcopal Church, for example, praised the Constitution in a letter to Washington as "at present the admiration of the world, and may in future become its great exemplar for imitation." Washington himself had used similar language in his letter to the Hebrew Congregation of Savannah: "Happily the people of the United States of America have, in many instances, exhibited examples worthy of imitation."

22. Washington's aside concerning toleration has long puzzled scholars, for the Jewish com-

one class of people, that another enjoyed the exercise of their inherent natural rights.[23] For happily the Government of the United States, which gives to bigotry no sanction, to persecution no assistance,[24] requires only that they who live under its protection should demean themselves as good citizens,[25] in giving it on all occasions their effectual support.

It would be inconsistent with the frankness of my character not to avow that I am pleased with your favorable opinion of my Administration, and fervent wishes for my felicity.

May the Children of the Stock of Abraham, who dwell in this land, continue to merit and enjoy the good will of the other Inhabitants; while every one shall sit in safety under his own vine and fig-tree, and there shall be none to make him afraid.[26]

---

munity made no mention of toleration in their letter to him. Moreover, the indulgent religious "toleration" practiced by the British and much of enlightened Europe was generally viewed with favor by Jews, especially when contrasted to the intolerant treatment and second-class legal status that plagued them elsewhere in the world. The idea that toleration was inadequate, implying less than complete religious freedom, is more closely associated with Thomas Jefferson than with George Washington. For this reason, the editor of Jefferson's papers suggests that Jefferson himself added these words to the letter. Yet in 1789, in corresponding with Quakers, Washington also had made clear that liberty of worship belonged to the category of "rights" and not just of "toleration."

23. The language of "inherent natural rights" distinguished religious liberty in the United States from Jewish "emancipation" in Europe. In Europe, emancipation was generally a quid pro quo arrangement. It assumed that Jews would change their ways and left open the possibility (often later realized) that privileges granted to Jews would be taken away if they did not sufficiently "improve." Washington, by contrast, described religious liberty as an "inherent natural right" that can never be taken away.

24. This phrase became the most frequently quoted passage from the letter. It improved upon a phrase used by Newport's Jews in their letter to the president.

25. Some scholars argue that Washington's use of the phrase "demean themselves as good citizens" actually conditioned his promise of religious liberty, as if it would hold only as long as Jews maintained appropriate behavior. Others point to the fact that Washington frequently linked discussions of liberty with the need for Americans to "demean themselves as good citizens." In the wake of widespread resistance to federal taxation, as evidenced by Shays' Rebellion (1786–87) in Massachusetts and the Whiskey Rebellion (1790s) in western Pennsylvania, his concern for responsible citizenship is perhaps unsurprising. In his letter to the United Baptist Churches of Virginia (May 1789), he made clear that he held people of every faith to the same standard of good citizenship: "I have often expressed my sentiment, that every man, conducting himself as a good citizen, and being accountable to God alone for his religious opinions, ought to be protected in worshipping the Deity according to the dictates of his own conscience."

26. A close study of this phrase revealed that this particular biblical passage, that of the ancient Hebrew blessing and prophetic vision of the New Jerusalem in which every man sits safely

May the father of all mercies scatter light and not darkness in our paths, and make us all in our several vocations useful here, and in his own due time and way everlastingly happy.[27]

G. Washington

"under his vine and under his fig tree," was employed by Washington in his own writings more than any other passage. Like the Puritans, he evokes the idea of Zion being in America, as if the prophet's vision would find its fulfillment in the United States. That he applied his own favorite scriptural phrase to the Jewish people is extraordinary.

27. The Declaration of Independence had declared "life, liberty and the pursuit of happiness" to be "unalienable rights." Happiness, at that time, implied not just an emotional state but a deeper sense of well-being.

3

"AND MADE THEM WEAR A HAT"

Isaac Harby Asserts the Authenticity of Bareheaded Jewish Prayer (1826)

◇◇◇

GARY PHILLIP ZOLA

The Reformed Society of Israelites (RSI), formally established in Charleston, South Carolina, in 1825, was the first organized attempt to reform Judaism in the United States.[1] This historic initiative began on November 21, 1824, when forty-seven Charlestonian Jews gathered to discuss their growing dissatisfaction with what they considered to be the outmoded character and impenetrable style of the worship services conducted at the city's congregation, Kahal Kadosh Beth Elohim. Isaac Harby (1788–1828), a prominent local writer, educator, editor, and intellectual, was present at this organizational meeting, and he quickly emerged as one of the reforming group's most distinguished figures.

The members of the RSI initially hoped to modify many of the liturgical customs that came from the traditional Spanish-Portuguese prayer service, which the congregation had used from its inception in 1749. The complainants conveyed their ideas about how the services could be improved in a "Memorial" that they placed before the temple's *adjunta* (Spanish and Portuguese for "assistants" or "deputies," in this instance the term refers to the board of trustees). The *adjunta* refused to entertain any of the group's liturgical reforms, so Harby, along with two other RSI leaders—Abraham Moïse II (1799–1869) and David Nunes Carvalho (1784–1860)—began offering Charleston's Jewish community a new and reformed Jewish liturgy. Together these men compiled a new prayer service. The liturgy they produced constituted the first effort to reform the Jewish prayer book in American history.

Many of the liturgical reforms initiated by Charleston's Jewish reformers can

1. On the history of the Reformed Society of Israelites, see Gary Phillip Zola, *Isaac Harby of Charleston: Jewish Reformer and Intellectual* (Tuscaloosa: University of Alabama Press, 1994).

be documented in the pages of the various collections of RSI prayers that have survived. The reformers composed and recited original English prayers. They prayed in both Hebrew and English. Men and women sang hymns together, and the service itself was abbreviated and conducted with deliberate solemnity and decorum. One of the most important innovations was the introduction of a weekly sermon or educational address, delivered in English from the speaker's platform. These liturgical innovations were the first expressions in the United States of Jewish prayer book reform, a trend that had emerged fifteen years earlier in Europe.

The surviving records enable historians to document many of the reforms introduced by the members of the RSI, yet there are questions about the precise nature of the group's ritual practice that cannot be answered authoritatively. Did men and women sit together during worship? Were women involved in leading any aspect of the religious service? Was an organ played during Sabbath services or on Jewish festivals? We may never be able to definitively answer such questions.

In 1856, nearly three decades after the RSI had ceased meeting, Moritz (Maurice) Mayer (1821–1867),[2] the rabbi of Kahal Kadosh Beth Elohim, published the first historical account of how Reform Judaism evolved on American shores, "A History of the Religious Reform among the Israelites of North America."[3] Mayer's chronicle appeared in three successive issues of the German newspaper Sinai, published in Baltimore, Maryland, by the Reform theologian David Einhorn (1809–1879). According to Mayer, the RSI constituted "the light [from which Jewish Reform in America] was ignited." He praised "Charleston's Reformed Society" as a group that "consisted of honorable and brave men" who sincerely believed in "the principles of reform."[4]

Mayer's description of the RSI is particularly valuable because he incorpo-

2. Moritz (Maurice) Mayer (1821–1867) received his legal education in Munich. After participating in the German revolution of 1848–49, he immigrated in 1850 to the United States. Though lacking ordination, he served as hazan (1852–59) of Kahal Kadosh Beth Elohim. In 1853, he married Rachel Ottolengui (1822–1895). He also served as grand secretary (1863–67) of the Independent Order of Bnai Brith.

3. For the original German version, see Moritz Mayer, "Geschichte des religiösen Umschwunges unter den Israeliten Nordamerika's," Sinai [Baltimore, MD] 1 (1856) 101–7, 171–81, 197–205, and 241–45.

4. The quotation comes from pages 6–7 of Anton Hieke's unpublished translation and annotation of Mayer's history of the RSI (2016), edited by Alisa Rethy. The unpublished translation is in the Jacob Rader Marcus Center of the American Jewish Archives, Cincinnati, Ohio.

rates many colorful details regarding its rituals that he surely must have learned about from surviving RSI members who were his contemporaries. One of the RSI's founders, Abraham Moïse II (1799–1869), remained devoted to the RSI long after it ceased functioning. In 1830, Moïse published an abbreviated collection of its prayers in the hope of providing the "enlightened and pious Israelite" with a form of worship that was aligned with their "feelings, opinions, and dispositions."[5] There can be little doubt that Mayer's favorable and complimentary assessment of the ambitions of the Charleston reformers reflected the thoughts and opinions of aging RSI partisans like Moïse, who were eager to memorialize the history of their pioneering initiative.

Mayer contended that the worship service of the RSI "included all the elements we find, more or less, in our [contemporary] reformed congregations: sermon, singing, instrumental music, etc. *In addition, they would pray bareheaded*" (emphasis added). Until recently, there was no way of corroborating this assertion with primary source documentation dating back to the time when the RSI was active. Yet thanks to a recently discovered 1826 letter from Harby to Esdaile P. Cohen (1792–1856), another of the RSI's founding members, we can be certain that some members favored bareheaded prayer and believed this practice to be a religiously legitimate reform.

Writing on May 5, 1826, when the RSI was at its zenith, Harby offered Cohen two explanations as to why there was no religious reason for Jewish men to cover their heads while praying. First, Harby points out that the Torah specifically enjoins only the high priest—not all Israelites—to wear a hat while performing religious duties (Exod. 28:1–43 and 29:29–30). Second, the practice of wearing a hat while praying was a foreign custom borrowed from the Greeks during the Maccabean period (167–60 BCE). Thus, Harby asserted that bareheaded prayer was in fact the oldest and most authentic form of Jewish worship.

Praying with one's head uncovered never became the dominant practice of Reform Judaism in Europe. In America, however, bareheaded prayer became such a common practice that it was an identifying feature of the Reform synagogue during the late nineteenth and early twentieth centuries.[6] Rabbi Aaron Chorin of Arad, Hungary, is generally credited with being the first to defend the propriety of bareheaded worship, in 1826. In America, Baltimore's Har Sinai (established in 1842) was believed to be the first to adopt the practice of bare-

5. Barnett A. Elzas, *The Sabbath Service and Miscellaneous Prayers, Adopted by the Reformed Society of Israelites, founded in Charleston, S. C., November 21, 1825* (New York: Bloch Publishing, 1916), 5.

6. See W. Gunther Plaut, *The Rise of Reform Judaism* (New York: World Union for Progressive Judaism, 1963), 178–80; *The Reform Jewish Reader: North American Documents*, ed. Michael A. Meyer and W. Gunther Plaut (New York: Union of American Hebrew Congregations, 2001), 59–62.

headed prayer.[7] Harby's letter to Cohen proves that the Charleston reformers debated the authenticity of bareheaded prayer in the synagogue at the same time that Chorin made his opinion public. This new document also lends considerable credence to Mayer's 1856 claim that the members of the RSI prayed without covering their heads, thereby proving that the first manifestation of what would eventually become a broadly accepted practice in American Reform Judaism may be traced back to Charleston and the leaders of the RSI.

◇◇◇

Letter from Isaac Harby to the Reformed Society of Israelites, May 5, 1826

Source: A photostat copy of Harby's letter is preserved at the Jacob Rader Marcus Center of the American Jewish Archives, Cincinnati. The author wishes to thank Arnold Kaplan for providing a copy of the letter. The original letter is in the Arnold and Deanne Kaplan Collection of Americana, in the University of Pennsylvania's Kislak Center for Special Collections, Rare Books and Manuscripts, Philadelphia.

Charleston 5th May 1826

Dear Sirs,

I have no desire, at present, to convince any Israelite, not a member of the "Reformed Society" that the practice of *wearing hats* in the Temple of God is a badge of *slavery* and a sign of *irreligion*. That subject, and one or two others, rather startling to the bigot and the uninformed, will be treated *at large* in the preface to the Book of Prayers we are about to publish.[8]

But as you ask for the *facts* on which I grounded my reasoning, I will here, with pleasure, furnish you with two, containing a *negative* and a *positive* testimony on the subject.

The 21st chap. Leviticus contains the items of the Priests' mourning costume, marriage blemishes, etc. It speaks *particularly* of what he / the Priest / shall do — and none other.[9] In the 10th verse, same chapter, it says "And he that is the *high*

7. See "Head, Covering of," in *Universal Jewish Encyclopedia*, ed. Isaac Landman (New York: Universal Jewish Encyclopedia, 1941), 262–63.

8. The prayers of the RSI is the first example of Jewish prayer book reform in North America, as noted above, and the third oldest Reform liturgy in modern history. On the significance of the RSI's prayers, see Gary Phillip Zola, "The First Reform Prayer Book in America: The Liturgy of the Reformed Society of Israelites," in *Platforms and Prayer Books: Theological and Liturgical Perspectives on Reform Judaism*, ed. Dana Evan Kaplan (Lanham, MD: Rowman and Littlefield, 2002), 99–117.

9. This refers to Leviticus 21:1: "And the Lord said to Moses, Speak to the priests, the sons of Aaron, and say to them...." Harby cites this passage to underscore his argument that the verses pertain to the priests—the sons of Aaron—and no one else.

Priest among his brethren, *upon whose head the anointed oil was poured*, and that is consecrated to *put on the garments*, shall not uncover *his head nor rend his clothes*" [Lev. 21:10], etc. It goes on to tell who are really entitled to be priests (*Koanim*) [*sic*][10] the sons of Aaron & their descendants, etc. and what other things *they* shall do, and what *omit to do, as Priests. The law extends to nobody else.* The whole regulations in the passage about defilement of the dead, marrying a virgin etc. is [*sic*] expressly intended for *the sons of Aaron.*

Inference.

As the Laws of Moses, particularly the *ceremonial observances*, are all *positive* and *explicit* to a letter, it is evident he[11] would not have omitted to render the wearing of a hat or turban, or some such head-covering, *obligatory* on all the Israelites, if the thing had ever been *intended*. But it never was *the law.* The exclusive custom as above seen was *confined to the Priests;* the consequence is irresistible, it was not the custom of *the People!* When the Constitution of the U. States says "it shall be the duty of the President by and with the advice of the Senate, to appoint *ambassadors* to foreign powers,"[12] etc. — Every man in possession of common judgment knows that this power does not belong to the House of Representatives; nor the legislatures of the different states, nor to *the people*; but is *limited* and *confined*, only to the *Executive* as it is *expressed.*[13] Apply this plain fact to the priest being covered and nobody else *mentioned.*

This is the proof *negative.*

Now for the proof *positive:*

To be *covered* in a place or worship, whether in a temple of *Jupiter*[14] or *Ceres*,[15] was in many places, and on various occasions with however exceptions and alterations a *heathen* practice. The Jews were always, by Moses, by the Judges, and by the prophets, warned to eschew and abhor all *heathen customs.* They were never

10. Harby's transliteration reminds us that the Charleston Jews used the Sephardic pronunciation of Hebrew, wherein the Hebrew letter "hay" was left unsounded. The Ashkenazic pronounced the letter as if it was the letter "h" in English. It is for this reason that Harby transliterates the Hebrew word for priests as *koanim* instead of *kohanim.*

11. Moses.

12. See Article II, Section 2, Clause 1, of the U.S. Constitution.

13. It is interesting to note that in making his point, Harby compared the Torah to the U.S. Constitution. One can surmise that he viewed the two legislative texts to be comparable documents.

14. In Roman mythology, Jupiter is the king of the gods who ruled over the sky and thunder. Pluto, the god of the underworld, is Jupiter's brother.

15. Ceres, the Roman goddess of the harvest, fertility, agriculture, vegetation, and soil, is Jupiter's protector and sister.

covered in the place of worship, until they were *under Antiochus*;[16] & even then, only those who *derided* the religion of their country *wore their hats.*[17] The most patriotic period of Jewish History was in the time of the Maccabees.[18] They struggled like men. Read the whole of both books.[19] But particularly the 4th chap. of 2nd Maccabees. You will there find what havoc in the Jewish religion was made (after the death of Seleucus[20] by Jason[21] the brother of Onias[22] — the latter was, by right, high Priest; but the former succeeded by irreligion, flattering Antiochus, and "training up the Jewish Youth in the *fashions of the Heathen*" to make himself high Priest. After describing many of his heathenish and impious acts, the Scripture goes on to say "He put down the Government which was *according to the Law*,

16. Antiochus IV Epiphanes (c. 215–164 BCE) of the Seleucid empire spent much of his reign engaged in warfare, including as part of his rule over the Jews of ancient Palestine. In response to the persecution of the Jews of Judaea and Samaria, Judah Maccabee (fl. second century BCE) led an armed uprising against the Seleucid regime in 167–160 BCE. The minor Jewish holiday of Hanukkah, which stems from this historical event, celebrates and mythologizes the Maccabean revolt.

17. Harby bases his argument on the fourth chapter of 2 Maccabees, which specifies some of the ways that Jason championed Hellenization in Jerusalem. According to the text, the Jews who embraced Hellenic customs began wearing the *petasos* — wide-brimmed hats worn by the ancient Greeks. These hats are also described as "Hermes hats" because of their similarity to the headgear worn by Hermes, the patron god of athletics. For more on what the wearing of these hats might have indicated, see Benjamin Edidin Scolnic, *Judaism Defined: Mattathias and the Destiny of His People* (Lanham, MD: University Press of America, 1998), 117–20. See also Albert T. Olmstead, "Wearing the Hat," *American Journal of Theology* 24, no. 1 (1920): 94–111.

18. On the Maccabees, see note 16.

19. Harby relies entirely on the history contained in the Books of the Maccabees to argue his point that wearing a hat during prayer was a custom that came into vogue as a result of the Hellenization process that was rampant during the time of the Maccabean revolt. Despite the fact that the Books of the Maccabees are part of the Apocrypha and not in the Jewish Biblical canon, Harby considers them to be historically accurate. He tells Cohen to "read both books." It should be noted that II Maccabees describes an array of miraculous and supernatural occurrences that do not appear in I Maccabees. Most modern scholars agree that that both books were written in relatively close proximity to the events they describe and therefore contain valuable historical data worthy of study. On the historicity of the Books of the Maccabees — particularly II Maccabees — see Daniel R. Schwartz, *2 Maccabees* (New York: Walter de Gruyter, 2008).

20. After the death of Alexander the Great, Seleucus I Nicator (the last word means "victor") (c. 358 BCE–c. 281 BCE), a Macedonian army officer, rose to prominence and founded the Seleucid kingdom.

21. Jason was the Hellenistic high priest in Jerusalem under the Seleucid king Antiochus IV Epiphanes.

22. Onias III was a high priest during the Second Temple period who reputedly opposed the Hellenization of Judaea. Onias's brother Jason succeeded him as high priest.

and brought up new customs *against the Law*" [2 Macc. 4:10–11 AV].[23] And, as an example of what *new* custom was *against the Law*, he immediately after read the following:

"*For* he built gladly a place of exercise under the town itself, and brought -the chief young men under *his subjection* and made them *wear a hat*" Macc. 2nd. *Chap 4 v. 12*.[24]

Here is the *positive* argument or proof. This wearing the hat, among other things enumerated in the chapter referred to was *against the law*. What was begun by *impiety*, is continued through *custom*! The fact is irresistible. Let the old lights bring something stronger than this on the *covered side* of the question and I will confess they have more *sabby*[25] [sic] than I ever thought them to possess.

Yours truly, Isaac Harby

E. P. Cohen. Esq.[26]

23. Here Harby is referring to the King James Version of II Maccabees, 4:10–11. The uncited verse that Harby quotes (verse 11) is more comprehensible once it is set in context: In the preceding verse, the text declares that "when the king had granted [the post of high priest to Jason], and he had gotten into his hand the rule he forthwith brought his own nation to Greekish fashion. And the royal privileges granted of special favor to the Jews by the means of John the father of Eupolemus, who went ambassador to Rome for amity and aid, he [Jason] took away; and putting down the governments which were according to the law, he brought up new customs against the law." See II Maccabees 4:10–11 (King James Version).

24. See note 17.

25. Harby employs a popular Americanism heard in his region: "sabby" means "to know" or "to comprehend" (as in "savvy"). According to a glossary of American colloquialisms published in 1848, "sabby" was "a word of extensive use whenever a lingua franca has been formed of the Spanish or Portuguese language in Asia, Africa, and America. It is used by the negroes [sic] in some of the Southern States" (John Russell Bartlett, *Dictionary of Americanisms: A Glossary of Words and Phrases Usually Regarded as Peculiar to the United States* [New York: Bartlett and Welford, 1848], 283–84).

26. Esdaile P. Cohen (1792–1856) was one of the founding members of the RSI. Raised in Charleston, he married Frances Hays (1790–1865) in Montreal, Canada, in 1829. In 1830 he was an officer of Charleston's "Friendship" Masonic Lodge No. 9. See *American Masonic Record; Albany Saturday Magazine* (1830) 3:42 and 330.

4

"THE KINGDOM RESTORED TO ISRAEL"

Mormon Apostle Orson Hyde's Reflections on Judaism[1] (1841)

◇◇◇

JASON M. OLSON

Mormonism grew out of Protestantism—particularly Methodism—in the early nineteenth century. A new form of American religious expression, Mormonism quickly diverged from other brands of Christianity due to the mystical experiences of its prophet Joseph Smith Jr. (1805–1844) and its claims to be not a protest of Catholicism but rather a restoration of the Christian church of the first century. Animated by a distinctive nontrinitarian and restorationist theology, the Mormon church (which came to be known as the Church of Jesus Christ of Latter-day Saints) developed a unique dispensational attitude to the Jewish people.[2] Dispensational Protestantism, as developed by the Anglo-Irish cleric John Nelson Darby (1800–1882) and the American theologian Cyrus Scofield (1843–1921), asserts that the era of Jesus's apostles constituted the end of prophetic dispensations and that the restoration of the Jewish people to the Land of Israel in the latter days would usher in a final dispensation. By contrast, Mormonism asserts the final dispensation began with the advent and visions of Joseph Smith (beginning with his first vision in 1820) and that subsequent unfolding of human experience would include the restoration of the Jewish people to the Land of Israel. Mormonism also asserts that Jewish restoration would

1. My thanks to Mason Kamana Allred and David M. Whitchurch for their advice on selecting this document as well as their work on the background of Orson Hyde and his relations with the Jewish people. Note: The products (services) offered by Jason M. Olson, Mark A. Raider, and Gary Phillip Zola are neither made, provided, approved, nor endorsed by Intellectual Reserve, Inc., or The Church of Jesus Christ of Latter-day Saints. Any content or opinions expressed, implied, or included in or with the goods (services) offered by Jason M. Olson, Mark A. Raider, and Gary Phillip Zola are solely those of Jason M. Olson, Mark A. Raider and Gary Phillip Zola and not those of Intellectual Reserve, Inc., or The Church of Jesus Christ of Latter-day Saints.

2. Dispensationalism is the belief that God works in history through prophets who lead dispensations (periods in history when a prophet is called to teach God's word by God's authority) and proclaim God's truth on earth. When prophets have no ministry on earth, history will enter a period of apostasy.

not result from historical forces alone but would be aided by the agency and authority of the Mormon priesthood.

Smith believed that the Christian faith was in apostasy before the advent of his prophetic calling, but that Judaism was a viable and valid expression of faith and covenant for the Jewish people. It is useful to note that Smith's conception in this regard bears a striking resemblance to that of Martin Luther (1483–1586), the seminal German theologian who initiated the Protestant Reformation. However, unlike Luther—who, when faced with the Jews' refusal to convert to his version of reformed Christianity, concluded that God had annulled his covenant with the Jewish people—Smith did not require the Jews to convert to Mormonism. In other words, Smith, who viewed all forms of Christianity before the Latter-day Saints as apostasy, believed that Jews practicing Judaism were fulfilling their faith in covenant, including the idea of the return to the Land of Israel. As Smith stated in an 1842 Mormon periodical, the Jewish people "inculcate attendance in divine worship" and manifest to any "disinterested reader . . . true piety, real religion, and acts of devotion to God."[3]

Though Mormonism's founder wanted European Jews who converted to Mormonism to immigrate to America, he wished European Jews who remained faithful to Judaism to fulfill a theologically inspired proto-Zionist vision of returning to the Land of Israel. Smith tasked Orson Hyde (1805–1878), an early Mormon apostle, with using the priesthood's authority to dedicate the Land of Israel to the return of the Jewish people. Smith's personal writings contain explicit instructions in this regard, including the following item pertaining to Hyde and John Edward Page (1799–1867), who were members of the Mormon church's governing body known as the Quorum of the Twelve Apostles: "He [Hyde] requested to know in his letter if converted Jews are to go to Jerusalem or to come to Zion [America]. I therefore wish you to inform him that converted Jews must come here [America]. If Elder Hyde's & Page's testimony to the Jews at Jerusalem should be received, then they may know 'that the set time hath come' [for the return of European Jewry to the Land of Israel]."[4]

After proselytizing and raising funds throughout the eastern United States for several months, Hyde arrived in Liverpool, England, on March 3, 1841. On June 15, he wrote a letter to Smith from London, reporting on his assignment to serve as an "ambassador to the Jews abroad."[5] Hyde sent the letter to Smith

3. Joseph Smith, "The Jews," *Times and Seasons*, June 1, 1842, 810 (for an online version, see https://www.josephsmithpapers.org/paper-summary/times-and-seasons-1-june-1842/12).

4. Joseph Smith, *The Personal Writings of Joseph Smith*, ed. and comp. Dean C. Jessee (Salt Lake City, UT: Deseret Book, 1984), 486.

5. Letter from Orson Hyde to Joseph Smith (June 15, 1841), *Times and Seasons*, October 1,

in Nauvoo, Illinois, the headquarters of the Mormon church in this period, and intended it for publication in the monthly Mormon periodical *Times and Seasons* (1839–46). The letter was the second one Hyde had sent to Smith from Europe, and it detailed his efforts to meet with the leaders of London's Jewish community and his authorship of materials describing the origins and beliefs of the Mormon church. Hyde reported to Smith on his attempts to fulfill his assignment of seeking information regarding the "views and movements of the Jewish people."[6] After requesting a visit with the chief rabbi of Great Britain, Solomon Hirschell (1762–1842) of the Great Synagogue of London, Hyde was informed that the rabbi had suffered injuries in a recent accident and was unable to grant him an audience. In response, Hyde penned a letter to the rabbi (featured here)—which he copied into his letter to Smith—informing Hirschell of his "divine appointment" to meet with the Jewish communities in several major European cities.[7] There is no evidence that Hirschell responded to Hyde's letter.

The letter is one of the few instances of correspondence available between the first generation of Mormons and their Jewish contemporaries. It demonstrates a peculiar Mormon version of Christian proto-Zionism that, while affirming the integrity of Judaism, illuminates an important facet of Jewish-Christian relations in the early nineteenth century. In his letter to the rabbi, the Mormon apostle Hyde is clearly more concerned with the Jewish people's ingathering to the Land of Israel than he is with proselytizing. Hyde also warns the rabbi—against the backdrop of rising antisemitism in the West—of a coming "destroyer of the Gentiles" who will seek to annihilate the Jewish people. Most telling, however, is Hyde's accepting view of Judaism and affirmation that it is God's will the Jews be preserved as a nation until the time of their return to the Land of Israel. Viewed historically, this is a highly unusual stance for an American Christian in the early nineteenth century. By suggesting that practicing Jews are faithful to God through Judaism—irrespective of the theological requirements of Christianity—Hyde demonstrates the degree to which, very early on, Mormonism diverged from traditional American Protestantism in its views of dispensationalism, Judaism, and proto-Zionism.

◇◇◇

———
1841, 551–55 (for an online version, see https://www.josephsmithpapers.org/paper-summary/letter-from-orson-hyde-15june-1841/2).

   6. Ibid.

   7. Ibid.

Letter from Orson Hyde to Joseph Smith, June 15, 1841

Source: Letter from Orson Hyde (London, England) to Joseph Smith (Nauvoo, IL) (June 15, 1841), *Times and Seasons*, October 1, 1841, 551–55. Joseph Smith Papers Project, (c) by Intellectual Reserve, Inc. Used by permission. All rights reserved. www.josephsmithpapers.org.

London, June 15th, 1841.

REV. DR. SOLOMON HIRSCHELL,[8]

Pres't Rabbi of the Hebrew Society in England.

Rev'd Sir,

I cannot but express my sorrow and regret at the misfortune under which you labor, in consequence of the severe accident which befel you; and by which you are confined to your room. Please accept Sir, the sincere wishes of a stranger, that you may speedily recover from the injury you sustained in consequence of the accident; and resume the labors which your high and responsible station calls you to perform.

Feeling that I may not enjoy the privilege and happiness of a personal interview with you, I hope you will indulge the liberty which I now presume to take in addressing a written communication to you, embracing some of those things which I had fondly hoped, would have been the foundation of a mutual interchange of thought between us: But as Providence has laid an embargo upon that distinguished privilege, I must forego, at this time, the pleasure of a verbal relation of those things pertaining to your nation, with which my mind is deeply affected.

Since I have arrived to years of more mature reflection, and become religiously inclined, the writings of the Jewish prophets have won my affections;[9] and the scattered and oppressed condition of that people,[10] has enlisted the

8. Hirschell served as chief rabbi of Great Britain in 1802–42. A traditionalist and vocal opponent of liberal trends in European Jewish life, he excommunicated the British leaders of nascent Reform Judaism. Hyde's effort to engage Hirschell may reflect Mormonism's preference for Orthodox Judaism or, possibly, a lack of awareness about Reform Judaism.

9. Recognizing the ethnic and religious differences between himself and Hirschell, Hyde here seeks to affirm the idea that the Hebrew Bible was written by "Jewish prophets" while stressing his acceptance, as a non-Jew, of these teachings.

10. Hyde believed antisemitism to be a phenomenon at odds with God's will and asserted that "it was by a political power that the Jewish nation was broken down and her subjects dispersed abroad" (Orson Hyde, *A Voice from Jerusalem, or, A Sketch of the Travels and Ministry of Elder Orson Hyde: Missionary of the Church of Jesus Christ of Latter Day Saints, to Germany, Constantinople, and Jerusalem* (Boston: Albert Morgan, 1842), 14–15.

finest sympathies of my heart. Believing therefore, that the words of Hosea the prophet 2.23 [sic],[11] connected with your magnanimity, will prohibit the indulgence of any prejudice in your feelings against the author of this production, in consequence of his not being able, by any existing document or record, to identify himself with your nation.

About nine years ago, a young man [Joseph Smith] with whom I had had a short acquaintance, and one, too, in whom dwelt much wisdom and knowledge—in whose bosom the Almighty had deposited many secrets, laid his hands upon my head, and pronounced these remarkable words: "In due time, thou shalt go to Jerusalem, the land of thy fathers, and be a watchman unto the house of Israel; and by thy hands, shall the Most High do a good work, which shall prepare the way, and greatly facilitate the gathering together of that people."[12] Many other particulars were told me by him, at that time, which I do not write in this letter: But sufficient is written to show that divine appointment is claimed as the main-spring that has sent me forth from the embraces of an affectionate family, and kind friends as well as from the land that gave me birth.[13]

My labors since that period, have been bestowed upon the Gentiles. In various countries, and on both sides of the Atlantic, until, in the early part of March 1840, I retired to my bed one night as usual; and while meditating, and contemplating the field of my future labors, the vision of the Lord, like clouds of light burst into my view. (See Joel, 2.28).[14]

The cities of London, Amsterdam, Constantinople, and Jerusalem, all appeared in succession before me; and the spirit said unto me, "Here are many of the children of Abraham whom I will gather to the land that I gave to their fathers; and here also, is the field of your labors. Take therefore proper credentials from my people, your brethren, and also from the Governor of your State

11. Per the Christian Bible (AV King James Version) the passage in Hosea 2:23 reads: "And I will sow her unto me in the earth; and I will have mercy upon her that had not obtained mercy; and I will say to them which were not my people, Thou art my people; and they shall say, Thou art my God.'" The equivalent lines in the Hebrew Bible appear in Hosea 2:25.

12. This is one of Joseph Smith's prophecies. See Hyde, *A Voice from Jerusalem*, 14–15.

13. Hyde emphasizes that he is not on a proselytizing mission but rather has been tasked with gathering the remnants of the Jewish people in Europe to their ancient homeland in Palestine.

14. Per the Christian Bible (AV King James Version), the passage in Joel 2:28 reads: "And it shall come to pass afterward, that I will pour out my spirit upon all flesh; and your sons and your daughters shall prophesy, your old men shall dream dreams, your young men shall see visions." Hyde's reference exemplifies Mormonism's self-aware tradition as a mystical form of Protestantism, including the use of visions and dreams recounted in the biblical narrative to obtain guidance for the mission of the Mormon church.

with the seal of authority thereon,[15] and go ye forth to the cities which have been shown you, and declare these words unto Judah, and say,

"... Blow ye the trumpet in the land; cry, gather together, and say, assemble yourselves and let us go into the defenced cities. Set up the standard towards Zion—retire stay not; for I will bring evil from the north, and a great destruction. The lion is come up from his thicket, and the destroyer of the Gentiles is on his way—he is gone forth from his place to make thy land desolate, and thy cities shall be laid waste, without an inhabitant.'" [Jer. 4:5-7].[16]

"Speak ye comfortably to Jerusalem, and cry unto her, that her warfare is accomplished—that her iniquity is pardoned for she hath received of the Lord's hand double for all her sins" [Isa. 40:2].[17]

"Let your warning voice be heard among the Gentiles as you pass and call ye upon them in my name for aid and for assistance. With you, it mattereth not whether it be little or much; but to me it belongeth to show favor unto them who show favor unto you."

The vision continued open about six hours, that I did not close my eyes in sleep. In this time, many things were shown unto me which I have never written, neither shall I write them until they are fulfilled in Jerusalem.

It appears, from the prophets, that Jerusalem has none to guide—none to take her by the hand among all the sons whom she hath brought forth and reared: But these two sons are come unto thee! The sons of strangers shall build up thy walls.[18]

---

15. In April 1840, both Joseph Smith and Thomas Carlin (1789–1852), then governor of Illinois, gave Hyde letters of recommendation for his mission. See Hyde, *A Voice from Jerusalem*, iv–v.

16. This text is quoted from the Christian Bible (AV King James Version). In this passage, the prophet Jeremiah speaks about the coming of the Babylonian emperor Nebuchadnezzar (see chapter 36, note 8) who would lay waste to Jerusalem in 586 BCE. Hyde interprets the prophecy in a modern context to suggest that a "destroyer of the Gentiles" will bring destruction to the whole of European Jewry.

17. Hyde quotes the prophecy of Isaiah 40:2 to assure Hirschell and any Jews who might follow him that they may return to the Land of Israel and that God does not require their conversion to Christianity.

18. Hyde's explanation draws on Isaiah 51:18 in the Christian Bible (AV): "There is none to guide her among all the sons whom she hath brought forth; neither is there any that taketh her by the hand of all the sons that she hath brought up." Hyde apparently believed that since the Jewish people had no prophets at this time, it was necessary for him, as an ordained Mormon apostle, to "guide" the Jewish people to Palestine. As a gentile "son of a stranger," he intended to build up Jerusalem's walls (Orson Hyde, extract of a letter from Orson Hyde [Franklin, OH] (July 7, 1840), *Times and Seasons*, August 1840, 156–57 (for an online version, see https://content dm.lib.byu.edu/digital/collection/NCMP1820-1846/id/9338).

Permit me now Rev. Sir, to trouble you with the reflections of a mind that feels completely untrammeled from every party interest, and from every sectarian influence.[19] When I look at the condition of your fathers in the days of David and Solomon, and contrast that with the present condition of their descendants, I am led to exclaim, "How are the mighty fallen!" [2 Sam. 1:27].

Then they possessed a kingdom—a land flowing with milk and honey—then the strong arm of Jehovah taught the surrounding nations to pay tribute and homage to them—then their standard was raised high, their banner floated on every breeze; and under its shade, the sons and daughters of Israel reposed in perfect safety; and the golden letters of light and knowledge were inscribed on its folds. But now, no kingdom—no country—no tribute of gain or honor—no standard—no security: Their scepter has departed! And instead of that light and knowledge which once gave them a transcendent elevation above other nations, the height of their ambition, is now, (with some honorable exceptions) the accumulation of sordid gain, by buying and selling the stale refuse with which their fathers would never have defiled their hands.[20]

Why this wonderful change? Is the God of Abraham, Isaac, and Jacob, a just God? Most certainly he is. If, then, he is a just God, of course, he will mete out and apportion the chastisement or peanlty [sic: penalty], to the magnitude of the offence or crime committed. Allowing, then, the law of Moses to be the standard by which actions are weighed: Were not idolatry and the shedding of innocent blood, the greatest sins which your fathers committed? And was not the penalty inflicted upon them for that transgression, captivity in Babylon seventy years? Have they ever been guilty of idolatry at all since their return from Babylon?[21] No! Have they been guilty of shedding innocent blood, to that extent, since their return that they were, before they were taken captives by Nebuchadnezzar? The Jew says no. Very well: there [sic] will none deny, with any claim upon our credulity, but that the disaster and overthrow that befell the Jewish nation in the days of Vespasian,[22] very far exceeded in severity, in almost

19. Given Mormonism's claim to be a restoration of the original church of Christ, Hyde believed that he was untarnished by the history of Catholic and Protestant antisemitism.

20. Hyde here repeats a common trope about diaspora Jewry—namely, that once exiled from the Land of Israel, the Jewish people became detached from its natural existence and turned to banking and mercantilism, which were among the few economic activities permitted to Jews in premodern Europe.

21. Hyde believed that post-Babylonian Judaism was engaged in the true worship of God.

22. A successful military strategist and leader, the emperor Vespasian (c. 9–79 CE) is credited with consolidating and stabilizing Rome's vast empire. During the first Jewish-Roman War (66–73 CE), he was the general responsible for the capture of Judaea.

every particular, the disaster and ouerthrow [sic] that befel them in the days of Nebuchadnezzar.[23]

Now, then, if God be just, and mete out and apportion the chastisement or penalty to the magnitude of the offence or crime committed, it follows, of course, that your fathers committed some far greater crime subsequent to their return from Babylon, than ever they before committed. Be that crime whatever it may: Know ye, that for it, or because of it, the Roman armies were permitted to crowd their conquests to the heart of your city—burn your temple—kill your men, women and children, and disperse your remnant to the four quarters of the earth. The fiery storm that burst upon your nation at that time, and the traces of blood which they have, ever since, left behind them in their flight and dispersion, together with the recent cursed cruelties inflicted upon them in Damascus[24] and Rhodes,[25] but too plainly declare that the strong imprecation which they uttered on a certain occasion, has been fulfilled upon them to the letter. "Let his blood be on us and on our children" [Matt. 27:25]. If condemning and crucifying Jesus of Nazareth was not the cause of this great evil; what was the cause of it?[26]

Aware that I have written very plainly upon those points that have come within my notice; yet believe me, Sir, when I assure you, that my pen is pointed with friendship, and dipped in the fountain of love and good will towards your nation. The thoughts which it records have proceeded from a heart grateful to the Almighty, that the time has arrived when the day-star of your freedom already begins to dispel the dark and gloomy clouds which have separated you from the favor of your God. Ere long it will be said to you; "Arise, shine, for thy light has come, and the glory of the Lord has risen upon thee" [Isa. 60:1].[27]

23. Hyde believed that the duration of the Jewish people's Roman exile was longer than the Babylonian exile due to the Jews' alleged responsibility for Jesus's crucifixion.

24. In 1840, the Jewish community of Damascus was falsely accused of ritual murder. Known as the Damascus affair, this antisemitic blood libel resulted in attacks on the local synagogue and the imprisonment and torture by the Ottoman officials of Jewish community members. The incident became an international cause célèbre.

25. The Jewish community of Rhodes was also falsely accused of ritual murder in 1840. Local authorities interrogated the chief rabbi about the accusation. It took the intervention of the sultan of Constantinople to denounce the blood libel as false, but the damage had already been done. See Richard A. Freund, *The Archaeology of the Holocaust: Vilna, Rhodes, and Escape Tunnels* (London: Rowman and Littlefield, 2019), 112.

26. Hyde views the Jewish people's exile from the Land of Israel, the rise of antisemitism, and contemporary anti-Jewish hostilities as a result of the Jews' alleged crucifixion of Jesus.

27. Rather than require Jewish belief in Christianity to qualify for a return to Palestine, Hyde indicates the restoration of apostleship in the Church of Jesus Christ of Latter-day Saints has

The morning breaks, the shadows flee,
Lo! Zion's standard is unfurled;
The dawning of a brighter day
Majestic rises on the world.
The Gentile fullness now comes in,
And Israel's blessings are at hand:
Lo! Judah's remnant cleansed from sin
Shall in their promised Canaan stand.[28]

Now, therefore, O ye children of the covenant! Repent of all your backslidings, and begin, as in days of old, to turn to the Lord your God. Arise! Arise! And go out from among the Gentiles; for destruction is coming from the north to lay their cities waste. Jerusalem is thy home. There the God of Abraham will deliver thee. (See Joel 2, 32). There the bending heavens shall reveal thy long-looked-for Messiah in fleecy clouds of light and glory, to execute vengeance upon thine enemies; and lead thee and thy brethren of the ten tribes to sure conquest, and certain victory. Then shall thrones be cast down, and the kingdoms of this world become the kingdoms of our God. Then will they come from the east, west, north and south, and set down in the kingdom of God with Abraham, Isaac, and Jacob. But the children of the kingdom [gentiles] shall be cast out, and the kingdom restored to Israel.[29]

With sentiments of distinguished consideration, I have the honor, Sir,
to subscribe myself,
Your most ob't. servant, ORSON HYDE

---

broken the "curse" upon the Jewish people and presents them with an opportunity to return to the Holy Land.

28. The quote is from "The Morning Breaks," a hymn composed by the Mormon apostle Parley P. Pratt (1807–1857). First published in the inaugural issue of the Millennial Star (May 1840), it was included in the same year in the Mormon church's hymnal. See Parley P. Pratt, "Morning Hymn," Millennial Star, 1:24 (London: May 1840), 5–6 (for an online version, see https://contentdm.lib.byu.edu/digital/collection/MStar/id/8).

29. Rather than heralding the end of the Jewish people, Hyde believed the new messianic kingdom would restore the Jews as an ethnic and national polity in Palestine.

5

"A UNION OF HEART, A UNION OF ACTION"

Isaac Leeser and the Challenge of Jewish Education
in Nineteenth-Century America
(1843)

◇◇

JEFFREY HAUS

Isaac Leeser (1806–1868) was born in the small village of Neunkirchen in Westphalia. At the age of eighteen, he moved to Richmond, Virginia. In 1829, he accepted the office of *hazan* (ritual leader) at Congregation Mickveh Israel in Philadelphia, and he eventually became one of the foremost American Jewish leaders of his day. In addition to his congregational duties, Leeser helped pioneer the creation of an American Jewish institutional infrastructure, through which he intended to improve religious knowledge and unity among American Jews. Along with many other accomplishments, he published English translations of the Jewish liturgy and the Hebrew Bible, founded the Jewish Publication Society of America, and supported Rebecca Gratz's (1781–1869) efforts to establish the first Jewish Sunday school in Philadelphia.[1]

Leeser believed that American Jews could best address the forces that threatened their survival as a small minority by banding together. Toward this end, in April 1843, Leeser launched a monthly periodical, the *Occident and American Jewish Advocate*. Through this journal, Leeser sought to educate American Jews on religious subjects and mitigate the isolation many of them experienced as they followed American expansion to more remote parts of the country. He also hoped that the *Occident* would serve as a bulwark against Christian proselytizing efforts among Jews. The first half of the nineteenth century saw the rise of the secular press in the United States and, with it, a specifically Christian religious press aimed at spreading the gospel. The *Occident* represented a Jewish response to this trend and epitomized Leeser's broader mission of increasing the quality

---

1. See Lance J. Sussman, *Isaac Leeser and the Making of American Judaism* (Detroit, MI: Wayne State University Press, 1995). On the founding of the Hebrew Sunday School specifically, see Dianne Ashton, *Rebecca Gratz: Women and Judaism in Antebellum America* (Detroit, MI: Wayne State University Press, 1997), 144–66.

and reach of Jewish religious education in America. Its pages contained editorials, sermons, and news reports calling attention to events affecting different Jewish communities both in the United States and abroad. By educating and informing American Jews, Leeser worked to connect them to each other and the broader Jewish world.

The unifying bent of Leeser's journal was evident early on. In September 1843, the *Occident* published a missive from the American Jewish publicist Mordecai Manuel Noah (1785–1851) calling for the creation of a Hebrew College that would combine secular and Jewish religious instruction. Leeser chimed in with two subsequent editorials of his own, the first of which is included below. Here, he characterizes the ignorance of religious tradition as a "disease" weakening Jews in the West and one that threatens to cultivate laxity and "indifference" within their ranks. Invoking biblical and liturgical references, Leeser exhorts America's Jews to unite across religious, cultural, and class divisions to combat this problem. As Leeser concludes, no such unity could be achieved without an ability to compromise for the greater good. In this statement, Leeser identifies what continues to be one of the central challenges of American Jewish communal affairs.

◇◇◇

Statement by Isaac Leeser on Jewish Education, November 1843

Source: Isaac Leeser, "Public Religious Education," *Occident* 1, no. 8, (November 1843), 361–64. Klau Library, Hebrew Union College-Jewish Institute of Religion, Cincinnati.

Heshvan 5604, November 1843

Isaac Leeser, "Public Religious Education"

It admits of no doubt, that in a well-organized community the different members composing the same have certain duties to perform towards each other. Individual enterprise, when blessed from above, does not rarely effect a great deal in benefiting the public; but no permanent good will ever result from any undertaking, if the people do not take sufficient interest in it to foster it with their countenance and support. If the body public is sick, and is not sufficiently alive to its disease to apply the necessary remedies, it is in vain that skillful men urge it to guard against the baleful result of the unhealthy state under which it labors; it imagines that all is well, and heeds not the voice of admonition. But once convince it that there are plague-spots visible upon its surface, make it conscious that there is a burdensome sore which requires to be cut out: and you have already half cured the evil which but lately was not thought to exist. For you will soon find that every one who is desirous of life will ask you, "What he is to do in order that he may live?" and what means he is to resort to roll from himself, as one, the fatal disease which afflicts him no less than others. And when this result has been brought about, the progress to a healthy state is very rapid; and reformations have in this manner been produced which in their commencement were ridiculed by the common crowd, and thought beyond the scope of probability by the intelligent even.

Do our readers know that we Israelites,[2] living in England, America, and the West India Islands, are laboring under a fatal disease which has destroyed many a precious soul, and threatens still to carry its havoc much farther than it has done? We allude to the great ignorance which prevails among us with respect to the tenets of our religion, and the language in which the Bible was communicated to our forefathers. There is, we acknowledge, an ardent devotion among most of us to the name of Israel; but unfortunately there is little else to designate the character which this feeling should establish. And how can it be otherwise? Where are our teachers? Where our schools? Our colleges?[3] They have indeed been spoken of, and now and then projected; but they have unfortunately never been well established, and where they do exist, they have not been resorted to by all the classes of the community. We will not deny that of late years some little has been done to promulgate a knowledge of our religion; a few—but few indeed,—elementary books have been written to be used as manuals for beginners in the sacred study;[4] yet all this only proves how deeply seated the disease has been and is to this day, and how much remains to be achieved which has not yet been attempted. The indifference, therefore, which we witness, is in many cases the legitimate result of an ignorance of the duties and doctrines which Jews ought to perform and believe in; and the apostasy of a few by inter-

2. The term "Israelites" was adopted by Jews to defuse charges of dual political loyalty to a Jewish nation and to the land of their birth and gained wide use in nineteenth-century Europe and America. It connoted a purely religious connection among Jews, signaling the compatibility between Judaism and the expectations of modern citizenship.

3. At this date, no rabbinical training school existed in the United States, and the first ordained rabbi had arrived in the country only two years earlier. As Leeser points out, Jewish religious education was localized and haphazard. In 1867, he attempted to fill this gap by creating a rabbinical seminary, Maimonides College, in Philadelphia. The college closed shortly after Leeser's death in 1868.

4. Leeser had written some of these materials—notably, a Jewish catechism used by Rebecca Gratz's Hebrew Sunday School in Philadelphia.

marriages with the gentiles, or the adoption of the belief of the stranger, must be charged to the same cause, that when they sinned they knew not what they should do that they might live, and were perhaps unconscious of the enormity of their transgressions. It must be observed, that he who knows not what his religion demands of him, will hardly make any sacrifices in its favor, nor will he hesitate seeking his own pleasure and advantage, though he may be warned by a fellow-Israelite of the sinfulness of his contemplated course. But make him feel that religion is the life of his soul, and its observance the path to eternal salvation, and he will not readily fall into the snares of death, nor let his feet glide down the path of perdition.

Do our readers feel the force of these remarks? Have they seen with sincere regret the backsliding of some friend or beloved relative? Have they found themselves powerless to recall to the path of religion one for whose happiness they would have sacrificed their life to purchase his peace? Have they themselves experienced the trials of an inward struggle against temptation, and felt the weakness of a reliance based upon worldly wisdom to resist the evil? If so, let them hasten to do something for the promotion of the diffusion of the knowledge which is to banish this deplorable ignorance from themselves and those they love; let them, in the full confidence that the Lord will aid them, endeavor to contribute their share to promote a general religious education among us; for if ignorance is the disease which afflicts us, if want of a knowledge on religious matters is a reproach to us from the gentiles, it is evidently acting only in conformity with common sense to do all we can to scatter this ignorance, and to prove to the world at large that we too are fully alive to the necessity of a religious education.

Individuals can do but very little if they act singly; but if they combine their efforts, call each other in council, draw in the experience of the well-informed and righteous, who love their brothers, and seek not their own gain, the work will go bravely on, and in a little while a general acquaintance with the details of our beautiful system of faith will render its precepts loved and obeyed, instead of the general indifference with which they are now regarded. The disease of Israel, our readers may believe us, is not incurable, though it shows now many symptoms of inveteracy; it requires only the skill of a physician "who is yet in Gilead,"[5] and a readiness on the part of our associates in faith and hope to act unitedly and firmly, to cause healing to come to our wounds, and to bind up the limbs which now throb under the pain of the disease which afflicts them.

5. Leeser here refers to Jeremiah 8:21–22: "Because my people is shattered, I am shattered; I am dejected, seized by desolation. Is there no balm in Gilead? Can no physician be found? Why has healing not yet come to my poor people?"

In this effort every Israelite has a right to look to the other for assistance; and those who have the means would be acting but as good neighbors to open their hand wide and scatter some of the bounty which a kind Father has so abundantly conferred on them. But it must be understood, that the education should not be supplied to the poor only, but to all. The rich require a religious training equally with those in a humble sphere of life, wealth confers no immunity from sorrows, and is no safeguard against temptation. They, therefore, who have received riches at the hand of God, should also hasten to drink from the waters of salvation which He has poured out for all in the words of his law; and only thus can they become properly qualified to enjoy their superfluous wealth, when they know and feel that it is of God's stores they have received it, and that its best enjoyment is to spend it measurably in his service. Indeed, it would be useless to think of establishing schools where the rich and the poor should not both be taught alike; there is between them a bond of humanity; both are liable to sorrow, to disease and death; let both, therefore, have the same bond of joy, the same stay in happiness, the same support in the hour of sorrow, of sickness and of death. This bond is our heaven-born religion, the law of Sinai, the treasure of Israel.[6] Let all, then, be enabled to come and eat of this bread of wisdom;[7] and let us not rest in our efforts, till every child of Jacob be made familiar with its duties, and be rendered firm in faith, to resist, through the aid of a pious instruction, the temptations which on all sides are constantly ready as lures to draw off the sons of Israel from the path which leads to heaven. Other religions, we confess, have their temptations to encounter; but ours in particular is beset with the greatest dangers, as its professors are the few and the afflicted, whilst the followers of the others are the many, and in the enjoyment of all the worldly happiness which their situation allows them. It is, therefore, the more incumbent on all descendants of Abraham to place themselves around the heavenly treasure they have received as its faithful defenders; and to show others not so firm as themselves how they in their turn can become equally firm in the defense of the sacred cause, when the old combatants for the law and its purity have left this earthly life for the abode of the everlasting reward for their righteousness.

We will not prescribe any particular method to effect this good result, but merely to call the attention of others who are acquainted with the wants and the wishes of the people to speak understandingly on the subject; in the full

6. In this instance, Leeser challenges the developing view of charity as flowing in one direction from the rich to the poor. Religious education is not merely a charitable object, he asserts, but a communal responsibility that transcends class. He also argues against the reformist tendencies that had taken root among more prosperous and integrated Jewish communities.

7. A reference to the Passover liturgy that states, "Let all who are hungry come and eat."

persuasion, that the best interests of Israel are safest in the hands of the Jewish community, much more so, indeed, than with those who are self-constituted leaders. But, above all things, union is requisite: a union of heart, a union of action. No one can expect that his views shall alone be adopted; no one can hope that his advice will alone be taken. Therefore, let us have the united efforts of all those who wish well to the house of Jacob; and with the full assurance that divine blessing will not be withheld, we can then look forward to a happier state of religion among us than we now witness.

6

"THAT WE MIGHT BECOME A SHINING EXAMPLE"

The Innovations of David Einhorn's Prayerbook *Olat Tamid* (1858)

◇◇

PHIL M. COHEN

David Einhorn (1809–1879) was born in Dispeck, in the kingdom of Bavaria. He was educated at the *yeshivah* of Fürth and from 1828 to 1834 took classes at universities in Erlangen, Munich, and Wurzburg. There is no evidence that he earned a doctorate at any of these universities, but he generally used the title Rabbi Doctor. Though *yeshivah*-trained, Einhorn fell under the influence of the burgeoning Reform movement in Germany. Reform Judaism emerged initially in Germany and grew out of a number of factors—among them, the Jews' departure from a ghettoized life and emergence into general society in much of western Europe and the influence of Enlightenment ideas upon society generally.

The leaders of the Reform movement grappled with a large number of ideas, but in the main the core of the movement may be characterized as a struggle to understand the role of traditional Jewish doctrine in a newly conceived Judaism that disputed the absolute power *halakhah* had previously maintained in Jewish life. Thus, under consideration, inter alia, were the dietary laws (*kashrut*), the language of prayer, the relationship of contemporary Jews to the Holy Land, second-day observance of Jewish holidays, the role of women, and the permissibility of using instrumental music during religious services.

This new movement attracted a large number of important intellectuals, among them Samuel Holdheim (1806–1860)—with whom Einhorn formed a close relationship and whose pulpit in Mecklengberg-Schwerin he occupied after Holdheim's departure in 1847. In 1851 Einhorn was invited to serve as the rabbi in the Reform synagogue in Pest, Hungary, but his views were considered so radical by the government that it closed the synagogue two months after his arrival. Einhorn remained in Pest until his immigration to the United States in 1855. In his time in Pest he wrote his only major work of theology, *Das Prinzip des Mosaismus* (The principle of Mosaism; 1854). Upon his arrival in America, he assumed the pulpit of Har Sinai Congregation in Baltimore, Maryland.

Almost immediately after his arrival, Einhorn found himself in conflict with

Isaac Mayer Wise (1819–1900), who had recently accepted a lifetime appointment as rabbi of the Bene Yeshurun Congregation in Cincinnati. A rabbinical synod convened by Wise and Isaac Leeser (1806–1868), a champion of modern Orthodox Judaism, was held in Cleveland. It attempted to establish a platform of ideas upon which all of American Jewry could agree. One plank established the Talmud as one of the eternal foundations of Judaism—an idea Einhorn found abhorrent, believing instead that history had taken Reform Jews beyond the Talmud's protective shell. Thus the conference concluded with Einhorn, who had been in the country only a matter of weeks, quarreling with Wise, an adversarial relationship that would continue until Einhorn's death in 1879.

Another conflict Einhorn entered into concerned slavery. In 1861 Morris Jacob Raphall (1798–1868) published an article titled "Bible View of Slavery" in the *New York Herald*, explaining that although the Hebrew Bible recognized and countenanced slavery, biblical law and American law differed significantly, therefore the bible could not be used to endorse slavery in the American South or its abolition.[1] Einhorn vociferously countered Raphall, asserting that "it has ever been a strategy of the advocate of a bad cause to take refuge from the spirit of the Bible to its letter."[2] Despite local opposition, Einhorn continued to write and openly preach the idea that Judaism does not support slavery. He further asserted he would resign his pulpit should Maryland withdraw from the Union. When a pro-secession riot erupted on April 19, 1861, an angry and violent mob threatened pro-Union community members. Fear that Einhorn's life was in danger and rumors he might be tarred and feathered prompted loyal members of his congregation to spirit him and his family out of the city. Einhorn next settled in Philadelphia, where he became rabbi of Reform Congregation Keneseth Israel (1861–66). Thereafter, he left Philadelphia for New York City to assume the pulpit of the newly established Congregation Adath Yeshurun (1866–79), where he served as rabbi until his death.

In the nineteenth century, liberal-minded Jews in Europe began composing prayer books reflective of the spirit of the newly developing Reform movement. The first such prayer book appeared in 1816. These evinced in liturgy theological ideas that were under discussion throughout these early years. Such works appeared in the nineteenth century, many reflecting the ritualistic norms of the

1. See Morris Jacob Raphall, "'Bible View of Slavery,' a Discourse by Rabbi Morris Jacob Raphall at Bnai Jeshurun, New York on the National Fast Day, January 4, 1861," in *A Documentary History of the Jews in the United States, 1654–1875*, ed. Morris U. Schappes, rev. ed. (New York: Citadel Press, 1952), 405–18.

2. Quoted in Bertram W. Korn, *American Jewry and the Civil War*, reprint (repr., New York: Atheneum Press, 1951), 20.

region for which they had been composed, though they had a recognizable common core.[3] Einhorn brought this literary form with him to America, creating in 1858 a prayer book that reflected his own theology, a fervent messianism in which Jews in the diaspora are God's messengers. Titled *Olat Tamid* (Hebrew for "Daily Whole Offering"), the prayer book generally conformed to the European model and was used by several American congregations. What differentiates Einhorn's work from its predecessors is the large number of original prayers. About half of the book consists of readings composed by Einhorn. The original text was followed by two English translations: in 1872, Einhorn translated the text with emendations by Bernhard Felsenthal, and in 1896, Einhorn's son-in-law Rabbi Emil G. Hirsch (1851–1923) of Chicago's Sinai Congregation published a second English translation of the prayer book. The text reprinted below, Einhorn's reading for Shabbat Shekalim, demonstrates his theology at work and exemplifies his attempt to take a traditional Jewish observance and reframe its meaning for modern times.

◇◇

David Einhorn's Prayer for the Sabbath Service of Parashat Shekalim, 1858

Source: David Einhorn, *Olat Tamid: Gebetbuch für Israelitische Reform-Gemeinden* (Baltimore, MD: C. W. Schneidereith, 1858), 32–33. Trans. Phil M. Cohen.

Prayer for the Sabbath of Parashat Shekalim[4]

With pious feelings, oh God, do we remember today Your word proclaimed through Moses, that everyone in Israel, rich and poor alike, is obligated to offer his half *shekel* in the sanctuary in order to support the needs of the community as a rescue of his soul.[5] With pride and jubilation we also remember the pious will-

3. See Jakob J. Petuchowski, *Prayerbook Reform in Europe: The Liturgy of European Liberl and Reform Judaism* (New York: World Union for Progressive Judaism, 1968), chapters 1, 3, and 4.

4. The title of the prayer refers to one of the four special Sabbaths that occur in the Jewish calendar: Shabbat Shekalim, Shabbat Zakhor, Shabbat Parah, and Shabbat Hahodesh. According to biblical tradition, it was obligatory for adult males to bring a half shekel, worth perhaps two day's labor, to the ancient Temple in Jerusalem. The money, collected on or before the onset of the month of Adar, was used for Temple upkeep. It is noteworthy that Einhorn expands this notion to include "the needs of the community." He uses this special Sabbath to connect Israel's premodern history to his own day and as a metaphor for the life and mission of contemporary Jews.

5. The reference is to the beginning of the Torah portion Ki Tisa (Exod. 30:11–34:35), in which God describes the tabernacle to Moses, the ancient Israelites worship the golden calf, and

ingness with which Israel always fulfilled this Your holy will. Not only when the holy Temple[6] still stood, given annually shortly before the first of the month,[7] when our nation [Stamm][8] celebrated the memory of its birth as a godly and priestly people, [but also] when new offerings for the religious salvation for the entire community [Gesamtheit] were contributed. As well, during the course of the many, many centuries of our dispersion throughout all parts of the earth did your commandment find a powerful echo in our midst! Not merely a half-shekel was offered in these countless years of great difficulty; rather, the sacrifice included enduring unflaggingly the bitterest decline of [our] life, in the willing surrender of property and blood for the preservation of Your teaching. Allow us, oh Lord, their fortunate descendants, this unprecedented spirit of sacrifice of our forebears that we might become a shining example and a most solemn portent![9] Grant that every member of our community, out of gratitude for Your grace which has allowed us to live to see a better day, offer with joy a much smaller sacrifice that the present requires, because of the advancement of the times, Jeshurun,[10] at the time that it benefits from the fat of the land, will not forget that for which our ancestors renounced all earthly good and the walls were pierced by hostile armies.[11] One day we must all be brought before Your majestic throne of judgment and our deeds counted and weighed. Allow then the gifts which we have brought for the glorification of Your Name not be deemed insufficient. Amen.

Moses subsequently pleads with God to forgive the people. In citing the biblical phrase "rescue of his soul," Einhorn refers to the power of expiation and atonement.

6. According to the Hebrew Bible, the Temple in ancient Jerusalem included a shrine for the Ark and priestly offerings to God. It served as the primary edifice for the Jews' worship of God until 70 CE. The biblical narrative relates that King Solomon, who ruled ancient Israel from approximately 972 to 931 BCE, built the First Temple. It was subsequently destroyed in 586 BCE by the Babylonian king Nebuchadnezzar (634–562 BCE). Cyrus the Great of Persia (c. 600–529 BCE), who founded the vast Achaemenid empire (c. 550–330 BCE), supposedly authorized reconstruction of the temple in 538 BCE, and the Second Temple stood until it was destroyed in 70 CE, during the Roman siege of Jerusalem.

7. The month of Adar is the twelfth month of the Hebrew calendar, corresponding roughly to the month of March in the civil calendar.

8. Einhorn's use of the German word Stamm, which may be translated as "nation" or "tribe," signified his belief that the Jews are an ethnos or religious civilization.

9. Einhorn's prayer asserts historical continuity not only between ancient and modern Jewish history, but also with respect to the American Jewish experience.

10. A poetic term used in the Hebrew Bible to refer to Israel.

11. The reference here is to the destruction of the ancient Temple in Jerusalem by imperial Rome (see note 6). The worshipper is adjured to honor the suffering of ancient Israel and not to let the past fade from modern memory.

7

"A JEWISH CHAPLAIN FOR THE CAMERON DRAGOONS"

The Real Chaplaincy Controversy of the Civil War
(1861)

◇◇

ADAM D. MENDELSOHN

For two brief moments during the Civil War (1861–65), Jews qua Jews became the focus of national attention. The first moment was in the fall of 1861. In October of that year, Arnold Fischel (1830–1894)—a minister at Congregation Shearith Israel in New York City, one of the country's most distinguished synagogues—applied for the vacant position of regimental chaplain of the 5th Pennsylvania Cavalry. When he was rebuffed by Secretary of War Simon Cameron (1799–1889) on the basis of his religion, the case became a cause célèbre in the pages of Horace Greeley's (1811–1872) crusading *New-York Tribune*. And almost exactly a year later, in December 1862, General Ulysses S. Grant (1822–1885) issued an extraordinary military order banishing "Jews as a class" from the vast swathe of territory under his command.

These two moments have often been understood as dyadic wartime tests of the U.S. commitment to core principles of religious and civic equality in the midst of a national crisis. While the second of these episodes has been properly revisited—expertly explained by Jonathan D. Sarna in *When General Grant Expelled the Jews* (2012)—the "chaplaincy controversy," as the first episode has been named, becomes murkier upon closer inspection.

General Order 15, issued in May 1861, granted regimental officers in the Union Army the authority to elect a chaplain of their choosing to minister to the men of their units but limited the chaplaincy to "regularly ordained minister[s] of some Christian denomination." This order was later entrenched by Congressional statute. Though there was precedent for the chaplaincy to be restricted—only after the Mexican-American War (1846–48) was eligibility expanded to include Catholic clergy—such restrictions had broader implications during the Civil War. The Union Army depended on mass enlistment, filling its ever-growing ranks with volunteers recruited from natives and newcomers alike—including thousands of Jews who had flocked to the United States in the two decades before the war. To accept state-sanctioned discrimination might set a pattern that would persist long after the conflict was over.

One such regiment, the 5th Pennsylvania Cavalry, has been heralded for challenging this law. According to the version in the *New-York Tribune*—excerpted below—a "large portion of the rank and file" of this Philadelphia-raised regiment were Jews, as was also the case with its officers. These men had already seen their first regimental chaplain depart when Michael M. Allen (1830–1907) resigned, shortly after the law took effect. Now they elected Fischel as their chaplain. Whereas Allen was not an ordained minister, all that Fischel was lacking in the eyes of the law were the religious convictions of a Christian. Here, in other words, was an ideal test case. Or so the story goes.

When Fischel's application to the War Department was predictably rejected on the basis of his religion, Jewish organizations launched a public campaign to change the Congressional statute. They succeeded, after a sustained period of lobbying, in replacing an unjust law with one that opened the chaplaincy to all.

A second newspaper clipping—from the Baltimore *Sun*—below suggests a less familiar version of this same story. Colonel Max Friedman (1825–1901), traditionally cast as one of the heroes of the chaplaincy controversy, "called upon us yesterday to say that his regiment had never expressed a desire to have a Jewish chaplain, and that there are not more than twenty Jews in his whole corps, and that the whole story, as published in the *Tribune*, is without foundation."

Friedman's version is closer to reality than the conventional narrative. Only eighteen soldiers and officers (out of roughly seven hundred men) in the regiment were Jewish, and there is no evidence that they sought to appoint Fischel as their chaplain. Fischel appears to have acted entirely on his own accord when writing to the secretary of war: his contract with his synagogue was expiring in a matter of weeks, and he was in search of work.

Why was Friedman so eager to dispute the version in Greeley's newspaper? Far from being a heroic figure seeking to challenge an unjust law, Friedman was likely motivated by more prosaic concerns. There is some evidence to suggest that he had recruited phantom soldiers to pad his regimental rolls and appointed Allen, who had earned his living selling liquor before the war, to corner the profitable market of wine and whiskey sales to his troops. He had no desire to attract unwanted attention to him and his regiment, and he acted quickly to stifle the story.

A straightforward story is thus instead revealed to be a tangled tale. Allen, Fischel, and Friedman, in other words, seem to have been less fearless advocates of religious freedom than fictions of the *Tribune*'s imagination and our desire for a neat narrative. The truer tale does not diminish the justice and worthiness of the cause and course pursued by aggrieved Jewish groups. But it does reveal a past at once messier and more interesting than the received version.

◇◇

Letter from Simon Cameron to Arnold Fischel of October 23, 1861, *New-York Tribune*, October 31, 1861

> Source: Letter from Secretary of War Simon Cameron to Arnold Fischel, *New-York Tribune*, October 31, 1861, 4.

The following letter from the Secretary of War relates to a subject which we have already had occasion briefly to discuss:

"WAR DEPARTMENT, OCT. 23, 1861.

Rev. A. Fischel,[1] *Rabbi Jewish Synagogue, No. 5 Carroll-place, New-York.*

SIR: Your communication of the 17th inst., inclosing a letter from the Hon. F.A. Conkling,[2] in reference to the Chaplaincy of the Cameron Dragoons, has been received.

In reply, you are respectfully informed that by the 9th section of the act of Congress, approved July 22, 1861, it is provided that the Chaplain appointed by "the vote of the field officers and company commanders must be a regular ordained minister of some Christian denomination." A like provision, also, is made in the 7th section of the act of Congress, approved Aug 3, 1861. Were it not for the impediment thus directly created by the provision of these two acts, the department would have taken your application into its favourable consideration.

I have the honor to be, very respectfully,

SIMON CAMERON,[3] Secretary of War."

1. Hired in 1856 by Shearith Israel, the prominent New York synagogue, to serve as "lecturer and teacher," Arnold Fischel was one of several religious functionaries lured across the Atlantic by the offer of better pay. After his rebuff from the U.S. secretary of war (and the decision of his congregation not to renew his contract), Fischel worked for several unsatisfactory months as chaplain to Jewish soldiers around Washington. By the end of 1862 he was back in Europe.

2. Frederick Conkling represented New York's sixth district in Congress during the Civil War. In 1861 he served briefly as colonel of the 84th Regiment of New York Volunteers and thus may have had firsthand experience with appointing a regimental chaplain.

3. A longtime senator from Pennsylvania prior to the war and a contender for the leadership of the Republican party before the 1860 election, Simon Cameron (1799–1889) was one of the less successful members of what the historian Doris Kearns Goodwin has dubbed Abraham Lincoln's (1809–1865) "team of rivals" cabinet (*Team of Rivals: The Political Genius of Abraham Lincoln*

—What renders this case one of peculiar hardship is that the officers of the Cameron Dragoons[4] are generally, if not altogether, Jews, while a large portion of the rank and file are of that religion. There are also thousands of Jews in the army, and it is very desirable that such of them as may be sick, wounded, or dying in the hospitals should be able to procure the attendance of a minister of their own faith. We presume that on the meeting of Congress the unconstitutional and unwise provision of the act of June last will be rescinded.

"The Jewish Chaplain," *Sun*,[5] November 6, 1861

Source: "The Jewish Chaplain," *Sun*, November 6, 1861, 1.

THE JEWISH CHAPLAIN—We copied an article from the *New York Tribune*, a few days ago, on the subject of a Jewish Chaplain for the Cameron Dragoons, which, according to that paper, were mostly composed of members of the Jewish faith, and had expressed a desire to have their own chaplain, which drew forth a letter from the Secretary of War, showing the impossibility of such an arrangement— We are inclined to think that the whole matter is a hoax, and that the Secretary has been imposed upon by some person not connected with the regiment.

Col. Freidman [*sic*],[6] of the Cameron Dragoons, called upon us yesterday to say that his regiment had never expressed a desire to have a Jewish chaplain, and that there are not more than twenty Jews in his whole corps, and that the whole story, as published in the *Tribune*, is without foundation.—*Wash Rep.*

[New York: Simon and Schuster, 2006]). Dogged by rumors of graft and questions of his competence, Cameron was dismissed in January 1862 from the vital position of secretary of war and exiled to become minister to Russia.

4. Named in honor of Simon Cameron and raised in Philadelphia, the 5th Pennsylvania Cavalry had an undistinguished war record. According to one chronicler, the unit "achieved a record of failures, defeats, setbacks, and disasters probably unequalled by any other regiment, Federal or Confederate" (Edward J. Longacre, "The Most Inept Regiment," *Civil War Times Illustrated* 8, no. 7 [November 1969], 4).

5. Founded in 1837 by Arunah S. Abell (1806–1888) in Baltimore, Maryland, the *Sun* was originally a penny paper with a Jacksonian orientation and working-class readership. The Abell family owned and controlled the newspaper until 1910.

6. Not much is known about Max Friedman (1825–1901), the Bavarian-born colonel who was instrumental in raising the Cameron Dragoons and served as its first commanding officer. Friedman had some military experience from his membership in the prewar Pennsylvania militia, but this was likely of limited use when commanding a cavalry regiment. Whether because of stress, scandal, or ill health, Friedman resigned his commission and left the army in March 1862.

8

"IN THE STRICTEST JEWISH ORTHODOX STILE"

A Contract between Isaac Wolf and Congregation Etz Hayim
(Pittsburgh, PA)
(1864)

◇◇

SHARI RABIN

Between 1820 and 1880, the American Jewish community expanded
dramatically in terms of numbers and geographic spread. A mass migration
from German-speaking lands fueled an increase in the number of American
Jews from around 3,000 to 250,000. At a time when European countries were debating emancipation and the granting of citizenship rights to Jews, the United
States proved an alluring option, especially for young single men in search of
economic opportunity. By 1848, the U.S. pursuit of continental dominance had
largely been achieved, leading to the rapid development of new cities and towns.
Central European Jewish immigrants, many of them working as peddlers and
merchants, joined this move westward, away from the eastern port cities where
Jews had previously lived.

Under the American system of voluntarism, religious life was not funded
or overseen by the government. As they settled in new places, Jews of diverse
backgrounds and religious preferences had to put their own efforts and funds
into the creation of Jewish institutions, which came to include boardinghouses,
benevolent societies, fraternal lodges, and congregations. For instance, Pittsburgh, Pennsylvania, was by the 1850s a bustling midwestern city, thanks in part
to its location on a number of important steamboat and railroad lines and the
development of nearby oil fields. There were Jews in Pittsburgh at least as far
back as 1839, but the first congregation, Shaare Shamayim (Gates of Heaven),
was not founded until 1848.

Abraham Rice (c. 1800–1862), the first European rabbi to settle in the United
States, did not arrive until 1840, and only a small number followed his lead
before the Civil War. To enable worship and the proper observance of Jewish practices such as kosher slaughter and Jewish burial, most congregations
hired nonordained functionaries, usually referred to as *hazanim*, prayer leaders
who frequently functioned as religious ministers. In Pittsburgh, conflicts over

whether or not to retain the *hazan* led in 1855 to the creation of a new congregation, Rodef Shalom (Pursuit of Peace), but the city was too small to support two congregations, and they merged in 1860.

Among popular rabbis and Jewish communal leaders like Isaac Leeser (1806–1868) of Philadelphia and Isaac Mayer Wise (1819–1900) of Cincinnati, debates raged in this period over efforts to modernize Judaism through religious reforms, including mixed seating of men and women, family pews, and the abolition of the second day of festivals. In 1863, soon after a visit by Wise to Pittsburgh, Rodef Shalom voted to embrace some reforms. Congregation Etz Hayim (Tree of Life), an orthodox synagogue with a large Polish contingent, was created in protest. In October 2018, the Tree of Life synagogue, now known by the English translation of its name, was targeted by an antisemitic white nationalist who murdered eleven of its members.[1] Before this tragic event, however, it had a long and rich history as a site where generations of Pittsburgh Jews worked to enact an American Judaism.

The document reprinted here is an employment agreement between Etz Hayim and its first *hazan*, Isaac Wolf (spelled "Wollf" in the document; dates unknown), who was hired in 1864—as the Civil War raged—to serve the congregation "in the strictest orthodox stile [*sic*]." With no government involvement or denominational infrastructure in place, the hiring of religious functionaries was ad hoc, unregulated, and subject to the norms of American employment law. Leaders like Leeser, Wise, and New York's Samuel Myer Isaacs (1804–1878) used their personal correspondence and their newspapers to assist in making employment matches, but tensions flourished anyway. Congregations worried about fraudulent or unscrupulous ministers, while *hazanim* complained of exploitation. Contracts were one way to ameliorate these concerns.[2]

It is unclear how Etz Hayim came to hire Wolf, but the contract shows that it had the upper hand. His tasks went well beyond that of a service leader, including those of kosher meat slaughterer, janitor, marriage officiant, and grave digger. The contract guaranteed employment for only one year, asserted lay control over Wolf's activities, and stipulated that he could be fired at any time for a breach of morality, Jewish law, and/or honor, however construed by the congregants. His salary of $400, plus ritual fees, was one-fifth of what neighboring Rodef Shalom offered its minister.

1. Campbell Robertson, Christopher Mele, and Sabrina Tavernise, "Rampage Kills 11 at a Synagogue in Pittsburgh," *New York Times* (October 27, 2018), 1.

2. Shari Rabin, "Working Jews: Hazanim and the Labor of Religion in Nineteenth-Century America," *Religion and American Culture* 25, no. 2 (Summer 2015), 178–217.

Little information about Wolf is available, but congregational minutes indicate that he had resigned the position by January 1865, less than seven months after signing the contract. Eventually, those concerned about the challenges of religious leadership, among other issues, would found Hebrew Union College in Cincinnati, in 1875, and the Central Conference of American Rabbis, in 1889. Although in 1885 Pittsburgh became famous as the setting for Reform Judaism's pivotal Pittsburgh Platform, which called for the modernization and Americanization of Jewish practice and observance, Etz Hayim would continue to reject Reform Judaism, eventually becoming aligned with the Conservative movement.

◇◇

Contract of Employment between Isaac Wolf and Congregation Etz Hayim (Pittsburgh, PA), 1864

Source: Minutes Book, 16, Folder 2, Congregation Tree of Life (Pittsburgh, PA) Records, 1858–1917, MS-531, the Jacob Rader Marcus Center of the American Jewish Archives, Cincinnati.

ARTICLES OF AGREEMENT.

Made this day between the *Kahal*[3] Etz Hayim of the first part and Mr. Isaac Wollf on the second part.

Firstly, Mr. Isaac Wollf agrees to act in the capacity of *Chasan*,[4] *Shochet*,[5] *Shamas*[6] and *Baal Koreh*[7] in the strictest Jewish orthodox stile [sic].[8]

Secondly, Mr. Wollf agrees to read all prayers in the Synagogue excepting those which the President may allow to be read by any other.

Thirdly, As *Shochet* Wollf agrees to kill [at the] butchers[—]such one which the *Kahal* have selected[—] according to Jewish Rites in the following months[:] May June July + August and September three times and the other months twice a week[;] further to cleanse the meat vaines [sic] in the market house from five to

3. Meaning "community," often used to refer to a Jewish congregation.

4. A *chasan* (also spelled *hazan*) is a Jewish prayer leader or precentor who is trained and practiced in leading a congregation in worship. More generally, the term may also refer to a nonrabbinic religious functionary.

5. A kosher meat slaughterer.

6. A beadle (*shamash* in Hebrew) is someone who assists in the running of synagogue services.

7. The individual responsible for reading the lectionary portions of the Torah in synagogue worship services.

8. The many errors in spelling and grammar indicate that the contract's author was not a native English speaker.

seven in the months of May June July and August, from half past six to half past eight in the months September October Marz[9] and April and from six to eight in the months of November and December January + February A.M. O'clock[;] and whenever the meat is brought to his dwelling house further to kill all fowls in his house in summer time from six to eight and winter from five to six P.M. o'clock[. A]nd in case should Mr. Wollf live [at] such a distance that it is not convenient for members or seat holders to bring such Fowls to his house, it shall be the duty if requested from members and seat holders to call at their residences, to kill all fowls which is laid before him.

Fourth, To act as *Baal Koreh* in all its branches.

Fifth, As *Shamas* Mr. Wollf agrees to collect all moneys belonging to *Kahal* whenever he receives the bills from the Treasurer and [as] soon as said money [is] collected to hand the same to the Treasurer[;] further whenever requested by the president to carry invitations to each member for the meetings of *Kahal*[;] also to see that the synagogue shall be kept in good cleaning orders and in winter that fire be made in the stove and the bill for such charges do hand to the President[;] further to call the *mizvas*[10] and be present by opening and closing the synagogue and when requested by the President for the keys to give the same at once.

Sixth, Mr. Wolff further agrees to unite each couple that is Bride + Groom whenever permission by the President is granted[. I]n case of death in the familie [*sic*] of members or seat holders when requested to have somebody to sitt [*sic*] and watch by a corpse and do the diging [*sic*] of a grave[;] further, by the *shivah*[11] mornings and evenings when requested to attend to *minyan*[12] excepting only that it interferes with noteworthy duties.

Seventh, Mr. Wolff agrees to visit the burial ground at least every two months and to see whether everything is in good order.

Eighth, Mr. Wolff agrees to make a list on the 15th of Schwat[13] so as to see how many matzos [*sic*] shall be baked for Pesach[;][14] also do have the manage-

9. The German and Yiddish term for the month of March.

10. This refers to the practice of auctioning off liturgical honors to supplement congregational funds.

11. The seven-day period after a death marked by gatherings and communal prayer at the home of the mourners.

12. A prayer quorum, traditionally of ten adult Jewish men.

13. The fifth Hebrew month, according to the lunisolar calendar, usually corresponding to January or February of the civil calendar.

14. "Matzos" (*matzot*) are unleavened bread consumed during the spring holiday of Passover (Pesach).

ment of the same and do see that the matzos are baked according to the Jewish rites and so send to the dwelling houses.

Ninth. Mr. Wollf agrees whenever he morally[,] according to the Jewish Law[,] leaves the Path of Duty, and that he so far forgot himself what belongs to the honor of his situation he must leave at once without any compensation.

Tenth, The congregation Etz Hayim agrees to pay four hundred dollars per annum[,][15] Thirty three dollars and thirty three cents per month by order from the President [or] the treasurer[;] further the congregation will see that Mr. Wollf shall receive from the Butcher for the killing of beef cattle fifty cents per head also for sheep, calfs etc. Ten or twelve and ½ cents per head[;] further for uniting bride + groom not less than five dollars[;] for watching by a corpse not less than one dollar, for attending to everything by a corpse, not less than two dollars[. A]lso for every pound of matzos what goes through the supervision of Mr. Wollf he shall receive one cent[;] he shall further receive five percent for all mony [sic] collected by him.

Eleventh, This agreement comencing [sic] on the Twelfth of August Eighteen Hundred and Sixty Four, and shall expire on the twelfth of August Eighteen hundred and sixty five.

This agreement was read by both parties and found correct and in the first part the Ez Chayim congregation binds herself through the signature of the Gentleman and the second part through the handwriting of his signature which will be considered binding.

Pittsburgh, August 19th, 1864

Isaac Wolf

15. In present-day money, equivalent to roughly $6,000 per year. The highest paid rabbinic salary of the day was the lifetime contract of $8,000 per year (over $100,000 today) reportedly offered to Isaac Mayer Wise (1819–1900) in 1873 by Anshe Chesed of New York City.

9

"SOLICITED ON THE GROUND OF HUMANITY, RECOGNIZED AS A NATIONAL DUTY"

The Board of Delegates of American Israelites and the Rise of American Jewish Politics (1872-73)

◇◇

SETH KORELITZ

Created in 1859, the Board of Delegates of American Israelites was American Jewry's first political organization. The Board's founders were spurred, in part, by disquiet resulting from the Mortara Affair of 1858—an infamous controversy regarding Edgardo Mortara (1851–1940), an Italian Jewish child secretly baptized by his nursemaid and subsequently kidnapped by the Catholic Church. The Board's constitution called for the organization to gather statistics on American Jews, serve as a nonbinding arbitrator for its constituent congregations, promote religious education, protect Jewish civil and religious rights at home and abroad, and communicate with similar Jewish bodies throughout the world. Notwithstanding the Board's quasi-democratic framework and pledge to represent "every congregation of Israelites in the United States," it was, in reality, a largely self-appointed body of elite Jewish communal leaders.[1] It never developed a robust mechanism for enfranchising the constituency on whose behalf it claimed to speak. Throughout the 1860s and 1870s, however, the Board honored its commitment to keep "a watchful eye on occurrences at home and abroad" and called attention to events that threatened the "civil and religious rights of Israelites."[2] The Board's efforts emphasized a range of domestic civil rights issues (for example, challenging General Ulysses S. Grant's Civil War order expelling Jews from his jurisdiction due to alleged smuggling activity and lobbying for the appointment of Jewish chaplains in the U.S. military) and communal needs (such as helping establish Philadelphia's Maimonides College and

1. *Constitution and By-Laws of the Board of Delegates of American Israelites* (New York: Jewish Messenger, 1860), 4, series I: Records, 1859–77, box 1, folder 3: By-Laws and Constitution (drafts and five printed versions), undated, 1860, American Jewish Historical Society, New York City.

2. Ibid.

the Lower East Side's Hebrew Technical Institute and Educational Alliance).[3] In general, however, the Board had an international focus, and it became deeply involved in the struggle for Jewish emancipation and civil liberties abroad, particularly in Morocco, Turkey, Romania, and Ottoman Palestine. By the time the Union of American Hebrew Congregations absorbed it in 1878, the Board had established a durable albeit self-limiting style of American Jewish politics.

A long-standing interpretation of America as God's new Promised Land helped shape the Board's choice of tactics: as the first nation to be founded on principles of liberty and equality, the United States had a sacred duty to defend liberty and champion the oppressed. The Board appealed to humanitarian values when securing the rights of Jews at home and when lobbying the U.S. government to intervene on behalf of Jews abroad (and, occasionally, even in addressing foreign powers directly). It was America's mission, the Board constantly pointed out, to assist those suffering under the unmodern oppression of religious prejudice.

Yet the Board was also hesitant to take stands that seemed too sectarian. American Jews wanted to be accepted as Americans, and lobbying for the rights of foreign Jews could easily have been construed as their being more concerned with their relations to foreign Jews than with their responsibilities as Americans. By using the idea of mission and claiming that American ideals obligated action, Jews were able to simultaneously defend Jewish rights and claim that they were acting according to American values. This is not to say that the Board relied solely on the mission idea to achieve its goals. Its tactic was to justify U.S. action with the rhetoric of mission, but to secure American involvement by lobbying Congress and the executive branch. This use of rhetoric backed by pressure constituted the Board's method in politics.

Judged by later standards, the Board of Delegates' nineteenth-century tactics may appear timid. The Board made little or no use of the press to advocate for its causes, nor generally of the wealth of its supporters to influence decision

---

3. In 1867, the Board of Delegates helped establish Maimonides College. After merging in 1878 with the Union of American Hebrew Congregations, the organization was renamed the Board of Delegates of Civil and Religious Rights. Thereafter, it helped create the Hebrew Technical Institute in 1883 and the Educational Alliance in 1889. The Board of Delegates was officially dissolved as an entity in 1925. See Joseph Buchler, "The Struggle for Unity: Attempts at Union in American Jewish Life, 1654–1868," *American Jewish Archives* 20, no. 1 (June 1949), 32; Allan Tarshish, "The Board of Delegates of American Israelites, 1859–1878," *Publications of the American Jewish Historical Society* 49, no. 1 (September 1959), 22–24; Albert Isaac Slomovitz, *The Fighting Rabbis: Jewish Military Chaplains and American History* (New York: New York University Press, 1999), 16–18.

makers. Rarely did it raise the specter of a Jewish vote.[4] Instead, the Board referred to its concerns as consonant with true American values and maintained a posture least likely to make its causes seem like peculiarly Jewish ones. At the same, it also engaged in sophisticated political tactics. It lobbied Congress and used personal relationships with members of Congress on behalf of persecuted Jewish communities. It asked the U.S. government to pressure foreign regimes and even attempted to have its counterparts in Europe (especially the Alliance Israélite Universelle and the Board of Deputies of British Jews) lobby their respective governments. The most common practice of the Board was to establish contacts with key politicians and impress on them the congruence of the Board's wishes with American values. Given the context in which it operated, it is remarkable that the Board, essentially a voluntary undertaking propelled by a small group of committed activists, so successfully elevated nationwide discourse concerning Jewish affairs while creating a nimble framework to advocate for Jewish interests and causes.

As the American Jewish community grew in size and wealth, so did its potential to influence Washington and the country. The waves of mass migration to the United States from eastern and southern Europe, which brought some 2.5 million new Jewish arrivals to the so-called *goldene medine* (Yiddish for "golden land") between 1880 and 1924, ultimately reshaped American Jewish life and American society writ large. In the turbulent decades of the late nineteenth and early twentieth centuries, however, when American Jewry's cultural and political capital was still raw and unformed, its communal leadership largely adhered to the pattern pioneered by the Board of Delegates. In 1906, for example, Jacob Schiff (1847–1920), Louis Marshall (1856–1929), and other elite New York Jewish figures, following in the Board's footsteps, founded the American Jewish Committee (AJC). Even as the AJC introduced a new generation of American Jewish leaders, it bore the imprint of the Board's high-minded sensibility and cautious approach to domestic and international issues of Jewish concern. The AJC, too, was characterized by a decorous public profile, high reliance on personal contacts with non-Jewish power brokers, and public avowal of the congruence of Jewish causes and American values. Not until World War I was this model of elite political behavior seriously challenged. During the sea change in American Jewish life, Yiddish-speaking immigrant groups and leaders, middle-class Jewish women's organizations, and other nonelite forces called for the

4. For a useful discussion of Jews and American politics in the early nineteenth century, see Jonathan D. Sarna, *Jacksonian Jew: The Two Worlds of Mordecai Noah* (New York: Holmes and Meier, 1981), 4–5, 43–47, 81–90, 99–105, and 148–52.

nationwide democratization of Jewish public life. The challenge to the AJC and American Jewry's elite establishment climaxed in 1918 with the American Jewish Congress, a wartime plenary of 367 delegates representing eighty-seven cities across the country, which signaled a new era in organizational Jewish politics.

◇◇

Memorial of the Board of Delegates to Grand Duke Alexis, December 1, 1871

Source: "Memorial of the Board of Delegates to Grand Duke Alexis" (December 1, 1871), Board of Delegates of American Israelites Records, I-2, box 2, folder 12, Correspondence, A, Oversized Materials, American Jewish Historical Society, New York City. Emphasis in the original.

To His Imperial Highness, The Grand Duke Alexis,[5]

In common with other bodies of Citizens of the United States the *Board of Delegates of Israelites* proffer your Imperial Highness a Cordial welcome to these shores.

Requiring of the Emperor of Russia, your august father,[6] a sovereign who has devoted himself to the welfare of his people and under whose reign the *blessings of liberty* have been extended to millions and the conditions of our brethren in faith has perceptibly improved, we pay our respects to you as the representative of the Czar and endowed by Heaven with great opportunities for the good of Mankind.

The *progress* made in the imperial dominions since the accession of the good Czar, your father, encourages us to hope that every vestige of discrimination against the Jews of Russia will soon be swept away, and that relieved from the prejudice against them which yet lingers in the minds of the populace in some of the provinces, our brethren will occupy a position commensurate with their morality and intellectual ability.

We pray that you will preserve with other recollections of your sojourn in our Country, the impressions conveyed of the capacity of Israelites to become useful

5. Grand Duke Alexei Alexandrovich (1850–1908), son of the Russian tsar Alexander II (1818–1881), led a goodwill delegation to the United States from November 21, 1871, to February 22, 1872. During his visit, he met with President Ulysses S. Grant (1822–1885) as well as a variety of American officials and business leaders. He traveled extensively throughout the country, visited several major U.S. cities, and spent a brief time in Canada.

6. Alexander II maintained a relatively liberal attitude to Russian Jewry. Among his reforms were abolishing the system of military conscription for Jewish youth and easing restrictions on Jewish settlement outside the Pale. However, these changes were reversed after Alexander's assassination in 1881.

citizens, and that on your return to your home, your generous influence will be exerted to second the Imperial measures for the complete emancipation of the Jews of Russia.

From the Executive Committee of the Board of Delegates of American Israelites, Meyer S. Isacs,[7] Secretary.

Letter from Myer S. Isaacs to Simon Wolf, March 29, 1872

Source: Letter from Myer S. Isaacs to Simon Wolf (March 29, 1872), Board of Delegates of American Israelites Records, I-2, box 3, folder 3, American Jewish Historical Society, New York City.

Board of Delegates of American Israelites
Office of the Executive Committee
New York March 29 5632 1872

Hon. Simon Wolf,[8] Vice President
My Dear Sir,
The Executive Committee would feel obliged for information as to whether our Government, having received a communication representing the outrages against the Jews in Roumania [sic],[9] have replied to the U.S. Consul General at Bucharest[10] approving of the protest addressed to the Roumanian authorities

---

7. An active American Jewish communal leader, Myer S. Isaacs (1841–1904) was a philanthropist, real estate lawyer, judge, and newspaper editor. Together with his father, Rabbi Samuel Myer Isaacs (1804–1878), he established the *Jewish Messenger* (1857–1903), a traditionalist New York–based weekly.

8. Simon Wolf (1836–1923) emigrated in 1848 from Bavaria to the United States. He settled in Ohio, where he practiced law, before moving in 1862 to Washington, D.C. Thereafter, he became acquainted with several presidents, including Grant (in office 1869–77) and served as recorder of deeds for the District of Columbia (1869–78). Wolf participated in a variety of Jewish educational and charitable activities, and he served as president of the Independent Order of Bnai Brith, a Jewish fraternal society.

9. Starting in the 1860s, Romanian Jewry suffered from severe legal restrictions imposed by the tsarist regime and a series of regional physical attacks that culminated in the 1870s with a wave of pogroms. The "outrages against the Jews" noted here refer to anti-Jewish riots in Ismail, Bessarabia (today, Ukraine), and Cahul, Romania (today, Moldova), based on false accusations against the Jewish communities of stealing from and desecrating a cathedral in Ismail.

10. Benjamin Franklin Peixotto (1834–1890), a journalist and lawyer active in Jewish communal affairs, who was appointed by President Grant as U.S. consul to Romania (1870–76) and France (1877–85). As a result of Peixotto's diplomatic positions, he became a visible and influential Jewish figure.

by the Consular body.[11] If the Department of State has not yet taken action on the matter the Committee urge upon you to see the Secretary[12] and present the case, so that the persecution of our brethren in Roumania may be at least partially checked by the moral influence of foreign governments represented at Bucharest. The intervention of the United States (as of France, Great Britain & Germany already accorded) is solicited on the ground of humanity, and we are assured will be promptly and fully recognized as a national duty.

Respectfully yours, M.S. Isaacs, Secy

Letter from Simon Wolf to Myer S. Isaacs, May 12, 1873

Source: Letter from Simon Wolf to Myer S. Isaacs, May 12, 1873, Board of Delegates of American Israelites Records, I-2, box 3, folder 3, American Jewish Historical Society, New York City. Emphasis in the original.

Simon Wolf, Recorder,
Office of Recorder of Deeds
Washington, D.C.

Myer S. Isaacs Esq.
Sec'y of Board of Delegates

Dear Sir,

Business of a pressing character prevents me from being present at our annual meeting, but be assured that I heartily sympathize in and with every movement made by the organization tending towards the amelioration of our Coreligionists, not only in the distant Orient, *but also among our* people at home, for it seems to me that there ought to be a more healthy and vigorous sentiment right at our doors for if faithful men are suffering, men who have, and are, devoting their best years in behalf of a great Cause, it is not alone sufficient that

11. In the aftermath of the events in Ismail and Cahul, Peixotto had coordinated with the consuls from France, Great Britain, Germany, and other countries to send identical letters of protest to the Romanian government. Peixotto (and through him, the Board of Delegates) was anxious to secure a strong statement of support for this letter from the U.S. State Department.

12. Hamilton Fish (1808–1893), a New York lawyer and politician, was U.S. secretary of state in 1869–77. Fish initially opposed Peixotto's appointment as American consul, in large part because Fish objected to the notion that humanitarian interests should influence U.S. foreign affairs. For a brief overview of Peixotto's mission, including Grant's desire to placate American Jews through his appointment to a diplomatic post, see Jonathan D. Sarna, *When General Grant Expelled the Jews* (New York: Schocken, 2012), 103–16.

we rejoice at his or their success but we should also aid him or them materially. Nothing so cheers and animates as the "*nervus rerum*," especially when away from Home & friends.[13] I therefore most respectfully but Earnestly hope, nay beg, that the Board will take immediate action to sustain *our* Representative.[14] [Benjamin Franklin] Peixotto, as far as I Could control has been cheerfully and substantially rendered, and without Egotism Can say if he has not starved at his post it is Certainly *not the fault of those who* ought to have sustained him.

The Government of the United States does not need him there at all and only permits us the shield of a Consulate to aid *our* stricken friends. Therefore do not grumble at the Government but act for yourselves, and stay not in your deeds, not of Charity to Peixotto but of Benevolence to Humanity.

After discharging this duty do not forget it is high time that this Board be enlarged in power and usefulness. If we are to exercise any influence at all, it must be through the medium of those proven by which Everything in this Country is moved. The Jew must enter more largely into the area of Statesmanship, we must have more American Representatives, young men should be Encouraged, not only to be rich, but also to be honored for their political worth and character.

If we have not so far been capable of exercising a decided influence on the Body Politic, whose fault is it?

To be enabled to Enjoy you must be able to Command.

The Board could give a decided impulse without being sectional or local. Another point. You were to meet here this year. You have decided different and perhaps wisely this time, *but next year*, when we have the Long session of Congress, I deem it of the very first importance that you should meet here, and that we should be largely represented, for if we show by numbers and intellect that we are in Earnest, we will exert a greater influence in one day, than years of protests and Criticism.

There are many points which I would like to touch, but want of time prevents.

Very kindly yours, S. Wolf

13. The phrase *nervus rerum* (Latin for "nerve of things" or "sinews of war") derives from the Fifth Phillippic (43 BCE) of the Roman statesman Cicero (106–42 BCE), an oration attacking Marcus Antonius (83–30 BCE), a Roman general and autocratic protégé of Julius Caesar (c. 100–44 BCE). As a Roman triumvir, Antonius defeated the republicans at the battle of Phillipi (42 BCE), which led to Cicero's banishment and murder.

14. Peixotto's unsalaried consular appointment was a concession to American Jews. This diplomatic post was not a priority of the U.S. government.

10

"AS TO THE VALIDITY OF THE TRIBAL LAWS OF THE JEWS"

The Fascination of the American Press with
East European Jewish Marital Life
(1883–1902)

◇◇◇

GERALDINE GUDEFIN

Between the 1880s and the 1920s, millions of eastern European Jews left their homes in search of better economic prospects and greater religious tolerance. While these Jews followed various migration routes, the largest group of migrants settled in the United States. Starting in the 1880s, the American press displayed much interest in the newcomers and regularly commented on their foreign customs. Newspapers across the United States, especially in the urban centers where most Jewish immigrants resided, showed a particular fascination with Jewish marital practices, such as divorce.

The three newspaper articles presented here discuss the legal and cultural aspects of marital breakdown related to three eastern European Jewish men recently arrived in the United States.[1] The first two cases focus on the extralegal nature of Jewish divorce. In the absence of civil divorce, Jewish divorces had legal validity in the Russian empire but not in the Jews' new country. Because religious divorce was not a legal procedure in the United States, Jewish men and women who remarried after obtaining a ritual divorce (but not a civil one) became liable to prosecution on the ground of bigamy. Whereas the recently divorced Duroffsky (no first name is known) was warned against the legal ramifications of entering into a new marriage without a prior legal divorce, the marital status of his coreligionist Morris Kroner came under judicial scrutiny when his wife, Rosa, initiated a trial to annul their marriage. Arguing that his Russian Jewish divorce was devoid of legal validity on American soil, Rosa sought to convince the court that Morris was still wedded to his first wife, and that consequently his second marriage (to Rosa) was null and void. While these two stories

---

1. The articles' original orthography has been retained to preserve the cultural and historical context of the items.

focus on inadvertent bigamy resulting from the discrepancies between legal systems, the third article centers on a case of intentional bigamy, as Motke (known only by this name) had not been ritually divorced from his wife, whom he left behind in eastern Europe, when he sought to wed again. Instead of exploring the encounter between the newly arrived immigrants and American legal institutions, the Boston Daily Globe article recounts how Motke's shameful violation of the moral norms of his community landed him with a harsh physical punishment from his foreign coreligionists.[2]

Although they drew on existing and in fact quite widespread problems in the Jewish immigrant community, these articles displayed a shallow understanding of Jewish law and communal life. For instance, by resorting to Christian terminology to describe the Jewish procedure of divorce, they misrepresented eastern European Jewish life as far more organized, centralized, and hierarchical than it was in reality. Perhaps more problematically, these articles also tended to essentialize and exoticize the newcomers by emphasizing their religious, cultural, and even physical differences from the rest of the population. The three overlapping themes in these articles (disregard for the law, greed, and the mistreatment of women through forced divorce and infidelity) converged to present eastern European Jews as a menace to the American public order.

Absent from these articles was a description of the broader socioeconomic and cultural context that led the newcomers to violate American law, especially the impact of migration on Jewish family life, and the differences between the American legal landscape and its Russian counterpart. Even before the beginning of mass migration, Jewish family life in eastern Europe had been profoundly disrupted by the modernization of the tsarist empire in the nineteenth century. The increasing encroachment of the Russian state on Jewish communal autonomy, the weakening of rabbinical authority, and the growing pace of internal and external migration all resulted in disruptions in marital and family life such as divorce, spousal separation, bigamy, and husbandly desertion. Mass migration increased tensions between husbands and wives. Unlike many groups of foreigners in the United States, Jews from eastern Europe frequently migrated as entire families and settled in their new environment with no intention of returning to their hometowns. However, all family members did not come at the same time. Typically, the husband paved the way for his family's immigration, while his wife and children stayed behind for several months or even years. In numerous cases, this forced physical separation led couples to divorce, either while the wife was still in eastern Europe or after the spouses were reunited on

2. Detailed information concerning the parties noted in the articles is unknown.

American soil. Furthermore, the wives' delayed immigration encouraged the phenomenon of husbandly desertion, as myriad married men entered into new marriages on American soil while severing all contact with the families they had left behind. Once these marriages unraveled, the eastern European Jewish men and women who sought to divorce in the United States found themselves likely to violate American marital laws owing to a mixture of legal, cultural, and financial reasons—such as the fact that it was much easier to obtain a divorce under Jewish law than under American state law (especially in New York State, which considered adultery the only acceptable ground for divorce).

Despite their silence on broader issues, these articles illuminate both the attempt by the American state to discipline the marital practices of recent Jewish arrivals and the varied ways in which immigrants took action themselves, either individually or collectively—for example, by chastising the rule breakers in their midst through physical force, strategically invoking state law when deemed beneficial, or (in the case of an accused person) even moving to a different state.

◇◇◇

"A Jew Who's Got a 'GET'—Extra Legal Divorces Given by the Russian Church," *Boston Daily Globe*, November 12, 1883

> Source: "A Jew Who's Got a 'GET'—Extra Legal Divorces Given by the Russian Church [Special Despatch to the *Boston Globe*]," *Boston Daily Globe*, November 12, 1883, 1.

TROY, N.Y., November 11.—A conflict between the Russian Jewish Church[3] and the law officers of this country is imminent, and the 500 or more Polish and Russian Jews living in Troy are much worked up over the prospect. Duroffsky, a Polish Jew and merchant doing business in River Street, gave notice last week that he had obtained an ecclesiastical *get*[4]—a church paper allowing him to put

---

3. The term "Russian Jewish Church" is misleading, as Judaism does not have a centralized and hierarchical structure along the lines of Catholicism's papacy or the Russian Orthodox Church's Holy Synod. It is true that throughout the nineteenth century tsarist authorities attempted to assert more control over Jewish religious life by creating a state rabbinate (or chief rabbinate) that was integrated into the imperial administrative structure. These efforts were largely unsuccessful, as many Jews throughout the empire refused to accept the religious leadership of state-appointed rabbis. The decentralized nature of Jewish communal life was further exacerbated by immigration to the United States, which was a religious marketplace characterized by voluntarism and a lack of religious hierarchy. In fact, the lack of state control over Jewish life raised endless and heated questions about who qualified as a rabbi, possessed the authority to lead a congregation, and was considered fit to speak on behalf of all Jews.

4. *Get* is the Hebrew term for divorce. More specifically, it refers to the document that a Jew-

away his wife, and that he would in a few days wed the daughter of a wealthy compatriot residing in New York. This announcement reached the district attorney, and an investigation which was at once instituted brings out for the first time the fact that this church has a law of divorce under which a husband may appear before a tribunal of the church,[5] complain that he is dissatisfied with his wife, and after obtaining her consent, which is usually secured by intimidation or purchase, be divorced and privileged to take another wife. Dozens of the *gets*, it was found, have been issued in Troy, and men are living here in marital relations who have wives in the country.[6] In a few cases both the man and wife live in Troy in relations that are bigamous under our laws. District Attorney [La Mott W.] Rhodes[7] has notified the Jew in question that he will be prosecuted if he takes another wife, and threatens to lay the facts of the investigation regarding the illegal divorce tribunal before the grand jury at its next session. The head of the church in Troy, who is a sort of rabbi, referred to the matter in today's sermon, and advised that the case be made a test one. He characterized the district attorney's action as a piece of persecution like that which the Mormon church had withstood, and throve in spite of, for fifty years.[8] He declared further that it

---

ish husband presents to his wife to terminate their marriage. Although a woman can refuse the *get*, the gendered nature of this procedure overwhelmingly disadvantages women, who cannot initiate a divorce. This gender imbalance has its roots in the biblical origins of Jewish divorce, which allowed husbands to divorce women against their will. To remedy biblical laws, the central European rabbi Gershom ben Judah (c. 960–1040 CE) ruled that a divorce could not be finalized without the wife's consent.

5. According to Orthodox custom, a rabbinical court (*beit din* in Hebrew), composed of three learned Jewish men, supervises the divorce procedure. In the absence of civil divorce proceedings in the tsarist empire, Jews were subject to their confessional laws in the spheres of marriage and divorce. In the United States, by contrast, the government did not recognize the authority of Jewish law, and Jews were expected to conform to the requirements of civil divorce.

6. In the first decades of the twentieth century, several American courts probed the legality of the *get*. While they considered a Jewish divorce obtained in Russia valid, owing to its legality in the Russian empire, rabbinical divorces effectuated on American soil lacked such validity. Similarly, in a case from 1911, the New York Supreme Court ruled that a writ of divorce sent from the United States to Russia did not constitute a valid divorce according to state law. In Duroffsky's case, it is not clear whether the wife received the *get* in the United States or if Duroffsky sent it to her via a third party, while she remained in Europe.

7. La Mott W. Rhodes (1843–1890), a Democratic lawyer from New York State, was elected district attorney in 1881 and served in this role for six years.

8. The "Mormon question" was sparked by the Mormon Church's public announcement of its doctrine of polygamy in 1852. The right of Mormons to practice polygamy became a major constitutional question in the second half of the nineteenth century, as it pertained to the limits of religious freedom and the nature of the separation of church and state. In 1862, Congress

was a matter of church discipline, purely, and that the law officers had no constitutional warrant for interference. The merchant promises to sit in church here in Troy with his bride, from New York next Sunday.

"Tribal Laws—Appealed to by a Brooklyn Cigar Maker—The High Priest of Russia Grants Morris Kroner a Divorce which the Local Courts will Probably Ignore," *Brooklyn Daily Eagle*, December 17, 1885

Source: "Tribal Laws—Appealed to by a Brooklyn Cigar Maker—The High Priest of Russia Grants Morris Kroner a Divorce Which the Local Courts Will Probably Ignore," *Brooklyn Daily Eagle*, December 17, 1885, 4.

Morris Kroner, a cigar maker, of Fifth Avenue, was arrested some months since and charged before Justice [Frederick Sterling] Massey[9] with marrying his second wife, Rosa, while his first wife was alive. The second Mrs. Kroner is the daughter of a well-known tobacco leaf dealer and cigar manufacturer. This morning Mrs. Kroner and her father, a patriarchal looking Hebrew, paced up and down the corridor in the Court House, awaiting the calling of the suit for the annulment of the marriage between Morris Kroner and Rosa. Mrs. Kroner is a typical Jewish woman, petite in figure, with oval face, olive skin, and large black eyes. It was not expected the case would be reached today. The defendant was formerly a soldier in Russia, where he married a widow. He is a Cohen [sic] of the tribe of Levi.[10] The laws of the latter decree that no male of that tribe who claims special priestly privileges shall marry either a widow or a divorced woman. Kroner left his wife in Russia and settled here, where he made the ac-

---

passed the Morrill Act, making bigamy a federal crime, with the aim of curbing polygamy among Mormons. In 1878, the U.S. Supreme Court confirmed the illegality of polygamy in the landmark case *Reynolds v. United States*, leading to a wave of antipolygamy sentiment in subsequent years.

9. In 1884, Frederick Sterling Massey (1839–1895) was appointed judge of the First District Police Court in Brooklyn, NY; he served for two terms. He was an important figure in Brooklyn politics.

10. A *kohen* (transliterated in the original as "Cohen") is a member of the priestly class in the Jewish tradition. The division of Jews into three groups (Kohen, Levi, and Israel) dates back to ancient Israel, when the Second Temple was still standing in Jerusalem. All the direct patrilineal descendants of Levi, one of the twelve sons of the patriarch Jacob, belong to the tribe of Levi, the priestly tribe whose members served in the Temple. The term "Kohen" refers specifically to the direct patrilineal descendants of Aaron, Moses's brother. "Israel" refers to the rest of the Jews. Although these distinctions largely lost their meaning after the destruction of the Second Temple in 70, Jews from the Kohen group continue to enjoy some privileges in Jewish ritual life, and according to rabbinical law, they are not allowed to marry divorced women or converts.

quaintance of Rosa. Rabbi [Abraham Joseph] Ash,[11] of New York, was consulted by Kroner, and he in turn communicated with the High Priest of Russia,[12] who granted a divorce on the ground that the marriage between Kroner and his first wife was contrary to the tribal laws of the Levis. Among Russian, Turkish, and other Eastern Jews, the High Priest of the church is the only recognized authority to grant divorces, the various governments recognizing their authority.[13] But the second Mrs. Kroner, living under the laws of the United States, claimed their protection, and the question as to the validity of the tribal laws of the Jews will have to be passed upon by the Supreme Court.[14] Kroner belonged to the high priest's family, for which cause the Russian divorce was the more readily granted.

Kroner, who has been at large on nominal bail, has not been seen in Brooklyn for several weeks and did not put in an appearance in the Supreme Court this morning, for which reason Colonel R. Johnson, Mrs. Kroner's counsel, believes that he will merely have to argue that the laws of this country override the tribal laws of the Levis to secure the annulment of the marriage.

"Soundly Spanked—Would-Be Hebrew Bigamist Got Good Lesson—
Motke Had Wife in Warsaw, But Eye For Bank Books—Prepared to
Wed Boston 'Fiancee,' but Found 'She' Was a Man in Disguise—'Bride'
Assisted in Castigation—Grim Joke Served Its Purpose and Victim Left
City," *Boston Daily Globe*, July 8, 1902

> Source: "Soundly Spanked—Would-Be Hebrew Bigamist Got Good Lesson—Motke Had Wife in Warsaw, But Eye For Bank Books—Prepared to Wed Boston 'Fiancee,'

11. Rabbi Abraham Joseph Ash (1813–1888) was one of the earliest ordained Orthodox rabbis in the United States. He was born in Siemiaticze, in Polish Russia, and immigrated to New York in 1852. A staunch defender of Orthodoxy, he was one of the founders of New York's first congregation of eastern European Jews, Bet Hamidrash Hagadol. Ash served the congregation, situated on the Lower East Side, intermittently from 1860 until his death. As one of few Orthodox rabbis in America in the 1880s, Ash frequently prepared bills of divorce, which brought him into conflict with the civil courts.

12. Such a position did not exist in the Russian empire, but there were crown rabbis appointed by the Russian government. In Judaism, there is no figure akin to the pope in Catholicism. Ash probably corresponded with an authoritative eastern European rabbi.

13. In both the Russian and Ottoman empires, Jewish communities benefited from a large degree of communal and legal autonomy, and their personal status (such as married and divorced) was subject to Jewish law.

14. In New York State, the Supreme Court is not the court of last resort but a trial court.

but Found 'She' Was a Man in Disguise—'Bride' Assisted in Castigation—Grim Joke Served Its Purpose and Victim Left City," *Boston Daily Globe*, July 8, 1902, 12.

The cooling of the ardor of a would-be bigamist, a young Hebrew but three months in the country, is the latest joke in Jewish circles in this city.

About three months ago, a young man known at home as "Motke," which is [a] pet name for Mordecai, arrived in Boston via New York, from Warsaw. Motke has a number of friends in Boston who knew him in the old country.

When the new arrival first landed in Boston, he made his home in the B'naith Israel Sheltering home[15] for a few days, after which he secured lodgings with a private family in the neighborhood of Salem Street.[16]

In response to the questions by the landlady, Motke stated that he was a shoemaker, single, and would get married if he could find a suitable "Shidach" [sic], or match.[17]

The landlady knew of a girl who had $600 in the bank and thought that she could make a match between the two. The girl in the case was communicated with and given the opportunity to view the lodger without him knowing of the inspection.

The girl wrote her brother, who lives in Lowell [Massachusetts], that an offer of marriage was being made to her by a recent arrival, and in reply he told her to visit some of the "landslite" [sic] [countrymen] of her intended and find out something about his reputation.

This the sister thought to be a very wise suggestion, and she commenced to carry it out within an hour. It took but few calls on some people from Warsaw, who are in Boston, to inform the young woman that this Motke, when he left

15. Established in 1891 by Russian Jewish immigrants, the Benoth Israel (Daughters of Israel, spelled here as "B'naith Israel") Sheltering Home was a philanthropic organization in Boston's North End, the heart of Jewish immigrant life in the city, to assist recently arrived coreligionists. Among other services, it provided newcomers with temporary shelter and food and helped them secure housing and employment. Communal institutions like this played a crucial role in helping Jewish immigrants adjust to the conditions in their new country.

16. To limit housing costs, many immigrants took up residence in boardinghouses, which provided lodgers with food and a private room.

17. The term *shidukh* (Hebrew and Yiddish for "arranged marriage," is transliterated here as "Shidach"); the term for matchmaker is *shadkahn* (spelled below in the article as "shadchon"). Matchmaking was an important component of traditional eastern European Jewish life, as marriages cemented alliance between families. In the United States, these arranged marriages came into tension with the ideal of love marriage, leading myriad young Jewish immigrants to choose their own spouses. In the general American press, matchmaking was often used to illustrate the unique and distinctive marital practices of eastern European Jews.

home, also left a three-months' bride, whom he promised to bring over here as soon as he should be able.

Of course the young woman became indignant and refused to have anything more to do with the would-be bigamist. The Warsaw people, whom the young woman visited in her inquiries, however, thought that some punishment ought to be meted out to the "adventurer," "swindler," and many other fancy names that they called him at an indignation meeting in one of the Sfard synagogues[18] on Leverett Street and after due deliberation a plan was thought out, and the scheme acted upon. This culminated with great success last Sunday, and the plotters are going about chuckling, each claiming the credit of forming the plan.

About four weeks ago the plan was first put in action by a man who presented himself as a "shadchon" calling on Motke, and telling of a fine match that he had in view for him. As commission the "shadchon" claimed the modest sum of $25, $10 after the engagement and $15 at the time of the wedding.

A meeting between the young people was arranged, and it was also whispered in Motke's ear that the prospective bride had about $1000. Motke, however, would not take hearsay evidence and asked the girl plainly how much she had at their second meeting.

She answered him, $740 in the bank, and debts of about $80 coming to her from various persons, and showed Motke her bank book to bear out the statement. Motke could not read English, but he could tell figures, and the last line, $740, spoke for itself.

One thing about this new girl pleased Motke. She did not care to go out for a car ride nor to the theater. She even refused two invitations to matinees.

Two weeks ago the engagement took place, about 35 or 40 of their friends being present. The matrimonial agent was there to collect the $10, as a matter of course.

Last Sunday was to be the wedding day, and the prospective groom after insisting that the wedding should take place in a hall where he could invite all the friends he had made in Boston and give them a good time, allowed himself to become convinced that a home wedding was best, because it was cheapest, and a number of articles of furniture was counted off by the bride, which she said she could buy for the money that the hall rent, music, chickens, etc., would cost.

18. The concept "nusakh Sefard" (literally, "Sephardic rite") refers to the style of ritual practice, including liturgical and melodic elements, adopted in the eighteenth and nineteenth centuries by central and eastern European Jews who embraced aspects of Jewish mysticism (kabbalah) practiced by the centuries-old Jewish community of Safed in the Galilee region of Ottoman Palestine. Despite the confusing terminology, nusakh Sefard is actually a branch of Ashkenazic Jewish tradition and is primarily associated with Hasidic Jewish practice.

Sunday came, and Motke dressed in gala array, and armed with a large bouquet of bride roses called on his prospective bride at her room on North Margin Street.

There was a large number of people present, but all males, except the bride, and Motke thought that this was rather strange, but refrained from making any remarks. One of the young men asked Motke whether he was all ready, and Motke said "yes."

"He is all ready boys," shouted the young man.

This evidently was a prearranged signal. An onrush was immediately made on the unfortunate Motke, and while the bride was taking off her bridal gown, and appeared as a man, an acquaintance of Motke, the others strapped Motke to a form, and after undressing him, spanked him good and hard, using leather thongs with little knots at the end, something similar in appearance to the Russian knout.

Owing to the yells and shouting for mercy that Motke gave vent to it was found necessary to gag him while forty strokes were counted out to him.[19] The "bride" had the honor of tendering the first five, after which the "shadchon" and others took their turn.

After the operation, Motke threatened to prosecute his tormentors but when he was informed that in that case they would prefer charges of an attempt at bigamy against him, Motke thought better of it and departed for New York yesterday.

It is doubtful if he will try to marry in New York, as the lesson he received in Boston was very painful, and it is stated that it will be at least a month before he will forget it.

It is rather peculiar that although Motke had met the young man who acted as "bride" many times in the street he did not recognize him. Motke had made four calls on the "bride" prior to the "wedding" day.

19. This is a highly symbolic number, as the standard punishment for offenses in biblical law is forty lashes.

11

"FOR THE DEFENSE OF OUR JEWISH INTERESTS"

Henry Pereira Mendes's Call for an International Synod (1886)

◇◇

ZEV ELEFF

In May 1886, Rev. Henry Pereira Mendes (1852–1937) wrote to Chief Rabbi Nathan Marcus Adler (1803–1890) of the British empire. In the thirteen-page handwritten letter, Mendes reveals just how overwhelmed he and his Orthodox rabbinical colleagues were in the final decades of the nineteenth century. The English-born Mendes occupied a unique position in American Jewish life. He was a scion of a British rabbinic family and the religious leader of New York's Shearith Israel. His congregation was one of the few remaining centers of the Spanish-Portuguese tradition (Sephardic) that had established the Jewish enclave in North America during the colonial period. In addition, he had much to do with the subsequent waves of central and eastern European Jewish (Ashkenazic) settlement in the nineteenth century. A self-described leader of Positive-Historical Judaism, Mendes played a pivotal role in the formation of the Jewish Theological Seminary (established in 1886) to secure a brand of traditional-minded Judaism and then served as the founding president of the Orthodox Union (established as the Union of Orthodox Jewish Congregations of American in 1898). His deep involvement in Jewish life made Mendes anxious about the future of his faith community during the turbulent 1880s.

Owing to his British background, Mendes shared his concerns with England's ranking rabbi, hoping to enlist Adler's support in creating an international rabbinical council to provide stability and clarity to tradition-bound Jewry. Mendes also wrote to other rabbinic leaders, but not in such detail. The conference never materialized. To Adler, Mendes described the continued rise of Reform Judaism. In November 1885, a group of Reform rabbis had held a conference at the Concordia Club House in Allegheny City, just a few miles outside of Pittsburgh. The ensuing Pittsburgh Platform affirmed Reform Judaism's break from orthodox observance.[1] The vociferous public discussion of the con-

---

1. On the Pittsburgh Platform, see chapter 16, note 10.

ference and its outcomes troubled Mendes, who believed that Jews and Christians alike would take it to mean that Reform Judaism was the official creed of the Hebrews in the United States.

It was more than current events that suggested religious upheaval. Just as concerning to Mendes were advances in technology that threatened the status quo of traditional Jewish life. The New York preacher shared his frustrations over his "advanced civilization" and the wider use and dissemination of electricity. For example, he was unsure how to engage congregants who desired to ride streetcars on the Sabbath. More importantly, new forms of motorized transportation increased mobility and transformed New York from a walking city to a more capacious metropolis. More frequently, the well-heeled members of Shearith Israel desired to live in better neighborhoods beyond walking distance from the synagogue. Mendes recognized the changing nature of space and "community" and sought answers to cope with the dynamic reality of American society. His letter to Adler throws light on the complexities of religious and social change in the final decades of the nineteenth century.

◇◇

Letter from Henry Pereira Mendes to Nathan Marcus Adler, May 27, 1886

Source: Letter from Henry Pereira Mendes to Nathan Marcus Adler (May 27, 1886), ACC/2805/02/01/093, London Metropolitan Archives, London, United Kingdom. Reprinted by permission of Office of the Chief Rabbi, London, United Kingdom.

22 Iyar 5646
Rev. N. Adler[2]
Chief Rabbi

Rev. and dear Sir,

If I address you upon the subject of this letter my excuse is the grave importance of what I offer for your consideration, and the firm belief that the interests of Judaism are dear to your heart and paramount in your eyes.

---

2. Nathan Marcus Adler (1803–1890), originally from Hanover, served as chief rabbi of the British empire from 1844 to 1890. A leading representative of enlightened Orthodox Judaism, Adler was regarded as one of Europe's premier Jewish legal and spiritual authorities. During Adler's lifetime, British Jewry became completely emancipated by the state, and Adler played a key role in shaping organized British Jewry's communal institutions. In 1870, Parliament mandated the establishment of the United Synagogue as British Jewry's authoritative body, and Adler became the first chief rabbi of the United Hebrew Congregations of the Commonwealth.

In the last fifty or sixty years the Jewish population in America has vastly increased in numbers, wealth and influence.[3]

In or about 1824 the congregation of which I have the honor of being minister was the only one in New York City, and although Hebrews have been in the country since the middle of the 17th century, yet the Jewish population of the United States up to the first quarter of this century was perhaps no more than 1,500.[4] Now there are from two to three hundred congregations in New York alone, varying in type from a minyan [prayer quorum of ten adult men] to several hundred heads of families; and the Hebrew population of all the states is today estimated at from three to five hundred thousand.

The religious condition of so large a population of our people cannot but profoundly interest you, and I believe that you will not hesitate to show that your interest is practical rather than superficial. The American atmosphere of Liberty has appeased our religion: but liberty has become license. Were this evidenced by the lives of individuals only, I might not intrude this letter upon your valuable time. But in the years that I have been here, a minister loving our grand faith, I have thought much and constantly upon the outlook for Judaism in this land.

I see the gradual and steady approach of Unitarian Christianity, especially in the part of that section of the Jewish Community known as Radical Reformers.[5] I see all boundaries thrown down and intermarriage between Hebrews and Unitarians facilitated. I mark fundamental doctrines of our faith such as circumcision, the seventh day Sabbath, the nationality of our people, Revelation, the Messianic hope, denied—not by individual laymen, though that would be matter enough for consideration, but by Jewish ministers, assembled in council:—

Is it not time to move for the defense of our Jewish interests? Thus at the Pittsburg [sic] Conference of Jewish ministers a few weeks ago, one declared cir-

3. In 1820, Jews numbered about 3,000 women and men in the United States. By the time of Mendes's writing, that figure had risen to approximately 250,000. For a useful table on the American Jewish population, see Jonathan D. Sarna, *American Judaism: A History* (New Haven, CT: Yale University Press, 2004), 375.

4. On the history of Mendes's congregation, Shearith Israel, and the eventual break-off synagogue, Bnai Jeshurun, in the 1820s, see David de Sola Pool and Tamar de Sola Pool, *An Old Faith in the New World: Portrait of Shearith Israel, 1654–1954* (New York: Columbia University Press, 1955).

5. On the attraction to Unitarianism of some elements of Reform Judaism, see Benny Kraut, "A Unitarian Rabbi? The Case of Solomon H. Sonneschein," in *Jewish Apostasy in the Modern World*, ed. Todd M. Endelman (New York: Holmes and Meier, 1987), 272–308.

cumcision unnecessary for proselytes.[6] Another that he did not believe in what is called Revelation, — "religion," said he, "is the result of evolution."[7]

In the manifesto which they then collectively and formally issued: Article III intimates that the Mosaic legislation is not binding on us now, and reflects all ceremonial laws which are judged inconvenient, — "not adapted to the views and habits of modern civilization." Article IV declares the dietary laws, Mosaic and Rabbinic, abolished; also all regulations as to dress [and] priestly purity.... Article V proclaims "we consider ourselves no longer a nation, but a religious community and therefore accept neither a return to Palestine, etc., etc. — nor the restoration of any of the laws concerning the Jewish State."

This manifesto of course enjoys the authority naturally resulting from united action on the part of the Jewish ministers, not only in the eyes of the Jewish laity, but in the eyes of the Christians.

Add to this action such public utterances of one Jewish minister that "the day/Seventh day-Sabbath" [sic] has lost its holiness with the Jews. It cannot be divine. The Sabbath of the Jews is actually Sunday. We shall in time not very far off adopt the Sundays as our Sabbath. We transfer all the blessings of the old historical Sabbath day to the public Sabbath."[8]

Add to this the action of another Jewish minister who on the evening of the last Pesach [Passover] married a Jewess to an unconverted Christian.

Add to this the inconsistency of a gathering of such Jewish ministers who assembled for the "interests of Judaism" as they call it, and after having publicly assisted at the graduation of young Hebrew ministers, sat down publicly to a banquet where Mosaic as well as Rabbinic dietary law was flagrantly broken.[9]

6. The Reform theologian Kaufmann Kohler (1843–1926), who in this period served as rabbi of New York City's Temple Beth-El, championed the view that male converts need not undergo circumcision. See "Authentic Report of the Proceedings of the Rabbinical Conference," *Reformer*, January 8, 1886, 4.

7. This position was articulated by the well-known preacher Emil G. Hirsch (1851–1923), rabbi of Chicago's Sinai Congregation and Kohler's brother-in-law. See "Authentic Report of the Proceedings of the Rabbinical Conference," *Jewish Reformer*, January 22, 1886, 3.

8. The reference here is to Kaufmann Kohler (see note 6). See Tobias Brinkmann, *Sundays at Sinai: A Jewish Congregation in Chicago* (Chicago: University of Chicago Press, 2012), 94.

9. On July 11, 1883, Hebrew Union College held a reception to honor the rabbinical seminary's first ordination class. The so-called Trefa Banquet flouted Jewish dietary laws, serving those in attendance shrimp, crab, and other nonkosher fare. Word of the affair spread in the Jewish press and emerged as a major point of contention between Reform leaders and their opponents. See Lance J. Sussman, "The Myth of the Trefa Banquet: American Culinary Culture and the Radicalization of Food Policy in American Reform Judaism," *American Jewish Archives Journal* 57, nos. 1–2 (2005), 29–52.

Add to this the expression of an essayist, a Jewish minister, in a publication issued with the names of fourteen other Jewish ministers on the cover (thus lending the weight of their names) to the effect that it "is a wide field open for discussion, whether for instance, Judaism would lose its historical identity with the past by the abolition of circumcision, by the transfer of the Sabbath to another day of public rest, or by the allowance of intermarriage with the Gentiles."

These examples will be sufficient to demonstrate to you that Judaism in this country presents the questions for solution, what shall be done, what ought to be done to preserve the interests of our religion now, when it is no longer the Jewish laity doing—ish kol hayashar beeinav [Hebrew for "a man is upright in his own eyes"][10]—but when the Jewish people in this land is tzon ovedot—roehem heteum [Hebrew for "lost sheep as their shepherds have caused them to go astray"] (Jer. 50:6). And the gravity of the situation is increased when I inform you that the Jewish ministers to whom I have referred are ministers of the largest and wealthiest and most influential congregations in the United States. I approach now to the second matter for your equally earnest consideration.

The increased resources of civilization suggest many questions concerning which our religious legislation is criticized either as not providing for them at all, or insufficiently. Thus, for example, the use of the railroad in the city; the cars are drawn by steam; they are raised high from the ground, tickets can be purchased any day in the week. There is no labor involved other than the guard who stands and to watch if all passengers drop their tickets in a glass box placed for the purpose, and a guard who opens the gate of the carriage at each station. It is urged that no extra labor is imposed on either guard by any Hebrew who uses the Railway.[11] Some Hebrews use the steam Railway and not the horse-car-railway which is below, on the surface of the street. Others use it only to go to Synagogue by its means, as they live far from their place of worship, and have no place near them where they can attend, for here nearly all congregations differ in their ritual and customs. Some have German or English prayers, others abolish talit [prayer shawl], some worship bareheaded, some have ladies and gentlemen sitting together, others have but a third of the parashah [weekly Torah portion] read, some read Haftorah [weekly portion drawn from the Prophets] in English,

10. This appears to be an inexact paraphrase of Judges 17:6 and 21:25: "bayamim hahem ein melekh beyisrael ish hayashar beeinav yaaseh" (Hebrew for "in those days there was no king in Israel; every man did as he pleased").

11. Orthodox Jewish authorities have long proscribed the use of machines that utilize electricity on the Sabbath and festival holidays. The reasons are complex and concern the use of combustible engines (igniting a flame) and completing a circuit (related to "creating" on the Sabbath), among other technical areas of Sabbath observance.

others abolish it altogether, some observe no special order of *parashah*, or read a few verses where the minister chooses, others have lady-voices in the choir, others have Christian singers, and many have organ music.[12]

But many Hebrews who are obliged to live at a distance from Synagogue, and who conscientiously object to riding either by steam-car or horse-car, and who cannot derive satisfaction or edification from attending any Synagogue near them, do not go to Synagogue at all, or sleep at a hotel [on Yom] Kippur [Day of Atonement] night near their own Synagogue to attend that day. Their children grow up alienated from much which should command their sympathies as Hebrews.

Other questions suggested by our advanced civilization and constant inventions are the use of electricity in private dwellings instead of gas, the use of hydraulic or steam elevators in private apartment houses, some with ten or eleven floors and in which Jews and Christians alike reside, the heating of some house by steam generated outside the apartments or outside even of the building, the ramifications of commercial usage, the extensive use of bone fertilizers in agriculture, the universal custom of sowing wheat with grass seed, other grain with peas, etc., etc., and the crops of which are exported to Europe and used throughout the world, the general castration of young animals reared for food and not breeding, the wide-spread system of grafting, these and a hundred other problems which affect the Jews throughout the world, and a hundred such devices as a patent-whiffle tree, which would affect Jewish agriculturists in a new settlement or primitive country—assuredly merit authoritative consideration. When the Second Temple[13] was destroyed [Rabbi Yohanan ben Zakkai][14] moved to establish a Sanhedrin[15] to show the scattered Hebrews that the religious heart of the nation was still beating [BT Gitten 56b]. So after the Hadrian[16] perse-

12. The activities and practices noted here contravene traditional interpretations of Jewish law and custom.

13. On the Temple in ancient Jerusalem, see chapter 6, note 6.

14. Rabbi Yohanan ben Zakkai (c. 30–90 CE), a sage of the Second Temple period, was inclined to pacifism. Ben Zakkai negotiated with Vespasian (c. 9–79 CE), then a Roman general, during the first Jewish-Roman War (66–73 CE), to transfer besieged Jerusalem's rabbinic sages to Yavneh, a city in the southern coastal plan of ancient Palestine (south of present-day Jaffa) and there establish a center of Jewish learning. After the destruction of the temple, Yavneh functioned as the seat of the Sanhedrin (see the next note).

15. The Great Sanhedrin of ancient Palestine was a Jewish legal and religious court. It is believed there were two Sanhedrins, one civil and political and the other religious in nature. The Sanhedrins emerged in the period before the destruction of the Second Temple in 70 CE. Along with the patriarchate, this body was abolished by the Roman authorities in c. 425 CE.

16. The Roman emperor Hadrian (c. 76–138 CE) suppressed the Bar Kokhba rebellion (132–

cution the seven disciples of R. Akiba:[17] — R. Meir, R. Judah ben Ilai, R. Jose b. Halfta, R. Jochanan of Alexandria, R. Simon ben Jochai, R. Elazar b. Jacob, R. Nehemiah[18] — met and the outcome was the Synod of Usha[19] [BT Rosh Hashanah 31a].

Cannot the few Hebrews who today enjoy each in his own country, the honorable but responsible title of Chief Rabbi, and who so command the respect of the Hebrews in their land and of the Christian government, meet to consider the aspects of affairs and take means accordingly? Their meeting could be only preparatory; they could resolve whom to call to work with them, and to establish an authoritative synod.

Moreover, suppose the moment came when the signal of Restoration were beheld, — and the prophesy fulfilled: *esah el goyim yadi veel amim arim nisi veheiviyu vaneikhah bekhotzen uvenotekhah al katef tinasenah* [Hebrew for "I will raise My hand to nations and lift up My ensign to peoples, and they shall bring your sons in

---

35 CE) in ancient Palestine. He changed the name of Jerusalem to Aelia Capitolina and built a sanctuary honoring the supreme Roman god Jupiter (Jove) on the ruins of the Second Temple.

17. Rabbi Akiba (Akiva ben Yosef), arguably the most important rabbinic sage of his generation, lived in ancient Palestine in the decades that spanned the first and second centuries CE. He played a significant role in systematizing the Mishnah. His approach to hermeneutics and exegetical analysis was critical to the development of the Talmud.

18. The rabbinic legend of the death of Rabbi Akiba's disciples stems from amoraic tradition (c. 200–500 CE). Setting aside questions of chronological and historical veracity, certain scholars understand the rabbinic lore as seeking to establish a religious context for and relationship between the Bar Kokhba rebellion (132–35 CE), Rabbi Akiba, and Akiba's disciples, who are characterized in the literature as being disrespectful and jealous of each other. For example, according to Genesis Rabbah 61 (ed. Theodor-Albeck, p. 660): "Rabbi Akiva had twelve thousand pairs of disciples, from Gevat to Antipatris; and all of them died at the same time. Why? Because their eyes were narrow with each other. In the end, he [Rabbi Akiba] taught/raised seven disciples: Rabbi Meir, Rabbi Yehudah, Rabbi Yose, Rabbi Shimon, Rabbi Elazar ben Shamua, Rabbi Yohanan the shoemaker, and Rabbi Eliezer ben Yaakov. Others say: Rabbi Yehudah, Rabbi Nehemia, Rabbi Meir, Rabbi Yose, Rabbi Shimon ben Yohai, Rabbi Hanania ben Hakhinai, and Rabbi Yohanan the shoemaker. He [Rabbi Akiba] said to them: My first sons died only because their eyes were narrow with each other in Torah. Be careful not to do as they did. They stood and filled all the Land of Israel with Torah" (quoted in Aaron Amit, "The Death of Rabbi Akiva's Disciples: A Literary History," *Journal of Jewish Studies* 56:2 [Autumn 2005], 269–70). Amit argues that the aforementioned literary tradition is not necessarily related to the Bar Kokhba rebellion (ibid., 282–84). For a useful discussion of Akiva and the Bar Kokhba rebellion, see Barry W. Holtz, *Rabbi Akiva: A Sage of the Talmud* (New Haven, CT: Yale University Press, 2017), 149–59.

19. In the middle of the second century (c. 135 CE), an important rabbinic synod (religious court) was convened in the western Galilee town of Usha. Premodern sources include various and inconsistent accounts of the synod, which aimed to reestablish the Sanhedrin after the destruction of the Second Temple.

their bosoms and carry your daughters on their backs"] (Isa. 49:22)—to whom, to what representative body of Hebrews would the powers address themselves? To the leading American Hebrews? Alas, they themselves have declared already against a return to Palestine or restoration of our State! And as time wears on, so Jewish patriotic sentiment in their spheres of influence wears out. How far Judaism would be benefited in your own country by such action as I suggest, how far patriotism throughout the world would be nourished and fidelity to Jewish law fostered, and dignity conferred upon our Religion by such an assembly which would meet periodically, I need not say.

I write a copy of this letter to the Chief Rabbi of England [Adler], to the Chief Rabbi of France,[20] the Chief Rabbi of Holland,[21] the Chief Rabbi of Belgium,[22] the Chief Rabbi of Denmark,[23] the Chief Rabbi of Greece,[24] [the Chief Rabbi] of Germany[25] and [the Chief Rabbi] of Austria.[26]

I ask you, as one of those I have named, whether you, or a delegate appointed by you, would meet in London or Paris or any city agreeable, next July or August to take action in this direction.

All expenses will be paid without publicity, even as we would meet if so desired, without publicity. I say "we," for though I am unworthy of participation

20. Rabbi Isidor Lazard (1813–1888) of Paris served as chief rabbi of France from 1867 to 1888.

21. This likely refers to Rabbi Joseph Hirsch Dünner (1833–1911) of Amsterdam, who served as chief rabbi of the province of North Holland from 1874 to 1888.

22. Rabbi Dr. Bernhard Loebel Ritter of Rotterdam (1855–1935) served as chief rabbi of Belgium from 1885 to 1928.

23. Rabbi Abraham Wolff (1801–1891) of Copenhagen served as chief rabbi of Denmark from 1828 to 1891.

24. In 1886, Greece did not have a sole chief rabbi. In Corfu, home to a sizable Greek Jewish community of approximately 5,000, Alexander De Fanos (d. 1887) served as the region's chief rabbi from 1871 to 1887. Mendes may also be referring to one or both of two chief rabbis in Thessaloniki (northern Greece remained under Ottoman rule until 1913): Rabbi Mair Nahmias (1804–1887) and Rabbi Shmuel Arditi (1811–1887). See also chapter 19, note 11.

25. Founded in 1871, Imperial Germany operated as a federal system, and religious affairs were controlled by the individual states. Owing to long-standing tradition, some territories had so-called Landesrabbiner (territorial rabbis), who represented regions within a state. In general, Jewish communities were autonomous but regulated by the state. Mendes may be alluding to Rabbi Azriel Hildesheimer (1820–1899) of Berlin, the most respected Orthodox leader in Germany in 1886.

26. This likely refers to Moritz Güdemann (1835–1918), a traditionalist Austrian rabbi who in 1866 became the spiritual leader of Vienna's Leopoldstadt synagogue. In 1891, he was officially appointed chief rabbi of Vienna.

in this institution of such an august assembly, I would place my services at its disposal.

Men can do no more than try to do their duty. God will do the rest. It is in the hope that I do my duty in thus acquainting you of what must indeed command your intense sympathy that I address you and earnestly beg that you will write me, so that I receive your reply in [the month of] Sivan,[27] this will give time to make all necessary arrangements.[28]

I have only to add that it is the clashing of diverse opinions of ministers in the country which cause the present religious *tohu vavohu* [Hebrew for "unformed and void" or "chaos"] (Gen. 1:2) in Judaism. The condemnation or the acceptance of any of the synagogal or doctrinal innovations would exercise a tremendous and sufficient moral weight and would be welcomed by the laity provided it came from a body of representatives and respected rabbis, not from one locality but representing countries.

I cannot, in a letter, describe to you as forcibly as the situation demands, the desirability and the necessity of some assertions on your part, as on the part of all our leaders. Not only Judaism in America is becoming different from Judaism in Europe, in practice, aspirations and doctrines, but to quote from the words of a most prominent Jewish minister here: "Mothers and children have unlearned how to pray. Sabbath rest with its cheering song has taken leave from our homes. The flower of piety has withered. Hence we see religion at the freezing point and the enlightened Jews at the brink of atheism. What is to be done in order to stem the tide of evil and to preserve our identity with the past? How shall we take hold of the young, who in appallingly increasing numbers, threaten to desert our lines and inspire them with zeal and enthusiasm for our mission?"[29]

H. P. Mendes

27. Sivan, the third month of the Hebrew calendar, generally corresponds to May–June in the civil calendar.

28. Adler replied to Mendes and indicated his willingness to participate in an international conference on pressing ritual matters. He also encouraged Mendes to organize a chief rabbinate in the United States. Neither the conference nor the rabbinate came to pass.

29. Kaufmann Kohler, "Old and Modern Judaism," *Hebrew Review* 1 (1880), 113.

12

"CONVERSIONS TO AND FROM JUDAISM"

Joseph Krauskopf on American Christian Missions to the Jews
(1891)

◇◇

LINCOLN MULLEN

Joseph Krauskopf (1858–1923) was the noted rabbi of Reform Congregation Keneseth Israel in Philadelphia from 1887 to 1923. Educated in the first class of Hebrew Union College and ordained in 1883, Krauskopf became a key leader of Reform Judaism in the United States. Besides holding a prominent rabbinical post, Krauskopf was active in social benevolence and philanthropy, a key organizer behind the Pittsburgh Platform (1885),[1] a founder of the Jewish Publication Society, and the founder of the National Farm School (today's Delaware Valley University).[2] At Keneseth Israel, Krauskopf instituted a Sunday service in addition to the traditional services on the Sabbath. At those Sunday services he gave educational lectures in English on a variety of topics—including religion, science, philosophy, and contemporary events—to large audiences of both Jews and non-Jews. Krauskopf published many of these lectures in both book and pamphlet form.

Krauskopf's *Jewish Converts, Perverts, and Dissenters* (1891) originated as a series of ten lectures delivered from January to March 1891. Taking up the perennial theme of conversions between Judaism and Christianity, Krauskopf addressed the question of whether such conversions could be considered sincere. He argued that conversions to Judaism were primarily the result of a free choice. Converts came "of their own accord, through conviction, despite obstacle, disadvantage, contempt, because Judaism came to them as a new Revelation, because they were attracted to it by the simple grandeur of its doctrines, [and] by the nobility of heart and soul, and mind which it fosters."[3] On the other hand,

---

1. On the Pittsburgh Platform, see chapter 16, note 10.
2. On the National Farm School, see chapter 32.
3. Lecture I, "True and False Converts," 3–12 (portions of this lecture are reproduced below).

he asserted, conversions from Judaism to Christianity or to other religions were seldom if ever "the result of conviction."

In the lectures, Krauskopf backed up the latter claim with several lines of argumentation. First, he strongly emphasized the inheritance of religious identity. "Strange and sudden conversions," like those expected by evangelical forms of Protestant Christianity, he considered unnatural. His emphasis on the "law of heredity" was indebted to nineteenth-century evolutionary science, a topic on which he published a separate lecture series.

Second, Krauskopf offered a reappraisal of Christianity. In a lecture that drew on the search by contemporary scholars for "the historical Jesus," Krauskopf argued that Jesus was a "patriotic" Jew, whose teachings were rooted in the Torah and Talmud.[4] Christianity, as distinct from the teachings of Jesus, Krauskopf attributed to Paul, whom he blamed for the "mystical and mythical doctrines of a Trinity . . . [and] Salvation by Faith" that became characteristic of Christianity. Krauskopf emphasized the compatibility of Judaism and Christianity as he understood them.[5]

And third, he pointed primarily to the long history of Christians who forced Jews to convert, to which he dedicated a lecture, while also attributing conversions to a lesser extent to the venality or suspect motives of Jews who apostatized to Christianity for "immediate worldly advantage."[6]

When speaking of apostates, Krauskopf used the term "pervert," a word likely to strike modern readers as offensive. That said, it is useful to consider the full context of Krauskopf's remarks. A "convert," he argued, is someone who joins a religion (in this case, Judaism), while a "pervert" is someone who leaves a religion. Krauskopf explained that people who left Judaism were better understood as "allured perverts not convinced converts." That pejorative usage of the noun as a synonym for apostate was standard if not very common, and it predates the word's association with sexual deviancy—though that usage had begun to be common in the middle of the nineteenth century.[7]

4. Lecture II, "Jesus—a Jew, and Not a Christian," 14.

5. Lecture III, "Paul, the Jew and the Gentile," 12.

6. Lecture I, "True and False Converts," 10.

7. For a contemporary discussion of this usage of the term, see "A Pervert," *Nation* 55, no. 1427 (November 3, 1892), 335, https://www.google.com/books/edition/The_Nation/OuJIAQAA MAAJ?q=pervert+convert&gbpv=1. See also "pervert," *Oxford English Dictionary*, https://www.oed .com/, or "pervert," *Online Etymology Dictionary*, https://www.etymonline.com/word/pervert. On changes in late nineteenth-century Western discourse concerning sexuality, see Paul A. Robinson, "Havelock Ellis and Modern Sexual Theory," *Salmagundi* 21 (Winter 1973), 27–33 and 61–62.

Krauskopf's lectures carried on a tradition of American Jewish responses to Christian missions. That tradition dated back at least to the exposé of Joseph Samuel C. F. Frey (1771–1850) for financial improprieties and misleading efforts to convert Jews as the first missionary to the Jews in the United States, published under the title *Tobit's Letters to Levi* (1816),[8] and to subsequent responses to the American Society for Meliorating the Condition of the Jews. Many American Jewish leaders published critiques of missionary Christianity, such as *A Defense of Judaism Versus Proselytizing Christianity* (1889) by the Reform leader Isaac Mayer Wise (1819–1900). Krauskopf's lectures were heavily indebted to earlier polemics against Christian missionaries. His lectures provided a plausible explanation as to why conversion from Judaism to Christianity was seldom if ever genuine. His lectures also identified Reform Judaism as a legitimate option to which non-Jews could convert.[9]

Krauskopf's lectures were similar in both form and topic to the later but more famous volume by the American psychologist and philosopher William James (1842–1910), *The Varieties of Religious Experience* (1902).[10] Both works were originally a series of lectures, and each offered a theory to explain the phenomenon of religious conversion. Both do so through presenting vignettes of converts. In Krauskopf's case, the vignettes were drawn from founding personalities in the Christian Bible; forced converts from the Middle Ages and the early modern period; and modern figures such as Baruch Spinoza (1632–1677), Heinrich Heine (1797–1856), and Benjamin Disraeli (1804–1881). Where James's lectures were derived from the new science of psychology, Krauskopf's leaned at least in part on evolutionary science. Both volumes paid attention to sudden conversions. James offered a theory of religious experiences that, though intended to be universal, was heavily indebted to the vaguely Protestant liberalism of his milieu. Krauskopf more straightforwardly offered a theory of conversion from a Reform Jewish perspective.

The excerpts below are taken from Krauskopf's introductory lecture, in which he most clearly states his thesis, and from the lecture on "Allured Perverts," where he most directly discusses Christian missions to the Jews.

◇◇◇

8. *Tobit's Letters to Levi; or, A Reply to the Narrative of Joseph Samuel C. F. Frey* (New York, 1816).

9. See Jonathan D. Sarna, "The American Jewish Response to Nineteenth-Century Christian Missions," *Journal of American History* 68, no. 1 (1981), 35–51.

10. William James, *The Varieties of Religious Experience: A Study in Human Nature* (New York: Longmans, Green, 1902).

Excerpts from Joseph Krauskopf, "Lecture I: True and False Converts," January 4, 1891

Source: Joseph Krauskopf, "Lecture I: True and False Converts" (January 4, 1891), in Joseph Krauskopf, *Jewish Converts, Perverts, and Dissenters: Eleven Sunday Lectures before the Reform Congregation Keneseth Israel* (Philadelphia: Oscar Klonower, 1891), 3–12.

A man's religious belief is his heritage, seldom his acquisition. Even before the dawn of consciousness, long before he can stammer a "yea" or "nay," at the very threshold of life, he is initiated into some particular religion, which, as a rule, accompanies him through life, till the end of consciousness, unto the threshold of his grave. Before yet he knows the meaning of his religion, or understands the doctrines he professes, or the rites he performs, he is convinced of their superiority over all others. Before yet he has learned to love his own religion he has learned to hate the religion of others. . . .

No man is an individual. He is a composite of a long line of ancestry, the microsm [sic] of his family's thoughts and beliefs, of their likes and dislikes. Be he yet so original and independent, he is still a sprout of his family-tree. The mind is a palimpsest. One generation writes its layer on the top of the other, without however succeeding in wholly effacing that which was written before. The ancestor speaks through the mouth of his descendant.

This is no new revelation. It is the *Law of Heredity* applied to the mind. It helps to explain the origin of some of our religious beliefs, the cause of some of our strong likes and dislikes, and the reason why the fewest only ever succeed in breaking away from them, for what the *Law of Heredity* plants before birth the *Law of Environment* ripens after birth. What our grandparents have done unconsciously becomes the conscious work of our parents. Their God becomes our God, as they worship we worship, what is comforting and elevating to them, becomes so to us, their conception of the true and false, of the sublime and ridiculous, becomes our conception of the proper and absurd, and long before we can inquire and examine and judge for ourselves. Even though we examine at a later age, it is rarely that we can overcome our inherited and acquired prejudice and bias.

As to suddenly and completely turning from what has hitherto been held as true and sublime to what has always been regarded as false and ridiculous, and, henceforth, invest the latter with the awe and love hitherto bestowed upon that faith, which is our heritage of ages, and to which we have been inured from our earliest infancy, that it is well-nigh impossible. If such a sudden change of mind and heart occurs, the conversion must be due to some sudden dawning of a light that never dawned before, to some sudden revelation of truth never heard before, to a sudden, mysterious, fanning into a brilliant flame of some glimmering spark, that had long and unconsciously awaited its opportunity. If not due to any of these causes, then it must be due to a diseased, or a scheming, or a coerced, or an unduly influenced mind. If true and rational and sincere, it may be due to a freak of nature; to a law of nature it cannot be due. Nature makes no leaps. She never hurries where haste is dangerous. She permits her *Law of Variation* to make gradual progressive, or retrogressive, changes, but never to pass with a single bound, from what was always held as true and sublime to what was always spurned as false and ridiculous.

But such sudden conversions have occurred. There have been those, who sacrificed to idols one day, and on the following day acknowledged the invisible and incorporeal God of Moses and Mohammed as Supreme. There have been [Muslims] and Jews, who, on Friday in their Mosque, or on Saturday in their Synagogue, worshipped the *One and Only God*, and on the very following Sunday confessed belief in a *Triune God*[11] in a Cathedral. There have been Christians who in their church on Sunday affirmed, in the Apostles' Creed, their belief in Jesus Christ, the only Son of God, "who was conceived by the Holy Ghost, born of the Virgin Mary; suffered under Pontius Pilate, was crucified, dead, and buried; he descended into Hell, the third day he rose from the dead; he ascended into heaven, and sitteth on the right hand of God the Father Almighty; from whence he shall come to judge the quick and the dead,"[12] and on the following day cast aside their belief in a Redeemer, in a Vicarious Atonement, or in a Hell, as irrational, and the stories of the Miraculous Conception and of the Resurrection, as mythical.

The causes of such strange and sudden conversions we propose to investigate today, to see whether such radical and organic changes are true or false, due to conviction, to sudden revelations of new light, or to a diseased mind, or to persuasion, or force, or policy. As the field is broad, and our time short, we shall confine ourselves to what concerns and interests us most, namely: to an inquiry into the causes that led to conversions to and from Judaism.

The History of Judaism records quite a number of converts from other faiths to its ranks. Whence, and why, and how, came they? Was their conversion true or

11. This refers to the Christian doctrine of the Trinity, defined as the belief that there is one God with one substance and three divine persons — namely, the Father, the Son, and the Holy Spirit.

12. The Apostles' Creed is commonly used in Western Christian liturgies. It likely dates to the third century CE.

false? Came they of their own accord, or were they allured or forced? Was their motive spiritual or material gain, heavenly or earthly reward? ...

When now we ask the question: Why they came? We will hardly be accused of favoritism to Judaism for claiming, that the attracting force must have been the simple grandeur of its doctrines, the nobility of the heart and soul and mind which it fostered, the divine halo which it shed about the rights and liberties of the individual, about the purity of the home, about the morality of society, and about the peace and prosperity of the community. When first brought to the notice of the converts it must have come to them as a new revelation; it must have fanned the glimmering spark that in them yearned, consciously or unconsciously, for the better and truer faith, into a brilliant flame. One all-good Father of All, One Brotherhood of All, One Law, One Right, One Duty for All, One Aim—the establishment of universal Peace and Love and Good Will—among All, here, indeed, were truths never heard before, blessings never seen and felt before, and followers of the New Truth they became....

Granted that these proselytes embraced Judaism from conviction, the question still remains: Came they of their own accord or did it require the service of missionary zeal to bring the new revelation to them? The proselytizing spirit was certainly not unknown among the Jews; and they must have excercised [sic] it considerably, for St. Matthew informs us that "they compassed sea and land to make one proselite" [Matt. 25:13],[13] the Roman poet Horace (65–8 BC)[14] satirizes their missionary zeal and Josephus' (39–95 AC)[15] statement that there is not "a single town among Greeks or barbarians or anywhere else, not a single nation to which the observance of the Sabbath as it exists among the Jews has not penetrated, and among whom other Jewish laws and ordinances are not observed"[16] leaves little doubt that there was considerable proselytizing zeal behind it all.

And there is no need of apologizing for that zeal. There is a missionary zeal that is right and imperative, as there is one that is wrong, insulting and harmful. It is humane to bring religion to those that either have it not, or have a very

13. While Krauskopf's footnotes have not been reproduced in full, key citations have been included in brackets. Interestingly, Krauskopf used the abbreviations "B.C." (before Christ) and "A.C." (after Christ) in his writing.

14. The Roman poet Quintus Horatius Flaccus (Horace) (65–8 BCE) included the line "like the Jews we shall force you to join our throng" in Satires 1.4.

15. Titus Flavius Josephus (c. 37 or 38–100 CE) was a Jewish historian and Roman citizen who wrote in Latin.

16. Titus Flavius Josephus, Against Apion 2.10.39. It is commonly believed that this work was produced after 94 CE.

poor specimen of it. It is philanthropic to bring truth to those that live in error, and light to those who walk in darkness, and virtue to those who live in vice and crime, and religious hope and comfort to those who are in despair. It were inhuman to be in the possession of what might cleanse the heart, and elevate the mind, and not share it with those in need of it. A true belief almost demands of the believer the bringing to the notice of the corrupt the advantages of that belief. It were a mockery to talk grandiloquently of "loving our neighbors as ourselves" [Mark 12:31], and then consciously keep from them that which might benefit them as it benefited us, or to declare that the aim of one's religion is to effect the federation of all peoples into one brotherhood, under the fatherhood of one God, and under the sway of universal peace and good will and enlightenment, and then never move hand or foot or lip for the realization of that aim.

But, whatever missionary zeal there was, was of short duration, and I am far from believing, that it was as excessive, or as successful as Matthew or Horace or Josephus would have us believe. Of all religions in the world, Judaism is the least adapted for proselytizing among Heathen people. Were not its abstracts and philosophical doctrines, its rigorous ordinances, its sober tone and appearance, often too much for the Jews themselves? How is it to be believed, that they would find favor among heathen people, who were accustomed to conceivable, and even visible, gods, to imposing and attractive ceremonialisms, to riotous orgies and licentious practices sanctioned by their religions! It was a religion for the cultured and half-cultured, as Prof. [Theodor] Mommsen[17] well discerned, but it was not plastic enough to adapt itself to the tastes and wants and needs of the masses. Besides, Judaism lacked, at that time, the cosmopolitan aspect. It was too intimately interwoven with the Jewish Nation. The acceptance of the one almost included the acceptance of the other, which offended the racial and national pride of the would-be converts. In addition to this, most of the Rabbis rigorously insisted upon the Abrahamic rite for every male proselyte, to which, of course, the fewest only would submit. It seems that while some of the Rabbis were very enthusiastic for conversion, others had little faith in it. One of them went so far as to declare that "proselytes are to Israel what a scab is to the skin" [Yevamos 48b]. They knew that Judaism was no religion for the ignorant, or for the novelty-seekers, like the one that asked Rabbi Shammai to be instructed in Judaism, "while standing on one leg" [Shabbat 31a].[18] They suspected their

17. Theodor Mommsen (1817–1903) was a celebrated German scholar of classics and ancient history. Krauskopf had previously cited Mommsen on why gentiles in the ancient world converted to Judaism.
18. Shammai (50 BCE–30 CE), a prominent rabbinical authority frequently mentioned in the

motives, or feared the reaction after the temporary religious enthusiasm had subsided, and, therefore, they placed every obstacle in their way....

These last remarks contain already the answer to the other two questions that may yet be asked, viz.: whether the converts to Judaism were forced into it or whether they were lured into it by the hope of immediate worldly advantage. From the guilt of coerced conversion Judaism is almost wholly free. Only twice, as far as I can remember, during its existence of over 5000 years, does this foul blot stain its history: the first time in the case of prince Shechem and his people,[19] and the second time, when the Asmoneans gave to certain conquered tribes the choice between banishment and conversion.[20] And these two cases, though wrong, are not even without extenuating circumstances. The first one was the method chosen by enraged brothers as an atonement for the insult offered to the honor of their sister and to the name of their family; the second case was entirely a war measure, and was resorted to as a means of self-protection.

And as to material advantages, if the Jews had any to offer to strangers prior to their exile from their home, there was no need of proselytizing for them. They extended almost full fellowship to those who, residing in Palestine, obligated themselves to obey the seven duties,[21] which they regarded as the foundation of civilization, viz.: "To obey those in authority, to worship God, to forsake idolatry, to commit no lewdness, not to murder, not to steal, not to eat living flesh" [Sanhedrin 56b]. If they but renounced idolatry they considered them Jews. Their law commanded them to love the stranger, not to vex, not to oppress, nor to deal unjustly with him, but to have one law for the stranger as well as for their own people. They declared that before God all are one, and all good people, no matter what their faith or race or nation, will have their reward in the life beyond. If Israel had any to offer after their dispersion, there was still less need of proselytizing for them. Whatever they might have done for the Non-Jews, and they turned Jews, their religion obliged them to do without conversion. "Whoever associates with us," taught their Rabbis, "let him be as a brother. Whoever

---

Mishnah, is cited here for a well-known story in the Talmud in which a potential convert asked Rabbi Shammai to teach him the Torah while standing on one leg.

19. In Genesis 34, Shechem rapes Dinah, daughter of Jacob the patriarch. In revenge, the sons of Jacob encouraged the Shechemites to join them by being circumcised and then, while they were disabled by the pain of the circumcision, killed them.

20. In the first century BCE, the Hasmonean dynasty in Judaea forcibly converted the Idumeans (Edomites) to Judaism, albeit with significant opposition from the rabbis.

21. The Seven Laws of Noah, promulgated in Genesis 9, were considered by the Talmud to be binding on all people, including the gentiles. In contrast, the Mosaic law was binding only on Jews.

acts dishonestly towards a Non-Jew desecrates God. Mislead no one design-
edly, be he a Jew or Non-Jew. Injustice must be done to none, whether he belong
to our religion or to another. Be equally as charitable to the Non-Jew as to the
Jew. Christians and [Muslims] are equally with us messengers of God, who are
spreading light and truth throughout the world."[22]

And after all is said, pray, tell, what worldly advantage could that religion
hold out, whose followers, for 1800 years were homeless and friendless the
whole world over, who everywhere heard the preaching of "do to others what
you would have others do to you" [Luke 6:31], "peace on earth and good will
to all men" [Luke 2:14], yet seldom saw it practiced on them, strangers everywhere, everywhere the barest human rights denied them, every where school,
society, the professions, the higher callings barred against them, everywhere
forced to the lowest trades, compelled to live apart from their fellowmen, ma-
ligned, lowered to the very filth of the earth, forced to wear an ostracizing garb
that they might the easier be singled out for public taunt and contempt, pray
tell: what worldly advantage could such a religion and such a people hold out? . . .

Now to the other part of our inquiry: What were the causes that led to conversions *from* Judaism? This, too, is a very wide field. Jews have apostatized to almost all the religions with which they came in contact, to the Egyptian, Syrian,
Persian, Greek, Roman, [Muslim], Christian, and others. Our time, however,
will not permit us to investigate the causes of all these apostasies. We shall
therefore, have to limit ourselves to what, owing to our present environments,
concern and interest us most, namely, to an inquiry into the causes that led to
conversions from Judaism to Christianity. . . .

How about the apostasies to Christianity? To answer this question intelli-
gently and impartially, we must do, as we did before, in the case of Judaism, inquire what Christianity is, whether its doctrines are superior or inferior to those
of Judaism, whether its mode of worship possesses great attractiveness, or its
followers such great power and honor and influence as to compel or to incite
apostasies from Judaism.

What is Christianity? After long search and study and inquiry, I find easier
to tell what Christianity is *not* than what it *is*. If I take the Catholic's definition,
the Protestant objects; if I take the creed of Calvin as the standard, [Emanuel]
Swedenborg[23] cries "nay;" if I take that of the Episcopalean [sic], the Quaker

22. Quoted from the Tanna Devei Eliyahu, a midrash from the tenth century CE.

23. This is a reference to the Swedish Christian theologian and philosopher Emanuel
Swedenborg (1688–1772), whose book on the afterlife, *Heaven and Hell* (1758), was widely influential in the West.

throws up his hands in horror; if I favor the Methodist creed, the Baptist tells me I am wrong; if I take the Unitarian's conception, all these, and a host of yet other Christian sects, indignantly and emphatically declare that, whatever else Unitarianism may be, it is not Christianity.[24]

It is not my intention to re-quarrel their quarrels. I am anxious to know what Christianity is. I search among them all for those essential points, which all hold in common, in which there is perfect agreement among them all, and which all value highest, and eliminate those few points concerning which there is dispute among them. The result I obtain is startling. *I started to find Christianity, and I find Judaism.* Here it is, the same Judaism that we found before: the same God, the same commandments, the same hope, the same effort, the same origin, the same goal. *In the essentials of one God over all, one brotherhood of all, one duty and one aim for all, there is perfect agreement between Christianity and Judaism.* The points wherein some of the sects differ from Judaism are the very points wherein they differ among themselves. Some place two coadjutors alongside of God, some only one, some none. Some believe that God, at one time, assumed the form of man, and walked the earth as a prophet, others believe that he that thus walked, was not God, but a man God-inspired, others regard him, either wholly or partially, as myth, as graft from heathen theology, dismiss him, as a supernatural being, from their theology, and yet regard themselves as Christians.

If these sects, who stand wholly upon the platform of Judaism, with few, or with none, of the superadded beliefs, regard themselves as Christians, it is plain that the difference between Judaism and Christianity is more in name than in doctrine. Judaism can not speak of Christianity as *inferior*, especially when stripped of its superadded material, and certainly can not regard it as *superior*, seeing that in all essentials, in all that is valued highest by both, there is perfect agreement among both, as it could not well be otherwise, since Christianity has taken these literally and bodily, from Judaism.

Remembering that a man's religious belief is often the heritage of generations of ancestry, interwoven with his every fiber, therefore, not easily cast aside, and seeing that, religiously and ethically, Judaism and Christianity are the same, that when they differ only in a few mooted theological points, which are entirely dispensable for leading a true and pure life on earth, it becomes evident, that, when we see apostasies from Judaism to Christianity, we can not attribute such

24. Disagreement among Christian denominations was a common piece of evidence invoked in defensive Jewish polemics like this lecture. Reform Jews often cited Unitarianism, a form of Christianity that denies the deity of Jesus and thus the doctrine of the Trinity, as a rational faith that had much kinship with Judaism.

conversions to some sudden dawning of a light that never dawned before, to some revelation of truth never heard before. Remembering also the strong in-born dislike, which hundreds of years of persecution and aversion have engendered in the hearts of the followers of both against each other, and consulting the official statistics of the governments, and seeing that the Jewish people as a body, the whole world over, demonstrate a more moral, a more intellectual, a more peaceful and industrious life than do the Christians as a body, it is impossible for me to believe that such conversions are true. I believe they are false. I believe they are due to other motives than those of conviction, either to persuasion or to force or to policy. If not due to any of these, then I believe them due to some aberration of the mind, or to sheer desperation, in consequence of persecution, or fanatical narrowness, within the fold. If due to none of all these causes, then they never were conversions at all.

This belief of mine I propose to prove in this series of lectures on "Jewish Converts and Perverts." I propose to investigate the life, and character, and deeds, and environing times and conditions, of some of the most notable professed, or nominal, or falsely named, Jewish Apostates. I propose to prove that some of them, yielding to force, or policy, became only *nominally* Christians, in their hearts they remained true to Judaism; that others, yielding to a spirit of ambition or adventure, were even greater perverts as Christians than they were as Jews; that others, though regarded as converts by Christians, never were converts at all, and still others, though regarded as apostates by Jews, lived and died as the most faithful Jews of all.

Excerpts from Joseph Krauskopf, "Lecture V: Allured Perverts," February 1, 1891

Source: Joseph Krauskopf, "Lecture V: Allured Perverts" (February 1, 1891), in Joseph Krauskopf, *Jewish Converts, Perverts, and Dissenters: Eleven Sunday Lectures before the Reform Congregation Keneseth Israel* (Philadelphia: Oscar Klonower, 1891), 3–12.

They were *allured perverts not convinced converts*. Their bitter hatred against the Jews is unnatural. We cannot alter our nature over night. Our beliefs are not garments that can be thrown off at will. We cannot erase mind-impressions as we do the writing on the slate. We can not be descendants of a people that has held one kind of belief, uninterruptedly, for hundreds of years, grow up in, and be environed by, that belief from the day of our birth, and, then, suddenly fling it aside for that, which has been always regarded as inferior to and as its bitterest enemy and henceforth, hate and pursue, as an enemy, that which we have always loved. The Laws of Heredity, of Conformity to Type, of Environment, are against such sudden and such diametrically opposite changes. If such changes are not due to aberrations of the mind, we must look for their true motive elsewhere than in conviction.

That true motive it is, in nearly every case, not difficult to find. It is sometimes revenge for real or imaginary abuse by the mother-church. Sometimes it is a spirit of adventure or eagerness for notoriety. But most always it is personal advantage. To a Jew, who was not very firm in his inherited faith, who was persecuted and degraded on all sides, who hungered after bread or after wealth or honor or public office or social station, and who could not satisfy that hunger as a Jew, but could have an abundance of it, by permitting a few drops of baptismal water to be sprinkled upon his head, apostasy was a mighty temptation.[25] Missionaries had a sharp eye for such Jewish perverts. From the very first the capture of a Jewish soul was regarded as a capital prize by the Church. The opportunities for advancement, gain, power, honor, station, title, were held out to them as tempting bait to lure them on. Suspected, despised, spurned, often even persecuted as perverts among their own people, —fondled, made much of, by Christian people, dazzled by the tempting bait, they bared their heads for the few drops of baptismal water, and attained the end of their conversion. Despised usurers became royal financiers. The excommunicated Talmudist Josua Lorqui[26] became, under the stunning name of Geronimo de Santa Fé, the body-physician of Pope Benedict XIII.[27] The unprincipled Rabbi Solomon Levi advanced, under the holy name of Paulus de Santa Maria,[28] to the position of Bishop of Cartagena, Chancellor of Castille, and private Counsellor to King Don Henry III.[29] [Johannes] Pfefferkorn,[30] the adventurer and fugitive from justice,

25. A very common line of argument was that Jews who converted to Christianity were incentivized to do so, or even paid outright.

26. Yehosúa ben Yosef ibn Vives (fl. 1400–1430), took the name Hieronymus de Sancta Fide (Jerome of the Holy Faith) after converting to Catholicism.

27. Born in the southern Italian town of Gravina in Puglia, Pietro Francesco Orsini (1649–1730) was elected pope in 1724. As Benedict XIII, he sought to rein in the Italian clergy's decadence. His rule was characterized by weak political leadership and fiscal mismanagement.

28. Paul of Burgos (c. 1351–1435) converted from Judaism to Christianity in Spain.

29. Henry III (1379–1406) was king of Castile.

30. Johannes Pfefferkorn (1469–1523) was a convert from Judaism to Christianity who became a theologian and actively sought to destroy copies of the Talmud.

had his sins washed away in the baptismal font, and was placed into a very comfortable office by the Mayor of Cologne.

Such honors, however, were not heaped upon them for their own individual benefit. They were intended to be alluring baits for other perverts. These apostates knew that a continuance of their honors depended not only upon their own faithful compliance with every requirement of the Church, but also upon their zeal in inducing other Jews to follow their example. Driven on by the fear of being suspected of hypocrisy—which was a fatal suspicion in the days of the Inquisition—by the allurements of still higher honors, by the contempt with which they were treated by the Jews, these apostates, once Jews themselves—now apostates, once perverts to Judaism—now converts to the religion of "peace on earth and good will toward men" [Luke 2:14], became the instigators of some of the most frightful cruelties that were visited upon the Jews in the name of Christianity.

I am far from entertaining even the slightest ill feeling against Christianity of today for any of the cruelties, which the Church visited upon the Jews during 1500 years of her unlimited supremacy, or for the allurements she employed to swell her numbers from the ranks of the Jews. I am too sensible of all the excellencies which Christianity possesses, when true to its professions and teachings, of its absolute religious and ethical identity with Judaism, barring the Christological addenda,—the same God, the same Commandments, the same origin and goal, the same hope and effort—to entertain for a moment the thought that it would sanction such proceedings today, or at all tolerate them.

Surprising, therefore, it is to me, knowing of her present greater tolerance towards other creeds, of the poor success she has had in her missionary work among the Jews, that most of her Jewish converts were allured perverts, and even more of a disgrace to their new faith, than they were to their former faith, that she should still permit her missionaries to harass and beset the Jews. It is not to her missionary work that I object. That is a noble work when rightfully used, when employed among savages and criminals, among the godless and the heartless. But it is an insult to Catholicism to send Protestant missionaries among them, or to Protestantism to pester them with Catholic missionaries, or to Judaism to harass it with Christian missionaries, when in all essential and fundamental religious principles, in the worship of God, in the obedience to His Commandments, in the effort to do the right and to shun the evil there is perfect unanimity among them.

If religion has for its object, to make man true and good, faithful and pious, wise and happy, a child of God and a brother to man, pray, tell me, good Christian friend, what has Christianity to offer in that line that Judaism has not, or what does it possess in that line, which it has not bodily taken from Judaism? Was not its founder Jesus a Jew,[31] were not its first planters, his disciples, Jews, was not Paul, its first propagator, a Jew, are not the Commandments it repeats, the Prophets it quotes, the Psalms it chants, all, all Jewish? Pray, good Christian friend, consult governmental statistics, visit the schools and the markets, the factories and the shops, visit the Penal- and the Corrective-Institutes, the Hospitals and Asylums and Almshouses, the dens and the dives, and tell me: do the Jews show, proportionately, as many paupers and drunkards and criminals, as many vicious and fallen and diseased, as many shiftless and thriftless and worthless, as do the Christians? Tell me are Christians more thrifty, more prosperous, more learned, than are the Jews, or are their homes happier, or their family relationships purer, or their marital ties more sacred than those of the Jews?

Recall, good Christian friend, your army of missionaries from among the Jews. Such zeal has caused much trouble in the past, for every religious persecution has sprung from the notion that it is one man's duty to make another believe like him. Such zeal causes irritation now. The Jew cannot be converted to Christianity. What 1500 years of cruelty, what fire and sword and rack, what cruel laws and still more cruel degredation [sic], could not accomplish, will never be accomplished by missionaries, who are frequently Jewish perverts,[32] whose character and motives can not stand much investigation. The History, the martyrology, the blood, the reason, of the true Jew revolts even against the thought of apostasy.

The few that are captured here and there are not worth the trouble, and certainly not the vast sums of money that are expended for their capture. Smalley's "Cost of the Gospel" tells us that it costs $2800 to convert one Jew.[33] One of the latest Reports of the Great Britain Society for the Promotion of Christianity[34]

31. Krauskopf used his second lecture to establish the Jewishness of Jesus, a claim that was aligned with contemporary scholarship on the historical Jesus.

32. A large proportion of Christian missionaries to the Jews were converts from Judaism.

33. Both Christian and Jewish publications had a curious fixation on the costs of missions to the Jews. Christian missionary publications divided the amount spent on missions by the estimated number of Jews in the United States or the world to emphasize how little Christians spent per Jew on efforts to convert them, while Jewish publications divided the amount spent by the number of converts claimed by missionaries to emphasize the extraordinary ineffectiveness of the missions.

34. A reference to either the British Society for Propagating the Gospel among the Jews, founded in London in 1842 by Presbyterians and other dissenters from the Church of England, or the better known London Society for Promoting Christianity among the Jews, founded by the Church of England in 1809 (now known as the Church's Ministry among Jewish People).

among the Jews tells us that its 141 missionaries among the 7,000,000 Jews of Europe, Asia, and Africa, converted 34 children and 60 adults, at the expense of $188,141, — $2000 for every Jewish soul, and not even one convert for every missionary, and seldom a sincere convert among them all, for most of them regard the conversion as a hoax, as a shrewd scheme to get themselves helped out of straits, or into comfortable positions. Practical and sensible Christians are beginning to see through the farce. But recently Bishop [Henry Codman] Potter[35] of the Diocese of New York formally requested, that the Good Friday collections, that were formerly taken up for the conversion of the Jews, be henceforth devoted to Church work among the colored people.

Recall your army of missionaries from among the Jews, and spend their labor and your money where they are needed. With that labor and that money wipe out your White-Chapel[36] districts, tear down your tenement-barracks, eradicate your nurseries of vice and crime, bring a breath of pure air, a ray of sunshine, to those that rot in cellars and alleys, save men and women from moral pollution, save children from foul contamination, bring bread to those that are starving, and employment to those that are driven to crime by the moaning of wife and children for food and shelter, soften the hearts of employers, convert your corrupted officers and legislators, convert professing Christians into acting Christians, do the thousand other things which the needs of civilization and humanity demand, and which your religion commands. Make such use of your labor and your money, and you will have no time for trying to allure Jews from a religion, which in its results proves itself as good as yours. You will have no time for trying to convert those to your faith, who have a history of 5000 years, and an array of lawgivers and prophets and bards, and philanthropists to whom the whole civilized world does homage, to prove that the Jew can live a godly life by faithful obedience to the teaching of his own religion. You will have but time for living and acting the pure religious and ethical precepts of Jesus. You will find these not only Christian but also Jewish; and not only Christian and Jewish but also humanitarian; broader than Christianity, broader than Judaism, — as broad as all Humanity.

35. Henry Codman Potter (1834–1908) was bishop of New York for the Episcopal Church.
36. The reference is to Whitechapel, an impoverished section of London.

13

"A CAREFUL STUDENT OF THE RELIGION OF THE EAST"

Charles T. Strauss Converts to Buddhism at the
World's Columbian Exposition (Chicago, IL)
(1893)

◇◇

EMILY SIGALOW

On September 26, 1893, following the conclusion of the World's Parliament of Religions (convened as part of the World Columbian Exposition in Chicago, Illinois), Charles Theodore Strauss (1852–1937), a wealthy haberdasher of Jewish descent, took on the Five Precepts of Morality—Buddhist vows to abstain from harming living beings, stealing, sexual misconduct, lying, and intoxication—as part of a lay Buddhist initiation rite called *Pansil*.[1] In doing so, he became the first American and the first Jew known to have converted to Buddhism in the United States. Strauss was a dedicated student of Buddhism and an admirer of the teachings of the Buddha. Born in St. Gall, Switzerland, in 1852, he had emigrated to the United States at age of eighteen. Alongside his brother, he worked in his father's lace goods business. After his father died, Strauss and his brother inherited the business and carried it on under the firm name of Charles T. Strauss and Bro. At the time of his conversion, Strauss owned one of the oldest and largest wholesale lace-curtain manufacturing companies in New York City.[2]

Strauss had attended the World's Parliament of Religions to learn more about Buddhism from the prominent international Buddhist delegates in attendance—especially Anagarika Dharmapala (1864–1933), an outspoken Buddhist revivalist and Strauss's friend from Sri Lanka (then Ceylon). After the parliament's proceedings ended, Dharmapala lectured to a large audience about the principles of Buddhism. At this lecture, he introduced Strauss, a man of forty-one, to the audience as an earnest student of Buddhism. On stage in front of

---

1. "Embraced the Faith of Buddha," *Atlanta Constitution*, September 28, 1893, 3.

2. For more information about Strauss's family life, see "Married—Strauss-Agatz," *New York Times*, April 23, 1879, 5; "Convert to Buddha," *Chicago Daily Tribune*, September 28, 1893, 2. See also note 11.

the audience, Strauss publicly declared his intention to become a disciple of the Buddha. Dharmapala recited the Five Precepts of Morality in Pali, the classical language of Theravada Buddhism, and Strauss repeated them after him. Strauss's conversion to Buddhism caught the attention of many leading American newspapers, Jewish and otherwise. In a note in the *American Israelite*, one reader confessed that, "having traveled all over the world including the entire Orient, this incident whereby one of our co-religionists became a Buddhist was certainly novel and perplexing."[3] He added, "I do not believe that such a ceremony has ever before taken place, and in order to have it recorded I will ask you if space admits to insert this letter in your paper."[4] Other newspapers declared the event truly historic. The *Galveston Daily News* of Houston, Texas, described Strauss as the "first American to break down the barriers that have stood for centuries between Buddhism and the people of the West."[5]

Strauss's turn to Buddhism marked the first time in history when converting to Buddhism became a serious religious possibility for Jews in America.[6] His conversion was most certainly the nineteenth century's most famous example of Jewish involvement in Buddhism. It was also an indication of broader Jewish interest in Buddhism in the late nineteenth century, a trend that mirrored American society's growing fascination with Buddhism in this period. As the historian Thomas Tweed has observed, at the height of the tradition's popularity in nineteenth-century America, the "historical relation and relative merits of Christianity and Buddhism were discussed by Congregationalists and Methodists as well as Ethical Culturalists and Unitarians."[7] Tweed also points out that "no single event had more impact" in the American setting on Buddhism's development and credibility "than the World's Parliament of Religions."[8]

Strauss's relationship with Buddhism was transplanted overseas in 1908 when he moved his permanent residence to Leipzig, Germany. At that time, Leipzig was the center of the European trade market. Strauss helped establish

---

3. "Notes and Comments," *American Israelite*, October 5, 1893, 1.

4. Ibid.

5. "J.W. Strauss of New York Has Been Converted to Buddhism," *Galveston Daily News*, October 2, 1893, 4. The reporter used the wrong initials for Strauss in the article.

6. The word "conversion" is used here in the original sense of the term: to refer to someone who turned his or her heart and mind toward the teachings of a new religious tradition—in this case, Buddhism. See Richard Seager, *Buddhism in America*, rev. ed. (New York: Columbia University Press, 2012), 15.

7. Thomas A. Tweed, *The American Encounter with Buddhism, 1844–1912: Victorian Culture and the Limits of Dissent* (Chapel Hill: University of North Carolina Press, 2000), 33.

8. Ibid., 31.

a Buddhist community in Leipzig, the first Buddhist community in Europe. He traveled to Sri Lanka several times and established relations between the Buddhist community in Leipzig and the Maha Bodhi Society.[9] He fled Germany in 1916, just prior to America's entry into World War I, and spent his final years in Zurich, Switzerland.

◇◇◇

Newspaper Report of Charles T. Strauss's Conversion to Buddhism at the World's Columbian Exposition (Chicago, IL)

> Source: "Convert to Buddha: Act of Charles T. Strauss a Big Surprise in Gotham; Member of a Wealthy and Influential Hebrew Family—Said to Have Been a Student for Some Time of the Eastern Religion, but Keeps Secret His Intention of Embracing the Faith . . . ," *Chicago Daily Tribune*, September 28, 1893, 2.

NEW YORK Sept. 27.—[Special.]—The reported conversion to the Buddhist faith[10] in Chicago yesterday of Charles T. Strauss[11] of this city has created great interest here, where he is well known. Mr. Strauss is related to some of the wealthiest and most exclusive Hebrew families in New York City, and his father before him was a strict observer of the Jewish ritual. They are astonished as well as indignant over Mr. Strauss's abjuration of the faith of his fathers, and they cannot understand his move toward the effete religious mysticism of the East.

Charles T. Strauss is the head of the oldest and largest wholesale lace curtain house in this city, with headquarters at No. 466 Broadway. The business was followed by his father many years ago and bequeathed to two sons, who now carry it on under the firm name of Charles T. Strauss & Bro. Mr. Strauss is re-

9. For information about Strauss's work in Europe and Asia, see Heinz Muermel, "Carl Theodor Strauss, Buddhist Activist and Author (1852–1937)," unpublished speech at the 11th Annual International Conference on Sri Lankan Studies, n.d.

10. Buddhism, a major global religion with a complex belief system, considers existence as a totality and seeks to explain the persistence in the human experience of suffering and its cessation. Buddhism was founded by the Indian religious leader Siddhartha Gautama (c. 563–483 BCE)—known by the title Buddha (Sanskrit for "enlightened one")—and Buddhist belief, scripture, and practice derive from the account of Buddha's life, teachings, and monastic rules.

11. Born to a secular Jewish family in Switzerland, Charles T. Strauss (1852–1937) immigrated to the United States at age eighteen and became a successful business entrepreneur. In 1879, he married Katie Agatz (1860–1924), a Jewish woman of German ancestry who died young. At the time of Strauss's initiation into Buddhism, he was a widower with three children. Strauss never sought formal ordination but became an active expositor of the Maha Bodhi Society, a South Asian Buddhist association founded by Dharmapala. Strauss authored *The Buddha and His Doctrine* (1923), in which he affirmed a rationalist and ethical approach to the Buddhist tradition.

lated by marriage to Isaac Stern,[12] head of the well-known retail dry good firm of Stern Bros.[13]

Mr. Kugelman,[14] of the firm, said he was astonished to learn that Mr. Strauss had actually embraced the religion of Buddha. He added: "However, I suppose there is no reason for surprise, for although I know him slightly I have always understood he was a careful student of the religion of the East. He reads constantly and deeply and takes few persons into his confidence. I have no direct information that he has been converted."

At Mr. Strauss's residence, No. 264 West Fifty-Seventh Street, it was learned he had not yet reached home. Mr. Strauss is a widower and lives in a flat at the above address with his two young children, girls, and a housekeeper. The latter said she knew Mr. Strauss was interested in the tenets of Buddha, but that he had not told her he was going to embrace that faith during his visit to Chicago. She was not surprised, however, to hear that he had done so.

12. Born in Ziegenhain, Prussia, Isaac Stern (1844–1910) was brought to the United States in 1855 as a child with his family. In 1880, he married Virginia J. Michaels (1860–1927), and the couple had three children. Rising from humble origins to considerable wealth, the success of Stern Brothers Department Store (see the next note) eventually propelled the Sterns into the ranks of New York's elite Jewish families.

13. Founded in 1867 by Isaac (1844–1910), Louis (1847–1922), and Benjamin (1857–1933) Stern, the sons of German Jewish immigrants, Stern Brothers Dry Goods (later the Stern Brothers Department Store) became a flagship of New York City's burgeoning merchandising industry. In time, Stern's became a sizable chain in New York and New Jersey. In 1951, Federated Department Stores acquired Stern's; in 2001, the Stern's chain was closed, and its stores were converted to Macy's and Bloomingdale's.

14. The identity of this individual is unknown.

14

"WITHOUT SACRIFICING THE RIGHTS OF OUR CITIZENS"

Concerning the Ottoman Empire's Restrictions on American Jews Entering Palestine (1899)

◇◇

SUSANNA KLOSKO

In the waning decades of the nineteenth century, the Ottoman empire grew increasingly wary of widespread Jewish colonization in Palestine, much of which was spearheaded by early Zionist settlers from tsarist Russia. As a result, the Sublime Porte outlawed Jewish immigration to Palestine in 1881 and adopted strict visa laws for Jews who visited the country. Owing to a standard body of irregular enforcement procedures, however, including the sale by absentee landlords of tracts of land in Palestine to the fledgling Zionist Organization, Ottoman control of the reality on the ground was lax and fluid. Against this backdrop, the nascent Yishuv (Jewish society in Palestine before the creation of the State of Israel in 1948) continued to grow. Between 1882 and 1918, when the region came under British control in the aftermath of World War I, the Jewish community of Palestine increased from 24,000 to 90,000 — that is, from roughly 8 percent to 9 percent of the total population.[1]

The United States had extraterritorial privileges in the Ottoman empire as a result of an 1830 commercial treaty between the two governments. This meant that American citizens were entitled to live under American jurisdiction on Ottoman soil. Anxious to protect its privileges, the U.S. government resisted attempts by Ottoman authorities to restrict American activities in Palestine and to discriminate against American Jews and naturalized Americans of Ottoman birth by placing limits on their residence in the empire.

In August 1898, the American consul in Jerusalem, Selah Merrill (1837–1909), sent a telegram to Charles M. Dickinson (1842–1924), the U.S. consul general

---

1. See "Appendix 5. Jewish and Non-Jewish Population of Palestine-Israel, 1517–2004," in *Israel in the Middle East: Documents and Readings on Society, Politics, and Foreign Relations, Pre-1948 to the Present*, ed. Itamar Rabinovich and Jehuda Reinharz, 2nd ed. (Waltham, MA: Brandeis University Press, 2008), 571.

in Constantinople, informing him that the governor of Palestine "has strict orders to treat American Jews like Russian Jews, guaranteeing departure in one month." The following January, Oscar Straus (1850–1926), the U.S. minister to the Ottoman empire, wrote to Dickinson that he had made it clear to the Turks that "my government would not admit the right of the Ottoman government to discriminate between our citizens on the basis of race or religion, such power my government had no right to exercise under the Constitution and would not concede to any other government." Straus added that only those Jews who came "en masse" as colonists should be forbidden from settling in Palestine.[2]

What followed was a drawn-out correspondence among Merrill, Straus, and Dickinson on the rights of naturalized Russian Jews. Merrill and Straus could not have been more inclined to disagree on this topic. Straus—who would later cofound the American Jewish Committee in 1906 and serve as secretary of commerce and labor under President Theodore Roosevelt (1858–1919), becoming the first Jew to be appointed a cabinet secretary in U.S. history—was an ardent defender of Jewish rights at home and abroad. In contrast, Merrill, a Congregationalist clergyman and scholar of biblical Hebrew, did not hide the fact that he barely considered naturalized Jews to be American citizens and thus were undeserving of the protection he was required by law to provide. In an ironic twist of historical fate, Straus and Merrill proved to be unusual political bedfellows. Notwithstanding their disparate views on the principle of religious equality and the protection of American rights abroad, they both believed Jewish settlement in Palestine to be a misguided and economically harmful venture.

◇◇

2. Letter from Oscar S. Straus to Charles M. Dickinson (January 30, 1899), Consular Posts, Jerusalem, Palestine, Record Group 84, enclosure to no. 18, vol. 16, entry number 453, National Archives and Records Administration, College Park, MD.

Letter from Selah Merrill to Oscar S. Straus, August 21, 1899

Source: Letter from Selah Merrill to Oscar S. Straus (August 21, 1899), Consular Posts, Jerusalem, Palestine, Record Group 84, no. 10, vol. 14, entry number 453, National Archives and Records Administration, College Park, MD.

United States Consulate

Jerusalem, Syria, Aug. 21, 1899

Hon. Oscar S. Straus[3]

United States Minister

Constantinople

Sir:

On the 17th of August I telegraphed you as follows: "Jews continue to come, some enter by deposite [sic].[4] Others not pay deposite and passports and baggage taken in pledge to return. Some cases Hardegg[5] gives bail so that poor Jews shall not starve and die on the beach. We have no power to enforce return. Shall we tell Jews that our Government will not help them? Things getting very bad."

The next day I received the following telegram: "Inform Governor Turkish Government has no right to prohibit entrance nor to exact deposite from American citizens be they Jews or Christians. You are not authorized to say our government declines protection to its citizens. Your detailed report awaited so I can take action at Sublime Porte.[6] Straus."

My telegram covers the ground in the main, but I will go over the matter more fully and of course must state some things that I have repeatedly men-

---

3. Oscar Solomon Straus (1850–1926), a native of Bavaria, immigrated to the United States as a child with his family. The Straus family initially settled in antebellum Georgia but later moved to New York, where they opened a successful crockery business and bought the R. H. Macy and Company department store. After graduating from Columbia Law School in 1873, Straus practiced law and became a merchant. He served as U.S. minister to Turkey (1887–90 and 1898–1900), U.S. ambassador to Turkey (1909–10), President Theodore Roosevelt's secretary of commerce and labor (1906–09), and U.S. representative to the International Court in the Hague (1902–26).

4. Jews arriving in Palestine were required to submit a deposit that they could retrieve upon leaving the country.

5. Ernst Hardegg (1840–1911), a member of the Protestant pietistic German Templer Society and owner of Jaffa's American-German colony hotel, served as the American vice consul in Jaffa from 1871 to 1909.

6. A French translation of the Ottoman Turkish Bâbıâli, meaning "high gate," this term was used to refer to the Ottoman regime.

tioned before in communications to the Department of State or to the Legation at Constantinople.

The Turkish regulation requiring Jews arriving at Jaffa to leave the country again in thirty or ninety days, if they come as visitors, has, I understand, been agreed to by our Government. No provision, however, is made by either government, so far as I have been informed, as to how these people are to be made to return. . . .

As the Turks do not accept the word of these people on landing a system of money pledges has been resorted to; this may be called "fine," "tax," "deposite," "*bakhshish*," "bail," or "pledge"; it is a money guarantee that the parties will carry out the requirements of the Turkish Government which has been assented to by their own Government. . . .

A very limited number cannot pay the fine; in most cases they do not pay because they will not. They come to the Consulate, implore, beg, cry, and make a great scene hour after hour. "Sick children," "hunger," "poverty," and all sorts of arguments are used to induce the Consul to help them. Rather than see them starve or sent back to the steamer which probably would not receive them again, the Consul, out of simple pity for the wretched people, gives his word as security that they will leave the country at the expiration of the specified time according to the Turkish regulation. The parties then enter and make their way to Jerusalem or to other places to which they may be destined. . . .

In my judgment the cases now mentioned and in fact most of the cases that come before us and demand so much of our time and demand likewise our utmost ingenuity to cope with the Turkish authorities, ought never to occur. They occur because the rights of Jews entering this country are not strictly defined. I have urged the Department of State and the Legation to have this matter corrected by the two governments interested, to have the regulations and signed by the highest authorities, so that the Consul may not act blindly. For example, have the Turks a right to demand a guarantee of these people that they will return in a specified time? The Legation says "No,"—the Turks say "Yes." What is the Consul to do? . . .

The Consulate at Jaffa exists largely for the purpose of helping into the country a class of persons whom the Turkish government does not want upon its soil. More than half the time of the Jerusalem Consulate is spent in helping Jews out of trouble. . . . It is high time for the rights of both resident and immigrant Jews to be carefully defined.

My strong feeling is that notwithstanding all my communications upon this subject to the Dept. of State and to the Legation, the Jewish question in Palestine is not, in either place, thoroughly understood. In both places there is in mind, apparently, only "respectable American Jews who wish to visit Palestine and Jerusalem."—I wish this were true. Hence it may serve to throw light upon the matter if I say that respectable American Jews coming here as bona fide travellers, there is no trouble about any more than this is about Christian travellers. It is the immigrant class which the Dept. of State and the Legation do not understand or appreciate; ignorant, degraded, filthy Russian or Polish Jews who by hook or crook—ways well known in New York and Chicago[7]—have obtained passports from our government and as "American Citizens" demand our protection—but who cannot speak a word of English and therefore they are suspected, and who come here, the authorities are certain, to swell the ranks of the colonists.

Allow me to repeat my question: Cannot the United States and the Turkish governments come to some definite understanding upon this matter? Cannot well defined regulations be written down and furnished to the Consulate and to the Governor of Jerusalem? When that is done the Consulate[s] at Jerusalem and Jaffa will be relieved from a very great and constantly increasing burden and annoyance, —a very great relief it would likewise be to yourself and the Legation which you ably represent.

Respectfully Your obedient servant
(signed) Selah Merrill[8]
U.S. Consul

7. The reference is to political bosses in the United States such as William M. Tweed (1823–1878) and Richard Croker (1843–1922), who dominated New York City's Tammany Hall network, and Chicago's mayor William H. Thompson (1869–1944), who openly collaborated with the notorious gangster Al Capone (1899–1947). Tweed, Croker, and Thompson became notorious symbols of American municipal corruption and were accused of assisting illegitimate naturalizations to gain voters and other supporters.

8. The clergyman and archaeologist Selah Merrill (1837–1909) hailed from Canton, Connecticut. A graduate of Yale University, Merrill was ordained as a Congregational minister and trained as a lawyer. He served as chaplain of the Forty-Ninth Regiment of U.S. Colored Infantry at Vicksburg and later taught Hebrew at the Andover Theological Seminary. He served as American consul in Jerusalem (1882–85, 1891–93, and 1898–1907) and played a key role in the discovery and excavation of the second wall of Jerusalem (the area between the Jaffa Gate and the Temple Mount). In 1907, he was appointed American consul in British Guiana.

Letter from Oscar S. Straus to Selah Merrill, September 12, 1899

Source: Letter from Oscar S. Straus to Selah Merrill (September 12, 1899), Consular Posts, Jerusalem, Palestine, Record Group 84, no. 113, vol. 16, entry number 453, National Archives and Records Administration, College Park, MD.

United States Legation
Constantinople, September 12, 1899
Selah Merrill, Esquire,
United States Consul
Jerusalem. (Syria)
Sir:

... I certainly appreciate the difficulties you are laboring under, and the unfortunate and miserable condition of affairs brought about by this influx of Jews many of whom appear to be paupers. It is indeed a deplorable situation for the Jews themselves, impelled by an *exalté* religious sentiment to reenter the Holy Land, some even resorting to every subterfuge and sacrificing their last dollar to carry out this purpose, some impelled by religious fervor, and others by the desire to enroll themselves among those who receive a part of the charity fund sent by their coreligionists from other lands.[9] I also understand that the Turkish Government, as a matter of self-protection, in order to prevent complications in the future should wish to interdict the further immigration by Jews into Palestine. From your several graphic reports in this matter and from other information that has from time to time reached me, I am inclined to think it would be best for the Jews themselves if this immigration, from an economical point of view could be stopped, to prevent the aggregation of a large poor class into a province where the opportunities for earning a livelihood are not sufficient for those now in Palestine.

I believe I also fully understand the difficulties you are contending with, and the efforts you are making, with the help of our Consular-Agent at Jaffa, to relieve the situation, as individual cases present themselves. I also appreciate your request for more precise instructions based upon clearly defined arrangements with the Imperial Authorities. ...

The subject has had my serious and deliberate thought, with the hope of discovering some method which would have the desired result without infringing upon the rights of our citizens under our laws; and at the same time without

9. The reference is to the centuries-old *halukah* (Hebrew for "division") system whereby Jews in diaspora communities channeled charitable contributions to rabbinic authorities in Jerusalem, Safed, and Tiberias for the support of Jewish communal life and institutions in the Land of Israel.

establishing a dangerous precedent, which the Imperial Authorities would certainly not be slow to avail themselves of in curtailing the rights of American Citizens, naturalized and native born, in other parts of the Empire. Only recently I had a very acute question growing out of the effort of the Imperial Authorities to expel all the American Missionaries in the Vilayet[10] of Diarbekir [sic],[11] by reason of an alleged plot of certain Armenians, some of whom were connected with the Mission work of Rev. Dr. [Alpheus N.] Andrus,[12] the leading American Missionary in that Vilayet, the authorities had gone so far as to indict Andrus, and the line of argument employed for their action was that our Government had consented to their right to exclude and expel such foreign subjects, as the authorities believed to be dangerous.[13]

I refer somewhat in detail to this subject, that you may appreciate the difficulties I find in the way of arriving at a clearly defined arrangement and of giving specific instructions.

If we acquiesce in the claim of the Turkish authorities to prohibit the landing of American citizens of the Jewish race at Beirut, Jaffa, etc., it will certainly follow this prohibition will be applied to other American citizens; on the other hand by what authority under our laws can we consent to such prohibition regarding any class of our citizens. Of course if we had the same laws as England respecting its naturalized subjects, who on the return to their country of origin have no claim to British protection, then to that extent, the question would yield to easy solution.[14]

If we consent that after three months the Turkish police have the right to arrest American citizens and expel them, we thereby yield all our rights claimed by our treaty of 1830,[15] which we have strenuously upheld for many years.

10. A Turkish administrative province or district.

11. Diyarbekir province is located in southeastern Turkey. In 1895, the Turks massacred an estimated 25,000 Armenians and Assyrians in the district.

12. Alpheus N. Andrus (1843–1919), an employee of the American Board of Commissioners for Foreign Missions, was an American missionary who provided religious, medical, and educational assistance to local Protestant converts in Diyarbekir province.

13. The Sublime Porte frequently accused American missionaries of shielding and supporting Armenian nationalists, which created tension between the United States and the Ottoman regime.

14. Britain's Naturalisation Act of 1870 stipulated that naturalized British subjects were entitled to British consular protection in all foreign countries except their country of origin. By citing this law, Straus conflates the issue of American citizens who were formerly Ottoman subjects and who returned to the Ottoman empire with the issue of American Jews who were born in Russia and went on to settle in Palestine.

15. The Treaty of Commerce and Navigation, negotiated by an American commission consist-

If we give our consuls the right to arrest American citizens and expel them for no crime committed, we will be acting not only contrary to our laws, but as the executioners for the Turkish Criminal Courts.

I also observe the additional objections you raise, regarding the difficulties surrounding such cases, where the immigrant has not the means to pay for his return passage, and your statement that the number of such is comparatively large.

I have been careful in renewing passports, and whenever the facts justified a refusal, I have declined a renewal.

I have also written to America, to persons having influence among this class of Jews to discourage emigration to Palestine, and I am in hopes this will soon bear result in lessening the number.

So long as our laws remain as they are, guaranteeing equal protection to native and naturalized, whether within or beyond the limits of the United States, certainly no diplomatic or consular officer has a right to contravene these laws. I refer you to Sections 872 and 873 of the Consular Regulations, embodying Sections 2000 and 2001 of the Revised Statutes, which provide that all naturalized citizens while in a foreign country shall receive the same protection in person and property as is accorded to native born citizens etc.[16]

However much it may be desirable to relieve ourselves of the burdens and vexations complained of, so long as the law stands as it is, our duty is plain and we must endeavor to do the best we can in each case as it arises without sacrificing the rights of our citizens under our laws.

If it should appear that any persons claiming citizenship, have obtained their naturalization by fraudulent means, these cases should be promptly reported so suitable action can be taken as provided by law, or if citizens by the fact, for example, of permanently locating in Palestine, give evidence of abandoning their acquired citizenship this should be reported, so that a decision on that point may be arrived at....

Since writing the foregoing: I have had a conference with the Minister[17] and

---

ing of James Biddle (1783–1848), David Offley (fl. 1811–1838), and Charles Rhind (fl. 1810–1845), established formal diplomatic and economic relations between the United States and the Ottoman empire.

16. Appendix No. II, Title XXV: Citizenship, 872 Sec. 2000. United States Department of State, Regulations Prescribed for the Use of the Consular Service of the United States (Washington, D.C.: Government Printing Office, 1896).

17. Ahmed Tevfik Pasha (1845–1936), the Turkish minister of foreign affairs from 1899 to 1909, later served as grand vizier (a position akin to prime minister) of the Ottoman empire in 1909, 1918–19, and 1920–22.

he says he will at once give orders to the Governor of Jerusalem[18] to admit immigrant American Jews without requiring deposit of money or retention of baggage, but simply upon a visa by our consul stating "good only for three months" or something to that effect.

I am in hopes that after the three months, when the authorities demand the departure many will obey, if they do not obey and the authorities give you notice, you will be able to summon the persons in question, and impress upon them, the advisability of leaving, you will be able to influence many to obedience. This would leave yet a remaining number, probably a small number, who would not obey for various reasons, lack of means, etc. I am unable to give you instructions as to these last named, as the question arises, upon your making [a] report. I will submit it to the Secretary of State[19] for his further Instructions.

I am Sir,

Your obedient servant,

Oscar S. Straus

---

18. Mehmet Tevfik Biren (1867–1956) served as governor of Jerusalem from 1897 to 1901.

19. The American author and diplomat John M. Hay (1838–1905) served as secretary of state (1895–1905) under Presidents William B. McKinley (1843–1901) and Theodore Roosevelt (1858–1919). Hay was the architect of America's Open Door policy toward China (1899–1900) and negotiated the Hay-Pauncefote Treaty (1901) between the United States and Great Britain, which led to the building of the Panama Canal.

15

"MOSES PRESENTS THE TEN COMMANDMENTS TO THE CHILDREN OF ISRAEL"

Emile Pissis's Stained Glass Window of Congregation Sherith Israel (San Francisco, CA)

(1904–5)

◇◇◇

JOELLYN WALLEN ZOLLMAN

American Jews helped build and shape the state of California. They were pioneers present at the creation of the state in 1850, founding families living and working in every settlement of significant size from Sacramento to San Diego. American Jews came to the edge of the United States looking for adventure, good weather, better health, and above all an opportunity to make the American dream their own. California's early Jewish settlers were double immigrants, having come to America from Europe and then deciding to uproot themselves again to go west. They endured a risky journey by land or sea to reach the western United States. This journey required physical and mental agility, financial resources, and considerable latitude with respect to religious and ritual observance, as kosher food, minyanim (pl., the quorum required for Jewish worship), and other expressions of traditional Jewish life and culture were not always available.

San Francisco was the center of Jewish life in nineteenth-century California: it was the largest, best organized, and wealthiest Jewish community in the state.[1] In the 1870s, some 16,000 Jews called San Francisco home, making it America's second city in terms of Jewish population. Jews held important positions in the civic and commercial life of the city. U.S. Representative Julius Kahn (1861–1924),[2] a Jewish immigrant from Baden who represented northern

---

1. Los Angeles surpassed San Francisco in terms of Jewish population in the early twentieth century. In general, Los Angeles proved an attractive place for Jewish settlement as the city grew and developed, particularly after the discovery of oil, the dredging of a deepwater port at San Pedro, and the development of the Hollywood movie industry.

2. Julius Kahn (1861–1924) represented California's fourth district in the U.S. House of Representatives in 1899–1903 and 1905–24. His wife, Florence Prag Kahn (1866–1948), succeeded him in office, becoming the first Jewish woman to serve in Congress (1925–37).

California in Congress for more than twenty years, expressed the commitment, comfort, and confidence that characterized much of the community when he said, "The United States is my Zion and San Francisco my Jerusalem."[3]

Two congregations stood at the center of Jewish religious life in San Francisco: Emanu-El and Sherith Israel. Both congregations were founded in 1851 and remain active today.[4] Sherith Israel grew with the city, moving several times before building its current home in 1905 at the corner of California and Webster Streets in the affluent Pacific Heights neighborhood. Situated at the top of a commanding ridge, Sherith Israel is designed to see and be seen. The renowned San Francisco architect Albert Pissis (1852–1914) created the imposing Greek Revival structure that stands 120 feet above California Street, with a domed roof that stretches 60 feet in diameter. A modern architect described the synagogue's shape as "a box with a hat."[5]

◇◇

Emile Pissis, "Moses Presents the Ten Commandments to the Children of Israel," c. 1904–5

Source: "Moses Presents the Ten Commandments to the Children of Israel" (c. 1904–5), stained glass window, design by Emile Pissis, Congregation Sherith Israel, San Francisco, CA. Image reproduced with permission of Congregation Sherith Israel. Photograph by Maurice L. Kamins.

Albert Pissis, born in Mexico and trained in Paris, built several other notable San Francisco structures, including Hibernia Bank, the Flood Building, and the Emporium Department store. Pissis's buildings are known for their stability. Sherith Israel was the largest public space standing after the 1906 earthquake, a distinction that led to the use of the building as the city's superior court from 1906 to 1908. Pissis was not Jewish. He was, however, married to San Francisco native and Sherith Israel congregant, Georgia (Parquer) Stein (1870–1930). All of these factors—the prominent location on the corner of California Street, the size of the building, the use of a celebrated local architect (not to mention the fact that the non-Jewish architect was married to a Jewish congregant), the em-

3. Quoted in Bobbie Malone, *Rabbi Max Heller: Reformer, Zionist, Southerner, 1860–1929* (Tuscaloosa: University of Alabama Press, 1997), 184.

4. Emanu-El has its own notable architectural history. See David Kaufman, "Early Synagogue Architecture," in *California Jews*, ed. Ava F. Kahn and Marc Dollinger (Waltham, MA: Brandeis University Press, 2003), 40–56.

5. Quoted in Tafline Laylin, "San Francisco's Sherith Israel to Become Seismic-Safe," April 21, 2010, https://www.greenprophet.com/2010/04/san-franciscos-sherith-israel-updated-building/.

"Moses Presents the Ten Commandments to the Children of Israel"

ployment of the building as a city court—point to a congregation that felt strong and secure in San Francisco.

The interior of Sherith Israel is spectacular. If the exterior is "a box with a hat," then the interior is a bejeweled crown, with seating for 1,400 people, a 3,500-pipe organ, 89 leaded glass windows, and 1,100 decorative lights. The local artist Attillo Moretti (1852–1915) painted the floral and geometric frescoes on the walls and ceiling, using a warm, vibrant color palette of reds and golds with accents in green and blue. Under the direction of the congregation's rabbi, Jacob Nieto (1863–1930), Moretti also painted various Jewish symbols, including the Ten Commandments, the Torah, a *shofar* (ram's horn trumpet), *lulav* (closed frond of the date palm tree), *megillah* scroll, and a Hanukkah menorah inside the rim of the dome. The Italian-born Moretti gained notoriety as a religious painter who worked chiefly on the interior design of Catholic churches in northern California. Sherith Israel is his only known Jewish project. A painted interior is an unusual form of decoration for an American synagogue. Sherith Israel originally followed a Polish Jewish *minhag* (Hebrew for "custom"), so it is possible the painted interior is a nod to the Polish practice of painted synagogues. However, the style of the painted decoration is decidedly Spanish, which could indicate a connection to another American congregation called Shearith Israel—a Sephardic congregation located in New York City that was the first American synagogue. In any case, the synagogue's decorative interior cements San Francisco's Sherith Israel synagogue's role as a local landmark and a national treasure of American Jewish architecture.[6]

The most striking feature of the sanctuary is the stained glass on the west wall, designed by the architect's brother, Emile Pissis (1854–1934). A co-founder of the San Francisco Art Association, Emile Pissis trained in Paris, but made the Bay Area his home and the favorite subject of his art. This half-circle shaped window depicts a well-known biblical scene: Moses descending with the Ten Commandments for the Israelites. Typically, artistic renderings of this scene feature the biblical Mt. Sinai in the background. Sherith Israel's window design is distinguished by the fact that Moses has descended into California's Yosemite Valley, with the recognizable rock formations El Capitan and Half Dome in the background. Emile Pissis's skill in depicting the local landscape is evident here in his successful translation of granite formations into glass, so that the scene is identifiable to anyone familiar with these iconic images from California's first national park, Yosemite. Located just two hundred miles east of San Francisco, Yosemite was a popular destination for San Franciscans at the turn of the nineteenth and twentieth centuries, who traveled by train, stagecoach, and horseback to see giant sequoias, majestic waterfalls, and mountain vistas.

The congregation's archives are quiet regarding the selection, installation, and reaction to this unique American Jewish stained glass scene. Still, the window stands as visual testimony to the creation of a significant Jewish community in California as well as a tribute to a golden age for Jews in the Golden State. Moses's presence in the Yosemite Valley offers a blessing to the community and underscores the rootedness and constancy of Jewish life in California. Congregational lore identifies the small child in the lower right corner of the window, the one facing the congregation, as Rabbi Jacob Nieto's son. Generations of congregants have seen the window as a powerful statement of belonging. Not only does California's seaside-to-desert topography resemble that of the Land of Israel, but many Jews, including the synagogue's founders, have experienced San Francisco as a sort of new Promised Land.

Sherith Israel's cornerstone was laid on February 22, 1904, the 172nd anniversary of George Washington's (1732–1799) birthday. At the cornerstone ceremony, Nieto connected the two events: "We have selected for our cornerstone laying the natal day of that great man that laid the cornerstone of the most magnificent nation in the world's history. The difficulties we have met in build-

6. In 2012, Sherith Israel of San Francisco was added to the National Register of Historic Places.

ing this congregation and synagogue are as nothing [compared] to the heroic labors of the father of our land. Let us remember his example and build not for ourselves but for posterity and country, for faith and freedom."[7] Sherith Israel's foundation stands on faith in the freedom of America, and its windows reflect the congregation's belief that Jews could happily call California home.

7. Quoted in "Congregation Sherith Israel Lays Cornerstone of Splendid Temple," *San Francisco Call*, February 23, 1904, 8.

16

"FOR THE WELFARE OF ISRAEL IN THIS COUNTRY"

Cyrus Adler, Henry Pereira Mendes, and the Creation
of the United Synagogue of America
(1913)

◇◇

MICHAEL COHEN

In the early decades of the twentieth century, the term "conservative Judaism" was vague and undefined. It did not represent an ideologically coherent movement, nor did it have distinct boundaries. Though its adherents may have defined themselves in opposition to the strict orthodoxy practiced by American Jewish immigrants, and in contradistinction to Reform Judaism's Pittsburgh Platform (1885), most of those who identified with the movement sought to attract people in the broad center. They hoped to reach a rising generation of American Jews who were put off both by an immigrant orthodoxy that they viewed as antithetical to America and by a Reform movement that they believed had gone too far in its adaptation to America. Though ideological clarity would have defined the boundaries of a clear Conservative movement, the movement's founders instead chose to advocate for a broadly defined traditional Judaism that adapted to its American milieu. Solomon Schechter (1847–1915), the celebrated rabbi and scholar of the Cairo Geniza who served as president of the recommenced Jewish Theological Seminary (JTS) from 1902 to 1915, famously articulated this sensibility in the notion of "the collective conscience of Catholic Israel."[1] A unified American Judaism committed to tradition, Schechter asserted, "must avoid every action of a sectarian or of a schismatic nature" and seek to adapt to "the ideal aspirations and religious needs of the age."[2]

This central tension—between an emphasis on similarities and inclusivity and exclusive boundaries and ideological coherence—lay at the heart of the 1913 debate over the nature of the United Synagogue of America, an organization

1. Solomon Schechter, introduction to *Studies in Judaism* (Philadelphia: Jewish Publication Society, 1911), xviii.

2. Solomon Schecter, "Altar Building in America," *Jewish Exponent* 34, no. 20 (September 2, 1904), 1; Schechter, introduction, xviii.

founded by JTS rabbinical graduates to disseminate their message to American Jewry. The following 1913 exchange between Henry Pereira Mendes (1852–1937), a rabbi who had been active in JTS during its early years and who was a leader in the Orthodox Union, and Cyrus Adler (1863–1940), a leader of the JTS and president of Dropsie College for Hebrew and Cognate Learning in Philadelphia, reflects this tension.

To determine who should be included in the United Synagogue, Mendes found it necessary first to articulate the contours of the American Jewish spectrum in the early twentieth century. Beyond self-identification with competing forms of Jewish religious expression, there was no consensus understanding at the time as to what the terms used by different groups meant. Nonetheless, Mendes did his best to divide the American Jewish spectrum into five rough categories that had a significant amount of overlap and few clear distinctions among them. He divided orthodoxy into two camps to distinguish his own brand of (modern) orthodoxy from the "Russian Orthodoxy" of immigrant rabbis who he believed failed to sufficiently adapt Judaism to American life — particularly on women's issues. He also distinguished his own "modern orthodoxy" from "conservative" Judaism with a vague definition, noting only that conservative Judaism "permits some of the innovations" resisted by modern orthodoxy — without attempting to offer the last word in this regard. Finally, Mendes drew distinctions between competing camps of Reform Judaism, ultimately splitting the movement into "reform" and "radical reform" wings. Thus, while Mendes's definitions are hardly satisfying to anyone hoping to clearly define the contours of American Judaism in this period, they reflect the fluidity and diversity of an American Judaism struggling to define itself and its emerging institutional culture.

Responding to Mendes, Cyrus Adler laments the need to provide labels for the various streams of American Judaism, arguing that he identifies as part of the "mainstream" of American Judaism and noting that he hopes the United Synagogue will not represent a separate "party." He emphasizes the need to bring the center — what Mendes termed modern orthodox and conservative — into a single group, to save Judaism from the extremes of the American Jewish spectrum. In sum, while Mendes affirms the similarities between conservative and modern orthodoxy by his inability to express a clear difference, Adler's words reflect the widespread belief that whatever differences there may have been between modern orthodoxy and conservativism should not stand in the way of common action.

Taken together, the two documents reveal just how undefined Conservative Judaism actually was in this era and that the United Synagogue of America was not intended to be a third movement in American Jewish life. Rather, as its name reflects and as Adler hoped, it was an attempt to unite the broad center of American Judaism to perpetuate Judaism in America.

◇◇◇

Letter from Henry Pereira Mendes to Cyrus Adler, February 14, 1913

> Source: Letter from Henry Pereira Mendes to Cyrus Adler (February 14, 1913), Henry Pereira Mendes Papers, MS-39, box 1, folder 3, the Jacob Rader Marcus Center of the American Jewish Archives, Cincinnati.

New York

February 14, 1913

My dear Dr. Adler,[3]

Dr. [Solomon] Schechter[4] and Rabbi [Jacob] Cohn [sic][5] have both had several interviews with me concerning the proposed Agudath Jeshurun or Union for Promoting Traditional Judaism in America.[6] I have carefully examined the Preamble to the Constitution and the sketch of the constitution sent to me. I understand that you are Chairman of the Constitution Committee and I therefore write you.

In order to explain my views to you let us for the moment agree to the following definitions, even if they are not exactly correct:

First: Russian [Jewish] Orthodoxy. This is the Orthodoxy which insists upon a certain ritual and certain forms, but objects to English sermons, has little or no

---

3. Cyrus Adler (1863–1940), a semitics scholar and librarian of the Smithsonian Institution (1892–1905), was a founder of the Jewish Publication Society of America (1888); the American Jewish Historical Society (1892); and the American Jewish Committee (1906), on whose behalf he attended the Paris Peace Conference after World War I. He was editor of the *American Jewish Year Book* (1899–1905) and *The Jewish Encyclopedia* (1901–6). Active in the leadership of the Conservative movement's Jewish Theological Seminary, he helped found the United Synagogue of America (1913) and served as acting president of JTS (1915–24) and then president (1924–40). He was also president of Dropsie College for Hebrew and Cognate Learning (1908–40).

4. Trained as a rabbi and scholar, Solomon Schechter (1847–1915) garnered international acclaim for his recovery in 1896 of the Cairo Geniza records, a collection of rare premodern Hebrew religious texts and manuscripts preserved at an Egyptian synagogue. He served as president of the Jewish Theological Seminary (1902–15) and was a founder of the United Synagogue of America and an early proponent of Zionism.

5. Jacob Kohn (1881–1968), ordained in 1907 by the Jewish Theological Seminary, served as rabbi of New York City's Ansche Chesed Congregation (1911–31) and Los Angeles's Sinai Temple (1931–57). Author of several works on Jewish theology, he was active in American Jewish affairs and played a key role in shaping the Conservative movement's prayer books.

6. In 1913, this proposed organization was created as the United Synagogue of America. In 1991, its name was changed to the United Synagogue of Conservative Judaism.

decorum, fails to hold its young men and young women, refuses in its schools Hebrew and religious education to girls and cares little whether women and girls attend religious service or not. It also insists upon such customs as the *shaitel*[7] and, in a word, degrades womanhood as you and I understand it.

Second: Modern [Jewish] Orthodoxy, as represented by, for example, your and my congregation and several Ashkenazic congregations such as those in Baltimore, Philadelphia, and Montreal. This Orthodoxy resists innovations such as organs, pews,[8] disuse of *talit*, female voices in the choir, Christians in the choir, etc.

Third: Conservative Judaism. Let this term mean the Judaism which permits some of the innovations named.

Fourth: Reform Judaism, which in addition to such innovations, rejects certain historical beliefs and aspirations, such as restoration, etc.[9]

Fifth: Radical Reform [Judaism], which publishes a Pittsburgh Platform,[10] or a Programme of the Cincinnati Teachers Association,[11] which presents the Bible as myth and folklore, an epic like the *Iliad*.[12]

7. Yiddish term for the traditional Jewish woman's head covering.

8. The reference here is to the concept of mixed seating of men and women in American synagogues, a modernizing practice that was the subject of considerable controversy in the late nineteenth and early twentieth centuries.

9. In general, Reform Judaism posits that Judaism is dynamic and ought to be updated to provide Jews with opportunities for engagement with and participation in the modern world. It views traditional Jewish law as a source of inspiration and the process of selectively emphasizing some aspects of premodern Jewish literature — as well as reevaluating and reinterpreting extant Jewish liturgy, rabbinic law, and religious practice — as a legitimate and necessary step in the evolution of contemporary Jewish life and culture. Isaac Mayer Wise (1819–1900), the principal founder of Reform Judaism in the United States, spearheaded the creation in 1873 of the Union of American Hebrew Congregations, a nationwide framework for the emerging movement of Reform Judaism. In 1875 Wise created Hebrew Union College in Cincinnati to train and ordain Reform rabbis. In 1889 he founded the Central Conference of American Rabbis, the central rabbinic authority of Reform Judaism in the United States.

10. Created in 1885 at a meeting of Reform rabbis, the Pittsburgh Platform called for the modernization of American Jewish belief and practice. The document — which codified the principles of classical Reform Judaism — rejected traditional Jewish doctrine, affirmed the notion of Jews as a religious community, and explicitly renounced Zionism. For the text of the platform, see Paul Mendes-Flohr and Jehuda Reinharz, eds., *The Jew in the Modern World: A Documentary History*, 3rd ed. (New York: Oxford University Press, 2011), 521–22.

11. Founded in 1893, the Cincinnati Teachers Association emphasized a variety of issues, including local teachers' relationships with the superintendent, school management, disciplinary mastery by students, "ethical training," and civics. See John Brough Shotwell, *A History of the Schools of Cincinnati* (Cincinnati: School Life Company, 1902), 434–36.

12. The epic Greek poet Homer (fl. eighth century BCE) is commonly credited with the author-

Which of these Judaism [sic] will the proposed Union countenance? Can a scheme be adopted which by the moral force of its reasonableness shall attract Orthodox [Jewish] congregations, shall appeal to Russian [Jewish] Orthodox congregations, and shall strengthen and increase the Jewish loyalty of the Conservative congregations? . . .

With kindest regards,

Faithfully yours, Rev. [Dr.] H. Pereira Mendes[13]

Letter from Cyrus Adler to Henry Periera Mendes, February 17, 1913

Source: Letter from Cyrus Adler to Henry Pereira Mendes (February 17, 1913), Henry Pereira Mendes Papers, MS-39, box 1, folder 3, the Jacob Rader Marcus Center of the American Jewish Archives, Cincinnati.

February 17, 1913

My dear Doctor Mendes,

I have your letter of the 14th. I consider myself as purely a tentative Chairman to draw up a purely tentative Constitution for the proposed Agudath Jeshurun. I have always resisted any adjectives to my Judaism, believing that I belong to the mainstream of Judaism which meant an orderly and regularly [sic] development in accordance with our laws and traditions. I have always been willing to let other people give themselves adjectives, orthodox, conservative, reform, radical or even Zionist. To that extent, therefore, I am a Jewish man and not a party man. Now as far as I have any voice, this will be the attitude of the new organization. I thought that the main cleavages among Jews in America had been fairly settled when the Seminary was founded. The original Advisory Board of Ministers included Doctor Kohut, Doctor Jastrow, Henry S. Jacobs, your brother and Doctor Aaron Wise in addition to Doctor Morais, yourself, your father, Doctor Schneeberger and Doctor Drachman and later Doctor Szold was added to

---

ship of two of the oldest extant works of Western literature, The Iliad and The Odyssey, which were likely composed in the late eighth century BCE. The Iliad, set during the Trojan War (c. twelfth or thirteenth century BCE), describes the conflict and struggle between King Agamemnon and the warrior Achilles. The Odyssey tells the story of the Greek hero Odysseus's journey home after the fall of Troy.

13. Henry Pereira Mendes (1852–1937), scion of a Spanish and Portuguese rabbinic family, was trained as a physician. In 1877, he became the preacher and cantor of New York City's Congregation Shearith Israel. Active in a variety of American Jewish communal projects, he was among the founders of the Jewish Theological Seminary, Union of Orthodox Jewish Congregations, and Federation of American Zionists.

the Advisory Board.[14] Now I mean by this to recall to you that twenty-five years ago those of us who were interested in maintaining traditional Judaism were entirely prepared to bring about an amalgamation of what in your classification is called modern Orthodox and Conservative[15] and I believe that it is greatly for the welfare of Israel in this country and in all countries that these two tendencies should unite if they are not ultimately to be destroyed. I have not changed my form of worship since I have been a boy nor has the Congregation since I belonged to it and I suspect that it will not, but there are not enough of your mind and my mind to stem the tide which runs straight from Russian [Jewish] orthodoxy to radical reform. I believe it is a matter of duty as well as of wisdom, in which there is no sacrifice of principle involved, to create an organization which will conserve and as I hope even advance a traditional Judaism in America. I am entirely willing to let the platform be that of the Seminary and to have the Seminary [be] the rallying point for our effort. I hope that you and your Congregation will make common cause with us and that nothing will be allowed to stand in the way. It was for lack of organization sixty or seventy years ago that the Reform movement was allowed to gain the strength and headway which it has secured. Traditional Judaism now through numbers has a great advantage if it knows how to use that advantage,[16] and the attempt that is now being made

14. Rabbis Frederick De Sola Mendes (1850–1927), Bernard Drachman (1861–1945), Henry S. Jacobs (1827–1893), Marcus Jastrow (1829–1903), Alexander Kohut (1842–1894), Abraham P. Mendes (1825–1893), Henry Pereira Mendes, Sabato Morais (1823–1897), Henry W. Schneeberger (1848–1916), and Aaron Wise (1844–1896) were members of the Jewish Theological Seminary's Advisory Board of Ministers at its founding in 1886. The historian Abraham J. Karp notes: "Of the rabbis, five—Sabato Morais (president of the faculty), Henry P. Mendes, Bernard Drachman, Henry W. Schneeberger, and Abraham P. Mendes—were traditionalists who comfortably termed themselves Orthodox; and five—Alexander Kohut, Marcus Jastrow, Henry S. Jacobs, Frederick De Sola Mendes, and Aaron Wise—had broken with traditional Judaism and were considered by their congregations and themselves as adherents of [Positive-Historical] Judaism at the border (which side of the border is open to dispute) of Reform Judaism" ("The Conservative Rabbi—'Dissatisfied But Not Unhappy,'" *American Jewish Archives* 35, no. 2 (November 1983), 199).

15. In large measure, the founding of the Jewish Theological Seminary was a response to the developing strength of the Reform movement in the United States. Many contemporaries viewed the seminary as a vehicle capable of uniting adherents who viewed themselves as to the right of Reform Judaism, including so-called modern Orthodox and Conservative Jews.

16. The creation of the Union of American Hebrew Congregations (established in 1873), Hebrew Union College (established in 1875), and the Central Conference of American Rabbis (established in 1889) strengthened Reform Judaism across the United States. In parallel, as the numbers of Jewish traditionalists declined, traditional Jewish leaders lamented that their general lack of structure prevented their voices from being heard. A veritable sea change in Ameri-

is to properly employ our advantages. Vaguely I have the idea of the creation of an organization whose membership shall include clergymen and laymen but in which there shall be a sharp differentiation of functions so that no question pertaining to Rabbis shall be exercised [sic] by others. I have not framed anything yet but will try to do so in the course of the next few days but I most earnestly hope that you and your Congregation will affiliate with this movement as our own Congregation has readily and without hesitation.

Believe me as ever,

Faithfully yours, Cyrus Adler

can Jewish life occurred, however, with the mass waves of eastern European Jewish immigration in the late nineteenth and early twentieth centuries. Traditional American Jewry's ranks were now reinforced by millions of Yiddish-speaking Russian and Polish Jews, and the dynamic situation spurred the creation of a plethora of new organizational structures.

17

"THEY CAN SHIP ME ANYWHERE"

An Ottoman Jewish Immigrant in the American Heartland
(1913)

◇◇◇

AVIVA BEN-UR

Mass migration from the Ottoman empire, primarily to western Europe and the Americas, began in 1860. Forty years later, the largely dismembered empire was still home to approximately 350,000 Jews, representing more than 3 percent of the world's Jewish population and the fifth-largest Jewish community in the world (following the communities in Russia, Austria-Hungary, the United States, and Germany, in that order). In the early twentieth century, mainstream newspapers and American Jewish organizations began to take notice of a sizable influx in the United States of Ottoman Jews fleeing the Balkan wars, economic hardships, and natural disasters. The majority were Jews whose ancestors had been expelled from Spain in 1492 and who had developed an exilic language called Ladino. Also known in scholarly circles as Judeo-Spanish, Ladino is a fusion tongue based on early modern Spanish with elements from Arabic, Aramaic, Bulgarian, French, Greek, Hebrew, Italian, Portuguese, and Turkish and traditonally written in Hebrew letters. The *kolonia* (colony) that Ladino-speaking immigrants established in the United States became the most important Sephardic community that originated in the Ottoman empire. Its mostly impoverished members gravitated to the cities and eked out a living as peddlers and factory workers, but some became affluent factory owners, carpet dealers, and restaurateurs. Their intellectual elite, hailing primarily from the Greek city of Thessaloniki, became the mouthpiece of the community through a vibrant Ladino press. Between 1910 and 1948, they published nineteen Ladino periodicals, all but one in New York City.[1]

Most of what we know about the American Sephardic immigrant community derives from these newspapers. Archival sources—letters, postcards, diaries,

---

1. "Jewish Statistics," *American Jewish Year Book* 3 (1901–2), 159; Aviva Ben-Ur, "In Search of the American Ladino Press: A Bibliographical Survey, 1910–1948," *Studies in Bibliography and Booklore* 21 (Winter 2001), 10–52; reprinted in *Neue Romania* 28 (2003), 177–234.

and other documents in Ladino—have hardly been investigated. These materials are written in Ladino in a special Sephardic script known as *soletreo*, a word derived from the verb *seletrear* (meaning to correspond). This now virutally obsolete writing system evolved from a cursive employed in the Middle Ages by Jews in the Iberian Peninsula. The extent and range of archival documents written in this script can hardly be estimated, given that they are scattered and buried in diverse repositories and private collections and often emerge in unexpected places.[2] The first document below is one example.[3]

It derives from the records of the Industrial Removal Office (IRO), a Jewish organization founded in 1901 to decongest the impoverished immigrant neighborhoods of New York City by transferring newcomers to the interior of the United States and to Canada. During its first ten years of existence, the IRO relocated 54,374 people, mostly Jews, to 1,326 cities in forty-nine states or provinces within the United States and Canada.[4] The largest group of beneficiaries were eastern European Jews, but an important minority were Ottoman Jews (or "Turks," as they were called). Between 1907 and 1913, 36,685 people were removed from New York. Of these 28,773, or 78 percent, were Russians, followed in frequency by Austrians (3,327, or 9 percent). In addition, 181 Turks, many of them Ashkenazic, were removed, representing 0.005 percent of the total beneficiaries transferred in that time period.[5]

One of these beneficiaries was Ye'uda Gabai, who signed his name in Latin letters as Juda Gabay and was born in Izmir on November 18, 1889. According to his "Declaration of Intention" to become a citizen of the United States, filed in 1924, Gabay arrived at the port of New York in February 1913.[6] Gabay's case pro-

2. Descendants of Ladino speakers in the United States sometimes preserve postcards or letters written in the early twentieth century in *soletreo* by relatives living either locally or abroad.

3. The author has examined all 124 boxes of the Records of the Industrial Removal Office in the archives of the American Jewish Historical Society, New York City (hereafter AJHS).

4. *Tenth Annual Report of the Industrial Removal Office for the Year Nineteen Hundred and Ten* (New York: Industrial Removal Office, 1911), 5; Records of the Industrial Removal Office, 1899–1922 (I-91), box 5, AJHS.

5. *Thirteenth Annual Report of the Industrial Removal Office for the Year Nineteen Thirteen* (New York: Industrial Removal Office, 1914), 14; Records of the Industrial Removal Office, 1899–1922 (I-91), box 1, folder 5: "I-4: Annual Reports," AJHS.

6. "Index to Petitions for Naturalizations Filed in Federal, State, and Local Courts in New York City, 1792–1906," NAI Number 5700802, Record Group Title: Records of District Courts of the United States, 1685–2009, Record Group Number: RG 21, National Archives and Records Administration, Washington, D.C., Ancestry.com; New York, U.S., State and Federal Naturalization Records, 1794-1943 [online database], Provo, UT, USA, Ancestry.com, 2013; U.S. Department of Labor, Naturalization Service, United States of America, Declaration of Intention,

file was somehow never recorded in the IRO account books. However, from his letter of November 20, 1913, we know that he was "removed" first to Pittsburgh, Pennsylvania, and then to the town of New Kensington, fifteen miles northeast of the city. Gabay complained that the factory that employed him operated only seasonally and had shut down, leaving him with no further prospects for employment in the area until the factory's reopening, slated for May. He appealed to the IRO in the hope that it could send him to another, more auspicious, locale anywhere in the United States.

His letter is attached to an English translation by Albert Amateau (1889–1996), a native of Milas in the Ottoman empire who volunteered his services to aid fellow Ottoman Jewish immigrants. Although in his cover letter to the IRO official, Amateau claimed that his translation was literal, close analysis reveals strategic doctoring. In the original *soletreo* version, for example, Gabay wrote that he was willing to go anywhere the IRO would send him and alluded to a doctor's visit, which suggested that he was recovering from an illness. Amateau's "correction" has Gabay asserting that he did not want to return to New York and that the examining physician had declared him to be "strong like Iron."

David M. Bressler (1879–1942), the IRO's general manager, may have suspected a mistranslation and concluded that the factory would likely soon reopen. His response may also reflect a broader policy of the IRO against further investing in immigrants already removed to the country's "interior."[7] The interchange illuminates an intra-ethnic dynamic that the Ladino press did not capture. Amateau's translation shows how Sephardic immigrant officials exploited linguistic barriers to advocate on behalf of their misunderstood constituents

---

No. 155448, Juda Gabay, November 24, 1924. I am grateful to Devin Naar for sharing with me this apparently corresponding document and for his assistance with the *soletreo* transcription.

7. This policy mirrors—and may be a successor of—the practice of the *despacho*, a word in Portuguese and Spanish meaning "dispatch," in the sense of sending away. Jewish leaders of the Atlantic world and beyond implemented the *despacho* as a way to regulate the circulation of impoverished Jews, most of whom were of Iberian origin, and to prevent financial strain on local charity organizations. Individuals subject to the *despacho*, whether voluntarily or under coercion, were typically newcomers who were temporarily housed and fed by the Portuguese Jewish community before being redirected to other Jewish communities as far away as possible, with the mandate not to return for one or more years. For more on the *despacho*, see Tirtsah Levie Bernfeld, *Poverty and Welfare among the Portuguese Jews in Early Modern Amsterdam* (Oxford: Littman Library of Jewish Civilization, 2012), 16–17; Robert Cohen, "Passage to a New World: The Sephardi Poor of Eighteenth Century Amsterdam," in *Neveh Yaakov: Jubilee Volume Presented to Dr. Jaap Meijer on the Occasion of His Seventieth Birthday*, ed. Lea Dasberg and Jonathan N. Cohen (Assen, the Netherlands: Van Gorcum, 1982), 30–42.

and to portray them in the best possible light. In this case, however, the ruse did not work.

◇◇

Letter from Ye'uda Gabai to Joseph Gedalecia, November 20, 1913 (Transliteration and Translation from *Soletreo*-Scripted Ladino)

Source: Letter from Yeuda Gabai to Joseph Gedalecia (November 20, 1913), Records of the Industrial Removal Office, 1899–1922, I-91, box 22, folder 39, American Jewish Historical Society, New York City.

TRANSLITERATION

New Kensington, 20 November 1913[8]
Senior Josef Gedalecia, yihié,[9] en Nu
   York

Onorado Senior!
Usted ya se akodra komo antes
2 mezes fui mandado al interior por
el Rimuvel Ofis.
   Apenas ariví a Pitsburg el ajente
del Rimuvel Ofis me trusho akí
a Nu Kensington en una kaza de
un dzudío[10] donde yo iva tardar
i iva pagar 5 dolares ala semana
empesando del dia ke yo arriví,
kerendo dizir ke alos dias ke estuvi
batal sin topar echo, devía komer
amis gastes.
   Despues de 5 a 6 semanas de
lavoro oy me dieron estap[11] por
un tiempo indeterminado. Viejos
lavoradores dizen ke esta faktoría es
en Mayo loke empesa a tomar jente.

ENGLISH TRANSLATION

New Kensington, 20 November 1913
Mr. Joseph Gedalecia, may he live
   long, in New York

Honorable Sir!
You will recall that two months
ago I was sent to the interior by the
[Industrial] Removal Office.
   Hardly had I arrived in Pittsburgh
when the agent of the Removal Office
brought me here to New Kensington
to a [boarding]house of a Jew, where I
was to reside and pay 5 dollars a week
beginning on the day that I arrived,
meaning that on the days that I was
unemployed, without finding any job,
I had to eat at my own expense.
   After 5 or 6 weeks of work, they
let me go today for an indeterminate
time. Veteran laborers say that only
in May does this factory begin to hire
workers.

8. This line appears in Latin letters.

9. This appears to be the Hebrew letter ׳ followed by an apostrophe (׳), indicating the abbreviation for the word יחיה, denoting the traditional Hebrew form of address "may he live long."

10. This is a traditional Ladino pronunciation of the word denoting "Jew." The first letter followed by its diacritic (ז׳) is pronounced like the j in the French word *bonjour*.

11. From the English word "stop," indicating that he was suspended or temporarily laid off.

Dunkue i kon 5/6 semanas de lavoro ya se aze una idea ke apenas eskapí de pagar loke komí mientres el tempo ke estuvi batal[12] dunkue kualo devo yo azer? Akí en un lugar ke no tengo ni konosido ni amigo ni moneda.

Si el Rimuvel Ofis tiene algun lugar otro para mandarme yo esto dispuesto a irme onde fuese, visto ke el doktor ya me egzaminó i yo ya puedo lavorar kualunke lavoro i ya konosko muy poko el Inglés.

Asperando kon grande despasensa su repuesta lo saludo distinktamente.

Adereso

Ye'uda Gabai [signature in *soletreo*]

Juda Gabay [in Latin script]

General Delivery

New Kensington Pa [address in Latin script]

Therefore, even with 5 to 6 weeks of work, you can already imagine that I had hardly finished paying for the costs of my food during my unemployment. So what shall I do, here in a place where I have no aquaintances, friend, or money?

If the Removal Office has someplace else to which to send me, I am ready to go wherever it may be, given that the doctor already examined me and I am now able to work any job and I already know a little English.

Awaiting your reply most anxiously, I greet you attentively.

Address

Ye'uda Gabai

Juda Gabay

General Delivery

New Kensington, Pennsylvania

12. From Hebrew, Turkish, and Arabic, indicating, in this case, inactivity or unemployment.

Letter from Albert Amateau to David M. Bressler, November 24, 1913, Written on Federation of Oriental Jews of America Letterhead[13]

Source: Letter from Albert Amateau to David M. Bressler (November 24, 1913), Records of the Industrial Removal Office, 1899–1922, I-91, box 22, folder 39, American Jewish Historical Society, New York City.

Nov. 24, 1913

Mr. D. Bressler, General Manager,

Ind. Rem. Office,

172 2nd Ave, City.

My Dear Mr. Bressler: —

The inclosed [sic] is a letter written to us by Mr. Juda Gabai, of New Kensington, where he was sent by I.R.O. and its translation is self-explanatory.

"Two months ago I was sent to the Removal Office to Pittsburgh, and their agent took me to New Kensington, where he introduced me to a Jewish boarding house. I was there two weeks before I could get a position. I have worked for 6 weeks, and now the factory shut down, and people here say that it would no [sic] open for [sic] before May. I paid my board at the house up to date, including for the first two weeks, when I did not work. I have very little money left, and I am writing you this letter, that you should be kind enough, and ask the Removal Office, whether this report about the factory is true. And if so, whether they have any jobs for a man like me, at any other part of the country. I am willing to go anywhere that they send me to. I do not want to return to New York. Tell them that I am at their disposal, and that they can ship me anywhere in the United States. The Doctor, (he means Physician [sic]), when he examined me said that I was strong like Iron, and I know that I can do any kind of work. I know a little English, and I am sure that wherever I am sent I will give satisfaction.

"Awaiting your answer with impatience, I am your respectfully, Juda Gabai."

I tried my best to make a litteral [sic] translation, so that you can read his words as much as possible.

Yours Truly,

A. J. Amateau, Secretary

13. The Federation of Oriental Jews of America was established in 1912 in New York City to represent Jews of Ottoman origin in the United States. Most of its members were Ladino speakers, but a minority came from Arabic- and Greek-speaking backgrounds. Its stated purpose was "to improve the material, intellectual, and civic status of the Levantine Jews in America and to better their religious conditions by the establishment of Talmud Torahs" (David de Sola Pool, "The Levantine Jews in the United States," *American Jewish Year Book* 15 [1913–14], 218–19).

Letter from David M. Bressler to Albert Amateau, November 25, 1913

Source: Letter from David M. Bressler to Albert Amateau (November 25, 1913), Records of the Industrial Removal Office, 1899–1922, I-91, box 22, folder 39, American Jewish Historical Society, New York City.

Nov. 25, 1913
Mr. A. J. Amateau
356 Second Avenue
New York City.

My dear Mr. Amateau:

I have your letter of the 24th instant concerning Judah Gabay and have carefully noted your translation to [sic] the letter he sent you. It would not be advisable to suggest to Gabay to try some other locality at this time because from the reports at hand we find that the condition of the labor market for unskilled laborers is universally unfavorable. It is not unreasonable to assume that Gabay has somewhat exaggerated the length of time that will elapse before the factory re-opens. Of course, it seems hardly likely that in a large city like Pittsburgh, teeming with thousands of industries, that any factory would close from November until May. It is therefore fair to assume that within a few weeks Gabay should be at work again.

Very truly yours, Industrial Removal Office

18

"THE ORIENTAL SPANISH JEWISH JOURNAL" *LA AMÉRIKA*

The First Enduring Ladino Newspaper of the United States (1913–14)

◇◇◇

AVIVA BEN-UR

Between 1880 and 1924, 50,000–60,000 Levantine Jews immigrated to the United States from the Ottoman empire and its successor states (the Anatolian Peninsula and the Balkans). Most of these immigrants (approximately 35,000 by the early 1920s) settled in New York City. Although they included Greek- and Arabic-speaking Jews, the majority spoke Ladino, or Judeo-Spanish, the language their ancestors had developed after their exile from the Iberian Peninsula four hundred years earlier. Ladino, a language whose creation is identified primarily with the Spanish Expulsion (1492), developed in the Ottoman empire and is based on early modern Spanish with elements of Arabic, Aramaic, Bulgarian, French, Greek, Hebrew, Italian, Portuguese, and Turkish. Until the early twentieth century, Judeo-Spanish was almost always written in Hebrew, as opposed to Roman, letters.

One of the most important literary achievements of the Judeo-Spanish people is the Ladino press. The American Judeo-Spanish press, printed in Hebrew letters and founded primarily by immigrants from Salonika, was originally created to assist new immigrants in their cultural and economic adjustment to the United States. The difficulties common to Jewish immigrants in that country were more numerous in the case of Sephardic newcomers from the Middle East and the Balkans, since—due to their unfamiliar physiognomy and language and their ignorance of Yiddish—many of the existing Ashkenazic communal organizations did not recognize them as Jews. Moreover, many of these Ashkenazic organizations did not meet the cultural, linguistic, and religious needs of the Sephardim. For these reasons, Sephardic Jews found employment particularly difficult to secure and struggled to form their own religious, cultural, and political organizations.

Launched in 1910, *La América: The Oriental Spanish Jewish Journal*[1] published a list

---

1. On the masthead reprinted here, the Ladino name of the newspaper is transliterated as La America. The transliteration of Ladino to Latin letters has never been standardized.

of its agents in 1915 that reveals a readership as widespread as Havana (Cuba), Rio de Janeiro (Brazil), Buenos Aires and Santa Fe (Argentina), Mexico City (Mexico), Salisbury (now Harare in Zimbabwe), Vienna (Austria), London (the United Kingdom), Belgrade (Serbia), and Jerusalem. A "national, literary, political, and commercial weekly" designed to appeal to Sephardic Jewish immigrants from the Ottoman empire and its successor states, La Amérika was published in Hebrew-scripted Ladino, with occasional articles in Yiddish and English. The newspaper served as an educational, informational, and cultural vehicle for a diverse array of Sephardic Jewish readers. During its fifteen-year run, La Amérika taught immigrants about American culture and society while providing news about social, economic, and political developments in the United States and around the globe. Moshe (Moise) Gadol (1874–1971), a multilingual Bulgarian Jewish immigrant and founding editor of La Amérika, increased the magazine's weekly circulation to over a thousand readers.[2] Given that La Amérika's audience was centered in New York, whose Jewish community swiftly became the largest in the world, the magazine's impact on Sephardic Jewish readers and the American Jewish scene at large was significant.[3]

2. Owing to advances in the wood-pulp paper industry, the American newspaper arena grew at a phenomenal rate in the late nineteenth and early twentieth centuries. The Jewish press benefited in this regard no less than others. Though the circulation data about American newspapers before World War I are inexact, observers of the ethnic and immigrant press estimate that each newspaper purchased in this period generally was read by three or more people. In 1916, the American Yiddish press reached its peak: eleven daily newspapers with a total circulation of approximately 650,000. See The Jewish Communal Register of New York City, 1917–1918, ed. Samuel Margoshes, 2nd ed. (New York: Kehillah [Jewish Community] of New York City, 1918), 612–14; Robert E. Park, The Immigrant Press and Its Control (New York: Harper and Brothers, 1922), 89–110; Arthur Goren, "The Jewish Press in the U.S.," Qesher 6 (November 1989), 6e; David C. Smith, "Wood Pulp and Newspapers, 1867–1900," Business History Review 37, no. 3 (Autumn 1964), 328–45.

3. In 1918, contemporary observers estimated that New York City's Jewish community included 20,000 Sephardic Jews. See The Jewish Communal Register of New York City, 1917–1918, ed. Samuel Margoshes, 2nd ed. (New York: Kehillah [Jewish Community] of New York City, 1918), 611.

La Amérika: The Oriental Spanish Jewish Journal, 1913–14

Source: Image from the Jewish Historical Press/Creative Commons. Prefatory
note adapted from Aviva Ben-Ur, "In Search of the American Ladino Press:
A Bibliographical Survey, 1910–1948," *Studies in Bibliography and Booklore*
21 (2001), 10–52.

The image reprinted here titled "Kalendario La Amérika" (Ladino for "La Amérika
Calendar"), a supplement created to celebrate the Jewish New Year in 1913–14
(corresponding to the Hebrew year 5674), incorporates a variety of visual cues
and linguistic elements in a mix of Hebrew and Ladino that highlight ideas
about America's golden door, the diversity of Jewish culture, and the place of
Sephardic Jewish immigrants in the American setting.[4] At left, a group of cheerful well-dressed Americans stand at the water's edge. The figure in the top hat
holds a briefcase with the words "La Federasión," a reference to the Federation
of Oriental Jews,[5] while the immigration official grasps a scroll reading "Buro
Oriental del *hakhnasat orkhim*" (Oriental Bureau of Charity Institution), a reference to the Hebrew Immigrant Aid Society.[6] Arms outstretched, the Americans appear eager to greet the would-be newcomers. To the left of the Americans, the Statue of Liberty beckons with a lit torch and the words "La Libera
Amérika" ("America the free") on its pedestal. A passenger ship heading for
America anchors the vast expanse of ocean separating the figures on either side
of the illustration, while a rising sun illuminates the horizon. At right, a devil-

4. See also chapter 17.

5. On the Federation of Oriental Jews, see chapter 17, note 13. The Federation of Oriental Jews
of America was established in 1912.

6. The reference is to the Hebrew Immigrant Aid Society (HIAS). Created in 1881 to aid
eastern European Jewish refugees, HIAS merged in 1909 with the Hebrew Sheltering Aid Society (established in 1884) to become the Hebrew Sheltering and Immigrant Aid Society. Moshe
(Moise) Gadol (1874–1971) served as the HIAS Oriental Bureau's first secretary.

ish creature representing the Ottoman empire brandishes a large sword (with the words "Oriental politics" and "antisemitism") and banishes three harried yet thoroughly modern and self-possessed figures, one of whom clutches a box of belongings. The inference on display here is clear—namely, the coming Jewish new year promises haven and hope in America to Sephardic Jews seeking refuge from the imploding Ottoman regime's anti-Jewish hostility.

Viewed as a totality, the Ladino press in the United States, bearing both Hebrew and Spanish legacies, challenged the definition of what it meant to be "Jewish" and "Hispanic" in the modern era. Many of the ensuing conflicts and quandaries in this regard are vividly reflected in the pages of La Amérika and other contemporaneous Sephardic periodicals. The American Ladino press— and those men and women who produced and contributed to it—radically modify our understanding of the "eastern European period" of American Jewish history. Moreover, as exemplified by La Amérika, close investigation of Ladino-speaking Jews and their relations with the peoples with whom they most closely interacted prompts a reconsideration of American Jewish history and the history of American ethnic groups.

19

"THE NEW JERUSALEM"

A Gentile Perspective on New York's Jews at the Turn
of the Nineteenth and Twentieth Centuries
(1914)

◇◇◇

DAVID E. KAUFMAN

In the history of American Jews, New York City looms large as the "city
of dreams," the so-called new Jerusalem of America.[1] Colonial New Amsterdam
saw the first group settlement of Jews in North America, and for three centuries
thereafter New York City continued to be the main port of entry for generations of Jewish immigrants. Though rivaled by Charleston, South Carolina, and
Philadelphia, Pennsylvania, in the early nineteenth century, New York's dominant position in American Jewish life was well established by the Civil War. In
the late nineteenth and early twentieth centuries, some two and a half million
eastern European Jews immigrated to the United States, the great majority of
whom arrived by steamship in New York Harbor.[2] Given its explosive growth
and emergence as America's premier cosmopolis, it is perhaps unsurprising that
New York also became home to the largest urban Jewish community in history.[3]
Less commonly observed, however, is what this unprecedented phenomenon
meant for the social and psychological experience of New York Jews themselves.

1. See Tyler Anbinder, *City of Dreams: The 400-Year Epic History of Immigrant New York* (Boston:
Houghton Mifflin Harcourt, 2016).

2. It has been observed that "close to 85 percent of [eastern European Jewish immigrants]
landed in New York City, and approximately 75 percent of those settled initially on the Lower
East Side.... Unlike many of their fellow immigrants, Jews intended to stay. Strikingly, 33 percent of the total immigrant population returned to their old homes, while only 5 percent of Jews
made that decision" (Deborah Dash Moore, Jeffrey S. Gurock, Annie Polland, Howard B. Rock,
and Daniel Soyer, *Jewish New York: The Remarkable Story of a City and a People* [New York: New York
University Press, 2017], 79).

3. In 1910, when the number of New York Jews approached one million, the largest urban
Jewish populations of Europe were: Warsaw, with 306,061 Jews; Budapest, with 203,687; and
Vienna, with 175,318. See Paul Mendes-Flohr and Jehuda Reinharz, eds., *The Jew in the Modern
World: A Documentary History*, 3d ed. (New York: Oxford University Press, 2011), "Table VIII. The
Urbanization of European Jewry: The Six Most Populous Jewish Cities in Europe," 884.

"The New Jerusalem"—a 1914 article written by Stanley Went for the *Bell-man*, a literary magazine in Minneapolis—opens a window on New York's stunning transformation. In the tradition of the Swedish explorer Peter Kalm (1716–1779), who marveled at the adaptation of Jews to life in colonial North America, and Hannah Adams (1755–1831), the philosemitic American Christian chronicler of Jewish history, Went describes Jewish life in America from the vantage point of a gentile. The title of his piece alludes to the Christian Bible's "vision of the New Jerusalem" (Rev. 21:9–22:7). Writing for a Midwest publication, Went's observations of the burgeoning New York Jewish community bear a distinctive outsider's perspective: he was neither a Jew nor a New Yorker. Though at times patronizing and exaggerated, his analysis is nonetheless discerning and insightful. The historical timing of Went's piece is also noteworthy, as it comes after the peak of the mass waves of eastern European Jewish immigration but before World War I (1914–18) and the rise of American Zionism as a potent political force. Prior to the Balfour Declaration of 1917, only a minority of American Jews took the Zionist claim to Palestine seriously. Indeed, it made some sense, in that interim moment, to declare New York to be the "new Jerusalem" rather than envision the actual Jerusalem as the heart of a future Jewish state. The latter proposition, as Went incisively observed from the Minnesota heartland, required a leap of imagination and turning a blind eye to facts on the ground.

The gist of Went's article is not an account of population statistics but rather an intriguing analysis of a characterological phenomenon: the New York Jew. Went begins by observing that "the New York Jew is a type apart," distinct from Jews in other parts of world by virtue of his or her comfort in being a Jew. While European Jews, he explains, reacted to the Old World's antisemitic environment by overcompensating with pride or shame, New York Jews faced no such predicament. In multicultural New York, where they made up a quarter of the population, Jews felt at home and comfortable in their skin. The notion of such a fully adjusted and self-confident Jew was, to be sure, an exaggeration and a stereotype—as was Went's contention that the Jews had "conquered" the city and made it their "own" in economic, political, and social terms. But his basic observation that Progressive-era New York City had become a Jewish center of unprecedented scale and historic import—and had thus fostered the emergence of a new type of Jew—was entirely on the mark.

The heart of Went's piece is a provocative comparison of the inadvertent Jewish "colonization" of New York with the more ideologically driven movements to solve the "Jewish problem" of diaspora existence by creating a Jewish homeland in Palestine or elsewhere. Why resort to such chimerical schemes, Went opines, when a Jewish New York is a fait accompli? We need not accept Went's view that by 1914 New York had become a "Jewish city" to appreciate the implications of his assessment. How, after all, did the experience of Jews in New York compare with that of Zionist settlers in the Ottoman empire and their vision of a Jewish majoritarian society in the making? What does the stunning rise of New York's Jewish community illustrate about the nature of modern Jewish culture and national identity? More pertinent to the study of American Jewry as a whole, how was the New York case distinctive or exceptional in contrast to other American communities with a lower Jewish population density? Went's thought-provoking essay offers a useful and generative starting point to investigate such questions.

◇◇

Stanley Went, "The New Jerusalem," *Bellman*, January 17, 1914

Source: Stanley Went, "The New Jerusalem," *Bellman*,[4] January 17, 1914, 82–83.

The New York Jew is a type apart, like yet unlike his coreligionists scattered about the rest of the world. He is not, as so many Jews [are], acutely conscious of his race.[5] He is not particularly proud of it, for pride implies the opposite possibility of shame; and it would certainly never occur to the typical New York Jew to be ashamed of his origin. Indeed, I have only met one of his kind who took the trouble to disclaim his ancestry, and he was on board an Atlantic liner returning from Europe; so perhaps he had been contaminated by Gentile influence. He declared his name was O'Flannigan, a transparent piece of disingenuousness to which speech and features gave the lie.

The Jew of Europe is roughly divisible into two classes: the respectable Jew and the detestable Jew. The former is rather aggressively proud of his Hebraism; the latter is as pathetically anxious to conceal it. In New York a man is able to be frankly accepted as Jew, neither boasting nor extenuating his origin, for the simple reason that there he is among his own kind. New York, in fact, is the New Jerusalem, and for the first time since the troops of Trajan[6] burned the Temple

---

4. Established in 1906 by William C. Edgar (1856–1932), the *Bellman* was a popular Minneapolis-based literary magazine; it ceased publication after 1919. For a full description of the magazine, see John T. Flanagan, "Early Literary Periodicals in Minnesota," *Minnesota History* 26, no. 4 (December 1945): 303–11.

5. On the question of Jewish "racial" identity in the American context, see Eric Goldstein, *The Price of Whiteness: Jews, Race, and American Identity* (Princeton, NJ: Princeton University Press, 2006).

6. A successful ruler and military strategist, Trajan (c. 53–117 CE) presided as emperor (98–117 CE) over the greatest period in imperial Rome's development and territorial expansion.

and profaned the Holy of Holies,[7] the Jew has found a resting place which he can call his own.

Hither he comes, dirty, greasy, garlic-smelling, from every ghetto of Europe. On landing from the steamer, he disappears for a time into the great melting-pot of the East Side, and thence, after a year or two, he emerges into the light of day, washed and cleaned and groomed, shampooed and manicured, with gold fillings in his teeth and the light of conquest in his eye. His command of the English language is fluent and perfect; his command of American slang amounts to genius. His clothes are of the latest cut; his linen immaculate. His daily bath is not merely a measure of expediency, it is an absolute necessity for his comfort, which is proof enough that he has done more than just adapt himself to new conditions; he has absorbed them into the very marrow of him. He marries a buxom maiden of his own race, who thereafter takes on *embonpoint*[8] with startling rapidity; and the pair, in the cozy apartment within a block or two of Riverside Drive, inculcate in their children, of whom they are prolific, the principles of personal cleanliness and a respect for the American flag.

It is a little startling to realize that this exceedingly prosperous citizen is identically the same person in whose interest philanthropic people have been excogitating the "Zionist Movement"; that only a few years and the diligent application of soap and water, with all the attendant influences that are implied thereby, separate this independent American citizen from the suitable object of experimental benevolence.

Quite recently another most interesting suggestion for settling the "Jewish question" was made by J. L. Garvin,[9] editor of the London *Observer*, and endorsed by Israel Zangwill.[10] It was to re-create Salonika[11] and the isthmus on which it stands, out of the wreck of the Turkish empire, as the Jewish capital of the world. The suggestion opens up some fascinating possibilities and a field of speculation that is almost limitless. How would the Jewish people, as a nation,

7. The reference is to the Tabernacle, considered to be God's earthly dwelling place, in the Israelites' ancient Temple in Jerusalem.

8. A French term for plumpness, a sign of prosperity.

9. James L. Garvin (1868–1947), a British journalist and editor, assumed control in 1908 of the *Observer*, a liberal Sunday newspaper with a national readership in the United Kingdom.

10. The Anglo-Jewish writer Israel Zangwill (1864–1926) was best known for his acclaimed play *The Melting Pot* (1909). Originally a committed Zionist, Zangwill converted in 1905 to territorialism and thereafter promoted the idea of a Jewish homeland outside of Palestine.

11. Salonika (Thessaloniki), Greece, was a major center of Sephardic Jewish life and known as the "Jerusalem of the Balkans." In the early twentieth century, its community of over 60,000 Jews represented nearly 40 percent of the total population.

solve the problem of self-government? How would the revival of the city-state, as a political unit, succeed? Assuming the success of the experiment, would the artificially created state achieve a genuine national sentiment and patriotism, apart from a merely economic cohesion, in which coreligionists throughout the world would share? And if so, would not dreams of territorial expansion follow as a matter of course?

It is a far more attractive plan than the old one for the purchase of Palestine as the home of the Jewish race, for the conception of a Europeanized Palestine, despite the enterprise of Thomas Cook & Son,[12] is all unfamiliar to the mind, while Salonika is a busy modern mart, with the Jewish race already preponderant in its population. So interesting, indeed, do the possibilities of the scheme appear that one almost wishes it might have been tried in earnest, simply for the satisfaction of a philosophical curiosity.

The project, however, is destined to remain in the regions of speculation, for neither this nor the former Zionist experiment is likely to be put into effect. A thousand reasons could be urged against them, but the sufficient one is that they are not necessary. While Mr. Zangwill and other distinguished leaders of thought have been debating the "Jewish question," the question, if ever there was one, has quietly settled itself, as in the end such questions usually do. Without definite consciousness or volition the Jewish race has been shaping its own destiny. Its people have ever been citizens of the world: French, German, English, Italian, Spanish—owning allegiance to the flag of the nation that accords them hospitality, but always and everlastingly Jews. And now, for the capital of their race, by a purely spontaneous movement, they have selected the old Dutch settlement which has become New York.[13] It is an unofficial capital and no char-

---

12. Thomas Cook and Son, an international British tourism company, was founded in 1841.

13. In 1654, with the recapture by the Portuguese of Dutch colonies in Brazil, including Pernambuco (Recifé), the local Sephardic Jewish community there disbanded. Not only did the Jews wish to flee from the Inquisition, but they also feared Portuguese retribution for having aided the Dutch in the development of the colonies. Those with means escaped to Amsterdam and London, but twenty-three Jewish refugees aboard the St. Catherine eventually landed in Dutch-controlled New Amsterdam. The New Netherland colony had only approximately 750 people. Though the Jewish refugees were technically Dutch subjects, Peter Stuyvesant (c. 1612–1672)—a staunch defender of the Dutch Reformed Church and director-general of the New Holland colony in North America—sought to deny the Jews entry, arguing that they would defile the New World. Meanwhile, Amsterdam Jews interceded vigorously on behalf of the refugees. In the end, the Dutch West India Company decided to permit the Jews to remain in New Amsterdam, and Stuyvesant reluctantly acquiesced. Thus, the Jews gained a foothold in the New World. See documents 1.03–1.05 in American Jewish History: A Primary Source Reader, ed. Gary P. Zola and Marc Dollinger (Waltham, MA: Brandeis University Press, 2014), 10–12.

ter gives them title of possession, but it is theirs nevertheless, the chosen city of this indomitable people.

What will the Jew do with his possession now that he has achieved it? And is this in truth the Promised Land which he has reached after all the centuries of Ishmaelitish wandering?[14] More important still, what will his possession do to him? New York is by no means the first city that the Jew has owned. At one time and another he has owned many of the great cities of the Old World. But his possession has been purely an economic one. Now, for the first time, it is social and political as well, and in that fact lies the interest of the problem of the New York Jew.

Hitherto, wherever the Jew has wandered, he has preserved his racial characteristics, to a large extent even his racial customs. Circumstances have been particularly favorable in contributing to this result. Generally speaking, the Jew has been an alien, a social outcast living among, but apart from, a population that half-feared and wholly despised him. He has mingled perforce with his own kind and with no others, and so his identity has been preserved. Added to this has been the binding force of his religion, thriving, as all religions do thrive, on persecution, cemented by the authority of the rabbi and the strictness of its dogma. Only within the last century, even in the most enlightened countries, has there been any real bridging of the gulf that has kept Jew and Christian apart; and even now the bridge is a narrow one over which not all may pass. France has had her Dreyfus case;[15] when [Ernetso] Nathan[16] was elected mayor of Rome there were many who hurled at him the word "Jew" as a term of opprobrium; there is a club in London whose members felt that somehow they had

14. The term "Ishmaelite" derives from Ishmael, the oldest son of the biblical patriarch Abraham, who is considered to be the father of the Arab peoples (Gen. 16:11–16). The biblical narrative relates that Abraham gave Ishmael and his mother, Hagar, a supply of bread and water and sent them into the wilderness (Gen. 21:8–21).

15. The Dreyfus Affair centered on Captain Alfred Dreyfus (1859–1936), an assimilated French Jew and career military officer who in 1894 was falsely accused of espionage. Dreyfus's accusers manufactured evidence to support the charges against him, and he was convicted of treason. The French public generally applauded his sentence, and he was imprisoned, languishing in jail until 1899. The affair, which became a *cause célèbre* and a watershed in the history of antisemitism, stunned many in the West and shook the confidence of Jews in the liberal order. In 1906, Dreyfus was fully exonerated following a protracted legal battle, a vigorous public debate championed by the French writer Émile Zola (1840–1902), and an investigation that proved French military officers had framed Dreyfus by suppressing and falsifying evidence.

16. Ernesto Nathan (1848–1921), a British-born Italian Jewish politician, served as mayor of Rome (1907–13).

been caught napping when a scion of one of the first Jewish families in the land was elected to its membership.[17] The prejudice against the race is weakened, perhaps moribund, but it still survives.

In New York there may be prejudice, but if there is it does not matter, for here the Jew walks with the proud mien of a conqueror. He has subdued the defenses one by one: economic, political, social, the last the key to the position, and the fortress is won. Even if there is a society which closes its doors to him it does not matter, for he has no desire to enter; it is not worth his while. He can make society for himself; he is master of the situation and he knows it. This is where the Jew of New York differs from the Jew of Europe: he is free from self-consciousness because he has no doubts as to his standing. He says frankly, "I am a Jew," and omits to add, as does his European brother, the defiant "What are you going to do about it?" not from any delicate perception of the elegancies of speech, but because defiance is unnecessary.

Perhaps another century must elapse before the Jew has finally worked out his destiny in the land of his choice. In the meantime he is unconsciously engaged in the greatest struggle of his existence, the struggle for the preservation of his type, and the outcome of it is still in doubt. At present we can only see the effect of the new influences on two, or at most three, generations; and if three generations go to the making of a gentleman, it is very sure that more than that number are required for the unmaking of a Jew. The New York Jew of the second or the third generation is still true to type, but there are indications that the bonds that bind him to his past are slackening, and chief among these indications is his attitude toward his faith. His parents that came over from Europe in the steerage of a liner were of the strictest sect of the Pharisees,[18]

17. This may be a reference to the British Jewish financier Baron Nathaniel Mayer de Rothschild (1840–1915), scion of the wealthy European Rothschild family, who in 1885 became a member of the House of Lords. His father, Lionel de Rothschild (1808–1879), was the first practicing Jew to be seated as a member of Parliament. The historian Cecil Roth reports that at a 1909 meeting in London's fashionable Holborn Restaurant, David Lloyd George (1863–1945), then Chancellor of the Exchequer, publicly lamented Rothschild's involvement in a parliamentary debate about the Liberal government's proposed "People's Budget": "I really think we are having too much Lord Rothschild. Are we to have all ways of reform, financial and social, blocked, simply by a notice-board; 'No Thoroughfare. By Order of Nathaniel Rothschild?'" (Cecil Roth, *The Magnificent Rothschilds* [London: R. Hale, 1939], 130–32). George's comments were widely reported at the time.

18. Went employs the term "Pharisee" here to suggest a primitive and antimodern sensibility. In fact, the Pharisees were one of two dominant Jewish religious and political sects that arose during the Second Temple period; they were opposed by the Sadducees. The Pharisees emerged

holding tenaciously to the rabbinical law and being governed by it in the minutiae of their daily life. Their children, led by the exigencies of business and gentile intercourse, have departed from this straight and narrow path. If they continue the practice of their religion and hold to its traditions, they have joined the sect of the "Reformed Jews," professing a monotheistic faith and a belief in the messianic age and in the destiny of the children of Israel as the chosen people, through whom human perfection will ultimately be attained.

If that be so, then what is the force of calling New York the "New Jerusalem," and of what avail is it for the Jew to have entered into the Promised Land if he is to be swallowed up by the population that he finds there? It may be that, in the most literal sense, in losing his life he shall save it. It may be that, in mingling with that conglomeration of races which has become the American people, and leavening the lump with his magnificent qualities, the Jew will bring about the realization of his ancient promise. It is at any rate an interesting thought that perhaps by sacrifice, the sacrifice of his individual type to the betterment of the race, the Jew is destined at last to attain the New Jerusalem.

---

as a distinct group around 165 BCE and insisted on the strict observance of Judaism's doctrines and practices. After the destruction of the Second Temple in 70 CE, the Pharisees' worldview influenced the development of diaspora Jewish traditionalism.

20

"THE GENTLEMAN BEING BOTH A GERMAN AND A JEW"

B. H. Roberts Nominates Simon Bamberger as Democratic
Candidate for Governor of Utah[1]
(1916)

◇◇

AMBER TAYLOR

In September 1916, Brigham Henry Roberts (1857–1933), a prominent
historian, politician, and leader of the Mormon church, nominated the Jewish
business and political leader Simon Bamberger (1845–1926) as the Democratic
candidate for governor of Utah. Bamberger's nomination and subsequent electoral victory is significant for various reasons, perhaps most notably because it
broke the "unwritten law" that any governor of Utah must be a member of the
Church of Jesus Christ of Latter-day Saints. Utah was originally settled by Mormon pioneers in the mid-nineteenth century and admitted to the union in 1896,
and a vast majority of the state's population was made up of the church's rank
and file. A president in the church's First Council of the Seventy, Roberts stood
near the top of the church's hierarchy. As a Democrat, he often found himself
in political opposition to many of his coreligionists, and in 1916 he relished the
opportunity to shatter that "unwritten law."

Bamberger, a Darmstadt-born German-speaking Jew who had immigrated
to the United States in 1859 and settled in Utah after the Civil War, moved from
business to Utah politics when he was asked in 1898 to join the Salt Lake City
Board of Education. He served on the board until 1903. He was a strong supporter of free universal education, and early in his service, he donated a large
sum of his own money and then worked for weeks to raise the remainder of the
needed funds to keep the city's public school system solvent. Later, as a representative in Utah's legislature, he was known for his good-natured, witty an-
tics. After a particularly heated debate, he reportedly hid the speaker's gavel so
it would be safe for the Democratic majority he predicted for the next session
of the legislature.

---

1. The author wishes to offer special thanks to the Utah State Historical Society for providing
an original copy of the published Democratic party nomination proceedings.

As a historically insular people, Latter-day Saints were wary of outsiders, yet they have always maintained a certain affinity for Jews. Thus, Bamberger's Jewish heritage came into play only minimally in the election. When he traveled to an area of rural Utah's Sanpete County, which was dominated by Scandinavian Latter-day Saint immigrants, Bamberger was reportedly greeted with the taunt, *"Ve don't vant any damned Yentile for governor."* His reply—"I'm no gentile, I'm an Israelite"—won over the suspicious locals, and he was welcomed as a fellow Israelite.

Despite not being a member of the Mormon church, local church leaders supported Bamberger instead of the Latter-day Saint Republican candidate, Nephi Morris (1870–1943). This was largely because Bamberger was a Prohibitionist, whereas Morris and the Republican party supported a statewide law that prohibited the manufacture and sale of alcohol but provided for a "local option" (most rural towns adopted "dry" laws, while Salt Lake City and other urban centers remained "wet," or alcohol-friendly). In the nomination speech, Roberts discusses Bamberger's business acumen and prior public service, as well as his reputation for honesty and fairness in both business and politics. He also addresses the issue of Bamberger's being a German and a Jew. Roberts counters the latter concern by referring to Latter-day Saints' theological views of themselves as descendants of the Israelite tribe of Ephraim and thus being kin to Jews.

Bamberger easily won both the Democratic nomination for governor and the election, making him the second practicing Jew to serve as governor of a U.S. state; the first was Moses Alexander (1853–1932) of Idaho. In 1917, as governor, Bamberger helped achieve the passage of a workers' compensation act, and he worked to implement various other progressive measures in Utah.

150 NEW PERSPECTIVES IN AMERICAN JEWISH HISTORY

Speech by B. H. Roberts Nominating Simon Bamberger as Democratic Candidate for Governor of Utah, 1916

Source: Democratic State Committee, *Proceedings of the Democratic State Convention Held at Ogden, Utah, August 18, 1916* (Ogden, Utah: Democratic State Committee, September 1916), 15–22.

Speech of Hon. [Brigham Henry] Roberts[2] Nominating Hon. Simon Bamberger for Governor of Utah[3]

Mr. Chairman, Ladies and Gentlemen of the Convention:

There never was a time when the United States of America was so honored among the nations of the earth as she is today....

And all this, fellow citizens, at a time when the Democratic party has been in control of the affairs of the nation for three and a half years,[4] and has put into effective operation that legislative and administrative program of policies[5] promised four years ago.

Amid the world's greatest political upheaval, and the world's mightiest cataclysmic war,[6] America's ship of state has been made to keep an even keel, and

2. Brigham Henry Roberts (1857–1933) was a prominent figure in the political and religious landscape of Utah in this period. A leading member of the First Quorum of the Seventy, the third-highest governing body in the Church of Jesus Christ of Latter-day Saints, he was noted for his intellectual and progressive approach to theology and scripture. He was also a commanding presence in Utah's Democratic party, and he ran against the grain of the church leadership's tendency to support, sometimes overtly, Republican policies and candidates. In 1898, Roberts was elected to Congress as a Democratic representative from Utah, but he was denied his seat because he practiced polygamy (which was still common among church members).

3. Originally settled as a U.S. territory in 1850, Utah did not achieve statehood until 1896. On the eve of World War I (1914–18), the state's population was approximately 374,000 and consisted overwhelmingly of members of the Church of Jesus Christ of Latter-day Saints. By 1916, Utah had had three elected governors (prior to statehood, its governors were presidential appointees), all of whom were Republicans. Throughout the rest of the twentieth century, only five more Democratic governors were elected.

4. Roberts is referring to the fact that President Woodrow Wilson (1856–1924), a Democrat, had enjoyed a solid Democratic majority in both the House and Senate since 1912.

5. Some of the most fundamental parts of the national Democratic platform in 1912 were a campaign for tariff reform, which was believed would help alleviate the high cost of living, and effective antitrust laws. In 1914, Congress passed two antitrust laws, the Clayton Act and the Federal Trade Commission Act.

6. By 1916, World War I had been raging in Europe for two years. In accordance with isolationist attitudes among most Democrats of the era, Wilson had largely worked to keep the United States out of the war—an effort in which he had the support of Congress. However, Wilson was also affected by the preparedness movement that arose after German U-boats in 1915

under the guidance of the most masterful statesmanship of modern times, there has been preserved both the nation's peace, and what is yet more important, the nation's honor. This [is] at once the effort and the achievement of a Democratic administration, at the head of which, as chief, and beloved leader, is PRESIDENT WOODROW WILSON.[7]

POLITICAL ISSUES

... Whether Utah shall give such moral support to the national administration or not depends upon the success of the Democratic party in this state in the pending election; for I am assuming the success of the Democratic party in the national election. ... Nominate a man our party can elect as governor of this state, and he will carry with him the whole state ticket, the senators, the congressmen, and the presidential electors.

WHAT DEMOCRATS MUST DO

The Republican party convention of this state, which met in this very hall ten days ago, has placed at the head of their ticket for the office of Governor a factional candidate,[8] and has formulated a platform that will scarcely be recognized as an expression of standard Republican principles. So that very many Republicans feel that in this state they have neither a candidate nor a platform;

---

sank the British passenger ship *Lusitania*, which was carrying both British and American passengers (as well secret American munitions intended to aid Britain's war effort). Supporters of America's military preparedness saw themselves as realists who understood the United States would inevitably join the war. The United States did so in 1917, after a year-long political effort by Wilson toward that end.

7. Wilson saw his contribution to the war effort, both before and after the United States declared war and joined the Allied Powers (Britain, France, Italy, Russia, and others), primarily as a peace broker. Part of his impetus to enter the war was the hope that he might implement his plan for a League of Nations. The League's success was undermined by refusal of the U.S. Congress to support the initiative, but it nevertheless became a worldwide intergovernmental effort. In 1919, Wilson was awarded the Nobel Peace Prize for his efforts to create and implement the League.

8. Roberts is referring to Nephi L. Morris , the Republican candidate and a prominent figure in the Latter-day Saint Church leadership as well as Utah politics. Although Morris had recently jumped on the Prohibition bandwagon, he and most Republican leaders in Utah had only reluctantly done so. They instead preferred the "local option" of municipalities choosing to be either "wet" (alcohol-friendly) or "dry." Specifically, Morris's campaign was hampered by the perception of him as heir apparent to Utah's Republican Governor William Spry (1864–1929), a staunch anti-Prohibitionist and controversial governor.

and neither the party nor the candidate will make a strong appeal to the independent voters of the state.

The plain duty of the Democratic party in the face of such conditions is to nominate a candidate for Governor who will be entirely satisfactory to the Democracy of the state, and at the same time will make a strong appeal to dissatisfied Republicans and draw to his support the independent voters; who, as already stated in speeches from this platform today, are the determining factors in our elections.

Mr. Chairman, and Ladies and Gentlemen of the convention, I have such a candidate to present to you; and as I am unskilled in the art of maintaining suspense, I shall take you at once into my confidence by saying that my candidate for the high office of Governor of Utah is [the] HON. SIMON BAMBERGER of Salt Lake City.

BUSINESS CAREER

Mr. Bamberger is a native of Germany, but came to America about fifty years ago, and to Salt Lake City forty-eight years ago, where he engaged for a time in the hotel business, but in 1872 took to mining....[9]

In 1879 he became active in developing the coal fields of Sanpete valley, and later went to Europe and financed the construction of the Sanpete Valley Railroad, running from Nephi, in Juab county, to Sanpete valley points. In 1890 Mr. Bamberger began the construction of the Salt Lake and Ogden Railroad, which became the pioneer electric interurban system of the Rocky Mountains, and which with its connections link together the most fertile and populous parts of the valleys of Utah and Idaho, greatly facilitating travel and marketing possibilities of the richest sections of our state. He is also recognized as the promoter and founder of many industries in the state, such as coal companies, stone quarries, brick yards, lime kilns, etc. It will be observed that these business enterprises are all in the direction of the industrial development of the state, such kinds of business as give employment to men, that establish pay rolls, the steadiness and largeness of which, better than any other thing make

---

9. Mining had become a major part of Utah's economy by this period. With nearly every county in the state claiming some sort of mining enterprise (most notably the mining of copper and coal, but also of silver), it was an important and well-known sector of the economy. Bamberger rose to prominence in part for his success in revitalizing seemingly depleted mines, as well as through his efforts at building up the railroad network that could transport mined products more easily and cheaply.

for the prosperity of a community. . . . You never heard of a strike on the part of Mr. Bamberger's workmen; and it must have been the cause of extreme pleasure to Mr. Bamberger to receive, as he did only last night, the endorsement of a number of the prominent labor organizations[10] of the state to his candidacy for Governor of Utah. . . .

PUBLIC SERVICE

In the midst of this absorbing business career Mr. Bamberger has found time to render to the public valuable civic service. He has served two terms as a member of the Salt Lake City School Board. And when in 1903 the schools of our city were likely to be cut down a portion of the school year for lack of funds, it was Mr. Bamberger who headed a subscription list which ultimately amounted to $10,000 to keep the schools from closing a month before the legal term expired. He also served a term of four years as state senator in the Utah Legislature; so that he is already familiar with legislative processes. . . .

PROHIBITION

Your committee on platform and resolutions, Ladies and Gentlemen of the convention, have [sic] exhausted [its] ingenuity in the use of terms to make clear, and positive, and emphatic your declaration respecting the enactment of state-wide and nation-wide Prohibition.[11] My candidate, without hesitation or mental reservation, under-writes your declaration—subscribes to it in full, as an economic and efficiency necessity. No one can do more. Mr. Bamberger has given good earnest of his conviction in this matter of Prohibition by making financial sacrifice in the furtherance of it. Last year, on his own volition, at the request of prominent citizens of Davis county, he made Lagoon,[12] a pleasure resort on the

---

10. Bamberger was a progressive businessman, noted for championing fair wages and care for employees, both in his business and political pursuits.

11. In 1916, U.S. society was in the midst of a fierce debate over Prohibition. A cause that enjoyed prominence at various times and varying degrees of popularity in the country's history, Prohibition had recently taken root among factions in both the Republican and Democratic parties. Even in Utah, where Latter-day Saint leaders admonished against the use of alcohol through their own particular religious lens, the distillation and export of alcohol, especially to mining towns in the state and its environs, was a profitable business.

12. Lagoon, now a major amusement park, began as a kind of lakeside resort. It may be one of Bamberger's most prominent legacies, although most patrons today hardly know his name, let alone his association with the popular attraction.

line of his electric railroad, absolutely dry, though it materially depreciated the leasing value of the restaurant and other concessions of the pleasure resort....

The people of Utah have arisen in their majesty on this subject of state and nation-wide Prohibition, and no party or administration dare further attempt to thwart their clearly declared will. My candidate stands prepared to carry into complete effect their supreme mandate....

OBJECTIONS TO MR. BAMBERGER

Here Mr. Chairman I should be pleased to close my task and leave my candidate in the hands of this convention, but I should fail of my duty to my friend and fail in my service to this convention and to the Democratic party if I did not take note of the objections that are urged against Mr. Bamberger's candidacy— objections against his nationality, his race and religion—the gentleman being both a German and a Jew.[13] I am proud to know that such objections as can be made to my candidate can only be made on these grounds . . . only against his nationality, his race and religion.

It is suggested that since Mr. Bamberger is of German birth, that possibly such conditions might arise in case of a crisis between the United States and Germany, and Mr. Bamberger being governor of Utah, might have such pro-German sympathies that he would fail to bring the full moral and effective support of Utah to the side of the United States....

. . . Mr. Bamberger came to this West-World Republic in his young manhood, drawn hither by the advantages promised in this land of opportunity— opportunity promised by her limitless natural resources, but made available and secure to all her citizens by reason of the free institutions of the country. These Mr. Bamberger considered, and to them, and to the country through them, pledged his solemn allegiance bound by his oath and covenant. And here let me say that the religion of the Jew rises to give a special solemnity to his act. For it is a cardinal principle, and a divine injunction to the Jew that, "Thou shalt not foreswear thyself, but shall perform unto the Lord thine oaths" [Matt. 5:33].[14]

13. It is hard to say which was more objectionable in this period—Bamberger's German or his Jewish heritage. In the midst of World War I, anti-German sentiment was strong. Some Utahans objected to his Jewish ancestry although, significantly, the issue seems to have been more animated by the fact he was not a member of the Church of Jesus Christ of Latter-day Saints.

14. Here is a bit of unintended irony in Roberts's speech. The passage he quotes is from the Christian Bible (Matt. 5:33), in which Jesus presumably refers to ancient Jewish texts in order to then provide a higher law. Yet although the sentiment is easily recognizable (see, for example,

... In addition to this, here in America, and chiefly in Utah, are all his interests, his property, his family, his home, his future hopes, his fifty years of residence, with all the fond associations of his life for that time—every tie that can bind a man to home, family, and country binds this man in loyalty to America and to Utah. In the presence of these considerations how weak and silly appear the objections based on his nationality!

As to objections to my candidate on the ground of his race and religion—and one necessarily goes with the other—proudly here I take my stand by his side to defend him against this objection, and I never knew a prouder moment of existence than now, and while performing this act. Here and now I rebuke—and I hope this convention will rebuke—those who raise objection on this ground of race and religion. Such objection violates in letter and spirit the express provision of our state Constitution, which declares that—

"THE RIGHTS OF CONSCIENCE SHALL NEVER BE INFRINGED ... NO RELIGIOUS TEST SHALL BE REQUIRED AS A QUALIFICATION FOR ANY OFFICE OF PUBLIC TRUST, OR FOR ANY VOTE AT ANY ELECTION."[15]

The people of Utah should be the very last to make objections to the candidates for office on such grounds as race and religion.[16] And most of all they should not raise objections to a Jew. When our ancestors, my friends of Anglo-Saxon antecedents, in ancient times, were living in a state of savagery on the plains and in the forests and mountains of northern and central Europe, and drinking "vodka" or its equivalent from the skulls of their slain enemies, the an-

---

Deut. 23:21 in the Hebrew Bible), the text as written is not found in the Hebrew Bible. Thus, Roberts quotes a passage that is, in fact, an interpretation of a presumed Jewish religious obligation through a Christian, and then, even more specifically, a Latter-day Saint lens.

15. From their earliest days, Latter-day Saints were concerned about freedom of conscience and religion. The idea was given expression and made an essential aspect of the church's theological outlook through its inclusion as one of thirteen Articles of Faith penned in 1842 by the founder Joseph Smith (1805–1844). The eleventh article reads, "We claim the privilege of worshiping Almighty God according to the dictates of our own conscience, and allow all men the same privilege, let them worship how, where, or what they may" (A of F 1:11)

16. As a group that experienced painful persecution for much of its early history—which ultimately led to the Mormon exodus to the Great Basin of what would become Utah—Latter-day Saints, Roberts claims, should be much more tolerant than those who made religion the basis of their unfair judgment and poor treatment of Latter-day Saints and other groups. He is also referring to Mormons' still-fresh bitterness at being finally forced to acquiesce to the U.S. government's insistence that Latter-day Saints end the practice of polygamy (see also chapter 10, note 8). in 1898, Roberts himself had been refused his elected seat in the U.S. House of Representatives because of his refusal to separate himself from two of his three wives and their children.

cestors of Mr. Bamberger, the Jew, were living in Syria and Palestine in a highly developed state of civilization, under an enlightened system of legislation, and forming a literature in historical writings, in prophecy and poetry, that has instructed and refined all subsequent ages, and survives to this day; while the Mosaic code of legislation has become largely the ground-plan of all Anglo-Saxon civil law. If ever a man had reason to be proud of his racial origin, that man is the Jew, and for reasons, besides those I have urged, too sacred to be invoked here, and I shall not name them. Let it suffice to say, that I had hoped that here in Utah such a question would not have arisen. I had hoped that here we should have realized in a small way, at least, the fulfillment of one of the Hebrew prophecies, viz., "The envy of Ephraim shall depart, and the adversaries of Judah shall be cut off: Ephraim shall not envy Judah, and Judah shall not vex Ephraim" [Isa. 11: 13];[17] but together they should work for the accomplishment of high purposes. And I still look forward to the achievement of these good things through the agreement and co-operation of these forces.

We have an anomalous condition existing here in Utah—it exists nowhere else in the United States,[18] and we must be rid of it. Heretofore we have thought we must name candidates because they are Mormons or non-Mormons, instead of upon the basis of American citizenship, and their fitness and capacity for the service. Thus the "unwritten law" in Utah in relation to political preferment is that the governor must invariably be "Mormon"; the United States Senators for the state shall be one "Mormon" and one "Gentile: and a like division shall obtain as to the Congressmen....

Is not such an arrangement absurd, as well as anomalous and utterly un-American? Should not such an "unwritten law" be smashed? ... One of the attractive elements to me in the candidacy of Mr. Bamberger for Governor is the possibility that he might take the first step towards smashing this "unwritten law"; and the first step would also be the last. ... Revolutions achieving just ends go not backward.

---

17. Latter-day Saints consider themselves literal members of the House of Israel, through the tribe of Ephraim. They generally interpret this passage as a prophecy of themselves (as Israelites) joining with Jews as heirs of the covenant working together to bring about the prophecies of latter-day restoration and righteousness on earth.

18. The "anomalous condition" is the unspoken law that state leaders must be members of the Church of Jesus Christ of Latter-day Saints. Although Roberts claims that this is an "anomalous condition," American politics has historically embraced similar unwritten laws—or at least cultural expectations—dictating that U.S. political leaders embrace some form of basic Christian belief. In this, then, Utah may be considered more local than anomalous in its preferences.

My candidate, Mr. Chairman, and Ladies and Gentlemen of the convention, completes the circle of requirements of a candidate, touching it at every point.

Do you want a Governor who will give us the highest assurance of a business-like management of the State's affairs? . . .

Do you want a candidate who will be a guarantee that the sovereign will of the people shall be enacted into law and enforced in respect of Prohibition? . . .

Do you want a Governor who throughout gives good, earnest that there shall be an honest enforcement of all laws and the enactment of needed legislation without regard to creed, color, race, sex, or religion? . . .

Do you want a Governor whose domestic life is of a kind that does credit to the state and that will command the respect of the home-loving people of Utah? . . .

Do you want a consistent, continuously faithful Democrat for your candidate? Mr. Bamberger is such a candidate, members of this convention; and in conclusion let me say I HAVE THE HONOR TO PRESENT TO THIS CONVENTION AS ITS CANDIDATE FOR THE HIGH OFFICE OF GOVERNOR OF UTAH, HON. SIMON BAMBERGER, WHO BELONGS TO THE PEOPLE OF UTAH — TO ALL THE PEOPLE OF UTAH.

You can elect him Governor of this state, and with him carry the whole state ticket, the congressional candidates, and the national ticket, and thus place Utah in the column of triumphant Democratic states of the American Union.

21

"WHAT JUSTICE OR REDRESS CAN BE GAINED"

East European Jewish Immigrants and Legal Aid
(1917)

◇◇

GERALDINE GUDEFIN

The last decades of the nineteenth century saw the flourishing of legal aid societies. Staffed by lawyers and social workers, these institutions offered legal support to those who could not afford the prohibitive cost of legal representation in U.S. civil courts. As the article reprinted here highlights, securing access to legal support was especially important to the immigrant men and women of all nationalities who settled in the United States during the era of mass migration (1880–1924). First, immigration was paved with myriad obstacles, as their lack of familiarity with English and limited literacy made the recent arrivals highly vulnerable to exploitation in all areas of life—including housing, employment, and personal finances. Second, the discrepancies between the legal systems of their home countries and their host society, combined with their widespread ignorance of the American legal landscape, led numerous newcomers to inadvertently come into conflict with the law. In this context, the legal aid society offered crucial assistance to foreigners by defending the rights of those who had suffered emotional or financial exploitation in their new society or who had mistakenly breached American laws.

In response to these challenges, Jewish communal authorities set out to provide legal aid for the newcomers from eastern Europe, instead of relying on the services provided by non-Jewish legal societies. In part, the decision to offer legal representation to members of their own community stemmed from the belief that non-Jewish society largely lacked the linguistic and cultural awareness necessary to adequately help eastern European Jews. In New York City, this belief was compounded by the fact that Jewish applicants routinely experienced antisemitism in their encounters with the mainstream Legal Aid Society of New York. Additionally, the sense of alienation they felt in their dealings with non-Jewish organizations led many foreign-born Jews to embrace the damaging advice of "shyster [fraudulent] lawyers" from their own immigrant community.

Consequently, in 1902 the Educational Alliance, a Jewish settlement house located on the Lower East Side, the heart of New York's Jewish immigrant life, established a Legal Aid Bureau. This institution soon became central to the lives of thousands of eastern European Jewish men and women seeking not only legal but also moral and emotional redress, as a result of the injuries they had suffered at the hands of family members, fellow community members, or strangers.

The staff of the Legal Aid Bureau of the Education Alliance witnessed first-hand the gendered effects of migration. In addition to the challenges faced by their male counterparts, numerous Jewish women experienced husbandly desertion, a phenomenon that heightened their vulnerability even further. In a society that considered men to be the family's breadwinners, women were paid only a fraction of a man's salary, and they often single-handedly carried the burden of child care. As a result, many abandoned women fell into extreme destitution. In the most extreme cases, financial desperation even led mothers to entrust their children to the care of orphanages. Desertion was so widespread as to elicit strong responses from Jewish communal authorities. In New York, the United Hebrew Charities established a National Desertion Bureau in 1911, tasked with locating absconding husbands, bringing them back to their families, and reuniting the estranged spouses. The Yiddish-language press, including the Forward's "Gallery of Missing Husbands," participated in such efforts by publicizing the names and photographs of the deserters. From the perspective of Jewish communal leaders, family desertion was particularly problematic, not only due to the harm it inflicted on women and children but also because the widespread disappearance of the breadwinner put a great deal of strain on the finances of Jewish charities. This explains why Jewish communal institutions devoted so much local, national, and transnational effort to returning husbands to their families.

The work of the Legal Aid Bureau of the Educational Alliance formed part of the efforts of American Jewish institutions to Americanize Jewish men and women from eastern Europe. The Educational Alliance was one of many institutions that were founded by the Jewish community to facilitate the integration of the newcomers, including through teaching them the language, history, and norms of their host society. As the creation of the Legal Aid Bureau attests, Jewish communal leaders viewed the immigrants' acculturation to American legal norms as imperative. Providing an additional motive for the formation of Jewish legal aid was the desire to keep the newcomers' petty litigation out of court. In an era of increasing nativism and xenophobia, negative depictions of Jews in the American press became a source of concern for American Jewish communal leaders wary of an escalation of antisemitic sentiments and anxious that the country might soon close its border to eastern European Jews. Therefore, rather than air the community's internal disputes in American courts, Jewish institutions favored private arbitration within a communal framework. Yet while the staff of the Legal Aid Bureau succeeded in keeping myriad cases out of the courtroom, it had no impact on the U.S. government's immigration policies, and in 1924, the Johnson-Reed Act put a definitive end to the mass Jewish migration from Europe.

◇◇

Celia Silbert,[1] "Legal Aid for the Immigrant Jewess," *American Jewish Chronicle*,[2] February 9, 1917

Source: Celia Silbert, "Legal Aid for the Immigrant Jewess," part 1, *American Jewish Chronicle* 2, no. 14, February 9, 1917, 439.

"Do you know that there are scoundrels who travel from town to town marrying ignorant women, wherever they go, only to decamp with their savings? Have you heard of the fake dispossess notices served on the non-English speaking and reading East Sider? Have you any idea of the number of immigrant young women employed as servants who, when their wages become due, are thrown out bodily?" These are some of the questions that Dr. Henry Fleischman[3] asks in discussing the work of Legal Aid for the immigrant Jewess, and they are only a few of the embarrassments that involve her in America.

All countries are governed by laws, but the same laws do not govern all countries. One is expected to conform to the laws peculiar to the country he inhabits, but no matter how familiar one may be with the prevailing laws of his country and no matter how law-abiding, one may yet be guilty of clashing with the law inadvertently. When this occurs legal advice becomes necessary. If legal aid is a necessity to the law-observing and law-abiding man and woman in his own country, how much more so is it necessary to the newly arrived immigrant, who, on coming to a strange country, is confronted by new conditions and unfamiliar laws. An ignorance of the new laws not only brings the immigrant into con-

1. Celia (Silbert) Kamelmann (1882–1948) emigrated from tsarist Russia in 1884 with her family and grew up in the United States. As a young adult, she became active in social affairs on behalf of New York's immigrant population. She worked as a librarian at the Educational Alliance and as an independent journalist.

2. The *American Jewish Chronicle*, an English-language Jewish newspaper, was published in New York City between 1916 and 1918.

3. The Viennese-born Henry Fleischman (1878–1961), who immigrated to the United States at the age of seventeen, was trained as a physician but devoted his career to Jewish communal life. He was executive director of the Educational Alliance from 1905 to 1938.

flict with them, but often he is unable to secure the proper redress after having been victimized.

That the immigrant should encounter legal difficulties during the process of habilitation in the new country is not surprising, but to what extent these difficulties beset him can only be ascertained by paying a visit to one of our leading Legal Aid Bureaus. One that is doing effective work in giving legal aid to immigrants is that of the Educational Alliance. In speaking of this bureau, Dr. Fleischman said:

"It is the clinic to which is brought for expert examination, diagnosis and treatment every conceivable phase of 'man's inhumanity to man' and to woman."

"The state promises justice and legal redress of wrongs to all," he [Fleischman] continued, "It is curious to note, however, that the proper and effective performance of this state function depends on private philanthropy.

"One would suppose that the atmosphere of a bureau in which hundreds of applicants daily clamor for the righting of their wrongs, would be surcharged with emotions and passions. You picture to yourself glaring eyes, stern, set faces, clenched fists. The Legal Aid Bureau of the Educational Alliance presents a scene the very opposite of this. Meek, depressed and impassive old men, stolid young men and women, sorrow-burdened, careworn mothers, all give you impressions of anything but grievances that stir the emotions or drive the blood faster in the veins. It would seem as if the continual struggle for their due, for justice, for humane consideration had bred in these people a patience born of untold tribulations, a spiritual unassertiveness the result of years of repression, a furtiveness the result of efforts not to obtrude.

"The lines and wrinkles and hollows in their faces are the hieroglyphics which, deciphered, unfold the history of the Jews in Russian ghettos. If you interpret the signs you will do so in terms of cruelty, oppression and persecution."

Dr. Fleischman, who is the administrator of the Educational Alliance, has been connected with the Educational Alliance for the past twelve years. A thorough student of social and economic conditions, he is fully acquainted with all problems touching the immigrant Jew and his struggle for civic adjustment in the new land. The occupancy of the office of administrator of the Educational Alliance, the great social center of the East Side, brings him in direct contact with thousands of East Side men, women and children. He is their friend, philosopher and guide. And therefore he, more than anyone else, is in position to speak of the legal difficulties that confront the immigrant who comes to our shores.

"Men and women seek the bureau for redress not always measurable in dollars," he said. "It is a mistake to assume that all the troubles that come here can be disposed of by making Peter pay Paul the coin of the realm. Over thirty thousand individuals called at the bureau last year and it should not be difficult, without statistical enumeration, to conceive of the vast amount of effort involved in adjusting more than five thousand cases, each often involving correspondence for weeks or days of patient investigation and research, with perhaps a trial in court. Lawyers must be paid for their services just like other folks, and hence the necessity for our bureau. If you have been wronged criminally, there is the district attorney. If your injury is of a civil nature you must go to a lawyer, or to the legal dispensary.

"It is difficult to know what explanations ought to be but are not unless you have tried to make clear to an applicant that although the court has rendered judgment against a defendant, that, although the judgment has been handed to a marshal, and that, although the defendant is apparently prospering in his own establishment, he is judgment-proof and execution-proof."

Celia Silbert, "Legal Aid for the Immigrant Jewess," *American Jewish Chronicle*, February 23, 1917

Source: Celia Silbert, "Legal Aid for the Immigrant Jewess," part 2, *American Jewish Chronicle* 2, no. 16, February 23, 1917, 499.

Many are the abuses to which the immigrant Jewess is subjected on coming to our shores. A wanderer from home, a stranger in a strange land, its laws, regulations and institutions alike unknown to her, she offers a ready prey to unscrupulous individuals, evil-doers and schemers of all kinds. Were it not for the active interest and effective work of such Legal Aid Bureaus as that of the Educational Alliance, rallying to the assistance of the immigrant Jewess in her difficulties, her wrongs would go unrighted and she would remain a helpless victim of miscreants owing to her ignorance of the law.

With litigation expensive and many lawyers unethical in their practices, what justice or redress can be gained by a weak, frail little woman burdened with four or five children and abandoned by her husband? How can such a woman find means to engage detectives to locate the runaway and engage counsel to espouse her cause? How can a poor shop girl earning from five to eight dollars a week seek the help of a lawyer to collect the five dollars long overdue from her erstwhile employer? The Legal Aid Bureau of the Educational Alliance is the Bureau where all these wronged ones come in their search for redress.

Dr. [Henry] Fleischman, in continuing his remarks touching on the work of Legal Aid for the immigrant Jewess, said: "Advice in many cases is what is most sorely needed. In a strange land, unaccustomed to any but ghetto ways, not knowing where to go, many of the people come to us as they would to a friend to tell their troubles or to ask for sympathetic advice.

"The cases brought to our Bureau comprise claims for wages, marital troubles, non-support, juvenile commitments, petty frauds, charges against attorneys, matters affecting emigration, small collections and many complaints of desertion. Advice suffices for many; correspondence disposes of many more.

"Here, for instance, is an old woman of seventy, with a claim against a steamship company because her baggage has not been delivered. Only a short time ago the Bureau helped to unearth an organized band of swindlers who saw to it that the immigrant and her baggage were separated just as soon as she landed. Do you know that even our banking system has given rise to imposition on the immigrant? Have you heard of the fake dispossess notices served on the non-English speaking and reading East Sider? Have you any idea of the number of the immigrant young women employed as servants who, when their wages become due, are thrown out bodily?

"The Legal Aid Bureau has dealt with many of these chronic offenders who hire girls as servants and discharge them upon the flimsiest of pretexts and without pay. By the way, some offenders are practicing lawyers and physicians. The average amount of the thousands of claims made was seven dollars. The greater number of cases really involve less than five dollars—a paltry sum but the difference between a home and homelessness in very many cases. Scoundrels there are who travel from town to town marrying ignorant immigrant young women wherever they go, only to decamp with their savings as domestics or sweatshop operators. What does the comfortable public know of the appalling extent of wife desertion? Within the last six months over 250 complaints of this character have come to the Bureau. It is a wonder that when an immigrant finds himself surrounded by these new trials and troubles and worries, that when you speak of America, the land of milk and honey and the fig tree[4] (as they speak of it in his native village), he shakes his head and with a queer shrug of his shoulders implies that—well, perhaps?

"Is it, after all, so very surprising that the immigrant distrusts our institutions when his first experiences with America are of the kind that require the intervention of the Legal Aid Bureau? But the most unpalatable fact of all remains to be told; some of the oppressors of today were the oppressed of the years before, and it is probable that some of the very present day applicants will be the defendants in cases similar to their own a few years hence.

4. A common reference to Palestine in the Hebrew Bible.

"The evils of our banking system were mentioned as touching the humble sphere of the immigrant, and would you imagine that with only a few months of American residence to her credit, she has already felt the effect of our method of issuing checks? For instance, here is the case of a woman who was here last week with a check for six dollars paid her husband for six days' work. This check had been cashed by a grocer who, when it was returned by the bank with a slip attached reading 'insufficient funds,' threatened the poor laborer's wife with the most awful consequences if reimbursement was not made at once. He [the laborer], of course, sought his employer, a clothing sub-contractor, who with profuse apology, and explanations that did everything but explain, changed the check for another, only in turn to come back with a slip bearing the legend 'account closed.' Positive now that a swindle has been perpetrated in the most cold-blooded fashion, the grocer also rushes to this Bureau, and there he sits not far from the laborer who innocently contributed to the loss. And this theme with many variations is played continually.

"The Legal Aid Bureau of the Educational Alliance exerts its utmost to make litigation unnecessary. In its last annual report it is shown that of 5,402 cases only 303 were taken to court. The Bureau proceeds with a complaint on the general assumption that a misunderstanding was the cause of the trouble. The other side is at first invited to aid us in straightening out the tangle. It is made clear to him that the purpose is not to sue; on the contrary, to prevent suit and to that end his co-operation is asked. Both sides of the case having been presented in an informal kind of arbitration, those in charge do not hesitate to tell the defendant that he is right and the applicant wrong if that is their judgment; on the other hand, they do not fail to insist on prompt payment of the amount due if convinced that the facts warrant it. In the efforts to avoid litigation the Legal Aid Bureau goes still further. Often the failure of a defendant to respond to letters is due to an inability to read or write English, or for a petty employer to call may necessitate the complete closing up of his business while away. Realizing all these things, it is the duty of an assistant to visit employers who fail to answer letters. Many cases are thus settled in the employer's office which would otherwise have to be taken to court for adjudication. Last year there was paid out to clients of the Bureau nearly $18,000.

"If the city realized the work that is being done in the Legal Aid Bureau of the Educational Alliance and legally could appropriate money for these purposes, it would subsidize this work to a considerable extent.

"It is not always possible to straighten out these tangles satisfactorily, but suppose that is accomplished in only one-fifth or one-tenth of the cases, how much hard cash has been saved to the city?"

22

"A PRINCE IN ISRAEL"

S. Felix Mendelsohn's Eulogy for Jacob H. Schiff
(1920)

◇◇◇

MINA MURAOKA

Rabbi Samuel Felix Mendelsohn (1889–1953) of Temple Beth Israel, a leading Reform congregation in Chicago, Illinois, gave the following eulogy for the celebrated American Jewish financier and philanthropist Jacob H. Schiff (1847–1920).[1] At first glance, Mendelsohn and Schiff do not seem to have had much in common. They were born more than forty years apart. Schiff was of central European origin and Mendelsohn, despite his Germanic sounding surname, hailed from eastern Europe. Both men, however, were raised in traditional Jewish households, and both immigrated to the United States in their late teens. Though Schiff rejected Orthodox Judaism, as an adult he was known to be a relatively observant member of the affluent German Jewish circle grouped around Reform Judaism's New York City flagship Temple Emanu-El. He generously supported the Reform movement's key institutions, including its rabbinical school (Hebrew Union College) and the nascent Conservative movement's Jewish Theological Seminary. Ordained in 1917, Mendelsohn, who served as Temple Beth Israel's rabbi for thirty-four years, became a key communal leader in Chicago and a keen observer of the city's Orthodox Jewish community.[2] In addition to four books on humor, Mendelsohn frequently published editorials in Chicago newspapers that sought to explain Jewish perspectives on contemporary issues and events.

Mendelsohn's eulogy of Schiff illustrates the complex nature of American Jewish identity in the early decades of the twentieth century. Though Mendelsohn's adulatory remarks are in many respects unsurprising, they nonetheless hint at the delicate balance between lay leaders and rabbis and throw light on

---

1. For a useful scholarly biography, see Naomi W. Cohen, *Jacob H. Schiff: A Study in American Jewish Leadership* (Waltham, MA: Brandeis University Press, 1999).

2. See Zev Eleff, ed., *Modern Orthodox Judaism: A Documentary History* (Philadelphia: Jewish Publication Society, 2016), 159.

the new Jewish communal relationships developing in the midst of mass waves of eastern European Jewish immigration to the United States. Successful Jewish business leaders, Mendelsohn argues, should take their cues from Schiff's example and invest their talents and resources in helping newcomers become productive and loyal members of the American Jewish community. It is also interesting to consider the ways Mendelsohn's eulogy casts a sidelong glance at non-Jewish perceptions of Judaism and American Jewish culture. Unlike many of Schiff's contemporaries—who assimilated into the American scene to gain acceptance by non-Jewish society—Schiff, as Mendelsohn points out, bestrode the public arena on his own terms: he refused to sacrifice his Judaism or turn away from his responsibilities as a communal steward. It is perhaps in this regard that the younger Mendelsohn understood himself as proximate to the senior Schiff. In short, for neither man did questions of religious observance and/or denominational affiliation supersede concerns about the survival of American Judaism; the continued adaptation of Jewish life to the dynamic American setting; and the development of a wide range of Jewish religious, communal, and political activities. The document below underscores Schiff's outsize impact on American Jewry and American society. It also highlights the abiding liberal worldview that the historian Jonathan D. Sarna has referred to as the "cult of synthesis," which characterized American Jewish life in the twentieth century.[3]

◇◇

Sermon of Rabbi S. Felix Mendelsohn, Temple Beth Israel (Chicago, IL), Friday evening, October 8, 1920

Source: S. Felix Mendelsohn, *Jacob H. Schiff: A Prince in Israel* (Chicago: Temple Beth Israel, 1920), 3–8; American Jewish Historical Society, New York City.

... On Saturday afternoon, September 25 [, 1920], the soul of Jacob H. Schiff was translated to the Academy on High. The deceased was undoubtedly the greatest American Jew of his day. He was great only because his life mirrored that which is best and noblest in the name Jew. While the Rabbis of the Talmud said that no eulogies are necessary in order to point out the merits of the righteous, yet we deem it advisable to devote our discourse tonight to a brief review of the salient qualities of the life of Jacob H. Schiff. For, to be sure, we the living can indeed derive much moral instruction from following the career of a

3. Jonathan D. Sarna, "The Cult of Synthesis in American Jewish Culture," *Jewish Social Studies* 5, nos. 1–2 (Fall 1998–Winter 1999), 52–79.

great and noble character, since this may urge us, too, to endeavor to embody his qualities into our lives.

DEDICATED HIS WEALTH TO GOD

... Jacob H. Schiff, as is well known to all, was a multi-millionaire. ...[4] We must bear in mind, however, that the reason why we are delivering addresses in memory of Jacob H. Schiff is not because he knew how to accumulate money, but rather because he knew how to spend it.[5] Many a Jewish magnate died and the pulpit did not have a word of praise about him, since he dedicated his wealth to Baal and not to the God of Israel.[6] The memory of Schiff is dear to us not because he was the richest but rather the greatest American Jew of his generation.

STROVE AND CONQUERED

... He struggled against nature, for it is not natural for a foreign youth, who comes to this country at the age of eighteen, to rise within a short time to the position of one of the world's leading bankers and financiers.[7] He has also striven with men, for the path of the Jew has never been strewn with roses, since he is always exposed to prejudices and misunderstandings. Yet Jacob H. Schiff has never lost his head, and never has he even for a moment forgotten his Jewish origin. Jacob H. Schiff, like the patriarch Jacob of old, has striven with God and with men and has prevailed. He was indeed the righteous man of his generation, and his death is an irreparable loss to all Israel.

... Jacob H. Schiff was a master of his human passions. Wealth never dazzled his eyes. Although one of the richest men of his day, he never forgot the moral phase of his life. He always remembered the doctrine of Judaism that man, whether rich or poor, has work to do in this world. You must make of your life a masterpiece or else you are a failure. ...

---

4. At the time of his death, Schiff's private fortune was estimated to be as much as $100 million (roughly equivalent to $1.3 billion today).

5. On Schiff's considerable largesse, see Cohen, *Jacob H. Schiff*, 23 and 55–81.

6. "Baal" (Hebrew for lord) is a term used in Hebrew Bible to describe false pagan gods.

7. In 1875, Schiff joined the investment firm Kuhn, Loeb and Company. Shortly thereafter, he married Therese Loeb (1854–1933), the daughter of Solomon Loeb (1828–1903). Schiff became head of Kuhn Loeb in 1885 and subsequently built it into one of country's premier investment companies. By 1901, the firm was second only to J. P. Morgan and Company (also known as the House of Morgan) in financing the nation's burgeoning railways.

The greatest and most outstanding character of Schiff was the fact that he never forgot his Jewishness. He was very proud of the fact that he descended from a prominent family of Rabbis.[8] He was anxious for the whole world to know that he was a Jew. This is why the entrance of his palatial home on Fifth Avenue had a mezuzah, in conformity with the Biblical command: "And thou shalt write them upon the doorposts of thy house and upon thy gates" [Deut. 6:9].[9] Many Chicago Jews, who make money, immediately move to Evanston or to Highland Park, and try to forget their Judaism, but not so Jacob Schiff. He supported two Temples in New York only because he himself found interest in the message and mission of the Synagogues.[10] I myself met many a Jew who told me: "I belong to a Temple which costs me several hundred dollars a year, but I never go there." Not so Jacob H. Schiff. He himself went to Temple Emanuel on Sabbaths [sic]. He studied the Bible and knew it, and not a day passed without his reading some traditional prayers. It was his aim to remind his brethren that Judaism was the concern of the Jew, not of the Rabbi alone.

JUDAIZED HIS FINANCES

His large financial interests did not interfere with his Judaism. In fact, he tried to Judaize his finances. He never went into any financial enterprise which would in any way harm the Jew. During the Russo-Japanese war[11] he refused to give assistance and discouraged other bankers from financing the rotten government of the tsar. A government which is based upon tyranny and pogroms cannot endure long, he asserted. Future developments in Russia corroborated his

8. On Schiff's rabbinic ancestry, see Cohen, *Jacob H. Schiff*, 2.

9. A mezuzah (Hebrew for "doorpost") is a small box affixed to the right side of a doorpost that contains a parchment on which is inscribed a prayer with biblical verses from Deuteronomy 6:4–9 and 11:13–21. When entering or leaving a home, it is customary to touch the mezuzah and, after doing so, kiss one's hand.

10. The Schiff family belonged to New York's prestigious Upper East Side congregations, Temple Emanu-El and Temple Beth-El. In 1927, the synagogues merged.

11. The Russo-Japanese War (1904–5) between tsarist Russia and imperial Japan grew out of rival claims to Manchuria and the Korean Peninsula. In 1905, Japan attacked and destroyed the Russian fleet at Tsushima. President Theodore Roosevelt (1858–1919) mediated a successful end to the conflict and helped forge the Treaty of Portsmouth. The war marked Japan's emergence as a global power and was the first Asian military victory in modern times over a European power.

prophecy. . . .[12] Many other Jews will for the sake of a dollar sell their God and their people. Adolph S. Ochs,[13] publisher of the *New York Times*, who could have influenced public opinion in this country against Poland, is nevertheless defending her cause, because he is afraid of a decline in the circulation of his paper.[14] Indeed, in memory of Schiff we may well exclaim: "Alas for the departed whose equals are not to be found!"

Jacob H. Schiff was a reform Jew. Yet he was very conservative in his beliefs and practices. He felt that without Jewish life our religion could not survive. He was therefore very fond of observing all Jewish ceremonies in his home. He thus managed to repudiate the idea that reform is synonymous with license. Reform is simply the modern way of living Judaism, and if you do not live your religion you are not much of a Jew.

GREAT LOVER OF LEARNING

. . . He respected particularly Jewish learning. He felt that the greatest curse of Judaism in this land was ignorance. . . . Hence in order to revive Judaism in this country Jacob Schiff felt the necessity of educating Rabbis who could teach the people Judaism and its history. He therefore endowed heavily the Jewish Theological Seminary of New York and the Hebrew Union College of Cincinnati. He also felt the need of training teachers for our Sabbath Schools, and it was through his generosity that two Teachers' Colleges were organized in this country. He also financed the publication of the new Jewish translation of the Bible and of the Jewish Classics. . . .[15]

Jacob H. Schiff was very progressive in his thoughts. For a long time he opposed the Zionist movement. In recent years, however, he realized that there was no hope for the Russian and Polish Jews in their native lands, and that the

12. Schiff played a critical role in the American government's abrogation of the U.S.–Russia commercial treaty of 1832. See Cohen, *Jacob H. Schiff*, 29 and 145–52.

13. Adolph S. Ochs (1858–1935), an American newspaper publisher and owner of the *New York Times*, hailed from Cincinnati. He married Effie Wise (1860–1937), daughter of Isaac Mayer Wise (1819–1900), and actively participated in American Jewish affairs—particularly the fight against antisemitism.

14. For a contemporaneous perspective on Ochs's "refusal to print [reports] on the Polish pogroms," see Oswald Garrison Villard, "Adolph S. Ochs and His Times," *Nation*, August 31, 1921, 222.

15. See note 5 in this chap.

possibilities of the Balfour Declaration were tremendous.[16] He therefore became an ardent follower and a heavy supporter of the Zionist movement.[17]

"GIVE UNTIL IT HURTS"

He was a great philanthropist, but he did not want to appropriate philanthropy for himself. He urge[d] others to give. During the recent drive in behalf of Jewish War Relief,[18] Jacob H. Schiff issued a slogan: "Give until it hurts, and then give again!" If you do not do that you are not a good Jew, he asserted. Indeed, he practiced this doctrine, and he wanted others to follow his example.

... For many years he was the national treasurer of the American Red Cross.[19] He also supported heavily many educational institutions such as Harvard, Cornell, and Barnard Colleges [sic]. He offered as a donation a quarter of a million dollars to the university of his native town, Frankfurt-am-Main, but he withdrew it upon learning that this institution discriminated against Jewish professors. Yet in spite of his intense Jewishness he was highly respected by all Gentiles, as was evidenced from the telegrams of condolence which President [Woodrow] Wilson[20] sent to Mrs. Schiff immediately upon the death of her husband. His financial interests were heavy indeed; yet he found time for everything and in this respect he was surely different from most Jewish businessmen who always complain of a lack of time.

16. Following a series of protracted negotiations, on November 2, 1917, the British government issued the Balfour Declaration (a letter from British Foreign Secretary Arthur James Balfour to Lord Rothschild) expressing "sympathy with Jewish Zionist aspirations" in Palestine (Paul Mendes-Flohr and Jehuda Reinharz, eds., *The Jew in the Modern World: A Documentary History*, 3d ed. [New York: Oxford University Press, 2011], 660). The declaration, which marked a pivotal shift in Zionism's political fortunes, catapulted Chaim Weizmann (1874–1952) into the international limelight as the Zionist movement's premier leader.

17. On Schiff's attitude toward Zionism and the Balfour Declaration, see Cohen, *Jacob H. Schiff*, 224–37.

18. On Schiff's leadership of Jewish war relief efforts during and after World War I, see ibid., 206–7; Caitlin Carenen, "Complicating the Zionist Narrative in America: Jacob Schiff and the Struggle over Relief Aid in World War I," *American Jewish History* 101, no. 4 (October 2017): 41–63.

19. The American Red Cross, a branch of the international Red Cross humanitarian organization founded in 1864 by the Swiss activist Jean-Henri Dunant (1828–1910), was organized in 1881 by Clara Barton (1821–1912).

20. Woodrow Wilson (1856–1924), twenty-eighth U.S. president (1913–1921), was a leader of the Democratic party and a key figure in the Progressive movement.

Jacob H. Schiff left instructions with his family that no eulogy should be delivered at his funeral. . . . The Rabbis said that the Patriarch Jacob never died [BT Taanit 5b], and this may be said also of Jacob H. Schiff. His good deeds have won him an immortal place in the hearts of Jewry and humanity. . . . Every American Jew can best honor the memory of Jacob H. Schiff by continuing, be it even in a modest way, the work which he endeavored to do. By doing this we shall be worthy children of our race, and like the Jacobs of all times, we may hope to be able to strive with God and with men and yet prevail.

23

"THE LADIES, GOD BLESS 'EM, USED TO HOLD BAZAARS, BUT NOT NOW"

American Jewish Women and Philanthropy (1920)

◇◇◇

DEBORAH SKOLNICK EINHORN

In the late nineteenth and early twentieth centuries, Jewish Federations[1] depended on a very small number of elite donors. In the first Jewish Federation campaign, the Federation of Jewish Charities of Boston received funds from only 489 donors in 1895.[2] But during World War I, Jewish Federations turned to popular philanthropy—striving for universal giving—as a means of creating communal solidarity and serving dramatically increased needs through the collective power of small donations. The shift from elite, patrician philanthropy to popular giving remains one of the most critical turning points in Jewish organizational history.

During World War I, American Jewish women followed the lead of President Woodrow Wilson (1856–1924), responding with pluck and determination to the nationwide campaign to support the American war effort.[3] Their service on the home front—replacing men in the workforce, conserving resources, embracing public efforts aimed at keeping morale high—was the result of extensive propaganda and a huge culture shift with significant implications for middle-class white women, whose status was historically conditioned by the domes-

---

1. On the history of the Jewish Federation system, see chapter 33, note 3.

2. The creation of successful financial federations at the turn of the nineteenth and twentieth centuries was part of a broad national trend embraced by Protestant, Catholic, and Jewish communal leaders. The first American Jewish efforts to federate fund-raising occurred in Boston (1895); Cincinnati (1896); Chicago (1900); and Philadelphia, Detroit, and Cleveland (1904). See Olivier Zunz, *Philanthropy in America: A History*, rev. ed. (Princeton, NJ: Princeton University Press, 2012), 51–53.

3. Tax returns for the period demonstrate that the American public was "trained to give 'something' almost irrespective of income, during the war, and that [subsequently] the habit had been established," in *Community Chest: A Case Study in Philanthropy*, ed. John R. Seeley, Buford H. Junker, R. Wallace Jones Jr., N. C. Jenkins, and M. T. Haugh, rev. ed. (Piscataway, NJ: Transaction Publishers, 1989), 21.

tic sphere. Likewise, American Jewish women's "war-born spirit of service" extended into fund-raising campaigns for social causes, selling war bonds, and campaigning for the relief of refugees and those suffering closest to the conflict. Owing to the efficacy and value of such undertakings, American Jewish women's groups became central to Jewish communal fund-raising efforts during the war.

The changes wrought by necessity during World War I were, in part, fueled by the Progressive era's idealistic emphasis on democracy and universal suffrage. A singularly dramatic shift in this regard was the ratification in 1920 of the Nineteenth Amendment to the Constitution, which gave women the long-awaited right to vote.

In the postwar era, American Jewish women strove, together with their male counterparts, to ensure *every* American Jewish family would continue contributing to Jewish social and political causes in accordance with its means. As American Jewish communities adopted formal, scientific, and year-long Jewish Federation campaigns, women sought to find their place in the evolving system of American Jewish philanthropy. Accustomed to the expanded responsibilities of wartime and bolstered by their hard-won enfranchisement, Jewish women's groups sought to build on and maintain their vigorous fund-raising capacity. They also pushed to continue serving their communities in new ways. Having demonstrated their innovative mettle during the war and the campaign for universal suffrage, they now sought recognition "as the equals of men, in federation as at the polls." Unwilling to be relegated to the task of coordinating social events, members of New York City's Jewish women's groups took to the streets, canvassing for prospects with the goal of subscribing "each member of the family upon whom she calls. One hundred per cent is the goal of the women workers." On the basis of such collective efforts, New York Jewish women—in parallel with their compatriots in other U.S. cities—assumed the lead in creating the women's division of the Jewish Federation system.

In the article reprinted below, the journalist and fiction author Zelda F. Popkin (1898–1983)[4] celebrates the acumen and triumph of American Jewish women's organizational and fund-raising efforts. She deftly plays on societal expectations, entertains with her hyperbole, contextualizes events within history, and marks a critical watershed for American Jewish women of her class.

---

4. A journalist and fiction author, Popkin wrote short stories, articles, mysteries, and novels of Jewish and Zionist interest. At the age of seventeen, she became the first woman hired as a general-assignment reporter by the *Wilkes-Barre Time Leader*. In addition to her writing career, Popkin worked in public relations for the Jewish Joint Distribution Committee and American Friends of Hebrew University.

She also acknowledges the limitations of the new structure, citing women's "supplementary" roles in raising an "exact" (but not equal) portion of the necessary funds. What is especially revealing, however—notwithstanding wider society's "return to normalcy" and the resurgence of traditional middle-class male and female roles after World War I—is the extent to which Jewish women labored to usher in a new era of inclusive American Jewish philanthropy. On a variety of fronts, they created new strategies and systems—even eschewing Popkin's hated "fancy work"—and employed sophisticated fund-raising methods. Not since the late nineteenth century, when the shift from elite patrician philanthropy to popular giving portended a major change in Jewish organizational history, had such a dramatic change in American Jewish organizational life and American Jewish philanthropy occurred.

◇◇◇

Zelda F. Popkin, "Women to 'Sell' Philanthropy: The Ladies, God Bless 'Em, Used to Hold Bazaars, But Not Now," *American Hebrew,* September 10, 1920

Source: Zelda F. Popkin, "Women to 'Sell' Philanthropy: The Ladies, God Bless 'Em, Used to Hold Bazaars, But Not Now," *American Hebrew,* September 10, 1920, 440 and 482.

In the good old days before the war,[5] when kind-hearted ladies and gentlemen came together to gather a few paltry thousands of dollars for the poor, the blind, or the orphan, this was their modus operandi: "The gentlemen of the committee will hold a dinner at headquarters, and will invite the city's most prominent citizens. Mr. Brown, who knows the financial status of every man, will be chairman, and Mr. Smith, who is the wealthiest and most charitable man in town, will start off the subscription list with a large donation. Mr. Brown will call upon each gentleman present and secure a contribution from him, according to his estimated means. Of course, there will be a few teams, who will report a few hundred dollars from the 'general public.' And the ladies—God bless 'em—they will make fancy work and hold a bazaar or bake cakes for a Kaffee Klatch or card party. That will be enough for them to do."[6] But the war, which changed many things, changed all this, too.

5. The reference is to World War I (1914–18). The United States entered the war in 1917 on the side of the Allies.

6. Popkin here mocks both the conventions of Jewish communal fund-raising as well as how such efforts are discussed by local Jewish newspapers.

The day of the drive commenced,[7] and a new era was begun in American philanthropy—an era in which the raising and distributing of charitable funds ceased to be a haphazard, hand-to-mouth business, and took its place among the sciences, regulated by laws of demand and supply. Huge, tremendously successful Liberty Loan, Red Cross, soldier welfare and War Relief drives set a new standard and replaced the antebellum personal methods with a substitute that wrought millions where thousands had been raised before—publicity and organization—popular appeal and systematic, thorough, expertly managed campaigns.[8] And in those days, when the whole philanthropic system was undergoing a shake-up, new fields of women's usefulness were discovered. The ladies put aside their embroidery[9] and sold Liberty Bonds—billions of dollars worth. They invaded office and store for war relief. They toured the country in the interests of Americanization and food conservation. They learned the meaning of social service. And the unsystematic "sweet charity" of their grandmothers was shed like an outmoded garment.

It remained, however, for the Federation for Support of Jewish Philanthropic Societies to utilize the war-born spirit of service in such a manner that the Jewish women of New York were given an opportunity to stand shoulder to shoulder with the men of this community and share equally with them the huge task of raising the millions which are needed each year to support the ninety-two leading Jewish philanthropies, that are affiliated through [the] Federation. By organizing its Business Men's Council, the Federation enlisted the support of busy businessmen and taught them that philanthropy was a duty and not merely a hobby. In the same manner, through its Women's Division of the Ways and Means Committee, the Federation has given the women of New York's Jewish community an opportunity to succeed [in] the man-made world of business organization.

The program of the Women's Division—which was organized during the summer months, for a whole year of work in [the] Federation's "drive to end

7. The reference is to the New York Jewish Federation's postwar campaign, which reflected the new American trend toward professionalizing fund-raising.

8. Wartime relief campaigns, which centered on patriotic expectations of universal participation, set new standards for reaching donors and systematically resulted in a huge uptick in American philanthropy.

9. This turn of phrase is rhetorical. In addition to innovations in fund-raising, many women participated in the American Red Cross's wartime knitting program. Posters called for volunteers ("Our Boys Need Sox—Knit Your Bit") and encouraged women to conserve resources on the home front and send garments to troops abroad.

drives"[10]—is the most ambitious task ever undertaken by the Jewish women of New York. Its field of operations is the entire city—every street and house of Manhattan, the Bronx, and nearby localities in which are located Federation institutions. The goal of the Women's Division is the enrollment of an annual contributor to [the] Federation of every Jewish resident of New York.

Just as ambitious and unique as its program is, so interesting were the methods by which the organization was effected. Plans were formulated, discussed and carried out around festive tea tables, and a cup of tea helped to bring workers into the fold.[11] The summer hotel porch rocker was a medium for the spread of propaganda and the dances and parties in boarding house parlors were seized upon by relentless Federation enthusiasts as occasions to tell about [the] Federation's needs, and to recruit works and secure contributions. The Jersey shore, the Westchester hills, the Long Island resorts all heard and answered the call of [the] Federation and the result was an inpouring of pledges and assistance to [the] Federation's headquarters at 114 Fifth Avenue.

The program of the Women's Division is supplementary to that undertaken by the men through their Business Men's Council, and its significance is that an exact division of the burden of raising [the] Federation's annual four million dollar budget has been made and women are recognized as the equals of men, in [the] Federation as at the polls.[12] To the men has been assigned the canvass of every member of every industry—the spreading of the message of [the] Federation to their business associates. . . . The women's task is to bring [the] Federation into the homes of New York Jewry, as the men bring it to factory and office.[13]

Mrs. Sidney C. Borg[14] heads the Women's Division and assisting her are a

10. After World War I, the New York Jewish Federation shifted its fund-raising activity to a year-round campaign, with "persistent continuous work" and "all-year-around propaganda" displacing previous "sporadic efforts" ("Federation to Eliminate Campaigns," *American Hebrew*, May 21, 1920, 3).

11. Note the use of traditionally female spaces and strategies to launch a campaign that expanded the sphere of women.

12. In this instance, Popkin evokes New York State's recent ratification, on June 16, 1919, of the Nineteenth Amendment.

13. In using class-appropriate rhetoric to describe gender norm challenges, Popkin redefines "the world as home-enlarged" and legitimates Jewish women's participation in postwar fund-raising efforts. On this rhetorical shift, see Beth Wenger, "Beyond the Myth of Enablers," *American Jewish History* 79, no. 1 (Autumn 1989), 17.

14. Madeline B. Borg (1878–1956) founded the Big Sister movement in 1912 and the Jewish Big Sister movement in 1914 in the United States. In 1939, she became one of the first women

group of women who have achieved notable records in patriotic and philanthropic work. These workers have agreed to act as district chairmen. The city is divided into 65 districts, each in [the] charge of a chairman and her committee of ten or more workers. The plan of work has the marks of thorough organization and is so "business-like" that milady before the war would have shrunk from it in fright and given up the task before it was begun.

The district chairman assigns a specific number of blocks to each worker in her district. The worker takes a census of every man, woman, and child in her district, including neighborhood shops and business houses. She lists the names of every Jewish resident and shopkeeper, calling to her aid apartment house superintendents, storekeepers, sympathetic neighbors, and even friendly policemen. Her list compiled, she returns it to [the] Federation office, where it is regularly rechecked to ascertain whether the persons are already members, and how much each member contributes to [the] Federation. Thus in addition to the preparation for all-year-round Federation activity the women workers expect to secure the first complete census of New York Jewry. The lists, when re-checked, will be returned to the worker, who will at some time during the twelve-month-drive call upon each of her "prospects," taking a morning, afternoon, or evening to tell the family about [the] Federation, employing for this work whatever leisure she may have, suiting her hours to her convenience. In addition the worker will call into play her latent powers as a saleswoman, to secure a new or increased Federation subscription from each member of the family upon whom she calls. One hundred per cent is the goal of the women workers. They have pledged themselves not to cease their efforts until New York Jewry supports [the] Federation with the full contributing strength of every man, woman, and child.

True indeed, the one-time methods of entertainment and social function will not be altogether spurned. The institutions affiliated with [the] Federation will, throughout the year, be centers of gaiety, fostered by the Women's Division for the purpose of arousing interest and raising funds. Neighborhood parties for [the] Federation will furnish a common ground upon which the strangers who dwell next door may meet and become friends.

The spiritual bond of service and fellowship, which has linked together ninety-two institutions and has brought forth the cheerful sacrifice and effort of busy men and women, will be strengthened through the efforts of the Women's Division. The contribution of these workers will be more than time and dollars.

---

to serve as president of the New York Jewish Federation. She received an honorary doctorate of humane letters from Columbia University.

It will be a proof of women's ability in hitherto untried fields, with new working methods. It will be a gift of service and devotion that New York will long remember and strive to emulate. Among the women who have volunteered to serve as chairmen, vice-chairmen, or members of the committees for the "sale," are ... [Here follows a list of sixty-eight names, including the well-known activist and educator Rebecca Kohut (1864–1951), representing many of New York City's elite Jewish families.].

24

"NO ARISTOCRACY AND NO SNOBOCRACY"

Samuel H. Goldenson and the Democratization
of the Synagogue
(1922)

◇◇◇

DAN JUDSON

The following document comes from the archives of Rodef Shalom
Congregation in Pittsburgh, Pennsylvania, a Reform synagogue founded in
1855.[1] The congregation gained national renown in 1885 when it hosted a gathering of Reform rabbis who produced the first comprehensive statement of
American Reform Judaism, known as the Pittsburgh Platform.[2] After the turn of
the nineteenth and twentieth centuries, the synagogue grew rapidly and swiftly
emerged as one of the country's leading congregations.[3] In 1907, Rodef Shalom
built a new sanctuary that was large enough to accommodate 1,200 worshippers. In 1909, President William H. Taft (1857–1930) paid a visit to the congregation and spoke from the pulpit during Shabbat services.

The document below reflects the moment, about a decade later, when Rodef
Shalom, which stood at the forefront of modernizing practices, moved from
financing itself by selling reserved seats in the sanctuary to charging dues. The
congregation's success in this regard proved to be a catalyst for other synagogues across the country to follow suit. The change to Rodef Shalom's dues
structure was not simply a matter of financial concern. As the report reprinted
here illustrates, the change reflected ethical and cultural concerns as well as
economic ones. At this juncture, World War I (1914–18) was still a recent event,
and the public arena was suffused with rhetoric concerning democracy, equality,
and liberty. Against this backdrop, it became untenable for synagogues to perpetuate a financial system in which wealthier congregants' social status and de-
sires outweighed those of poorer congregants.

1. The author acknowledges with great appreciation Martha Berg, archivist of Rodef Shalom,
for invaluable research assistance.

2. On the Pittsburgh Platform, see chapter 16, note 10.

3. For a useful history of the congregation, see Barbara Burstin, *Steel City Jews: A History of Pittsburgh and Its Jewish Community, 1840–1915* (Pittsburgh, PA: self-published, 2008).

Prior to the structural changes initiated by Rodef Shalom, almost every synagogue in America funded itself primarily through the sale of reserved seats. For most synagogues, membership required owning or renting a seat. Purchasing a seat meant that the buyer legally owned the seat and no one could sit in it without the owner's consent. In fact, like other property, one could sell or inherit the seat. To sell congregants seats, synagogues divided their sanctuaries into different sections, with the seats closest to the front of the sanctuary being most desirable and costly. In general, members paid the total cost for their reserved seats up front and thereafter annually paid 10–12 percent of their value to the congregation. Synagogues also rented seats. To encourage ownership, however, rental prices were higher than the annual fees associated with ownership.[4]

This revenue-generating system worked well for American synagogues for more than a hundred years. At the beginning of the twentieth century, however, voices arose decrying this economic structure as problematic and inequitable. "In God's house all must be equal," asserted Leo M. Franklin (1870–1948), rabbi of Detroit's Temple Beth El and an advocate of the move to free seating. "There must be no aristocracy and no snobocracy."[5] In 1906, Stephen S. Wise (1874–1949) created the Free Synagogue in New York and went a step further: the congregation was built around the concept of free seating, no membership fees were required, and congregants instead paid dues voluntarily to the synagogue. To do otherwise, Wise insisted, introduced into "the democratic fellowship of religious communion all the unlovely differentiation of the outside world."[6]

The countrywide shift of American synagogues away from the prevailing financial models of seat ownership came after World War I. The move was inspired by practical and moral considerations. In practical terms, as Samuel H. Goldenson asserts in the document reprinted here, ending the practice of seat ownership would invite and prompt wider participation in worship services and synagogue life. Rodef Shalom itself reported a net increase of 53 percent in attendance at worship services following the elimination of seat ownership, a development Goldenson attributes to the new system's "greater hospitality." This trend, which was also noted by congregations across the country, demonstrated that a modified dues system eliminating seat ownership could work.[7]

4. See Dan Judson, *Pennies for Heaven: The History of American Synagogues and Money* (Waltham, MA: Brandeis University Press, 2018), 34–44.

5. Leo Franklin, "A New Congregational Policy," *American Israelite*, November 17, 1904, 4.

6. Stephen Wise, *Challenging Years: The Autobiography of Stephen Wise* (New York: G. P. Putnam's Sons, 1949), 99.

7. See, for example, "Temple Israel May Adopt New Pew System," *Jewish Advocate*, February 17, 1921, 1.

Goldenson also made a forceful moral argument: "Do you or do you not think that there ought to be at least one place on earth where a poor man may enter without fearing that he will be penalized for being poor?"

In sum, the World War I era, replete with affirmations of democracy—consider, for example, President Woodrow Wilson's (1856–1924) dictum that America sought to make the world "safe for democracy"; the campaign for the Nineteenth Amendment (ratified in 1920), which codified universal suffrage; and W. E. B. Dubois's cri de coeur on behalf of black soldiers who "fought for America and her highest ideals" ("We return from fighting. We return fighting. Make way for Democracy.")[8]—opened wide the door to the democratization of American Jewish life. Meanwhile, Jewish public discourse, including the notions that synagogues should be democratic and all congregants ought to be equal in God's house, profoundly influenced and shaped the way American Judaism evolved and operated. Rodef Shalom was a pathfinder in this regard, and in its wake synagogues across the country gradually eliminated seat ownership and adopted more equitable financial models. The transition from seat ownership to dues is thus an intriguing case study in the interrelationship of religion, culture, and economy, as well as important indicator of a fundamental shift in the trajectory of the American Jewish experience.

◇◇

Samuel H. Goldenson,[9] "An Announcement Concerning the Unassigned Pew System," March 26, 1922

> Source: *An Announcement Concerning the Unassigned Pew System: Made by Rabbi Samuel H. Goldenson to the Congregation Rodef Shalom, Pittsburgh, PA*, Sunday, March 26, 1922; Archives of Rodef Shalom Congregation, Pittsburgh, PA.

... You know we have been conducting this congregation under what is known as the unassigned pew system, as a trial for two years. The period of trial ends the first of April, and naturally I want the members of the congregation to be advised of this fact, and to give earnest thought and consideration to it. Let me read you an important statement with reference to this trial. . . . The board of

8. W. E. B. Du Bois, "Returning Soldiers," *Crisis* 18, no. 1 (May 1919), 13–14.

9. Born in Kalvaria, Poland, Samuel H. Goldenson (1878–1962) immigrated to the United States in 1890 with his parents. Ordained by Hebrew Union College in 1904, he served as rabbi of Congregation Adath Israel in Louisville, Kentucky (1904–6); Congregation Beth Emeth in Albany, New York (1906–18); Temple Rodef Shalom in Pittsburgh, Pennsylvania (1918–34); and Temple Emanu-El in New York City (1934–47). He also served as president of the Central Conference of American Rabbis (1933–35).

trustees, on March 7th, 1920, made a report and in this report the following was stated:

"An unassigned pew system shall be made effective . . . beginning with the new fiscal year on April 1, 1920, and continuing for at least two years." The second statement: "If after two years, the majority of the present owners of pews, based not on the majority of the members of the congregation, but the majority of the present owners of pews should decide that the continuation of the unassigned pew system is detrimental to the highest interests of the congregation, the system shall be discontinued. If, on the other hand, the said owners of pews do not so decide, then the system shall continue in force."

Within two weeks . . . there will be called together the owners of the pews of the congregation, those who owned pews in the congregation two years ago, and they will be requested to consider and decide whether the continuation of the unassigned pew system is detrimental to what? — to the highest interests of the congregation, then we shall not continue the unassigned pew system. If they do not so decide, the unassigned pew system shall become a permanent feature in the congregation, and men and women thereafter shall be seated in the Temple in accordance with the available seats at any time at the services, and not according to whether one has rented or purchased or owned his seat. That is the question before us. . . .

Now, friends, I wish to make a statement in connection with this matter. . . .

What are the highest interests of the congregation? In order to understand what the phrase, "the highest interests of the congregation" means, it is well to be reminded of a few simple or rather important facts about the nature and purpose of a congregation in Israel, or of the function of a Temple in Israel. First negatively — that the Temple is not a social club. In a social club class distinctions may play a part. I do not say they should, but they may play a part in a social club. The second is, a Temple in Israel is not a commercial enterprise. In a business financial . . . considerations may control and usually do control. This is not a business. A Temple in Israel is not a house of amusement. In the management of a theatre, questions of personal pleasure or convenience may become and usually do become of primary importance, but the Temple in Israel is a place dedicated to the worship of God and consecrated in the study of the moral law. The moral law requires the practice of righteousness, of justice, of mercy, of humility, of tolerance, of sympathy, of high mindedness, of generosity and loyalty, and of many other virtues. That is what a Temple is. . . .

If our interpretation of the meaning and the function of a Temple in Israel is a correct one, the following questions become pertinent:

Do you think that our religion would be served best by administering the congregation in such a way as to seat our members in the house of worship in accordance with what each man paid for his pew, thus classifying them on the basis of the amount of personal property owned in the Temple, and thus creating in the Temple a rich man's section here and a poor man's section there?

Do you or do you not think that there ought to be at least one place on earth where a poor man may enter without fearing that he will be penalized for being poor? I would like to read that question once more. Do you or do you not think that there ought to be at least one place on earth where a poor man may enter without fearing that he will be penalized for being poor, and do you not think that that place should be the house of God? Do you or do you not think that in order to prove the sincerity of our convictions and professions that we should make the administration of our Temple affairs as much as possible in harmony with the teachings of our age-old religion, and thus cooperate to make the preachments of the pulpit effectual in the lives of those children we are trying to bring up under the laws of Israel?

Do you or do you not think that in the proposed consideration we should be interested in the fact that the attendance of our Sunday services during the last two years have increased over 50 percent?[10] It is certain that many of these have been attracted to the Temple by reason of the greater hospitality made possible under the new system. Now, I am talking about figures, and I shall give you figures. The average attendance, during the first year of my incumbency, on Sunday mornings was 296. Let me tell the members of the congregation that we have kept a careful record of the attendance of each Sunday morning service for three years. The average for the first year was 296. The average of the second year was 381. During the first and second year no unassigned pew system had been adopted. There was an increase in the attendance, a normal and natural increase, of 29 per cent. Last year, after the unassigned pew system had been adopted, the average jumped to 580 during the Sunday season, from 381 to 580. That means an increase of 53 percent over the previous year, or 96 per cent over the first year. This year our attendance is about the same as last, thus far. So we are holding the 53 percent since we have introduced the unassigned pew system. I am asking the members of the congregation whether it is important, as a religious organization, to take this fact into consideration? Do you want our religion to reach 53 percent more persons in Pittsburgh?

There is one more question. . . . Do you or do you not think that loyalty to

10. In this period, Sunday services were not uncommon in Reform synagogues. See Kerry Olitzky, "The Sunday-Sabbath Movement in American Reform Judaism: Strategy or Evolution?," *American Jewish Archives* 34, no. 1 (1982), 75–88.

our religion as well as loyalty to our country demands that we do not perpetuate upon American soil all those misunderstandings and prejudices that have
played such an unhappy part among the European Jewish settlements? ... I have
written out [my] questions. They are the expression of my deliberate consciousness on these matters and my convictions. . . . Do you or do you not think that
here in a liberal American congregation, we should conduct our affairs as a solidarity, a religious Jewish solidarity, among American Jews? — loyalty to religion;
loyalty to country.

And now I shall read you the last part of the report which you will receive in
a few days.

"Our congregation stands at the cross-roads. There are two paths, the one
backward, the other forward, the one backward to old traditions, old prejudices, old habits, reasonable at the time because of the restricted conditions
of the Jews' existence. The other is forward—with broad vision, great liberty
and absolute freedom in which to cultivate new ideals for the inculcation and
dissemination of a religion knowing no distinctions except those based upon
righteousness and justice. Many cities have their eyes upon us, this Congregation Rodef Shalom of Pittsburgh, watching which road we shall choose. Your
committee is confident that the choice will be in accord with the best traditions
of the congregation, which has always been ready to lead in social and moral
movements. This congregation will not now, on this momentous question, be
untrue to itself."

To this I want to add my personal faith in you and my confidence in you. I
believe there is enough vision among you and enough generosity among the
members of our congregation; I believe there is enough of the spirit of self-
sacrifice among the members of this congregation of Rodef Shalom to adopt
this system by a very, very large majority, if not a unanimous vote. I again say
to the members of the congregation that I congratulate you now upon rising to
the occasion and leading in this very great cause, in the reconstruction of the
life of Israel in America.

25

"TO MAKE THEM POSITIVE, SELF-CONSCIOUS JEWS"

The Shift in Reform Judaism to a Pro-Zionist Jewish
Educational Agenda
(1922–40)

◇◇

JONATHAN B. KRASNER

Emanuel Gamoran's (1895–1962) appointment as educational director of the Reform movement's Commission on Jewish Education (CJE) in 1923
augured an ideological reorientation of the Reform movement and a remaking
of its approach to Jewish education. The former, which engendered a rapproche-
ment with more traditional streams of Judaism, saw the movement revisit and
amend the radical positions that its rabbinical leaders articulated in the 1885
Pittsburgh Platform,[1] including a rejection of Zionism and the abandonment
of particularistic rituals and ceremonies. The latter involved a vigorous initiative to standardize curricula, improve educational materials, and increase contact hours in the one-day-a-week schools. Lying at the nexus of these trends
was Gamoran's commitment to a philosophy of American Jewish life grounded
in cultural pluralism, religious reconstruction, and a commitment to Jewish
national revival.

Gamoran's immigrant Hasidic background made him an unlikely choice to
head the Reform movement's educational program. While earning a teaching
degree at the Jewish Theological Seminary's Teachers Institute, he was influenced by Mordecai M. Kaplan (1881–1983), an American Jewish theologian and
the founder of Reconstructionist Judaism, who instilled in him both a conviction that Judaism was not merely a religion but an evolving civilization and a
commitment to its reconstruction and harmonization with modern beliefs and
values. Gamoran continued his studies at Columbia University's Teachers College, where he wrote his doctoral dissertation under the supervision of the progressive educational reformer William Heard Kilpatrick (1871–1965). From Kilpatrick and the progressive educational philosopher John Dewey (1859–1952),
Gamoran developed an appreciation of the social function of education and a

1. On the Pittsburgh Platform, see chapter 16, note 10.

belief that students learned best when they were engaged and invested in their own learning.

Gamoran's formative experience was his apprenticeship at the New York Bureau of Jewish Education (BJE)—under the supervision of Samson Benderly (1876–1944), an ardent champion of educational reform and Jewish national and cultural renascence. Benderly believed that the future of Jewish education in the United States depended on the propagation of a third option that split the difference between the minimalist Sunday school and the traditional Talmud Torah, with its long hours, immigrant sensibility, and neglect of girls' education. Serving in a variety of capacities at the BJE, Gamoran acquired experience teaching and administering supplementary schools, organizing club work and extension activities, and writing educational materials. He also imbibed the Safed-born Benderly's enthusiasm for cultural Zionism and commitment to Hebrew as a living language.

A straight line can be drawn from Benderly's school modernization, teacher professionalization, and curricular standardization efforts in New York City (including his training of dozens of Jewish educators) to the establishment of modernized Jewish supplementary schools and central Jewish educational agencies in Jewish communities across the United States. Benderly's acolytes entered the Jewish education field after World War I at a time when many younger Reform rabbis were expressing dissatisfaction with the state of Reform Jewish education. These rabbis faulted the movement's congregational arm, the Union of American Hebrew Congregations (UAHC), for not having a professional educator on its staff.

When Rabbi George Zepin (1878–1963), secretary of the UAHC's Department of Synagogue and School Extension, set out to find an educational director who was knowledgeable about Judaism and conversant in progressive educational methods, he had a hard time finding qualified candidates within the ranks of the Reform movement. After consulting with John Dewey, Zepin concluded that the ripest recruiting ground was Benderly's BJE. Recognizing the probable reluctance of Benderly's protégés to accept a position at the UAHC, a bastion of classical Reform Judaism, Zepin enlisted the assistance of Henry Slonimsky (1884–1970), a Russian-born professor of Jewish education and ethics at Hebrew Union College, who viewed classical Reform Judaism as emotionally hollow. Slonimsky in turn reached out to the BJE's assistant director, Alexander Dushkin (1890–1976), one of the "Benderly boys." Slonimsky's plea not to "give up on the Reform camp" and his reassurance that an endeavor to intensify Reform education would find support among the Reform clergy helped convince Gamoran to accept the directorship of the CJE, a newly organized body under the aegis of the UAHC and the Central Conference of American Rabbis (CCAR), the movement's rabbinical organization. Spreading the BJE's educational reforms to the Reform movement appealed to Benderly disciples like Dushkin, who privileged Jewish unity over denominationalism.

During his thirty-six-year career directing the CJE, Gamoran distinguished himself as an indefatigable advocate of curricular reform and religious school improvement. The graded curriculum that he unveiled soon after his appointment emphasized customs and ceremonies, history, Hebrew, and music over catechisms and moralistic Bible stories. Gamoran traveled to Reform temples across the country, promoting the CJE's curriculum, introducing progressive instructional approaches, and advocating for additional instructional time. But his ideological commitments and curricular innovations were most effectively disseminated through the line of textbooks that he edited and published. Under Gamoran, the UAHC emerged as a leading Jewish educational publisher.

Throughout the 1920s and 1930s, as illustrated in the documents excerpted below, the Zionist sympathies of Gamoran and other activists proved to be a major sticking point for Reform Judaism's establishment. As a result of Gamoran's persistent efforts, however, the Reform movement's curriculum and line of textbooks steadily introduced a rising generation of Reform Jews to concepts like Jewish peoplehood, home-based rituals, Hebrew songs, holiday observances associated with the Land of Israel, and stories of heroic *haluzim* (Hebrew for "Zionist pioneers") making Palestine's desert bloom. Thus, a decade before the Reform movement's Columbus Platform (1937), which officially signaled a new openness to ritual practice and support for "upbuilding Palestine as a Jewish homeland,"[2] Gamoran proved to be a crucial amplifier of a new pro-Zionist Jewish educational agenda, engineering a shift in educational emphasis from universalism to particularism and from sectarianism to Jewish transpartisan identification.

◇◇◇

2. For the text of the Columbus Platform (1937), see Paul Mendes-Flohr and Jehuda Reinharz, eds., *The Jew in the Modern World: A Documentary History*, 3d ed. (New York: Oxford University Press, 2011), 575–76.

Letter from Henry Slonimsky[3] to Alexander Dushkin,[4] May 19, 1922

Source: Letter from Henry Slonimsky to Alexander Dushkin (May 19, 1922), Alexander Dushkin Papers, P-134, folder 9, Central Archives for the History of the Jewish People, Jerusalem, Israel.

I write to you on a matter of a confidential character in which I trust you will be able to give me some help and advice. . . . You know the educational system in the Reform camp:[5] it is in a perilous state, and something will have to be done to reform this Reform. The day school[6] in one form or another must come; and the content must be made more richly and distinctively Jewish. We haven't any central agency to take charge of and direct the school work of the Reform temples. There is something in the nature of such an agency in the "Synagog [and] School Extension Dept"[7] located here; but only part of the time of one of the men in the office is devoted to it and his work is not of a directing or initiating kind, but merely of the nature of collecting illustration material and of advising occasionally about textbooks, and the work is of a very haphazard kind.[8]

I can see only one way out. We need a man here (one man to start with) to specialize on the problem of our Jewish and religious education. We need a man who shall, in the first place, be thoroughly conversant with educational theory — one who has done work at Teachers College;[9] and one who is in the

3. Henry Slonimsky (1884–1970) earned a doctorate in 1912 at the University of Marburg, under the tutelage of the neo-Kantian German Jewish philosopher Hermann Cohen (1842–1919). After serving on the Hebrew Union College faculty (1922–24), he became dean of the Jewish Institute of Religion (1926–50) — founded in 1922 by Stephen S. Wise (1874–1949; see note 33). With the Jewish Institute of Religion's merger in 1950 with Hebrew Union College, he continued serving as dean until his retirement in 1952.

4. Alexander Dushkin (1890–1976) directed the Bureau of Jewish Education in Chicago (1921–36) and the Jewish Education Committee of New York (1939–49). He was also the founding editor (1929–35) of *Jewish Education* (later renamed the *Journal of Jewish Education*).

5. One-day-a-week Sunday or Sabbath schools, inspired by the Protestant Sunday school movement, had become the dominant model of Reform Jewish education in the 1860s and 1870s.

6. Slonimsky is likely referring to the afternoon supplementary religious school rather than to the all-day Jewish private elementary school model, also known as the *yeshivah ketanah*.

7. A division of the Union of American Hebrew Congregations (UAHC), the Department of Synagogue and School Extension was established in 1903 and tasked with facilitating and promoting religious education for children.

8. The pressure to hire a full-time educational director was acute, coming mainly from the members of the Central Conference of American Rabbis (CCAR). The establishment of the Commission on Jewish Education (CJE), in 1923, was a joint venture of the CCAR and the UAHC.

9. Founded in 1887, Teachers College serves as the graduate school of education, health,

second place thoroughly imbued with Jewish feeling and Jewish knowledge—i.e., one who has grown up in the [Samson] Benderly[10] atmosphere or in something equivalent.

His work will be of a practical and constructive character. He must work out plans for the reconstruction of the religious school system. I need not tell you that it is a task of the most far reaching significance and of statesmanship in the preeminent sense of the term. He will have help and encouragement—first of all from myself, and I'll engage to rally forces behind him. I of course am engaged primarily in an academic task; but I will be with him and at his disposal in every possible way.

I wish you could realize the importance of this whole undertaking. The old alignments—Reform, Orthodox, etc., etc.—are bound to be obliterated. We must have Jews and we must do our best to make them positive, self-conscious Jews. You must not give up on the Reform camp and simply leave it out of your account. They represent the elite in wealth, prestige and ... what is more, in Jewish possibilities, at any rate through their children. Furthermore, if something is not done for them, then of an inevitable sociological law ... our Russian brothers[11] will follow in their footsteps, so that everything will be lost.

To come down to the concrete situation, I have not been authorized to ask you for a man, I have not even been asked to approach you informally, and I wouldn't particularly want it to be known; but I want you to look for such a man and to write to me about it. I am being put on the various commissions and committees and if I can't place him now I can place him later.

Of course there are great difficulties in the way. They[12] will be reluctant be-

---

and psychology of Columbia University. In the early twentieth century, the college acquired a reputation as a center of progressive education, boasting such marquee faculty members as John Dewey (1859–1952), Edward Lee Thorndike (1874–1949), and William Heard Kilpatrick (1871–1965).

10. Samson Benderly (1876–1944) was the first director of the New York Bureau of Jewish Education (BJE) and a charismatic champion of the modernized Jewish supplementary school; progressive methods; and the teaching of modern Hebrew through immersion, using the natural or direct method. Benderly mentored a generation of Jewish educators (known as the "Benderly boys") who eventually led a variety of central educational agencies, schools, camps, and Hebrew teacher colleges throughout North America. These people typically combined paid internships at the BJE with academic study at Columbia University Teachers College and the Jewish Theological Seminary's Teachers Institute.

11. The term "Russian Jews" was commonly used in this period to refer to eastern European Jewish immigrants to the United States.

12. Slonimsky is referring to the membership of the CCAR and the leadership of the UAHC, both of which included outspoken anti-Zionists.

cause it is a confession of poverty; and above all, above all, there is the question of Zionism! Now you must help me to get a man who while not officially and notoriously a Zionist is nevertheless such a good and positive Jewish patriot that we can use him. I will say nothing further, you will understand.

Letter from Alexander Dushkin to Henry Slonimsky, August 10, 1922

Source: Letter from Alexander Dushkin to Henry Slonimsky (August 10, 1922), Alexander Dushkin Papers, P-134, folder 9, Central Archives for the History of the Jewish People, Jerusalem, Israel.

As an organization, the Bureau of Jewish Education[13] has never been more interested, theoretically, at least, in Orthodox Jews than in Reform Jews. The fact that we have hitherto worked so much more with the Orthodox element than with the Reform was caused rather by the conditions in the field than by any avowed purpose on our part. The Orthodox Jews and their Talmud Torahs and Hebrew schools offered a richer, more fertile, and easier field for trying out certain of the basic ideas in our program of Jewish education than did the Reform Jews and their institutions.

You will be interested in knowing that some 7 or 8 years ago, the Bureau supplied most of the teachers in the Sunday School of Temple Emanuel of New York;[14] that I was one of the teachers; and that at the time, our effort was to see to what extent we could shape the work in that influential Sunday school nearer to our hearts' desire. Dr. [Hyman G.] Enelow[15] was at that time altogether with us. Unfortunately, owing to financial difficulties in the Bureau and to personal prejudices and quarrels in Temple Emanuel, that work was gradually decreased and later altogether abandoned. Of course, we have done but little for the Sunday schools in this country, but the above is a rather tan-

13. Founded in 1909 as a branch of the New York Kehillah, a nonsectarian citywide effort to create an all-inclusive Jewish communal structure that lasted from 1908 to 1922, the BJE was the first central Jewish educational agency in North America. Directed by Samson Benderly until his retirement in 1941, the BJE was charged with professionalizing Jewish education. It also ran model Jewish schools in the 1910s.

14. Founded in 1845, Temple Emanu-El of New York City is often referred to as the flagship of Reform Judaism on the eastern seaboard. In the early twentieth century, its membership included New York's elite Jewish leaders Jacob H. Schiff (1847-1920), Louis Marshall (1856-1929), and Felix Warburg (1871-1937).

15. Hyman G. Enelow (1877-1934), ordained in 1898 at Hebrew Union College, served as the rabbi of Temple Emanu-El from 1912 until his death.

gible expression of our desire to be of service to the Reform schools as well as to the Orthodox ones.

I agree with you that the problem is for you, as it is in general, one of personnel. I shall certainly keep your request in mind. What adds to the difficulty is this: Among certain of our younger men there is, I must confess, a suspicion of the Jewish sincerity of Reform education; perhaps, to an unwarranted degree. However, I shall be very eager indeed for you to keep me in touch with the situation in Cincinnati[16] as it develops. From my side I assure you of my interest and my desire to help. Perhaps when the time is ripe, the right person may be found.

Letter from Samuel Schulman[17] to Emanuel Gamoran,[18] March 19, 1924

> Source: Letter from Samuel Schulman to Emanuel Gamoran (March 19, 1924), Emanuel Gamoran Papers, SC-3857, the Jacob Rader Marcus Center of the American Jewish Archives, Cincinnati.

In reply to yours of the 12th inst., I beg to say that I cannot give you any opinion of the fitness of Dr. [Samuel] Margoshes[19] to write a book on "Modern Jewish History" for children of high school age. . . . I would therefore suggest to you, since you have been negotiating with him, that you arrange for him to meet me. You will readily understand that the book which Dr. Margoshes is to write is perhaps the most important book in the high school curriculum from the point of view of Reform Judaism and the needs of the schools connected with the Temples for which our curriculum has been laid out.

A book on "Modern Jewish History" will have to deal fully with the rise and growth of the Reform movement in Judaism. It will have to touch on all the ques-

16. Cincinnati had been the epicenter of Reform Judaism in the United States since the mid-nineteenth century, and until 1951 it was the headquarters of the UAHC.

17. Samuel Schulman (1864–1955), senior rabbi of Temple Emanu-El (1899–1934), served as chair of the Committee on Youth Education of the Reform movement's joint CJE and in 1939 was a founder of the National Federation of Temple Youth. He was an outspoken critic of Zionism and defender of classical Reform Judaism.

18. Emanuel Gamoran (1895–1962), a protégé of Samson Benderly served as director of the CJE of the UAHC and the CCAR from 1923 to 1958. See the headnote for additional biographical information.

19. Samuel Margoshes (1887–1968), ordained at the Jewish Theological Seminary (JTS) in 1910, was a member of Benderly's inner circle. In 1916, Margoshes earned separate doctorates at Columbia University and JTS. From 1926 to 1942, he was editor of the Yiddish newspaper Der tog (The day). He also worked for many years as the Jewish National Fund's public relations director.

tions which have been debated during the last one hundred years. I assume that as far as knowledge and research are concerned, that [sic] you have assured yourself of the ability of Dr. Margoshes, who as you tell me, is a graduate of the Jewish Theological Seminary and holds the degree of H.L.D.[20] from that seminary. . . .

You will however admit that we cannot prepare a book for our young people that will not enthusiastically present the justification of the Reform movement in Judaism, while at the same time it can speak with perfect objectivity of every other phase of Judaism. You might turn around and say to me what is needed in a history is merely the true statement of facts. And you might say that you vouch for Dr. Margoshes. . . . Nevertheless, I must say that I have yet to meet historians who write interestingly, who are not influenced by their own personal convictions.

I do not hesitate to say that for just such a book as this, I would have preferred a writer who in life is identified with the Reform movement in Judaism. But I have no prejudice against Dr. Margoshes. I only cannot recommend him at present until I know more about his point of view and the manner in which he intends to treat the subject. So please see to it that a meeting is brought about between him and me. . . .

If as chairman of the Committee on Youth Education, I am to make a recommendation to the members of my committee, I must have knowledge upon which to base such a recommendation. I may say that I take my Chairmanship seriously. And if I am to advise in the matter, I must have facts upon which to base my advice.

Letter from Samuel Schulman to David Philipson,[21] March 19, 1924

Source: Letter from Samuel Schulman to David Philipson (March 19, 1924), David Philipson Papers, MS-035, box 2, folder 1, the Jacob Rader Marcus Center of the American Jewish Archives, Cincinnati.

Enclosed I send you a copy of my answer to Dr. [Emanuel] Gamoran, so that you have it for your information. If in addition to the executive director, we are going to have [as] all our writers men who cannot be presumed to be in sympathy with what our temples and schools stand for, I fear we will have a great dif-

20. The degree Doctor of Hebrew Letters (H.L.D.) was awarded by the Jewish Theological Seminary.

21. David Philipson (1862–1949), ordained in 1883 at Hebrew Union College, served as rabbi of Congregation K. K. Bene Israel (Rockdale Temple) in Cincinnati (1888–1938). An ardent anti-Zionist and a champion of classical Reform Judaism, he chaired the UAHC's board of editors of Religious School Literature (1903–24) and the Reform movement's joint CJE (1924–43).

ficulty in carrying out our curriculum. And it would be a fine irony (this I say in strict confidence) if through the pressure brought to bear by the manager of the Synagogue and School Extension[22] in these appointments, the Judaism of our temples would get to be incorporated by men who are not in sympathy with it.

I have been very liberal thus far, but I think the whole thing needs watching, especially when I am informed the new expert for youth education is to be appointed and he too, will probably come from the same group (one of Dr. Benderly's pupils)[23] from which we have thus far received our principal[24] for the Hebrew Union College School for Teachers and our educational director[25] for the Commission of Education. I certainly enjoy humor. But this is becoming a scream....

Letter from Louis Wolsey[26] to Emanuel Gamoran, August 26, 1930

Source: Letter from Louis Wolsey to Emanuel Gamoran (August 26, 1930), Emanuel Gamoran Papers, SC-3857, the Jacob Rader Marcus Center of the American Jewish Archives, Cincinnati.

This is to acknowledge your kind letter of August 19. In response thereto let me cite the following instances from Mrs. [Elma Ehrlich] Levinger's[27] book concerning which I took the exception....

22. The reference is to George Zepin (1878–1963) (see chapter 27, note 15). With Slonimsky's assistance, Zepin hired Gamoran and supported his educational efforts.

23. Schulman is referring to Israel Chipkin (1891–1955), a Benderly protégé, who led the Jewish Education Association (1921–44), the American Association of Jewish Education (1944–49), and the Jewish Education Committee of New York (1949–55). Schulman ultimately scuttled both Chipkin's appointment as director of the UAHC's youth education department and Margoshes's selection as author of the modern Jewish history textbook.

24. The reference is to Abraham N. Franzblau (1901–1982), who served as founding principal of the Hebrew Union College School for Teachers, located in New York from 1923 to 1931. Trained in education and pastoral psychiatry, Franzblau relocated to Hebrew Union College in Cincinnati, where he served as professor of pastoral psychology. Returning to New York in the mid-1940s, he helped reorganize the college's School for Teachers into the School of Education with the merger in 1950 of Hebrew Union College and the Jewish Institute of Religion. After retiring in 1958, he devoted the remainder of his career to psychiatry, research, and lecturing.

25. The reference is to Gamoran.

26. Louis Wolsey (1877–1953), senior rabbi at Philadelphia's Congregation Rodeph Shalom (1925–47), was active in several Jewish organizations and Republican politics. In 1942, he was a founding member of the anti-Zionist American Council for Judaism, but he withdrew from the organization after the establishment of Israel in 1948.

27. Elma Ehrlich Levinger (1887–1958), a 1912 graduate of Radcliffe College, was an edu-

Every bit of nationalism referred to above (and in other places of the book also) are [sic] a deliberate attempt to violate every commitment of Reform Judaism, and to make propaganda for this radically different interpretation—alas, with the machinery of the very organization under whose auspices the book is issued. I consider the whole procedure a bit of treason. I have no objection to Zionistic organizations or Zionistic adherents publishing that kind of propaganda. In fact, I think it would be their duty to do so, but to insinuate that kind of doctrine into the Reform Sunday schools of America, under the guise of Reform Judaism, savors of nothing less than a conspiracy within the ranks of Reform Judaism. You certainly have not read Mrs. Levinger's book or you would not have made the statements you do in the second paragraph of your letter. Judging from the citations I have made, it is fair to infer that your reading committee either was composed of Zionists or the committee did not read it. I remember the manuscript coming to my desk and that I was altogether too busy to read it. I greatly regret now that I did not make the sacrifice. I certainly would have protested most vigorously against the propaganda of what otherwise is a helpful book.

I take it that Reform Judaism and the Reform Synagog [sic] have dedicated themselves to the preservation of Judaism and Jewish culture in the Diaspora. The danger of Zionism which we have foreseen for the last quarter of a century is now beginning to manifest itself not alone in the impoverishment of the material resources of Diaspora Judaism, but unfortunately of its spiritual life as well. The Union of American Hebrew Congregations, which pays you your salary, has a deficit of $160,000, while you, one of its paid workers, are making propaganda with the Union's constituency to divert their resources to Palestine instead of to their own immediate needs. This is a perfectly absurd paradox. This is in harmony with the recent agitation of the *Jewish Forum*[28] where it was suggested that the American Jews declare a moratorium for the next five years in the building of synagogues and devote that money to Palestine. I might say in passing that it is quite amusing to note the support given the suggestion by Zionistic Reform rabbis who have already built their million dollar synagogues.[29]

------

cator and prolific author who published over thirty books for children and adults, including a number of textbooks for the UAHC's CJE. In 1930, the UAHC published her *Entertaining Programs for the Assembly in the Religious School*, which is the subject of this letter.

28. The *Jewish Forum* (1918–62), a monthly periodical founded by Solomon T. H. Hurwitz (1886–1920) and edited for forty-four years by Isaac Rosengarten (1888–1961), promoted Jewish ideas and culture from a modern Orthodox perspective.

29. Wolsey is likely referring to, among others, Rabbi Abba Hillel Silver (see note 34) of the Temple-Tifereth Israel in Cleveland, Ohio, which in 1924 completed a cathedral-like struc-

This destruction of our Jewish life and the Diaspora has now come to such a pass that someone must cry a halt. If we must neglect America to build up Palestine, then we must dismiss Palestine. We must maintain a Jewish life in the Diaspora. You will some day wake up to discover that your Zionistic propaganda is self-defeating.

Letter from Emanuel Gamoran to Louis Wolsey, September 5, 1930

Source: Letter from Emanuel Gamoran to Louis Wolsey (September 5, 1930), Emanuel Gamoran Papers, SC-3857, the Jacob Rader Marcus Center of the American Jewish Archives, Cincinnati.

I have your letter of August 26th, which was forwarded to me while I was down South lecturing at the Teachers Institute....[30] I must confess to great disappointment as a result of reading your letter.

... Your letter is particularly surprising, as it comes so soon after the last sessions of the Central Conference of American Rabbis, in which, by a big majority, "Hatikvah" was inserted into the *Union Hymnal*.[31] It seems to me that you and those who share your outlook should be reconciled to the thought first, that American Reform Jewry is by no means unanimous on the question of Jewish nationalism; secondly, that if we are to take the Jewish Agency seriously, those who are not Zionists will also have to develop favorable attitudes to Palestine on

---

ture; Rabbi Joseph Silverman (1860–1930) of New York City's flagship Temple Emanu-El, which in 1927 moved to a grand Upper East Side edifice; and Rabbis Jonah B. Wise (1881–1959) and Henry J. Berkowitz (1894–1949), who presided over the 1928 opening of Congregation Beth Israel's Byzantine-style home in Portland, Oregon.

30. The reference is to the Teachers Institute of Hebrew Union College. Founded in 1909 by Rabbi Louis Grossman (1863–1926), who served as its principal (1909–18), the institute was made possible by the philanthropist Jacob H. Schiff, whose gift of $100,000 for teacher training was split between the college and the JTS.

31. In 1930, the Central Conference of American Rabbis narrowly approved a resolution (by a vote of 65–59) offered by Stephen S. Wise (see note 33) to include the Zionist anthem "Hatikvah" (Hebrew for "the hope") in the forthcoming revised edition of the Reform movement's *Union Hymnal*, a compilation of hymns designed to "stimulate congregational singing, inspire Jewish devotion, revive the value of Jewish melody, make use of neglected Jewish poetry . . . and encourage in the religious schools an earnest study of Jewish music," in *Union Hymnal: Songs and Prayers for Jewish Worship*, ed. Abraham Wolf Binder (New York: Central Conference of American Rabbis, 1932), 311–12. Wolsey, who chaired the committee tasked with revising the hymnal, was incensed by the anthem's inclusion, which he viewed as antithetical to Reform theology. Gamoran evidently mentioned the CCAR vote here to be provocative.

the part of the young in order to elicit from them the support which is needed to build up that country. In any case, on a number of occasions the Commission on Jewish Education has taken the attitude, through its committees, that those people who do not want to use certain elements in our books are free not to use them. However, that does not mean that Rabbi [Morris S.] Lazaron[32] and Rabbi [Stephen S.] Wise[33] and Rabbi [Abba Hillel] Silver[34] and Rabbi [Barnett] Brickner,[35] and a host of others, are not entitled to have a Chamisha Asar[36] [sic] program if they wish to celebrate it in their religious schools. Your attitude appears to me exceedingly illiberal. . . .

However, I now want to call your attention to the manner in which your letters were written. Your second letter especially illustrates a new method of procedure. First, you assume that everything that is nationalistic in Judaism must be condemned; second, you proceed to label a few things nationalistic that are

32. Morris S. Lazaron (1888–1979), ordained in 1914 at Hebrew Union College, served as rabbi of the Baltimore Hebrew Congregation (1915–46) and was a prolific author. Initially non-partisan vis-à-vis Zionism, in 1942 he became a founder of the anti-Zionist American Council for Judaism.

33. Stephen S. Wise (1874–1949), a leading and controversial rabbi, social progressive, and Zionist leader, was active in a variety of American and Jewish political and social causes. He founded New York's Free Synagogue (1907), the American Jewish Congress (1920), the Jewish Institute of Religion (1922), and the World Jewish Congress (1936). He was instrumental in the campaign for Jewish statehood and the anti-Nazi boycott of the 1930s, and sustained contact with many key U.S. officials on behalf of American Jewry, including Presidents Woodrow Wilson (1856–1924) and Franklin D. Roosevelt (1882–1945).

34. Abba Hillel Silver (1893–1963), rabbi of the Temple-Tifereth Israel in Cleveland, Ohio, and a Zionist leader, was one of American Jewry's most influential figures. Active in an array of Jewish social and political undertakings, Silver served as president of the Zionist Organization of America (1945–46), president of the CCAR (1945–47), and chairman of the American section of Jewish Agency for Palestine (1946–49). A brilliant orator, Silver presented the Jewish Agency's case to the United Nations in 1947 for an independent Jewish state. In 1952, he gave the benediction at the inauguration of President Dwight D. Eisenhower (1890–1969).

35. Barnett Brickner (1892–1958), ordained in 1919 by Hebrew Union College, served as rabbi of Holy Blossom Temple in Toronto, Canada (1920–25) and Anshe Chesed Congregation in Cleveland, Ohio (1925–58). He and his wife, Rebecca Ena (Aaronson) Brickner (1894–1988), a founder of the Hadassah Women's Zionist Organization, were protégés of Samson Benderly. Both were active in Jewish communal and educational affairs and played leading roles in the American Zionist movement.

36. The reference is to the holiday Hamishah Asar Bishvat (Hebrew for the fifteenth day of the Hebrew month Shvat), also known as Tu Bishvat—a minor holiday related to the agricultural cycle and first-fruit offerings of the harvest season in the Land of Israel. With the advent of Zionism, Tu Bishvat became invested with contemporary cultural significance related to land reclamation, afforestation, and modern Jewish colonization in Palestine.

not so; third, you proceed to condemn these passages. Don't you recognize the old adage of giving a dog a bad name and hanging him?

However, besides your method, which I think is in itself unjustifiable, the tone of your letters is most insulting ... [and your accusations] are a sad reflection, both on your ideals of "ethics" and on your "good taste." I shall keep both of these letters!

26

"CONSCIOUS OF THEIR IDENTITY, THEY MARRY WHOM THEY CHOOSE"

The Elopement of Irving Berlin and Ellin Mackay (1926)

◇◇

When twenty-two-year old Ellin Mackay eloped in 1926 with Irving Berlin (né Israel Baline, then age thirty-seven), news of the Catholic socialite's civil marriage to the famous Jewish songwriter and composer ignited a firestorm of controversy—and Mackay's father disinherited her for marrying outside her faith. The couple's elopement (they are pictured here en route to their honeymoon in Atlantic City, New Jersey) prompted a front-page *New York Times* article proclaiming "Surprises Father" and "Parent Disapproves Society Girl's Marriage to Jazz Composer."[1]

Mackay (1903–1988), heiress to an upper-crust Republican family whose enormous wealth derived from mining and communications, was a successful writer known for her *New Yorker* articles. Her father, Clarence H. Mackay (1874–1938), president of the Mackay Radio and Telegraph Company and chairman of the board of the Postal Telegraph Company (later purchased by IT&T), was one of America's richest men until the Wall Street crash of 1929. Berlin (1888–1989), the son of Yiddish-speaking Russian Jewish immigrants who arrived penniless in New York in 1893, grew up in the rough-and-tumble of Manhattan's Lower East Side ghetto. Berlin had pluck and considerable talent, and his meteoric rise as a darling of vaudeville, Tin Pan Alley, and Broadway made him into an iconic American celebrity. His fellow composer George Gershwin (1898–1937) later dubbed Berlin "America's Schubert" and "the greatest songwriter that has ever lived."[2] In his lifetime, Berlin produced a considerable body of beloved Americana, including the songs "Alexander's Ragtime Band" (1911), "Easter Parade" (1933), "God Bless America" (1938), "White Christmas" (1942), and "There's

1. "Ellin Mackay Wed to Irving Berlin; Surprises Father," *New York Times*, January 5, 1926. 1 and 3.

2. Quoted in *The George Gershwin Reader*, ed. Robert Wyatt and John Andrew Johnson (New York: Oxford University Press, 2004), 116.

News of the Elopement of Irving Berlin and Ellin Mackay, 1926.
Source: Bain News Service, "Irving Berlin & wife (Ellin Mackay),"
George Grantham Bain Collection, Prints and Photographs
Division, Library of Congress, Washington, D.C.

No Business Like Show Business" (1946); musical theater productions such as
"Ziegfeld Follies" (1919), "As Thousands Cheer" (1933), and "Annie Get Your
Gun" (1946); and numerous scores for Hollywood films, including *Holiday Inn*
(1942), starring Bing Crosby (1903–1977), Marjorie Reynolds (1917–1997), and
Fred Astaire (1899–1987)—all of which helped to shape the "Great American
Songbook."

Intermarriage between Jews and Christians was not unheard of in early
twentieth-century America. As early as 1908, Israel Zangwill's celebrated Broadway production, *The Melting Pot: The Great American Drama*, loosely based on William Shakespeare's *Romeo and Juliet* (1597), enchanted American audiences. In

Zangwill's play, which depicts an interfaith love affair between a Russian Jewish composer and the daughter of an antisemitic Russian Christian aristocrat, ancestral boundaries are transcended, past misdeeds are forgiven, and the young lovers are united. Following a performance in Washington, D.C., President Theodore Roosevelt (1858–1919) is reported to have leaned over the rim of his box and exclaimed: "That's a great play, Mr. Zangwill, that's a great play!"[3]

Viewed in cultural and historical perspective, what makes Mackay and Berlin's 1926 union so remarkable, apart from their celebrity status, is that it signaled the growing "cultural clout" of "the companionate marriage ideal" and the modernizing notion of matrimony as "an arrangement intended for personal and sexual fulfillment."[4] In a New Yorker article published a year earlier, Mackay herself dismissed the forced social conventions of matchmaking—that is, fashionable New York society's distinction "between a brilliant match and a mésalliance'"—in favor of individual choice.[5] "Modern girls," she declared, "are conscious of their identity and they marry whom they choose, satisfied to satisfy themselves."[6] Likewise, the abovementioned New York Times article quoted Berlin as saying "the question of religion in connection with the marriage ... would be considered later, if at all."[7] A friend of the couple added, "it was his [Berlin's] understanding that although a religious ceremony would be performed later, the couple would continue their individual faiths."[8]

The Berlin-Mackay marriage lasted sixty-two years and produced three children and nine grandchildren. Throughout their lives, Berlin and Mackay remained identifiable, respectively, as a Jew and a Catholic, and their household was ecumenical on matters of religious observance. Berlin never shied away from his Jewish identity or his secular disposition, and he remained a visible

3. Quoted in Joseph Leftwich, Israel Zangwill (New York: Thomas Yoseloff, 1957), 252.

4. Lila Corwin Berman, "Sociology, Jews, and Intermarriage in Twentieth-Century America," Jewish Social Studies 14, no. 2 (Winter 2008), 39.

5. Ellin Mackay, "The Declining Function: A Post-Debutante Rejoices," New Yorker, December 12, 1925, 15. Commenting on Mackay's article from Paris, F. Scott Fitzgerald (1896–1940), a chronicler of the Jazz Age, observed: "Chicago, like London, has personality, whereas New York society has always been imitative and most conspicuously anemic.... Dullness is natural among people like New York society, too stupid to find interest outside.... The innocent middle westerners of Yale and Princeton must also escape the interminable engraved cards informing them that their presence is requested" (quoted in Henry Wales, "Scott Fitzgerald Puts Barb on Ellin's Shaft at Society," Daily News, December 7, 1925, 102).

6. Mackay, "The Declining Function," 15.

7. Quoted in "Ellin Mackay Wed to Irving Berlin," 3.

8. Quoted in ibid.

supporter of a variety of Jewish organizations and causes. In many respects, what was seen in 1926 as a sensational event proved to be an occasion marking the normalization of interfaith marriage in twentieth-century America and a pathway to new manifestations of American Jewish identity.

—EDS.

27

"TO OBSERVE THE SABBATH IN ITS TIME-HONORED WAY"

Temple Adath Israel (Louisville, KY) Debates the Elimination of Sunday Worship Services
(1931)

◇◇

DAN JUDSON AND DEBORAH SKOLNICK EINHORN

The following is a report from a special committee convened by Temple Adath Israel in Louisville, Kentucky, to determine whether the congregation should shift from its long-standing Sunday morning service to a Friday evening Sabbath service. Temple Adath Israel, the oldest synagogue in Kentucky, was founded in 1842. In the mid-1850s it was one of the first Reform congregations in the United States, and later it became a founding member of the Union of American Hebrew Congregations. In 1873 it was the second largest Reform congregation in the country.[1] By the end of the nineteenth century the congregation was firmly in the camp of classical Reform Judaism led by Rabbi Adolph Moses (1840–1902), who was known for his strident commitment to the universal spirit of Judaism.[2] Adath Israel was one of approximately forty Reform congregations that would institute Sunday services. Most of these synagogues turned to such services as a supplement to Shabbat morning services to allow

---

1. Lee Shai Weissbach, *The Synagogues of Kentucky* (Lexington: University Press of Kentucky, 1995), 17–18; Mark W. Gordon, "Rediscovering Jewish Infrastructure: Update on United States Nineteenth Century Synagogues," *American Jewish History* 84, no. 1 (March 1996): 13 and 22; "Louisville: Historical Overview," *Encyclopedia of Southern Jewish Communities*, https://www.isjl.org/kentucky-louisville-encyclopedia.html.

2. See, for example, Adolph Moses's speech at the 1894 Hebrew Union College graduation, where he suggested that the name "Judaism" be replaced with "Yahvism." He wrote: "In the mind of the Gentiles, this name [Judaism] indissolubly associated our religion, which is universal in its deepest sources and universal in its scope and tendency, with the Jewish race, and thus stamps it as a tribal religion" (Adolph Moses, *Yahvism and Other Discourses*, ed. H. G. Enelow [Louisville, KY: Louisville Section of the Council of Jewish Women, 1903], 1–10). For more on Moses, see note 8.

congregants to participate in worship services who could not otherwise attend due to the six-day work week.[3]

The special committee tasked with deciding the fate of the Sunday morning service was split almost evenly, with the barest majority voting to maintain the service. The divide in the congregation between those who wanted a return to tradition in the form of a Shabbat evening service and those who wished to maintain the classical Reform approach of a Sunday morning service reflected the broader split in Reform Judaism at this time. Following the radical stance on traditional observance institutionalized in the Pittsburgh Platform (1885),[4] the movement began to modulate its approach to ritual. By 1937 the Pittsburgh Platform had been superseded by the Columbus Platform, which called for "the preservation of the Sabbath, festivals, and Holy Days" as well as the use of Hebrew together with the vernacular.[5] Adath Israel's Sunday service dispute came in the midst of these changes as well as other cultural transitions regarding entertainment, technology, and social mores—all of which make appearances in the debate.

Without irony, Adath Israel's supporters of Sunday morning worship services relied on an argument advocating that tradition be restored and argued that Friday evening is "sacred as a home service" for Reform Jewish families. By contrast, the minority "decline[d] to do as Christians do" and proposed "to worship a Jewish God, on the Jewish Sabbath." In seeking to change the congregation's status quo, the minority argued that Friday night services would serve as a magnet to draw "cultured Jews unaffiliated with our Temple, or if, affiliated, wholly indifferent." Interestingly, as the document reveals, while the majority and minority factions relied on diverse (and often conflicting) justifications of their positions, there is a finger-wagging quality to the exchange. Both sides overtly criticized the priorities of their fellow congregants and questioned their choices, motives, and commitments. In particular, the holy grail of attracting the local Jewish community's fashionable younger set runs through the proceedings. At this moment in American Jewish history, as in so many others,

3. See Kerry Olitzky, "The Sunday Sabbath Movement in American Reform Judaism: Strategy or Evolution," *American Jewish Archives* 34 (April 1982): 75–88; Kerry Olitzky, "Sundays at Chicago Sinai Congregation: Paradigm for a Movement," *American Jewish History* 74, no. 4 (June 1985): 356–68.

4. On the Pittsburgh Platform, see chapter 16, note 10.

5. For the text of the Columbus Platform (1937), see Paul Mendes-Flohr and Jehuda Reinharz, eds., *The Jew in the Modern World: A Documentary History*, 3d ed. (New York: Oxford University Press, 2011), 575–76.

tradition—whether defined as a Friday evening or a Sunday morning worship observance—clashed with cultural norms, technology, and the expectations of the American workplace.

◇◇

Temple Adath Israel (Louisville, KY) Debates the Elimination of Sunday Worship Services, 1931

Source: "Board Minutes of Temple Adath Israel, 1931," 174–81. Courtesy of Archives of The Temple, Congregation Adath Israel Brith Sholom, Louisville, KY.

A meeting was called by Mr. M. F. Marx,[6] chairman of the special committee of 15, on Monday evening, Nov. 16, 1931.

This committee met for the purpose of considering the feasibility of holding services on Friday evening instead of Sunday morning.

A resolution was passed requiring that a majority and a minority report to be submitted. The following are the members constituting [the authors of] the majority report and are eight in number: Mr. Edward Sachs, Mr. Percy Loevenhart, Mr. Arnold Levy, Mr Wm. Trost, Mr. Melvin Meyers, Miss Minnie Baldauf, Mr. Sol Levy, [and] Mrs. Leon Goodman, Chairman.[7]

From members who spoke, your chairman has gleaned many reasons why Sunday morning Services should be retained by Congregation Adath Israel, Louisville, Ky.

(1) Temple going is largely a matter of will and desire. With rare exceptions one can always attend services when one wishes—it is only a matter of wanting to attend.

(2) Our present arrangement gives to everyone a chance to attend services—the most Conservative and the most Reform.

6. Moses F. Marx (1880–1963) and his brothers Frank L. Marx (1890–1960) and Solomon Marx (1893–1969) owned the Marx Hide and Tallow Company (Louisville, KY).

7. The congregants listed here are Minnie Baldauf (1871–1942), Barbara S. Goodman (1888–1948; wife of Leon Goodman, 1853–1908), Arnold Levy (1883–1969), Sol Levy (1865–1944), Percy J. Loevenhart (1875–1936), Melvin S. Meyers (1881–1946), Edward Sachs (1861–1938), and William Trost (1861–1943). On Barbara S. Goodman's leadership of the Reform movement's National Federation of Temple Sisterhoods (later renamed Women of Reform Judaism), see Jonathan D. Sarna, "'To Quicken the Religious Consciousness of Israel': The NFTS National Committee on Religion, 1913–1933" in *Sisterhood: A Centennial History of Women of Reform Judaism*, eds. Carole B. Balin, Dana Herman, Jonathan D. Sarna, and Gary P. Zola (Cincinnati: Hebrew Union College Press, 2013), 49–71.

(3) There is the Friday evening service from 5:45 to 6:10, giving to all so inclined an opportunity for meditation, for prayer and for *kaddish* and finally a chance to return for the traditional Friday eve, with the family in the home.

(4) The Saturday morning, or Sabbath service, in our Temple portrays all that tradition, beauty, spirituality and sacredness implies. It gives to everyone of our Faith—members or non-members—an opportunity to observe the Sabbath in its time-honored way.

(5) Many of our older men and women who will hesitate to go out at night, for whom cold, rain, snow and heat, make the Friday evening service positively prohibitive, look forward to the Sabbath in the Temple. There are younger women, without escorts and living at considerable distances from the Temple, who will not go out alone after dark; these too form a part of the Saturday and the Sunday congregation. Unfortunately, economic conditions are such that our men cannot be with us on Saturday and yet we have many retired businessmen who can find time for everything and anything save an hour in the Temple.

(6) The Saturday morning service enables the mother to come to Temple with her children, thereby inculcating in the young the habit of Temple attendance.

(7) Friday eve is sacred as a home service and our present Friday eve service makes it possible to have family reunions on this sacred eve.

(8) We changed from Friday night to Sunday because Friday eve was not a success. Many of you may not know that the Friday eve service in Adath Israel actually died because it was most fashionable to go to [the] theatre on Friday night. The writer recalls seeing our sainted Rabbi [Adolph] Moses[8] stand on the pulpit Friday night after Friday night, imploring the people to come; preaching with all of his strength and his philosophy, actually shedding tears and all to no purpose. Today we have the fashionable movies, the fashionable dinner parties, the fashionable social clubs and groups and all assisted by the untiring telephone operators and the automobiles and this program attracts

8. Originally from Prussia, Adolph Moses (1840–1902) studied at the University of Breslau and the local rabbinical seminary of Zacharias Frankel (1801–1875), a leading exponent of Positive-Historical Judaism (see chapter 16, note 15). Drawn to radical politics, Moses participated in, respectively, the Italian and Polish national struggles for independence between 1859 and 1864. After his release from imprisonment by the tsarist regime, he studied at Frankfort-am-Main under Abraham Geiger (1810–1874), one of the founders of Reform Judaism. In 1870, Moses immigrated to the United States. He served as rabbi of Congregation Shaarei Shomayim in Mobile, Alabama (1871–88), and Temple Adath Israel in Louisville, Kentucky (1882–1902). In 1885, he was one of the fifteen rabbis who created the Pittsburgh Platform.

our young people. Many of us who have studied the situation feel that conditions and interests in our Congregation are such that it does not warrant a change from Sunday morning to Friday evening.

(9) Friday evening service will seriously interfere with our excellent Saturday morning service and this in truth is admitted by some of those who make the most ardent plea for Friday night.

(10) It is surely unwise to spoil a well-attended service for an experiment.

(11) No change in the day will change the disposition to go, or not to go, to Temple.

(12) The Sunday service has a memory and a tradition in our midst that it is a pity to destroy.

(13) The leading Reform congregations in the country have Sunday services.

(14) From the latest available statistics, 17 congregations of the [Union of American Hebrew Congregations] have changed the day of their services in the last 20 years. Of these, 10 went from Sunday to Friday night and seven from Friday night to Sunday. On this basis of the hundreds affiliated with the Union we should make no change.[9]

(15) The parents who are inconvenienced by the calling for their children at the close of Religious School are comparatively few, despite the extravagant statement that was made at the congregation dinner.

(16) Our Sunday Service is perfectly timed. Sunday morning 11:00 AM to 12:15 PM enabling the tired businessman to sleep till 10:00 AM. The young people are the ones that we seek, and the Temple-going habit they learn from "Kehal Yisroel" [sic] — the congregation of Israel. One father and mother cannot accomplish this, nor can a dozen, but if the parents of Adath Israel Congregation will assume the responsibility and will not yield to every weak excuse—it is too hot or too cold, too wet or too dry, an extra hour or two at golf, etc.—our task will be an easy one, for our arrangement is perfect.

(17) With the fewest exceptions, no one can really say, "I can't come on Sunday" but very many can say, "I can't come on Friday evening."

(18) The people who have been attending Sunday services have shown a positive interest in the Temple; they are more numerous than those who have spoken for Friday evening and we must consider the businesswoman who is too tired after a day on her feet to rush out Friday evening.

9. On concerns in the Reform movement of the 1920s and 1930s about congregational membership and shifting norms of ritual practice, see Michael A. Meyer, *Response to Modernity: A History of the Reform Movement in Judaism* (New York: Oxford University Press, 1988), 303–9 and 322–25.

(19) Summed up:
  (a) Tired businessmen and women are less apt to attend Friday evening service than Sunday morning.
  (b) We feel that our beautiful Saturday morning service will be seriously impaired by the change from Sunday to Friday eve.
  (c) It is a farce and sacrilege to say, "Friday evening service may be worth trying if you close in time to attend the nine o'clock movie."
  (d) Friday night services [are] very difficult for older men and women because of darkness, weather conditions, etc. and for unescorted women who fear to be out alone.
(20) I am quoting Rabbi Philip Jaffe[10] who recently occupied our pulpit, who is Regional Rabbi for Kentucky, Ohio, North and South Carolina, and Wisconsin and whose home is in Cleveland, when I tell you that one of Cleveland's Temples gave up Sunday service for Friday night,[11] hoping thereby to gain the young people and they have failed. These groups look forward to Friday evenings for its social functions, for the basketball games, etc., and the Temple cannot compete. Working as he does primarily with the young people he feels that there are too many counter attractions to bring our youth to the Temple on Friday evening.

In closing, may I repeat, "We worship under ideal conditions and at an ideal time," so, "Come to Temple once a week if humanly possible."
Mrs. Leon Goodman, Chairman, Majority Report.

◊ ◊ ◊

Mr. Charles W. Morris,[12] Chairman of the Minority Committee, then read his report, as follows:

Mr. President, Ladies and Gentleman:
This minority report represents the conclusion of seven of the committee of 15 appointed by the president. The word "conclusion" is used because each of the seven members presented a different reason for the proposed change from Sunday morning to Friday evening services and may or may not have agreed with the reasons advanced by the other members. This report will attempt to convey

10. The identity of this individual is unknown.
11. The specific Cleveland synagogue referred to here is unknown.
12. The Louisville attorney Charles W. Morris (1892–1961) was a civic and political activist and a founder of the Louisville Conference of Jewish Organizations.

to you in a necessarily restricted form the various opinions of those committee members advocating the proposed change.

At the outset, let it be frankly stated that the predominant factor, the predominant motive actuating the minority committee is the hope for increased interest in our religion, expressed both by attendance at divine services and by the personal conduct and by the personal attitude toward extra Temple activities which should naturally follow such attendance. Unless the proposed change will quicken the interest of our active members and will create and arouse the interest of those who do not now participate in congregational life, we might as well leave things as they are. On the other hand, if, by changing our time for services, we could stimulate the loyalty and the religious consciousness of our community, and especially of our young men and women, then I am sure there is not a single member of this congregation who would not heartily endorse such a movement.

If we look at conditions honestly and frankly, we are forced to the inevitable and distressing conclusion that Reform Judaism is in a bad way. Let me give you some local examples:

The Reform Jewish community has grown considerably during the past five years. This is due not only to the arrival at maturity of young men and women at a rate exceeding the losses caused by death, but also by the advent of new families in excess of those who have moved away from our community, and by the wealth and social ambition of persons formerly affiliated with Orthodox groups. It would naturally follow that our membership should have increased proportionately, but, on examination, we find that during the last ten years we have lost twenty per cent of our members, fifty per cent of our pew owners, and a very considerable percentage of our income.

There are in this community today more intelligent and cultured Jews unaffiliated with our Temple, or, if affiliated, wholly indifferent to it than ever before in the history of this congregation. The speaker, himself, can name thirty men and women, all sons and daughters of former pillars of the Temple, some former members of our Board and even officers of our congregation, who belong in that menacing category; and the list is growing, for as our interested members die, no one steps forward to take their places, and that is not all.

We have a membership of something over four hundred. If we assume that each of these members has two other persons in his family, we have 1,200 potential [attendees] at divine services. Out of that possible 1,200 persons, less than ten per cent will be found in Temple at the average Sunday services, and of that ten percent, not ten members, other than Sunday School teachers, are under forty years of age. It is not the fault of the service, which is impressive and short;

it certainly is not due to the rabbi, who is beloved and admired by all; but something is lacking, and it is the duty of the few remaining interested members of the congregation to find out what that something is, if it is possible to do so.

Last Tuesday night, a distinguished authority on Jewish education speaking in this vestry room deplored the pitifully short Sunday School period of one and one-half hours, plus assembly, generally prevailing in other Jewish reform congregations. He ascribes to this deficiency a great part of the current indifference. He says that our children cannot acquire Jewish self-respect, Jewish knowledge, or Jewish ideals in a period of one and one-half hours a week. Our children come at 9:30 AM[,] have a twenty-minute assembly, and leave at 10:45 AM. In other words, instead of one and one-half hours deplored by Dr. [Abraham N.] Franzblau[13] as wholly inadequate, the children of Adath Israel have fifty-five minutes a week of classroom work. How can we expect them to grow up into loyal, informed and interested members? That, in a brief way, is the situation as it exists today. How would Friday night services help?

Let us begin with the Religious School. If we had no Sunday morning services, we could not only lengthen the hours of instruction, but we could have two assemblies—one for the older boys and girls, and another for the younger children. By giving our young people twice as much religious instruction, is it not possible that we may have a better chance to train them into loyal and interested adult members of our congregation?

On Sundays the average older man likes to take things easy; read his Sunday papers; call on the sick. The Temple does not pull him, partly because Sunday is not his Sabbath, partly, perhaps, because, as Dr. [Joseph] Rauch[14] has stated, the Sunday service is not a religious service. We know that the younger members invariably and inevitably sleep late on Sunday morning. Perhaps they should not. BUT THEY DO, and they won't come to Temple. Perhaps they would

13. On Abraham N. Franzblau (1901–1982), founding principal of the Hebrew Union College School for Teachers, see chapter 25, note 24.

14. Originally from Austria, Joseph Rauch (1880–1957) immigrated to the United States at the age of twelve and joined the members of his family who had preceded him in Galveston, Texas. The family next moved to Cincinnati, where Rauch studied at the University of Cincinnati and Hebrew Union College. Ordained in 1905, he served as rabbi of Mt. Sinai Temple in Sioux City, Iowa (1905–12), and Temple Adath Israel in Louisville, Kentucky (1912–57). He studied at the University of Chicago, Columbia University, Cambridge University, and the Southern Baptist Theological Seminary, where he earned a doctor of theology degree. He was active in religious, civic, and interfaith affairs and authored several articles, including "Apocalypse in the Bible," *Journal of Jewish Lore and Philosophy* 1, no. 2 (April 1919), 163–95. See also David L. Locketz, "Joseph Rauch: A Biographical Study," rabbinic thesis, Hebrew Union College–Jewish Institute of Religion, 2004.

not come on Friday nights, but they say they would. We have everything to gain and nothing to lose.

It has been said that we should not make our Temple a mere convenient interval between dinners and movies or card games; that the younger people should not be permitted to use it as a place for making engagements. This committee is unable to understand why the young people should use the Temple for such a purpose when the telephone is so handy—and this committee does not believe that the young people would do this, but, at any rate, it is difficult to conceive why it is any worse for people to come to Temple and then play cards or go to movies on Friday night than it is for them to stay away from Temple and then play golf or cards or go to the movies on Sunday afternoon.

This committee refuses to assent to the theory that men are too tired when they get home from business on Friday night to dress up and go to Temple. Unfortunately, the number of men whose business wears them out on Friday afternoon is so small as to be non-existent. Our businessmen are not too tired to go out in the evenings for recreation. Surely they are not too tired to spend an hour in the soothing and healing atmosphere of the Temple.

Recently the speaker has had occasion to visit temples in two other cities, both smaller congregations than ours. Each of these temples had Friday night services and we were impressed with two facts. First, the very large proportion of men in attendance, and, second, the distinctly JEWISH atmosphere. Both services were better attended than ours, one in actual numbers, the other proportionately, and it is impossible to escape the conclusion that one reason for this circumstance lies in the fact previously mentioned, namely, that our Sunday morning service is not essentially a religious one. Is it not possible that a Friday night service, on our Sabbath, and, frankly, a Jewish religious service, will be more attractive to persons seeking the warmth and the spiritual comfort of Judaism?

It has been stated that the unattached women, the old woman, or feeble women cannot come out on Friday nights, especially in bad weather. Our investigation leads to the conclusion that, excluding teachers in the religious school, not more than ten women of this category now attend Sunday services. Most of these could come equally well on Saturday, and the three or four working women could come to Temple on Friday nights as easily as they now go to lectures, concerts, and moving pictures.

Complaint is made that the length of time devoted to services on Friday night will be too short. Let us not forget that our Sunday services begin at 11:00 AM and end at 12:00 PM. Certainly, the proposed change will lengthen, not shorten, the period of worship.

It has been said that the more progressive cities have discarded Friday night services. Here are the facts, as stated by George Zepin,[15] Secretary of the Union of American Hebrew Congregations, in a letter dated November 2, 1931:

(1) During the past 5 years 6 congregations changed from Friday evening to Sunday morning services with [a] sermon. This is 5.9 percent of all Friday evening services five years ago.
(2) During same period 9 congregations changed from Sunday morning to Friday evening service with [a] sermon. This is 36 percent of all Sunday service congregations five years ago.
(3) According to office records, 104 congregations have Friday evening services and 22 congregations have Sunday morning services.

Moreover, it must not be forgotten that in those large centers which still maintain Sunday services, the worshippers must come from long distances, there is an enormous transient attendance, and that most of these congregations have Friday night services, too.

It is insisted that Friday night is not the traditional time for Orthodox religious services in the synagogue, but, on the contrary, is devoted to religious services at home. The answer to that objection is threefold. In the first place, this is not a traditionally Orthodox congregation, but the earliest and the finest traditions we have come from the times when we had our services on Friday nights, sixty years of glorious traditions emblazoned in the archives of Reform Jewish history, years when our Temple produced the greatest lay leaders it has ever had. In the second place, we challenge contradiction of the fact that every single one of the few members we have who still observe Friday night at home, are in favor of Friday night services in the Temple. In the third place, it is inconceivable that SUNDAY ever was, now is, or ever can be the traditional day for Jewish worship. Of the two days, who will deny that Friday evening is traditionally, historically, and logically the holier, the truer, and the most natural and consistent occasion for the expression of the faith of Judaism?

It has been said that the distractions of Friday night drew our members away from Temple and caused the change to be made thirty years ago. The truth is

15. George Zepin (1878–1963) was born in Kiev, Russia, and brought to the United States as a child by his family. In 1900, he graduated from the University of Cincinnati and was ordained at Hebrew Union College. After serving as a rabbi in Kalamazoo, Michigan (1900–1903), field secretary of the Union of American Hebrew Congregations (UAHC) (1903–5), superintendent of the Jewish Social Agencies in Chicago (1908), rabbi of Congregation Beth El in Fort Worth, Texas (1909), and director of the UAHC Department of Synagogue and School Extension (1905–6 and 1910–17), he became secretary of the UAHC (1917–41).

that Friday night in those days was the "theatre night," and the fashionable members of our congregation then, as now, desired to be seen in all their glory when society met together. But times have changed. No one night is any more important than the other in our community. The only factor which differentiates Friday night from other nights is that we would begin Friday night services with a nucleus of thirty to forty people who already attend the short mourning services now in practice.

The two objections most frequently and vociferously advanced are that we must not go backward and that we must not be un-American. This, we are told, is a Christian country, and we must do as the Christians do. The minority members of this committee absolutely refuse to concede that this is a Christian country so far as our religion is concerned, and they respectfully decline to do as Christians do, in the observance of the Jewish faith. On the contrary, we insist that in this country every man is guaranteed the right to worship God according to the dictates of his conscience, and we do not subscribe to the view that as Americans we must embrace the Christian Sabbath, any more than we embrace the Christian savior or the Christian's crucifix. Let us remind these objectors who wish to be as Christian-like as possible in their religious observances, that they had best begin their attack on Saturday services, which has always been and still is the principal day for the holding of religious services in this congregation; and if there are members of this congregation who feel that we would offend our non-Jewish friends by worshipping our God on Friday night rather than on Sunday morning, then they consistently advocate the abolition of Saturday services also. But we do not believe that non-Jews will have less respect for us because we observe our own Sabbath and the Sabbath of Jesus, rather than pretend to be half-Christian by holding one service on our Sabbath and one service on theirs.

Finally, it is urged that our rabbi is opposed to the change, and that we should back up our rabbi. Oh, that we might always be so eager to carry out our rabbi's wishes! For many years our rabbi has asked us to come to Sunday services too, but the rows of empty pews tell a shameful tale [of] the indifference of his wishes. We know that our rabbi, by reason of that very loyalty, fairness, and devotion which have always won our love and respect, will do his part to carry out the sincere and conscientious wishes of the congregation, so long as those wishes are moral in purpose and Jewish in principle. We want our rabbi to have the attendance he deserves, and we believe we can come nearer to that goal by following the example of Cincinnati and returning to our own Sabbath for worship.

We, of the minority committee, feel that Reform Judaism is in peril; that every possible step should be taken to combat the indifference, the ignorance, and the irreligious attitude of our young men and women. We feel that if we fail, they will be lost not only to Jewish worship but also to Jewish education, Jewish enterprise, and Jewish philanthropy. We view with dismay, akin to despair, the unfilled gaps in the ranks of Jewish leaders and workers, and we propose any change, any step, which holds the promise of recapturing their interest and loyalty. We feel that by increasing the hours of religious education, by making it easier for our young folks to come, by bringing back the inspiring spiritual atmosphere which is lacking in Sunday services, by meeting as Jews, in a Jewish temple, to worship a Jewish God, on the Jewish Sabbath, may help to preserve the strength, the dignity, and the glory of our people and of our ancient faith.

Charles W. Morris, Chairman, Minority Report.

28

"THE MAN WHO CRYSTALLIZES GREATNESS IN THE TWENTIETH CENTURY"[1]

Reform Congregation Keneseth Israel (Philadelphia, PA) Honors Albert Einstein

(1934)

◇◇◇

The leaders of Reform Congregation Keneseth Israel, meeting at the historic Bellevue Stratford Hotel in downtown Philadelphia, present a certificate of honorary membership to Albert Einstein (1879–1955). Left to right: William H. Fineshriber (1878–1968), senior rabbi (1924–49); Einstein; Julian B. Feibelman (1897–1980), assistant rabbi (1926–36); and Joseph H. Hagedorn (1873–1949), synagogue president (1922–38).[2]

Source: Photograph in "Minute Book" (1934). Courtesy of Archives of Reform Congregation Keneseth Israel, Elkins Park, PA. Photographic assistance provided by Marlene Adler.

—EDS.

1. This phrase derives from the document in chapter 29.

2. For information about Einstein, Fineshriber, Feibelman, and Hagedorn, respectively, see chapter 29, notes 6, 12, 7, and 15.

29

"DESTINY HAS BOUND US TOGETHER"

Albert Einstein Speaks to Reform Congregation Keneseth Israel (Philadelphia, PA)
(1934)

◇◇

LANCE J. SUSSMAN

On December 4, 1934, the eve of the fifth day of Hanukkah 5695, Albert Einstein (1879–1955) and his second wife, Elsa (1876–1936), were made honorary members of Philadelphia's Reform Congregation Keneseth Israel at the Bellevue Stratford Hotel, "the Great Dame" of South Broad Street, Philadelphia, on the occasion of the eighty-seventh anniversary of the synagogue's founding. The event, complete with dancing and the lighting of a Hanukkah menorah, was attended by over 1,200 people and widely covered in the local media.[1]

In 1934, Reform Congregation Keneseth Israel's impressive neoclassical structure filled most of a city block.[2] The synagogue's members included many of Philadelphia's elite Jewish families, including Adam Gimbel (1817–1896), founder of the Gimbels national department store chain; Lessing J. Rosenwald (1891–1979), a scion of the Sears, Roebuck and Company magnate Julius Rosenwald (1862–1932); Samuel Paley (1876–1963), founder of the Columbia Broadcasting System; Moses Annenberg (1877–1942), publisher of the *Philadelphia Inquirer*; and Albert M. Greenfield (1887–1967), a highly successful real estate developer and banker, who helped keep the congregation solvent during the Great Depression. Keneseth Israel's senior rabbi, William H. Fineshriber (1878–1968), had already distinguished himself in his former pulpit, at Temple Israel of Memphis, Tennessee, by debating the legendary American orator and politician William Jennings Bryan (1860–1925) on the subject of evolution and publicly condemning the Ku Klux Klan. By the mid-1930s, Fineshriber was deeply engaged with major Hollywood studios on behalf of the Central Conference of

1. See, for example, "Keneseth Israel Honors Einstein: Scientist Made Honorary Member at Congregation's 87th Anniversary," *Philadelphia Inquirer*, December 5, 1934.

2. To date, there is no scholarly history of Keneseth Israel. The most comprehensive work on the synagogue is Shelly Kapnek Rosenberg, *Reform Congregation Keneseth Israel: Its First 100 Years, 1847–1947* (Elkins Park, PA: Reform Congregation Keneseth Israel, 1997).

American Rabbis about the moral standards of the American film industry and its depiction of Jews.

The Einsteins had settled in Princeton, New Jersey, in 1933 and were still living on Library Lane when they accepted the synagogue's invitation. Although Abraham Flexner (1866–1959) — the leading reformer of American medical education in the period and the founder of the Institute for Advanced Study, where Einstein worked — was generally opposed to Einstein's appearing in the public eye, the winner of the 1921 Nobel Prize in physics continued to speak to groups and organizations whose values he supported, including ethical humanism, Zionism, pacifism, and civil rights. Einstein rarely spoke to synagogue groups, but he may have agreed to do so on this occasion at least in part because the central European Jews from the Stuttgart-Ulm area who founded the synagogue in 1847 included some of his ancestors.[3]

The document reprinted here that contains Einstein's remarks was published after the eighty-seventh anniversary event.[4] Einstein's address, written and delivered in German and English, emphasized the need for Jewish unity in times of peril. He did not express an explicitly ideological viewpoint, nor did he call directly for American Jewish rescue efforts. However, he did urge his audience to resist assimilation and break from the Jewish cultural isolation of previous eras. This was a message sure to resonate with Philadelphia's Reform Jewish community and, more generally, American Jewry's liberal-minded mainstream. He also boldly asserted that Jews should not view their heritage in purely religious terms but rather find individual spiritual purpose in a nontheistic fashion as a form of resistance to Nazi aggression.[5] As the text illustrates, notwithstanding the congregation's esteem and reverence for Einstein, its leaders did not uniformly agree with his perspective on Judaism and modern Jewish culture.

◇◇

3. There is no evidence that Einstein maintained any contact with the synagogue after the event.

4. See also the photograph of the synagogue's leaders presenting a certificate of honorary membership to Einstein (chapter 28). The photo appears to have been taken in a corridor of the Bellevue Stratford Hotel.

5. For other statements by Einstein on Judaism, see "Prof. Einstein Discusses Judaism," *Jewish Telegraphic Agency*, September 30, 1934, https://www.jta.org/1934/09/30/archive/prof-einstein-discusses-judaism; Hayim Greenberg, "Einstein Discusses Religion," in Hayim Greenberg, *The Essential Hayim Greenberg: Essays and Addresses on Jewish Culture, Socialism, and Zionism*, ed. Mark A. Raider (Tuscaloosa: University of Alabama Press, 2016), 158–66.

Albert Einstein's Address to Reform Congregation Keneseth Israel, Philadelphia, PA, 1934

Source: "Minute Book" (1934). Courtesy of Archives of Reform Congregation Keneseth Israel, Elkins Park, PA.

[The congregation's eighty-seventh annual meeting] was an occasion which, for all who attended, will forever stand forth as one unique in its brilliant proceedings. Our friends from other congregations, who attended as guests of our members, have been especially laudatory, and this, combined with the appreciation of our membership present that evening, makes the event which welcomed the distinguished scientist, Dr. Albert Einstein,[6] into our midst, one of unparalleled distinction.

It was just such an occasion which one might hope to derive but rarely achieves, and were we to set out to duplicate it, the elements of spontaneity and whole-heartedness would undoubtedly be absent. It is not alone that speakers were illustrious; that an honored guest, a "citizen of the world," brought a message of hope to his people; it was not alone that members gathered and friends mingled, and their spirit and interest went out. We say it is not one of those things alone; it is all of them. Where then, can we begin, or where end, in describing this significant event, so generally alluded to by contemporaries as "the most distinguished Jewish affair of the year"?

On the one hand, Rabbi [Julian B.] Feibelman[7] characterized our guest of

---

6. In 1905, the German Jewish scientist Albert Einstein (1879–1955) posited the general theory of relativity on the electrodynamics of moving bodies and the equivalence of mass and mechanical energy, subsequently distilled into the famous equation $E = mc^2$. Thereafter, Einstein rapidly became one of the world's leading scientists. In 1921 he was awarded the Nobel Prize in physics. Notwithstanding his nonobservant upbringing and background, Einstein remained strongly attached to Jewish culture throughout his life. In 1922, as part of a trip to Asia, he visited Palestine, where he was treated to a hero's welcome and saw the Jewish colonies of the Yishuv. This period also marked the start of his association with the Zionist movement. In February 1933, during a visit to the United States, he decided not to return to Germany owing to the rise of Adolf Hitler and the Nazi party. He spent time in Belgium and England before settling permanently in the United States in October 1933 and assuming a faculty position at the Institute for Advanced Study in Princeton, New Jersey. Though a pacifist, he understood the risk if Nazi Germany developed an atomic bomb before the Allies. Together with other American and émigré scientists, he urged the administration of President Franklin D. Roosevelt (1882–1945) to pursue uranium research, which ultimately led to the Manhattan Project. In 1952, following the death of Israel's first president, Chaim Weizmann (1874–1952), Einstein was offered the presidency of the Jewish state—a largely ceremonial post—which he declined.

7. Born in Jackson, Mississippi, Julian B. Feibelman (1897–1980) was ordained in 1926 by Hebrew Union College. After serving as assistant rabbi at Keneseth Israel (1926–36), during

honor (and our account will hardly do justice to the address he gave) when he asked his audience to "gaze upon an impractical man," and he developed his thesis as showing that, whereas the world generally bows before the practical and the realistic, Albert Einstein, the man who crystallizes greatness in the twentieth century, has none of these qualities. Rather does he dwell in silent modesty, and in an ether of thought so lofty that he places himself all unconsciously alongside the eloquence of the ages, and we are privileged today to have in our society [a man akin] in spirit and breadth of intellect [to] Galileo [Galilei], [Nicolaus] Copernicus, and [Isaac] Newton,[8] yet one who in his very greatness is the most humble of men.

Dr. Einstein presented his address in German,[9] then later read a translation of it, here given:

> I thank you for the evidence of sympathy and fraternal feeling which this cordial reception manifests. If we as Jews can learn anything from these politically sad times, it is the fact that destiny has bound us together, a fact which in times of quiet and security we often so easily and gladly forget. We are accustomed to lay too much emphasis on the differences that divide the Jews of different lands and different religious views. And we forget often that it is the concern of every Jew, when anywhere the Jew is hated and treated unjustly, when politicians with flexible consciences set into motion against us the old prejudices, originally religious, in order to concoct political schemes at our expense. It concerns every one because such diseases and psychotic disturbances of the folk-soul are not estopped by oceans and national borders, but act precisely like economic crises and epidemics.[10]

which time he earned a doctorate at the University of Pennsylvania, he became senior rabbi of Temple Sinai (1936–67) in New Orleans, Louisiana.

8. Galileo Galilei (1564–1642), an Italian mathematician, astronomer, and physicist, laid the foundations of modern experimental science through his investigations of natural law. His observations established the basis for the laws of motion identified by the English mathematician, astronomer, and physicist Isaac Newton (1642–1727). In 1609 Galileo constructed the first telescope, and his astronomical discoveries confirmed the theory of the solar system of the Prussian mathematician and astronomer Nicolaus Copernicus (1473–1543). Galileo was later forced by the Inquisition to recant his view that the earth orbited the sun.

9. The Keneseth Israel archives do not include the original German text of Einstein's talk.

10. Einstein's emphasis on global Jewish unity contrasted with Keneseth Israel's adherence to classical Reform Judaism, which was deeply anchored in ethical monotheism and deemphasized Jewish ethnicity in favor of a universalist sense of mission. While a review of Keneseth Israel's records during World War II (1941–45) reveals greater concern for security for the New Jersey shore than the rescue of European Jews, some Keneseth Israel members did privately arrange for German family members to resettle in the United States.

The most important lesson which we can learn from these tragic occurrences is, according to my view, the following: we must not conceive of the Jewish community as one purely of religious tradition; but we must so build it up that it still shall give to each individual composing it a spiritual purpose, protection against isolation, opportunities for educating the youth, and in times of individual need of [sic] external pressure, also the needed material protection.[11]

In this fashion we shall regain that spiritual balance and modesty which frequently we have lost in the isolation of the assimilation process. Self-respect, together with a modest reserve toward the outside world, instead of an inner isolation and characterlessness, in conjunction with external ambition and lust for power, must be our motto. In order to achieve such convalescence, we must give the individual, by the aid of the community, a definite spiritual purpose. If prudently and with enthusiasm we can learn to find this way, without falling into our earlier error of spiritual isolation from the outer world, not only will our children be made more secure and happier, but they will prove more useful for the larger human community than our present Jewish generation.

Dr. [William H.] Fineshriber,[12] in culminating this evening's exceptional program, struck the keynote so befitting the occasion, in summoning Israel to allegiance toward "passionate, aggressive peace, in contradistinction to passive expressions against the calamity of war." Dr. Fineshriber's words fell, as he is so gifted to have them do, like the great calm which soothes and gives surety to the listener. He referred to the sacrifices and sufferings of the Jewish people, not so much a race as a band consecrated to endure, and through endurance, humility and perseverance, to point the way, leading others by the inspiration of their steadfastness.[13]

11. Einstein's assertion that Judaism should not be primarily conceived of as a religion—a foundational teaching of classical Reform Judaism—but rather as way of achieving self-actualization, physical protection, and material support is striking. His remarks display a secular and vaguely nationalistic understanding of Jewish culture.

12. Born in St. Louis, Missouri, William H. Fineshriber (1878–1968) was ordained in 1900 by Hebrew Union College and initially served as senior rabbi of Temple Israel (1905–23) in Memphis, Tennessee, where he gained a national reputation owing to his anti-Klan and pro-evolution views. He was senior rabbi of Keneseth Israel in 1923–49.

13. Interestingly, in his remarks following Einstein's address Fineshriber defended Reform Judaism's mission doctrine and the argument that "Judaism is not a thing of the past, confined to the ghetto, but a living spirit for today and tomorrow, equally as needed in and equally as applicable to the new conditions in lands of freedom" (Samuel S. Cohon, "The Mission of Re-

On behalf of the congregation, Dr. Fineshriber made the presentation of an award of honorary membership in the congregation to Dr. and Mrs. Albert Einstein. This was set forth on a beautiful parchment scroll as follows:

Because of the epoch-making contributions to Science which Dr. Albert Einstein has made, and

Because of the quiet dignity and patience with which Dr. Albert Einstein has faced injustice and brutality, meted out to him and his family by the government of a nation of which he was one of the chief ornaments, and especially

Because, in his life and teachings he has always stressed the essentially Jewish outlook on life, in his reverence for the Eternal and Infinite, in his spiritual approach to the problem of the nature and a destiny of mankind, and his practical application in his own life of the ancient prophetic principle, that the universe is governed, "not by power nor by might," but by the Spirit of God,[14]

We, the Reform Congregation Keneseth Israel, of Philadelphia, Pennsylvania, in the United States of America, on the occasion of our Eighty-Seventh Annual Meeting, gratefully and joyously elect to Honorary Membership

Doctor and Mrs. Albert Einstein, and pray that they may continue to worship and work with us in devotion to the ideals of the good, the true and the beautiful, to which this Congregation is dedicated.

The president Mr. [Joseph] Hagedorn,[15] who also acted as toastmaster, in an eloquent address voiced his tribute to the guest of honor and a loving testimonial to the rabbis. He declared, "as Jews we can afford to give up many things, but not our membership in the synagogue. Our responsibility as members is to continue to support, with full heart and will, the program of the synagogue, which more than any other safeguards the interests of the Jew against prejudice,

---

form Judaism," *Journal of Religion* 2, no. 1 [January 1922], 39). He emphasized Reform's theological view of Judaism as a religion and, despite the Nazis' aggressive nature, reaffirmed the widespread Reform belief of the period in pacifism.

14. The proclamation incorrectly characterizes Einstein's connection to Judaism as "spiritual" and asserts that pacifism is a prophetic principle. In the wake of World War I, as many as 80 percent of Reform rabbis were pacifists until the late 1930s. See Michael A. Meyer, *Response to Modernity: A History of the Reform Movement in Judaism* (Detroit, MI: Wayne State University Press, 1995), 313. On Einstein and pacifism, see Virginia Iris Holmes, *Einstein's Pacifism and World War I* (Syracuse, NY: Syracuse University Press, 2017).

15. Joseph Hagedorn (1873–1949), a shirtwaist manufacturer, served as president of Keneseth Israel (1922–38) and held numerous leadership positions in the Philadelphia Jewish community.

so that its usefulness may not be curtailed, but may go forward with action and determination to enlarge its scope of service."

In introducing Dr. Fineshriber, Mr. Hagedorn referred to the completion of ten years of ministry as rabbi in Keneseth Israel, and announced that at a special meeting of the board, it had been unanimously voted to mark this occasion by tendering Dr. Fineshriber a "sabbatical" year. This came as a complete surprise to Dr. Fineshriber, who with great feeling thanked the congregation for its manifestation of loyalty and understanding with and devotion toward him during his ministry here, declaring these to have been among the happiest years of his life.

The business of the meeting was expeditiously and gracefully handled by Mr. Jerome J. Rothschild.[16] ... The program had been most auspiciously introduced with the beautiful chanting, by Cantor Benjamin Grobani,[17] of the blessings over the Hanukkah lights and the invocation....[18]

16. Jerome J. Rothschild (1884–1964), a successful Philadelphia lawyer and Jewish communal leader, was active in the American Jewish Committee and the National Conference of Christians and Jews. He served as a member of Keneseth Israel's board of trustees.

17. Born in Berdichev, Ukraine, Benjamin Grobani (1885–1987) had immigrated to the United States with his family as a boy. A talented musician, teacher, and composer, he served in the 1930s as Keneseth Israel's first cantor and subsequently moved to Baltimore, Maryland, where he became cantor of Congregation Oheb Shalom (1941–67).

18. Curiously, there is no other mention of Hanukkah in the pamphlet, nor was the holiday alluded to by any of the speakers that evening.

30

"DON'T HUSH ME!"

American Jewish College Students and Jewish Identity in the Interwar Period

(1939)

◇◇

KARLA GOLDMAN

The following items, published in the January and February 1939 issues of the monthly *Bnai Brith Hillel News* at the University of Michigan (UM), offer a provocative glimpse of the complex identities of interwar Jewish students at a moment of particular communal stress. These items responded to a December 1938 piece (not available in the current collection) by Morris Jampel (1920–1969), published immediately after Kristallnacht (November 9–10, 1938), when Nazi targeting of German Jews erupted into unrestrained violence.[1] The resulting destruction of synagogues, looting of Jewish stores, arrests and incarcerations of thousands of Jewish men, and a significant but undocumented death toll were reported in newspapers around the world, including the *Michigan Daily* (the university's student newspaper), on November 16.

For Jewish student leaders, the startling news of Nazi persecution of Jewish citizens threw long-standing tensions about their own belonging into stark relief. Like many American universities, UM provided a complicated setting for Jewish students hailing from Michigan and other communities around the country (most Jewish students at UM were from Michigan, other midwestern states, New York, or New Jersey). Although UM did not ask about religion on its admission forms (a notable omission compared to East Coast schools, which punctiliously tracked and limited their number of Jewish students), enrolled students did fill out religious preference cards. Based on this information, the *Bnai Brith Hillel News* in 1934 counted 1,400 Jewish students on campus (900 who identified themselves as Jews plus a "conservatively estimated" 25 percent of the 2,000 students who did not indicate a religious preference).[2] This number represented a smaller percentage (approximately 12 percent) of Jewish students than

1. See note 13.
2. "Jews on Campus," *Bnai Brith Hillel News*, November 3, 1934, 2.

was the case at many schools with active Jewish quotas (Harvard University's Jewish enrollment held steady at 15 percent, but Yale University had generally 9 percent or less). Still, given its large number of students, UM would have had one of the largest Jewish enrollments in the country.

Choosing to go to school in Ann Arbor, at a significant distance from one's own community (whether Detroit or New York City), represented an expensive and culturally challenging choice at a time when most Jewish college students took up studies closer to home. Enrolling at a school like UM offered students a fuller immersion in American youth culture and a potentially stronger validation of their authentic Americanness. Indeed, many Jewish UM students found their way to positions of campus prominence. Still, Ann Arbor's Jewish students had to navigate a range of social exclusions and prejudices. As on other campuses, discrimination by Christian fraternities and sororities at UM, like exclusionary quotas, reflected ongoing institutional anxiety over the demographic shift represented by a rapidly growing percentage of qualified Jewish applicants and students.

Tension related to Jewish difference on the campus found its fullest expression during the interwar years at UM in 1935, when four members of the National Student League (all Jewish men from New Jersey or New York) were expelled for behavior related to their radical activities. The student newspaper greeted their exile with pleasure, while campus deans considered establishing "quotas for out-of-state students."[3] Meanwhile, the campus Hillel director, Rabbi Bernard Heller (1897–1976), suggested that if Jewish students felt compelled to be radical, they should at least refrain from "protrud[ing] themselves to the leadership or forefront." With these comments, he reminded any campus radical who might think that "his demeanor is his own affair" that "all Jews . . . suffer by each other's actions."[4]

The belief that one Jewish individual's behavior could affect the perception of all campus Jews was echoed by Jampel in the exchange below. His concern was not with radical politics but with "obnoxiousness and personal over-aggressiveness," behaviors he associated with Jews who were not yet "thoroughly American." His interlocutors pushed back with assertions that to be truly American, Jews needed to participate in defending democratic civilization—including rejecting group stereotypes and refusing to hide or apologize for one's Jewishness.

---

3. "Good Riddance of Bad Rubbish," *Michigan Daily News*, August 1, 1935, 1; Minutes of the Conference of the President and Deans, May 15, 1935, Conference of Deans (University of Michigan) records: 1920–68, box 1, Bentley Historical Library, University of Michigan, Ann Arbor, MI.
4. Bernard Heller, "Director's Column," *Bnai Brith Hillel News*, April 15, 1935, 1.

The stakes were high, as was awareness of the brewing crisis in Europe. At a moment that Hillel's student director Ronald Freedman (1907–2007) declared to be "a critical turning point in the history of civilization," Jews were needed in the battle for democratic values. They could not afford to contort themselves to meet the expectations of others. "This is no time for palsied shrinking in the corner," Freedman argued. "This is the time to display some of the stuff from which the prophets were made." Jampel also believed that the times were too fraught for missteps. He feared the results of entering an open society or campus without first securing the "vital armor" of language, clothing, and behavior that conformed to societal niceties. It took only "one unpleasant experience with a single Jew," he observed, to convince potentially sympathetic gentiles of the wisdom of Jew-hatred, breaking open the way to "the onslaught of a vicious and militant antisemitism."

◇◇

Ronald Freedman,[5] "Don't Hush Me!" *Bnai Brith Hillel*[6] *News,* January 1939

Source: Ronald Freedman, "Don't Hush Me!," *Bnai Brith Hillel News,* January 1939, 2. Bentley Historical Library, University of Michigan, Ann Arbor, MI. Reprinted by permission of Michigan Hillel.

There is current in Jewish life the fallacious notion that if all Jews could only be hushed up, if they would maintain a "dignified" silence, if they would completely separate themselves from the present social-economic-political world, all would be well. This view expressed in a recent editorial of the *Hillel News* is a very dangerous approach to our present problems.

In the first place, it is founded on the erroneous notion that antisemitism is a result of the Jewish personality as it is expressed in action today. It seems hardly necessary to restate the old argument that antisemitism arises out of socio-economic forces over which the Jew has no control. The fact that Jewish perse-

5. At the time of this exchange, Ronald Freedman (1907–2007) was a graduate student at UM and student director of the Bnai Brith Hillel Foundation. He later became a noted demographer and founder of the university's Population Studies Center.

6. In 1924, the Independent Order of Bnai Brith (see chapter 43, note 18) adopted the nascent Hillel campus organization, giving rise a year later to the Bnai Brith Hillel Foundation, a pluralistic Jewish student organization. Colleges and universities across the country swiftly created Hillel chapters UM's chapter, the fourth to be created nationally, was established in 1926. The organization sponsors social, cultural, and religious programming for Jewish and non-Jewish college students.

cution is at its height in areas and times of economic distress should provide a clue to the uninitiated that antisemitism is for the privileged few a convenient deflection of the unrest of the underprivileged. It needs only an examination of the identity of the antisemites to discover that the idea of Jewish personality defects as a cause of antisemitism is a rationalization. The causes of antisemitism are far deeper.

In the second place, the "hush-hush" school does not seem to realize that the present situation is more than a temporary deviation from the course of a perfect world. More and more we are realizing that we are at a critical turning point in the history of civilization. The lines of battle today are being drawn on the basis of a dichotomy of forces: on one side, the democratic forces, on the other side the anti-democratic forces (not all of which are fully fascist). The situation is not yet completely one of a black-and-white division, but is sufficiently so to justify a determined stand. We must remember that the forces that are fighting against democracy are also fighting against the entire social heritage to which the Jews have contributed so much and for which they have suffered so much. It is for the defense of this heritage of civilization more than for the defense of their own group that the Jews must join with other democratic groups today. This is no time for palsied shrinking in the corner. This is the time to display some of the stuff from which the prophets were made.

In the third place, the advocates of "hush" confuse dignity with silence. As Abe Zwerdling[7] pointed out at [a] recent Hillel Forum, dignity consists in living by and for the principles in which one honestly believes. No one will quarrel with the idea that reasonable decorum is necessary and desirable; nor will anyone deny some of the simpler social conventions that make social living possible. What must be denied is the view that to prevent any adverse criticism we must live completely innocuous conventional lives, live according to accepted patterns, hold accepted beliefs. That would indeed display a lack of dignity which is on the face of every cringing hypocrite. We must live not only in the dignity of good manners but also in the higher dignity of consistency with what we believe. Anything less is moral suicide. Anything less is to abandon religion.

7. Born in Ann Arbor, Michigan, Abraham Zwerdling (1914–1987) was the son of immigrants Osias (1878–1977) and Hannah Zwerdling (1882–1963). Abraham Zwerdling graduated from UM in 1935 and received a law degree from the university's law school in 1939. He practiced law in Detroit and Washington, becoming a prominent labor and civil rights lawyer. He served as general counsel for the United Automobile Workers and the American Federation of State, County, and Municipal Employees. Osias Zwerdling was a leading figure in the creation of Ann Arbor's organized Jewish community—including the local Beth Israel Congregation and, via the sponsorship of Bnai Brith, UM's Hillel chapter.

Morton Jampel,[8] "No, Not I!," *Bnai Brith Hillel News*, January 1939

Source: Morton Jampel, "No, Not I!," *Bnai Brith Hillel News*, January 1939, 2. Bentley Historical Library, University of Michigan, Ann Arbor, MI. Reprinted by permission of Michigan Hillel.

We were highly pleased to see an editorial recently printed in the *News* raise a great deal of criticism, but we were strongly annoyed by the interpretations and inopportune reading between the lines.

In reply to the above-printed letter and editorial that maintains our philosophy is that of "*Sha, sha, yid!*"[9]—a very dangerous philosophy. . . . We are the last ones to stifle an aggressive Jewry, one that realizes it must fight to stay alive. We are the last ones to say, "*Sha, sha, yid!*"

But we also refuse to say that "personal idiosyncrasies" are not responsible in some part for antisemitic feeling.

We are fully cognizant of the fact that antisemitism, like any racial hatred, is basically caused by economic competition. We in no way meant to deny that fact. But we still maintain that a great deal of Jewish hatred is aroused, especially in countries like the United States, where there is no Jew-baiting as in Germany, by personal aggressive characteristics that many Jews maintain (and that even the most liberal gentiles are wont to use for generalizations concerning Jewry in general). Such traits, as we see it, are basically and merely superficial.

There are many young gentiles, neither Jew-baiters nor liberals, who are willing and ready to consider the Jew a fellow human being in all ways his [sic] equal. But after one unpleasant experience with a single Jew the gentile leaves the borderline category and enters the class of potential antisemite. He is then ready material for men like [Joseph] Goebbels[10] and [Charles] Coughlin. . . .[11]

Jews are a people, we maintain, bound by much more than a common religion, but not racially, biologically one group. The traits . . . described as inher-

8. Morton Jampel (1920–1969) graduated from UM in 1940 and was the editor of *Bnai Brith Hillel News*.

9. Yiddish for "hush, hush Jew," analogous to the "hush-hush" phrasing in the previous document.

10. Joseph Goebbels (1897–1945) was a key deputy of Adolf Hitler (1889–1945), Nazi Germany's dictator, and served as the regime's minister of propaganda.

11. The Canadian-American Catholic priest Charles E. Coughlin (1891–1979), known as the "radio priest," was one of the most influential American religious figures of the 1930s and 1940s. Operating from his church, the Shrine of the Little Flower, in Royal Oak, Michigan, Coughlin hosted a popular weekly radio program that featured vehement anticommunist, antisemitic, and pro-Nazi views for a nationwide audience of tens of millions of listeners.

ent, we say are mere superficial characteristics of a few (possibly many) but not all; characteristics that should be eradicated.

Bernard Friedman,[12] "Mail Bag," *Bnai Brith Hillel News*, January 1939

Source: Bernard Friedman, "Mail Bag," *Bnai Brith Hillel News*, January 1939, 2. Bentley Historical Library, University of Michigan, Ann Arbor, MI. Reprinted by permission of Michigan Hillel.

To the Editor:

The editorial "The Mark of the Ghetto" in the Hillel *News* for November expresses the kind of attitude that has vitiated so many of the protests against the Nazi persecution of the Jews. The writer indicates that the reason for the pogrom is the assassination of [Ernst Eduard] vom Rath,[13] that if the Jewish people were a united nation, they could relieve their oppressed minority, that we are attacked because our religion doesn't conform with Christianity, and that finally, we can prevent this sort of thing if, individually, we conduct ourselves with circumspection and decorum and (this wasn't mentioned in the editorial, but it has so frequently been said to me along with the others, that I suspect it was intended) we must never, never engage in liberal activity because that makes it conspicuous. This strikes me as naïve to the point of being harmful and I should like to object item by item.

First, Goebbels himself admitted that an anti-Jewish drive with intent of confiscation was already planned before the killing of vom Rath. And anyway, surely we have observed enough of the doings of Nazi Germany to realize that the people are stirred up not by news, which isn't printed as such, but by whatever means the government chooses to employ to stir them up. Vom Rath, by the way, was not a Nazi ... and could have been massacred with his whole family by a delegation of Jewish communists direct from Moscow without Hitler's turning a hair, if he didn't happen to be ready to.

Second, third, and fourth, antisemitism is not caused by religious differ-

12. Bernard Friedman (1917–1994) was a member of the Class of 1937 at UM and was a graduate student in philosophy in 1939. He later joined the Columbia University faculty, where he served as an economics professor and associate dean of the Graduate School of Arts and Sciences.

13. The assassination in Paris of Nazi German diplomat Ernst Eduard vom Rath (1909–1938) on November 9, 1938, by the Polish Jewish teenager Herschel Grynszpan (1921–1945) served as the pretext for a wave of organized anti-Jewish violence across Germany known as Kristallnacht ("the night of broken glass"). Historians generally view Kristallnacht as a prelude to the Holocaust.

ences, nor by the personal idiosyncrasies of individual Jews . . . ; its source is in more basic economic and social set-ups, of which antisemitism is only one epiphenomenon and, however deeply it may touch us, not the worst of them. Antisemitism and persecution of all kinds will arise wherever there is reaction of the type of which Nazism is an extreme, and the only way to alleviate and finally to remove such persecution is to fight reaction wherever it occurs and to fight it not only as Jews but in unity with every other progressive force. The only way to fight antisemitism is to fight fascism in every form, to preserve and strengthen democracy in the United States and to see to it that the United States fulfills its duty as a democracy in exercising all its peaceful means together with other democracies to prevent fascism from spreading and to eliminate it where it exists.

Isaac Rabinowitz,[14] "Director's Column," *Bnai Brith Hillel News,* February 1939

Source: Isaac Rabinowitz, "Director's Column," *Bnai Brith Hillel News*, February 1939, 2-3. Bentley Historical Library, University of Michigan, Ann Arbor, MI. Reprinted by permission of Michigan Hillel.

The editor has invited me to comment upon his editorial "No, Not I!" in the January issue of the *News*. . . . There are at least two implications of Mr. Jampel's point of view with which I find myself in disagreement. . . .

First, there is the implication, a product of *selbst-hass* [German for "self-hatred"], that antisemitism is justified to the extent that some Jews are aggressive or do have unpleasant "personal idiosyncrasies." "I don't like these Jews myself," so the familiar argument runs, "and I can't blame gentiles for being antisemitic so long as there are Jews like them." What this really [means] is, "I would be antisemitic myself if I were a gentile; we Jews are despicable." And that, in turn, means: "How I wish I were not a Jew! How much better to look down than to be looked down upon, to be superior and not inferior!" Thus Jewish inferiority-feeling and the self-loathing which accompanies it are the psychological roots of this view and are responsible for much of the intensity with which the attitude is maintained. For certainly the argument that antisemitism is justified to the extent that Jews have unpleasant "personal idiosyncrasies" is meretricious in its logic. To argue so would be to argue that we all

14. Isaac Rabinowitz (1909–1988) earned a PhD in 1932 from Yale University, served as the director of Hillel at UM (1935–40), and taught biblical and Hebrew studies at Cornell University (1957–75).

... know, universally and unfailingly, what a pleasant personal characteristic is. On such value judgments, however, there seems to be a wide variety of opinion. How then can one be sure that what one gentile thinks is a "personal aggressive characteristic," and therefore unpleasant, another gentile will not admire, or think to be humility? But even if there were such fundamental agreement, logic and ethics would combine to require us to condemn what is vicious and to extol what is virtuous, but they would certainly not admit of justifying blanket hatred of a human being on the ground of some reprehensible habits; for a human being, after all, has many habits and characteristics, not all of them reprehensible, and has, moreover, shown that he has the ability to change his habits. And if this be true in the case of a single human being, how much the more in the case of an entire group?

To all this, rejoinder may be made that ... gentiles do judge us by the bad habits and characteristics of some of us. This, however, is only true when antisemitism is already a configuration within a given social, economic, and political pattern.... The fantastic nature of the argument is further disclosed when we turn it around: whoever heard any gentile say he was a philosemite because he like[d] the way Jews combed their hair, wore their clothes, spoke English, etc.?

The second implication of the editorial with which I should like to deal is the proposition that bad habits among Jews are bad because they bring antisemitism down upon us. Of all the criteria which have been used to distinguish good from evil, surely this is the queerest not to say the least useful. It is very often the case that those who are most vociferous in proclaiming the view ... that antisemitism is attributable to the evil characteristics of the Jews, are not at all interested in combating evil itself. It is a curious coincidence ... that this view of antisemitism emanates most frequently from circles which are not averse to the exploitation of labor or even to the non-employment of Jews. And ironically enough, such folk defend their failure to hire co-religionists by the very same arguments which they use in advancing the view that antisemitism is caused by the badness of the Jews, i.e. "personal aggressiveness," "unmannerliness," "loudness," etc....

My conclusion? Fight all evil, including antisemitism; judge each man as though you were standing in his place; and strive after the good.

Morton Jampel, "For the People and of the People," *Bnai Brith Hillel News*, February 1939

Source: Morton Jampel, "For the People and of the People," *Bnai Brith Hillel News*, February 1939, 2–3. Bentley Historical Library, University of Michigan, Ann Arbor, MI. Reprinted by permission of Michigan Hillel.

The controversy we innocently started several issues back rages on! First a letter to the editor, then a rebuttal by Ronald Freedman, student director of the foundation, and now a refutation by Dr. [Isaac] Rabinowitz, director of the foundation. . . .

Dr. Rabinowitz bases his refutation of our previous editorial on two points, and we will treat [both of] them separately.

We object first to the deductions made from our statement that some Jews are obnoxiously aggressive. The charge that this is a product of *selbst-hass* and should be interpreted as meaning "I don't like these Jews myself, I would be antisemitic myself if I were a gentile, How I wish I were not a Jew!" is undeniably an *argumentum ad hominem* and must be rebutted as such.

Our statement (a product of *selbst-lieb*) [incorrect German for "self-love"] should be interpreted as meaning, "I don't like to see these obnoxious Jews hurting themselves. I am one of them, and being glad of it, feel I have the right to advise them to adopt means I happen to think best for preparing for the onslaught of a vicious and militant antisemitism."

This we hope clears up the misunderstandings concerning the actual meaning beneath the words. . . .

Then, the charge is made that our argument justifies antisemitism since we say attacks of antisemites have some logical basis. We never said that. We said that when the Jew does behave in a manner obnoxious to certain superficial American standards he is laying himself open to attack. That in no way justifies the attack, which is first and foremost barbaric and bigoted.

But that's the situation. The Jew is in the arena now, and he can't refuse to wear vital armor because the armor is artificial protection. Not if he hopes to survive.

As to just what these standards of behavior are—well, we all know what is meant by obnoxiousness and personal over-aggressiveness. . . . To put it tersely, when we talk about obnoxious (to the gentiles looking for a chance to criticize) Jews on campus, we mean that fraction of the Jewish student population that talks with a European Jewish intonation, that is loud, yes vulgar to the gentile, in dress, manner, and language. . . . There is absolutely no reason why American-born-and-bred boys and girls shouldn't be thoroughly American in behavior and habits. The truth may hurt, but it is our unpleasant duty to do the telling. We trust it is understood what is meant by American habits and manners.

Then the statement is made that gentiles will judge us only by our bad habits, by the exceptions, only when the existing social, economic, and political order is such that antisemitism is a part of it. Exactly! And that is just the set-up in this country now, although the antisemitism has not yet reached a vicious or militant form. Therefore, we say that the mark, unreasonable as it may seem, must be toed, as preparation to the struggle that will decide whether or not this country is to have a vicious antisemitism.

The criticism could then be made ... that this oppressing the Jew, is doing the job of the antisemite for him. This we deny. Such self-discipline as we prescribe we suggest as a means to an end. . . . Our advice is analogous to a rule of rigid silence imposed on an army preparing to advance on the enemy. The rank-and-file soldier may not want to be silent and [may] cry "Fascism!" when restrained. But the noise of one man would make the whole regiment vulnerable.

There is a strong distinction to be maintained between the vicious "Sha, sha, yid!" doctrine of those Jews, who feel themselves unfortunately a part of a race that is causing them only grief, and the doctrine of the Jew who says, "Will you please shut up while our army is marching! You'll gum [up] the works before we're ready to attack!" (And incidentally, this coming attack is not as figurative as it may seem, being the inevitable and ultimate conflict between fascism and liberalism.)

This we feel is the crux of the entire situation. The strong similarity between the condescending Jew who nervously tries to squelch his noisy brethren, and the Jew's Jew who is squelching his brethren so that they will be better prepared to fight against antisemitism and for freedom is a similarity that must not be confused. Suspiciousness and fear will readily confuse the latter with the former.

Dr. Rabinowitz's conclusion is fight all evil! Right you are, Dr. Rabinowitz! And fight it we will! Fight so that a Jew can be a Jew, and as aggressive and obnoxious a Jew as he wishes to be. But we cannot go to the battle until our army learns to march in step, wear the same uniform, and obey the discipline vital to success. Such orders coming from a fascist would mean something dangerous, something to be suspected. But we trust our motives are not questioned.

The essential difference, then, appears to be that we suggest eradicating the superficial obnoxiousness of the Jew before we can attack the evil of antisemitism itself, while Dr. Rabinowitz says that such a program is not only dangerous but actually is self-destructive. This contention we fail to see. We will let the matter rest there, and in future editorials will offer constructive suggestions for the step the Jew must take after his army is disciplined.

That will either prove the validity of this thesis or label us reactionary and false.

31

"ENSURING OUR FUTURE"

The Creation of the Emergency Committee for Zionist Affairs (1939)

◇◇◇

MARK A. RAIDER

The year 1939 was a crucial turning point in world and Jewish history. As war loomed, the Twenty-First Zionist Congress convened in August in Geneva, Switzerland. Caught between the millstones of Nazi Germany's persecution of European Jewry and the British government's antipathy to the Zionist movement, the congress decried the malevolent Hitler regime and lamented the British White Paper's proposal to severely curtail Jewish immigration to the Yishuv (Palestine's pre-state Jewish community) and establish "an independent Palestinian state" with the Jewish population fixed at a one-third minority.[1] The center of Zionist political authority now shifted from England, where Chaim Weizmann (1874–1952), had led the movement since the Balfour Declaration (1917),[2] to Jerusalem, where David Ben-Gurion (1886–1973)[3] presided over the labor movement–led Jewish Agency executive. In parallel, American Zionist leaders, seeking to rally American Jewish support for the embattled Yishuv and the campaign for Jewish statehood, created the Emergency Committee for Zionist Affairs (ECZA).

The document reprinted below recounts the launch of the ECZA and highlights American Zionism's transnational scope. It underscores the grave challenges faced by American Jewish leaders who sought to protect endangered Jewish communities in Europe and Palestine, and it highlights the fraught and perilous context in which American Zionists operated. American Zionist groups, which held various worldviews spanning the ideological and religious spectrum, traditionally worked in separate social and cultural spheres. The exi-

---

1. "Memorandum by the Chief of the Division of Near Eastern Affairs (Murray) to the Secretary of State," May 15, 1939, 867N.01/1599, in *Foreign Relations of the United States: Diplomatic Papers*, 1939, vol. IV, The Far East, The Near East and Africa (Washington, D.C.: Government Printing Office, 1955), 752–53.

2. See chapter 22, note 16.

3. See chapter 39, note 28.

gencies of wartime, however, prompted them to band together and establish the ECZA as a nonpartisan umbrella vehicle. Aimed at harnessing American Jewry's economic resources and cultivating the goodwill of American society at large, the ECZA sought to centralize the political capital of the Zionist movement in the United States. As was the case during World War I, when Louis D. Brandeis (1856–1941) and Julian W. Mack (1866–1943) led a Zionist coalition that helped govern American Jewish affairs and worked closely with the administration of President Woodrow Wilson (1856–1924), the ECZA sought to generate American support for the Zionist aims in Palestine and shape American Jewry's wartime agenda.

The ECZA (renamed the American Emergency Committee for Zionist Affairs in January 1942 and the American Zionist Emergency Council in the fall of 1943) initially elected Rabbi Stephen S. Wise (1874–1949) as its chairman. Composed of twenty-four members representing four major American Zionist groups—the centrist Zionist Organization of America (ZOA), the centrist Hadassah women's group, the labor-oriented Poalei Zion party, and the religious Mizrachi party—the ECZA included Nahum Goldmann (1895–1982) of the Jewish Agency in an ex officio capacity as well as nonvoting representatives of the communist Hashomer Hatzair party (which called for a binational Jewish-Arab state), the right-wing Revisionist group (which advocated a Jewish state on both sides of the Jordan River), and the Left Poalei Zion (a Marxist offshoot of Poalei Zion). As the official wartime voice of the Zionist movement outside of the Yishuv, the ECZA generally echoed the demands of the Jewish Agency and called for easing British White Paper restrictions and the creation of an independent Jewish military force in Palestine. It also mounted a nationwide campaign in support of Zionist-led relief and rescue efforts, and it spurred the creation of the non-Jewish and pro-Zionist American Palestine Committee in 1941 and the Christian Council on Palestine in 1942.

As the war unfolded, the ECZA collaborated with other American Jewish groups, particularly the nonpartisan American Jewish Joint Distribution Committee and the Orthodox-sponsored Vaad Hazalah (Rescue Council), to rescue Jews trapped in Axis-occupied Europe. After news of the Holocaust was publicly verified in the fall of 1942, American Jews steadily gravitated toward an activist and combative agenda centered on rescue, relief, and postwar reconstruction. In 1943, Weizmann, disappointed by what he perceived as the ECZA's slow pace and passivity, proposed reorganizing the group under the leadership of Rabbi Abba Hillel Silver (1893–1963). Silver was highly critical of Wise's faith in the administration of President Franklin D. Roosevelt (1882–1945), and his militant anti-British posture clashed with Wise's tempered political strategy. Long-suppressed tensions between the men surfaced, and the ECZA became engulfed in a public political feud. The conflict, which underscored a generational rift in American Zionism's ranks, anticipated American Jewry's emerging pro-Zionist consensus. It was ultimately resolved in 1943 at the American Jewish Conference, a wartime national plenary session over which the ECZA leadership—like the Brandeis-Mack group at the American Jewish Congress (1918)—had considerable sway. In the event, a broad coalition of Zionist and pro-Zionist forces crystallized around Silver, and the American Jewish Conference adopted an unprecedented resolution calling for the establishment of a Jewish commonwealth in Palestine. The latter signaled a watershed in American Jewish life, as Zionism came into view as the driving political force of the hour. Thereafter, Silver solidified his control of the ECZA (soon renamed the American Zionist Emergency Council, as noted above) and played a dominant role in the American Zionist campaign to win public sympathy and U.S. Congressional support for Jewish statehood. He worked closely with Ben-Gurion and other Yishuv leaders to accomplish this objective, and he represented the Zionist movement at the postwar deliberations of the United Nations. With the establishment of the State of Israel in 1948, the American Zionist Emergency Council's influence waned, and its functions were assumed by new organizations—including, in due course, the American Zionist Committee Public Affairs Committee, later renamed the American Israel Public Affairs Committee (AIPAC).[4]

◇◇

Transcript of Meeting of the Emergency Committee for Zionist Affairs, September 18, 1939

Source: Minutes of Inter-Party Committee Meeting, September 18, 1939, Stephen S. Wise Papers, 1874–1949, P-134, box 99, folder: American Zionist Emergency Council (I), American Jewish Historical Society, New York City.

Minutes of Inter-Party Committee Held on Tuesday, September 18, 1939, at 4:00 PM at the Offices of the Z.O.A.[5] 111 Fifth Avenue, New York.

4. See chapter 39.

5. The Zionist Organization of America (ZOA), established in 1898 as the Federation of American Zionists (FAZ), originated as an umbrella group of the fledgling Zionist movement in the United States. In 1918, the American Jewish jurists Louis D. Brandeis (1856–1941) and Julian W. Mack (1866–1943) assumed leadership of the FAZ. During World War I, a talented group of Brandeis loyalists known as the "Brandeis-Mack group" transformed the ZOA into a nationwide political organization with considerable political clout. In 1921, at the ZOA's national convention in Cleveland, Ohio, Brandeis and his adherents, who differed from Chaim Weizmann

Present: Dr. Solomon Goldman,[6] presiding; Leon Gellman;[7] Louis Lipsky;[8] Mrs. Bertha Schoolman;[9] Dr. Abba Hillel Silver;[10] Robert Szold;[11] David

---

(see note 30) and the world leadership in favoring a policy of private economic investment in Palestine, withdrew from the ZOA. Thereafter, Louis Lipsky (see note 8), representing Weizmann's American supporters, became ZOA president. The Lipsky administration was unable to sustain the ZOA's previous growth, but it successfully negotiated the 1924 merger of the major annual Zionist fund-raising efforts that led to the creation of the United Palestine Appeal (see note 39). In 1929, the Brandeis-Mack group regained leadership of the ZOA. The ZOA was never a mass organization, but together with the Hadassah Women's Zionist Organization (see note 23), it generally represented the mainstream of American Jewish opinion regarding Zionism and the campaign for Jewish statehood.

6. At the time of this meeting, the Russian-born Conservative rabbi Solomon Goldman (1893–1953) of Congregation Anshe Emet in Chicago, Illinois, served as both co-chairman of the United Jewish Appeal and president of the ZOA (1938–40). Closely associated with Stephen S. Wise (see note 13) and the American Jewish Congress, Goldman played a central role in wartime Zionist and interfaith activity in the United States.

7. The Russian-born Zionist activist and journalist Leon Gellman (1887–1973) served as president (1935–39) of the American branch of the Mizrachi religious Zionist party (see note 25). In 1949, Gellman immigrated to Israel, where he became chairman of the World Mizrachi Organization.

8. The Zionist leader, journalist, author, and translator Louis Lipsky (1876–1963) was managing editor of the *American Hebrew* and, under the aegis of the ZOA, editor of the *Maccabean* (later called the *New Palestine*). He was an important conduit between American Zionism and the secular press in the United States. During the Brandeis-Weizmann clash, Lipsky supported Weizmann concerning financial support and control of the Yishuv. He served as ZOA president (1921–29) and in 1929 played a key role in the creation of the Expanded Jewish Agency, a short-term effort to open the Jewish Agency's governing bodies to non-Zionist American Jewish representation and leadership.

9. The Hadassah leader Bertha Schoolman (1897–1974) was a Jewish educator, Zionist activist, and member of the Actions Committee of the World Zionist Organization (WZO). Schoolman played a critical role in the Hadassah Medical Organization, the Jewish National Fund, and Youth Aliyah. She was a founder of Neve Hadassah Youth Village in Palestine.

10. The Lithuanian-born Rabbi Abba Hillel Silver (1893–1963), a leader of Reform Judaism and Zionism in the United States, was a founder and co-chairman of the United Jewish Appeal (see chapter 43, note 29) and president of the United Palestine Appeal. Silver advocated a combative Jewish political agenda to achieve Zionist aims in Palestine. During World War II, he worked with David Ben-Gurion to oust Chaim Weizmann and Stephen S. Wise from positions of leadership in the world and American Zionist organizations, respectively. Although Silver was generally inclined to collaborate with Ben-Gurion's Labor-led WZO coalition, he was also sympatheic to the right-wing Revisionist Zionist party.

11. Robert Szold (1899–1977), a Zionist activist and lawyer, was aligned with the Brandeis-Mack group. He served as chairman (1929–32) of the ZOA administration. In 1942 he became an officer of the American Emergency Committee for Zionist Affairs.

Wertheim;[12] [Dr.] Stephen S. Wise;[13] Samuel Caplan,[14] secretary; Hayim Greenberg;[15] and Morris Margulies.[16]

Minutes of the Last Meeting: In connection with the minutes of the meeting of September 10th, Dr. Wise stated that upon receipt of a cable from Dr. Nahum Goldmann[17] asking for 8,000 pounds to charter a Yugoslavian boat for transporting stranded delegates in Geneva, he had been authorized to negotiate with the JDC [Joint Distribution Committee] to secure these funds. He reported that the JDC was prepared to render assistance which, however, was made unneces-

12. The Rumanian-born David Wertheim (1898–1953) served as secretary general (1930–45) of the American branch of the Labor Zionist party. After World War II, he served as the Hebrew Immigrant Aid Society's representative in Israel.

13. A key member of the Brandeis-Mack group, the Hungarian-born American Jewish and Zionist leader Rabbi Stephen S. Wise (1874–1949) founded the American Jewish Congress (1918); the Jewish Institute of Religion (1922), which merged in 1950 with Hebrew Union College; and the World Jewish Congress (1936). He served as president of the ZOA and the United Palestine Appeal. A leading liberal voice of the American Jewish establishment, during World War II Wise found himself in the challenging position of serving as an intermediary among American Jewry, the administration of President Franklin D. Roosevelt (1882–1945), and the Zionist movement. He vigorously opposed Vladimir Jabotinsky's (1880–1940) right-wing Revisionist Zionist party—including its American offshoot (known as the Bergson group), led by Hillel Kook (1915–2001), who operated under the name of Peter Bergson. At the American Jewish Conference (1943), together with Weizmann, Wise was dislodged from his dominant position in Zionist affairs by Ben-Gurion and Silver.

14. The Russian-born Samuel Caplan (1895–1969), a journalist and Zionist activist, edited the *New Palestine* and the *Congress Weekly*, the biweekly periodicals of the American Jewish Congress.

15. The Russian-born Labor Zionist leader Hayim Greenberg (1887–1953) served as editor of the American periodicals *Der yidisher kemfer* (The Jewish militant) and *Jewish Frontier* (1934–53). A noted Jewish public intellectual, Greenberg was Labor Zionism's unofficial spokesman outside of Palestine (and, later, Israel). During World War II, when Wise and Silver clashed over the direction of the American Zionist Emergency Council and resigned from their co-leadership positions, Greenberg served as the council's acting head. He played a key role at the Biltmore Conference (1942) and the American Jewish Conference (1943), and he is credited with winning the support of the Latin American delegations to the United Nations for the creation of the State of Israel (1948).

16. The Ukrainian-born Zionist activist and journalist Morris Margulies (1888–1967) was one of the organizers of the American Jewish Congress (1918) and the Keren Hayesod (1921; see note 39) and served as the ZOA's national secretary (1932–42).

17. In 1936, the Zionist leader Nahum Goldmann (1895–1982), together with Stephen S. Wise, founded the World Jewish Congress. Following the outbreak of World War II, Goldmann took up residence in New York City. He spent extended periods of time in Washington, D.C., during the war as a representative of the Jewish Agency for Palestine.

sary by the receipt of a subsequent cable from Dr. Nahum Goldmann advising that "Jugoslavia boat unnecessary as Italian boat sailing."[18]

The minutes were also corrected in respect to eliminating the paragraph dealing with the $500 advanced by Mrs. Alexander Lamport[19] in Geneva for the reason that this amount was not an obligation of the "Committee of Ten" but had to be repaid by the Washington Bureau or the Zionist parties.[20]

Organization of Committee: On behalf of the Poalei Zion,[21] Mr. Wertheim declared his objection to including official non-Zionists[22] in the committee and

18. The reference is to delegates to the Twenty-First World Zionist Congress, held in Geneva in August 16–25, 1939. Following Nazi Germany's invasion of Poland on September 1, 1939, British liners canceled their Atlantic sailings, leaving over 150 Palestinian Jewish delegates, 100 Polish Jewish delegates, and 100 American Jewish delegates stranded. To manage the crisis, the Joint Distribution Committee established a special office to assist the American and Palestinian delegates, most of whom left Europe on American and French liners. Goldmann interceded with the Italian consul to obtain passage for the Polish Jewish delegation via Italy. See "Americans To Get U.S. Cruiser If No Other Way Is Open," *Jewish Post*, September 1, 1939, 1; "Queen Mary, President Roosevelt Bring Jewish Leaders from Europe," *Jewish Post*, September 8, 1939, 1; "150 Leave Geneva for Palestine," *JTA Daily News Bulletin*, September 20, 1939, 5.

19. Esther H. Lamport (1897–1993), national treasurer of the Hadassah Women's Zionist Organization of America (see note 23), was married to Alexander Lamport (1886–1961), a wealthy textile manufacturer whose business specialized in synthetics.

20. The "Committee of Ten" included Nahum Goldmann, Louis Lipsky, Stephen S. Wise, Abba Hillel Silver, Robert Szold, Henry Monsky (see note 27), Cyrus Adler (see chapter 16, note 3), and one representative each from Hadassah, Poalei Zion, and Mizrahi.

21. The socialist Zionist party Poalei Zion (Workers of Zion) originated in tsarist Russia in the late nineteenth century and sought to combine the class interests of the Jewish proletariat with political Zionism and the realization of socialism. The American branch of the party was transplanted to the United States in the early twentieth century with the mass immigration of eastern European Jews to American shores.

22. In the pre-state era, American Jews who rejected the concept of Jewish sovereignty but supported the continued development of Jewish life in the Yishuv were referred to as non-Zionists. Meanwhile, those who identified as "anti-Zionists"—for either religious or ideological reasons—flatly opposed all efforts to bolster the Jewish nationalist cause. The American Jewish Committee (AJC), established in 1906 by affluent American Jews of central European ancestry, originally disparaged Zionism. Under the leadership of the New York lawyer Louis Marshall (1856–1929), it gradually adopted a supportive stance toward the Yishuv. In 1929, Marshall and Weizmann negotiated the creation of the Expanded Jewish Agency so as to include a sizable element of non-Zionist communal leaders and pursue joint fund-raising efforts. Despite such cooperation, the AJC remained opposed to the Zionist movement's political aims, and in 1943 it withdrew from the American Jewish Conference when the latter endorsed the creation of a Jewish commonwealth in Palestine. The breach between the AJC and Zionism was not healed until 1947, when the former changed its position and supported the United Nations partition plan.

requested that all Zionist parties be given two representatives on the committee instead of one. Mrs. Schoolman, on behalf of Hadassah,[23] felt that if non-Zionists were to be included, first place should be given to non-Zionist members of the Jewish Agency Executive[24] resident in New York. Mr. Gellman, on behalf of Mizrachi,[25] also objected to the inclusion of non-Zionists and concurred in the view that the parties should be allowed two representatives each.

23. The Hadassah Women's Zionist Organization of America began as the autonomous women's auxiliary of the ZOA but became a fully independent entity in 1933. Expanding its medical and health-related activity in the Yishuv—activity that began with the creation of the American Zionist Medical Unit (1918) and the Hadassah Nurses' Training School (1921)—Hadassah grew to provide a wide range of services, including infant welfare stations, school lunch programs, youth villages, and communal health and recreation centers. In 1936, the organization officially opened the Hadassah School of Nursing at the Hebrew University of Jerusalem, and in 1939 it established the Rothschild-Hadassah University Hospital, the Yishuv's first major medical research and care center. In the pre-state era, Hadassah, which became the largest American Zionist group and a fund-raising powerhouse, boasted a talented array of leaders including Szold, Alice Seligsberg (1873–1940), Irma (Rama) Lindheim (1886–1948), Zipporah "Zip" Szold (1888–1979), Rose G. Jacobs (1888–1975), Rose L. Halperin (1896–1978), Judith G. Epstein (1895–1988), and Tamar de Sola Pool (1890–1981).

24. The Jewish Agency was legally recognized by the League of Nations in the Mandate for Palestine as "a public body for the purpose of advising and cooperating with the Administration of Palestine in such economic, social and other matters as may affect the establishment of the Jewish national home and the interests of the Jewish population in Palestine, and subject always to the control of the Administration, to assist and take part in the development of the country" (Paul Mendes-Flohr and Jehuda Reinharz, eds., *The Jew in the Modern World: A Documentary History*, 3d ed. [New York: Oxford University Press, 2011], 670–71). In its first decade, the Jewish Agency was headed by Weizmann. Per an agreement ratified by the Sixteenth Zionist Congress (1929), the organization was reconstituted as the "Enlarged Jewish Agency" with an executive council ("one half shall be persons nominated by the non-Zionist members of the Council, and the remainder shall be persons nominated by the Zionist Organisation") forming "a single whole, with a collective responsibility to the Council" (Resolutions of the 16th Zionist Congress, Zurich, July 28th to August 11th, 1929, With a Summary Report of the Proceedings [London: Central Office of the Zionist Organisation, 1930], 14). Starting in the mid-1930s, the Jewish Agency was dominated by a Labor-led coalition under Ben-Gurion. With the establishment of the State of Israel in 1948, the Jewish Agency was reconstituted as a nongovernmental organization responsible for many of Israel's overseas activities, including education, fund-raising, and *aliyah*.

25. The religious Zionist movement Mizrachi (a Hebrew acronym for *merkaz ruhani*, meaning both "spiritual center" and "eastward") was created in Vilna in 1902 under the leadership of Rabbi Isaac Jacob Reines (1839–1915). Mizrachi dedicated itself to working within the structure of the WZO and promoting a Jewish nationalist agenda according to Orthodox Jewish values and principles. It proclaimed the slogan "the Land of Israel for the people of Israel according to the Torah of Israel." In 1939, the American branch of Mizrachi had 75,000 members.

Dr. Goldman explained that it was the intention to invite Dr. [Cyrus] Adler[26] and Mr. [Henry] Monsky[27] as individuals and not as representatives of non-Zionist groups. Mr. Lipsky, Dr. Wise, and Dr. Silver stated that there was no objection to giving the parties two representatives, but it was to be understood that the committee was functioning as the representative in the United States of the World Zionist Executive[28] and its decisions should be regarded as having within the scope of its authority the same binding effect as the decisions of the Executive of the Jewish Agency.

It was thereupon agreed:

(1) To allow the Zionist parties two representatives each on the committee.
(2) To invite Dr. Adler and Mr. Monsky to serve on the committee; Mr. Wertheim and Mrs. Schoolman being recorded in the negative.
(3) To postpone the decision with regard to the three non-Zionist members of the Jewish Agency Executive pending the arrival of Dr. [Chaim] Weizmann.[29]

26. See chapter 16, note 3.

27. The Russian-born Henry Monsky (1890–1947), a lawyer and American Jewish communal leader, served as president (1938–47) of the Bnai Brith organization. Despite Monsky's personal attachment to Zionism, he was nonpartisan in his communal activity—which included holding leadership positions in the Joint Distribution Committee, the National Conference of Christians and Jews, the Jewish Welfare Board, and the United Palestine Appeal. At the height of World War II, he played a key role at the American Jewish Conference (1943) and helped win the support of non-Zionists for a postwar vision of a Jewish commonwealth in Palestine. In 1945, he was a consultant to the U.S. delegation to the organizing conference of the United Nations.

28. The World Zionist Organization (wzo) was created in 1897 by the First Zionist Congress in Basle, Switzerland. The wzo was charged with the responsibility of coordinating and implementing the political, financial, and development strategies of the Zionist movement in the diaspora and Palestine. In time, the composition of the executive of the wzo became nearly identical with that of the Jewish Agency for Palestine. In practical terms, the former reflected the political priorities of the Zionist parties, while the latter served as a public body that managed the relationship between the British Mandatory government and the Yishuv. At the time of this meeting, Ben-Gurion was chairman of both executives (1935–48).

29. The Russian-born Chaim Weizmann (1874–1952), architect of the British government's Balfour Declaration (1917) that expressed "sympathy with Jewish Zionist aspirations in Palestine" (see chapter 22, note 16), was arguably Zionism's most important leader in the early decades of the twentieth century. Weizmann, who from 1892 to 1901 had trained in Germany and Switzerland as a scientist and emigrated in 1904 to England to assume a post at the University of Manchester, devised a synthetic method for producing acetone used by the British government to produce munitions during World War I. After the war, Weizmann assumed the leadership of both the Jewish Agency and the wzo, serving as president of the latter (1920–31). Following the White Paper of 1930, in which the British government withdrew its support from the Zionist movement, Weizmann resigned in protest from his position. When the Seventeenth Zionist

It was decided that the official name of the committee be "The Emergency Committee for Zionist Affairs"; further, that this committee take over the American Zionist Bureau at Washington, and that a subcommittee be named to prepare a budget for the next three months.

DR. WEIZMANN'S COMING: Dr. Silver raised the question of whether the time was now propitious for Dr. Weizmann to come to the U.S. in view of conditions which would not be favorable for the launching of the proposed loan,[30] and more particularly, in view of the special session of Congress to revise the neutrality laws.[31]

It was agreed to send the following cable to Dr. Weizmann:

LIPSKY SILVER WISE PREPARING FOR YOUR COMING BUT ALL BELIEVE ADVISABLE DELAY YOUR VISIT UNTIL SPECIAL CONGRESS SESSION BUSINESS CONCLUDED — SOLOMON GOLDMAN

DR. NAHUM GOLDMANN'S COMING: The chairman reported that he had received a cable from Dr. Nahum Goldmann, who is now in Paris, stating that he was awaiting our decision as to whether he should now come to the U.S.[32] It was decided that consideration of this matter should be deferred to a later meeting.

Congress (1931) convened it elected Nahum Sokolow (1859–1936) to serve as WZO president (1931–35). In 1935, with the backing of the Labor Zionist movement, Weizmann returned to the presidency of the WZO but his political stature and power was diminished. In 1948 he became Israel's first president.

30. At this juncture, Weizmann was making plans for an extended stay in the United States, starting in early October. The possibility of raising private funds and/or a U.S. government loan to assist with the resettlement of European Jewish refugees in Palestine was under consideration.

31. On September 21, 1939, President Franklin D. Roosevelt addressed a joint session of Congress and called for a revision of U.S. neutrality laws enacted in the early 1930s by isolationist forces, which asserted that American munitions manufacturers and banks had embroiled the country in World War I. Roosevelt reassured Congress and the public that he opposed entering World War II, but he argued that efforts to legislate neutrality undermined American interests. "Destiny first made us, with our sister nations on this hemisphere, joint heirs of European culture," Roosevelt stated. "Fate seems now to compel us to assume the task of helping to maintain in the Western World a citadel wherein that civilization may be kept alive" (quoted in Alonzo L. Hamby, *Man of Destiny: FDR and the Making of the American Century* [New York: Basic Books, 2015], 303). Following several weeks of stormy debate, Congress passed new legislation. Signed into law by Roosevelt on November 4, 1939, it permitted Great Britain and other allies under siege by Nazi Germany to purchase American munitions.

32. Acting on behalf of Weizmann, Goldmann — who was stationed in Geneva — conducted discussions with the French government about the status of European Jewish refugees and the possibility of forming Jewish military units (including American Jewish volunteers) under

"Sept. 12 [1939]

GOLDMAN LIPSKY SILVER WISE

NEW YORK

WEIZMANN DOUBTLESS TRANSMITTED YOU OUR APPRECIATION
POSITION URGENT REQUIREMENTS STOP EXTRAORDINARY FINAN-
CIAL EFFORT IMPERATIVE PLEASE CABLE YOUR ESTIMATE IMMEDI-
ATELY REALISABLE FUNDS FROM ALLOCATIONS COMMITTEE UJA[33]
LOAN ON ACCOUNT FUTURE RECEIPTS STOP ACCEPT YOUR SUGGES-
TION FUNDS BE RETAINED OUR ACCOUNT NEW YORK TO BE REMITTED
ACCORDING OUR TELEGRAPHIC REQUESTS WOULD APPRECIATE
YOUR CABLING US WEEKLY BALANCES REGULARLY STOP IMPORTANT
SHOULD BE REALISED WE MUST COPE 6500 MAAPILIM[34] LANDED
OFFICIALLY LAST QUARTER 1200 RELEASED HANDED JEWISH AGENCY
ONLY TODAY WHOM OF 650 CZECHS ALSO HOPE UTILISE FULLY OVER

French command. These discussions became moot in June 1940, after France fell to Nazi Germany.

33. Despite the widespread economic suffering of American Jewry during the Great Depression, philanthropy remained a central feature of American Jewish communal life throughout the 1930s. Meanwhile, Zionist groups, alarmed by the drop in American Jewish funding for the Yishuv—the combined income of the WZO's fund-raising arms, Keren Hayesod (see note 39) and the Jewish National Fund (JNF) (see note 38), dipped to $339,000 in 1933—waged a campaign to increase the proportion allotted to Palestine by the countrywide drives of the Council of Jewish Federations and Welfare Funds. In their attempt to increase the allocations to the Yishuv, Zionists encountered opposition from many major Jewish philanthropists who generally favored European relief and distrusted Zionist projects. In 1939, the United Palestine Appeal began independent national campaigns, with Silver as its principal tactician and orator. In 1939 it reached an agreement with the Joint Distribution Committee, which led to the creation of the United Jewish Appeal (UJA; see chapter 43, note 29). The UJA raised $7,000,000 in 1939 and $14,500,000 in 1940. However, the diminishing allocation to Palestine caused a rupture in 1941, which was healed by a 63:37 division of funds. During the 1940s, the UJA raised $638,000,000, and ultimately as much as 75 percent of its income went to Palestine. These sums established the UJA as one of the greatest voluntary fund-raising organizations ever known.

34. The Hebrew term maapilim, used to describe European Jewish refugees who immigrated to Palestine illegally in the 1930s and 1940s in defiance of the British Mandatory regime, derives from the biblical account of Israelite spies who entered the Land of Israel (Num. 13–14) and reported to Moses: "We came to the land to which you sent us; it flows with milk and honey" (Num. 13:27). An estimated 30,000 maapilim entered Palestine in 1938–39, including 10,000 in the few months preceding this meeting.

5000 CERTIFICATES[35] WHOSE HOLDERS YET UNARRIVED INCLUDING
1500 STILL IN GREATER GERMANY FOR WHOSE DEPARTURE ADMIS-
SION SPECIAL FACILITIES BEING SECURED THEIR ABSORPTION PRES-
ENT CIRCUMSTANCES WILL ENTAIL ADDITIONAL EXTRAORDINARY
EXPENDITURE TRUST YOU WILL DO UTMOST STOP REGARDING FOOD
VERY GRATEFUL YOUR OFFER POSITION FOLLOWING AMPLE FOOD-
STOCKS AVAILABLE FOR MONTHS NEGOTIATING GOVERNMENT RE-
GARDING ADDITIONAL PURCHASES NEIGHBOURING COUNTRIES STOP
PRESENT ACUTE DIFFICULTIES CAUSED FIRST BY PANIC CONSEQUENT
HOARDING WITHHOLDING OF SUPPLIES RISE PRICES SECONDLY BY
RESTRICTION CREDITS INSISTENCE CASH PAYMENTS MAKING POSI-
TION POORER PEOPLE UNTENABLE STOP IN ABSENCE QUOTATIONS
UNABLE JUDGE WHETHER PURCHASES AMERICA WORTHWHILE OUR
PRIMARY NEED IS ESTABLISHMENT STORES FOR SALE AT COSTPRICE
TO NEEDY FOR THIS REQUIRE SPECIAL FUNDS WHAT WE NEED IS
MONEY NOT GOODS EAGERLY AWAITING YOUR REPLY
  KAPLAN[36] EXECUTIVE"

"Sept. 14, 1939
ZIONIST ORGANIZATION AND UNITED PALESTINE APPEAL[37]
NEW YORK
JEWISH AGENCY JERUSALEM REPORTS GENERAL SITUATION MOST
GRAVELY AFFECTING ECONOMIC POSITION YISHUV VIZ DISTURBANCE

---

35. The reference is to the thousands of potential German and Czech Jewish immigrants seeking legal immigration certificates issued by the British Mandatory regime. Certificates were allotted to the Jewish Agency and subsequently distributed among potential immigrants.

36. The Russian-born socialist Zionist leader Eliezer Kaplan (1891–1952) immigrated to Palestine in 1920. He rose through the ranks of Palestine's Labor Zionist movement and became a key figure in the Histadrut trade union, the Mapai party, and the Tel Aviv municipal government. Known for his financial acumen, Kaplan served as treasurer (1933–48) and head of the Settlement Department (1943–48) of the Jewish Agency for Palestine. He favored Weizmann's moderate policies vis-à-vis the British government. After the establishment of the Jewish state in 1948, Kaplan became minister of finance (1948–52) in Israel's first government and helped shape the country's fiscal policies and emerging economy.

37. Established in 1925, the United Palestine Appeal (UPA) sought to unify American Jewish philanthropic and relief efforts on behalf of the Yishuv. In practice, it operated as the American branch of the Jewish Agency for Palestine's key fund-raising organizations, the Jewish National Fund and the Keren Hayesod. In 1939, the UPA partnered with the American Jewish Joint Distribution Committee to create the United Jewish Appeal. After the creation of the State of Israel in 1948, the UPA was renamed the United Israel Appeal.

FOOD GOODS MARKETS CAUSED RISE PRICES WHILE WITHDRAWAL
MILLION POUNDS BANK DEPOSITS RESULTED VIOLENT CONTRAC-
TION CREDITS STOP GENERAL DISLOCATION AND EXPORT UNCER-
TAINTY REDUCED ORANGE CULTIVATION TO MINIMUM STOP AS RE-
SULT STOPPAGE BUILDING INDUSTRY WHICH AGGRAVATING URBAN
UNEMPLOYMENT AND GRAVE PLIGHT ORANGE COLONIES SEVEN
THOUSAND LABOURERS LOST EMPLOYMENT SEVERAL THOUSAND
OTHER FAMILIES WITHOUT SUBSISTENCE TOTAL UNEMPLOYED NOW
SIXTEEN THOUSAND BESIDES NEEDY MIDDLE CLASSES STOP UNAB-
SORBED NEWCOMERS CONSTITUTE SPECIAL AGGRAVATION SITUA-
TION STOP AGRICULTURAL SETTLEMENTS REMAIN LEAST AFFECTED
BUT DEPENDENT CREDIT FACILITIES MANUFACTURING INDUSTRIES
LIKEWISE GOOD PROSPECTS BUT DEPENDENT CREDITS STOP POLITI-
CAL EXIGENCIES INCLUDING ENROLLMENT JEWISH AUXILIARIES
DEMANDING SPECIAL FUNDS STOP ALL THESE EMERGENCY NEEDS
PRESSING WHILST PALESTINE STILL ABLE ABSORB IMMIGRANTS
THOUSANDS FROM GERMANY CZECHOSLOVAKIA EXPECTED AS THEIR
LEAVING UNPREVENTED STOP KAYEMETH[38] COULD UTILISE UNIQUE
OPPORTUNITIES PURCHASES STOP INCOME NATIONAL FUNDS FROM
MANY COUNTRIES CUT OFF WE APPEAL TO JEWRIES WHICH STILL IN-
TACT CONCENTRATE THEIR EFFORTS MAINTAINING POSITION JEW-
ISH AGENCY YISHUV ENSURING OUR FUTURE
WEIZMANN"

UPA FUNDS: In view of the cable from Eliezer Kaplan on behalf of the Executive, advising that funds be retained in New York, to be remitted according to
telegraphic requests, it was decided to request the UPA to retain all funds intended for the Keren Hayesod[39] [KH] and Jewish National Fund [JNF], subject

38. The Jewish National Fund (JNF) (in Hebrew, Keren Kayemet Leyisrael) was founded at
the Fifth Zionist Congress in 1901 to facilitate and advance the Zionist movement's acquisition
of land for and the development of Jewish colonies in Palestine. After 1920, the JNF—led by
Menachem Ussishkin (1863–1941) from 1923 until his death—concentrated on purchasing large
tracts of land in the Haifa Bay area; the Jezreel, Hefer, and Beit Shean Valleys; and the Galilee.

39. Keren Hayesod (Hebrew for "Foundation Fund") was created by the WZO in 1920 to
finance the pre-state Jewish community's development in Palestine. Both nonprofit and nonpartisan, Keren Hayesod enlisted the support of Zionist and non-Zionist donors to facilitate a
variety of noncommercial and economic enterprises in the Yishuv, including public activities
related to immigration, housing, education, health services, social services, labor, and self-
defense. Registered in 1921 as a limited British company and initially based in London, Keren
Hayesod moved its headquarters in 1926 to Jerusalem. At this juncture, it also began coordi-

to directions of the Executive with regard to disposition of the funds. The KH and JNF are to be advised of this decision.

VISIT TO WASHINGTON: A memorandum describing the interview on September 11th [1939] by Dr. Goldman, Dr. Wise, and Mr. Lipsky with the British Ambassador[40] and the Secretary of State[41] was circulated among members of the committee and was made part of the record.

CABLE EXCHANGE WITH DR. WEIZMANN:
THE FOLLOWING CABLES WERE REPORTED:

"Sept 11, 1939

WEIZMANN

LONDON

ASSUMING AUTHORIZATION ACT IN USA FOR EXECUTIVE IN ALL MATTERS ARISING FROM WAR ALSO CORRESPONDENCE FOR EXECUTIVE WHEREVER YOUR COMMUNICATIONS IMPOSSIBLE FORMING COMMITTEE INCLUDING PARTIES PLUS SILVER SZOLD ADLER MONSKY STOP ESTABLISHED CONTACT TODAY HULL LOTHIAN BOTH DELIGHTED YOUR COMING

WISE LIPSKY GOLDMAN"

"Sept 14, 1939

GOLDMANN

ZIONIST ORGANIZATION

YOURS ELEVENTH AGREE YOUR COMMITTEE ACTING AS SUG-

---

nating fund-raising activities in the United States through the United Palestine Appeal. In the 1930s, Keren Hayesod played a central role in financing the Zionist movement's Youth Aliyah efforts aimed at rescuing European Jewish children and youth from the rising tide of antisemitism and Nazism and enabling their emigration to Palestine.

40. Philip Henry Kerr (1882–1940), the Eleventh Marquess of Lothian, served as British ambassador to the United States (1939–40). Kerr initially favored British appeasement with Nazi Germany but became an opponent of the Hitler regime following Germany's occupation of Czechoslovakia in March 1939. Kerr played a pivotal role in securing American support for the Lend-Lease program through which the United States provided aid and military materiel to the Allied forces.

41. The Tennessee politician Cordell Hull (1871–1955) served as secretary of state under President Franklin D. Roosevelt for eleven years (1933–44). To this day, Hull's indifference to the plight of European Jewish refugees during World War II remains a subject of historical controversy. In 1945, he was instrumental in creating the United Nations and was subsequently awarded the Nobel Peace Prize.

GESTED STOP PLEASE ESTABLISH CONTACTS IMMEDIATELY ESPE-
CIALLY POLAND POSSIBLE WITH ASSISTANCE DIPLOMATIC PHILAN-
THROPIC CHANNELS STOP INFORMING JERUSALEM COMPOSITION
YOUR COMMITTEE

    WEIZMANN"

SUPPLIES FOR PALESTINE: Upon the receipt of a report by Mr. Szold with regard to possible purchase of wheat supplies for shipment to Palestine, the committee authorized Mr. Szold to cable the necessary information to the Executive
in Palestine and to inquire what action is to be taken.

STATEMENT OF ZIONIST POSITION: It was proposed that a general statement
to the public, announcing the formation of a committee and outlining its scope
of activity, be made after the committee is fully organized.

NEXT MEETING: It was decided the next meeting will be held on Monday,
October 2 at 4:00 PM.

Respectfully submitted,

SAMUEL CAPLAN

Secretary

32

"FARMING AS A LIFE OCCUPATION"

Peter Salm and the National Farm School (Bucks County, PA) (1939–42)

◇◇

KERRY M. OLITZKY

In 1896, Rabbi Joseph Krauskopf (1858–1923), a prominent Reform rabbi and the spiritual leader of Congregation Keneseth Israel in Philadelphia (1887–1923), established the National Farm School in Doylestown, Pennsylvania. The impetus for the school came from Krauskopf's 1894 visit to Jewish rural colonies in the Russian Pale of Settlement and the Jewish Agricultural School in Odessa. Returning to Philadelphia, Krauskopf decided to found a similar vocational training institution in Bucks County, Pennsylvania, to help ameliorate the plight of eastern European Jewish immigrants to the United States.

Though the National Farm School was nonsectarian and devoid of any religious affiliation, its early ranks were composed primarily of Jewish students.[1] To support his vision of "science with practice," Krauskopf raised considerable funding from the Federation of Jewish Charities in Philadelphia and private donors—including the famous entrepreneur and philanthropist Andrew Carnegie (1835–1919)—which helped launch and sustain the school in its early years.[2] In 1946, the small farming institution changed its name to the National Farm School and Junior College. Accredited in 1948 as the National Agricultural College, it was subsequently renamed the Delaware Valley College of Science and Agriculture in 1960, and in 1969 it became a coeducational institution. Joshua Feldstein (1921–2018), an immigrant from Lithuania who attended the original National Farm School as a student, served as president of the college

---

1. According to the Registrar's Office records, of the 85 students who entered the National Farm School in 1939, 58 graduated in 1942. Though the early records do not include information concerning students' religious identification, of 133 total students enrolled in 1941, 95 identified as Jewish, and 38 were listed as gentile. In 1942, the school included 46 Jewish students and 18 students of other religions. With the onset of World War II, the percentage of Jewish students increased even as the class sizes decreased.

2. Quoted in "Dr. Krauskopf, Founder," Delaware Valley University Archives, https://library.delval.edu/archives/krauskopf.

from 1975 to 1987. In 1989, the school shortened its name to Delaware Valley College, and in 2014 it officially became Delaware Valley University.

The documents reprinted here, drawn from uncataloged student files of the National Farm School, provide insights into the plight of the European Jewish refugees and how this small institution helped open a pathway for the Americanization and vocational training of young Jewish men. Born in Hameln, Germany, Peter Salm (1919–1990) was one of many central European Jewish refugees admitted to the National Farm School. During Hitler's rise to power, Salm fled with his family in 1933 to Rome, where he completed high school. In 1938, he immigrated to the United States with his mother, Helen Salm Byrns, and stepfather, Harold Byrns (Hans Bernstein), the noted conductor and orchestrator who in 1949 founded the Los Angeles Chamber Symphony. Salm's application materials, which list "Protestant" as his religious affiliation, tell the story of his desire to take on "farming as a life occupation."[3] Unable to afford the National Farm School's tuition, which included room and board, Salm successfully applied to the National Council of Jewish Women and the National Refugee Service to fund his education. He finished the Farm School program in three years and enlisted in the U.S. Army. Owing to his mastery of German and Italian, Salm served as an interpreter and translator in the U.S. Army Counter Intelligence Corps (1942–46).

Following his military service, Salm pursued undergraduate and graduate studies at the University of California, Los Angeles and Yale University, respectively. In 1958, he earned a PhD in comparative literature; married June Macy; and joined the faculty of Wesleyan University, in Middletown, Connecticut. In 1963, he was appointed a professor of German at Case Western Reserve University, in Cleveland, Ohio. A specialist on the German writer Johann Wolfgang von Goethe (1749–1832), Salm published scholarly work on and translations of Goethe's tragic play *Faust* (1806–8) and other aspects of European literature.

◇◇

3. There is no indication that Salm converted to or practiced Christianity. It was not uncommon, however, for German Jews who enlisted in the U.S. military during World War II to identify themselves as Christian in case they were captured by the Nazi military forces or ended up as a prisoner of war. See Bruce Henderson, *Sons and Soldiers: The Untold Story of the Jews Who Escaped the Nazis and Returned with the U.S. Army to Fight Hitler* (New York: Harper Collins, 2017), 185–86 and 230–31. The quote is from Salm's one-line response to a question ("What is your purpose in wishing to enter the National Farm School?") in his admission application. See Correspondence re: Peter Salm and the National Farm School (1939–42), uncataloged documents from the National Farm School Student Admission Files, Registrar's Office, Archived Prewar Student Material, Joseph Krauskopf Memorial Library, University Archives, Delaware Valley University, Doylestown, PA.

Selections from Peter Salm's Student File, National Farm School, Doylestown, Pennsylvania, 1939–42

> Source: Selections from Correspondence re: Peter Salm and the National Farm School (1939–42), uncataloged documents from the National Farm School Student Admission Files, Registrar's Office, Archived Prewar Student Material, Joseph Krauskopf Memorial Library, University Archives, Delaware Valley University, Doylestown, PA.

Excerpt from Salm's Application for Admission to the National Farm School, March 12, 1939

I was born in Hameln, Germany as the second son of a prominent merchant who is still residing in Germany while awaiting his immigration into the USA.

I am at present making my home with my mother and stepfather and the family relation is most harmonious. Furthermore we are all on very friendly terms with my natural father.

I enjoyed the privilege of an excellent education in Germany and Italy, am an accomplished linguist and [have] travelled extensively. I possess a thorough knowledge of German, English, Italian, and French.

Interested in Natural Sciences since youth my love of nature prompted me to decide at an early age to turn to farming. I spent several summer vacations among farmers and felt perfectly at home with them.

Letter of Recommendation from Alice Guthrie,[4] March 12, 1939

It is my conviction that Peter Salm is well fitted for the training of farmer since he has shown an inclination towards country life for many years.

I know him to be a young man of fine make-up and of outstanding qualities devoted to his family and most attentive to his mother.

He should prove to be a desirable companion to his co-workers and will doubtlessly become an asset to your institution.

Letter of Recommendation from John A. Gutman,[5] March 12, 1939

The writer has known Peter Salm for quite a number of years, and counts his mother and step-father among his most intimate friends. He therefore is well

4. Biographical information about this person is unknown.
5. Biographical information about this person is unknown.

able to state that Mr. Salm come[s] from a family of high standing, that he has enjoyed an excellent education, and is, in any respect, a young man whom one can heartily recommend.

He has now decided that of all the professional possibilities available, he would like best to become a farmer in this country. As I know Peter Salm to be not only an intelligent man and one used to serious work but also a very healthy and strong person, I do think that his choice is the right one, and I feel sure that any school which would take him on as a pupil, would not be disappointed in him.

Excerpt from the *National Farm School Yearbook,* n.d.

Though Pete set his foot on Farm School grounds a total stranger to the American way of life, he quickly adapted himself to his environment. He became one of the best students and workers. Salm assumed the role of instructor in astronomy giving informal lectures to many of his fellow-classmates. On dance weekends, Peter went in for star-gazing with zest. Peter also did a neat job as top literary man on the *Gleaner.*[6] After one of Salm's thrillers appeared, many a spine had to be defrosted with a blow torch. Salm was one of our better barbers. Though he mauled quite a few heads at the outset, he finally mastered the tonsorial art, and gave quite a few excellent clip-jobs. Pete has now been classified 1-A in the army. He is most anxious to enter the service to protect the country which gave him a new lease on life.

Letter from H. B. Allen,[7] August 5, 1942

To the Officer in Charge:

Although it is with regret that we see Peter Salm leave us, we can only commend him, of course, for his desire to serve in the armed forces of the United States. . . .

Peter Salm has been a student of the National Farm School for three years and was one of the finest students in the class of 1942. He ranked first in his class and was, therefore, valedictorian. Not only was he an outstanding student in classwork, but he was known as an extremely fine worker in the practical work

6. The reference is to the monthly student newspaper of the National Farm School.

7. Harold B. Allen (1886–1958) served as president of the National Farm School from 1939 to 1943.

which forms a very important part of our program here. He has shown himself to be conscientious, honest, and loyal in all his dealings with students and faculty. He displays qualities of leadership, having been an officer in clubs and captain of the soccer team. After graduation in March of this year, Peter was kept on as a postgraduate assistant, which position he is leaving to enter the army.

In the estimation of all of us here, there is no question of the fine character and loyalty to the United States of Peter Salm. I should like to register my unqualified recommendation of Peter.

Letter from Peter Salm to H. B. Allen, October 31, 1942

... All I am able to report now [is] the fact that I am a member of the Army Air Corps. Aside from that I am still "unassigned." I was first classified as an airplane mechanic.... However, recently I found out that the men at the classification center are more interested my knowledge of German and Italian than in my mechanical aptitude. Before I do any work as an interpreter I shall no doubt be investigated with regard to my integrity and loyalty to this country. I would not be surprised if you had already received inquiries about me.[8] Naturally, I am very happy to have such a wonderful reference as the National Farm School.

Letter from H. B. Allen to Peter Salm, November 4, 1942

... It was very good of you to write me telling about your activities. I have shown your letter to two or three of your former classmates, and I shall probably read some of it in the assembly or at chapel.

I can quite understand how your knowledge of German and Italian may prove to be more useful to the country than any mechanical abilities that you may have. I also realize that you will be only too glad to use your talents wherever they prove to be most useful to the country. Thus far I have received no inquiries since you first made your application. Naturally, I shall be only too glad to speak for you the good word that you deserve.

---

8. Owing to Salm's German ancestry, the U.S. Selective Service System originally categorized him as an enemy alien. In 1942, when he received permission to join the U.S. military, he declined the National Farm School's offer of a postgraduate assistantship and enlisted in the military.

33

"CITIZENSHIP, CIVIC VIRTUE, AND SAFEGUARDING DEMOCRACY"

Israel S. Chipkin on American Jewish Education (1941)

◇◇

RONA SHERAMY

In this chapter, a memorandum addressed to Alexander Dushkin (1890–1976), director of Chicago's Bureau of Jewish Education from 1921 to 1949, Israel S. Chipkin (1891–1955) offers observations on the centralizing efforts within the Jewish communal world and Jewish education. This push to coordinate Jewish education distinguished the first half of the twentieth century from the decades preceding it, which had been characterized by highly localized, disparate, and mostly ineffective educational efforts (limited to "only Sunday School or 'Heder,' or only mechanical Hebrew reading, or prayers"). In New York City, where Chipkin spent his career, the impetus for coordination was sparked in 1909 by the police commissioner Theodore A. Bingham's (1858–1934) public critique of immigrant Jewish youngsters' alleged street crime and truancy. The comments stung Jewish leaders and spurred the greatest effort to date to fortify and organize Jewish education, culminating in the creation of New York's first Bureau of Education, led by Samson Benderly (1876–1944),[1] a charismatic champion of modern and progressive Jewish education methods. In subsequent decades, other Jewish communities created their own bureaus, as educators trained in Benderly's model—like Chipkin and Dushkin—fanned out over the mid-Atlantic states and the Midwest, bringing their coordinating skills, passion for Hebrew, and progressive theories with them.

Constant advocacy was needed to frame Jewish education as a community responsibility, meriting financial support from the new Jewish federations and welfare funds. This was even more the case in the wake of the stock market crash of 1929 and the onset of the Great Depression, a period when Jewish education was seen by some communal leaders as an expendable luxury. The selection below embodies the arguments in favor of communal oversight of and financial

1. See chapter 25, note 10.

support for Jewish education, as a means of both developing the individual Jew in society and reinforcing American democratic values: "Hence, the interest of Jewish education in child, youth and adult; in past and present, in personality and group life, in the quality of citizenship and civic virtue, in the safeguarding of American democracy." The argument that Jewish education was thoroughly compatible with and vital to American citizenship would become even more pressing in subsequent months. Less than six weeks after this memorandum was drafted, the Japanese bombing of Pearl Harbor on December 7, 1941, ushered the United States into World War II.

◇◇

Israel S. Chipkin, "Memorandum to Jewish Communal Executives and Jewish Educators," October 27, 1941

> Source: Israel S. Chipkin, Memorandum to Jewish Communal Executives and Jewish Educators (October 27, 1941), Records of the Board of Jewish Education of Greater New York, 1920–1982, MS-706, box 15, folder 7: Israel S. Chipkin, 1939–1949, the Jacob Rader Marcus Center of the American Jewish Archives, Cincinnati.

I. S. Chipkin[2]

October 27, 1941

Memorandum to Jewish Communal Executives and Jewish Educators

The number of Jewish Federations and Welfare Funds[3] in the United States is

2. Born in Vilna, Lithuania, Israel Chipkin (1891–1955) immigrated to the United States with his family as an infant. He was a pioneering American Jewish educator who advocated for a more centralized and systematized approach to educating Jewish children. Chipkin was a protégé of Samson Benderly (1876–1944), who sought to transform Jewish education through progressive educational ideas, professionalized approaches to pedagogy, and the revival of Hebrew. Like Benderly, Chipkin argued that the Jewish community should invest in and take responsibility for Jewish education, rather than leave the duty to parents and congregations. This vision reflects what would become the modern American Jewish educational system. An impassioned Zionist and Hebraist, Chipkin also advocated for offering Hebrew as a foreign language in New York public schools. He served in numerous capacities in the classroom, at the helm of schools and Jewish organizations, and as editor of the journal *Jewish Education*. An accomplished administrator, he led both the Jewish Education Association of New York (1921–44) and the American Association for Jewish Education (1944–49). He concluded his career directing research at the Jewish Education Committee of New York.

3. The first Jewish Federation (or "Welfare Fund," as it was called in some cities) was founded in Boston in 1895. Others were created in subsequent decades in cities with sizable Jewish populations: for example, New York's Jewish Federation was established in 1917. Philanthropists created federations to centralize fund-raising and the distribution of resources and to support a range of Jewish communal needs. Although Jewish education would become a substantial

growing. This fact reflects the growing responsiveness in many large and small communities to organized and responsible Jewish endeavor[s] for meeting the philanthropic, social, religious or educational needs of Jewish citizens as individuals or as communities.

Coincident with the increasing number of central philanthropic or community agencies is their widening scope of interest in the functional institutions and activities of the community. Prominent among the latter is Jewish education. Community interest in, and responsibility for, Jewish education is becoming more widespread.

Why is this community interest in, and responsibility for, Jewish education spreading? Because both the concept "Jewish community" and the concept "Jewish education" are assuming wider sociological significance. As an everwider number of individual Jews or Jewish families is sought out by central agencies to share in community responsibilities, the normal or abnormal social or cultural or philanthropic needs of these people are added to the list of communal interests, and their thoughts and attitudes towards various communal activities find their expression in the discussion of programs of central communal endeavor. Programs of Jewish Federations and Welfare Funds reflect not only a multiplicity of community institutions and activities but also a diversity of social, economic or ideological groupings within the community.[4] In other words, community responsibility for diversified interests and participation of diversified elements in a total community program seem to describe the newer

---

beneficiary of Federation dollars in the late twentieth century, Chipkin writes at a time when education was a low-priority recipient of allotments. Federations were focused at the time on providing social services and addressing the needs of Jews around the world. See also Harry L. Lurie, *A Heritage Affirmed: The Jewish Federation Movement in America* (Philadelphia: Jewish Publication Society of America, 1961), 3–158; Lila Corwin Berman, "How Americans Give: The Financialization of American Jewish Philanthropy," *American Historical Review* 122, no. 5 (December 2017), 1459–89.

4. By the middle of the twentieth century, the American Jewish community was multigenerational and diverse. Broadly, it consisted of descendants of Sephardic Jews (Jews who traced their origins to the Iberian Peninsula) who had settled in New Amsterdam (later known as New York) in the late seventeenth and early eighteenth centuries; Ashkenazic German-speaking Jews from central Europe, who arrived in large numbers in the first half of the nineteenth century; waves of eastern European Yiddish-speaking Jews who fled persecution in tsarist Russia in the late nineteenth and early twentieth centuries; and Jews from across Europe escaping antisemitism up until the outbreak of World War II (within the confines of strict immigration quotas put in place in the early 1920s). Ideologically, religiously, economically, and culturally, the Jewish community was heterogeneous. It therefore was no easy task for any one educational system to accommodate the needs of such a mixed population and broad cultural spectrum.

concept of "Jewish community." This representative responsibility and variety of activity should seem natural in an atmosphere of American democracy.

Just as the concept "Jewish community" has become richer and more complex in meaning and responsibility, so has the concept "Jewish education." No more can one use this term and mean only Sunday School[5] or "Heder,"[6] or only mechanical Hebrew reading, or prayers, or only poor children or bad children, or only the past and the pious. Jews in American communities are beginning to respect each other for their ideological differences. They are beginning to understand that as normal human beings Jews are entitled to a variation in their outlook on life, that the motivation for humanitarian impulses towards their own brethren or towards their neighbors and towards all peoples, springs from spiritual resources within their personalities and within their family or group life. These spiritual resources are drawn from religious faith and tradition, from historic and cultural experiences, from the cultural and social forces of the present day, from participation in the current life of particularistic and universalistic groups. In other words, "Jewish education" becomes the process by which individual personality is enhanced and the standards of Jewish community life or activity are improved. In such a process, experience, perspective, and prophecy must enter. Variety of form, expression, thought, program, and institution becomes a welcome manifestation of a normal functioning of community life. But respectful encouragement of variety invites greater desire for cooperative activity and the submission to democratic control and responsibility. From this point of view Jewish education becomes not only the spiritual resource for communal endeavor, but also the stabilizing, progressive and perpetuating process for carrying on Jewish communal activities. Hence, the self-interest of the cen-

5. Modeled after Christian Sunday Schools, the first Hebrew Sunday School was founded by Rebecca Gratz (1781–1869) in Philadelphia in 1838. Jewish communities along the eastern seaboard followed Philadelphia's model over the course of the nineteenth century, building one-day-a-week schools (also called Sabbath schools) that were staffed primarily by women. These schools played an important role for communities that lacked any structured Jewish education outside of the home. By the twentieth century, however, they were deemed inadequate by a new cadre of professional Jewish educators like Chipkin, who criticized the supplementary schools' limited meeting time and shallow curriculum.

6. In eastern Europe, heders were the primary setting for Jewish study for boys and, to a far more limited extent, girls. Eastern European Jewish immigrants transplanted this form of traditional Jewish schooling to the United States, with a focus on educating their sons in the basics of Torah, Talmud, and liturgy. As was the case in Europe, in the United States the quality of heder education varied greatly. Among the heders' weaknesses was a lack of trained teachers. Indeed, many heders had the reputation of hiring male instructors who could not find employment elsewhere.

tral communal agencies in the process and results of the several educational institutions in the community. Hence, the interest of Jewish education in child, youth, and adult, in past and present, in personality and group life, in the quality of citizenship and civic virtue, in the safeguarding of American democracy, in the welfare of Jews in Europe and in Palestine,[7] in the protection of minorities everywhere, in the spiritual life of all peoples.

It behooves these individuals who are charged with the responsibilities for carrying out general programs of communal endeavor or specific programs of Jewish education to understand each other better and to effect a greater mutual integration of their respective programs of communal endeavor in the light of the wider and more significant meanings of the concepts, "Jewish community" and "Jewish education."

Fortunately, in such coming together of persons or of minds, they need not confine their discussion to theocratic considerations alone. Thirty years of experience may be drawn on for lessons learned. More than a score of organized communities has served as laboratories. New needs and new demands confront community executive and educator. It is suggested that they get together for the sake of mutual enlightenment and for the general welfare of the community to explore and appraise the cooperative possibilities of the present and the future.

7. Like his peers among Benderly's protégés, Chipkin was an ardent Zionist who saw schools as a way to inculcate in American Jewish children love for the Zionist idea, Palestine as a Jewish national home, and the perpetuation of Hebrew language and culture.

34

"PILGRIMS," ALSO KNOWN AS "MAYFLOWER AND 'ILLEGAL' PASSENGER SHIP"

Arthur Szyk and the Twin Promised Lands of America and Palestine
(1946)

<><><><><><><><><><><><><><><><><><><><><><><><><><><><><><><><><><><><><><><><><>

KARLA GOLDMAN AND MARK A. RAIDER

It would be hard to overstate the impact of the Lodz-born Jewish artist and illustrator Arthur Szyk (1894–1951) on American Jewry's perception of Zionism and the campaign for Jewish statehood. In 1940, after spending the interwar years in Poland, France, and England, Szyk immigrated to the United States. Modeled on the work of medieval and Renaissance masters, Szyk's iconic style found a home in a variety of books, paintings, and illustrations focused on critical social, cultural, and political themes.

Szyk was already well-known at the time of his arrival in the United States. He had a repertoire including a series of twenty-three paintings on the Polish contribution to American history that had been displayed at the New York World's Fair of 1939, an illustrated *Haggadah* (1940), and a series of seventy-two anti-Nazi political caricatures titled "War and Kultur" (1940) that had been exhibited by the Fine Art Society in London. With the U.S. entry into World War II, Szyk's work assumed an explicitly patriotic American character. His design for the U.S. postal service of a series of stamps, inspired by the 1941 "Four Freedoms" speech by President Franklin D. Roosevelt's (1882–1945), made his art suddenly ubiquitous in the American public arena. Major exhibits in American museums and at the White House brought universal acclaim, and his work appeared in countless popular vehicles, including postcards, magazines, newspapers, advertisements, and posters. After the war, Szyk moved to New Canaan, Connecticut, where he continued work as a book illustrator, devoting considerable energy to promoting the Zionist campaign for Jewish statehood.

Arthur Szyk, "Pilgrims," also known as "Mayflower and 'Illegal' Passenger Ship," 1946

Source: Arthur Szyk, "Pilgrims," also known as "Mayflower and 'Illegal' Passenger Ship" (1946). Pen, ink, and pencil on board. Robbins Family Collection, Palo Alto, CA. Courtesy of Paul and Sheri Robbins. Photographic assistance provided by Irvin Ungar.

The illustration reproduced here, "Pilgrims" (1946), also known as "Mayflower and 'Illegal' Passenger Ship," depicts the 1620 voyage of the English Puritans to North America and the postwar journey of European Jewish refugees aboard a clandestine Aliyah Bet ship bound for British Mandatory Palestine.[1] Fusing the symmetrical images is an elaborate center panel dominated by a *magen David* (Hebrew for "shield of David," also called "Star of David") above a menorah. In the middle of the star, Syzk placed a royal crown inscribed in small letters with the Hebrew phrase *keter shem tov* (meaning "crown of the good name"). This idiomatic phrase, derived from the title of a book of teachings attributed to the founder of Hasidism, Israel Baal Shem Tov (c. 1698–1760), connects the American and Jewish "pilgrims"'—as refugees from oppression seeking to create a beacon of moral progress in a metaphorical Promised Land.

1. Aliyah Bet was the Hebrew code name used by Zionist activists who assisted Jewish refugees' and Holocaust survivors' entry into Palestine in defiance of the British White Paper of 1939 and the British blockade of Jewish immigration to the Yishuv.

This metaphor is reinforced by the inclusion in English in the lower left-hand corner of the site and date of the illustration's creation. Syzk's invocation of "New Canaan" ties the two ships to the Israelites' biblical journey toward old Canaan. In flight from oppression, both the seventeenth-century Puritans and the twentieth-century Holocaust survivors sought the redemption of themselves and the lands to which they were headed.

Below the star, in larger Hebrew letters in the center of the design, Syzk included the phrase "im ein ani li mi li" (meaning "If I am not for me, who will be for me?"), codified in *Ethics of the Sages* 1:14. This is the first part of a text that continues, "And when I am for myself alone, what am I? And if not now, then when?" By including just the first part of this phrase, Syzk emphasizes the imperative for self-interested action in the face of a world that responds to oppression with disinterest. A seven-branch menorah, part of the portable sanctuary used by the Hebrews in the wilderness and subsequently installed in the ancient Temple of Jerusalem, literally and figuratively anchors the scene.[2] To the left of the menorah is a ram; to the right is a lion wearing a crown—both generative symbols in Jewish tradition of fidelity to God and the promise of redemption.

To underscore the symmetry of the journeys of the *Mayflower* and the Aliyah Bet ship—and their respective journeys from totalitarian bondage to the Promised Lands of America and Palestine—the vessels are accented in the upper corners by American and Zionist flags and below by upraised anchors. No less important is the twin symbolism of the beleaguered but expectant Puritan and Jewish refugee travelers aboard the two ships—the one headed west, the other headed east—each facing an uncertain future and adorned, respectively, with Christian and Jewish flags lofted by the wind.

In sum, the perceived dual destinies of the Land of Israel and the United States—two Promised Lands anchored by the ideas of election, redemption, and the creation of a new Zion—come to full fruition in this work. Part homage and part propaganda, Syzk's illustration goes beyond the oft-used trope of depicting America's founding founders as a latter-day version of the biblical Israelites. By establishing the symmetry of the flight of contemporary Jews to Palestine with the journey of the *Mayflower*, Syzk depicts the quest for a Jewish state as an invocation of the same enterprise, hopes, and ideals that underlay the pilgrims' quest for America.

2. On the Temple in ancient Jerusalem, see chapter 6, note 6.

35

"THE GREATER SIN"

Jacob M. Rothschild's Yom Kippur Sermon on American Jews, the South, and Civil Rights (1948)

◇◇◇

MARK A. RAIDER

Jacob M. Rothschild (1911–1973) came to maturity in Pittsburgh, Pennsylvania, the "quintessential symbol of the American industrial city."[1] By the close of World War I, Pittsburgh's population had surged to over 590,000 inhabitants, with a local Jewish population of 60,000.[2] Witness to the industrial Midwest's fast-paced development, Rothschild's youth coincided with Pittsburgh's swift transformation owing to the Great Migration of disenfranchised black Americans fleeing the South's oppressive conditions and the region's magnetic attraction for hundreds of thousands of European immigrants seeking economic opportunity. Anchored at the turn of the nineteenth and twentieth centuries by Carnegie Steel (later U.S. Steel), the nation's largest steel company with over three million tons of capacity, the Pittsburgh-based steel industry harnessed the vast resources of the Appalachian basin's coal seam to produce nearly three-quarters of the country's steel output. The industry's stunning commercial success, which enabled the swift westward development of the country's railway system, was fueled by the exploitation of workers and the cheap labor provided by its subsidiaries, including those in the South where the victimization of prison labor and impoverished black workers was protected and bolstered by a mix of legal and civic constraints.

With the steel industry's meteoric growth and increasing demand for factory laborers, there arose a struggle between local steel workers and the industrial titans grouped around Andrew Carnegie (1835–1919), Henry Clay Frick (1849–1919), and other magnates. Starting with the bloody Homestead strike

---

1. John Bodnar, Roger Simon, and Michael P. Weber, *Lives of Their Own: Blacks, Italians, and Poles in Pittsburgh, 1900–1960* (Urbana: University of Illinois Press), 13.

2. Harry S. Linfield, "Jewish Population of the United States," *American Jewish Year Book* 24 (1922), 314.

of 1892, successive waves of labor unrest—stoked by social, economic, and political pressures that proliferated in the World War I era and climaxed in the
1930s, often resulting in episodes of brutality and violence—attracted nationwide attention to the desperate plight of America's industrial working class. It
was against this turbulent backdrop that the young Jacob Rothschild learned
about the everyday challenges of economic inequality and social injustice. In
this period, he was deeply influenced by Rabbi Samuel Goldenson (1878–1962),
the spiritual leader of Temple Rodef Shalom from 1918 to 1934. Goldenson
was a champion of workers' rights and a leading religious voice in the nation's
struggle against the exploitation of labor.

In 1927, Rothschild enrolled simultaneously at the University of Cincinnati
and Hebrew Union College where he completed his A.B. and rabbinic studies,
respectively. Ordained as a Reform rabbi in 1936, he served for brief periods as
the spiritual leader of synagogues in Davenport, Iowa, and Pittsburgh. In 1942,
he enlisted in the U.S. military and served as a chaplain in the Pacific theater, including an American relief mission to troops at the battle of Guadalcanal. After
the war, he assumed the pulpit of Atlanta, Georgia's, leading Reform synagogue:
the Hebrew Benevolent Congregation, known locally as "the Temple."

Arriving in postwar Atlanta, Rothschild was greeted by a prosperous community of more than 10,000 Jews, who accounted for roughly half of Georgia's Jewish population.[3] The scourge of racial injustice in the South and Jim Crow's hold
on Atlanta and its Jewish community was not lost on Rothschild. Like his predecessor—Rabbi David Marx (1872–1962), who served the congregation from 1895
to 1946—he supported racial equality and opposed violence against the black
community. Unlike Marx, he espoused untraditional Reform and Zionist views,
and he unabashedly insisted that American Jews shared responsibility for the
future of social and economic justice in the South. Keenly aware of the South's
vexed history of extralegal racial violence, Rothschild's unapologetic brand of
liberalism worried many Atlanta Jews who recalled Georgia's "most intensive
decade of lynching between 1910 and 1920," which claimed one of their own.[4]
In this period, Leo Frank (1884–1915), a Cornell-educated Jewish man from New
York who had married into an Atlanta family, was wrongfully convicted of raping
and murdering thirteen-year old Mary Phagan (1899–1913). Following Frank's
sham trial, which took place in a noxious and antisemitic public atmosphere,

3. Harry S. Linfield, "The Jewish Population of the United States," *American Jewish Year Book*
47 (1945), 645; Ben B. Seligman and Harvey Swados, "Jewish Population Studies in the United
States," *American Jewish Year Book* 50 (1948–49), 673.

4. Stewart E. Tolnay and E. M. Beck, "Black Flight: Lethal Violence and the Great Migration," *Social Science History* 14, no. 3 (Autumn 1990): 360.

Governor John M. Slaton (1866–1955) commuted Frank's death sentence to life imprisonment. However, a group of white men, many with ties to the Ku Klux Klan, abducted Frank from his prison cell; drove him east to Marietta, where an execution site had been prepared in advance; and lynched him. A crowd of men, women, and children had gathered to view the spectacle.

The sermon reprinted below, delivered two years after Rothschild's arrival in Atlanta, throws light on an intriguing moment in American Jewry's engagement with the challenge of creating "a more perfect union."[5] Set against the backdrop of Jim Crow's long history, the Leo Frank case, the tragedy of the Holocaust, and a spate of recent episodes of Klan terrorism and lynching, Rothschild's comments reveal the dynamic interrelationship of American Jews and southern culture in the 1940s, at the dawn of the integrationist era.[6] Illustrating the extent to which southern Jewry's postwar identity was as much a product of its privileged white status as a reflection of a distinctive ethnic and religious inheritance, Rothschild's proactive sensibility reveals a striking capacity to exceed the orbit of the regional Jewish community's self-imposed limitations. Anticipating key themes of the civil rights struggles of the 1950s and 1960s, when Rothschild worked closely with Rev. Martin Luther King Jr. (1929–1968), the sermon challenges southern Jews to live up to America's promise of equality for all.

◇◇◇

Sermon of Jacob M. Rothschild, "The Greater Sin," October 13, 1948

> Source: Jacob M. Rothschild, "The Greater Sin" (October 13, 1948), Civil Rights Sermons Collection, SC-8799, the Jacob Rader Marcus Center of the American Jewish Archives, Cincinnati.

> Yom Kippur [Day of Atonement], 5709[7]
> October 13, 1948

Judaism never put much stock in miracles. Our religion has always been too realistic for that. It has made no unattainable claims; set no unreachable goals.

5. Preamble to the U.S. Constitution.

6. Rothschild's use of the term "Negro" reflects the cultural and historical context of American society in the mid-twentieth century. Adopted in the 1930s as an endonym and exonym in place of "colored," which was by then widely perceived as pejorative, it was gradually supplanted by the descriptors "black" and "African American" in the late 1960s. See Ben L. Martin, "From Negro to Black to African American: The Power of Names and Naming," *Political Science Quarterly* 106, no. 1 (Spring 1991), 102–5; Tom W. Smith, "Changing Racial Labels: From 'Colored' to 'Negro' to 'Black' to 'African American,'" *Public Opinion Quarterly* 56, no. 4 (Winter 1992), 498–99 and 502–9.

7. The Hebrew date 10 Tishri 5709 corresponds to October 13, 1948, in the civil calendar.

To be a Jew does not require great leaps of faith. Ours has always been a down-to-earth, rational religion. The spirit of realism in Israel's faith becomes apparent in our observance of this Day of Atonement. This is the day set aside for self-examination, for searching the heart, for ridding our souls of sin. It is a solemn day, spent in prayer and observed by fasting, on which man admits his failure to live by God's law. No one really expects us ever to attain perfection. Psalmists long ago recognized the great gulf between the law of God and the acts of men. "As high as the heavens are above the earth, so high are God's ways above man's" [Isaiah 55:9]—so said the ancient poet. How comforting, then, this day might be. Here is the perfect opportunity to find ourselves forgiven. God's standard is too high for us. His law is too difficult. Our sins were just the expected failures of all mortals. All we need do, therefore, is come into His presence on each Yom Kippur, acknowledge our inevitable guilt, pray for forgiveness—and lo! We shall be forgiven.

But Judaism never put much stock in miracles—even the miracle of forgiveness. For Jews, life just isn't made that simple. We are held accountable for our conduct. We are responsible for our acts. So with great care the rabbis chose the scriptural portion to be read in synagogues on this day. You followed the English translation in your prayer books this morning. There was no word of "forgive them for they know not what they do" [Luke 23:34]. On the contrary, the very passage read on this day of forgiveness seeks to establish the responsibility of man for his acts. This commandment—"My law"—says our Heavenly Father, is not too hard for thee, neither is it far off. It is not up in heaven, nor is it across some remote sea. But the word is very nigh unto thee, in thy mouth, and in they heart that thou mayest do it. Here is the Jewish philosophy of life—a philosophy which says: Don't rationalize your guilt by claiming that morality is too difficult for attainment by mere man. Don't pretend helplessness because the right way to live is placed out of your reach. Don't for a moment think that you can blame your sinfulness on the fact that goodness is beyond your grasp. Quite the opposite is true. This law which you have abused, this way of life which you have forsaken, this word which you have ignored is very close to you. The law is in your hearts to understand—and in your hands to execute. Therefore, there will be no miracle of forgiveness upon request. You earn your right to be forgiven by your acceptance of the word of God which is written upon your heart.

Once we understand this Jewish point of view, the real significance of our Day of Atonement becomes clear. Our guilt becomes more profound than just committing acts which violate the moral law. Our basic sinfulness rests in the tasks we didn't do—in the failure to recognize the fact that the law of God works through us. Seen in this light, our failure to measure up to the challenge of life is even more glaring. Our sins become not mere acts of selfishness, of petty cruelty, or small dishonesty. Everywhere there is misery and unhappiness, fear and insecurity because millions of people just like ourselves have left unrecognized and unfulfilled the moral law that lies close at their hand. Let us, then, re-examine our hearts on this day of days and seek to find in them the key that will unlock for us the door to God's forgiveness.

I

We live in the South—a fact that somehow sets us apart from other Americans. Our problems are different; we are entitled to different rules. When our country seeks to implement the standards of equality set forth in the American Constitution, the South considers it an infringement of its way of life. When our federal government wants to ensure the safety of all its citizens, the South reacts as though such simple justice were an affront to its own moral code. There are some who have not yet become completely resigned to the kind of one-sided race-relations that alone is acceptable to the average Southern mind. Even they have by this time developed a sort of shock-proof covering which protects them against news that appears from time to time in our press: The utter and unreasoning stupidity of a Kiwanis Club[8] that refused to award a prize to the winner of a drawing because he was a Negro.[9] The white man who went, armed, to the home of a Negro who had dared to vote—despite a warning—and who was forced to kill the Negro in "self-defense."[10] We expect occasional outbursts such

---

8. Founded in 1915 in Detroit, the Kiwanis fraternal society, initially called the Supreme Lodge of Benevolent Order Brothers, originated as a local club for white businessmen. By the 1920s, the club had developed into a national organization, with the motto "we build" to signal its commitment to community service.

9. In 1946, Harvey Jones (1924–1996), a black Navy veteran and tenant farmer in Ahoskie, North Carolina, purchased a lottery ticket for a 1947 Cadillac automobile in a local Kiwanis club contest. Though Jones's ticket was drawn, he was declared ineligible because "the Kiwanians did not want a Negro to win" and "the lottery was for white folks" ("Harvey Jones and the New Car," *Life*, July 28, 1947, 36). The incident attracted national attention.

10. This is a caustic reference to the murder of World War II veteran Maceo Snipes (1909–1946) of Rupert, Georgia, who was shot in the back on July 18, 1946, by the white supremacist Edward M. Williamson (1914–1985) after voting in the state's gubernatorial primary election. After being shot, Snipes walked three miles to the home of a neighbor, who took him by wagon to the nearby Montgomery Hospital, in Butler, Georgia. Two days later, Snipes died from his injuries. Hospital staff members subsequently claimed that they did not have "black blood" for a transfusion. On July 29, 1946, Snipes's attacker, Williamson—claiming self-defense—was exonerated by a Georgia jury.

as these.[11] We can even read with a certain degree of equanimity the editorials that follow them.[12] They all say the same thing: Every right-minded Southerner deplores such acts. Sometimes we wonder where these right-minded people are—and even if the writer of the editorial is one of them.[13] This sort of thing, however, no longer shocks us.

But when an event occurs like the one in Milledgeville, [Georgia,] not long ago, then it is time to take stock of ourselves. Let me refresh your memories a bit. The president of the University System of Georgia[14] called a meeting of all school heads. There are Negro colleges in Georgia.[15] Representatives from

11. Rothschild's understated sarcasm betrays his alarm over white society's acceptance of the seeming normalization of racial violence perpetrated against black citizens. Indeed, as he was no doubt aware, on July 25, 1946, only a week after the Snipes murder, two black couples, World War II veteran George W. (1917–1946) and Mae Murray Dorsey (1926–1946) and Roger (1922–1946) and Dorothy Dorsey Malcom (1926–1946), were murdered in broad daylight by a dozen Klan members at Moore's Ford Bridge, linking Monroe and Watkinsville in Walton County, Georgia. Dorothy and George were siblings; Dorothy was seven months pregnant at the time of her death. The Snipes murder and the lynching of the Dorseys and Malcoms generated considerable national attention and outrage, including demonstrations outside the White House. In response, President Harry S. Truman (1884–1972) created the President's Committee on Civil Rights and proposed antilynching legislation to Congress, but the legislation failed owing to the resistance of southern Democrats. The confluence of events also prompted Martin Luther King Jr. (1929–1968), then a seventeen-year old student at Morehouse College, to write a letter of protest to the *Atlanta Constitution*.

12. The Snipes murder and Walton County lynching were extensively reported, and editorials about them appeared in multiple publications, including the *Atlanta Constitution*, *Augusta Chronicle*, *Chicago Defender*, *Macon Telegraph*, *New Republic*, *New York Times*, *Newsweek*, *Savannah Morning News*, *Savannah Tribune*, and *Time*. See Patrick Novotny, *This Georgia Rising: Education, Civil Rights, and Politics of Change of Georgia in the 1940s* (Macon, GA: Mercer University Press, 2007), 199–213.

13. On August 1, 1946, the *Butler Herald*, echoing southern white hostility to black voting rights, asserted: "The matter of opposing Negroes voting in the Georgia White Primary [sic] is not a fight against the Negro himself as against those with sinister motives who would use the Negro vote to attain their objectives. . . . There are largely those individuals and organizations outside Georgia of the agitator, radical types, such as Communists, and those who fail to understand the South regarding the two races" (quoted in Novotny, *This Georgia Rising*, 199n305).

14. Harmon White Caldwell (1899–1977) served as president of the University of Georgia (1935–48) and chancellor of the University System of Georgia (1948–64).

15. In 1948, approximately six thousand black students were enrolled at the following higher education institutions in Georgia: Albany State College (established in 1903), Atlanta University (1865), Atlanta University School of Social Work (1920), Clark College (1879), Fort Valley State College (1895), Gammon Theological Seminary (1883), Georgia Baptist College (1899), Georgia State College (1890), Morehouse College (1867), Morris Brown College (1881), Paine College (1882), Spelman College (1881), and State Teachers and Agricultural College (1902). See Willard

these schools were naturally included. Meetings were held at the Georgia State College for Women.[16] White visitors were housed and fed in dormitories on the school campus. The Negro educators lived in homes of Negroes; they ate their meals separately. But they did sit at the same meetings with their white colleagues. This affront to white supremacy was too much for certain citizens of our state. They burned up their fiery cross, intimidated the assembled college presidents—and amidst threats of violence, forced the three Negroes to leave Milledgeville,[17] even providing physical escort for them as they drove away.[18] Once again the inevitable editorials.[19] Writer[s] "viewed with alarm" and "pointed the finger of scorn." They enlisted the aid of "all right-thinking citizens" against such outrages to the good name of the South. But nothing was done. The law either could not or would not act.

We must do more than "view with alarm" the growing race hatred that threatens the South. First of all, we must make ourselves aware of what goes on. All over Georgia in the primary gubernatorial election just held,[20] the important

---

Range, *The Rise and Progress of Negro Colleges in Georgia, 1865–1949* (Athens: University of Georgia Press, 1951), 208 and 223–35.

16. The curriculum of the Georgia State College for Women—established in 1891 in Milledgeville as the Georgia Normal and Industrial College—emphasized "general culture, effective citizenship, and vocational competence" (*Georgia State College for Women Bulletin* 24, no. 10 [May 15, 1944], 2).

17. A reference to presidents Aaron Brown of Albany State College (1943–53), Cornelius V. Troup of Fort Valley State College (1945–66), and George M. Sparks of Georgia State College (1928–57).

18. Rothschild is referring to an annual meeting of Georgia's university system leaders, which included eighteen black educators and administrators and was held on the campus of the Georgia State College for Women in mid-September 1948. The *Savannah Tribune* reported that the black attendees at the "mixed race meeting" were given "the Ku Klux Klan treatment," including threats made to local hosts who provided home hospitality, causing them to take "sudden leave from town" (quoted in Novotny, *This Georgia Rising*, 308). Following the Klan's denunciation of the meeting as a "violation of state Jim Crow laws and Southern traditions," a cross was burned in front of the home of Guy H. Wells, president of the Georgia State College for Women (1934–53) (quoted in ibid., 308–9).

19. On September 19, 1948, the *Atlanta Constitution* described the Klan's harassment of the academic meeting as the "product of dim-witted, infantile, evil little minds," and Milledgeville's *Union Recorder* called the Klan's effort "to frighten and intimidate" the administrators "ridiculous" (quoted in ibid., 308–9).

20. Rothschild is referring to the statewide primaries leading up to Georgia's special gubernatorial election on November 2, 1948. The election was held in the wake of the so-called three governors' controversy, caused by the sudden death on December 21, 1946, of the state's governor-elect Eugene Talmadge (1884–1946). The competing claims of Talmadge's three

issues were ignored. There was only one real issue—civil rights. And there were tens of thousands of voters who had been indoctrinated with bias even on that issue. They were told that civil rights meant having to sit next to Negroes in public places of entertainment, in churches and schools. They believed that civil rights meant having Negroes in their homes and at their tables and marrying their daughters. It must be obvious that to people who cannot even countenance a meeting at which negroes are present, such an interpretation would be a spur to violent and unreasoning hate.[21]

The solution for the ills of the South rests with the people of the South. That much of its claim is valid. The law of justice is not [so] remote from us that we must look for others to impose it upon us. The law of righteousness is not up in heaven that we must wonder who will go there and bring it down for us and give it to us. The law is in our own hands—to invoke and to make effective. But the goddess of justice is blind indeed and her scales dishonest when the true facts are systematically denied those who must administer justice. Impartial consideration and unbiased action can never be achieved when truth is deliberately distorted and passions purposely aroused. Yet almost nowhere has the attempt been made to disprove the lying bigots who capitalize on festering hatreds. Millions of us must know the truth—but we keep silent even though the word is in our own hearts.

The problem is ours to solve—and the time for solution is now. We do not have the right to postpone and procrastinate. By our very delay, we invite the outside interference that we fear. If the people of the South are sincere in their oft-stated desire to solve their racial problems, then it is time for some concrete evidence of that fact. No one denies that the problem is a complex one, steeped in prejudice and made difficult by irreconcilable differences. But nothing can be gained by the constant and repeated side-stepping of the issue—side-stepping that is confined not to the bigoted and the hate-mongers but which is engaged in by our recognized civic leaders and citizens of vision as well. There are agencies at work in the South which attempt to come to grips with the problem. One

---

would-be successors led to a protracted legislative and legal battle. The state's supreme court eventually declared lieutenant governor–elect Melvin E. Thompson (1903–1980) governor until a special election could be held. In 1948, Herman Talmadge (1913–2002), son of the deceased former governor, won the special election and completed the term; in 1950, he was reelected to a full term as governor.

21. For a detailed analysis of the 1948 gubernatorial election and its impact, see Novotny, *This Georgia Rising*, chapter 3 ("1948's Governor's Race and the Politics of Change in Postwar Georgia").

of these is the Southern Regional Council.[22] It—and the others—receives the lip service of great numbers of our citizens—but the actual labors of a pitiful few. Yet their program not only is far from even the suggestion of revolution—it is all but innocuous as well. It patiently works out the slow and ever-evolving solution which alone can be effective—the solution based upon understanding the issues and making the necessary adjustments. The men and women who support such organizations are at least aware of the fact that God's law is not too remote from them—but is very near. They try at least to make it a part of their hearts.

On this Day of Atonement, let us face honestly the facts of our life in the South. We have committed no overt sin in our dealings with Negroes. I feel certain that we have treated them fairly; certainly we have not used force to frighten them. We have even felt a certain sympathy for their predicament—and perhaps a fleeting shadow of shame has flickered at our conscience. No, our sin has been the deeper one, the evil of what we didn't do haunts on this day of reckoning. We who take pride in our heritage as Jews, we who bask in the glory of Southern tradition have a greater responsibility for enlightened action. The burden is squarely upon us. It becomes increasingly obvious that unless decent people take up the burden, the South faces a return to the most primitive kind of bigotry and race hatred. Let us, then, be among those who are willing to do something. The time for pious utterances is past. Now is the time to act. We cannot expect to come before the tribunal of God's mercy and gain miraculous forgiveness for the sin of our neglect year after endless year. The law of justice, the law of decency is within our grasp. Let us find it in our hearts to tackle honestly the problem that keeps the South from real greatness.

22. Created in 1944 as the successor to the Commission on Interracial Cooperation (1929–44), the Southern Regional Council, headquartered in Atlanta, Georgia, brought together black and white moderates to promote regional economic development and pursue an agenda of making "separate but equal more equal" (quoted in Randall L. Patton, "Lillian Smith and the Transformation of American Liberalism," *Georgia Historical Quarterly* 76, no. 2 (Summer 1992), 377). A split developed between the council's gradualists (who advocated working for change within the constraints of society's civic, economic, and legal institutions) and political activists (who believed racial injustice to be paramount and called for the council to denounce Jim Crow and segregation). In 1949, the council adopted a resolution declaring that "the South's system of apartheid 'in and of itself constitutes discrimination and inequality of treatment'" (quoted in ibid., 379). At this juncture, many of the council's white members who supported racial equality but wished to pursue a gradualist strategy left the organization.

We Jews spend too much of our time worrying about how we look to other people. Each of us constitutes himself a one-man public relations committee and dutifully weighs every event on the scales of Jewish security. There is no lack of justification for such an attitude. It is an honest—and inevitable—reflection of the fact that our position is far from secure. We can sing the praises of American democracy in public, but in our hearts we still feel its weaknesses. We can exude confidence over our future, but we still support the Anti-Defamation League[23] and the American Jewish Committee[24] and all the others. It is this feeling of insecurity that added to our horror over the brutal slaying of [Count Folke] Bernadotte.[25] We, like all civilized people, registered shock when the

23. In response to the notorious Leo Frank case (1913–15), the Chicago attorney Sigmund Livingston (1872–1946) called for the creation of a watchdog organization "to stop the defamation of the Jewish people, and to secure justice and fair treatment to all citizens alike" (quoted in Abraham H. Foxman, "The Anti-Defamation League," in *Encyclopedia of American Jewish History*, ed. Stephen H. Norwood and Eunice G. Pollack (Santa Barbara, CA: ABC-CLIO, 2008), 1:243). With the support of Adolph Kraus (1850–1928), a fellow Chicagoan and president of the nationwide Jewish fraternal organization Independent Order of Bnai Brith (Sons of the Covenant), Livingston founded the Anti-Defamation League to combat antisemitism and other forms of bigotry and prejudice. See also "The Anti-Defamation League: A Statement of Policy (May 1915)," in Paul Mendes-Flohr and Jehuda Reinharz, eds., *The Jew in the Modern World: A Documentary History*, 3d ed. (New York: Oxford University Press, 2011), 566–67.

24. Established in 1906, the American Jewish Committee (AJC) aimed "to prevent infringement of the civil and religious rights of Jews, and to alleviate the consequences of [Jewish] persecution" ("Report of the American Jewish Committee," *American Jewish Year Book* 10 [1908], 238). Led by affluent American Jews of central European ancestry—notably Louis Marshall (1856–1929), Jacob Schiff (1847–1920), Mayer Sulzberger (1843–1923), Julian W. Mack (1866–1943), Julius Rosenwald (1862–1932), Joseph Proskauer (1877–1971), and other successful lawyers, bankers, and entrepreneurs—the AJC sought to act as the voice of American Jewry. Though the AJC swiftly developed into a highly effective organization for the protection of Jewish interests and rights, its authority was challenged in the United States by a broad spectrum of Jewish progressives, including labor, women's, and Zionist groups whose members objected to its conservative, oligarchic, and patriarchal approach to American Jewish affairs.

25. The Swedish diplomat Count Folke Bernadotte (1895–1948) played a key role in World War II in negotiating the release of prisoners from Nazi concentration camps. In May 1948, following the establishment of the State of Israel, the United Nations security council appointed Bernadotte to mediate the ongoing Arab-Jewish conflict and seek a regional peace agreement between Israel and the Arab League. While traveling in Jerusalem with Col. Andre P. Perot (1896–1948), commander of a detachment of French peacekeeping forces, Bernadotte was assassinated by members of the right-wing Zionist paramilitary group Lehi (also known as the

news was made known. We reviled the slayers, castigated them in strong language — just like everyone else. But we felt more than horror. We felt terror, too. No one started a pogrom against actors when Booth assassinated Lincoln[26] — but we were afraid that every Jew would bear the guilt of the slaying of Bernadotte.

We are equally sensitive to favorable propaganda. Recently in Atlanta a school burned down. Our county schools, already overburdened with large enrollments, could not absorb the pupils of E. Rivers School.[27] Over eight hundred children were threatened by a make-shift year of education. Our Temple . . . along with almost every church in the area, offered their facilities for use. Both Jewish buildings were found to have excellent facilities, and both are in daily use as public schools. We would be less than human if we did not feel some gratification over the opportunity thus given us for public service. I am certain that members of the church being used felt a similar glow of pride. But with us it went further. We looked upon it as a God-given opportunity to cement public relations. Now these people would see that we're just like they are — no horns, no beards — just nice, friendly people like themselves.

There's nothing wrong with this desire to safeguard our position in the community, only the emphasis is misplaced. The sin we commit is in thinking that the goal is unattainable by our own efforts. It isn't. The means of winning the esteem of others is not over the sea nor up in the heavens where only a miracle can make it effective. The means is very close to use — in our mouths and in our hearts. At the risk of alienating all the vast congregation of Israel whose faces are seen in the synagogue only these two days each year, it must be said that far more important than filling our school house with strangers is the need for filling our Temples with Jews. If we want our non-Jewish friends to respect us, then we must first respect ourselves. . . . A Jew, ignorant of the meaning of his

---

Stern gang). The Israeli government subsequently outlawed the Lehi group and prosecuted and jailed those responsible for the murders.

26. The American actor and Confederate sympathizer John Wilkes Booth (1838–1865) assassinated President Abraham Lincoln (1809–1865) on April 14, 1865.

27. On September 14, 1948, the E. Rivers Elementary School (originally the Peachtree Heights School, renamed in 1926 to honor Eretus Rivers [1872–1932], a philanthropic Atlanta railway executive and real estate developer) burned to the ground in an accidental fire. While a new school (designed by the firm Stevens and Wilkinson) was being built, classes were temporarily held at The Temple and the Second Ponce de Leon Baptist Church. When the new school opened its doors in 1950, the building was featured in Time magazine and acclaimed as an outstanding example of the International Style in architecture ("Better School for the South," Architectural Forum 94 [April 1951], 161–63).

faith, cannot expect to gain the admiration of his Christian friends.... When we know our religion, we may be moved to live nobler lives, to act more honorably, to love more sincerely.... We may well offer ourselves as an entirely new person to our non-Jewish neighbors—a person worthy of respect and deserving honor.

This is the Day of Atonement. We have neither time nor desire for subterfuge. Let us be honest with ourselves just this once. We want the good opinion of our neighbors. We need the security that their respect alone can give us.... Let us this day look into our hearts—admit the sin of neglect of which all of us are guilty. And pray that in the year to come we may by our devotion to our faith merit the forgiveness which we pray will be ours today....

36

"WHAT THE JEWS BELIEVE"

A Liberal Rabbi Explains Judaism to the Readers of
Life Magazine
(1950)

◇◇◇

RACHEL GORDAN

On September 11, 1950, *Life* published Rabbi Philip S. Bernstein's (1901–1985) featured article, "What the Jews Believe" (excerpted below). The Rochester rabbi's article spilled onto a dozen pages of the magazine and set out to answer typical questions about Judaism.[1] As John Shaw Billings (1891–1975), the magazine's first editor, wrote to Bernstein in January of that year: "The article we are looking for is primarily theological. It is not political; it is not cultural; it is not sociological. It answers in the simplest (and loftiest) terms the Christian questions 'What is a good Jew? What does he believe? Why does he believe it?' The article, for authority, should be written by a rabbi, but it is addressed to the non-Jews. Unless the non-Jew understands it and accepts it and warms to its exposition of a faith not his own, the article is a failure."[2]

Here, the *Life* editor made plain the goals of much post–World War II literature introducing readers to Judaism. This literature consisted of magazine articles and books that set out to explain what was called the "third side of America's religious triangle" in terms that the majority non-Jewish population would understand.[3] Previous decades had seen a few primers on Judaism published in the United States—the books by the Orthodox rabbi Leo Jung (1892–1987) about Judaism in the 1920s were among the best regarded

1. For the complete article, see Philip S. Bernstein, "What the Jews Believe," *Life*, September 11, 1950, 160–62, 164, 167–72, 174, and 179.

2. Letter from John Shaw Billings to Philip S. Bernstein, January 12, 1950, box 5: "What the Jews Believe" (*Life* article), folder: "Correspondence, PSB and John Shaw Billings of *Life*, January–February 1950," Philip S. Bernstein Collection, University of Rochester Rare Books, Rochester, NY.

3. Quoted in Kevin M. Schutz, *Tri-Faith America: How Catholics and Jews Held Postwar America to Its Protestant Promise* (New York: Oxford University Press, 2011), 76.

in their time[4]—but only in the postwar era do we find the flowering of such explanatory literature. Bernstein's cousin, the Conservative rabbi Milton Steinberg (1903–1950), authored another of the era's most popular texts, *Basic Judaism* (1948), and Herman Wouk—the modern Orthodox novelist and winner of the Pulitzer Prize—wrote another, *This Is My God* (1959). Indeed, authors in all of the major movements of mid-twentieth-century American Judaism contributed to this literature. Bernstein subsequently expanded his 1950 *Life* article and published a book in the following year by the same title.

Bernstein's article and book are notable because they demonstrate a number of important characteristics of the genre and the era out of which it emerged. As a *Life* article, "What the Jews Believe" was intentionally positioned as middle-brow literature and aimed to provide cultural uplift for a general lay audience. That in itself was notable: since when had learning about Judaism become a sign that one was an educated American? It would be difficult to find one event or figure to mark the beginning of this changed status for Jews and American culture. In the decades following World War II, however, we find evidence that while many Americans had entered the war with marked antipathy for this persecuted minority religion, whose adherents were regarded as alien and not quite white, they exited the war with new sympathy for Jews and a growing acceptance of Judaism. In the mid-twentieth century, the desire to know something about the religious group persecuted by America's wartime enemies became a sign of one's bona fides as a liberal American.

Two other striking features of Bernstein's *Life* essay are its focus on Judaism as a religion (it is evident that Bernstein followed Billings's editorial directions) and its use of Christian categories as starting points of explanation. From the beginning of the article, Bernstein answers an imaginary Christian's questions about Jewish religion: "The Jew has no single organized church. He has no priests. The concept of salvation by faith is alien to his mind." But Bernstein is also willing to proclaim the value and distinctiveness of Judaism: "Yet he has deep religious convictions which run like golden threads through all Jewish history. For him Judaism is a way of life, here and now. He does not serve his God for the sake of reward, for the fruit of the good life is the good life. Thus his answers about the nature of his religious beliefs are profoundly different from the answers made by Christians."

Although scholars of American religious history tend to draw a correlation

4. Leo Jung, *Essence of Judaism: A Guide to Facts of Jewish Law and Life* (Philadelphia: Little Blue Books, 1924), and *Living Judaism* (New York: Night and Day Press, 1927).

between American interest in the Jews' distinctive roots and heritage and the countercultural moment of the late 1960s and 1970s, the literature that introduced readers to Judaism, of which Bernstein's work is an important example, suggests that Americans—both Jews and non-Jews—were beginning to learn about, and even embrace, the distinctiveness of Judaism a decade earlier.

◇◇◇

Philip S. Bernstein, "What the Jews Believe," *Life*, September 11, 1950

Source: Excerpt from Philip S. Bernstein, "What the Jews Believe," *Life*, September 11, 1950, 160–62. Reprinted by permission of Alice B. Perkins.

The Jew has no single organized church. He has no priests. The concept of salvation by faith[5] is alien to his mind. Yet he has deep religious convictions which run like golden threads through all Jewish history. For him Judaism is a way of life, here and now. He does not serve his God for the sake of reward, for the fruit of the good life is the good life.[6] Thus his answers about the nature of his religious beliefs are profoundly different from the answers made by Christians.

Judaism around the world is marked by diversity of practice and latitude of faith. But for all the degrees of divergence on detail, a great common denominator of faith unites most American Jews. This unique agreement is not imposed from the top down upon the congregations because the Jew acknowledges no supreme ecclesiastical authority, but rather it wells up from the depth of the Jewish heart, nourished in the long history of an ancient people.

In the days of ancient Israel the priesthood at Jerusalem laid down the law for

5. Salvation by faith alone is a Christian theological doctrine that Martin Luther (1483–1546), the architect of the Protestant Reformation, used to make a central distinction between Protestantism and Catholicism. The doctrine asserts that humanity is fallen and sinful, unable to save itself, but that God grants pardon or justification solely by virtue of one's faith. In this pardoning, God imputes Christ's righteousness to the sinning believer.

6. Here, Bernstein glosses over the fact that many Jews do believe in an afterlife as part of the reward for this life, and that the resurrection of the dead is a core doctrine of Jewish theology. For more traditional Jews, the belief in a messianic era includes the belief that the bodies of the dead will be brought back to life. However, Bernstein's elision of Jewish belief in an afterlife reflects mid-twentieth-century liberal Reform (and, to some extent, Conservative) rabbinical thought that Jews' not believing in an afterlife was in keeping with Judaism as a more rational religion. In mid-century explanatory texts like Bernstein's, Catholicism was often the implicit negative foil to a modern, rational Judaism.

all Jews. Then in 586 BCE, Nebuchadnezzar[7] besieged Jerusalem,[8] demolished Solomon's Temple,[9] and carried the Jews into exile in Babylon.[10] With their Temple and their priesthood[11] gone, the Jews in the strange new communities where they found themselves formed voluntary assemblages for common worship and study of the law. These congregations were called synagogues, quite free and independent of one another. This institution proved so valuable that it has been continued to this day as the method of Jewish worship. It also provided the basic pattern for the churches which, after Paul, the Christians set up and developed along more unified lines.[12] Among the Jews, however, the synagogue has survived in its pristine form. Any adult male Jews today can establish a congregation.

The congregation's rabbi is a teacher, not a priest. Without any vested ecclesiastical authority, he is not even necessary to the functioning of the synagogue. Any male Jew with sufficient knowledge of the prayers and the laws can con-

7. Nebuchadnezzar II (605–562 BCE), the king of Babylon, succeeded his father who had defeated the Assyrians. Nebuchadnezzar expanded the Babylonian empire through conquest of Jerusalem and Judah and organized building projects, with the most effort directed at the city of Babylon—which became one of the wonders of the ancient world. Babylon and Nebuchadnezzar II are described negatively in the Book of Daniel, which describes Babylon as a city of sin and evil.

8. In 589 BCE Nebuchadnezzar II laid siege to Jerusalem, leading to starvation and disease among the inhabitants and culminating in the destruction of the city and Solomon's Temple in 586 BCE (see chapter 6, note 65). Selective about who was exiled and who was left behind, the Babylonians took the elite of Judah captive and left behind the lower classes. During the Babylonian exile (586–539 BCE), the Judaeans managed to preserve their religious identity, and the institutions they developed had a large influence on Judaism and religious thought.

9. Solomon's Temple was built in 957 BCE by King Solomon, who succeeded his father, King David. Solomon's Temple, also known as the First Temple, was the only place where Israelites could offer sacrifices. The Temple replaced the Tabernacle that had been constructed in the Sinai Desert.

10. Jews who had formerly resided in the Kingdom of Judah were exiled to Babylon, and Judah became a Babylonian province.

11. According to the Hebrew Bible, the priesthood of ancient Israel was composed of men who were patrilineal descendants of Aaron (the older brother of Moses), who served in the Tabernacle. The priests' temple role included offering animal sacrifices, priestly blessings, and purification rituals. A high priest was anointed to serve in certain functions, such as entering the Holy of Holies (the inner sanctuary first of the Tabernacle and then of the Temple) on Yom Kippur (the Day of Atonement) to offer an animal sacrifice to God. See Exod. 40:12–16 and Lev. 21.

12. Paul the Apostle, or Saint Paul, was born a Jew named Saul of Tarsus. He was both a Roman citizen and a Jew, and he became a Christian who taught Jesus's gospel and founded churches throughout the Mediterranean basin.

duct a religious service, officiate at marriages and bury the dead. During [World War II], although more than half the rabbis of the country volunteered to be chaplains and 311 actually served in uniform, they could not begin to cover the multitudinous units in which Jews were found. Consequently, on many of the battlefronts of Europe and on remote Pacific Islands, Jewish officers and enlisted personnel officiated at religious exercises.[13]

In the central fortress of Jewish spirituality, the Torah is the repository for the Law of Judaism. Torah embraces a triple meaning. Primarily it is the Sacred Scrolls found in every synagogue. These are contained in an ornamental ark which, whenever possible, is built into the wall of the structure so that when the congregation faces it they look toward Jerusalem's Holy Temple. This is an abiding reminder of the biblical Ark of the Covenant in which the Tablets of the Law were carried.[14] The Torah scrolls are written by hand on parchment, fastidiously and often beautifully done by one who is usually a descendant of generations of scribes. In 1908 when the synagogue of which this writer is now minister burned down,[15] an Irish policeman dashed to the ark and seized the Torah. He handed it to the rabbi who was rushing up to the building. "Here," he said, "I saved your crucifix." Well, the Jews have no crucifix, but the policeman had the right idea: the scrolls are the most sacred symbols of Judaism.

Torah has a second meaning: the Pentateuch, the first five books of the Bible: Genesis, Exodus, Leviticus, Numbers, Deuteronomy.[16] These books are the acknowledged foundation of Judaism, containing the principles of the faith, the Ten Commandments, the golden rule, the laws of holiness.[17] The Pentateuch is

13. Bernstein himself played a significant role in the military, serving as an official adviser on Jewish affairs to U.S. army commanders and helping find homes for displaced Jews after the war.

14. The Ark of the Covenant is described in the Book of Exodus as a gold-covered wooden chest with a lid that contained the two stone tablets on which the Ten Commandments were written. It was built according to specifications that God gave to Moses while the Israelites were encamped at the foot of Mount Sinai. The Ark was carried by the Levites.

15. Although Bernstein cites 1908 as the year of the Brith Kodesh fire in this *Life* essay, the historical record indicates that the fire actually occurred a year later. See "Fire Breaks Out in Selden Building, Sweeping Rapidly to All Adjoining Streets—Berith Kodesh Temple Destroyed," *Rochester Democrat and Chronicle*, April 14, 1909, 12; Kerry M. Olitzky and Marc Lee Raphael, *The American Synagogue: A Historical Dictionary and Sourcebook* (Westport, CT: Greenwood Press, 1996), 267–68.

16. Pentateuch is a Greek word meaning "five books."

17. The Golden Rule has its biblical source in Lev. 19:18, which states: "Thou shalt not avenge, nor bear any grudge against the children of thy people, but thou shalt love thy neighbor as thyself: I am the LORD." The New Testament includes a few variations on this Hebrew Bible

at once the biography of the greatest Jew of all time—Moses—and the history of the formation of the Jewish nation and the development of its faith. It runs the whole gamut of Jewish spiritual experience from the sublime poetry of the creation narrative to the minutiae of the dietary laws. So precious is the Pentateuch to the Jews that they divide it into fixed weekly portions and read them on every Sabbath and holy day in the year. When the sacred round is completed, there is the gay festival of Simchas Torah [sic] ("rejoicing in the law") at which the last verses of Deuteronomy are followed by the first verses of Genesis, symbolizing the eternal cycle of the law.[18]

Finally, Torah means teaching, learning, doctrine. If a Jew says, "Let us study Torah," he might be referring to the Pentateuch or to the Prophets or to the Talmud or any of the sacred writings. He is certainly referring to the first obligation of the Jew to study God's ways and requirements as revealed in Holy Writ.

For a Jew the educational process begins at the age of five. According to tradition, a drop of honey is placed on the first page the child is to learn to read; he kisses it, thus beginning an association of pleasantness which is expected to last through life. When most of the world was illiterate, every Jewish boy could read and by 13 was advanced in the study of a complex literature. Thus arose the love of learning, the keenness of intellect to be found among so many Jews.

For all his love of learning for its own sake, the religious Jew finds much more in the Torah than burdensome legalism.[19] It is an unending source of inspiration and practical help to him. He begins and ends the day with prayers. He thanks God before and after every meal, even when he washes his hands. All his waking day the traditional Jew wears a ritual scarf beneath his outer garments as

---

version of the Golden Rule. Bernstein's labeling of this teaching as the Golden Rule is a nod to Christian nomenclature, as it was Protestants who first called Jesus's teaching "Do unto others as you would have done to you" the Golden Rule. The "laws of holiness" refers to Lev. 17–26, in which the Israelites are told what the Lord expects of them.

18. On the holiday Simhat Torah, the final portion of the Book of Deuteronomy is read in the synagogue followed by the beginning of the Book of Genesis, allowing for the annual cycle of Torah readings to continue unbroken.

19. Bernstein's use of the term "burdensome legalism" is a response to the Christian attack on Judaism as a works-based religion in which salvation is earned by obedience to Jewish law, instead of by faith alone. This criticism has a Pauline genealogy in that the Apostle Paul was a Pharisee before he became a Christian, and his disillusionment with and critique of the Pharisaic sect's concern for legalism became the basis for this strain of anti-Judaism. After the destruction of the Second Temple in 70 CE, as Pharisaic beliefs became the basis for rabbinic Judaism, criticism of the Pharisees as overly concerned with law metamorphosed into criticism of Jews in general.

a reminder of God's nearness and love.[20] There are prescribed prayers for birth, circumcision, marriage, illness, death. Even the appearance of a rainbow evokes an ancient psalm of praise. In effect, law means the sanctification of life.[21]

Jews never regarded the codification of law as a strait jacket. One basic device keeps it fluid: the oral law which supplemented the written law and was subject to emendation, interpretation, adaptation.[22] For example the ancient Torah says, "An eye for an eye" [Exod. 21:24]. In itself this was an advance over the laws of the surrounding tribes [that] usually prescribed death for the taking of an eye. Nevertheless the sages were not content to let this law stand. They said that the intent of the law was to compel the offender to pay in damages the accepted equivalent for the loss of an eye. Thus the written law was not repudiated but became the basis of a sensible adaption to the realities of human society. As another example, the Torah proclaimed, "Remember the Sabbath day to keep it holy" [Exod. 20:8–11]. Jews observed this commandment with the greatest seriousness, but in the oral law the rabbis evolved a whole series of necessary exceptions. They said the Sabbath could be violated to bring help to the sick or to defend oneself against attack. They formulated it into a principle, stating long before Jesus was born that the Sabbath was made for man, not man for the Sabbath.

The central prayer of Judaism is the Shemah: "Hear, O Israel, the Lord our God, the Lord is One."[23] This is the heart of every Jewish service. More, it is recited by the Jew when he believes death is approaching. Together with "Thou

20. The talit katan (small prayer shawl) is a four-cornered talit, worn by boys as young as three underneath or over their shirts. This poncho-like garment has knotted fringes known as zitzit attached to its four corners. For this reason, it is sometimes called arbah kanfot (meaning "four corners"). The Torah does not mandate wearing a talit katan, but rabbinic law strongly encourages doing so.

21. Here, again, Bernstein responds, somewhat defensively, to Christian charges that Judaism is tied to legalism by explaining that Jewish law is for the purpose of making life more holy and not legalism for its own sake.

22. Oral law refers to the legal interpretations of the Torah and rabbinical ordinances, explaining how Jewish law is to be carried out. This commentary was not recorded in the Pentateuch (the written Torah) but is found in the Mishnah and the Gemara, which together constitute the Talmud. These were recorded after the destruction of the Second Temple. According to Jewish tradition, the oral Torah was passed from generation to generation in an unbroken chain starting with Moses, to whom God gave the oral Torah along with the written Torah at Mount Sinai.

23. The traditional Jewish prayer known as Shemah Yisrael ("Hear, O Israel"), derived from Deut. 6:4 ("Hear, Israel, the Lord is our God, the Lord is One"), is a cardinal expression of Judaism's monotheistic belief system.

shalt love the Lord thy God with all my heart," it is to be found in printed form in the *mezuzah*, the little tubed case placed on the doorposts of the homes of observant Jews, a constant reminder of God's presence and a sign of the Jewishness of the inhabitants.

The Shemah and its concomitant prayers, including "Thou shalt love thy neighbor as thyself," originated in antiquity. Originally this affirmation of God's unity was a protest against idolatry: the entire history of the Hebrews in Palestine is marked by the struggles between the prophets who spoke for one God and the backsliding people who preferred visible idols to the invisible Jehovah. Following Paul, the Shemah took on a new significance. Although Jews are able, if they wish, to understand Jesus, the Jew of Nazareth, they have never been able to understand or accept the idea of the Trinity.[24] Thus from the beginning of the Christian era to this day, the Shemah has been the rallying point of Jewish loyalty confronting the persecution or the blandishments of a daughter religion.

For the modern American Jew two meanings have emerged which, while not new, are current in their emphasis. The first, suggested by the writings of Albert Einstein,[25] is, in effect, the scientific confirmation of the unity of God which binds the atom to the stars in universal law. The advances in human knowledge, always welcomed by the Jews, seem to vindicate his basic belief in the oneness of the universe.

From God to Man, from his Fatherhood to our brotherhood—this is the second meaning of the Shemah to modern Jews. The concept of human oneness has always been an integral element in the Jewish religious outlook. Frequently this has been misunderstood because of the Jews' insistence on remaining a distinctive group. The Jew has never believed that brotherhood means regimentation, the elimination of differences or the stifling of minorities. Loving your neighbor as yourself, he believes, requires respect for differences. One of the great rabbis who lived more than two thousand years ago said that the most important statement in the Bible was not the Ten Commandments nor the golden rule but "This is the book of the generations of man" [Gen. 5:1].[26] To the Jews themselves the Scriptures were not the heritage of a single people but of all humanity.

24. The Trinity is the Christian doctrine that God is one God but also three coeternal consubstantial persons: Father, Son, and Holy Spirit.

25. On Albert Einstein, see chapter 29, note 6.

26. The rabbinic teaching referred to here is Sifra Kedoshim II 4:12: "And you shall love your neighbor as yourself. Rabbi Akiva says: 'This is an all-embracing principle in the Torah.' Ben Azzai says: 'This is the numeration of the generations of Adam' [Gen. 5:1]—This is an even greater principle."

37

"OUR SIMPLE DUTY AS JEWS"

Herbert A. Friedman's Radio Address for the
United Jewish Appeal
(1957)

◇◇

FELICIA HERMAN

The development of a robust Jewish communal philanthropic infrastructure has been one of the defining elements of Jewish life in America, inspiring pride in generations of American Jews, generating admiration from other
American ethnic and religious groups, and catalyzing untold amounts of money
and hours of volunteer and professional time to meet the massive challenges and
opportunities facing the Jewish people in the United States and around the world.

Far beyond being simply a financial instrument, Jewish philanthropy in
America has also served as a powerful community-building tool — even, as the
sociologist Jonathan Woocher has argued, a critical element of the community's
"civil religion."[1] Especially with the rise of professionalized, federated giving
in the early twentieth century[2] (a response to the need for more efficient fund-
raising mechanisms to meet the huge demands of mass immigration), Jewish
communities large and small across America have used philanthropy as a way
to build and strengthen their personal, professional, and philanthropic ties.
American Jews have gathered at organizational events, worked together at fund-
raising drives, built professional affinity groups, and even traveled together on
missions to Israel and Jewish communities around the world. This work has
immeasurably strengthened a sense of Jewish peoplehood for American Jews,
creating a tangible sense of connection to Jews in their own communities and
around the world, as well as an opportunity to act upon an age-old sense of collective responsibility for fellow Jews.

1. Jonathan Woocher, "'Sacred Survival' Revisited: American Jewish Civil Religion in the
New Millennium," in *The Cambridge Companion to American Judaism*, ed. Dana Evan Kaplan (Cambridge: Cambridge University Press, 2005), 283–98.

2. On the history of the Jewish Federation system in the United States, see chapter 33,
note 3. On the history of the United Jewish Appeal, see chapter 43, note 29, and Marc Lee
Raphael, *A History of the United Jewish Appeal, 1939–1982* (Chico, CA: Scholars Press, 1982).

Judaism's injunctions to care for the poor and needy date back to biblical times. A diverse array of institutions facilitating that care emerged over time, as Jews in different periods and regions adapted to local constraints, opportunities, and changing communal needs. This was especially true as different Jewish communities evolved and adapted to local cultures and circumstances.

Philanthropy formed a cornerstone of Jewish life in America from the first moments of Jewish settlement, with the so-called Stuyvesant Promise of 1655.[3] Rejecting a request from New Amsterdam's director-general, Peter Stuyvesant (1592–1672), to permit the expulsion of Jews recently arrived from Brazil, the Dutch West India Company allowed the refugees to remain "provided the poor among them shall not become a burden to the company or to the community, but be supported by their own nation."[4] In America, Jews' responsibility to care for their own dovetailed with what the French diplomat and political observer Alexis de Tocqueville (1805–1859) noticed as early as 1835 as Americans' "extreme skill" of founding social and civic associations to meet every conceivable communal need, and "inducing [people] to pursue it voluntarily."[5] Over time, American Jews created a panoply of philanthropic initiatives to address the core challenges facing not only their own communities but also Jews overseas: providing social services for the poor, elderly, orphaned, and infirm, as well as vocational training; absorbing and/or resettling millions of Jews fleeing persecution; fighting ever-evolving manifestations of antisemitism; building a Jewish national home in Israel; supporting Jewish education and spiritual communities; creating recreational facilities like community centers and summer camps; improving community relations; and even using the tools and values of Jewish giving to support non-Jews in need in the United States and around the world.

The heyday of American Jewish communal philanthropy was the 1950s and early 1960s—a "golden age," according to the historian Jack Wertheimer and others.[6] Demands for Jewish philanthropy were high, but they were met by an outpouring of giving that dwarfed anything any Jewish community had given

3. On the Stuyvesant Promise, see Beth Wenger, *New York Jews and the Great Depression: Uncertain Promise* (New Haven, CT: Yale University Press, 1996), 139–42.

4. Dutch West India Company, "Reply to Stuyvesant's Petition (April 26, 1655)," in *The Jew in the Modern World: A Documentary History*, ed. Paul Mendes-Flohr and Jehuda Reinharz, 3rd ed. (New York: Oxford University Press, 2011), 502.

5. Alexis de Toqueville, *Democracy in America*, vol. 2 (1840), in Alexis de Toqueville, *The Tocqueville Reader: A Life in Letters and Politics*, ed. Olivier Zunz and Alan S. Kahan (Malden, MA: Blackwell, 2002), 181.

6. Jack Wertheimer, "Jewish Organizational Life in the United States since 1945," *American Jewish Year Book* 95 (1995), 4.

in history. Between 1939 and 1967, the Jewish Federation system raised over $3 billion, more than half of which was sent to Jewish communities outside of the United States.[7] Within the broader American context of the postwar economic boom and an explosion of engagement in civic associations of all types, American Jews responded to the dramatic needs of the time with unprecedented generosity. Most of the remnant of European Jewry—including those now trapped behind the Iron Curtain—wanted to leave Europe and needed to be rescued and resettled. And the creation of the State of Israel led to other massive financial needs, both in terms of the general upbuilding of the state and the resettlement of nearly a million Jews from across the Middle East who fled or were expelled from their ancient communities in waves of violent antisemitism that swept Arab countries for decades after 1948.

Rabbi Herbert A. Friedman's (1918–2008) moving fund-raising speech for the United Jewish Appeal in 1957 offers a glimpse into this extraordinary time in American Jewish history. Using the innovative (though not unprecedented) technique of broadcasting a sectarian fund-raising appeal on a local radio station, Friedman invited his listeners to participate in the exciting—albeit tragic—events unfolding overseas. He was one of the foremost American Jewish leaders of the postwar period, a charismatic speaker with a colorful, daring background. He had served as a U.S. Army chaplain from 1944 to 1947, witnessing the horrors of the Holocaust and the need for refugee resettlement firsthand. Immediately after the war, while still a chaplain, he was recruited by the Haganah, the Jewish underground in Palestine, to help smuggle arms, Jewish displaced persons, and even medieval Jewish documents stolen by the Nazis into Palestine. The latter project, which he undertook at the request of the historian Gershom Scholem (1897–1982), was discovered by his superiors, and he was honorably discharged from the U.S. military.[8] He spent the next three-plus decades of his life leading and fund-raising for the United Jewish Appeal, galvanizing American Jews to donate hundreds of millions of dollars for fellow Jews abroad who were caught up in the historic upheavals and transformations of the latter half of the twentieth century.

◇◇

7. Daniel J. Elazar, *Community and Polity: The Organizational Dynamics of American Jewry* (Philadelphia: Jewish Publication Society, 1976), 220.

8. Herbert A. Friedman, *Roots of the Future* (New York: Gefen Books, 1999), 58–65, 102–5, 107–11, and 130–42.

Herbert A. Friedman's[9] Radio Address for the United Jewish Appeal, May 26, 1957

Source: Herbert A. Friedman, "Radio Address for Long Beach, California" (May 26, 1957), Rabbi Herbert A. Friedman Collection, 1930–2004, MS-763, Series H: United Jewish Appeal, 1945–1995, Subseries 1: Sermons, Speeches, and Writings, 1949–1982, box 22, folder 9, the Jacob Rader Marcus Center of the American Jewish Archives, Cincinnati.

. . . One of the most gratifying experiences I have encountered in traveling around the country on behalf of the United Jewish Appeal[10] has been the manner in which communities have been responding with an extraordinary display of devotion and ingenuity.

What is happening here today in Long Beach is a most spectacular demonstration of what I mean. This method of getting directly into each home in the community with so meaningful a message—and all in a space of a half-hour—is something almost unique in the history of local fund-raising. The splendid cooperation of this institution—KFOX—symbolizes the best tradition of American democracy with its historic concern for victims of persecution and injustice.[11]

9. A prominent American Reform rabbi and Jewish leader, Herbert A. Friedman (1918–2008) served as the executive vice-chairman of the United Jewish Appeal (UJA; see the next note). (1956–69). During Friedman's tenure, the annual amount of funds raised by the organization rose from $50 million to $450 million, supporting Jews in need around the world and in the State of Israel. Friedman developed activities that became regular features of the UJA's fund-raising strategy: donor mission trips to Israel and former Nazi concentration camps in Europe, emergency fund-raising campaigns, training programs for young lay leaders, and gala dinners honoring major donors. In 1985, he helped the philanthropist Leslie Wexner (b. 1937) create the Wexner Heritage Foundation, a training program for American lay leadership that has since trained nearly 1,800 American Jewish leaders.

10. The United Jewish Appeal for Refugees and Overseas Needs (UJA) was created in 1939 to serve as a core component of American Jewry's national fund-raising infrastructure. The UJA combined the efforts of relief agencies that aimed to help and support Jews abroad—namely, the American Jewish Joint Distribution Committee (which assisted Jews in Europe), the United Palestine Appeal (which promoted the immigration and settlement of Jews in pre-state Israeli society), and the National Coordinating Committee Fund (for European refugees arriving in the United States). In the decades following World War II, fund-raising for domestic Jewish needs— originally conducted at the regional level by some two hundred Jewish communities—was centralized by the Jewish Federation structure and the UJA. In 1999, the UJA combined with the Council of Jewish Federations and United Israel Appeal to become United Jewish Communities, later renamed the Jewish Federations of North America. See also chapter 43, note 29.

11. This is an interesting comment for Friedman to make, especially given that Jewish and other nonprofits had been using radio as a fund-raising mechanism for some time—airing

My warmest congratulations to all concerned in this humane and imaginative approach to campaigning. I wish you great success tonight. And now let me tell you what I have on my mind.

My friends, we have a tremendous task of life-saving this year, for which we are soliciting enormous sums of money.[12] Actually we are asking you for a double gift—one to the regular campaign and an extra one to the Emergency Rescue Fund (ERF). The monies of the regular campaign are used for the integration and absorption of hundreds of thousands of immigrants who have gone to Israel in the past several years, but who are not yet self-sufficient and who need further help on the road to independence. The regular monies are used also for the thousands who are in want and need in various countries of the world, where we maintain through the Joint Distribution Committee (JDC) feeding and health programs, hospitals, schools and all sorts of services for people who are underprivileged. For these two purposes, we ask you at least to repeat your regular campaign gift of last year.[13]

---

speeches, radio dramas on themes connected to fund-raising campaigns, and interviews, and even broadcasting the events at annual organizational dinners. Friedman had used an even more innovative technology (closed-circuit television) to broadcast what was likely a version of this same speech earlier in the year. He is likely referring here to the broadcasting of Jewish-specific causes on stations in smaller Jewish communities (for example, Long Beach's Jewish population was about 6,000). He had made the same comment one month earlier in a radio address to the San Bernardino Jewish community, consisting of four hundred Jewish families.

12. The overwhelming needs of international Jewry in the postwar era—and the greater ability to raise funds for such dramatic and historic needs as opposed to more quotidian local needs—profoundly shifted the focus of American Jewish philanthropy from domestic to overseas relief in this period. In the 1930s, 7 percent of Jewish philanthropy went to international needs. By the end of World War II, funds were divided between domestic and overseas (including Palestine) purposes, and throughout the 1950s more than 55 percent of the funds raised went overseas. The focus shifted over time from helping displaced persons in Europe to resettling them in Israel and building up the Jewish state itself. See Wertheimer, "Jewish Organizational Life," 16.

13. One of Friedman's fund-raising innovations was institutionalizing emergency campaigns that would raise additional funds for Jews overseas, primarily in Israel. This two-line strategy (named for the two separate lines on pledge cards, one where donors pledge an amount to the annual campaign, and one where they make a pledge to the special campaign) raised money for both through annual Jewish Federation campaigns (with 55–65 percent of funds raised allocated overseas) and through emergency campaigns. Fund-raising for the UJA reached peaks in 1946 with aid to Jewish displaced persons, in 1948 to support mass immigration to Israel, in 1956 for the Special Survival Fund ($17 million to finance the mass immigration of North African Jews to Israel), and in 1957 for the Emergency Relief Fund, which fell short of its stated $100 million goal but nonetheless raised $25 million to assist Hungarian, Polish, Egyptian, and North African Jews. For the data cited here, see S. P. Goldberg, "Jewish Communal Services: Pro-

What then is the purpose of the extra gift to the ERF? We are confronted this year with the massive problem of rescuing at least 100,000 Jews (and some observers including Mr. [David] Ben-Gurion[14] himself say there will be more) from lands where they are persecuted, in terror, under attack, and from which they are once again running for their lives. I think you should know that there are more Jewish refugees in flight on the roads again in 1957 than at any time in the last ten years.

Our experience has shown that it takes around $1,000 to save a person—to bring him out of a land of darkness somewhere to a new home somewhere in another part of the free world. The arithmetic is inescapable. To rescue 100,000 people at $1,000 per person will cost $100 million. That is the amount we are seeking to raise in the ERF, above and beyond the normal campaign. That is why our people all over America are stretching themselves to give large rescue fund gifts. Everyone realizes that when human life is at stake, money becomes secondary, and really the greatest value of money is that it can actually purchase life.

Where are all these Jews coming from? What are the areas of danger which we say involve 100,000 people[?] First of all, there is Egypt.[15] You all know by now that many ex-Nazis have found a welcome home in Egypt under the regime of dictator [Gamal Abdel] Nasser.[16] Those Nazis designed brutal plans against the

---

grams and Finances," *American Jewish Year Book* 59 (1958), 141–42, "Jewish Communal Services: Programs and Finances," *American Jewish Year Book* 60 (1959), 74, and "Jewish Communal Services: Programs and Finances," *American Jewish Year Book* 61 (1960), 66.

14. David Ben-Gurion (1886–1973), a founder of the State of Israel and its first prime minister and minister of defense (both 1948–54 and 1955–63). For more information, see chapter 39, note 28.

15. Jews had lived in Egypt since biblical times. Before 1948, the Egyptian Jewish community numbered about 75,000—one of many populous Jewish communities scattered across the Arab world. The creation of the State of Israel in 1948 led to a massive increase in hostility toward Middle Eastern Jews. In Egypt this included arrests and sentences to detention camps, violence (including murder), property confiscation, rioting, and harassment. About 20,000 Egyptian Jews fled or were expelled from Egypt in 1948, about three-quarters of whom found refuge in Israel. Emigration slowed during the first part of the 1950s but rose again during the Suez Crisis of 1956 (see chapter 38, note 9). Declaring all Jews to be Zionists and enemies of the state, Egypt expelled almost 25,000 Jews (about half of the remaining Jewish population) and imprisoned another 1,000. Again, most Egyptian Jews wound up settling in Israel. Almost all were penniless, being allowed to take only one suitcase and a small amount of cash out of Egypt, and being forced to sign documents declaring that they were leaving voluntarily and donating their property to the Egyptian government.

16. In 1952, the military officer Gamal Abdel Nasser (1918–1970) toppled the Egyptian monarchy in a coup (see chapter 38, note 10). The monarchy had cooperated heavily with the

Jews of Egypt, at the request of the Egyptian government. The plans they drew up are similar to the Nuremberg Laws and other Nazi edicts.[17] Since last November, when the plan was put into effect, thousands of Jews in Egypt have been arrested, thrown into concentration camps, beaten by police, had their businesses taken away, lost their jobs, had their bank accounts frozen, had their money stolen, and were actually deported from the country, many of them in handcuffs.

The International Red Cross has been chartering mercy ships which have carried Jews to European ports, and so far 20,000 people—almost half of the entire Jewish population of Egypt—[have] already left that unhappy land. Just the other day another vessel arrived in Athens with 604 on board, of whom 115 were sick and old. I have seen these people arriving in Naples, Rome, Paris—they are shocked, bewildered. This is reminiscent of the way Jews were treated in Nazi Germany fifteen and twenty years ago. I tell you it is like a nightmare. We have met these people and tried to assuage their pain. We have picked up the broken pieces and we try to rebuild the shattered lives. Most have gone on to Israel, but there are thousands in France, Italy and Greece who are absolutely penniless and who need help. These 20,000 who've come out are not the end. There are at least another 20,000 or perhaps more in Egypt, and I would venture to say that at the current rate of exodus, most of them will have left, and will thus become our responsibility, before many more months have gone by.

In addition to Egypt, there is Hungary. You all remember the saga of human heroism in which the courageous freedom fighters fled from Communism after the great revolution in Budapest last fall.[18] Among the refugees who fled from Hungary to Austria were about 10 percent who were Jews—1,700 persons. We set up swift emergency machinery in Vienna to care for them, and we have already spent many millions of dollars. I am happy to say that a large number have already been cared for successfully. About 4,000 came to the United States,

---

Nazis, finding common cause in antagonism toward the British and French (both of which were colonizing forces throughout the Middle East), as well as toward Jews and the prospect of a new Jewish state on its border. After the war, many former Nazis escaped Europe and found refuge in Egypt.

17. The Nuremberg Laws were antisemitic laws introduced in 1935 in Nazi Germany. They prohibited Jews from becoming German citizens, marriages and sexual intercourse between Jews and Germans, and the employment of German gentile women under the age of forty-five in Jewish households.

18. The Hungarian Revolution (1956) prompted some 20,000 Jews to flee Hungary—one-fifth of the country's Jewish population and roughly 10 percent of all people who fled Hungary at the time. Unlike Egyptian Jewish refugees, most of whom emigrated to Israel, most Hungarian Jews resettled in the West—about half in the United States, Canada, Australia, Latin America, or western Europe.

another 3,000 to Canada, 1,000 to Australia, several thousand to Israel—all at great expense. On the other hand, I must sadly report to you that there are still 3,000 in Austria—and once again we have opened DP camps for them.[19] I never believed that we would ever again see DP camps for Jews on the continent of Europe. I thought that after the sickening inhumanity of the Hitler period we would be finished with those terrible initials. But we must use the phrase DP again today—and we are all working feverishly to close those camps as quickly as possible. This can only be done by taking the people out and giving them new homes for resettlement. Israel is willing to take them all, and we must continue to find the money. That's as far as Egypt and Hungary are concerned.

I wish I could tell you the whole story of what is happening in certain countries of eastern Europe, behind the Iron Curtain. If I could, I know you would be thrilled to the marrow of your bones by the tale of human rescue which is going on.[20] This part of the story must remain untold, but I want you to ponder seriously the plight of people who are living under Communist dictatorship and who are trying to hold on to their religion and their faith against all pressures. Freedom of religion is one of the most important principles of American democracy. For Jews, I would say, freedom of religion is the most important principle. Our brothers behind the Iron Curtain are striving for and yearning to maintain their independence as Jews. This is another great part of the rescue story in which you have a direct role. More than this I cannot say.

And where is Israel in all of this—gallant, embattled, valiant Israel—who

19. Displaced persons (DP) camps were set up in the immediate aftermath of World War II to house and care for the millions of Europeans displaced by the war, largely Jewish survivors of concentration camps, labor camps, and prisoner-of-war camps. Most DP camps had been closed by 1952. While millions of DPs were repatriated to their country of origin, the vast majority of Jews refused to return to countries where their communities had been exterminated and where they feared continued persecution. Most Jewish refugees moved to Israel, at first clandestinely (with the help of the Zionist movement) and then openly after the Jewish state was created in 1948.

20. This reference is likely to the Joint Distribution Committee's (JDC) revived work in Poland, newly sanctioned by the Polish government, to help Jews suffering in the wake of a new wave of antisemitism and ongoing repression under communism. In the fall of 1957, Friedman frequently referred to the JDC in his speeches. In 1958–59, when a new Polish government allowed Jews to emigrate, over 50,000 left the country—a majority of whom settled in Israel. Friedman might also be referring to changes afoot in Romania, which would lead in 1958 to the emigration of thousands of Romanian Jews. See Herbert A. Friedman, "Notes for Recording for Fall Communities," October 7, 1957, Rabbi Herbert A. Friedman Collection, 1930–2004, MS-763, Series H: United Jewish Appeal, 1945–1995, Subseries 1: Sermons, Speeches, and Writings, 1949–82, box 22, folder 11, the Jacob Rader Marcus Center of the American Jewish Archives, Cincinnati.

must strain every resource to be on guard against an Arab world which is united within itself, true, but which is united on one platform—namely, the destruction of Israel and its obliteration from the map[?] Struggling with a crushing defense burden, Israel might well take the position that at this moment she cannot be saddled with the extra burden of tens of thousands of penniless immigrants.

But Israel does not say that. Instead she throws wide open her ports, her homes, her schools and welcomes happily with loving arms all who come crowding to her shores. Israel is playing most unselfishly the heroic role for which she was created.[21] If there ever was a time when we could take pride in that little state, this is the hour. She is true to the highest ideals and fondest hopes we had for her as a strong and safe harbor for Jews who are in trouble elsewhere. I wish to God there had been an Israel before. Not all the six million would have perished under Hitler.

I know it is hard to grasp the idea of 100,000 people from Egypt, Hungary, eastern Europe, North Africa. But I think it is easy to conceive of one person or a family of five, or two brothers, or three sisters. Think of a man, a woman, a child, and people like yourselves, who are not tonight in the comfort of towns like Long Beach but on trains or planes or ships, being brought to freedom in Israel or America or Europe. And think of what it means to rescue each person at an average cost of $1,000. Think of how much better you will sleep tonight if you help rescue one or two or ten people. And think of how some weary refugee will rest easier tonight if he knows you are worrying about him.

It is our simple duty as Jews who are our brothers' keepers—and as human beings who want our own children to be proud of us—it is our simple duty to respond to this urgent call. Let each man do his utmost, make his largest possible double gift, and we shall again write a shining chapter in the glorious annals of Jewish self-help.

May I thank you for listening.

21. Despite the extreme financial challenges Israel faced in the 1950s, Ben-Gurion was passionately committed to keeping the country's doors open to newcomers. While this policy helped build up Israel's Jewish population and fulfill the country's mission of being a homeland and refuge for Jews from anywhere in the world, the reality on the ground was extraordinarily complex. The combination of mass immigration, including a large influx of impoverished, unskilled, and illiterate people; the lack of infrastructure and finances to absorb and care for a population that doubled in the first years of Israel's existence; and the profound differences between Ashkenazic and Mizrahi Jews, who had barely encountered each other until then, led to an intense culture clash that profoundly shaped Israel's social, cultural, and political life. Today, more than half of Israelis are of Mizrahi heritage. Much has been written on this topic. See, for example, Anita Shapira, *Ben-Gurion: Father of Modern Israel* (New Haven, CT: Yale University Press, 2014), 174–80.

38

"VALIANT BUILDERS, FIGHTERS, AND DREAMERS"

Abba Hillel Silver on American Jewish Relations with Israel (1957)

◇◇◇

OFER SHIFF

Abba Hillel Silver (1893–1963), arguably one of the two or three most important American Jewish leaders of the twentieth century, has been the focus of renewed attention in recent decades. A formidable American Zionist strategist and scholarly Reform rabbi, Silver played a pivotal role in the 1940s in the international campaign for Jewish statehood. After the creation of Israel in 1948, Silver suddenly found himself in a new role—namely, that of a dedicated Zionist who fiercely opposed the Israeli leadership's assertion of *aliyah* (Jewish immigration to Israel) as the only legitimate expression of post-1948 Zionism. A purported binary choice between Jewish life in the diaspora and Israel, Silver recognized, fundamentally challenged the postwar reality of Israel-diaspora relations and underscored Israeli skepticism in American Jewry's belief in American liberalism as a viable basis for long-term Jewish existence.

Viewed historically, it is clear the clash between Silver and Israeli officialdom was partly philosophical and partly the result of a power struggle in the 1950s between American Zionists and the Israeli political establishment. Though the discord forced Silver to resign from most of his official positions in the Zionist movement, he nevertheless remained a potent and commanding presence in the Jewish public arena. By the time Silver gave the speech reprinted in this chapter, occasioned by the launch of the Jewish Welfare Fund of Cleveland's inaugural fund-raising drive, he had come to terms with his political defeat. It is evident, however, that the rough-and-tumble of the political battlefield did not obviate his philosophical principles and ideological worldview. Together with staunch support for Israel's diplomatic struggles, Silver's speech includes subtle criticism of Israel's pessimistic outlook regarding Jewish–non-Jewish relations. It also prefigures the mix of support and criticism that would not only persist but would come to characterize the core problematic of American Jewish–Israeli Jewish relations in the decades ahead.

Delivered seven months after the Suez Crisis (October–November 1956) and approximately one month after Israeli diplomatic efforts failed to counteract Israel's forced withdrawal from the Sinai Peninsula without prior guarantees from the United States or the United Nations, Silver's speech featured a bitter reaction to what he regarded as unfair American and international pressure. He claimed that such pressure played into Soviet hands just when it invaded Hungary to quell the popular Hungarian uprising of October 1956. He also deplored the fact that, in contrast to the policy toward the Hungarian refugees (who fled Hungary after the Soviet invasion), the United States had not eased its immigration restrictions in favor of the Egyptian Jews who were expelled by the Egyptian authorities, nor had it called for an investigation of Egypt's human rights violations regarding its Jewish citizens.

In many ways, the speech expressed grave disappointment with the administration of President Dwight D. Eisenhower (1890–1969) in a manner reminiscent of Silver's harsh denunciations in the 1940s of the administrations of Presidents Franklin D. Roosevelt (1882–1945) and Harry S. Truman (1884–1972). However, a more careful reading of the speech reveals that its main purpose was to refute any pessimistic conclusions that might be drawn regarding what seemed to be a recurrent Jewish impotence in the face of the U.S. government's willingness to sacrifice Jewish interests and Jewish refugees yet again—as it had done during World War II. Silver's main effort to communicate optimism went into the speech's opening and closing sections. In both places he presented this optimism with respect to Zionism's historic struggles and Israel.

In the speech's introductory portion, Silver welcomed Robert E. Briscoe (1894–1969), the Orthodox Jewish mayor of Dublin, Ireland, and the guest of honor of the dinner event. He drew a comparison between the longtime Irish struggle for sovereignty and the Zionist struggle for a Jewish state. He called attention to the optimism and readiness to apply public pressure on the U.S. government that had characterized both Irish and Zionist national endeavors. In the concluding section of the speech, he recalled a visit in 1935 to the Winter Palace in Leningrad—the former residence of the Russian tsars that had been turned into a museum. In the library adjacent to the tsar's bedchamber, Silver was amazed to find a copy of Israel Zangwill's *Children of the Ghetto* (1898). The plot of this novel stressed the dream of immigrant Jews in their western European and American ghettos to become fully integrated into their new modern environments while still maintaining their Jewish identity. Using this book as a point of reference, Silver noted the considerable irony to be found in the fact that Zangwill's celebratory vision of the Jewish diaspora and the possibility of a free and unfettered Jewish existence could find such an unexpected home in the crucible of medieval European autocratic rule.

This diaspora-Zionist interpretive stance replaced Silver's earlier approach (during the years immediately after Israel's foundation) of overtly criticizing Israel-centric Zionism, with its pessimistic prognostications for diaspora life. It should be noted, however, that an element of criticism still remained. This may be seen in the humorous tone taken by Silver in his welcoming remarks to Briscoe—which in fact called attention to very serious assumptions about the differences in mentality between the North American "New World" and the "Old World" of Europe and Israel. In Silver's eyes, the idea of an Orthodox Jew being elected mayor of a Catholic city in Europe, or of a Catholic being elected mayor of Jerusalem, was almost inconceivable. This was despite the fact that similar situations were by no means inconceivable in the United States. Silver's jocularity thus presupposed very different expectations regarding social reality in Europe and Israel compared with the United States. Similar to his "children of the ghetto" vision, Silver's humorous remarks underscored his critical view, according to which Jewish aspirations to integrate into the non-Jewish world were still inconceivable in Israel. However, rather than a head-on confrontation with Israel, Silver focused on reinterpreting the Zionist dreams around which American Jews rallied in solidarity.

◇◇◇

Abba Hillel Silver,[1] Keynote Address to the Jewish Welfare Fund Appeal, April 11, 1957

Source: Abba Hillel Silver, Keynote Address to the Jewish Welfare Fund Appeal (April 11, 1957), Abba Hillel Silver Papers, MS-4787, Series V: Writings, 1909–1963 undated, box 70, folder 955: Jewish Welfare Fund, Cleveland, 1957, Western Reserve Historical Society, Cleveland, OH.

My dear Friends, you have assembled here, in such large numbers, for two purposes: first, to pay honor to a brave man, whose Irish luck and Jewish *mazel* [Yiddish for "good fortune"], made him Lord Mayor of Dublin.[2]

Ireland, they say, is a country in which the probable never happens, but the

1. Abba Hillel Silver (1893–1963), rabbi of the Temple-Tifereth Israel (Cleveland, OH), one of the largest and most venerable Reform synagogues in the United States, was the foremost American Zionist in the second half of the 1940s. On May 8, 1947, Silver presented the case for an independent Jewish state before the General Assembly of the United Nations, which led to passage on November 29 of the partition resolution and provided the legal basis for the creation of the State of Israel. See also chapter 25, note 34, and chapter 31, note 10.

2. Robert Briscoe (1894–1969), the son of Lithuanian Jewish immigrants, served as Lord Mayor of Dublin from 1956 to 1961. Active in the struggle for Irish national independence, he was also a strong supporter of Zionism and advocate for the rights of Jewish refugees.

impossible always does. And what was more impossible in the minds of those who do not know the unpredictable Irish, than for an Orthodox Jew to be elected chief magistrate of the principal city of Catholic Ireland.

But there are two places in the world where miracles still happen—Ireland and Israel. Our tradition has it that the millennium, when it comes, will be preceded by two messiahs, one, the Messiah ben Joseph, and the other, Messiah ben David. Well, the election of a Jew to be Mayor of Dublin, means that the Messiah ben Joseph has come. When an Irishman will be elected Mayor of Jerusalem, it will mean that the Messiah ben David has come, and the millennium will have definitely arrived.

I am heartened and grateful for Mr. Briscoe's presence in our midst tonight, for Ireland was very much in our minds when we carried on our long, often bitter, struggle for the establishment of the State of Israel. The historic experience of the Irish people was so reminiscent of our own that their long uphill struggle for freedom was an inspiration and challenge to us, as was the loyalty of the Irish Americans to their ancestral home.

Centuries of brutal persecution and oppression—which in the early half of the nineteenth century sent tens of thousands of its impoverished and starved sons and daughters to leave their native land and to seek new homes—and a prolonged campaign of slander and revilement did not break the spirit of the valiant race. Their fortunes touched bottom when they began their heroic fight for freedom, for home rule and for their national dignity.[3]

Toward the close of the last century, the American poet, Walt Whitman,[4] spoke of Ireland as an "ancient sorrowful mother, once a queen, now lean and tattered, crouching over a grave."[5]

But the grave was not the goal of the Irish patriots, and many of them paid

3. The Irish Home Rule movement campaigned for self-government for Ireland within the United Kingdom of Great Britain and Ireland. It was the dominant political movement of Irish nationalism from 1870 to the end of World War I.

4. The poet and humanist Walt Whitman (1819–1892) is considered one of the greatest figures in American letters. Among his enduring works is the collection of poetic verse titled *Leaves of Grass* (1855).

5. The reference is to the first stanza of Walt Whitman's "Old Ireland" (1861): "Far hence, amid an isle of wondrous beauty, / Crouching over a grave, an ancient sorrowful mother, / Once a queen—now lean and tattered, seated on the ground, / Her old white hair drooping dishevel'd round her head; / At her feet fallen an unused royal harp, / Long silent—she too long silent— mourning her shrouded hope and heir; / Of all the earth her heart most full of sorrow, because most full of love" (Walt Whitman, "Old Ireland" (November 2, 1861), ed. Matt Cohen, Ed Folsom, and Kenneth M. Price, Walt Whitman Archive, https://whitman-prod.unl.edu/published /periodical/poems/per.00078).

with their lives, that Ireland might be resurrected. They fought valiantly, with pen and sword, above ground and underground. Many of them died, many were imprisoned, many were driven into exile, and their brothers and sisters, though loyal citizens of the United States, came to their aid, politically and materially. They invoked the support of both political parties in our own country. In May 1919 a resolution was adopted in the Senate of the United States:[6]

"Resolved that the Senate of the United States express its sympathy with the aspirations of the Irish people for a government of their own Choice."[7]

And the Irish people won through to victory. All this was very much in the minds of Jewish fighters for the freedom of the Jewish people and the reestablishment of the State of Israel.

I can understand clearly enough, therefore, why an underground fighter for the freedom of Ireland, like Mr. Briscoe, is such an ardent champion of the young state of Israel — and why those of us who have fought for the freedom of Israel are such admirers of Mr. Briscoe and such friends of free Ireland.

I said at the outset, that we are assembled here in such large numbers for two purposes. The second is to inaugurate our 1957 Campaign for the Jewish Welfare Fund. That you have inaugurated [it] most auspiciously, the figures which are recorded here this evening clearly indicate. You are living up to your noblest traditions and the high expectations which you have of yourselves. One should never lack confidence in our people. When Moses, commissioned by God to return to Egypt and to summon the people of Israel to freedom, expressed the fear, "They may not believe" [Exod. 4:1], the rabbis declared that "our Moses spoke not properly."[8]

The Heart of Israel is sound; its instinct for survival sure; the fundamental loyalties unchangeable. At times it is confused and sorely troubled. It is then the duty of its trusted leaders to give it light and to replenish its faith and courage, but never to doubt it.

Since we last met in 1956, events of gravest moment have transpired which put Israel and the Near East upon the front page of every newspaper in the world

6. Silver's reference to the 1919 resolution hints at the campaigns he had led to sway the U.S. Congress during the 1940s, invoking the support of both the Democratic and Republican Parties and often in defiance of the executive branch.

7. Quoted from the May 28, 1919 joint resolution passed by the 65th U.S. Congress (H. Con. Res. 57; House Report No. 1063). For the full text, see Éamon de Valera, *Ireland's Claim for Recognition as a Sovereign Independent State* (Washington, D.C.: Irish Diplomatic Mission, 1920), 41, https://babel.hathitrust.org/cgi/pt?id=mdp.39015027328197&view=1up&seq=47.

8. Silver is quoting a midrash in Shemot (Exodus) Rabbah 3:12.

and upon the lips of all men.[9] In a determined effort to put an end to an intolerable situation, brought about by the dictator of Egypt, [Gamal Abdel] Nasser,[10] that dwarf on the Nile, who was perched on the giant shoulders of Communist Russia, Great Britain, France, and Israel struck into Egypt, the former to take back the Suez Canal, which Nasser had illegally seized, the latter to smash the military forces of Nasser, which were mustered in large numbers in the Sinai peninsula, together with staggering arsenals of military equipment, poised to invade and destroy Israel. The campaign which Israel waged against Egypt was brilliantly successful, and in one hundred hours, the vaunted might of Nasser lay broken, scattered, and completely routed. The dwarf proved after all, to be only a dwarf, with great lung power. The forces of Great Britain and France proceeded systematically to the taking over of the canal when the United States intervened, as you well know, and in an outburst of righteous indignation, summoned the assembly of the United Nations and with the cooperation of the Soviet Union and the Asian-African bloc voted [for] a ceasefire order. Great Britain and France, responsive, as democracies must be, to world opinion, stopped their operations and withdrew from the canal—the Egyptian civil administration is back again in [the] Gaza [Strip], from which it had been expelled—and the dwarf is on the shoulders of the giant again, crowing about his great victories—laughing at the world and frightening it.[11]

Today, six months later, one wonders whether our government feels as righteous about its precipitous intervention in this affair. Some are inclined to recall

9. Silver refers here to the Sinai War, also known as the Suez Crisis (October 29, 1956–November 7, 1956). Following the nationalization of the Suez Canal by Egyptian president Gamal Abdel Nasser (see the next note), Israel invaded the Sinai Peninsula with British and French support, under a secret agreement with Britain and France that was supposed to allow the two powers to regain control of the canal. In the event, the Israeli military took control of the entire peninsula (including the Gaza Strip), but U.S. and Soviet pressure brought about a cease-fire followed by a full Israeli withdrawal.

10. In 1952, Gamal Abdel Nasser (1918–1970), a charismatic military officer, toppled the Egyptian monarchy in a coup and became president of Egypt. He promoted a pan-Arab philosophy, calling for political and cultural unity among Arab peoples, an anti-imperialist foreign policy agenda, and the destruction of Israel. In 1958, he engineered a political union between Egypt and Syria called the United Arab Republic, which lasted only until 1961. Nasser championed a series of wars against Israel: the Suez Crisis (1956), the Six-Day War (June 1967), and the War of Attrition (1969–70). He ruled Egypt until his death.

11. The American pressure to which Silver refers here included explicit threats by the Eisenhower administration to support proposed United Nations sanctions against Israel—which, in turn, precipitated a major crisis in U.S.–Israel relations.

the words of [Heinrich] Heine: [12] "For such a righteous act, men deserve to go to Heaven, and there be thrashed every day with rods."[13]

The past year was a very severe and trying one for Israel, one which tested it politically—its statesmanship—its maturity and, economically, its power of survival. Under terrific economic strain and reduced income, Israel met both tests successfully. Even while these unnerving and unsettling events were taking place (and they are still taking place) Israel was admitting thousands of new settlers—victims of Egypt's terror expropriation and expulsion.[14] In passing, it might be noted that our government did not ease its immigration restrictions to permit the entrance of these victims of political persecution, as it had done in the case of the Hungarian refugees, and no mercy airlift was provided for them. Nor did it [the U.S. government] call upon the United Nations to investigate Egypt's outrageous treatment of Jews—arrests, expulsions, economic strangulation, revocation of citizenship—as it did in the case of Hungary.[15]

And why, one wonders, is that prim legalist, the secretary general of the United Nations, Mr. [Dag] Hammarskjöld,[16] who has been and is so solicitous

12. Heinrich Heine (1797–1856), one of the greatest German lyric poets, was a significant figure in the revolutionary literary movement known as Young Germany. Despite converting from Judaism to Christianity, Jewish themes featured prominently in many of his best-known works.

13. Silver is paraphrasing a polemical statement from Heine's 1833 *Die Romantische Schule* (The Romantic school)—published in reaction to France's 1830 July Revolution—in which Heine discusses the obscurantist views of zealous partisans: "A pious Quaker went so far as to sacrifice his whole fortune in buying up and burning [the Italian architect and painter] Giulio Romano's [c. 1499–1546] most beautiful mythological paintings; truly he deserves for his pains to reach heaven, and there to be flogged." See Heinrich Heine, *The Prose Writings of Heinrich Heine*, ed. Havelock Ellis (London: Walter Scott, 1887), 68–141, https://www.gutenberg.org/files/37478/37478-h/37478-h.htm#THE_ROMANTIC_SCHOOL.

14. In October 1956, Nasser imposed a set of sweeping regulations enabling the Egyptian state to abolish civil liberties, stage mass arrests, and strip citizenship from any group it desired. Over 1,000 Jews were arrested, and 500 Jewish businesses were seized by the government. Jewish bank accounts were confiscated and many Jews lost their jobs. Some 23,000–25,000 out of 60,000 Egyptian Jews fled the country. Many were forced to sign declarations that they were "voluntarily" emigrating and "agreed" to the confiscation of their assets and property. By 1957, the Jewish population of Egypt had fallen to 15,000. See also chapter 37, note 15.

15. The Hungarian uprising (October 23–November 10, 1956), which began as a student protest against the country's communist-imposed policies, was violently suppressed by the Soviet regime. On November 4, Soviet troops invaded Hungary and crushed the rebellion. As a result, some 2,500 Hungarians were killed, and 250,000 refugees fled the country.

16. Dag Hammarskjöld (1905–1961) was a Swedish economist and diplomat who served as the second secretary general (1953–61) of the United Nations. He was killed in a plane crash.

about defending every jot and tittle of Egypt's sovereignty—why has he not spoken out in indignation, in the case of Egypt's clear violation of the United Nations' Declaration of Human Rights[17] which states that "no one shall be subject to arbitrary arrest, or deprived of his nationality, of his property."[18]

Israel has been admitting Jewish refugees from other countries—North Africa, Hungary, Poland—some 20,000 in the last two months alone. It is estimated that 100,000 will come to Israel this year![19] It constructed thousands of housing units for the new arrivals. It built and completed during these days of strain and tension, a pipeline, which will carry oil from Eilat on the Gulf of Aqaba to Beer Sheba, the metropolis of the Negev—and the construction of another line has been begun to carry oil from a port on the Mediterranean [Sea].[20] This opens a vast new vista upon the future economic growth and development of the young state.

What courage is here—and what vision: "No weapon that is formed against you shall succeed" [Isa. 54:17].

Israel's troubles are by no means at an end. For there will be no peace in the Near East until our government, which is today the most powerful factor in the Near East situation, adopts a clear policy in reference to the important region and assumes clear, just and unequivocal commitments there.[21] Such a clear policy has not yet evolved. What emerges, from time to time, is an unpredictable initiative, without careful consideration of consequences, such as the reversal of our stand on the building of the Aswan Dam,[22] or a total referral of

17. Formally proclaimed by the U.N. General Assembly in 1948, the Universal Declaration of Human Rights declares "the inherent dignity and . . . the equal and inalienable rights of all members of the human family [to be] the foundation of freedom, justice and peace in the world" (https://www.un.org/en/universal-declaration-human-rights/).

18. The declaration states: "No one shall be subjected to arbitrary arrest, detention or exile," "No one shall be arbitrarily deprived of his nationality nor denied the right to change his nationality," and "No one shall be arbitrarily deprived of his property" (ibid.).

19. Between 1955 and 1957, Israel absorbed roughly 166,000 immigrants, a majority of whom came from Morocco, Tunis, Egypt, Poland, and Hungary.

20. Due to international tensions before and after the Sinai War (1956), Israel searched for ways to secure its oil supply. In 1957, the Israeli government constructed oil tanks in Beer Sheva and Eilat and built a pipeline from Eilat to Beer Sheva. Trains transported crude oil from the south to Haifa.

21. Silver advocated for an American foreign policy in the Middle East designed to persuade the Arab states of the futility of defeating Israel and argued that the U.S. government should neither arm the Arab states nor forge regional alliances with them.

22. The American promise of economic aid for the Aswan Dam project was supposed to keep the Soviet Union from extending its regional influence in the area. On May 16, 1956, Nasser rec-

all Near East problems to the United Nations, or an isolated military commitment to the Baghdad Pact,[23] or an Airfield for Arms Pact with Saudi Arabia, by the terms [of] which the United States will continue to sell arms to Saudi Arabia and American officers will train the army, navy, and air personnel of Saudi Arabia—on condition, of course, that no American Jew is to be included among these American officers. President [Dwight D.] Eisenhower,[24] presumably to advance the cause of the American ideal of democracy and of the equal rights of all of its citizens, signed that agreement. I wonder if he would have signed such an agreement if it [had] called for a ban, not on American Jews, but on American Presbyterians, or American Episcopalians, or American Catholics. Presumably the red carpet is rolled out for those who can speak in the name of 3,000 barrels of oil. But the rug is pulled from under the feet of those who can speak only in the name of the equality of the American citizens and their inalienable human rights.

Israel, will, for some time to come, and until a clear policy emerges, have to rely on itself—on its own powers of self-defense—and build its strength. This is possible. And its recent experiences may justify a confident prospect for the future.

What you are doing in this campaign?—what the Jews of America are doing is helping Israel to build her strength.

It is good to have had the promise of the president of the United States, which was made at the time of the withdrawal of Israeli forces from Gaza and Sharm El Sheikh that, "Israel will have no cause to regret this step."[25] It is even better to know that a first-class Israeli fighting force is on hand to see that there will be no cause for regret. Legal experts can find loopholes in any pledge or promise which our government makes and there are plenty of them in our State Department. But men and women by the thousands and the tens of thousands and

---

ognized the People's Republic of China, a move that drove the United States on July 19 to withdraw its offer of a loan for the dam's construction. Great Britain followed suit and withdrew its offer of aid to Egypt.

23. The Baghdad Pact (1955), a defensive organization created by Turkey, Iraq, Great Britain, Pakistan, and Iran, promoted shared political, military, and economic goals. The group's chief goal was to foster peace and prevent the spread of communism in the Middle East.

24. Dwight D. Eisenhower (1890–1969) served as supreme commander of the Allied forces in Europe during World War II and subsequently as U.S. president (1953–61).

25. Quoted in Lucy S. Dawidowicz, "The United States, Israel, and the Middle East," *American Jewish Year Book* 59 (1958), 211. After Israel agreed to comply with the U.N. resolution demanding its full withdrawal from the Sinai Peninsula, Eisenhower sent David Ben-Gurion (1886–1973), then Israel's prime minister, a letter thanking him for his decision and promising that the United States would work to ensure that Israel's security needs were met.

hundreds of thousands, who are trained and prepared and equipped to defend their homeland, will act as a powerful deterrent to a political adventure in that part of the world.

The sympathy of the free world is with Israel. Israel seeks no one's territory. It is eager for peace with all its Arab neighbors. It is prepared to negotiate all outstanding issues with them. It will, however, insist on the same sovereign rights which it concedes to all its neighbors. It will, with our aid, win through. These valiant builders and fighters and dreamers, will win through—in spite of all hostility.

I recall a visit which I made to Russia in August 1935. I went to the Tsarskoye Selo—the Palace of the Tsars—on the outskirts of Leningrad. The palace had been converted by the Soviet [government] to a national museum and they kept it exactly as it was left by the tsar and his family, before they were carried off and executed.[26]

I passed through many rooms of the palace and finally came to a small library adjoining the bedroom of the tsar and the tsarina and there on one of the book-shelves, I was startled to see a copy of Israel Zangwill's *Dreamers of the Ghetto*.[27] You can imagine what thoughts ran through my mind at that moment: The tsar, the last of a long line of oppressors of the Jews, who denied them their elementary human rights, now long since dead, riddled with Bolshevik bullets—and here is this little volume, *Dreamers of the Ghetto*, the story of the indomitable faith and courage of the Jews whom the tsars persecuted, keeping, as it were, a lonely vigil over his vanished pomp and power and glory.

The tsars are dead. But the dreamers of the ghetto have left their many dark ghettos in the world and have, by their faith and courage and ideals, built for themselves, and those who will follow them, a land of their own and a free home of their own.

And we are determined to share in their hope and in their sacrifices, even as we share in their pride.

26. Following the Russian February Revolution (1917), the imperial Romanov family—Nicholas II (1868–1918), his wife Alexandra (1872–1918), and their five children—were imprisoned in the Alexander Palace before being moved to Tobolsk and then Yekaterinburg, where they were shot and bayoneted to death on the night of July 16–17, 1918.

27. *Dreamers of the Ghetto* (1898), a collection of essays by the Anglo-Jewish writer and playwright Israel Zangwill (1864–1926), explores the lives of famous historic Jewish figures including the German poet Heinrich Heine (see notes 12 and 13), the Dutch rationalist philosopher Baruch Spinoza (1632–1677), and the social democratic thinker and activist Ferdinand Lassalle (1825–1864). At the turn of the nineteenth and twentieth centuries, the book enjoyed widespread popularity and was the basis for dramatic productions and films.

39

"WE MUST CHANGE OUR LINE"

Will Maslow's Report on the Conference of the American Zionist Committee for Public Affairs[1]
(1960)

◇◇

MARK A. RAIDER AND GARY PHILLIP ZOLA

In 1859, a handful of American Jewish communal leaders — representing 50,000 Jews, or roughly 0.22 percent of the American population — created the Board of Delegates of American Israelites.[2] As Seth Korelitz explains in the headnote to chapter 9, the Board of Delegates, American Jewry's first communal relations body, was dedicated to protecting the civil rights of Jews at home and abroad.[3] A century later, five major American Jewish advocacy groups, purporting to represent some five million Jews (or roughly 3 percent of the country's population),[4] functioned as the nonsectarian guardians of the American Jewish scene: the Jewish War Veterans of America (established in 1896), the American Jewish Committee (1906), the Anti-Defamation League of Bnai Brith (1913), the American Jewish Congress (1918), and the Jewish Labor Committee (1934).[5] Against this backdrop, local Jewish community relations councils arose across the country in the 1930s; they united in 1944 to create the National

---

1. In 1963, the American Zionist Committee for Public Affairs was renamed and incorporated as the American Israel Public Affairs Committee (AIPAC).

2. See Jonathan D. Sarna, ed., "Appendix 1: The Growth of the American Jewish Population," in *The American Jewish Experience* (New York: Holmes and Meier, 1986), 296.

3. For more on the Board of Delegates of American Israelites, see chapter 9.

4. See Sarna, "Appendix 1," 296.

5. Discussions of the organizations noted here can be found in other documents in this volume (see the index). With respect to the Anti-Defamation League, it is important to note that the organization gradually became independent of its parent organization, Bnai Brith. The historian Jack Wertheimer notes that by the late 1980s, it "no longer received any funding" from Bnai Brith and by 1992 "it claimed a budget of $34.5 million, a staff of 350, and 30 regional offices" ("Jewish Organizational Life in the United States since 1945," *American Jewish Year Book* 95 [1995], 72). Under the leadership of Abraham H. Foxman (b. 1940), who served as the Anti-Defamation League's national director from 1987 to 2015, the organization formally separated from Bnai Brith.

Community Relations Advisory Council (renamed in 1968 the National Jewish Community Relations Advisory Council and in 1997 as the Jewish Council for Public Affairs.) In the early decades of the twentieth century, these organizations and their leaders differed, often fiercely, over the place of Zionism and the Yishuv (pre-state Israeli society) in Jewish public life. In the aftermath of World War II and the Holocaust, however, as the majority of American Jews rallied to the Zionist cause, so too did the aforementioned groups, together with American Jewry's synagogue movements and a host of other organizations. In sum, the creation of the State of Israel in 1948 prompted a sea change in American Jewish culture, resulting in a broad array of groups from all quarters of American Jewish life embracing fund-raising and political activity aimed at bolstering the fledgling Jewish state.

Though American Jewry's transformation provided the scope and inducement for a groundswell of countrywide pro-Israel sentiment and activity, it was hardly inevitable that a new group would take the lead to champion the nascent U.S.-Israel alliance. Indeed, such a development appears all the more striking when one considers that in addition to the five national organizations noted above, an array of well-developed American Zionist groups representing a spectrum of religious and political perspectives had taken root decades earlier in American soil.[6]

In 1951, Isaiah "Si" Kenen (1905–1988), a veteran of the Zionist political arena, established the American Zionist Committee for Public Affairs (AZCPA), initially the political arm of the centrist American Zionist Council. Conceived of as a nonpartisan pro-Israel watchdog group, the AZCPA separated from the council in 1963 and was renamed and incorporated as the American Israel Public Affairs Committee (AIPAC). In just a couple of decades, Kenen grew AIPAC into one of country's most prominent and influential lobbying organizations. By the turn of the twentieth and twenty-first centuries, AIPAC had become, in the words of Barack Obama (b. 1961), later president of the United States, the custodian of America's "bipartisan consensus to support and defend our ally Israel."[7]

The memorandum reprinted below is a report on the AZCPA's first annual conference in March 1960. The author, Will Maslow (1907–2000), executive director of the American Jewish Congress (AJC), composed this aide-mémoire to share his recollections of the AZCPA's first gathering with Rabbi Joachim Prinz

6. See chapter 31.

7. Barack Obama, "Obama's Speech at AIPAC," June 4, 2008, National Public Radio, https://www.npr.org/templates/story/story.php?storyId=91150432.

(1902–1988), president of the AJC and one of American Jewry's key leaders. The document sheds light on the AZCPA's early development, interlocutory role vis-à-vis American Jews and Israel, and the fledgling organization's trajectory as a political lobby for Israel. Set against the dynamic backdrop of the Cold War era and the 1960 U.S. presidential election season, the report underscores the complexity of both U.S.-Israel relations and the challenges that beset relations between American Jews and Israeli society. The report also reflects ongoing tensions that surfaced in the Suez Crisis (1956) when Egypt, emboldened by growing Soviet support, barred Israel from the Straits of Tiran as well as from the Suez Canal.[8] The crisis deepened as Arab fedayeen (paramilitary groups), based mainly in the Egyptian-held Gaza Strip, attacked Israel settlements and population centers. Late in 1956, Jordan and Egypt entered into a military alliance against Israel, one of the precipitating events of the Sinai Campaign—in which Israel won a swift victory. The United States and the Soviet Union then joined diplomatic forces to press Israel to withdraw from the occupied areas. In an effort to address strained relations between the Israel and the U.S. governments, the AZCPA mobilized American Jewish groups and individuals to lobby congressional representatives in Washington to support Israel's position. In March 1957, President Dwight D. Eisenhower (1890–1969) wrote to Israeli prime minister David Ben-Gurion (1886–1973) promising that "Israel will have no cause to regret" its withdrawal from the Sinai Peninsula.[9] Meanwhile, wary of political instability and the threat of communist influence in the Mediterranean basin, Eisenhower proclaimed a new American foreign policy, known as the Eisenhower Doctrine, to support "the independence and integrity of the nations of the Middle East."[10] The policy, which enjoyed broad American public support and to which Israel acceded, continued when John F. Kennedy (1917–1963) became president in 1961.[11]

In addition to outlining the contours of U.S.–Israel relations, the document

8. See chapter 38, note 9.

9. Quoted in in Lucy S. Dawidowicz, "The United States, Israel, and the Middle East," *American Jewish Year Book* 59 (1958), 211.

10. For a contemporaneous report on American society's response to the Eisenhower Doctrine, see ibid., 212–15.

11. During the Kennedy administration, the U.S. government sought to engage Arab leaders concerning the Palestinian Arab refugee problem. However, the League of Arab States (or Arab League; see note 27) refused to enter into negotiations. Meanwhile, Israel insisted a solution to the Arab-Israel conflict could be achieved only by direct Arab-Israel peace talks. When the Soviet Union provided Egypt with long-range bombers, MiG planes, and other modern arms, Israel renewed its appeal for U.S. weapons. In 1962, Kennedy lifted the American arms embargo and approved the sale of U.S. Hawk antiaircraft missiles to Israel.

below hints at the philosophical and ideological tensions that informed American Jewry's developing relationship with Israeli society in the decades following statehood. Primed to give generously to ongoing Zionist activities and invest in Israeli savings bonds, American Jews suddenly found themselves at odds with Israeli leaders who called upon young American Jews to immigrate to the Jewish state. "The recruitment of American Jewish youth for agricultural pioneering in Israel," Ben-Gurion and other government officials insisted, "should become the primary function of the Zionist movement in the United States."[12] Ben-Gurion's statements rankled American Jews and led to a public dispute with Jacob Blaustein (1892–1970), president of the American Jewish Committee, over the nature of modern Jewish life and the vitality of the American Jewish diaspora. Ostensibly resolved in the Blaustein–Ben-Gurion Agreement,[13] which held that "aliyah [Hebrew for "ascent to the Land of Israel"] with the free discretion of the American Jew himself: it is entirely a matter of his own volition,"[14] the underlying cause of the debate remained unresolved. The Zionist leadership in Israel continued to declaim the principle of shlilat hagolah (Hebrew for "negation of the exile"), arguing that diaspora Jewish life was ultimately futile and authentic Jewish life was possible only in the Jewish state.

World events in the late 1950s made it clear that American Jewry could not rely on the old understandings and rules of engagement that had characterized the American scene before the middle of the twentieth century. The AZCPA, devoid of the partisanship that shaped other American Jewish organizations, maintained a singular focus: to promote the development and security of Israel, irrespective of ideological or philosophical differences. The historian Isaiah Berlin (1909–1997) famously quoted the Greek poet Archilochus in his analysis of the Russian writer Leo Tolstoy and the French political thinker Joseph de Maistre: "The fox knows many things, but the hedgehog knows one big thing."[15] The AZCPA (later AIPAC)—the hedgehog of American Jewish politics—unswervingly devoted itself to advancing U.S.-Israel relations and the survival of the Jewish state.

◇◇

12. "U.S. Members of Jewish Agency Oppose Recruitment of American Jewish Youth for Israel," JTA Daily News Bulletin, August 7, 1951, 1.

13. For the text of the agreement, see "Blaustein-Ben-Gurion Agreement (1952)," in The Jew in the Modern World: A Documentary History, ed. Paul Mendes-Flohr and Jehuda Reinharz, 3rd ed. (New York: Oxford University Press, 2011), 581–84.

14. Quoted in "Appendix: An Exchange of Views: American Jews and the State of Israel," American Jewish Year Book 53 (1952), 564.

15. Isaiah Berlin, Russian Thinkers (London: Hogarth, 1978), 22.

Memorandum from Will Maslow to Joachim Prinz Concerning a Meeting of the American Zionist Committee for Public Affairs, March 29, 1960

Source: Memorandum from Will Maslow to Joachim Prinz (March 29, 1960), World Jewish Congress Records, 1918–1982, MS-361, box H8, folder 16: American Israel Public Affairs Committee, 1956–1963, the Jacob Rader Marcus Center of the American Jewish Archives, Cincinnati.

March 29, 1960

CONFIDENTIAL!

To: Dr. [Joachim] Prinz[16]

From: Will Maslow[17]

Cc: Judge [Justine] Polier,[18] [et al.]

16. A native of Prussia, Joachim Prinz (1902–1988) was introduced to Zionism through the Blau Weiss (German for "blue white") youth movement. He earned a doctorate in philosophy in 1921 from the University of Giessen and received rabbinic ordination in 1923 from the Jewish Theological Seminary of Breslau. In 1924, he assumed the pulpit of Berlin's Friedenstempel (Temple of Peace), where he developed a reputation as a captivating orator. In 1937, as a result of the Nazi regime's repressive laws, Prinz emigrated to the United States. He settled in Newark, New Jersey, and in 1939 became rabbi of Temple Bnai Abraham. Active in Zionist affairs, Prinz worked closely with Stephen S. Wise (see chapter 31, note 13) and participated in the leadership of the United Palestine Appeal, the American Jewish Congress (AJC), the Conference of Presidents of Major American Jewish Organizations, and the Conference of Jewish Material Claims against Germany. By the 1950s, Prinz had emerged as one of American Jewry's leading figures and spokespersons. As president of the AJC (1958–66), he played a key role in leading the organization into the civil rights movement of the 1960s and mobilizing the American Jewish community's campaign for social, economic, and racial justice. Prinz worked closely with Martin Luther King Jr. (1929–1968) and other civil rights leaders, and he spoke at the March on Washington for Jobs and Freedom, on August 28, 1963.

17. Born in Kiev, Ukraine, William Maslow (1907–2007) was brought by his parents to the United States in 1911. After earning a law degree in 1931 from Columbia University, Maslow worked in the 1930s and 1940s for the New York City Department of Investigation, National Labor Relations Board, and Fair Employment Practice Committee of the administration of President Franklin D. Roosevelt (1882–1945). In 1945, Maslow became general counsel for the AJC, for which he was later executive director (1960–72). Under Maslow's leadership, the organization became one of American Jewry's leading civil rights organizations.

18. Justine (Wise) Polier (1903–1987), daughter of Stephen S. Wise (see chapter 31, note 13), trained at Yale Law School and became a leading advocate for workers' rights, civil rights, and educational and health services for children. In 1935, Polier became the first female judge appointed to New York City's Domestic Relations Court. A close adviser of Eleanor Roosevelt (1884–1962), Polier was instrumental in creating New York State's antidiscrimination legisla-

Subject: First Annual Conference,
American Zionist Committee for Public Affairs[19]

I attended the conference which was held in Washington [D.C.] on Saturday night and Sunday.[20] There were about 100 representatives present who were members of the [American Zionist Committee for Public Affairs], representatives of friendly cooperating organizations or community leaders. The purpose of the conference was not to reach any policy decisions but apparently an effort by Si Kenen,[21] its executive director, to acquaint his lay leadership with some of the current problems involving Israel.

There were formal speeches by Armin Meyer,[22] director of the Near East Division of the State Department, [Israel] Ambassador [Avraham] Harman,[23] and Kenen himself. There was a vigorous and protracted question period after each

---

tion. As a judge, she was responsible for two landmark antidiscrimination cases, *In the Matter of Skipwith and Rector* (1958) and *Wilder v. Sugarman* (1974).

19. Established in 1951 by Isaiah Kenen (see note 21), the AZCPA originated as the political arm of the centrist American Zionist Council. In 1963, the group separated from the council and was renamed and incorporated as the American Israel Public Affairs Committee (AIPAC). In the 1970s and 1980s, AIPAC grew to become the country's most influential pro-Israel lobbying organization.

20. The conference was held on March 26–27, 1960.

21. Born in New Brunswick, Canada, Isaiah "Si" Kenen (1905–1988), son of eastern European immigrant Zionist activists, attended the University of Toronto. He subsequently moved to Cleveland, Ohio, where he studied law and became active in Zionist affairs. In the 1940s, he worked as the Jewish Agency for Palestine's information director. After the establishment of Israel in 1948, he became a registered foreign agent with Israel's foreign affairs ministry and a member of Israel's delegation to the United Nations. In 1951, Kenen organized the pro-Israel lobbying group AZCPA, the predecessor to the AIPAC. He served as AIPAC's director (1963–74).

22. Armin H. Meyer (1914–2006), an American diplomat of Lutheran descent, served as a member of the U.S. legation in Iraq (1944–48). He became a career foreign service officer in 1948. In the 1950s, he was stationed in Beirut and Kabul. During the Kennedy administration, Meyer was appointed deputy assistant secretary for Near Eastern affairs. He later served as U.S. ambassador to Lebanon (1961–65), Iran (1965–69), and Japan (1969–72). Following the 1972 Olympic Games in Munich, at which Israeli athletes were taken hostage and killed by a Palestinian terrorist group, President Richard M. Nixon (1913–1994) named Meyer to head a task force on international terrorism.

23. Born in London, Avraham Harman (1914–1992) trained as a lawyer before immigrating in 1938 to British Mandatory Palestine. With the establishment of Israel in 1948, he became an officer in the new state's foreign affairs ministry. He spent much of the 1950s and 1960s as an Israeli diplomat in North America and was stationed in Montreal and New York City. He served as Israel's third ambassador to the United States (1959–68) and president of the Hebrew University of Jerusalem (1968–83).

speech. [Sanford H.] Bolz[24] and I participated actively in the questioning. The speeches were off the record but I am reporting the highlights for your confidential information.

I. ARMIN MEYER

Mr. Meyer, who has been in the State Department for twenty years, is the staff person in charge of the day-to-day work of the Near Eastern Division. He is responsible to an Assistant Secretary of State, formerly [William M.] Rountree[25] and now [G. Lewis] Jones.[26] He impressed me as being extremely friendly to Israel. At the same time, he defended, sometimes vigorously, sometimes lamely, State Department policy during his informal remarks and in the question period. He made the following points:

1. If Zionists continue over-emphasizing the Arab boycott,[27] they will only encourage the Arabs to press forward more vigorously. [Prime Minister David]

24. Sanford H. Bolz (1915–1991) graduated from Cornell University Law School in 1938 and worked in the 1940s for the National Labor Relations Board and other U.S. government agencies. He served as counsel to the American Jewish Congress (1948–60) and the American Jewish Committee (1960–65). In the 1950s, he played an active role in several important desegregation and civil liberties cases.

25. William M. Rountree (1917–1995) entered U.S. government service in 1935 as an accountant in the Treasury Department. After playing a role in the Lend-Lease program (1941), Rountree joined the State Department in 1942 and was stationed in Cairo, Egypt, to assist with World War II aid activity. Following the war, he administered American aid programs in Greece, Turkey, and Iran and became a Middle East and South Asia specialist. In 1955, he was appointed deputy assistant secretary of state for Near Eastern, South Asian, and African Affairs, and in 1956, he was appointed assistant secretary. He served as U.S. ambassador to Pakistan (1959–62), Sudan (1962–65), South Africa (1965–70), and Brazil (1970–73).

26. A native of Baltimore, Maryland, George Lewis Jones (1907–1971) began his foreign service career in 1930 as a clerk in the U.S. embassy in London. Stationed in Athens and Cairo in the 1930s and 1940s, he rose through the ranks, and in 1950 he was appointed the State Department's director of Near Eastern affairs. He served as a senior American diplomat in Tunis (1951–53), Cairo (1953–55), and Tehran (1955–56). President Dwight D. Eisenhower (1890–1969) appointed him the first U.S. ambassador to Tunisia (1956–59). He served as assistant secretary of state for Near East and South Asian affairs (1960–61) and was stationed in the U.S. embassy in London (1961–64).

27. Established in 1945, the League of Arab States (or Arab League) sought to undermine the Yishuv's (and later Israel's) growth and economic stability by imposing a regional boycott of the Jewish state in the making. Though the boycott did not significantly hinder Israel's swift economic and national development, the Arab League was able to bring significant pressure to bear on Israel in the 1950s and 1960s. Tensions in this regard flared as a result of regional Arab mari-

Ben-Gurion[28] himself did not even raise this issue in his talks with the State Department.

2. The State Department is not looking for new projects or new initiatives. It is not pursuing the Arabs but merely trying to maintain correct political relationships.

3. Israel is doing extremely well economically. Its gross national product per capita is now larger than the Netherlands' or Italy's.[29] Nevertheless, the State Department favored a continuing program of economic aid for Israel.[30]

4. Ben-Gurion himself endorsed the idea of economic loans to the Arabs from the U.S. as tending to divert them from their warlike adventures.

------

time policy designed to impede the passage of goods and supplies to Israel through the Straits of Tiran and the Gulf of Aqaba. As the Cold War unfolded, the Soviet Union's alignment with Arab regimes across the Middle East and growing hostility toward Israel exacerbated the situation and stoked the escalation of military conflicts between Israel and the neighboring states of Egypt, Jordan, Lebanon, and Syria. The conflicts included the Suez Crisis (1956; see chapter 38, note 9.), the Six-Day War (June 1967), and the Yom Kippur War (1973). The Arab League's boycott, which remained intact for several decades, began to unravel in the 1980s following the Egypt-Israel peace accord (1979).

28. Born in Poland, David Ben-Gurion (1886–1973) joined the Zionist movement as a youth and was active in Russian revolutionary activity. In 1906, he immigrated to Palestine, where he became a laborer. In 1911 he temporarily relocated to Turkey, where he studied law at Istanbul University. During World War I he fought with the Jewish Legion, a British military regiment he helped organize with other Zionist leaders. In 1920, he was among the founders of the Histadrut trade union and became its secretary general. In 1930, he was a founder of the Palestine labor party Mapai and was elected as party chairman. In 1935, he became chairman of the Jewish Agency for Palestine. Following the establishment of the State of Israel, he served as the nation's first prime minister and defense minister (both 1948–53). In 1955, after a brief hiatus, he returned to government, was reelected prime minister, and again simultaneously served as defense minister (both 1955–63). He continued to play an active role in national politics as Israel's elder statesman until retiring in 1970.

29. In the 1950s and 1960s, Israel's economy developed at a rapid pace. The country's gross national product grew annually by an average rate of over 11 percent, and the per capita gross national product grew by over 6 percent. The country's growth was fueled, in large part, by the social democratic state-building ethos of Israel's governing coalition, under the leadership of Ben-Gurion and the Mapai party, which carried out a massive domestic investment and refugee absorption agenda. In this period, Israel's economy was also boosted by U.S. government aid, postwar German reparations to victims of the Nazi regime, the sale of State of Israel bonds, and the Jewish Agency's nongovernmental development activity.

30. Prior to the Six-Day War (1967), U.S. government aid to Israel (mostly in the form of loans) averaged about $63 million per year. In 1959, the Eisenhower administration created a modest military loan program to help supply Israel with advanced military equipment and technology.

During the question period, Meyer was asked about the denial of visas to Jews,[31] the transit of the Suez Canal,[32] the World Bank loan,[33] restrictions on American ships touching Israel ports,[34] the sale of Navy oil,[35] Arab [Jewish] refugees,[36] and Arab student propaganda.[37]

II. AMBASSADOR HARMAN

The Ambassador warned us not to be diverted from long-term views by short-term irritations and problems. He described the two primary problems facing

---

31. In this period, many countries in the Arab world and the Soviet bloc systematically denied their Jewish citizens visas. American Jewish groups rallied to the defense of these Jewish communities and lobbied the U.S. government to intervene on their behalf.

32. See the headnote to this document.

33. A World Bank report issued a few months before the conference noted Israel's "impressive achievement" and its "very rapid rate of expansion ... in the face of formidable obstacles." In one decade, the report noted, Israel, a World Bank member country since 1953, had produced "a modern economy and raised the standard of living within striking distance of that in more prosperous countries in Europe" ("The Economy of Israel," Department of Operations, South Asia and Middle East, International Bank for Reconstruction and Development, February 19, 1960, 40). The report stopped short of making a specific recommendation concerning World Bank loans to Israel.

34. In this period, the Arab League "blacklisted all American ships which have touched at Israeli ports of call," including "about 25 American-flag vessels" carrying military supplies and ships with "Israeli agricultural and industrial products, Jewish immigrants, or which were hired by Israeli companies" ("Arab Boycott—Resolution of New York Legislature," May 3, 1961, in *Congressional Record: Proceedings and Debates of the 87th Congress, First Session*, vol. 107, part 6: May 1, 1961–May 17, 1961 [Washington, D.C.: Government Printing Office, 1961], 7030–31).

35. Just a few weeks before the conference, the U.S. Navy rescinded the so-called Haifa clause of its protocol for delivering oil to American naval installations. The U.S. government, the clause stated, was "not responsible for any financial losses resulting from calls by tankers at Haifa which later called at Arab ports." In the wake of public criticism, the clause "was discontinued lest it be misconstrued as U.S. acquiescence in the Arab boycott" (ibid., 7031).

36. Between 1948 and 1960, approximately 850,000 Jews were forced to leave Arab countries, including 586,000 refugees who resettled in Israel.

37. In the course of the 1960 U.S. presidential campaign, Mustafa Kamel, the ambassador of the United Arab Republic to the United States, denounced "Zionist plots and games in the United States" ("Arab Ambassador in Washington Attacks American Jewish Community," JTA *Daily News Bulletin* 27, no. 168, September 1, 1960, 2) and called on Arab students at American colleges and universities to "spread pro-Arab propaganda among their American friends to counter pro-Zionist election statements" ("July–Nov: ME Aspects of the U.S. Presidential Campaign," in *Middle East Record*, ed. Yitzhak Oron [London: Israel Oriental Society, 1960], 1:108) by John F. Kennedy and Richard M. Nixon—respectively, the Democratic and Republican nominees.

Israel for the next decade. The first was the effort to transform its polyglot population into a unified people. He drew encouragement from the fact that no communal election list like the Moroccans or the Iraqis had been able to win any seats in the Knesset although such lists had been successful in some municipal elections.[38] The best way to achieve this assimilation, he argued, was to assure educational and economic equality.

The second great problem was that of economic development of the country. He stated that the rate of productivity of Israeli workers was increasing about three percent a year. Whatever new enterprises should be public or private was no longer an ideological controversy but a factual one.[39]

38. Throughout the 1950s and 1960s, local government in Israel was largely an extension of the national political scene and was dominated by Israel's Ashkenazic political establishment. By 1959–60, nearly a third of Israel's Jewish population (which grew in this period from 2,088,685 to 2,114,417) resided in Jerusalem, Haifa, and Tel Aviv and accounted for 76 percent of the country's total population. In the 1959 elections, voter turnout was 79.0 percent and 81.6 percent at the municipal and national levels, respectively (until 1973, municipal and national elections were held on the same day). As a result of the 1959 elections, a new national government came to power under David Ben-Gurion's Labor-led political coalition, and the Mapai party maintained political control at the municipal level.

Harman's comments illustrate the patronizing attitude of Israel's Ashkenazic political establishment vis-à-vis recent Mizrahi Jewish immigrants from Morocco, Iraq, and other Middle Eastern countries. In particular, he refers to the outcome of the 1959 elections, which did not include representation of Mizrahi groups, and the wave of unrest that swept Mizrahi immigrant communities in the months before the elections, including riots in Haifa's Wadi Salib quarter (July 9 and July 30), Migdal Haemek (July 19), and Beer Sheva (July 20)—all cities with sizable Mizrahi communities. The discord and violent episodes stemmed from discrimination against Mizrahi Jews by local and national government officials and agencies. Subsequently, an independent commission of inquiry recommended "more determined efforts to integrate such immigrants in the community and improve educational, employment, and housing opportunities for them" (Misha Louvish, "Israel," *American Jewish Year Book* 62 [1961], 314–17). In due course, the government also allocated special funding for large families, particularly new immigrants from Middle Eastern countries. See Daniel J. Elazar, "The Local Dimension in Israeli Government and Politics," in *Local Government in Israel*, ed. Daniel J. Elazar and Chaim Kalchheim (Lanham, MD: University Press of America, 1988), 3–40; Dana Blander, "Elections for the Local Authority—Who, What, When, Where and How?," November 5, 2008, 2008), especially "Chart 1: Voting Rates in Municipal and Knesset Elections, 1950–2003 (1949–2006)," https://cn.idi.org.il/articles/10198.

39. Harman is obliquely referring to the notion of *mamlakhtiyut* (Hebrew for "statism") as the paramount driver of Zionist political strategy. Ben-Gurion deployed this concept to denote a duality in which the cause of Jewish state building would take priority over all other interests, and diaspora Jewry would accede to the centrality of Israel in modern Jewish life. Notwithstanding Harman's comment, the concept generated fierce philosophical and ideological debates in Jewish public life.

Finally, he discussed the key political question: Where is [Egyptian president Gamal Abdel] Nasser[40] headed, towards internal economic development or towards external military adventures? Present Israeli appraisal is that Nasser has not changed and that his chief focus [is] external interests. Nasser still regards himself as the instrument of wide change outside of Egypt and is still consumed by the desire to remake the Near East and Africa under the hegemony of Egypt.[41] Israel's chief protection is that Israel's security and world stability are linked.

During the question period I asked [Harman] whether the economic loans and grants from the U.S. tended to divert Nasser to internal problems or only strengthened his hand for military adventures. Harman's answer was not clear but he seemed to indicate that Israel did not oppose economic loans except the recent World Bank loan for the improvement of the Suez Canal because Israel is denied the use of the canal.

III. *KENEN*

He began by stating there never had been a time when the U.S. Congress had been so friendly towards Israel. The surplus of oil on the world market has resulted in downgrading the Arabs although Nasser was still disturbing the State Department. He observed that the House Foreign Affairs Committee was much more friendly than the Senate Foreign Relations Committee.[42]

He then went on to state we must change our line and demand Middle East summit talks and a peace conference between the Arab states and Israel.

Getting down to more practical matters, Kenen reported that 19 of the 23

40. On Gamal Abdel Nasser, see chapter 38, note 10.

41. On Nasser's pan-Arab movement, see chapter 38, note 10.

42. Two weeks before the conference, Congress had considered modifying the U.S. government's mutual security assistance legislation to include an amendment "denying aid to nations that waged economic warfare against others by boycott, blockade, and restriction of international waterways" (quoted in Dawidowicz, "The United States, Israel, and the Middle East," *American Jewish Year Book* 62 [1961], 189). Sponsored by two members of the House of Representatives (Leonard Farbstein [1902–1993] of New York and Wayne Hays [1911–1989] of Ohio), the legislation, which sought to bolster Israel's maritime security needs, enjoyed the bipartisan support of the House Foreign Affairs Committee. In the Senate, however, J. William Fulbright (1905–1995) of Arkansas, chair of the Senate Foreign Relations Committee, "bitterly attacked the amendment" and attempted to weaken its pro-Israel orientation (quoted in ibid., 190). A somewhat softened version of the legislation was eventually adopted as part of the Foreign Assistance and Related Agencies Appropriation Act of 1962.

members of the House Foreign Affairs Committee had reported a rider to the Mutual Security Act in which they insist that the Suez Canal should be open to Israel. Kenen believed that this rider would be approved by the House without question and would not have great difficulty in the Senate. Finally, he stressed the importance of planning early campaigns for suitable planks in the Republic[an] and Democratic national conventions.[43] (A technical subcommittee of the conference will meet with Kenen in New York this Friday, April 1.)

At the closing session, the conference adopted a four-page policy statement which contained the following six-point program:

(1) Continued U.S. economic assistance to Israel and the Arab people to raise living standards.
(2) Full adherence to the U.S. policy to preserve "the independence and integrity of the nations of the Middle East."[44]
(3) Efforts to halt Soviet arms shipments to the Middle East and to prevent an arms imbalance in that region.
(4) No compromise with boycott, blockade, and other warlike acts.

43. This refers to the AZCPA's efforts to lobby both the Republican and Democratic parties to adopt pro-Israel language and positions in their national convention platforms. The final Democratic platform called for ensuring the "independence for all states" in the Middle East, "direct Arab-Israeli peace negotiations, the resettlement of Arab refugees in lands where there is room and opportunity for them, an end to boycotts and blockades, and unrestricted use of the Suez Canal by all nations" ("1960 Democratic Party Platform," July 11, 1960, in Gerhard Peters and John T. Woolley, the American Presidency Project, https://www.presidency.ucsb.edu /documents/1960-democratic-party-platform). The final Republican platform affirmed the importance of "the integrity and independence of all the states of that area including Israel and the Arab States," resolving "obstacles to a lasting peace in the area, including the human problem of the Arab refugees," and "an end to transit and trade restrictions, blockades and boycotts" ("Republican Party Platform of 1960," July 25, 1960, in ibid., https://www.presidency.ucsb.edu /node/273401).

44. Following the Sinai Campaign (1956), President Eisenhower recalibrated U.S. policy in the Middle East in an effort to extend American influence in the region, bolster the stability of pro-Western Arab regimes, and provide security assurances to Israel and her supporters. A key tenet of the Eisenhower Doctrine was that "the United States regards as vital to the national interest and world peace the preservation of the independence and integrity of the nations of the Middle East" and "if the President determines the necessity thereof, the United States is prepared to use armed forces to assist any such nation or group of such nations requesting assistance against armed aggression from any country controlled by international communism" ("Public Law 85-7, March 9, 1957," https://www.govinfo.gov/content/pkg/STATUTE-71 /pdf/STATUTE-71-Pg5-2.pdf).

(5) Resettlement of Arab refugees in Arab countries, with compensation from Israel for their abandoned property.[45]

(6) A U.S. initiative to promote direct negotiations between Israel and the Arab states.

45. On December 2, 1950, two years after Israel's War of Independence, the United Nations adopted General Assembly resolution A/393/5, calling for the resettlement and compensation of Arab refugees. To promote this effort, in 1955 U.S. Secretary of State John Foster Dulles (1888–1959) announced the American government's readiness to supply Israel with economic development loans. This concept, subsequently a touchstone of American Middle East policy, was also articulated in 1957 by Senator Hubert H. Humphrey (1911–1978) of Minnesota as follows: "Resettlement in Arab lands with compensation for property left in Israel is, in fact, the only effective and realistic way of solving the Arab refugee problem. The fact is that for ten years the Arab states used the Palestine refugees as political hostages. Nothing has been done to assist them in a practical way lest political leverage against Israel be lost" (quoted in "Mutual Security Act of 1960," in *Congressional Record: Proceedings and Debates of the 87th Congress, First Session*, vol. 106, part 7: April 20, 1960, to May 5, 1960 [Washington, D.C.: Government Printing Office, 1960], 9061).

40

"YOU DON'T HAVE TO BE JEWISH TO LOVE LEVY'S"

Levy's Real Jewish Rye Advertising Campaign (1961)

◇◇

Citing the famous French anthropologist Claude Lévi-Strauss (1908–2009), the historian Stephen J. Whitfield observes that "every culture is the result of a mishmash." "Even more so is America," Whitfield explains, "because its society is itself composed of minorities. . . . The modernity that Americans have found so congenial also tends to undermine the rigidity that separates Jews from others."[1]

Among the unusual but in some ways characteristic humorous manifestations of the nexus between Jews and American culture in the 1960s—akin to the artful but unapologetic Jewish sensibility displayed by the comedian Allan Sherman (1924–1973), the playwright Neil Simon (1927–2018), and the writer Philip Roth (1933–2018)—was the Doyle Dane Bernbach (DDB) advertising campaign (1961–73) that used the slogan "You don't have to be Jewish to love Levy's real Jewish rye." "We had a local bread, real Jewish bread, that was sold widely in Brooklyn to Jewish people," recalled Judy Protas (1923–2014), the DDB advertising executive who conceived not only of that slogan but also of the lyrics to the Cracker Jack jingle ("Candy-coated popcorn, peanuts and a prize").[2] "What we wanted to do was enlarge its public acceptance. Since New York is so mixed ethnically, we decided to spread the good word that way."[3]

1. Stephen J. Whitfield, *In Search of American Jewish Culture* (Waltham, MA: Brandeis University Press, 1999), 4 and 11.

2. Quoted in Margalit Fox, "Judy Protas, Writer of Slogan for Levy's Real Jewish Rye, Dies at 91," *New York Times*, January 12, 2014, 22.

3. Ibid.

You don't have
to be Jewish

to love Levy's
real Jewish Rye

Poster of New York Police Department Officer Depicted in
Levy's Real Jewish Rye Advertising Campaign, 1961

Source: Doyle Dane Bernbach, "You Don't Have to Be Jewish to Love Levy's Real
Jewish Rye: New York Police Department Officer," 1961. Courtesy of DDB Worldwide
Communications Group LLC. Image provided by American Jewish Historical Society,
New York City.

In collaboration with the photographer and television commercial artist
Howard Zieff (1927–2009)—who later became a director known for, among
other Hollywood movies, *Private Benjamin* (1980), starring Goldie Hawn
(b. 1945)—Protas affixed the slogan to portraits of New Yorkers from all walks
of life: a robed choirboy, a matronly figure at a kitchen table, an African American boy, an Asian boy, an Asian man, a Native American man, a police officer,
and the aging silent film star Joseph "Buster" Keaton (1895–1966), each delight-
ing in a sandwich made with Levy's rye bread. Initially displayed in the New

York City subway system, the ads became an overnight sensation and attracted national attention. Walter Winchell (1897–1972), the iconic New York critic, called the campaign "the commercial with a *sensayuma* (say it aloud fast)."[4] Even the famously controversial black civil rights activist Malcolm X (1925–1965) relished the ads: he was photographed beaming beside the one featuring the black child. In due course, DDB sold individual posters as collectibles to customers across the country.

Running from the mid-1960s through the early 1970s, the Levy's rye bread advertising campaign became an iconic American commercial phenomenon, much like ads for Coca-Cola, Campbell's Soup, and Coppertone sunscreen. What set the Levy's campaign apart, however, was the playful way it introduced ideas about Jewish culture and ethnic pride to the public arena in the midst of an era of increasing racial tensions and political polarization. "The Levy's ad," observed the historian Lawrence H. Fuchs, "aimed at selling more rye bread by tapping into the growing multiethnic consciousness of Americans."[5] It was both "an invitation to cross boundaries" and a vehicle "to enhance profits."[6] Relying on the viewer's cultural literacy and sense of humor, the ubiquitous ads celebrated America's diversity even as they reinforced the dynamic tension between Jewish distinctiveness and American belonging.

—EDS.

4. Quoted in ibid.

5. Lawrence H. Fuchs, *The American Kaleidoscope: Race, Ethnicity, and the Civic Culture* (Hanover, NH: Wesleyan University Press, 1990), 325.

6. Ibid.

41

"AN INTOLERABLE SITUATION AND A MORAL BLOT ON HUMANITY"

American Jews Respond to the Plight of Soviet Jewry (1964)

<<<<<<<<<<<<<<<<<<<<<<<<<<<<<<<<<<<<<<<<<<<<<<<<<<<<<<<<<<<<<<<<<

AMARYAH ORENSTEIN

Conventional wisdom identifies the Six-Day War of June 1967[1] as the critical turning point in American Jewry's awareness of the plight of Soviet Jewry and the start of the American Jewish movement to liberate the three million Jews trapped behind the Iron Curtain. In fact, however, though the Middle East crisis catalyzed a groundswell of American Jewish political activism, the two documents presented below make clear that a variety of factors, some indigenous to the Soviet Union and some to the United States, influenced the development of the Soviet Jewry movement before 1967.

American Jews became increasingly aware of the plight of Soviet Jewry throughout the 1950s but voiced only sporadic expressions of concern that failed to produce any change in the Kremlin's treatment of its Jewish population. Some American Jews, blinded by a romanticized vision of the Soviet Union, refused to see claims of anti-Jewish persecution as anything but another form of the red-baiting scare that swept the United States in the early years of the Cold War. Many others, motivated by the memory of their own insecurity and struggle against discrimination in the decades before World War II, focused much of their energy on their upward climb in postwar American society. Hesitant to raise their voices about Jewish issues, American Jewish organizations typically downplayed the Jewish dimension of the Soviet Jewish problem in favor of a general anticommunist line and prodded the free world to join in the condemnation of communism and communist antisemitism.

By the early 1960s, however, as Soviet antisemitism acquired a new virulence, many American Jews began to take increased action. In mid-1963, Jewish officials in the U.S. government brought this issue to the attention of President John F. Kennedy (1917–1963), while members of the Jewish establishment, rab-

---

1. See chapter 54, note 3.

bis, and individual citizens sought to move the issue of Soviet Jewry to the top of the American Jewish communal agenda.

The renowned rabbi, thinker, and scholar Abraham Joshua Heschel (1907–1972) was motivated by the civil rights movement, a cause in which he became increasingly involved throughout the 1960s, to speak out on the subject. "If we are ready to go to jail in order to destroy the blight of racial bigotry, if we are ready to march on Washington in order to demonstrate our identification with those who are deprived of equal rights, should we not be ready to go to jail in order to end the martyrdom of our Russian brethren?" he asked in a paper presented to the Conference on the Moral Implications of the Rabbinate at New York's Jewish Theological Seminary of America on September 4, 1963.[2] Moreover, in a letter dated December 31, 1963, he warned that unless the American Jewish establishment took immediate drastic action, he would have no choice but to launch his own national movement on behalf of Soviet Jewry.[3]

Aware of Heschel's threat and sensitive to the plight of Soviet Jewry, Lewis H. Weinstein (1905–1996), chair of the Conference of Presidents of Major Jewish Organizations (a coordinating body of Jewish establishment organizations commonly known as the Presidents' Conference) and Isaiah Minkoff (1901–1983), executive director of the National Community Relations Advisory Council (NCRAC), pledged to organize a national mobilization conference. They secured the cooperation of the American Jewish Committee, whose board had recently affirmed its duty "to arouse mankind to the plight of nearly three million Jews ... who are threatened with the destruction of their cultural and religious identity."[4] Thus, the first establishment-led organization devoted to the cause of Soviet Jewry, the American Jewish Conference on Soviet Jewry (AJCSJ), was born. Heads of every significant defense, cultural, Zionist, and religious organization in the American Jewish community attended the new organization's national convention at the Willard Hotel in Washington on April 5 and 6, 1964. So, too, did key non-Jewish figures—senators and congressmen as well as church, labor, and civil rights leaders. Delegates committed themselves to

2. Abraham Joshua Heschel, "The Jews in the Soviet Union," in Abraham Joshua Heschel, *The Insecurity of Freedom: Essays in Human Existence* (New York: Farrar, Straus and Giroux, 1966), 269.

3. Lewis H. Weinstein, "Soviet Jewry and the American Jewish Community," *American Jewish History* 77, no. 4 (June 1988): 602.

4. At the time, the American Jewish Committee was the only major Jewish community relations agency that belonged to neither NCRAC nor the Presidents' Conference. See Albert D. Chernin, "Making Soviet Jews an Issue: A History," in *A Second Exodus: The American Movement to Free Soviet Jews*, ed. Murray Friedman and Albert D. Chernin (Waltham, MA: Brandeis University Press, 1999), 34.

helping "the last remnant of the once great eastern European Jewish community" and called on the Soviet regime to restore religious and cultural rights to its Jewish subjects; end discrimination against them in all areas of public life; and permit, "on humanitarian grounds," the reunification of Soviet Jewish families separated during the Holocaust.[5]

In the meantime, however, a small but forceful group of activists outside the mainstream Jewish organizations became increasingly troubled not only by the growing campaign against Soviet Jews but also by what it perceived as American Jewish indifference to the condition of Soviet Jewry. Organized in late April 1964 and led by Jacob Birnbaum (1926–2014), a recent British immigrant who was "deeply discouraged by the lack of truly purposeful and dedicated activity" on the part of the establishment-led AJCSJ, the Student Struggle for Soviet Jewry (SSSJ, or Triple-SJ) reflected the broader culture of 1960s student protest, dedicating itself to less talk and more direct action.[6] Using the lessons of the Holocaust as a stark warning and the civil rights movement as a model of successful grassroots activism, the young Jewish activists of the SSSJ took to the streets, demonstrating, sitting in, and riding freedom buses to protest the treatment of Soviet Jewry.[7]

Dissatisfied and impatient with what it considered to be the special pleading of American Jewish communal leaders, the SSSJ aimed to rouse the American Jewish community as a whole—its leadership and laity—to take concrete action

5. American Jewish Conference on Soviet Jewry, Resolution, Records of the National Conference on Soviet Jewry, I-181 and I-181A, box 1, folder: AJCSJ, 1965–1967, American Jewish Historical Society, New York City.

6. Jacob Birnbaum, "The Student Struggle for Soviet Jewry," June 1964, 6, box 317, folder 12, Student Struggle for Soviet Jewry Records, Mendel Gottesman Library, Yeshiva University, New York City (hereafter SSSJ Records).

7. The AJCSJ embodied all that the SSSJ would stand against. Though the organizations that sponsored the creation of the AJCSJ pledged to use their resources and energies "to the fullest to bring to the attention of the world the facts about the oppression of Soviet Jewry, through every means at [their] command, through every channel of information available to [them], through every contact and association, in every place and in every season," they initially did no such thing (AJCSJ, "Declaration of Principles," April 1963, Records of the National Conference on Soviet Jewry, box 1, folder 1, American Jewish Historical Society, New York City). Rather, citing "ample precedent in American history," delegates simply asked that "the United States government use its good offices to make known to the Soviet government the extent of our government's concern for the situation and status of three million Jews in the Soviet Union" ("Statement to Secretary of State Dean Rusk," April 7, 1963, in ibid.). Moreover, the sponsoring organizations refused to empower the nascent AJCSJ, not supplying it with any budget, full-time staff members, or permanent home. See also Chernin, "Making Soviet Jews an Issue," 38–39; William W. Orbach, *The American Movement to Aid Soviet Jews* (Amherst: University of Massachusetts Press, 1979), 26.

on behalf of Soviet Jewry, sway the U.S. government to put political pressure on the Kremlin to change its anti-Jewish policies, lobby the Soviet government directly (insofar as possible), and boost the morale of Soviet Jews. Not only did the sssj's campaign play a critical role in securing the eventual freedom of Soviet Jewry, but it also posed a direct challenge to the traditional politics of the American Jewish community. Thus, in addition to shedding light on the early and lesser-known history of the American movement to liberate Soviet Jewry, the sssj's founding statement (reprinted below) also serves as a corrective to what the historian Michael Staub has referred to as the general neglect by scholars of the extent to which Jewish youth culture in the 1960s helped shape and revitalize the American Jewish community in the Cold War era.[8]

◇◇

Testimony before the U.S. House of Representatives by the American Conference on Soviet Jewry, April 16, 1964

Source: "American Jewish Conference on Soviet Jewry," in *Congressional Record: Proceedings and Debates of the 88th Congress, Second Session*, vol. 110, part 5 (March 19, 1964–April 6, 1964) (Washington, D.C.: Government Printing Office, 1964), 6899–901.

... Mr. RYAN of New York.[9] Mr. Speaker, last December I spoke on the floor of the house about the Soviet campaign of discrimination against Russian citizens of the Jewish faith. At that time I detailed the various methods, including the prevention of publication of books, the closing of synagogues, the prohibition against the baking of *matzoth* [*sic*], and the eradication of Jewish religious and cultural life. I have also called upon President [Lyndon B.] Johnson to use his good offices to appeal to Premier [Nikita] Khrushchev[10] to lift these religious and cultural restrictions.[11] Today and yesterday a conference

8. Michael Staub, introduction to *The Jewish 1960s: An American Sourcebook*, ed. Michael Staub (Waltham, MA: Brandeis University Press, 2004), xviii.

9. William Fitts Ryan (1922–1972), a Democrat, represented Manhattan's Upper West Side in the U.S. House of Representatives from 1961 until his death in 1972. A liberal crusader, Ryan was the first congressman to vote against funding the Vietnam War, and he marched in civil rights demonstrations throughout the South.

10. Nikita Sergeyevich Khrushchev (1894–1971) led the Soviet Communist Party and served as premier of the Soviet Union from 1957 to 1964.

11. Responding to the claim by Lewis H. Weinstein (1905–1996), chairman of the NCRAC and a personal friend of President John F. Kennedy (1917–1963), that no president since Theodore Roosevelt (1858–1919) had openly intervened with Russian authorities on behalf of the persecuted Jewish community, Kennedy agreed to meet with Jewish community leaders after his re-

on Soviet Jewry is being held in Washington, D.C., with over 500 persons in attendance....[12]

Mr. Speaker, Supreme Court Justice Arthur J. Goldberg[13] delivered a most thoughtful address to the conference in which he pointed out the reasons why all Americans must be concerned with Soviet antisemitism which constitutes a fundamental deprivation of basic human rights. I wish to bring to the attention of all my colleagues the address of Mr. Justice Goldberg:

ADDRESS BY THE HONORABLE ARTHUR J. GOLDBERG, ASSOCIATE
JUSTICE, U.S. SUPREME COURT, TO THE AMERICAN JEWS [SIC]
CONFERENCE ON SOVIET JEWRY, APRIL 5, 1964

... The denial of human rights by the Soviet Union to Jews is properly a matter of deep concern to all Americans of every religious persuasion. It is similarly a proper matter of deep concern to all Americans of the Jewish faith that the Soviet Union while professing in theory to permit the free exercise of religion to all people and groups in fact and practice is hostile to all religious faiths. The Soviet Union is avowedly a materialistic nation. Its government is not neutral in religious matters. Its policies and influence are directed against religious beliefs and practices. Therefore, in a conference of this kind we

---

turn from Dallas, Texas, in early December 1963. However, he was assassinated on November 22. Keeping his pledge to continue where the slain president had left off, President Lyndon B. Johnson (1908–1973) agreed to sit down with Jewish leaders. This meeting did not take place until April 8, 1964, and though he sanctioned the tactic of widespread public protest, insisting that it could sway the Soviet leaders, President Johnson refused to consider direct U.S. government intervention on behalf of Soviet Jewry.

12. The conference was sponsored by twenty-four Jewish organizations from across the political and denominational spectrum: the American Israel Public Affairs Committee, American Jewish Committee, American Jewish Congress, American Trade Union Council for Histadrut, American Zionist Council, Bnai Brith, Central Conference of American Rabbis, Conference of Presidents of Major American Jewish Organizations, Hadassah, Jewish Agency for Israel (American Section), Jewish Labor Committee, Jewish War Veterans of the U.S.A., Labor Zionist Organization of America, National Community Relations Advisory Council, National Council of Jewish Women, National Council of Young Israel, Rabbinical Assembly, Rabbinical Council of America, Religious Zionists of America, Synagogue Council of America, Union of American Hebrew Congregations, Union of Orthodox Jewish Congregations of America, United Synagogue of America, and Zionist Organization of America.

13. Arthur J. Goldberg (1908–1990) was appointed in 1962 to serve as an associate justice of the Supreme Court by President Kennedy. He resigned from the bench in 1965 when President Johnson asked him to serve as U.S. ambassador to the United Nations.

are not and cannot be unmindful of the plight of the great body of people in the Soviet Union whose human right to freedom of religious exercise is substantially curtailed. The discrimination against Jews by the government of the Soviet Union is an aspect of overall discrimination against all religious groups. It is, however, something more than a manifestation of religious repression by an atheistic state. The evidence is overwhelming that the religious and cultural freedom of Soviet Jewry is more severely limited than any other religious group and that discrimination against Soviet Jews has reached alarming proportions. The tragic experience of mankind with the cancer of antisemitism so fresh in the minds of all makes it imperative that those who believe in the dignity of man and in human rights speak out in vigorous protest.

I want to commend the sponsors of this conference for convening it. The meeting itself is a virtually unprecedented testimonial to the unity of Jewish opinion on this vital and important subject. I hope and trust that you will continue to protest against the virus of antisemitism in the Soviet Union until no vestige of it remains.

The 2 ½ to 3 million Jews of the Soviet Union, though classified by the Soviet Constitution and laws as a national group, are deprived of their national culture and the means of expressing it. Every other Soviet nationality is permitted the use of its national language and is granted support for its cultural institutions. But the teaching of Hebrew, the biblical language, is banned in the Soviet Union; [the use of] Yiddish, the tongue of 450,000 Soviet citizens, is discouraged; Jewish schools virtually prohibited and nonexistent; the once flourishing Yiddish theater scarcely tolerated; and Jewish literature and publications sharply curtailed.

The religious freedom of Soviet Jews is severely limited—more so than any other religious group; increasingly synagogues are closed and private worship restricted; both Bible and prayer books are denied printing; other necessary religious articles made unavailable; the last kosher butcher shop in Moscow closed down; the ancient Jewish cemetery in Kiev condemned; the state baking of matzoth [sic] discontinued; private baking discouraged by prosecutions;[14] the training of seminarians hampered; and religious exchanges discouraged.

Jews are vilified in the Soviet press and other mass media which reflect hostility to the Jewish people as such. This has reached such proportions

14. In July, 1963, authorities arrested four Jews on charges of "profiteering" in the sale of matzah.

that Western Communist Parties which generally slavishly follow the Kremlin line have been moved to protest the publication of a blatantly antisemitic book published last year in Kiev, copies of which have just come to light in this country and in the Western world. This book, *Judaism Without Embellishment*, is not just a privately printed tract. It was officially issued by the Ukrainian Academy of Science. . . .

Jewish emigration even for the limited purpose of reuniting families torn asunder by war and Nazi persecution is permitted only on the most insignificant scale.

There is increasing evidence of discrimination against Jews in employment and areas of public life.

Finally, there is also evidence that an undue proportion of Jews is being prosecuted and executed for economic crimes.[15]

Discrimination against Soviet Jews is not solely an internal matter for the Soviet Union. It is a proper concern for all in this country and elsewhere who believe in human values. Soviet mistreatment of the Jews violates [the] worldwide concept of human rights and human dignity; transgresses the United Nations Charter to which the Soviet Union is a party and violates the universal declaration of human rights which is morally binding upon all member states of the United Nations.

. . . In stating my views, I do so as an American citizen who supports the effort of our government, with due regard for our own security as a nation, to seek ways for better understanding between our country and the Soviet Union; one who shares with the great majority of our people the desire for an end to the Cold War and for a just and lasting peace.

In appealing for an end to governmental discrimination against Jews in the Soviet Union, I am mindful that as a nation our record is not perfect—we all too often fall short of realizing the great ideals of human liberty and equality embodied in our great declaration of human rights. I am also mindful, however, that our government policy is directed to ending rather than extending discrimination. . . .

15. As an extended economic crisis crippled the Soviet economy, authorities used the Jews as a scapegoat. Between July 1961 and August 1963, hundreds of people were tried for so-called economic crimes. Of the 163 people sentenced to death, 60 percent were Jews—though Jews made up just over 1 percent of the Soviet population. The disproportionate number of Jews accused of such crimes prompted protests against the antisemitic nature of the trials. In April 1962, for example, the world-renowned intellectuals Martin Buber (1878–1965), François Mauriac (1885–1970), and Bertrand Russell (1872–1970) issued a public appeal to Khrushchev, urging him to repeal the death sentences handed down to those found guilty of economic crimes.

Founding Statement of the Student Struggle for Soviet Jewry, April 1964

Source: Student Struggle for Soviet Jewry Records, box 1, folder 1, Yeshiva University Archives, Mendel Gottesman Library, New York City.

COLLEGE STUDENTS' STRUGGLE FOR SOVIET JEWRY[16]

Dear Friend:

There is overwhelming evidence to show that in recent years the Soviet government has greatly speeded up its attempts at forcible assimilation of Russian Jewry.[17] The screw is being turned swiftly and inexorably tighter. Just one example: in the last few years alone well over 300 synagogues have been closed

16. The word "College" was later dropped from the organization's title and the group was henceforth known as the Student Struggle for Soviet Jewry.

17. Though the issue of Soviet Jewry was spotlighted in the postwar period, its roots date back to the founding of the Soviet state. The Russian Revolution of 1917 had sparked hope that the official antisemitism of the tsarist regime, which not only deprived Jews of equal rights but also sanctioned anti-Jewish violence, would come to an end. Seeking to defuse nationalist sentiment, the Bolshevik party formulated a nationalities policy in the 1920s known as *korenizatsiya* (Russian for "putting down roots"), creating national republics and many autonomous regions, establishing national languages, and promoting the development of all national cultures. The Soviet regime officially recognized Soviet Jewry as a national minority with Yiddish as its national language, but the Jewish religion was persecuted along with all others, and Zionism and the Hebrew language were suppressed.

Following the Nazi invasion of the Soviet Union in 1941, the communist regime again allowed a modicum of national expression in an effort to mobilize all elements of Soviet society in what was known as the Great Patriotic War. However, the Soviet Jewish cultural revival of the war years, marked by the creation of the Jewish Anti-Fascist Committee to foster Western Jewish support for the Soviet war effort, proved fleeting. In the wake of the Holocaust and the Allied victory over Nazi Germany, Soviet Premier Joseph Stalin (1878–1953) initiated his own solution to the so-called Jewish problem. With the emergence of the Cold War and the very real possibility of an armed conflict with the United States, he feared that Soviet Jews, many of whom had family members in the West and whom he suspected of identifying with world Jewry, would not be loyal to the Soviet Union. Thus, even as the Soviet Union gave political assistance in 1947 to the creation of the State of Israel (in a bid to extend its sphere of influence to the Middle East), it intensified its campaign of intimidation and repression against its own Jews. The January 1948 murder of Solomon Mikhoels (1890–1948), a famous Yiddish actor and chairman of the Jewish Anti-Fascist Committee, marked the start of what Soviet Jews called *di shvartse yorn* (Yiddish for "the black years"). Shortly thereafter, Soviet authorities abolished the Jewish Anti-Fascist Committee and liquated all institutions of Yiddish culture, including the last remaining Yiddish schools, the Yiddish theater, and the Yiddish press. On August 12, 1952, thirteen members of the defunct Jewish Anti-Fascist Committee—who had been arrested in 1949, held incognito, and tortured—were executed following a secret trial in which they were charged with treason, espionage, and bourgeois nationalism for their alleged plot to establish a Zionist republic and U.S. military base in the Crimea.

down, leaving only 60 or so synagogues for a population of 3,000,000 Jews. Furthermore, autonomous cultural life is almost completely banned. By contrast, tiny Soviet minorities of less than half a million have flourishing cultural institutions of every kind, and most other religious denominations continue to lead a very visible and active, if limited, existence.

We are able to document a concerted effort at spiritual and cultural strangulation, very often shot through with a vicious antisemitism. The net result is that masses of Jews are in an increasingly ambiguous position, neither assimilating nor living self-respecting Jewish lives, nor yet being able to emigrate.

This is an intolerable situation and a moral blot on humanity. Justice is indivisible. Just as we, as human beings and as Jews, are conscious of the wrongs suffered by the Negro and we fight for his betterment, so must we come to feel in ourselves the silent, strangulated pain of so many of our Russian brethren. A recent visitor to Russia was approached by a man with glowing eyes, who whispered: "*Far voos shveigt ir?*" — [Yiddish for] "Why do you keep silent?"

We, who condemn silence and inaction during the Nazi Holocaust, dare we keep silent now?

The time has come for a mass grass-roots movement — spearheaded by the student youth. A ferment is indeed at work at this time. Groups of students all over New York are spontaneously coming together and hundreds of signatures have been collected.

There is a time to be passive and a time to act. We believe most emphatically that this is *not* a time for quietism. We believe that a bold, well-planned campaign, to include some very active measures, can create a climate of opinion, a moral power, which will become a force to be reckoned with.

A meeting has, therefore, been arranged of students from all parts of the metropolitan area.

Monday evening next — April 27 — at 8 P.M.[18]
at COLUMBIA UNIVERSITY

18. Approximately two hundred students — mostly from Yeshiva University, the Jewish Theological Seminary, Columbia University, Queens College, and Stern College — answered the call to action and organized themselves as the SSSJ, calling for immediate action. Half in jest, Birnbaum suggested the possibility of a May Day demonstration in the front of the Soviet mission to the United Nations. Students earnestly accepted his proposal and worked around the clock to organize, recruiting participants, designing placards, and making other necessary preparations. Held just four days after the organization's founding meeting, the May Day protest marked the first of the SSSJ's countless public demonstrations on behalf of Soviet Jewry. Between 700 and 1,000 students from thirteen universities in the New York metropolitan area picketed in front of the Soviet mission to the United Nations on May 1.

in the Graduate Student Lounge of PHILOSOPHY HALL

The agenda will be as follows:

After brief introductory remarks, the meeting will be thrown wide open for the purpose

    1. of clarifying the issues

    2. of examining possible courses of action, and

    3. of appointing a pro-tem city-wide college committee for Soviet Jewry.

Your care, your concern for a suffering portion of *klal yisroel* [Hebrew for "all of Israel"] united with the concern of your fellows, will surely wing its way through the ether, leap over frontiers, and penetrate into the heart of many a discouraged Russian Jew.

COME! BRING YOUR FRIENDS!

Jacob Birnbaum[19]

Moses Stambler[20]

Bernard Caplan[21]

James Torczyner[22]

---

19. Jacob Birnbaum (1926–2014) was the grandson of Nathan Birnbaum (1864–1937), whose personal odyssey led him from a proto-Zionism to identification with the movement for Jewish cultural autonomy in the diaspora, and finally to becoming a penitent who joined the Orthodox anti-Zionist ranks of Agudat Yisrael. Jacob was also the son of Solomon Asher Birnbaum (1891–1989), a scholar of Hebrew paleography and epigraphy, as well as the Yiddish language. During World War II, Jacob Birnbaum worked in the Uncommon Languages Department of Britain's national censor. From 1946 to 1951, he lived in France and worked with Holocaust survivors. In the spring of 1963, intent on raising awareness of the "spiritual genocide" being perpetrated against Soviet Jewry, he immigrated to the United States to devote himself to the creation of an American Jewish campaign to alleviate the plight of Soviet Jews (Jacob Birnbaum, "The Student Struggle for Soviet Jewry," June 1964, 6, box 317, folder 12, SSSJ Records).

20. At the time, a Yeshiva University student.

21. At the time, Bernard Caplan was chair of the Social Action Committee of the national Orthodox Jewish student organization called Yavneh.

22. A Yeshiva University student suspended for his Soviet Jewry activism, James Torczyner advocated for more militant action in planning the SSSJ's inaugural protest. Following a heated three-hour phone conversation, however, he and fellow Yeshiva student Glenn Richter (who would become the SSSJ's national coordinator) relented and threw their support behind the May Day rally in lieu of a "militant and illegal 3 A.M. action" against the Soviet mission to the United Nations (Glenn Richter, "A Student Organization: Birth to Bureaucracy," unpublished sociology paper, Queens College, New York, May 8, 1964, n.p., box 56, folder 5, SSSJ Records).

42

"ISRAEL'S ESSENTIAL EMISSARY"

Golda Meir on the Cover of *Time* Magazine (1969)

◇◇

When Golda Meir (1898–1978) appeared in 1969 on the covers of *Time*, *Life*, and *Look* magazines and the front pages of every major American newspaper, shortly after being elected Israel's fourth prime minister, it was not the first time that her visage had adorned the public arena. A frequent visitor to the United States, Meir was already a visible and familiar presence in the American setting. A veteran spokesperson for the Zionist cause, she would crisscross the country on speaking tours; giving countless interviews to the press; meeting with Jewish, Zionist, and pro-Israel groups; and raising funds for the Jewish state. The arresting 1956 portrait of Meir by the photographer Burt Glinn (1925–2008), used by *Time* when she became Israel's foreign minister, earned her the moniker "Israel's essential emissary."[1] A decade later, Boris Chaliapin (1904–1972), an illustrator for *Time*, produced a magazine cover to mark Meir's ascension to the pinnacle of Israel's political establishment. Indeed, for most of her adult life, even after the debacle of the Yom Kippur War (1973),[2] she remained a celebrated and beloved figure in the United States. The subject of numerous biographies, plays, films, and other expressions of fandom—for example, the artist Andy Warhol (1928–1987) included Meir in his silkscreen pantheon titled "Ten Portraits of Jews of the Twentieth Century"—Meir's iconic image endures as a symbol of Israel in the American mind.[3]

---

1. Burt Glinn's portrait of Golda Meir, first published by *Time* in 1956, was reprinted in 2020 as part of its "100 Women of the Year" initiative. Inspired by *Time*'s long-standing "Person of the Year" selection (known until 1999 as "Man of the Year") and timed to commemorate the one hundredth anniversary of the Nineteenth Amendment to the U.S. Constitution (1920), Meir was selected to represent the year 1956. See "The 100 Women of the Year," *Time*, https://time .com/100-women-of-the-year/; "100 Women of the Year: 1956: Gold Meier," *Time*, March 5, 2020, https://time.com/5793561/golda-meir-100-women-of-the-year/.

2. See chapter 43, note 49.

3. In addition to Meir, Warhol's portraits of people he called "Jewish geniuses" (quoted in

Meir was born in Kiev, on the eve of tsarist Russia's implosion; endured poverty, the fear of pogroms, and the arrest of a sibling; and as a child immigrated to Milwaukee, where her family lived in "straitened, but steadily improving" working-class conditions.[4] She Americanized swiftly and enjoyed access to a variety of educational opportunities. Inspired by Labor Zionism's romantic ethos—the building of a socially just Jewish workers' society in Palestine—she gravitated to the American branch of the Poalei Zion (Workers of Zion) party.[5] She studied to become a teacher and worked in both the Milwaukee public schools and the local Labor Zionist *folkshul*, a supplementary Yiddish-language school with afternoon and evening classes. In 1921, she immigrated to Palestine with her husband, Morris Meyerson (1893–1951). There she joined a kibbutz and became a labor movement activist.

Rising through the ranks of the pre-state Zionist establishment and the Histadrut trade union, Meir developed a strong track record as a public servant. At a time when English-language skills and the talent for charming reporters were in strikingly short supply, she became a singularly important interlocutor with British Mandatory authorities, American officials, and the media. Nowhere was her skill set more productively deployed than in the United States. In 1948, for example, as Israel's War of Independence loomed, she undertook an emergency fund-raising mission in her capacity as acting head of the Jewish Agency's Political Department. Barnstorming the country, she raised more than $50 million—a staggering sum that financed roughly a third of Israel's wartime costs.[6]

In the early years of Israel's statehood, Meir proved to be an especially effective labor minister (1949–56), crafting legislation to protect Jewish and Arab workers, spearheading efforts to build the country's roads and new housing to accommodate the mass influx of new immigrants from Middle Eastern and

Ken Johnson, "Funny, You Don't Look Like a Subject for Warhol," *New York Times*, March 28, 2008, E35) were of the actress Sarah Bernhardt (1844–1923); U.S. Supreme Court justice Louis D. Brandeis (1856–1941); philosopher Martin Buber (1878–1965); Nobel prize winner Albert Einstein (1879–1955); founder of psychoanalysis, Sigmund Freud (1856–1939); jazz composer George Gershwin (1898–1937); modernist writers Franz Kafka (1883–1924) and Gertrude Stein (1874–1946); and the Marx Brothers comedians, Chico (1887–1961), Harpo (1888–1964), and Groucho (1890–1977).

4. Michael Brown, *The Israeli-American Connection: Its Roots in the Yishuv, 1914–1945* (Detroit, MI: Wayne State University Press, 1996), 162.

5. See chapter 31, note 21.

6. Brown, *The Israeli-American Connection*, 195.

African countries, and promoting civic equality. As foreign minister (1956–66), she drew on her intimate knowledge of American society and long-standing relationships to help build close ties between Israel and the United States. In 1969, she became Israel's fourth (and to date only female) prime minister (1969–74), as well as the third female prime minister in the history of the family of nations.

It is important to note that Meir was an outlier in the rough-and-tumble of the twentieth-century political arena. In an era dominated by powerful patriarchs—consider, for example, Charles de Gaulle (1890–1970), Lyndon B. Johnson (1908–1973), and David Ben-Gurion (1886–1973)—and pulsating with dashing mavericks who represented generational change—John F. Kennedy (1917–1963), Che Guevara (1928–1967), and Moshe Dayan (1915–1981), to name but a few—Meir cut an unusual political profile. Throughout Meir's career, as the historian Anita Shapira points out, she was forced to navigate the suspicions, jealousies, and bruised egos of the many strong and willful men around her.[7] Her unassuming demeanor and affable nature—she wore sensible shoes, carried her own handbag, and entertained guests in her kitchen—masked her keen political instincts, steely resolve, and partisan ambitions.

The *Time* cover art reprinted here presents a snapshot of Meir at the height of her political power. A banner ("Middle East: Toward the Brink") in the upper left corner a conveys a sense of dramatic urgency, while a resolute Golda Meir, with a Star of David in the background, confronts the viewer. In its exquisite simplicity, the illustration captures the dynamic tension of the War of Attrition (1967–70), when Israel faced hostility at its borders and the emerging threat of the nascent Palestine Liberation Organization. It also hints at the bonds between American Jews and Israel as well as the implications of U.S.-Israel relations for the future of the Middle East. Ongoing violent skirmishes between Egypt and Israel, including an Israeli ground offensive known as Operation Raviv in early September 1969, prompted Meir's official U.S. visit and a series of White House meetings, where she presented President Richard M. Nixon (1913–1994) with an Israeli request to purchase advanced military aircraft. Following two days of meetings (September 25–27), Nixon and Meir reported to the press that the matter was under serious consideration. Thereafter, Meir met with cabinet officers and a variety of Congressional leaders.

From Washington Meir traveled to New York City (September 29), Los Ange-

7. Anita Shapira, "Golda: Feminism and Femininity," in *American Jewish Women and the Zionist Enterprise*, ed. Shulamit Reinharz and Mark A. Raider (Hanover, NH: University Press of New England, 2005), 301–12.

"Israel's Golda Meir," *Time*, September 19, 1969. Source: "Israel's Golda Meir," *Time*, September 19, 1969, cover. Artwork by Boris Chaliapin. Reprinted with permission.

les (October 1), Milwaukee (October 3), and Atlantic City (October 6) before returning to Israel. In each city, she was greeted by local officials and crowds of enthusiastic well-wishers, including thousands of cheering and singing American Jews. During her New York visit, Mayor John Lindsay (1921–2000) hailed Meir as "a gallant woman and a gallant leader" and saluted "the men, women, and children of brave, beleaguered Israel." Meir wept "when the crowd broke into [Israel's national anthem] 'Hatikvah' [Hebrew for the hope]," and she subsequently spoke about her family's history of having fled tsarist Russia in 1906 for the United States. "The first lesson of what democracy really means, I learned here," she said. She emphasized that she had "left America for Palestine in 1921 neither because [I] did not like the country nor because of antisemitism. It was because [I] had accepted Zionism and wanted to bring to Palestine" the values and ideals "I learned in this wonderful country."[8]

8. "'New York Is Yours!' Says Mayor Lindsay in Welcome to Golda Meir," *JTA Daily News Bulletin* 36, no. 184, September 30, 1969, 1.

It is worth observing that history has not been kind to Meir, often derided as "the Old Lady" by detractors. Particularly in Israel, Meir—once lionized and venerated—is now disparaged for allegedly failing to prevent the outbreak of the Yom Kippur War, which led to a devastating loss of Israeli life and imperiled the Jewish state. The contrast between Israeli and American perspectives of Meir, however, could not be more stark. The *Time* cover presented here invites us to step back from the realm of polemics and consider from a macrohistorical perspective—that is, the historian's privileged viewpoint of hindsight—what Meir represented and represents in terms of American Jewish identity and the development of U.S.-Israel relations.

—EDS.

43

"TO SECURE ISRAEL'S SURVIVAL AND SECURITY"

President Gerald R. Ford and Secretary of State Henry
Kissinger Meet with American Jewish Leaders
(1976)

◇◇

MARK A. RAIDER

In the mid-twentieth century, the Middle East, characterized by a
patchwork of postcolonial Arab regimes, rich oil resources, and intricate political rivalries, swiftly became a microcosm of the Cold War between the United
States and the Soviet Union. Israel's military victories in the Sinai campaign
(1956) and the Six-Day War (1967), albeit an existential matter in terms of its
own national security, had the effect of checking Soviet influence in the Middle
East. Some Washington circles favored the maintenance of a strong Israel to
achieve a balance of power in the region. Others, including State Department
analysts and officials, believed that the U.S. government should deploy economic incentives to sway Arab regimes and undermine growing Soviet influence. An overt pro-Israel American strategy, it was feared, could be counter-
productive and drive Egypt, Saudi Arabia, Jordan, and Lebanon into the Soviet
orbit. This line of thinking was aligned with both powerful American business
interests and the historic investment of U.S. capital in Arab lands with vast oil
reserves.

The high level of engagement of Jews in the American political scene also
influenced U.S. policy in the Middle East. No less than other minority groups,
American Jews amounted to a significant constituency with a distinctive set of
interests. Candidates for local, state, and federal office in the 1960s and 1970s
courted their support. In addition, the number of Jews holding public office in
the United States in this period rose, with many elected as mayors, governors,[1]

---

1. The American Jews elected to governorships in 1960–80 were Frank R. Licht (RI), Marvin
Mandel (MD), Abraham Ribicoff (CT), Samuel Shapiro (IL), and Milton Shapp (PA).

and members of the U.S. House of Representatives[2] and the Senate.[3] Others were appointed to cabinet-level positions by Presidents John F. Kennedy (1917–1963), Lyndon B. Johnson (1908–1973), Richard M. Nixon (1913–1994), Gerald R. Ford (1913–2006), and Jimmy Carter (b. 1924).[4]

The cases of Philip M. Klutznik (1907–1999) and Henry Kissinger (b. 1923)[5] (who became figures in the Democratic and Republican party establishments, respectively) are in many ways emblematic of American Jewish political success in this period. Klutznik's involvement in American Jewish affairs included serving as national president of the fraternal organization Bnai Brith (1953–59) and international president of the World Jewish Congress (1977–79). He began his career in public service as commissioner of Federal Public Housing under Presidents Franklin D. Roosevelt (1882–1945) and Harry S. Truman (1884–1972), served as U.S. representative to the United Nations in the Eisenhower, Kennedy, and Johnson administrations, and was appointed secretary of commerce in the Carter administration. Kissinger, a refugee from Nazi Germany and Harvard-trained scholar, rose to become Nixon's national security adviser in 1969 and was appointed secretary of state in 1975, a role he retained under Ford. The ending of the war in Vietnam, the normalization of relations with China, the con-

---

2. The American Jews elected to the U.S. House of Representatives in 1960–80 were Bella Abzug (NY), Anthony Beilenson (CA), Mickey Edwards (OK), Joshua Elberg (PA), Jacob Gilbert (NY), Ben Gilman (NY), Martin Frost (TX), Dan Glickman (KS), Bill Gradison (OH), Bill Green (NY), Elizabeth Holtzman (NY), Charles Joelson (NJ), Ed Koch (NY), Ken Kramer (CO), John Krebs (CA), William Lehman (FL), Eliott Levitas (GA), Allard Lowenstein (NY), Marc Marks (PA), Ed Mezvinsky (IA), Abner Mikva (IL), Richard Ottinger (NY), Ben Podell (NY), Joseph Resnick (NY), Fred Richmond (NY), Benjamin Rosenthal (NY), Jim Scheuer (NY), Stephen Solarz (NY), Gladys Spellman (MD), Sam Steiger (AZ), Herbert Tenzer (NY), Henry Waxman (CA), Ted Weiss (NY), Lester Wolff (NY), and Howard Wolpe (MI).

3. The American Jews elected to the U.S. Senate in 1960–80 were Rudolph "Rudy" Boschwitz (MN) Howard Metzenbaum (OH), Abraham Ribicoff (CT), Richard Stone (FL), and Edward Zorinsky (NE).

4. Kennedy appointed Arthur J. Goldberg (see chapter 41, note 13) secretary of labor and Abraham A. Ribicoff secretary of health, education, and welfare. Johnson appointed Goldberg U.S. ambassador to the United Nations and Wilbur J. Cohen secretary of health, education, and welfare. Nixon appointed Walter Annenberg U.S. ambassador to Great Britain, Arthur Burns chairman of the Federal Reserve Board, Edward H. Levi attorney general, and Herbert Stein chairman of the president's Council of Economic Advisers. Ford appointed Edward H. Levi attorney general. Carter appointed Harold Brown secretary of defense, W. Michael Blumenthal secretary of the treasury, Neil Goldschmidt secretary of transportation, and Philip Klutznick secretary of commerce.

5. See note 44.

clusion of the Yom Kippur War,[6] and the attempt to find a Middle East settlement were among the activities that made him one of the most iconic holders of this office. Speaking at a farewell luncheon given in his honor in 1977 by the Conference of Presidents of Major American Jewish Organizations, Kissinger declared, "I have never forgotten that thirteen members of my family died in concentration camps, nor could I ever fail to remember what it was like to live in Nazi Germany as a member of a persecuted minority."[7] The meteoric trajectory of Klutznik, Kissinger, and a handful of other Jewish political figures, for which there are precious few parallels in American history, is truly remarkable.

The early 1970s brought many dramatic changes as well as insecurity and anxiety to the forefront of American society. The fraught Vietnam War's conclusion, as tragic and humiliating as the war itself, left an indelible impact of American culture. The shootings of student protesters at Kent State University and Jackson State College in 1970 shocked the nation. The Watergate scandal (1972–74) revealed the extent of Nixon's corruption and undermined the public's confidence in government. The Arab oil embargo (1973–74), targeting countries that had supported Israel during the Yom Kippur War (1973), quadrupled oil prices, negatively affected the American economy, and exposed the vulnerability of the U.S. energy security policy.

For American Jews, notwithstanding the general trend of the Jewish community's upward economic mobility and successful acculturation at all levels of society, the uncertain social, economic, and political climate of the early 1970s heightened concerns about Israel's prospects for survival. Responding almost reflexively to the shock of the Yom Kippur War, American Jewish organizations and communal institutions immediately began to coordinate a national emergency fund-raising campaign on Israel's behalf, convince local entities to support Israel's war effort, and lobby American policy makers. Thus, on October 6, 1973—within hours of the war's outbreak and even as a sizable portion of American Jewry observed the Yom Kippur holiday—American Jewish leaders mobilized to secure political support for Nixon's request for a $2.2 billion appropriation of funds by Congress that would allow Israel to purchase American military supplies. The United Jewish Appeal[8] pledged to raise $900 million, and the Israel Bond's organization and a plethora of Jewish and Zionist groups initiated emergency fund-raising initiatives. The Conservative synagogue move-

6. See note 49.

7. Quoted in Harvey Starr, *Henry Kissinger: Perceptions of International Politics* (Lexington: University Press of Kentucky, 1984), 31.

8. See note 29.

ment alone raised a total of $82 million. Finally, some thirty-five thousand prospective American Jewish volunteers inundated the offices around the country of the Jewish Agency for Israel, a nongovernmental organization that works with diaspora Jewish communities. The volunteers included a large number of doctors with prior experience in the Vietnam War. Only a few thousand volunteers were actually sent to Israel in the first weeks of the war, and most paid for their own airfare.

The Yom Kippur War's dramatic trajectory and Israel's hard-won victory, aided by a massive American airlift of military supplies, came at a cost of heavy Israeli casualties and swept away the memory of Israel's stunning triumph in the Six-Day War. When the Yom Kippur War ended on October 24, 1973, a flurry of disengagement and ceasefire negotiations ensued, brokered by the United States and the United Nations. Kissinger's famous "shuttle diplomacy" played a pivotal role in this regard. Meanwhile, public outrage in Israel over the government's lack of military preparedness led to a commission of inquiry, the resignation of Prime Minister Golda Meir (1898–1978), and new elections. Although Meir remained a beloved figure in the American Jewish arena, her standing in Israeli society was severely battered (see chapter 42). In June 1974 Yitzhak Rabin (1922–1995), a former chief of general staff and, most recently, the Israeli ambassador to the United States, succeeded Meir as the head of a new government.[9] Notably, he was the first sabra (native-born Israeli) to become prime minister.

When Ford became U.S. president in August 1974, he faced a highly volatile international and domestic landscape. On the one hand, Ford made it clear to the Soviet Union that despite Nixon's resignation, the United States still intended to pursue the policy of détente—an easing of relations between the countries, with an eye toward mutual arms reduction. The high stakes in this regard were obvious: less than a year before, the Yom Kippur War had nearly resulted in a nuclear showdown between the superpowers. On the other hand, Ford was required to work on the domestic front within parameters established by several U.S. politicians led by Senator Henry "Scoop" Jackson (1912–1983), who linked American trade with the Soviet Union to the relaxation of its emigration policies, thus enabling Soviet Jews (known as "refuseniks") to immigrate to Israel. Against this charged backdrop, U.N. Resolution 3379 (1975) condemning Zionism "as a form of racism and racial discrimination" resounded like a thunderclap.[10] In the event, Chaim Herzog (1918–1997), Israel's ambassador to

9. See note 51.

10. United Nations General Assembly, "Resolution Adopted by the General Assembly,"

the United Nations and later its sixth president, famously ripped up the text of the resolution while delivering a blistering response from the General Assembly hall's podium. Though the United States decried the U.N. vote—which was supported by the Soviet bloc; many Arab, Muslim-majority, and African countries; Mexico; Portugal; and others—the impact of the debacle on Israel's American supporters, particularly American Jewry, was profound. As the document below illustrates, American Jewish leaders, who were keenly aware that Israel's survival depended upon the U.S. government's support—particularly the good graces of the occupant of the Oval Office—recognized that any deflection of American support from a pro-Israel foreign policy would be perilous.

◇◇

Transcript of Meeting of President Gerald R. Ford and Secretary of State Henry Kissinger with American Jewish Leaders at the White House, March 17, 1976

Source: Memorandum, Robert B. Oakley for the President's File, Meeting with American Jewish Leadership Group, on Wednesday, March 17, 1976, 3:15–4:45 p.m. in Cabinet Room, folder: March 17, 1976—Ford, Kissinger, American Jewish Leadership Group, box 18, National Security Adviser. Memoranda of Conversations, Gerald R. Ford Presidential Library.

SUBJECT

Memorandum for the President's File by Robert B. Oakley[11] of the National Security Council Staff,[12] March 17, 1976

A/RES/3379 (XXX), November 10, 1975, https://unispal.un.org/UNISPAL.NSF/0/761C10635307 66A7052566A2005B74D1. The resolution was revoked in 1991; see United Nations General Assembly, "Elimination of racism and racial discrimination," A/RES/46/86, December 16, 1991, https://unispal.un.org/UNISPAL.NSF/9a798adbf322aff38525617b006d88d7/0aea0b9fe5c99b0 885256a9b0061300c?OpenDocument.

11. Robert B. Oakley (1931–2014), a career officer with the U.S. State Department, served on the National Security Council's staff as senior director for Middle East and South Asia Affairs (1974–77). He was later appointed U.S. ambassador to Zaire (1979–82), Somalia (1982–84), and Pakistan (1988–91) and U.S. special envoy to Somalia (1992–93).

12. Established in 1947 under President Harry S. Truman (1884–1972), the National Security Council (NSC) aimed originally, in large part, to centralize the U.S. government's efforts to contain the Soviet Union and the Cold War. Bringing together officers and appointees of the executive branch, the Central Intelligence Agency, and the leadership of the U.S. air force, army, marine corps, and navy, the NSC operated in the 1950s and 1960s as a clearinghouse for American foreign affairs intelligence and planning. Under President Nixon (who in 1969 ap-

Meeting with American Jewish Leadership Group, on Wednesday, March 17, 1976, 3:15–4:45 p.m. in Cabinet Room

PARTICIPANTS

* Mr. Max M. Fisher[13]
* Rabbi Alexander M. Schindler,[14] Chairman, Conference of Presidents of Major American Jewish Organizations[15] and President, Union of American Hebrew Congregations[16]
* Mr. David M. Blumberg,[17] President, Bnai Brith[18]

------

pointed Henry Kissinger [see note 44] national security adviser), the NSC became an influential and powerful instrument guiding American foreign policy, often bypassing the secretaries of defense and state when it came to the overall coordination of the president's policy-making agenda.

13. Max M. Fisher (1908–2005), an American Jewish businessman and philanthropist, was one of the dominant Jewish communal leaders of his generation. A staunch advocate for Israel, Fisher advised the administrations of Republican presidents from Eisenhower (see chapter 38, note 24) through George W. Bush (b. 1946) on U.S.-Israel relations and Middle Eastern affairs.

14. Born in Germany, Alexander M. Schindler (1925–2000) fled Europe in 1932 and settled in the United States. Ordained in 1953 by the Hebrew Union College–Jewish Institute of Religion in Cincinnati, Schindler became president of the Union of American Hebrew Congregations (1973–95). In 1976–78, he served as chair of the Conference of Presidents of Major American Jewish Organizations (see the next note). For more on Schindler, see chapter 46.

15. Established in 1956 to represent American Jewry to the executive branch of the U.S. government, the Conference of Presidents of Major American Jewish Organizations, is an umbrella group for the forty largest American Jewish religious and secular bodies.

16. Founded in 1873 by Isaac Mayer Wise (1819–1900), the principal founder of the American synagogue movement known as Reform Judaism (see chapter 16, note 9), the Union of American Hebrew Congregations was renamed in 2003 as the Union for Reform Judaism.

17. David M. Blumberg (1911–1989), of Knoxville, Tennessee, was a prominent civic leader, philanthropist, and president of Bnai Brith (1971–78).

18. The Independent Order of Bnai Brith (Sons of the Covenant), a Jewish fraternal organization founded in New York in 1843, originally modeled itself on the Jewish communal associations characteristic of European Jewry. It swiftly became a regional and then nationwide network of lodges dedicated to social, philanthropic, and political work among American Jews. In response to the notorious Leo Frank case (1913–15; see the headnote to chapter 35), Bnai Brith created the Anti-Defamation League (see chapter 35, note 23). Though formally non-Zionist in the nineteenth and early twentieth centuries, Bnai Brith's support of Jewish communal life in Palestine dated back to the 1860s. After World War I, the organization helped bolster Zionist settlement throughout the Yishuv. In the 1940s, Bnai Brith became openly Zionist in its political orientation.

* Mr. Yehuda Hellman,[19] Executive [Vice Chairman], Conference of Presidents of Major American Jewish Organizations
* Rabbi Arthur Hertzberg,[20] President, American Jewish Congress[21]
* Mr. Jerold C. Hoffberger,[22] President, Council of Jewish Federations and Welfare Funds[23]
* Mr. Harold Jacobs,[24] President, Union of Orthodox Jewish Congregations[25]
* Mrs. Charlotte Jacobson,[26] Chairman, World Zionist Organization— American Section[27]

19. Yehuda Hellman (1921–1986) was executive vice chairman of the Conference of Presidents of Major American Jewish Organizations (1959–86).

20. Arthur Hertzberg (1921–2006), a prominent Conservative rabbi, civil rights activist, and scholar, served as president of the American Jewish Congress (see note 21). His published works include *The French Enlightenment and the Jews: The Origins of Modern Anti-Semitism* (1968), *The Zionist Idea: A Historical Analysis and Reader* (1970), and *The Jews in America: Four Centuries of an Uneasy Encounter* (1989).

21. Organized in 1922 by Stephen S. Wise (1874–1949) as an independent group, the American Jewish Congress grew out of a national democratic assembly of American Jewry that had the same name and was convened at the end of World War I. In the 1930s, the organization championed a nationwide anti-Nazi economic boycott and fought against British restrictions on Jewish immigration to Palestine. For most of the twentieth century, it operated as the liberal flagship of American Jewry's Israel advocacy and civil rights activity.

22. Jerold C. Hoffberger (1919–1999), of Baltimore, Maryland, was president of the National Brewing Company (1946–73); an owner of the Baltimore Orioles baseball team (1954–79); and president of the Council of Jewish Federations and Welfare Funds (1975–78).

23. Established in 1932, the Council of Jewish Federations and Welfare Funds (renamed in 2009 the Jewish Federations of North America) is a national body of more than 450 metropolitan Jewish Federations and smaller "network communities" (see chapter 33, note 6) that collectively serve over eight hundred communities in the United States and Canada.

24. Harold M. Jacobs (1912–1995), a successful manufacturer of kitchen cabinets and an Orthodox Jewish lay leader, served as president of the Crown Heights Yeshiva (1953–68), the Union of Orthodox Jewish Congregations (1973–78), and the National Council of Young Israel (1981–92).

25. Founded in 1898, the Union of Orthodox Jewish Congregations, the central organization of Orthodox Judaism in North America, is a traditionalist religious movement that affirms the divinity of the Hebrew Bible, the authority of the homiletic and rabbinic literature produced in the postbiblical and premodern eras, and strict adherence to *halakhah*. The union's authoritative rabbinic body, the Rabbinical Council of America, was established in 1923.

26. Charlotte Jacobson (1914–2010), a prominent American Jewish communal leader, was national president of Hadassah (1964–68) and chair of the American Section of the World Zionist Organization (1971–82). In 1981 she became the first woman to serve as president of the Jewish National Fund.

27. The American Section of the World Zionist Organization, consisting of representatives

* Mr. Frank R. Lautenberg,[28] General Chairman, United Jewish Appeal[29]
* Mr. Arthur Levine,[30] President, United Synagogue of America[31]

---

of different American Zionist groups, coordinates the affairs of the Zionist movement in the United States.

28. Frank R. Lautenberg (1924–2013), CEO of the payroll management company Automatic Data Processing, Inc. (known as ADP), served as general chairman of the United Jewish Appeal from 1974 to 1976. A longtime Democratic party activist, Lautenberg was appointed as executive commissioner of the Port Authority of New York and New Jersey (1978–82) and was elected five times as U.S. senator from New Jersey (1982–2001 and 2003–13).

29. Until the 1930s, American Jewish groups competed to allocate philanthropic funds generated by a variety of welfare fund drives in cities across the country. In 1939 the United Palestine Appeal (UPA), led by Rabbi Abba Hillel Silver (see chapter 25, note 34, and chapter 31, note 10), reached an agreement with the Joint Distribution Committee and its allied National Refugee Service to create the United Jewish Appeal (UJA). In successive decades, the UJA became American Jewry's primary mechanism for raising and allocating funds for domestic and international purposes. Despite the Great Depression, the UJA raised $124 million between 1939 and 1945, including $42 million for the "upbuilding, defense, and war mobilization" of the pre-state Jewish community in Palestine (Marc Lee Raphael, *A History of the United Jewish Appeal, 1939–1982* [repr., Providence, RI: Brown Judaic Studies, 2020], 13). Throughout the 1950s and 1960s, the UJA continued to raise hundreds of millions of dollars annually. In the wake of the Six-Day War (June 1967), a UJA emergency drive raised $173 million in donations, and a concurrent State of Israel bonds campaign generated $428 million in sales. During the Yom Kippur War (October 1973), the UJA raised $686 million. In 1999, the UJA merged with the Council of Jewish Federations and the United Israel Appeal to form the United Jewish Communities (renamed in 2009 the Jewish Federations of North America; see note 23). The data are derived from Menahem Kaufman, "From Philanthropy to Commitment: The Six-Day War and the United Jewish Appeal," *Journal of Israeli History* 15, no. 2 (1994), 180–82, and Jack Wertheimer, "Current Trends in American Jewish Philanthropy," *American Jewish Year Book* 97 (1997), 18–19).

30. Arthur J. Levine (1916–2002) was president of the United Synagogue of America in 1973–77.

31. Founded in 1913, the United Synagogue of America emerged in the United States in the early twentieth century as a new form of traditional Jewish belief and practice that came to be called Conservative Judaism. Among its founders were Solomon Schechter (1847–1915), the first president of the Jewish Theological Seminary of America, and Mordecai M. Kaplan (1881–1983), who later created a splinter movement known as Reconstructionist Judaism. The term "conservative" was intended by the founders to convey the importance of conserving traditional Judaism as a totality while adapting its religious beliefs and practices to modern American society. In contrast to Orthodox Judaism, the Conservative movement does not subscribe to the literality of the Hebrew Bible or the idea that all premodern Jewish beliefs and practices have remained valid and binding up to the present. Although Conservative Judaism adopted many innovations characteristic of Reform Judaism (for example, the full-fledged participation of women in religious life, including worship services and serving as rabbis, cantors, and synagogue officers, mixed seating of men and women, and use of the vernacular), it views the Torah as divinely inspired and subscribes to many traditional Ashkenazic beliefs (such as the centrality of *halakhah*,

* Mrs. Rose Matzkin,[32] President, Hadassah[33]
* Rabbi Israel Miller,[34] Immediate Past Chairman, Conference of Presidents of Major American Jewish Organizations
* Mr. Edward Sanders,[35] President, American Israel Public Affairs Committee[36]
* Mr. Jacob Sheinkman,[37] President, Jewish Labor Committee[38]

---

observance of dietary laws, and importance of Hebrew). The Rabbinical Assembly of America, the organization's authoritative rabbinic body, was founded in 1901.

32. Rose Ellis Matzkin (1914–2002), of New York City, was president of Hadassah (1972–76) and a member of President Ford's Task Force on Women.

33. See chapter 31, note 23.

34. Israel Miller (1919–2002), ordained in 1941 as an Orthodox rabbi, was senior vice president of Yeshiva University (1979–84) and active in American Jewish communal affairs. President Johnson appointed Miller in 1964 to the National Citizens Committee for Community Relations to help implement civil rights legislation. Miller held key positions with the American Israel Public Affairs Committee, the American Zionist Federation, the Conference on Jewish Material Claims against Germany, the Conference of Presidents of Major American Jewish Organizations, and the Rabbinical Council of America.

35. Edward Sanders (1922–2009), of Los Angeles, was a Democratic party activist and American Jewish communal leader. He held key positions in the American Israel Public Affairs Committee, the Conference of Presidents of Major American Jewish Organizations, the National Conference of Christians and Jews, and the Urban League. Appointed senior adviser on Middle Eastern affairs (1978–80) by President Carter, he helped to shape the Camp David Accords (1978).

36. On the American Israel Public Affairs Committee (AIPAC), see chapter 39, note 19.

37. Jacob Sheinkman (1926–2004), of New York City, was a lawyer, human rights activist, and general counsel of the Amalgamated Clothing Workers of America (ACWA) (1958–72). As president of the Jewish Labor Committee (1974–80), he worked to strengthen U.S.-Israel relations. He later served as president of the Amalgamated Clothing and Textile Workers Union (1987–95), a product of the 1976 merger of the ACWA and the Textile Workers Union of America, and was an outspoken opponent of President Ronald Reagan's (1911–2004) policy of U.S. military intervention in El Salvador and Nicaragua.

38. Founded in 1934, the Jewish Labor Committee (JLC) originally was a broad coalition of left-wing Jewish representatives of the Amalgamated Clothing Workers of America, the Forverts Association, International Ladies' Garment Workers Union, Jewish National Workers' Alliance, Poalei Zion party, United Hebrew Trades, and Workmen's Circle (Arbeiter Ring). With the rise of Nazism, the JLC sought to provide aid to liberal and socialist victims of the Hitler regime. It also sought to educate members of the general American labor movement about the plight of European Jewry and to raise funds for rescue and relief activity during World War II. Though officially non-Zionist, the JLC gradually moderated its stance and became an overseas partner of the Histadrut trade union in Palestine (and later Israel). In the 1940s, the JLC mobilized American Jews to support the emerging civil rights movement and prompted the creation of the American Federation of Labor's civil rights division. In the 1950s and 1960s, the JLC played a leading

* Dr. Joseph P. Sternstein,[39] President, Zionist Organization of America[40]
* Mr. Elmer L. Winter,[41] President, American Jewish Committee[42]
* The Honorable Gerald R. Ford,[43] President of the United States
* The Honorable Henry A. Kissinger,[44] Secretary of State
* The Honorable Brent Scowcroft,[45] Assistant to the President for National Security Affairs

---

role in organizing civil rights demonstrations, including the March on Washington for Jobs and Freedom (1963); campaigning for fair employment legislation; and supporting the creation of the United Farm Workers.

39. Joseph P. Sternstein (1925–2006), a Conservative rabbi and American Jewish leader, served as president of the Zionist Organization of America (1974–78), American Zionist Federation (1979–82), and Jewish National Fund (1985–89).

40. On the Zionist Organization of America (ZOA), see chapter 31, note 5. In 1948, the American Zionist movement's membership rolls peaked with the establishment of the State of Israel. At this juncture, one out of five American Jews belonged to a Zionist group, and the ZOA alone boasted roughly 250,000 dues-paying members. In subsequent decades, membership in American Zionist groups fell dramatically. For example, the ZOA had fewer than 25,000 members in the mid-1950s. Paradoxically, even as the ranks of American Zionist groups in the 1960s and 1970s shrank considerably, the development and security of Israel became a pervasive philanthropic, political, and cultural concern of American Jewry as a whole.

41. Elmer L. Winter (1912–2009), a Milwaukee businessman who founded the international temp agency Manpower, served as president of the American Jewish Committee in 1973–77.

42. On the American Jewish Committee (AJC), see chapter 35, note 24. In the 1960s the AJC was active in the American civil rights movement. It also sponsored research on the image of the Jew in Catholic teaching and liturgy that informed the church's doctrinal review process and the framing of Vatican II's (1962–65) declaration "Nostra aetate" (Latin for "in our time") that rejected the centuries-old charge of deicide against the Jews.

43. Gerald R. Ford (1913–2006), a moderate Republican, served in the U.S. House as a representative from Michigan (1949–73) and minority leader (1965–73), as well as U.S. vice president (1973–74). With the resignation of Richard M. Nixon (1913–94), Ford became the thirty-eighth president of the United States (1974–77).

44. Henry A. Kissinger (b. 1923), a Jewish refugee who in 1938 fled Nazi Germany and immigrated to the United States, was drafted into the U.S. military in 1943. After World War II, he completed his studies at and became a faculty member of Harvard University. He later worked as a research director at the Council on Foreign Relations (1954–56) and consultant to the U.S. State Department (1965–69). Nixon appointed him national security adviser (1969–75). He also served as secretary of state under Nixon and Ford (1973–77). Following the Yom Kippur War (see note 49), Kissinger conducted what was called shuttle diplomacy between Jerusalem, Cairo, and Damascus, which yielded a series of cease-fire and disengagement agreements between Israel, Egypt, and Syria.

45. Brent Scowcroft (b. 1925), from Utah, held a variety of operational and administrative positions in his military career, including in the Long Range Planning Division of the U.S. Air Force (1964–66) and as a special assistant to the director of the Joint Chiefs of Staff (1970–72).

* Mr. David H. Lissy,[46] Associate Director, Domestic Council[47]
* Mr. Robert Goldwin,[48] Special Consultant to the President
* Mr. Robert B. Oakley, Area Director for Middle East and South Asian Affairs, National Security Council Staff

Max Fisher: Mr. President, I would like you to meet Rabbi Schindler, the new Chairman of the Conference of Presidents of Major American Jewish Organizations. We all welcome this opportunity for an exchange on the concerns we have.

President: Let me make a few general observations first, then Henry Kissinger and I will deal with specific questions. Let's review the developments in the Middle East since I became President. After the Yom Kippur War[49] the

---

He later served as military assistant to the president (1972); deputy national security adviser (1973–75); and national security adviser (1975–77 and 1989–93) under Presidents Ford and George H. W. Bush (1924–2018), respectively.

46. David H. Lissy (b. 1943) graduated from the University of Pennsylvania law school, entering government service in 1969. After serving in the State Department (1970–73), he joined the Domestic Council (see the next note) as associate director for education, labor, and veterans issues (1975–77). In 1976, he transferred to the White House staff as a special assistant for domestic affairs, to concentrate on mobilizing Jewish support for President Ford's reelection campaign — including the coordination of meetings among Jewish groups, administration officials, and the president. See David Lissy Files, 1974–77, boxes 38–43: "Jewish Affairs," Gerald R. Ford Presidential Library and Museum.

47. Under Presidents Nixon and Ford, the Domestic Council (the predecessor of today's Domestic Policy Council) was a large White House office with jurisdiction over economic and domestic policy. Initially, Ford named some trusted aides to important staff positions but kept several Nixon appointees in key positions. Though Ford signaled a desire under the leadership of Vice President Nelson D. Rockefeller (1908–1979) to strengthen the Domestic Council, making it equivalent to the National Security Council, political infighting among Rockefeller, Secretary of Defense Donald Rumsfeld (b. 1932), and Chief of Staff Dick Cheney (b. 1941) undermined the vice president's agenda. In due course, Rockefeller resigned from the Domestic Council and announced that he would not join the 1976 presidential ticket as Ford's running mate.

48. Robert Goldwin (1922–2010), a political scientist, served as a special consultant in the Ford administration (1974–76).

49. The Yom Kippur War (October 6–25, 1973) erupted with a surprise Egyptian-Syrian military invasion of Israel; Jordan subsequently joined the combined Arab forces. When the war started, much of Israeli society was observing Yom Kippur (the Day of Atonement), which in Israel is both a religious and a national holiday. Relying on the Israeli intelligence assessment of a "low probability" of war and mistaking Egyptian and Syrian troop movements for military exercises, the cabinet of Prime Minister Golda Meir (1898–1978) and the Nixon administration were largely unprepared for the attack by surprisingly strong Soviet-supplied Arab forces. In the first few days of the war, Israel was dealt a heavy psychological blow, as Egyptian forces in the Sinai Peninsula and Syrian forces in the Golan Heights outmaneuvered and overpowered Israel

U.S. was helping rebuild Israel, providing large amounts of economic and military assistance. Then in March 1975 the negotiations fell apart and we had a period of uncertainty before they were concluded in September 1975, with the historic Sinai Agreement.[50] Now the U.S. and U.N. observers are in place—I just saw a report on that today—and both sides are carrying out their part of the bargain. It took great courage by both sides to reach this agreement. More recently we have had the visit of my friend, Prime Minister [Yitzhak] Rabin.[51] We had three meetings and a dinner together and came to an understanding on some ideas of how to proceed in trying to get negotia-

---

Defense Force (IDF) positions in the north and south. By the fourth day of the war, Israel had sustained such significant losses that its very survival appeared to be in jeopardy. The critical turning point in the war's progress occurred on October 16, following a massive airlift of American supplies to Israel, when the IDF crossed the Suez Canal and began overtaking the Egyptian forces. By October 21, the tide of the war had shifted to Israel's advantage. At this juncture, the Nixon administration used its leverage to pressure Israel to halt its military progress, accept a proposed American- and Soviet-sponsored cease-fire agreement, and preserve the geopolitical status quo. When the war ended on October 25, Israel's Arab neighbors viewed it as a victory, in contrast to their humiliating defeat in 1967. Thus, their military losses were offset by a restored sense of national pride. Notwithstanding Israel's demonstrated ability to defend itself and America's commitment to its security, the path remained open for a political resolution to the Israel-Arab conflict.

50. Signed on January 18, 1974, the Egypt-Israel Separation of Forces Agreement (also known as the Sinai I Agreement) facilitated the redeployment of Egyptian and Israeli military forces west and east of the Suez Canal, respectively. It also created a buffer zone on both sides of the canal that was to be monitored by U.N. peacekeeping troops. The agreement specifically stated it was "not regarded by Egypt and Israel as a final peace agreement" but rather as "a first step toward a final, just, and durable peace according to the provisions of Security Council Resolution 338" ("Separation of Forces Agreement Between Israel and Egypt," January 18, 1974, https://ecf.org.il/media_items/598). A similar disengagement agreement between Israel and Syria was signed on May 31, 1974. No agreement was reached between Israel and Jordan. The Sinai II Agreement, negotiated by the Ford administration and signed in Geneva on September 4, 1975, further delineated the scope of the original ceasefire agreement, including that "non-military cargoes destined for or coming from Israel shall be permitted through the Suez Canal" and the creation of an "early warning system . . . entrusted to the United States" ("Egyptian-Israel Disengagement Agreement," Department of State Office of the Historian, September 1, 1975, https://history.state.gov/historicaldocuments/frus1969-76v26/d226).

51. Yitzhak Rabin (1922–1995), previously chief of the general staff during the Six-Day War (June 1967) and Israel's ambassador to the United States (1968–73), had by this time succeeded Golda Meir, becoming Israel's fifth prime minister (1974–77) following a storm of postwar political controversy. A key issue that occupied the Rabin government after the Sinai II Agreement was the question of maintaining Israel's qualitative military superiority in the region and its ability to purchase advanced U.S. military technology and weaponry.

tions started again.[52] This is not easy but the Prime Minister recognized the danger of doing nothing.

It is of great importance to us to secure Israel's survival and security. In the current fiscal year we have requested $1.5 billion in military assistance—50 percent of it in grants—and $800 million in economic aid for Israel. We have asked [for] about $700 million for Egypt and smaller amounts for other Arabs. In fiscal year 1977 we have requested one billion dollars in military aid for Israel and $780 million in economic aid. There is about $650 million for Egypt. We are working in a constructive way to see that Israel has a military capability adequate to meet any contingencies. That and the favorable developments in Egypt give brighter prospects for the future than in the past.[53]

Sadat[54] has taken a strong position toward the USSR. In his speech he

52. Ford met with Rabin on January 27, 28, and 29, 1976.

53. American geopolitical priorities in the Middle East in the 1950s and 1960s centered on supporting the development of oil-producing countries, preventing the spread of Soviet influence in the region, and supporting Israel's security while maintaining an impartial stance in the Israel-Arab conflict. Within this context, successive American administrations tried unsuccessfully to court the Arab states with moderate economic aid. In particular, Egypt received surplus U.S. wheat under the Food for Peace Program. A host of factors, including the Six-Day War (1967) and the cost of the Vietnam war, led the United States to generally reduce aid to the Arab states in the late 1960s. Anwar Sadat (see the next note), who became Egypt's president in 1970, worked to improve Egypt-U.S. relations and reduce his country's dependence on the Soviet Union. The U.S. government meanwhile increased economic and military aid to Jordan after its civil war (1970–71), known as Black September, in which Palestinian guerrillas were expelled from the country.

For much of the 1960s, the U.S. government provided Israel with moderate economic aid (mostly loans), while France supplied it with advanced weaponry and technology. The shift in U.S. military aid to Israel began in 1962, when the Kennedy administration made possible the sale to Israel of Hawk antiaircraft missiles. After the Six-Day War (1967), French president Charles de Gaulle (1890–1970) protested Israel's preemptive strike by refusing to provide the country with further military aid. In 1968, the Johnson administration approved the sale of Phantom jet fighters and established the precedent of U.S. support for Israel's qualitative military superiority in the region. In 1971, the Nixon administration, with broad public and Congressional support, committed to improving Israel's security, increased U.S. military loans to Israel to $545 million, and created a new line item in the U.S. foreign aid budget for Israel. In 1974, following the Yom Kippur War (1973), the United States provided emergency aid and a military aid grant to Israel. Since 1976, Israel has been the largest recipient of U.S. foreign assistance.

54. Anwar Sadat (1918–1981), a former Egyptian military officer, president of the national assembly (1960–68), and Gamal Abdel Nasser's vice president (1964 and 1969–70), served as Egypt's third president (1970–81). Following the Sinai Agreements (see note 50), Sadat steered Egyptian foreign policy toward increased engagement with the United States and, at least indi-

cut off all relations with them.[55] It took a lot of courage and I applaud it. It turns Egypt more our way. We should welcome and support this evolution.

That provides a rough estimate of where we are. Now, I understand that you have some questions about the C-130 propeller aircraft[56] we intend to sell to Egypt. This is fully justified. It provides no offensive military capability. You must look at the total picture of aid to Israel, both military and economic, compared to our aid for Egypt. No one should object to the division of support. The planes should go to Egypt. If you disagree, I want to know why. If you have questions, please ask. I am firmly convinced this is the right move for Israel as well as the U.S.

Now I will ask Henry to give you his ideas.

Kissinger: We must take the strategic view, look at what has been created and where the greatest danger to Israel lies. The greatest danger is a unified Arab front backed by the Europeans and the Soviets, isolating the U.S. and Israel. So we want to disentangle the situation and eliminate this threat. The security of Israel is strategic and not tactical. At the end of the October War everyone was united in opposition to Israel and they were all pressing the U.S. to pressure Israel for an immediate return to the 1967 boundaries.[57] Our desire

---

rectly, created conditions that made reconciliation with Israel a possibility. Egypt's dramatic realignment with the West reached a climax in 1975 with the collapse of several interlocking Soviet-Egyptian military equipment, loan, and trade agreements. Sadat's abrogation of the Egyptian-Russian Treaty of Friendship and Cooperation (1971) in a speech to the Egyptian parliament on March 14, 1976, signaled the collapse of Egypt's alliance with the Soviet Union.

55. For a transcript of Sadat's speech in which he explains his request to abrogate the 1971 Soviet-Egyptian treaty, see "Address by President Anwar El Sadat before the People's Assembly, Cairo, March 14, 1976," 201–56, Anwar Sadat Chair for Peace and Development, Presidential Addresses, University of Maryland, https://sadat.umd.edu/sites/sadat.umd.edu/files/Address%20 to%20the%20People%E2%80%99s%20Assembly.pdf.

56. After the Yom Kippur War, the Nixon and Ford administrations worked to encourage and then reinforce Egypt's pivot away from the Soviet Union. With the completion of the Sinai II Agreement (see note 50), the Ford administration considered selling Egypt combat aircraft, including F-5 fighter jets. Congressional opposition, however, augmented by strenuous American Jewish criticism, scuttled the administration's plans. U.S. arms sales to Egypt were limited to so-called nonlethal equipment such as C-130 transport aircraft and reconnaissance planes.

57. The term "1967 boundaries"—synonymous with the terms "1949 armistice border," "pre-1967 border," and "Green Line"—refers to Israel's de facto borders from the conclusion of its War of Independence (May 15, 1948–March 10, 1949) until the Six-Day War (June 5–10, 1967). Israel's military conquests in 1967 led to its occupation of the Golan Heights, Gaza Strip, Sinai Peninsula, and West Bank. Soon thereafter, Israel annexed east Jerusalem and deemed the united city its capital. The future of the occupied territories remained in question. It was

to maintain a special relationship with Sadat is not naive, but to buy time so we can bring about a better situation. This is why we propose C-130s. Sadat is having a tough time with his army who could throw him out and open the way for a massive influx of Soviet arms. We must remain in control of the diplomatic situation. There is no danger of large-scale U.S. arms sales to Egypt. You must keep in mind the overall strategic considerations.

President: The breach in Egypt's relationship with the USSR followed Soviet pressures. They cut off spare parts and maintenance for Egyptian weapons and equipment.

Kissinger: Egypt's MiGs[58] fly only six hours a month. We want to keep Egypt neutralized but no army can be expected to accept the prospect of no weapons at all.[59]

President: If we cut off Israel's spare parts, their military capability would go down. But selling six C-130s[60] will not affect Egypt's military capability.

Someone mentioned to me your interest in the Sheehan article.[61] Our

---

widely believed their status would be determined as part of peace agreements between Israel and neighboring Arab countries.

58. A reference to the Russian-made Mikoyan-Gurevich (MiG) jet fighter and interceptor aircraft. During the Cold War, the MiG jet played a critical role in the Soviet air force and the militaries of countries allied with the Soviet Union.

59. Sadat's strategic realignment with the West and the cooling of Egypt-Soviet relations made it difficult for the Egyptian military to purchase replacement parts for its Soviet-made weapons system. Lacking the ability to maintain its planes and missiles, military analysts argued, Egypt's army and air force would become significantly inferior to those of Israel.

60. First produced in 1956 by the American Lockheed Corporation, the C-130 Hercules is a four-engine military transport plane designed to carry up to 42,000 pounds; operate on rough, dirt strips; and drop troops and equipment into hostile areas. In March 1976, the Ford administration announced plans to lift the U.S. military embargo against Egypt and sell the country six C-130 aircraft at a cost of roughly $65 million. Despite opposition to the sale from American Jewish groups as well as Israeli and some American officials, it was formally approved by Congress the following month. The U.S. government had previously sold the C-130 to Iran (1962), Kuwait (1970), and Jordan (1973).

61. Edward R. F. Sheehan (1930–2008), a Harvard research fellow and a foreign correspondent specializing in Middle Eastern affairs, published a lengthy article in the quarterly journal *Foreign Policy* that contained excerpts from hitherto highly secret records of exchanges between Kissinger and Arab and Israeli leaders as well as U.S. government officials' statements about the Israel-Arab conflict. Sheehan's article, which generated a public furor, included the following disclosure: "Kissinger consistently refused to promise the Arabs that the United States would push Israel back to its 1967 borders, but in June 1974 and June 1975, Presidents Nixon and Ford secretly assured the Arab leaders that the United States favored substantial restoration of the

position is firm and clearly understood by both Sadat and Rabin. We stand by
Security Council Resolutions 242 and 338, period.[62] They provide for negotiations and secure and recognized boundaries. We stand for that.

Kissinger: We have a problem. We cannot comment on every book or article that
appears. There are so many, and full of distortions. Look at Matti Golan[63] and
Admiral [Elmo] Zumwalt.[64] We cannot contradict or correct all the errors but
the U.S. position is as the President has stated and we have never deviated

---

1967 frontiers—a position Washington has so far declined to make public" (Edward R. F. Sheehan, "How Kissinger Did It: Step by Step in the Middle East," Foreign Policy 22 [Spring 1976], 5).

62. U.N. Security Council Resolutions 242 and 338 were passed following the Six-Day War
(1967) and the Yom Kippur War (1973), respectively. Resolution 242 (reaffirmed in 338) pro-
poses a framework for Middle Eastern peace negotiations between Israel and her Arab neighbors based on a "land-for-peace" formula (United Nations Security Council, "Resolution 242
(1967)," S/RES/242, November 22, 1967, https://unispal.un.org/unispal.nsf/0/7D35E1F729DF49
1C85256EE700686136). The resolutions call for the withdrawal of Israeli forces "from territories
occupied in the recent conflict," an Arab "termination of all claims or states of belligerency,"
recognition of the State of Israel and its "right to live in peace within secure and recognized
boundaries free from threats or acts of force," and "achieving a just settlement of the [Pales-
tinian] refugee problem" (ibid.).

63. In 1976, Matti Golan (b. 1936), a political correspondent for the Israeli newspaper
Haaretz, published The Secret Conversations of Henry Kissinger: Step-by-Step Diplomacy in the Middle East,
first in Hebrew and then in an English translation. Golan's book, initially censored in Israel because it included classified material leaked to Golan by Israeli officials, generated considerable
public controversy in Israel and the United States. Tracing the arc of American involvement in
the Yom Kippur War, from its outbreak through the Sinai I and II Agreements (see note 50),
Golan offered a searing indictment of both Meir's government and the Nixon administration.
Kissinger, in particular, was singled out as the cause of Israel's misfortune. "Till the very outbreak of the fighting," wrote Golan, "Kissinger remained more concerned with the possibility
of an Israeli preemptive strike than an Egyptian-Syrian attack." Golan also asserted that Kissinger instructed Kenneth B. Keating (1900–1975), the U.S. ambassador to Israel, to personally deliver "a presidential entreaty" to Meir "not to start a war" (The Secret Conversations of Henry Kissinger:
Step-by-Step Diplomacy in the Middle East, trans. Ruth Geyra Stern and Sol Stern [New York: Quadrangle, 1976], 41).

64. Elmo Zumwalt (1920–2000), a decorated career officer in the U.S. Navy who reached the
rank of rear admiral in 1965, served in World War II (1941–45), the Korean War (1950–53), and
the Vietnam War (1955–75). In 1976, Zumwalt published a contentious memoir titled On Watch,
that included a highly critical account of the Nixon administration's Cold War policies. Zumwalt
also accused Kissinger of delaying supplies to Israel during the Yom Kippur War (1973) and of
blaming Secretary of Defense James R. Schlesinger (1929–2014) for the delay. "It was Henry
himself who stalled the [American] airlift," Zumwalt claimed. "I do not mean to imply that he
wanted Israel to lose the war. He simply did not want Israel to win decisively. He wanted Israel
to bleed just enough to soften it up for the post-war diplomacy he was planning ... to 'create a
new reality' and no more" (On Watch: A Memoir [New York: Quadrangle, 1976], 433).

from it. The Arabs complain that they are never able to get a commitment from us on the 1967 boundaries. Had we wished to pursue the 1967 boundaries, we could have done it much more easily without any need for ambiguity. We could have joined the [European Economic Community] in October 1973 and done it directly.[65] Instead we decided upon the step-by-step approach to avoid just this and ease the pressure on Israel. We have always said that the location of secure and recognized boundaries is to be negotiated by the parties. We stand on Security Council Resolutions 242 and 338.

Fisher: Some would say this meeting has a Teutonic aspect with Kissinger and Schindler.

Kissinger: I would say it is a Harvard aspect.[66]

Schindler: Mr. President, I want to thank you for receiving us and for your past affection for the Jewish community. Because we are Americans we also thank you for the way you have conducted yourself in office. And we thank you for the overall thrust of U.S. foreign policy in the Middle East—to separate the moderates and the radicals and to drive out the Soviets. There has been more progress in containing confrontation in the past two years than during the preceding twenty years. So we support your overall policy. We also agree that six C-130 aircraft will not affect the military balance of power. Still we are afraid and we are apprehensive. We fear it is the beginning of a process. The symbolic aspect scares us. We buy the overall approach of supporting moderates so we support economic aid to Egypt and we do not oppose the nuclear agreement.[67] But we are worried about the six C-130s as being the start of

65. Kissinger is obliquely referring to the indifference of the European Economic Community (EEC) to Israel's precarious position in the Yom Kippur War (1973). When the war broke out, the EEC proclaimed its support for U.N. Security Council Resolution 242 (see note 62) but did nothing practical to address the situation. No European country joined the United States in providing military aid to Israel, nor did any EEC member state permit American planes used in the airlift of supplies to Israel to use its airspace or territory for landing and refueling.

66. Kissinger's friendly quip suggests that it is his Harvard academic training, not his shared German ancestry with Alexander M. Schindler (and, by implication, other delegation members), that is most salient in his thinking and policy-making efforts.

67. In 1972, the United States and the Soviet Union initiated the Strategic Arms Limitation Talks (SALT) in an effort to reach a permanent accord and curtail the development of the American and Soviet nuclear arsenals and the proliferation of strategic offensive arms. Continued negotiations and interim SALT agreements focused on efforts to achieve a comprehensive nuclear test ban, the reduction of American and Soviet forces in Europe, and a prohibition on the development of chemical weapons. Though the effort to ease relations between the United States and the Soviet Union, known as détente, became a hallmark of the Nixon and Ford administrations, U.S. officials remained dubious about the idea of achieving nuclear parity

a much larger process. Why does Egypt need arms? Its only enemy is Israel. Israel must fear not only Egypt but all the Arabs. Arms can be transferred from one to another. Last year Israel got $1.3 billion in arms but the Arabs got between $14 and $15 billion worth of arms.[68] There is also a qualitative imbalance, the superiority of American equipment. That is why we do not want American equipment going to Egypt. Israel needs to maintain qualitative superiority with planes like the F-15.[69]

President: Let me comment. If we look back at the four wars Israel has fought[70] and the tragic loss of life, perhaps we can agree that the best way to alleviate the fear of another is to have Egypt dependent upon the U.S. rather than the Soviets or even Western Europe. It is better for us to be able to turn them on and off than for others to be in that position. Also, you cannot dismiss

---

with the Soviet Union. Despite episodic successes over the next couple of years, the SALT efforts stagnated, and the global arms trade increased quickly. Meanwhile, the Nixon and Ford administrations adopted strategies related to nuclear planning, intelligence analysis of the nuclear balance, and nuclear weapons innovation and modernization aimed at securing qualitative strategic superiority vis-à-vis the Soviet Union. During the 1976 presidential campaign, Governor Ronald Reagan (1911–2004) of California, who challenged Ford for the Republican party's nomination, declared détente under the Ford administration "a one-way street" that advantaged the Soviet Union and failed the United States (Ronald Reagan, "Tactics for Détente," Wall Street Journal, February 13, 1976, 8). Responding to Reagan's criticism on February 13 at a press conference in Orlando, Florida, Ford defended his administration's Cold War policies, championing the country's "growing relationship with the People's Republic of China" as well as efforts to "relax tensions" and "negotiate with strength with the Soviet Union" (Gerald R. Ford, *Gerald R. Ford, 1976–77: Containing the Public Messages, Speeches, and Statements of the President* [Ann Arbor: University of Michigan Library, 2005], 1:268). "It is my duty," Ford stated, "to do all that I can to reduce the level of danger by diplomatic means. So my policy for national security can be summed up in three words: peace through strength. I believe it is far better to seek negotiations with the Soviet Union ... than to permit a runaway nuclear arms race and risk a nuclear holocaust" (quoted in "Arms Control and the 1976 Presidential Election," *Arms Control Today* 6, no. 10 [October 1976], 1).

68. As indicated above (see note 53), beginning in 1976, Israel became the largest annual recipient of U.S. foreign aid.

69. Produced by the American company McDonnell Douglas, the F-15 Eagle is a twin-engine tactical fighter jet with a high payload capacity. In 1976, shortly before the presidential election, Ford promised to sell Israel the aircraft. Israel initially purchased twenty-five jets from the United States at a cost of $625 million. Capable of reaching an altitude of 67,000 feet and with a range of 3100 miles, the F-15 became a staple of the Israeli air force.

70. Ford is apparently referring to the Sinai Campaign (1956), the Six-Day War (1967), the War of Attrition (1969), and the Yom Kippur War (1973). During this period, Israel was also threatened by low-level guerrilla warfare conducted by the Palestinian Liberation Organization and other paramilitary groups, which maintained bases in Jordan and later in Lebanon.

the problem between Libya and Egypt.[71] Egypt is a much better friend of the U.S. than Libya which is getting huge amounts of military assistance from the USSR. That is creating a serious problem for us.

Kissinger: Egypt will not allow itself to be totally disarmed. Either Sadat gets some arms from the U.S. or he will go elsewhere or he will be thrown out. Do not drive him to despair. The problem of more arms for Egypt may come back in a year or two but by then we will have gained time for more peace moves. The President is speaking theoretically when he talks of the U.S. having the ability to control Egypt's supply of arms. There is no plan for a significant supply of U.S. arms. You spoke of the F-15 but we have no intention of supplying sophisticated arms to Egypt. The transfer of equipment is a very difficult question. We have no fixed program except the C-130s and the training of ten to fifteen Egyptian officers at our military schools. If we felt the need to move past this to another phase of arms supply we would be obliged to consult Congress but we do not wish to reach this point. On the other hand, we do not wish to go back to the point we were at in 1969 when we had to talk to the Egyptians through the Soviets. Last year there was an influx of Soviet arms to Egypt prior to the expected visit of Brezhnev[72] but we stopped it by Sinai II.[73]

Rabbi Hertzberg: We are sympathetic to your policy. But you are going from a little bit pregnant to more pregnant. How can you stop the process? Egypt is very hungry for arms. If the military is that strong within Egypt, it will have to come back again for more arms. If we agree to six C-130s as a symbolic act, then it is the symbol of more, but how much more and when? There is a

71. Ford is referring to escalating tensions between Libya under Colonel Muammar Gaddafi (1942–2011), who seized power in a 1969 military coup, and Egypt under Sadat. Relations between the leaders deteriorated after Sadat rebuffed Gaddafi's entreaties to unify their nations and began to disengage from the Soviet Union. Strife between the countries—including foiled assassination plots, an aircraft hijacking, embassy closings, and border clashes—erupted in late July 1977 into a full-scale war. Following an Egyptian military incursion into Libya, international pressure prompted Sadat to unilaterally declare a cease-fire. Egypt-Libya relations collapsed entirely in 1977 when Sadat began to pursue diplomatic negotiations with Israel leading to the Egypt-Israel peace agreement (1978).

72. Leonid Brezhnev (1906–1982), secretary general of the Soviet Communist Party, was the dominant political leader of the USSR from 1964 to 1982. Under Brezhnev's leadership, the Soviet Union modernized its military, achieved parity with the United States in nuclear weaponry, and bolstered its aerospace program. In the 1970s, Brezhnev sought to ease tensions with the West through a policy of détente with the United States and committed the Soviet Union to the SALT agreements.

73. See note 50.

theory that Israel is so dependent upon the U.S. that it means parameters are set for Israeli policy. But what about U.S. influence on Sadat's policy? What will bring Egypt and the Arab moderates closer to the U.S. and Israel? What will Egypt do in return for the C-130s? What do we get in exchange?

President: One thing has already occurred, the breaking of Egyptian military relations with the Soviets. Closing the port of Alexandria to Soviet naval vessels deprives the Soviet fleet of valuable repair and maintenance facilities. They can go to Libya, maybe, but it is not as good. You cannot develop installations overnight to meet the Soviet needs. There are also two ports in Syria, but they are not as good as Egypt. That is already a big dividend.

Kissinger: Another dividend is the peace process. So long as Egypt adheres to its present policy we can withstand Arab/Soviet pressures to move too fast toward peace. With Sadat we can move at a pace Israel can accept. We told Rabin to think about what Israel could do next. He sent us some ideas on non-belligerency. We took them to Sadat but to no other Arab.

Mrs. Matzkin: Mr. President, you want to know what the people think. Well, the question I get all the time is if the U.S. supplies both Israel and Egypt, how do you cut off supplies if there is a war? Does the U.S. take sides? U.S. arms will be tested on the battlefield where we do not want them tested. You asked if Egypt did not deserve a reward. I reply that they have a reward. They have most of the Sinai back, they have the oil fields and they are getting large amounts of economic aid. Egypt has internal problems yet it is spending its money on arms and is not committed to peace.

President: It is our hope that military and economic aid will allow the U.S. to avoid another war. Having both dependent upon the U.S. gives us leverage to preclude it. Although Sadat is an outstanding leader, he does have to contend with military leaders who see the Soviets cut off supplies and look to see what the U.S. will do. There is a theoretical potential of military leaders who might want to take charge in Egypt. We must deal with reality and keep Sadat in office. He has done more than anyone since I have been President to try and find a non-military understanding with Israel.

Kissinger: You talk as if Egypt were to be fully rearmed. If the President made such a decision and Congress approved it, there would still be five years or more needed to replace Egypt's present weapons due to production and training problems. But let's be realistic. We are not interested in replacing Soviet equipment with U.S. equipment. That is not our problem. Our problem is to keep the peace process alive. The situation you describe would probably take ten years to achieve even at top speed. But that is not what we are talking about.

Hoffberger: The President and the Secretary of State mentioned Egyptian military influence and the threat to Sadat. Are you telling us Sadat is in a precarious position?

President: My impression—and Henry can supplement it—is that Sadat is in a strong position. He has given the kind of inspirational leadership Egyptians like. Yet there is a history of military rule in Egypt and the army taking power. This was true of both Nasser[74] and Sadat. We must be alert to contingencies. Egypt has an enormous debt and a huge military supply problem. There are great pressures to do more economically and militarily. We see no immediate threat but we must be realistic as to what could happen if the economy were to collapse or military supplies [were] totally cut off. Then there is the threat of Libya and [Gaddafi].[75]

Winter: I have just come from a meeting of the Business Council.[76] I am troubled by what you say. Secretary Kissinger says we will not be the chief suppliers of both sides, so where does Egypt turn for the bulk of its arms? To Europe? So how are we going to get them wholly into our camp without a full military relationship which we do not want?

President: The same delay Henry spoke of about U.S. deliveries applies to Europe. It would take five years or more as Henry stated and this applies to the Europeans. Personally, I agree with you and would prefer to have Egypt dependent upon the U.S. rather than Europe. But we have not made that commitment. Practically, I would prefer this but we have not done it.

Kissinger: I understand the dilemma you pose. There is no good answer. We cannot accept either to supply nothing or to be the chief supplier. If we are either one or the other, it would be too much. So we will find a path in between and try to gain time. I do not think we are in a position to make an absolute decision. We do not want to be the main supplier nor to decide to do nothing more, even than the C-130s. But there is no great speed in doing more. We want to be able to move the peace process along.

Rabbi Miller: Mr. President, we all know of your friendship with the American Jewish community. So we will speak with candor based on respect and show you the deep worries of that community. We are profoundly worried, not about six lousy planes but about what you and the Secretary here have said. We are concerned about tomorrow. We recognize what you are saying

---

74. On Gamal Abdel Nasser, see chapter 38, note 10.

75. On Muammar Gaddafi, see note 71.

76. Headquartered in Washington, D.C., the Business Council is a nonpartisan association and lobbying organization of elite leaders of multinational businesses.

is that the U.S. must gamble, that there is no guarantee. We recognize this since the situation cannot remain static. Our concern is that the U.S. will become a supplier to Egypt which will have a mixed source of supply—from France and others—and Saudi Arabia will have a substantial amount of arms, which it can supply to Egypt. Realistically, in another conflict, Egypt will not stand away and it will have many sources of supply. As to negotiations, your gamble on supplying arms to generate movement will necessarily become a fixed commitment. As negotiations progress, another allocation of more advanced and sophisticated weapons will be requested by Egypt as a price for continuing. You will say, we have gone so far so we must go a bit further to keep negotiations going. The American Jewish community worries about this scenario. We worry also about the Sheehan article. We worry about the billions and billions of dollars in arms for the Arabs. Where are we going? We worry about what is going to happen tomorrow.

President: You expressed the same concerns a year ago prior to the negotiations in March and then after the March negotiations failed. Yet by developing the trust of both Israel and Egypt we were able to obtain the Sinai II Agreement. It is an achievement of great significance. You were concerned throughout the past year but the movement has been a success so your legitimate fears have been eliminated by the results. I believe in Security Council Resolutions 242 and 338. There must be progress within the confines of these resolutions. We cannot eliminate your concerns and apprehensions. They will always be present. But you must have faith and trust. This is not the ideal world but the real world. We are making headway on getting trust between the U.S. and Egypt and the U.S. and Israel and Egypt and Israel. Lots of progress. It should not be underestimated.

Miller: We are expressing the fears of our people. You all must deal with this and get it across to our people. Mr. Jacobs will talk to you about aid, about the fifth quarter. There are certain ways to explain trust. It is not enough to say "trust us."

Mrs. Jacobson: We appreciate your comments on the Sheehan article. I would like to set the record straight on leaving here by saying that you have told us the U.S. position does not go beyond supporting Resolutions 242 and 338. It seems to me that we need an additional step by Egypt toward peace. Sadat dismissed the Soviets because they were not giving what Egypt wants. It is a golden opportunity to move towards peace. Let us make a new effort with Egypt. A major breakthrough on the Sinai. The word peace is still missing.

President: We are always ready to begin negotiations if Israel and Egypt are ready. It is not up to us. But you cannot make overall headway by concentrating exclusively on Israel and Egypt. We are working with Prime Minister Rabin to find ways of further progress. It is up to Israel and the Arabs but we will continue our mediating role.

Kissinger: The Israeli government is telling us constantly not to go too fast, not to try for overall peace now. We have an agreed strategy with Israel to try for an end to the state of war. But the gamble of turning back on C-130s for Egypt would be extremely dangerous. We asked Israel to do a bit on the West Bank before Rabat to preclude the PLO, but it did not work.[77] The Israelis are nostalgic for Jordan today. I am not sure your idea would be greeted with joy in Jerusalem since Israel would need to spell out its position on final boundaries if it were to negotiate for peace.

Jacobs: I saw your wife in California, campaigning for you, Mr. President.[78] She makes an excellent impression.

President: I am trying hard to get my votes up to her polls.

Jacobs: What about the fifth quarter funding for Israel, are you going to support it or not?

77. Ford is referring to Kissinger's intensive efforts at shuttle diplomacy involving Egypt, Jordan, Syria, and Israel and possible arrangements and compromises between the countries concerning the status of territories occupied by Israel in the Six-Day War (1967), including the West Bank. Within this context, the Nixon and Ford administrations tried to persuade Israel to come to terms with Jordan as quickly as possible. However, the possibilities in this regard were severely curtailed after the Seventh Arab Summit Conference, meeting in Rabat, Morocco, in October 1974, recognized the Palestine Liberation Organization (PLO) as the sole representative of the Palestinian people and affirmed the PLO's right "to establish an independent national authority over all liberated territory" (League of Arab States, "Seventh Arab League Summit Conference, Resolution on Palestine," October 28, 1974, https://unispal.un.org/UNISPAL.NSF/0/63 D9A930E2B428DF852572C0006D06B8). In effect, the Rabat resolution sidelined King Hussein bin Talal (1935–1999) of Jordan and potential Jordan-Israel negotiations concerning the future status of the West Bank and East Jerusalem. The tense political situation was further complicated in November 1974 when the United Nations granted the PLO observer status and in November 1975 with the passage of U.N. Resolution 3379 (revoked in 1991), which declared that "Zionism is a form of racism and racial discrimination" (see note 10). Against this backdrop, the Ford administration adjusted its overall strategy and emphasized a second Egypt-Israel disengagement agreement concerning the Sinai Peninsula that was codified in the Sinai II Agreement. The agreement resulted in the eastward redeployment of Israeli forces, the creation of a U.N. buffer zone along the border between Egypt and Israel, and the construction of an advanced U.S. monitoring system.

78. Betty Ford (1918–2011), wife of Gerald R. Ford and First Lady of the United States (1974–77), was an outspoken supporter of the Equal Rights Amendment, abortion rights, and breast cancer awareness. In 1982, after years of battling substance abuse and addiction, she created the Betty Ford Center for the treatment of chemical dependency.

President: We did not recommend any funds for the 5th quarter. We recommended $2.3 billion for FY [fiscal year] 76 and $1.8 billion for FY 77, with $1.0 billion in military aid. Based upon the analyses of all the reports in the U.S. government, this is plenty to keep up with Israel's modernization needs. It is not as much as their Matmon-B plan,[79] but it is enough. The technicians actually recommended $.5 billion, but I upped it to $1.0 billion. In all honesty, during my talks with Rabin there was no sign they were disappointed. Maybe he tells you something he does not tell me but he said he was content. They had a much longer shopping list but a lot of it was filled.

Now the Senate Appropriations Subcommittee has increased the aid bill by one billion dollars, $500 million of it for Israel for the fifth quarter. I am trying hard to get the budget under control. I am squeezing every Department except Defense. So now you want me to approve another one billion. How can I justify that when people complain about how heartless and cruel I am for cutting food stamps, HEW [Department of Health, Education, and Welfare], and other programs. This is a very significant increase for the Middle East, especially when I am told by the technicians in [the Central Intelligence Agency] and [Department of Defense] that $500 million would be enough for Israel. I recommended $1.0 billion. I must relate domestic programs to foreign programs. We must stop the growing deficit and inflationary pressures. I think it is wrong to ask for this and I feel strongly about it.

Fisher: To sum up, the six planes to help Sadat is not really a concern. The concern is over the U.S. eventually becoming a major supplier. This year you have to gamble with six planes. Next year, you may have to gamble again, but if so, you will go before Congress. You do not want the U.S. to be a major supplier. You are playing for time. We understand this.

On aid, I know your problem but what will happen if Congress passes the bill? That is a real problem. There is a lot of sentiment in Congress for an increase across the board for Israel. I would not be frank if I did not tell you of our concern that this be approved.

President: I get bill after bill from Congress, they add $1.2 billion to HEW, $1.0 billion to [Housing and Urban Development], more to Interior. Look at the totals and see where this would take us. So I veto. We must get a handle on the rate of growth. If we did not change a law, there would be a $50 billion increase in FY 77 expenditures. This country simply cannot afford it. Look at the projections. Already the Congressional Committees have sent increases

79. *Matmon* is Hebrew for "treasure." The Matmon-B plan, proposed after the Yom Kippur War (1973), was a multiyear list of military equipment Israel sought from the United States.

to the Budget Committee totaling over $20 billion without the increase for foreign aid. How do I answer those who say I am hard-hearted on domestic programs if I go along with greater foreign aid and military assistance? You need to look at all this in context. My job is a tough one, but I can face it.

My fundamental view is the same today as for twenty years in Congress and it will not change. We will deal with day-to-day problems in a frank and candid way. You need to trust me. My view will be the same in the future as in the past on Israel.

Fisher: Thank you for this meeting, Mr. President.

44

"POWER IN THE PROMISED LAND"

The Incredible Hulk and Sabra
(1981)

◇◇

The importance of comic books to American society cannot be over-stated. "Few enduring expressions of American popular culture," observes the historian Bradford W. Wright, "are so instantly recognizable."[1] Since the 1930s, when Joe Shuster (1914–1992) and Jerry Siegel (1914–1996) of Cleveland, Ohio, the sons of eastern European Jewish immigrants, created the iconic hero Super-man, American Jews have played a central role in the comic book industry. In 1962, Stan Lee (1922–2018) and Jack Kirby (1917–1994), also sons of Jewish immigrants, created the Incredible Hulk, a tormented figure loosely based on the Gothic psychological thrillers *Frankenstein; or, The Modern Prometheus* (1818) by Mary Shelley (1797–1851) and *The Strange Case of Dr. Jekyll and Mr. Hyde* (1886) by Robert Louis Stevenson (1850–1894).

In 1980, as Israel, Egypt, and the United States opened a bold new chap-ter in Middle Eastern history following the Camp David Accords (1978), re-newed hope for a peaceful resolution to the Israel-Arab conflict took center stage. In the same year Marvel Comics, no stranger to the challenge of explor-ing complex social and political themes, introduced a new Israeli superhero to the comic book world: Sabra (the alias of the fictional Israeli policewoman Ruth Bat-Seraph). The Hebrew word *sabra*, as the comic book explained, "denotes a native-born Israeli" and is "derived from an indigenous form of fruit—a prickly pear possessed of a sweet interior and a spiny outer surface to protect it from its enemies."[2] Raised on a kibbutz, Sabra possesses mutant superpowers and secretly works as a Mossad agent. She springs to the fore in the dramatic 1980 issue "Power in the Promised Land" when she mistakes the Hulk's sudden ap-pearance in the Tel Aviv port as part of a terrorist attack. A tangled narrative

---

1. Bradford W. Wright, *Comic Book Nation: The Transformation of Youth Culture in America* (Balti-more, MD: Johns Hopkins University Press, 2001), xiii.

2. Sal Buscema, Bill Mantlo, Allen Milgrom, Jim Novak, Bob Sharen, and Jim Shooter, "Power in the Promised Land," *Incredible Hulk* 1, no. 258, February 1981 (New York: Marvel Comics), 16.

The Incredible Hulk and Sabra in "Power in the Promised Land," February 1981. Source: Sal Buscema, Bill Mantlo, Allen Milgrom, Jim Novak, Bob Sharen, and Jim Shooter, "Power in the Promised Land," *Incredible Hulk* 1, no. 258 (February 1981), New York: Marvel Comics, 16. Reprinted by permission of Marvel Comics.

ensues in which a Palestinian Arab boy is killed, resulting in a climactic battle royale between Sabra and the Hulk during which the green monster reveals the truth of their encounter: "Boy died because boy's people and yours both want to own land! Boy died because you wouldn't share! Boy died because of two old books that say his people and yours must fight and kill for land. . . . Hulk came looking for peace—but there is no peace here!"[3] The Hulk's revelation halts their fighting and prompts both Sabra's sudden epiphany and the comic book's final moment: "For an instant, Sabra prepares to give chase. She is, after all, an Israeli super-agent . . . a soldier . . . a weapon of war. But she is also a woman capable of feeling, capable of caring. It has taken The Hulk to make her see this dead Arab boy as a human being. It has taken a monster to awaken her own sense of humanity."

The adventures of Sabra, including future encounters with the Hulk, the Fantastic Four, and Black Panther, continued into the 1990s. Possessed of superhuman strength, extraordinary combat skills, and a distinctive superpower that enables the transferrance of her so-called life energy to save dying victims of evildoers, Sabra's profile as a fierce warrior and savior echoes the myth of the Israeli hero that permeated American culture in the mid- to late twentieth century.[4] Injecting a sizable quotient of moral complexity, political ambiguity, and self-reflection into the comic book arena, Sabra also reflects ideas and perceptions that informed the American public discussion of the Israel-Arab conflict and U.S.-Israel relations in the 1980s and 1990s.

—EDS.

3. Ibid., 30.

4. See Mark A. Raider, "Moshe Dayan: 'Israel's No. 1 Hero' (in America)," *Journal of Israeli History* 37, no. 1 (2019): 21–61.

45

"OVERLOOKED, OUT THERE ON THE RIM, IN THE SOUTHERN PART OF AMERICA"

Eli N. Evans, Macy B. Hart, and the Project of Southern Jewish History

(1987)

◇◇

SHARI RABIN

The 1970s and 1980s brought tremendous change to the American Jewish community in general and to Jewish life in the South in particular. Jews achieved new heights of social acceptance and economic status, as American culture moved to celebrate ethnic pride and cultural pluralism. The transformation produced a groundswell of communal interest in history and memory, verging on the nostalgic and centered disproportionately on the experiences of urban eastern European Jewish immigrants at the turn of the nineteenth and twentieth centuries. At the same time, changes in tax policy fueled a rise in private foundations and individual donors, leading to a nationwide surge of charitable giving that significantly influenced Jewish organizational life beyond the conventional role played by local community Jewish Federations. As a result, new Jewish institutions flourished, including those focused on Jewish cultural preservation and public history. The National Yiddish Book Center, founded in Amherst, Massachusetts, in 1980, and the Lower East Side Tenement Museum, founded in Manhattan in 1988, are only two of the most prominent examples.[1]

Meanwhile, Jewish communities in small southern towns saw their numbers dwindle, falling victim to upward social mobility and the region's broader demographic and economic transformations after World War II. The children of small-town shopkeepers became doctors and lawyers and moved to cities like

---

1. Jack Kugelmass, "Turfing the Slum: New York City's Tenement Museum and the Politics of Heritage," in *Remembering the Lower East Side: American Jewish Reflections*, ed. Hasia Diner, Jeffrey Shandler, and Beth Wenger (Bloomington: Indiana University Press, 2000), 179–211; Joshua B. Friedman and Moshe Kornfeld, "Identity Projects: Philanthropy, Neoliberalism, and Jewish Cultural Production," *American Jewish History* 102, no. 4 (October 2018), 537–61; Lila Corwin Berman, "How Americans Give: The Financialization of American Jewish Philanthropy," *American Historical Review* 122, no. 5 (December 2017), 1459–89.

Atlanta, New Orleans, or even Chicago. One such southerner was Eli N. Evans (b. 1936)—the son of Emanuel J. "Mutt" Evans (1907–1997), a former mayor of Durham, North Carolina—who moved to New York City as a young man. In 1973 he published *The Provincials: A Personal History of Jews in the South*, a pastiche of travel writing, history, and autobiography that launched the widespread awareness of and interest in southern Jewish history. A few years later the Southern Jewish Historical Society was founded to foster historical research on southern Jews.[2]

The document reprinted below is a letter written by Eli Evans in 1987 to Macy B. Hart (b. 1947), a native of Winona, Mississippi, and the long-time director of the Reform movement's Henry S. Jacobs Camp. The camp had been founded in Utica, Mississippi, in 1970 for Jewish children in the surrounding region. Sometime thereafter, according to Hart, families from small and declining Jewish communities started dropping off Judaica artifacts at the camp, hoping they would be used and/or preserved. In 1986 Hart secured a grant of over $500,000 from the Abraham Plough Foundation of Memphis, Tennessee, to build a home for these objects on the grounds of the camp, to be called the Museum of the Southern Jewish Experience.[3]

In the letter, Evans explains his support for—and his concerns about—the museum. He recognizes the recent move toward embracing southern Jewish heritage and describes it as a necessary corrective to the prevailing trends in American Jewish culture that are centered almost exclusively on the North. Advocating a new narrative of southern Jewish history, Evans argues for a museum that "not only collects but celebrates," and he points to the possibilities for encouraging genealogical work and highlighting Jewish contributions to southern history and culture. Of particular interest to Evans were notable businesspeople, politicians, and artists, including a number of people who were supporters of slavery and the Confederacy. At the same time, he raises concerns about the viability of the project, pointing to the competitive fund-raising marketplace and rising standards of professionalism and technological savvy in public history.

2. Stuart Rockoff, "The Rise and Fall of the Jewish South," in *Jewish Roots in Southern Soil*, ed. Marcie Cohen Ferris and Mark I. Greenberg (Waltham, MA: Brandeis University Press, 2006), 284–303; Mark K. Bauman, "A Century of Southern Jewish Historiography," *American Jewish Archives Journal* 57, nos. 1–2 (2007), 20.

3. Materials from the museum's early years are currently unprocessed and located at the offices of the Goldring/Woldenberg Institute of Southern Jewish Life (ISJL) in Jackson, Mississippi. Many thanks to Joshua Parshall, director of the ISJL's Department of History, for providing generous access to this archive. Additional material can be found on the Museum of the Southern Jewish Experience in the Nearprint Special Topics File at the Jacob Rader Marcus Center of the American Jewish Archives, Cincinnati.

Launched in October 1989 with much fanfare, the Museum of the Southern Jewish Experience was designed in the shape of a Star of David and contained 7,330 square feet, including space for galleries, a sanctuary, and administrative offices. Under Project Director Marcie Cohen Ferris (b. 1957), later a professor of American studies at the University of North Carolina at Chapel Hill, the museum undertook a wide range of projects focused on preservation, documentation, and education. Despite public enthusiasm for the museum, attracting visitors to remote Utica and the persistent complexity of its institutional relationship to the camp and, by extension, the Reform movement proved challenging. In 2000, Hart left his position at the camp and launched the Goldring/Woldenberg Institute of Southern Jewish Life (ISJL) in Jackson, Mississippi, with the museum as one part of a more ambitious effort to support small Jewish communities in the region. In 2013 the museum left the camp, and its collections were put in storage. In 2017, it was legally separated from the ISJL, and as of 2020 plans are under way for it to reopen in New Orleans. The following document opens a window on the museum's early history and the development of southern Jewish history and memory. It also sheds light on the challenges of Jewish organizational fund-raising in the donor-driven philanthropic culture of the late twentieth century.

◇◇

Letter from Eli N. Evans[4] to Macy B. Hart, April 30, 1987

Source: Letter from Eli N. Evans to Macy B. Hart, April 30, 1987.
Courtesy of Museum of the Southern Jewish Experience, New Orleans, LA.

Dear Macy:[5]

Thank you for coming by and sharing with me the master plan for the Museum of the Southern Jewish Experience. As I told you, it is unfortunately a

---

4. Eli N. Evans (b. 1936), president emeritus of the Charles H. Revson Foundation, was raised in Durham, North Carolina. He earned a BA from the University of North Carolina and a JD from Yale Law School, and he served as a speechwriter on the White House staff of President Lyndon B. Johnson (1908–1973). The author of *The Provincials: A Personal History of Jews in the South* (New York: Atheneum, 1973), *Judah P. Benjamin: The Jewish Confederate* (New York: Free Press, 1988), and *The Lonely Days Were Sundays* (Oxford: University of Mississippi Press, 1993), Evans made a considerable impact on the field of southern Jewish history.

5. Macy B. Hart (b. 1947) was raised in Winona, Mississippi, served as director of the Henry S. Jacobs Camp from 1971 to 1999, and founded the Institute for Southern Jewish Life in 2000. For more information, see Zeev Chafets, *Members of the Tribe: On the Road in Jewish America* (New York: Bantam Books, 1988), chapter 1 ("Macy B. and the Dixie Diaspora").

project that the Charles H. Revson Foundation[6] cannot help because this kind of an entity is not on our agenda. However, it is an idea that personally resonates with me because of my own involvement in writing about Southern Jewish history and traveling 7,000 miles across the South in the 1970's interviewing all ages of Southern Jews for my book.[7] I want to congratulate the Abraham Plough Foundation[8] for having the imagination to make a generous grant to launch such a far-reaching idea.

I say "far-reaching" because we Jews born and raised in the South have just recently, in the last ten or fifteen years, become aware of the depth and dignity of our own history. Up until then, center stage was always the Northeast, where the great immigrant stories commanded such attention and applause that historians have never bothered to look elsewhere. We have languished on the periphery, like country cousins or "The Provincials" (if you will pardon the reference), not destined to triumph but to survive, overlooked, out there on the rim, in the Southern part of America where our history and our accomplishments did not count. Now, that impression has been somewhat corrected with a growing body of literature and new philanthropic attention. But the sense of inferiority still lingers among the young, who still harbor these impressions of inadequacy from earlier times.

The Museum of the Southern Jewish Experience could be the centerpiece of a new movement of Southern Jewish pride, and harness this new excitement and interest to make a real difference in the attitude of Southern Jews—young and old—about themselves. The museum could collect family diaries and letters; show families how to do oral and video histories; develop and display photographic projects and turn them into books and/or documentary films (like the recent book[9] of photographs of Mississippi Jewish communities). It should stimulate the display and collection of family photograph albums; encourage putting family trees on a computer in the museum and then hook them into the genealogical project of the Museum of the Diaspora [Museum of the Jew-

6. The reference is to a private family foundation founded in New York City in 1956 by Charles H. Revson (1906–1975), who also founded Revlon Cosmetics. Evans served as the foundation's president from 1977 to 2003.

7. Evans is referring to his popular book, *The Provincials* (1973).

8. A private family foundation, the Plough Foundation was established in 1960 in Memphis, Tennessee, by Abraham Plough (1891–1894), founder of Plough Chemical Company—later the Schering-Plough Corporation—a pharmaceutical company that eventually merged with Merck. In 2019, the foundation announced plans to disburse its remaining funds and close its doors.

9. The reference is to Leo Turitz and Evelyn Turitz, *Jews in Early Mississippi* (Jackson: University Press of Mississippi, 1983).

ish People at Beit Hatfutsot] in Israel.[10] It could encourage community histories, centennial celebrations, and collect community, state, and regional material and develop books, teaching materials, and traveling exhibitions. It could research and do exhibitions on notable families—the Ploughs;[11] the Thalhimers[12] in Richmond: the Neiman and Marcus families[13] in Texas; Judah Touro[14] of New Orleans; the Massells[15] of Atlanta; the Sulzbergers[16] of Chattanooga. It could promote exhibitions on the lives of political figures (such as Judah P. Benjamin,[17] Gustavus Myers[18] who for thirty years served on the City Council in Richmond, and the hundreds of office holders who have been elected to public office in the last fifty years). It could display photographic studies of the works of artists like the sculptor ([Moses] Ezekiel)[19] and writers (Phoebe Pember,[20]

10. Founded in 1978 on the campus of Tel Aviv University, the Museum of the Jewish People at Beit Hatfutsot focuses on the "unique and ongoing 4,000 year-old story of the Jewish people— past, present and future" (Museum of the Jewish People at Beit Hatfutsot, "About the Museum of the Jewish People at Beit Hatfutsot," https://www.bh.org.il/about-us/about-beit-hatfutsot/).

11. See note 8.

12. The reference is to the family of William Thalheimer (1809–1883), an antebellum Jewish migrant to Richmond, Virginia, who in 1842 founded Thalheimer's, which became a major department store in the city.

13. The families of Abraham Lincoln Neiman (1875–1940), Carrie Marcus Neiman (1883–1953), and Herbert Marcus (1878–1950), Jewish entrepreneurs who were connected through the marriage of Abraham and Carrie, opened the first Neiman Marcus Department Store in 1907 in Dallas, Texas.

14. Judah Touro (1775–1854), a Jewish merchant and businessman born in Newport, Rhode Island, was an important philanthropist who made generous bequests to Jewish causes in his will.

15. The reference is to the family of Samuel A. Massell Jr. (b. 1927), who served as mayor of Atlanta from 1970 to 1974.

16. The reference is to the family of Arthur Hays Sulzberger (1891–1968), publisher of the *New York Times* from 1935 to 1961. Sulzberger did not actually live in Chattanooga. His father-in-law, Adolph Ochs (1858–1935), lived in Chattanooga from 1878 to 1896. While a resident of the city, he purchased the *Chattanooga Times*, and he later purchased the *New York Times*.

17. Born to a Sephardic Jewish family in the Caribbean, Judah P. Benjamin (1811–1884) was an antebellum U.S. senator from Louisiana who, following the outbreak of the Civil War (1861–65), served as attorney general, secretary of war, and secretary of state of the Confederate States of America. At the end of the war, he fled to England.

18. Gustavus Myers (1801–1869), born in Richmond, was an attorney, city council member, and Jewish leader.

19. Moses Ezekiel (1844–1917), born in Richmond, was a Confederate veteran and an acclaimed sculptor.

20. Born in Charleston, South Carolina, Phoebe Yates Pember (1823–1913) was the first female administrator of the Confederate Chimborazo Hospital during the Civil War.

Ludwig Lewisohn,[21] etc.) and poets and painters. It could be a place that not only collects but celebrates the Southern Jewish experience. It could be not only a building at the camp that people visit but the "earth station" that radiates materials outward to an audience of thousands across the South, the nation, and the world.

However, the most difficult step is the next one. With almost twenty years of philanthropic experience, I can tell you that the problem I think you will have in raising other funds is that the project is not laid out precisely enough to give other funders any confidence in it. You need a more detailed plan, some originality, and the thinking and advice of the best people in America and abroad, consulting with scholars in the field, to help plan such a project. It won't be done again on this scale and it should be done right. It should be a detailed plan— physically and substantively—that will give potential contributors the opportunity to participate and name exhibitions, rooms, activities, and programs in their own states and cities. There should be a way for thousands of families to contribute photographs to a video disc project, include a contribution when they send the photographs, and then be able to summon those photographs from the video disc when they visit the museum with their families (the Statue of Liberty[22] did this very successfully).

I hope the Plough Foundation will release some funds to enable you to take that next step in developing a more detailed plan. Some funds released now would enable you to engage people to advise you and come up with an exciting and imaginative project, beautifully described and illustrated, that could be circulated widely to several thousand potential contributors. People would want to contribute because they would sense that the idea could matter—to themselves, their families, their communities, states and regions.

My feeling is that there is a considerable amount of money in the South for the right idea if it is developed with flair, imagination, sense of participation and a carefully conceived and feasible plan. But make no mistake about it: the idea and its conception is central because few people will contribute major monies to a static, old-style museum which will only act as a repository for Southern Judaica or an attic that collects objects from vanishing congregations which will be seen just by campers and visitors to Utica. It must be a "big idea"—a 21st cen-

21. Ludwig Lewisohn (1882–1955) emigrated from Germany to Charleston as child with his family. A significant American Jewish writer, Zionist publicist, and scholar of literature, he was one of the founding professors of Brandeis University, where he taught comparative literature from 1948 until his death.

22. This is a reference to the American Museum of Immigration, a predecessor to the Ellis Island Immigration Museum, which opened in 1990.

tury museum anchored in new technologies and committees to a regional and national educational and cultural mission.

Without this next step of creativity and detail, the idea will just remain a dream and the Ploughs could well be disappointed that others did not come forward, when indeed, the project and you need some funds to take the idea to the next level of specificity and presentation. I know you have been talking to Jocelyn Rudner[23] about next steps and I would be happy to talk with her as well, if she wishes to do so.

Thank you again for coming by and please know that you can count on my personal support in seeing the idea through to its completion.

With best wishes, Eli Evans

23. Jocelyn Plough Rudner (1923–2017), daughter of Abraham Plough (see note 8), served as chair of the Plough Foundation board from 1985 to 1995.

46

"A NATURAL ALLIANCE"

Alexander M. Schindler on Black-Jewish Relations (1987 and 1992)

◇◇

GARY PHILLIP ZOLA

Blacks and Jews have been both "strangers and neighbors" to one another in America, and the interrelationship between these two minority groups, which may be traced back to the colonial period, has been complicated and inconsonant.[1] There were times when blacks and Jews saw one another as allies and coworkers in the battle for justice and equality. At other times, ambivalence or even antipathy best described the two groups' attitudes to one another. However, it was not until the late nineteenth and early twentieth centuries that interactions between America's black and Jewish groups took on a sustained and politically significant dimension. Over the course of American history, it is the civil rights movement of the 1950s and 1960s that is widely viewed as the apex of black-Jewish relations—and for good reason.[2]

American Jews played an outsize role in the civil rights movement, particularly during the decade that followed the U.S. Supreme Court's 1954 watershed ruling in Brown v. Board of Education of Topeka. Jews raised significant funds for civil rights organizations such as the Congress of Racial Equality, the Southern Christian Leadership Conference (SCLC), and the Student Nonviolent Coordinating Committee (SNCC).[3] Young northern Jews actively participated in an ongoing

1. Maurianne Adams and John H. Bracey, *Strangers and Neighbors: Relations between Blacks and Jews in the United States* (Amherst: University of Massachusetts Press, 1999).

2. Scholarship on the history of black-Jewish relations in the United States is extensive. See, for example, Cheryl Lynn Greenberg, *Troubling the Waters: Black-Jewish Relations in the Twentieth Century* (Princeton, NJ: Princeton University Press, 2006); Yvonne Patricia Chireau and Nathaniel Deutsch, eds., *Black Zion: African American Religious Encounters with Judaism* (New York: Oxford University Press, 2000); Jack Salzman and Cornel West, eds., *Struggles in the Promised Land: Towards a History of Black-Jewish Relations in the United States* (New York: Oxford University Press, 1997); Jack Salzman, Adina Back, and Gretchen Sullivan Sorin, eds., *Bridges and Boundaries: African Americans and American Jews* (New York: George Braziller, 1992); Hasia Diner, *In the Almost Promised Land: American Jews and Blacks, 1915–1935* (Westport, CT: Greenwood Press, 1977).

3. According to an unpublished memoir written by the New York real estate developer

array of civil rights marches, sit-ins, and voter registration campaigns in the American South. Some historians have asserted that half of the white students who served as volunteer participants in the Mississippi Freedom Summer of 1964 were Jews.[4] The appalling murders of James Chaney (1943–1964), Andrew Goodman (1943–1964), and Michael Schwerner (1939–1964) in Philadelphia, Mississippi, in that summer has become a prooftext illustrating the prominent role that Jews played in the movement.[5] Several Jewish houses of worship were bombed in the South during the 1950s and 1960s, and many American rabbis marched with Martin Luther King Jr. (1929–1963) during those years.[6] American rabbis were jailed, harassed, and in some instances physically injured.[7] In a high-profile *Playboy* interview published in January 1965, King noted the important role that Jews played in the civil rights movement: "It would be impossible to record the contribution that the Jewish people have made toward the Negro's struggle for freedom — it has been so great."[8]

This remarkable civil rights alliance did not come to life fully formed in the 1950s. The making of the black-Jewish alliance of the 1950s and early 1960s grew

---

and philanthropist Daniel Rose (b. 1929), Martin Luther King Jr. told him on August 27, 1963, "that of all the contributions of $1,000 or more he had ever received for the Southern Christian Leadership Conference, some 90 percent had come from Jews involved in the Civil Rights movement" ("Dr. Martin Luther King, Jr. & the March on Washington," 2020, SC-17374d, the Jacob Rader Marcus Center of the American Jewish Archives, Cincinnati). For more on the SNCC, see note 22.

4. Launched in June 1964, the Freedom Summer (also known as the Mississippi Summer Project) was a national campaign that brought volunteers to Mississippi in the hope of registering as many black voters as possible. On Jewish participation in the campaign, see Edward S. Shapiro, *A Time for Healing: American Jewry since World War II* (Baltimore, MD: Johns Hopkins University Press, 1992), 223; Debra L. Schultz, *Going South: Jewish Women in the Civil Rights Movement* (New York: New York University Press, 2001), 18 and 39.

5. The fact that Goodman and Schwerner were Jewish is repeatedly stressed as this incident is told and retold. See Kimberly Marlowe Hartnett, *Carolina Israelite: How Harry Golden Made Us Care about Jews, the South, and Civil Rights* (Chapel Hill: University of North Carolina Press, 2015), 222; Seth Cagin and Philip Dray, *We Are Not Afraid: The Story of Goodman, Schwerner, and Chaney and the Civil Rights Campaign for Mississippi* (New York: Macmillan, 1988).

6. On temple bombings in the South during the 1950s and 1960s, see Melissa Fay Greene, *The Temple Bombing* (Reading, MA: Addison-Wesley, 1996); Clive Webb, *Fight against Fear: Southern Jews and Black Civil Rights* (Athens: University of Georgia Press, 2001); Allen P. Krause, Mark K. Bauman, and Stephen Krause, *To Stand Aside or Stand Alone: Southern Reform Rabbis and the Civil Rights Movement* (Tuscaloosa: University of Alabama Press, 2016).

7. Christopher M. Richardson and Ralph Luker, *Historical Dictionary of the Civil Rights Movement* (Lanham, MD: Rowman and Littlefield, 2014), 247–48.

8. Alex Haley, "Playboy Interview: Martin Luther King," *Playboy: Entertainment for Men* 12, no. 1, January 1965, 76.

out of a long history of organizational interrelations that began in the early years of the twentieth century. Blacks and Jews worked together in the National Association for the Advancement of Colored People (NAACP) and the National Urban League—organizations that subsequently partnered in the 1920s and 1930s with leading Jewish communal organizations such as the Anti-Defamation League of Bnai Brith, the American Jewish Committee, and the American Jewish Congress.

During the first half of the twentieth century, blacks and Jews experienced similar manifestations of institutionalized discrimination and bigotry. Restrictive housing covenants prevented members of both minority groups from purchasing homes in certain neighborhoods, and both blacks and Jews were prominent targets of a resurgent Ku Klux Klan during that period. Both groups suffered from unfair hiring practices that hampered vocational opportunities for well-qualified applicants. In spite of the fact that black citizens suffered from the shameful history of slavery and the subsequent cruelties imposed on them by an intransigent American racism, these two groups found ways to collaborate in a common cause before World War II. As one influential black newspaper, the *New York Age*, noted as early as 1889, there was "a similarity between the Jew and the Negro. One is despised almost as much as the other."[9]

Conditions changed, however, after World War II. American Jews had become increasingly aware that their coreligionists in Europe had been brutally obliterated while the entire world stood by in silent apathy. There was no sustained effort by any nation to help the imperiled Jews of Europe in the 1930s. At this same time, blacks had become increasingly resentful of the fact that even after fighting and, in many instances, dying valiantly for the United States during World War II (and in previous wars), they remained second-class citizens when they returned home. These conditions set the stage for a celebrated black-Jewish alliance that took shape during the early years of the civil rights era. Many American Jews were motivated to fight for civil rights for blacks because the world had been silent during the Holocaust, and blacks were determined to fight for their rightful dignity and equality that America had persistently withheld.

Yet the shared vision that enabled blacks and Jews to work shoulder to shoulder during the civil rights era had already begun to fade by the mid-1960s.[10]

9. Quoted in Philip S. Foner, "Black-Jewish Relations in the Opening Years of the Twentieth Century," *Phylon: The Atlanta Review of Race and Culture* 36, no. 4 (Winter 1975), 360.

10. Even during the high-water mark of black-Jewish collaboration, there were always intergroup conflicts. See Marc Dollinger, *Black Power, Jewish Politics: Reinventing the Alliance in the 1960s* (Waltham, MA: Brandeis University Press, 2018).

Many factors contributed to the growing rift that occurred in the years following King's assassination in 1968. First, the Civil Rights Act of 1964 and the Voting Rights Act of 1965 did not produce the results anticipated by the black community. This important legislation did not successfully curtail the racism that was so deeply embedded in American society. While blacks continued to suffer from economic disadvantages, many members of the Jewish community began to advance economically after World War II. Jews abandoned the inner cities and settled in newly established suburban communities, while a majority of blacks remained mired in depressed urban centers. Although Jews moved to the suburbs, their businesses often remained in the cities. Many blacks were served by Jewish merchants, and these encounters were mixed. Some Jewish store owners developed warm and close relations with their black customers, while others were viewed as uncaring merchants who neither lived in nor cared about the black community and were interested primarily in making money. During the race riots in the 1960s, many of these stores became the targets of angry rioters. When King was asked if the looting of so many Jewish stores during the riots was indicative of a rise in black antisemitism, he demurred: "No, I do not believe that the riots could in any way be considered expressions of antisemitism." King answered: "It's true, as I was particularly pained to learn, that a large percentage of the looted stores were owned by our Jewish friends, but I do not feel that antisemitism was involved."[11] In spite of King's assurances, Jews began to wonder if they were targets of black antisemitism.

At the same time a younger generation of black activists began to insist that black organizations should be led by black leaders. These activists pointed out that blacks were capable of advocating for themselves; they did not need to depend on well-meaning whites to liberate them. Some Jews who had long been active in the NAACP and other civil rights organizations felt bruised by these changing attitudes, and these hard feelings only intensified with the rise of black leaders who advocated a form of black nationalism that rejected King's teachings about universal love and "the beloved community."[12] These voices called upon the black community to become economically self-sufficient on its own terms and by its own efforts. The Nation of Islam, for example, insisted that blacks take pride in themselves and reclaim their African heritage. In 1967, Louis

11. Haley, "Playboy Interview," 76.

12. Martin Luther King Jr., "'The Birth of a New Nation,' Sermon Delivered at Dexter Avenue Baptist Church," April 17, 1957, Martin Luther King Jr. Research and Education Institute, Stanford University, https://kinginstitute.stanford.edu/king-papers/documents/birth-new-nation -sermon-delivered-dexter-avenue-baptist-church.

Farrakhan (b. 1933) became the national spokesman for the Nation of Islam. In those early years of his national prominence, he began attacking Jews by insisting that they controlled the media. Farrakhan's bigoted accusations marked the beginning of his long and continuing history of anti-Jewish rhetoric.[13]

Finally, the rise of the Black Power movement in the mid-1960s sparked a new interest in ethnicity and ultimately gave birth to a new phenomenon: identity politics. Historians have noted that the American Indian Movement (known by the acronym AIM), the Chicano civil rights movement (referred to as El Movimiento), the gay liberation movement, and many other group identity and liberation movements arose in rapid succession on the heels of the Black Power movement. This cultural transformation prompted many Americans to begin "unearthing buried roots and occluded histories as well as celebrating [their own] distinctive heritages."[14]

American Jewry was also influenced by the rise in ethnic and group identity movements. Not surprisingly, Jews, too turned inward and began to concern themselves with specifically Jewish causes. In the aftermath of the Six-Day War of 1967, for instance, the American Jewish community experienced a tremendous burst of national pride as a result of Israel's astonishing military achievements. Israel's accomplishments bolstered Jewish self-respect in America, and many American Jews became politically active in support of Israel's long-term security interests.[15] Similarly, as liberation movements abounded in America, Jews increasingly took interest in the movement to free Soviet Jewry. In a sense, that movement provided American Jews with a meaningful outlet for the spirit of liberation that flourished in the United States during the late 1960s and early 1970s.[16]

13. The militant black religious leader Louis Farrakhan (b. 1933), head of the Nation of Islam, is a leading voice of antisemitism in American society. See Nathaniel Deutsch, "The Proximate Other: The Nation of Islam and Judaism," in *Black Zion: African American Religious Encounters with Judaism*, ed. Yvonne Patricia Chireau and Nathaniel Deutsch (New York: Oxford University Press, 2000): 91–117; "Nation of Islam," Southern Poverty Law Center, https://www.splcenter .org/fighting-hate/extremist-files/group/nation-islam.

14. Marilyn Halter, *Shopping for Identity: The Marketing of Ethnicity* (New York: Schocken Books, 2000), 4.

15. See Michael L. Morgan, *Beyond Auschwitz: Post-Holocaust Jewish Thought in America* (New York: Oxford University Press, 2001), chapter 5 ("The Six-Day War and American Jewish Life"); Marc Lee Raphael, *A History of the United Jewish Appeal* (Chico, CA: Scholars Press, 1982), chapter 8 ("The American Jewish Philanthropic Response to the Six-Day and Yom Kippur Wars"); Lawrence Grossman, "Transformation through Crisis: The American Jewish Committee and the Six-Day War," *American Jewish History* 86, no. 1 (March 1998), 27–54.

16. See chapter 41. See also Stuart Altshuler, *From Exodus to Freedom: A History of the Soviet Jewry*

By the mid-1980s, the black-Jewish alliance of the civil rights movement had become a nostalgic and distant memory, as an array of controversial incidents put blacks and Jews at odds with one another. Many historians and commentators tried to explain what seemed to be a "broken alliance." What had happened to the black-Jewish coalition? Did blacks and Jews still have a common cause?[17]

These are the very questions that Rabbi Alexander M. Schindler (1925–2000), one of the most significant leaders of American Jewry in the last quarter of the twentieth century, confronted in two public addresses he delivered in 1987 and 1992, respectively. Schindler had fled Germany in 1932 and settled in the United States shortly thereafter. Upon receiving his rabbinical ordination in 1953 from the Hebrew Union College–Jewish Institute of Religion in Cincinnati, Schindler spent most of his professional career working for the Reform movement's congregational body, the Union of American Hebrew Congregations (UAHC). In 1973, when he became the president of the UAHC, his public profile grew dramatically. During 1976–78, Schindler became the first Reform Jewish leader to serve as chair of the Conference of Presidents of Major American Jewish Organizations, an organization established in 1956 to provide the executive branch of the U.S. government with a consensus voice representing American Jewry as a whole. In this period, Schindler spoke out regularly on matters of social justice, human rights, and liberal causes in both Jewish and secular communities, becoming one of the leading Jewish voices of his era.[18]

In the two addresses presented below, Schindler examined the tensions that

---

Movement (Lanham, MD: Rowman and Littlefield, 2005); Murray Friedman and Albert D. Chernon, eds., *A Second Exodus: The American Movement to Free Soviet Jews* (Waltham, MA: Brandeis University Press, 1999).

17. Jonathan Kaufman, *Broken Alliance: The Turbulent Times between Blacks and Jews in America* (New York: Scribner, 1988). Many authors have written about the breakdown in black-Jewish relations during the 1980s and 1990s. In addition to Kaufman's *Broken Alliance*, see, for example, Ethan Goffman, *Imagining Each Other: Blacks and Jews in Contemporary American Literature* (Albany: State University of New York Press, 2000); Seth Forman, *Blacks in the Jewish Mind: A Crisis of Liberalism* (New York: New York University Press, 1998); Michael Lerner and Cornel West, *Jews and Blacks: A Dialogue on Race, Religion, and Culture in America* (New York: Plume, 1996); Saul Berman, *Blacks and Jews: Alliances and Arguments* (New York: Delacorte Press, 1994).

18. A much-deserved full-scale biography of Schindler has not yet been written. However, there are two useful theses on Schindler: Karen Companez, "Alexander Schindler: A Thematic Biography," MA thesis, Hebrew Union College–Jewish Institute of Religion, 2002; and Lynne Goldsmith, "Bridge to the Future: Alexander Schindler and His Influence on the Development of Reform Judaism's Outreach Program," MA thesis, Hebrew Union College–Jewish Institute of Religion, 2007. See also Aron Hirt-Manheimer, *The Jewish Condition: Essays on Contemporary Judaism Honoring Rabbi Alexander M. Schindler* (New York: UAHC Press, 1995).

b

characterized black-Jewish communal relations during the 1980s and early 1990s. The first speech was delivered in 1987 at Central State University (CSU) a public historically black university located in Wilberforce, Ohio. CSU was commemorating the centennial anniversary of its founding, and the school's president invited Schindler to speak on the history of black-Jewish relations in America.

In 1992, Schindler chaired a large conference on "Racism, Antisemitism, Xenophobia, and Other Forms of Intolerance" sponsored by the World Jewish Congress. He was asked to introduce Rev. Jesse Jackson (b. 1941), who had been invited to address the gathering. Jackson, a veteran American civil rights activist and former associate of King, had become a highly controversial figure in the Jewish community in 1984 when the *Washington Post* reported that Jackson, who at the time was seeking to become the Democratic Party's candidate for president, had referred to Jews as "Hymies" and New York City as "Hymietown" in a private conversation with news reporters.[19] Many in the conference's audience had a jaundiced view of Jackson's propriety as a speaker.

In both speeches, Schindler surveyed the controversies that collectively had driven a wedge between the black and Jewish communities in the years following King's assassination. Schindler's analysis of the relationship is noteworthy: he criticized both sides and emerged as an impassioned advocate for black-Jewish reconciliation. He criticized those who wanted to dwell on their hard feelings and allow past misunderstandings to distract them from the core values that the communities shared. He urged his listeners to return to the important work that they should be doing together. Schindler prioritized a universal moral idealism that blacks and Jews have in common. "In addition to our common nightmares," Schindler eloquently concluded, "we Blacks and Jews dream common dreams. We share a vision of a just and open and generous society. We agree that it is the foremost task of governments to protect the weak and the stranger, to achieve social and economic and political justice. We are both committed to the need for change, in our country, in the world. We see our common dream not in the valley of the status quo, but on Martin Luther King's mountain top."

19. See note 26.

Alexander M. Schindler, Central State University Centennial Address, February 3, 1987

Source: Alexander M. Schindler, Central State University Centennial Address (February 3, 1987), Alexander Moshe Schindler Papers, MS-630, box 24, folder 8, the Jacob Rader Marcus Center of the American Jewish Archives, Cincinnati.

It is a privilege which I greatly appreciate to be here and to help you celebrate this great university's centennial. I am particularly pleased to be invited during "Black History Month"—a month that persists in reminding us of the magnificent contribution which Blacks have made to American life, even though, as most such celebrations go, that contribution escapes the awareness of Americans during the rest of the year.

The man for whom this performing arts center was named, Paul Robeson,[20] was a human being of awe-inspiring powers, not the least of which was his compassion, his sense of identification with all peoples whose lives and cultures were endangered by injustice. Thus, in 1949, at the height of Joseph Stalin's vicious campaign against Soviet Jews and their culture, Paul Robeson ended his concert in a great concert hall in Moscow with a special encore.

Robeson's choice was a Yiddish song, "The Partisan Song," that had become the hymn of the Jewish resistance to Nazism. By singing this anthem, by expressing his respect and, yes, his love for the Jewish people whose flesh and whose soul had been seared by the genocidal assault of the Nazis, Paul Robeson managed to freeze the growing antisemitism of the Stalin era at least for as long as his sonorous voice echoed in that concert hall. Robeson succeeded in uniting his audience, Russians and Jews, by reminding them of their shared anguish, their survival, and their resistance to a common enemy.

I pray that my voice today might echo that spirit of unity within our own American landscape. Mine is the voice of an American Jew whose civil and religious convictions closely coincide. As an American, I believe that our country will not be whole[,] will not be capable of healing its social ills and fulfilling its highest potential[,] until it comes to terms with our society's continuing oppression of Blacks. And as a Jew, I have been taught by precept and by my people's historic experience to recoil against bigotry and to fight against injustice. I have been instructed to internalize the superbly concise teaching of Rabbi Hillel, our sage of 2,000 years ago, who summed up the quest for liberation with

20. Paul Robeson (1898–1976) was an internationally acclaimed American bass-baritone concert artist and actor who was recognized for his political activism as well as his contributions to American culture.

three questions: "If I am not for myself, who will be for me? If I am only for my-self, what am I? And if not now, when?" [*Ethics of the Sages* 1:14].

Perhaps it is this coincidence of the American and Jewish ideal that led the president of your university to request that I speak about Blacks and Jews in America, that I trace the story of our mutual relationship on these shores. It is a relationship which was never dispassionate, always oscillatory, pendulous, swaying from harmony to discord and back again.

In the [19]50s and [19]60s, American Jews responded passionately to the fight against racial segregation. In the heat of that climactic struggle, the Black-Jewish alliance was at the heart of the civil rights movement. When the Mississippi summer was organized to break the back of the then most savagely resistant state of the Union, more than 50 percent of the young people who volunteered from all parts of the U.S. were Jewish youngsters. Two of the three martyrs of that struggle killed by mobs in Mississippi, Michael Schwerner and Andrew Goodman, were Jewish, the third, James Chaney, was a Black. Most of the funds raised by such organizations as the NAACP, the [Southern] Christian Leadership Conference and SNCC[21] were secured from Jews, both rich and poor. Rabbis marched with Martin Luther King throughout the south; many were jailed, some were beaten. Jewish political leverage—often in a three-faith setting—helped to produce the landmark civil rights laws of the '60s.

Those were days of vision and of courage—the courage not only to face a common enemy, but to face one another eye-to-eye, to see more deeply into one another's hearts than we can in less extraordinary circumstances. We who participated in the movement were transformed by it in greater measure than the country itself was transformed. Such was our reward.

Ah, but then our gazes faltered. An alienation between Blacks and Jews developed during the decade following the assassination of Martin Luther King—a falling out that has been dissected often enough for me to spare you another sketch of its sorry history. Ocean Hill–Brownsville,[22] the Andrew Young

21. The Student Non-Violent Coordinating Committee (SNCC) was a grassroots civil rights group formed in the early 1960s by younger blacks who sought to have a more prominent voice in the civil rights movement. Ella Josephine Baker (1903–1986) was one of the founders of the SNCC.

22. "Ocean Hill-Brownsville" refers to a bitter controversy that arose in 1968 in the Ocean Hill–Brownsville school districts of Brooklyn, New York, when the school board—controlled by the local black community—dismissed school workers who were almost all white and Jewish. This action led the teachers' union to call a citywide strike, which lasted for more than a month. The affair led to bitter tensions between blacks and Jews in New York City. See Jerald E. Podair,

affair,[23] vocal Jewish opposition to affirmative action in the Bakke[24] and De-funis cases.[25] And then there were Black militant rallies against Zionism and in support of the terrorist PLO, Jackson's "Hymietown,"[26] and Farrakhan's un-diluted antisemitic venom.[27] Each of these events deepened the gulf between our peoples. We stopped [looking] at one another or if we did, we did so only in mutual distrust and with a growing hostility. Why? Why this sudden alien-ation, this rapid descent from Martin Luther King's mountaintop to the vale of suspicion and rancor?

I suppose that journalistic histrionics had something to do with it all, for each of the events to which I alluded suffered media sensationalism, and from

The Strike That Changed New York: Blacks, Whites, and the Ocean Hill–Brownsville Crisis (New Haven, CT: Yale University Press, 2002).

23. "The Andrew Young affair" refers to the forced resignation in August 1979 of Andrew Young (b. 1932) from his position as President Jimmy Carter's (b. 1924) ambassador to the United Nations. Young resigned after the public learned that he had met privately with a mem-ber of the Palestine Liberation Organization (PLO)—a meeting that violated what was then U.S.foreign policy. A second "Andrew Young affair" took place in August 2006, when the former ambassador was working as a consultant to help Walmart improve its image in the community. Young was forced to resign his Walmart post after making racially insensitive remarks about Jews, Arabs, and Koreans—whom he accused of having been "overcharging us, selling us stale bread, and bad meat, and wilted vegetables" (quoted in Michael Barbaro and Steven Green-house, "Wal-Mart Image Builder Resigns," _New York Times_, August 18, 2006, C00003).

24. Allan Bakke (b. 1940), a white California man who had twice unsuccessfully applied for admission to the University of California medical school, filed suit against the university, claiming that he was the victim of so-called reverse discrimination because his grades and test scores had surpassed those of many minority students who had gained admission. On June 28, 1978, the U.S. Supreme Court decided that affirmative action was constitutional, but it simulta-neously invalidated the use of racial quotas.

25. In 1971, Marco DeFunis Jr. (1950–2002) gained national attention when he challenged the admissions policies of the University of Washington Law School. The DeFunis case was one of the first attempts to challenge the constitutionality of affirmative action in higher education. On April 23, 1974, the Supreme Court decided that the case was moot because DeFunis had nearly completed his education at the school.

26. On February 13, 1984, as noted above, the _Washington Post_ reported that Jackson had called Jews "Hymies" and New York City "Hymietown" in a private conversation with news re-porters. After initially saying that he could not recall using those terms, Jackson publicly apolo-gized. See Kathy Sawyer, "Buoyant Jackson Finds Forgiveness, Questions," _Washington Post_, Feb-ruary 28, 1984, A6.

27. See note 13. See also Robert A. Rockaway, "'The Jews Cannot Defeat Me': The Anti-Jewish Campaign of Louis Farrakhan and the Nation of Islam," Tel Aviv: Tel Aviv University, Faculty of Humanities, 1995.

the self-same media, mind you, that consistently ignored hundreds of projects and activities of Black-Jewish cooperation throughout our country and through all these stormy decades.

Prejudice also came into play, with the damnable exaggeration given voice by extremists in both camps. For example, seizing on a picture of Lowery embracing Arafat,[28] Jews began to condemn all Black leaders as being "anti-Israel" while ignoring the excellent pro-Israel voting record of the Black Congressional Caucus.

Black extremists, in turn, painted the entire American Jewish community as opposed to affirmative action, and this despite the fact that most American Jewish organizations actively and consistently champion affirmative action goals and timetables, and even quotas in cases of proven prior bias. Countless other examples of such stereotyping, of blaming an entire community for the failings of individuals[,] could be adduced. Thus, some Blacks see all Jews as rich, privileged, powerful, bigoted. And some Jews see all Blacks as poor, violent, living on welfare, and seething with anti-Jewish hatred. And so it goes.

Still another factor speeding the process of our alienation was an increasing ethnic assertiveness. A spirit of group autonomy awakened in the America of the late sixties. Even before King's assassination, many Black leaders were resolved to take control of their own destiny. They spoke of Black power and Black separatism and began to displace Jews, who on their part became ever more preoccupied with their own agenda, with Soviet Jewry and with the struggle to secure Israel's safety.

This inward turning of both groups may have been due to the fact that their relationship during the preceding decades had been inherently unequal, and that some Jews, let it be confessed, were patronizing in their attitude. Black leaders had good reason to resent such contumely, but all too often they drove Jews from the activist front with calumnies against Israel and Zionism, and with harsh words better reserved for the Ku Klux Klan than for erstwhile liberal and faithful allies.

Be that as it may, in the '70s and '80s resurgent ethnic identity began to hold sway in America. The sense of overarching community began to fade. Jews and

28. One month after Young was forced to resign as U.S. ambassador to the United Nations for meeting privately with a representative of the PLO, Rev. Joseph Lowery (1921–2020), president of the SCLC, led an SCLC delegation of black leaders to Lebanon to meet with Yasser Arafat (1929–2004), the leader of the PLO. A photo was taken of the two men embracing. See Murray Friedman, *What Went Wrong? The Creation and Collapse of the Black-Jewish Alliance* (New York: Free Press, 1995), 327–28.

Blacks drifted apart. Each group went its own way, fighting its own battles, and sometimes fighting each other in a fractured and tribal America.

Last, but not in the least, in that earlier golden era of our unity the moral issues were more clear cut, infinitely simpler to grasp. The scales of justice were clearly weighted. On the one side non-violent Blacks sought the elementary right to vote, to be treated without discrimination in hotels, stores, restaurants or on public transportation. On the other side were bloody-minded mobs armed with police dogs, cattle prods, high pressure hoses and even rifles. Who could fail to distinguish between them, to know who is right and who is wrong? The moral equation was obvious to all.

Today, the moral problems in the continuing quest for racial decency are much more confused, ambiguous and controversial. Men and women of good will stand on both sides of many thorny topics and foremost among these is affirmative action, which more than any other issue divided our respective communities. Initially American Jews joined Blacks in advocating programs designed to bring disadvantaged minority men and women into the mainstream of American life. They recognized the need to correct and compensate for past and present discrimination by programs of outreach, recruiting, training and compensatory education. But then a new word was introduced into the debate and it proved to be the rock on which our alliance split.

I refer to the word "quota" which frightened many Jews primarily because they remembered quotas only as restrictive barriers, means used in the old country and the new to keep Jews out of schools and out of jobs and out of pleasanter living areas. Such restrictive covenants still obtain and are entered into, as we have seen[,] even by candidates for the Supreme Court (Rehnquist).[29] Thus frightened, some Jews emerged as the vocal opponents of "quotas." They

29. Schindler's written text leaves Rehnquist's name in parentheses, suggesting that he merely mentioned the jurist's name in connection with restrictive covenants. The reference here is to a kerfuffle that arose in 1986 when Associate Supreme Court Justice William H. Rehnquist (1924–2005) was nominated to become the Court's chief justice. During Senate hearings, it was disclosed there was a deed restriction on a property he had purchased in Vermont in 1974 stipulating that "no feet of the herein conveyed property shall be leased or sold to any member of the Hebrew race" (quoted in Matthew L. Wald, "Rehnquist Hearing Turns Town to Deed Pondering," New York Times, August 2, 1986, A12). Similarly, there was a restriction written in 1928 on a home Rehnquist sold in Phoenix, Arizona, in 1969 stating that the property was not to be sold, transferred, leased to, or inhabited by "any person not of the White or Caucasian race" (quoted in Robert Lindsey, "Rehnquist in Arizona: A Militant Conservative in '60s Politics," New York Times, August 4, 1986, A7). Rehnquist testified that he was unaware of these restrictions on his properties.

labeled them a form of "reverse discrimination" and joined in opposing the civil rights community in several major court cases.

Not all Jews did, of course. Thus in the DeFunis case, the National Council of Jewish Women, and my own organization, the Union of American Hebrew Congregations, the largest of all American Jewish organizations, entered an *amicus curiae* brief in favor of the University of Washington against DeFunis, and this even though DeFunis was a member of one of our West Coast congregations. (Admittedly that fact came as something of a surprise to us. Names are so confusing nowadays. I mean who would know that a guy named Marco DeFunis is Jewish, and a Reform Jew to boot. But it wouldn't have mattered anyway.) We took our lumps with pride, assured that we were on the side of justice.

Blunders were made by both communities in this realm. Jews failed to distinguish between quotas that exclude and quotas designed to bring the excluded into the mainstream. Blacks in turn made quotas a synonym for all affirmative action. They responded to Jewish press releases with rhetorical bombs of their own when somebody should have said: "Wait a minute. Let's sit down and hammer out a definition of affirmative action that we both can support."

Continuing clashing rhetoric to the contrary notwithstanding, the Jewish community has become substantially supportive here. As I have already indicated, most American Jewish organizations today actively and consistently champion affirmative action; yes, with goals and timetables, and even with quotas in cases of proven prior bias. How is affirmative action working out?

The early fears of Jews certainly proved unfounded. Affirmative action has scarcely transformed America into a quota society. As for the hopes of the Black community, let us admit these too were not fully realized. Affirmative action may have opened the doors to the middle class for some Blacks and it has expanded their entry into the professions. But it has not served to alleviate what is undoubtedly the most urgent problem of racial justice today: the plight of the Black urban underclass, those wretched millions whose state is desolate, who have no homes, no food, no jobs, and who have lost all hope that this is a society which gives a damn for them. If nothing else, this desperate need should move both Blacks and Jews to reweave a meaningful political relationship.

The truth of the matter is that we need each other. And what is required to re-forge our alliance? For Jews this means stemming the flight from coalition involvement; we have to learn that we cannot protect Israel or help Soviet Jews without allies in this land. For Blacks this means emerging from angry isolation. While nourishing their pride and self-worth they must nonetheless realize that they too cannot prevail alone, that they will not be able to change America without allies.

It is a natural alliance, for we Blacks and Jews are essentially kindred in spirit. Our commonalities exceed our differences by far. We share a vision of a just, generous and open society. We both recoil against the stench of bigotry. We both wish to see government help to solve social inequity. We vote more alike than any other racial or religious groups; look at the last presidential election and see: in the year of a Reagan landslide only Blacks and Jews gave a majority of their votes to Walter Mondale.[30]

Ours are the two American peoples who are committed to the idea of change in our country, who see the American dream not in the valley of the status quo but on Martin Luther King's mountain top. Only our common enemies, the enemies of freedom, rejoice when we square off against each other. What was lost during the era of our face-off—look at Howard Beach and Forsyth County and see![31]

No longer do we stand on the ground of a socially progressive era. Indeed, the ground on which we have stood in the past is crumbling beneath us. Six years of trickle-down Reagonomics have deepened the sense of danger and despair in America. Six years of assault on social welfare programs have raised the poverty indices of the Black urban underclass to unpardonable levels. Six years of an adversarial Justice Department, of relentless federal attacks on municipal affirmative action, have poisoned the public consciousness against Blacks and other minorities. Far right demagoguery has infected the wounded places

30. In the 1984 presidential election, the Republican incumbent Ronald W. Reagan (1911–2004) faced Democratic challenger Walter Mondale (b. 1928), who had served as Jimmy Carter's vice president (1977–81). Reagan won the election in a landslide, garnering 525 out 538 electoral votes—and winning 58.8 percent of the popular vote to Mondale's 40.6 percent. Historically, American Jews vote overwhelmingly for the Democratic party, but in the mid-1980s Jewish identification with the Republican party reached a peak of 29 percent.

31. Schindler is referring to the death of Michael Griffith (1963–1986), an immigrant from Trinidad, who was murdered in Howard Beach, Queens, New York, on December 20, 1986, in a racially charged incident. Griffith was the third black man to be murdered by a white mob in New York in the 1980s. Schindler is also referring to January 1987, when an integrated crowd of two thousand peaceful demonstrators entered the small town of Cumming, in Forsyth County, Georgia (outside of Atlanta). Forsyth's reputation as an "all-white county" and "racist legacy" prompted the organization of a "walk for brotherhood" (quoted in Dudley Clendinen, "Thousands in Civil Rights March Jeered by Crowd in Georgia Town," *New York Times*, January 25, 1987, A1). The demonstrators were greeted by thousands of angry whites shouting hateful epithets. The following week, more than fifteen thousand people joined a second march led by Coretta Scott King (1927–2006), Martin Luther King's widow; Mayor Andrew Young of Atlanta; Jackson; the Rev. Ralph David Abernathy (1926–1990); the comedian Dick Gregory (1932–2017); Benjamin Hooks (1925–2010), executive director of the NAACP; U.S. Senators Sam Nunn (b. 1938) and Wyche Fowler (b. 1940); and U.S. Representative John Lewis (1940–2020). Despite the star-studded cadre of leaders, the second demonstration was greeted with jeering and invectives.

of America with racism and antisemitism both. The media has become flabby, content to ignore the unsightly and to mimic the Reagan administration's false tune of "Happy Days Are Here Again." What hypocrisy this! What a perversion of the truth!

And we Jews and we Blacks we stand frozen in a wrestler's clench when we should be surging forward like two running backs on the same team. Aye, we Jews and we Blacks sit like a couple of Jonahs in the belly of a whale, when we should be doing God's work together, calling great cities—nay, a great nation—to repentance.

This is our mutual sacred task.

Alexander M. Schindler, Introduction of the Rev. Jesse Jackson to the Conference on Racism, Antisemitism, Xenophobia, and Other Forms of Intolerance, Brussels, Belgium, July 7, 1992

Source: Alexander M. Schindler, introduction to the Reverend Jesse Jackson delivered at the Conference on Racism, Antisemitism, Xenophobia, and Other Forms of Intolerance (July 7, 1992), Alexander Moshe Schindler Papers, MS-630, box 5, folder 5, the Jacob Rader Marcus Center of the American Jewish Archives, Cincinnati.

As chairman, it is my task to set the theme and to introduce the speaker. In setting the theme of this session, it is important to reassert what we heard last night in several versions, that antisemitism is not an isolated disease. It has its tragically unique dimensions, yet it is not totally unrelated to other maladies afflicting humankind; it is one most virulent manifestation of that unreasoned hatred which finds divergent expressions in our world: the "ethnic cleansing" that is ravaging Sarajevo, the xenophobia that fuels violence against immigrants in Austria and West Germany, Gypsies threatened in eastern Europe, a Pat Buchanan[32] whose presidential campaign was unruffled by the snide antisemitism of the candidate himself, a former imperial grand wizard of the Ku Klux Klan garnering a majority of white votes in Louisiana.[33]

32. The conservative American pundit and politician Patrick Buchanan (b. 1938) has a long track record of Holocaust denial and antisemitic statements. In Buchanan's 1992 campaign for the Republican presidential nomination, he blamed the Gulf War (1990–91) on "the Israeli Defense Ministry and its amen corner in the United States" (quoted in A. M. Rosenthal, "Forgive Them Not," *New York Times*, September 14, 1990, A33).

33. Schindler is referring to the American white supremacist David Duke (b. 1950), a former Grand Wizard of the Ku Klux Klan, who campaigned unsuccessfully to become a U.S. senator in 1990 and the governor of Louisiana in 1991.

From the Urals to the Ozarks, so it seems, the toxic waters of racism are rising, and a common effort is required to stem the blood-soaked tide. The victims of this unreasoned hatred are all dependent on one another. If we do not stand united, we will surely fall. In our most recent past, Blacks and Jews came together in the recognition of a shared fate. We recoiled again at the stench of bigotry and resolved to resist it together. Together we forged a Black-Jewish alliance that demanded racial justice, an end to discrimination at lunch counters and in the voting booth, in public schools and public accommodations. Together we changed the course of American history.

It is tempting to dwell on those earlier days, when our quotient of mutual pain was far higher than our quotient of mutual distrust. Nostalgia is comforting, it eases the spirit, does is it not?

Certainly, it is more comforting to remember the quality of leadership offered by a Bayard Rustin,[34] than to attend to the words of a Farrakhan[35] or Jeffries.[36] Surely it is more inspiring to recall the sight of a Martin Luther King flanked by Rabbis Abraham Joshua Heschel[37] and Maurice Eisendrath,[38] walking at the head of tens of thousands of civil rights marchers, than it is to think about the death of a Yankel Rosenbaum and the cries of "Hitler was right!" in Crown Heights.[39]

34. Bayard Rustin (1912–1987), a civil rights organizer and community activist, served as one of King's key advisers in the 1950s and 1960s.

35. On Louis Farrakhan, see note 13.

36. Leonard Jeffries (b. 1937) was head of the Black Studies Department at the City College of the City University of New York. In 1991, it was publicly reported that Jeffries, speaking at the Empire State Black Arts and Cultural Festival in Albany, New York, asserted that "Jews and Italians in Hollywood conspired to denigrate blacks in the movies and that rich Jews played a key role in helping to finance the slave trade" (quoted in Denise K. Magner, "Controversial City College Professor Is a Study in Contradictions: Hero of Afrocentrism or Flamboyant Racist?," *Chronicle of Higher Education*, December 18, 1991, https://www.chronicle.com/article/controversial -city-college-professor-is-a-study-in-contradictions/). In October 1992, the City University of New York board of trustees voted to remove Jeffries from his position. Jeffries subsequently sued City College in federal court for violating his freedom of speech. He won a $400,000 settlement and was reinstated to his position. See Richard M. Benjamin, "The Bizarre Classroom of Dr. Leonard Jeffries," *Journal of Blacks in Higher Education* (Winter 1993–94), 91–96.

37. Rabbi Abraham Joshua Heschel (1907–1972), a Polish Jewish refugee who immigrated to the United States in 1940, was one of twentieth century's towering Jewish theologians and philosophers. He played an instrumental role in the civil rights struggles of the 1950s and 1960s.

38. Rabbi Maurice Eisendrath (1902–1973), a prominent social activist, served as president of the Union of American Hebrew Congregations from 1943 until his death.

39. Yankel Rosenbaum (1962–1991), an Australian Jew and member of the Chabad Jewish community, was stabbed to death in New York on August 19, 1991, by a young black man named

But nostalgia goes lighter on our Jewish consciences too, let us admit it, for it is easier to remember that we Jews had everything to gain from toppling the barricades of discrimination in America than it is to confront the fact that our gains have wedded too many of us to the status quo in which we care more about tranquility shattered than justice denied. It is easier on our conscience to recall brave Jewish participation at the front lines of the civil rights movement than it is to confess our failure effectively to challenge the Reagan-Bush policy of urban neglect.[40]

Aye, it is easier to make an equation between Black-Jewish suffering based on our burning memories, than it is to reckon with the truth of the vast difference today between American Jewish empowerment and material well-being on the one hand and the ongoing disempowerment and poverty endured by Black Americans on the other.

Our speaker, the Reverend Jesse Jackson, was active in the glory days of the Black-Jewish alliance which we now so nostalgically recall, and as a Martin Luther King aide he was a key player in that coalition of decency in which Blacks and Jews were such indispensable partners. But times and events have led us to view him as having contributed to those tensions that now divide our communities, even as he has a unique potential to be a bridge between us.

This changing perception comes as no news to him. He hears our plaints wherever and whenever he encounters us in the public arena. Little purpose will be served in rehearsing the litany of our plaints. He knows them. We know them. The wounds will never heal if we keep on re-opening them. There is a need for a new beginning. We can't remain mired in the past but must move forward.

Jesse Jackson, on his part, has certainly endeavored to do so but honesty com-

---

Lemrick Nelson (b. 1975). Rosenbaum's murder was in retaliation for the death of Gavin Cato, a seven-year-old black boy tragically killed in a car accident involving a Hasidic Jew. These events were followed by four days of rioting, which reflected long-standing bitterness between the black and Chabad communities in the Crown Heights neighborhood. See Edward S. Shapiro, *Crown Heights: Blacks, Jews, and the 1991 Brooklyn Riot* (Waltham, MA: Brandeis University Press, 2006).

40. Asserting that small government and personal responsibility were the cornerstones of American prosperity and freedom, the Reagan administration (1981–89), strove to reverse decades of U.S. policy of providing federal aid to America's cities and disenfranchised populations. Under Reagan and Vice President George H. W. Bush (1924–2018), the federal government divested itself of responsibility for a variety of social programs. Meanwhile, what is known as "Reaganomics" provided unprecedented tax breaks for affluent Americans and the corporate sector. Many urban centers, sagging under the weight of racial tensions, industrial decline, and aging infrastructure, experienced a vicious downward spiral. Economic disparity and inner-city hardship accelerated at an alarming pace.

pels us to admit that we on our part have failed to respond to or even acknowledge his efforts over the past six years to repair the breach. He has been speaking of "secure borders" for Israel, and he has openly supported the Camp David accords and all the approaches embodied in it. He confronted Gorbachev[41] in Geneva on the issue of Soviet Jewry. He was ready to travel to Syria to intercede for the Israeli MIA's [troops missing in action]. Indeed, during the past months he was tireless in his efforts to gain freedom for Syrian Jews—and he made no fanfare about it. He did it because it was right.

To protest the Bitburg obscenity,[42] he visited concentration camps and since then he has spoken eloquently on the unique meaning of the Holocaust. He has repeatedly denounced the singling out of Israel for obloquy because of its trade with South Africa. He has consistently called for improved relations with the Jewish community, telling coalitional leaders that Blacks and Jews must play a key role in any joint effort to rebuild America's cities. Most significantly so, he has stood his ground against those in his own community who accuse him of selling out because of these things.

All of this and more was widely reported by the Black media. But it was scarcely mentioned in the Jewish or Israeli press. His many efforts to reach out to us were ignored and met with suspicion and silence. Justice demands otherwise. Let us therefore enter into today's dialogue openly, sensitively, and candidly. Let us not nurse our wounds and translate difference into a grievance. Let us not turn every controversy into combat, every disagreement into a bloodletting. Jews can't afford it. Blacks can't afford it. America and the world can't afford it. Only our common enemies, the enemies of freedom, rejoice when Blacks and Jews square off against each other.

We meet today on the very edge of a historic turning point—in Europe, in Israel, in America, in the world. At such a moment, we must look beyond the hurts and grievances to the desperate needs we share for *tikkun olam*, [Hebrew] for the repairing of our fractured world!

41. Mikhail Gorbachev (b. 1931), the Communist Party leader and premier of the Soviet Union from 1985 until 1991, pursued a policy of reform and oversaw the dissolution of the Soviet regime in 1991.

42. In May 1985, President Reagan's planned official visit to a cemetery in Bitburg, Germany, sparked a bitter outcry around the world when it was discovered that Nazi SS soldiers were buried there. Many people called on Reagan to cancel his trip because the Nuremburg Trials (1945–46) deemed the SS to be a criminal organization. Reagan attended the Bitburg ceremony nonetheless, but he added a visit to the Bergen-Belson concentration camp to his itinerary. See Richard J. Jensen, *Reagan at Bergen-Belsen and Bitburg* (College Station: Texas A&M University Press, 2007).

This above all, let us remember that our commonalities exceed our differences by far. For you see, the fear of common enemies does not mark the boundary of our necessary alliance. In addition to our common nightmares, we Blacks and Jews dream common dreams. We share a vision of a just and open and generous society. We agree that it is the foremost task of governments to protect the weak and the stranger, to achieve social and economic and political justice. We are both committed to the need for change, in our country, in the world. We see our common dream not in the valley of the status quo, but on Martin Luther King's mountain top.

It is with this understanding that we will listen to our speaker. He is an eloquent spokesman for our shared vision, a man who has done much to make it a reality. He is the most widely acknowledged leader of America's Black community, a staunch defender of his people's rights and dignity. But more, transcending race, he has earned the respect of millions of other Americans, as a leader of political, intellectual and moral power on the great and vexing issues of our time.

I present to you, the Reverend Jesse Jackson.

47

"TO SHIFT FROM THE CHILD TO THE FAMILY"

American Jews and the Challenge of Continuity (1988)

◇◇

BETH COUSENS

Launched in 1895, the Jewish Federations' philanthropic efforts were initially focused on the human service needs of a growing immigrant population. By the mid-twentieth century, the Jewish Federations turned to the needs of the developing State of Israel and the global Jewish population in crisis. Support for Jewish education in this period remained a secondary or tertiary concern. In the latter decades of the century, however, as immigrant needs diminished and U.S.-Israel relations became robust, Jewish Federations increasingly spent fund-raising dollars on Jewish educational efforts aimed at learners of all ages in a variety of settings and using mixed pedagogies.[1] Combating the perceived threat of Jewish assimilation and sustaining "Jewish continuity" emerged as key issues in a continent-wide discussion about the quality of American Jewishness.[2] By the late 1980s, Jewish Federation leaders and other makers of Jewish communal policy were ready to take concrete action to privilege and expand Jewish education as a strategy to support and build up Jewish life.

In the late 1980s, the Jewish Community Federation of Cleveland initiated a plan to focus on Jewish education and its potential to strengthen Jewish identity. Fueled in large part by the successful businessman and philanthropist Morton L. Mandel (1921–2019) and the Cleveland-based Mandel Foundation, this local work reflected broader conversations and interventions occurring across the country.[3] Though the agenda taken up by Cleveland's Commission on Jew-

1. Some examples of innovative Jewish educational undertakings that emerged in the latter decades of the twentieth century, supported by the private philanthropic sector in partnership with Jewish Federations, are Birthright Israel, PJ Library, Jewish Student Connection, Moishe House, Interfaith Family, OneTable, and Honeymoon Israel.

2. Jonathan Rosen, "Abraham's Drifting Children," March 30, 1997, *New York Times Book Review*, 7.

3. See Jack Wertheimer, "Jewish Education in the United States: Recent Trends and Issues," *American Jewish Year Book* 99 (1999), 3–115; Jonathan Woocher and Meredith Woocher,

ish Continuity was not new, the way the organization conducted its work and the strategy that work yielded were novel and innovative. First, the Jewish Federation broke new ground by convening the commission jointly with synagogue leaders. In fact, Cleveland's relatively high synagogue affiliation rate (an estimated 75–80 percent of Jewish households were affiliated with a synagogue) made the synagogues a natural focus of the commission's work.[4] Second, the commission determined that the Jewish educational landscape needed to be expanded beyond synagogue schools and updated to include a broad spectrum of children and families. To this end, the commission organized conversations about the need for new educators, settings, and initiatives; ideas for parent and family education; and organized activity "beyond the classroom."

The Cleveland commission garnered widespread attention and acclaim. So-called continuity commissions were created by other Jewish Federations, leading to new family engagement initiatives, the expansion of financial incentive programs for Israel youth experiences,[5] investments in professional development for teen educators, new experiential and immersive programs, and more. As the landscape of Jewish Federation activity became more complex, so did Jewish educational planning—with the lay process, Jewish Federations' philanthropic work, and professional staffing all becoming more intertwined and robust. In sum, the document reprinted here illustrates the pathfinding work of the Jewish Community Federation of Cleveland as well as a paradigm shift in the American Jewish scene writ large.

◇◇

―――――

"Jewish Education in the Twenty-First Century: An Ecosystem in Transition," *American Jewish Year Book* 113 (2013), 3–57.

4. Statistics for Cleveland's Jewish population in the 1980s are varied. A 1987 population survey indicated a steady decline in the community's overall size since the 1950s to a low of 65,000, but a 1996 survey estimated the population was 81,500. In general, it appears that despite the general contraction of Rust Belt Jewish communities since midcentury, Cleveland's Jewish population remained robust. Recent studies suggest that 81,500 Jews live in the metropolitan Cleveland area, and 61.5 percent of them (compared to a national average of 46.0 percent) belong to synagogues. See "2004 Jewish Cleveland—A Demographic Profile of Our Community Survey," Berman Jewish Databank, https://www.jewishdatabank.org/databank/search-results/study/403.

5. Among the many incentive programs created by Jewish Federations across the country, Cleveland's Israel Incentive Savings Plan served as an important model. See note 21.

Report of the Joint Federation and Congregational Plenum Commission on Jewish Continuity, Jewish Community Federation of Cleveland,[6] December 1988

Source: Report of the Joint Federation/Congregational Plenum Commission on Jewish Continuity, Jewish Community Federation of Cleveland (December 1988), Jack, Joseph and Morton Mandel Foundation Records, MS-831, Series B. Commission on Jewish Education in North America, 1980–1993, the Jacob Rader Marcus Center of the American Jewish Archives, Cincinnati.

December 1988

Dear Rabbi Silver[7] and Milt,[8]

It is with great honor and pride that we are able to submit to you the report of the Joint Federation/Plenum Commission on Jewish Continuity. The report [is the] culminat[ion of] three years of intensive work. Its recommendations are the most comprehensive attempt by a North American Jewish community to confront the challenges of ensuring Jewish continuity. The report also represents a significant evolution in the partnership between Federation and the synagogues, a partnership which strengthens Jewish communal life in Cleveland to a very great extent.

In the late 1980's we are 40 years from the transforming events of Jewish life in the twentieth century—the Holocaust and the rebirth of the State of Israel.[9] And these events, for our children and grandchildren, do not and cannot evoke the same powerful emotions of horror, wonder, and awe as they do for those who experienced these historic times. For many, the Holocaust is already as distant as the exodus from Egypt,[10] and Israel is one of over 150 nations in the

---

6. Established in 1903 as the Federation for Jewish Charities, the Jewish Community Federation of Cleveland (today called the Jewish Federation of Cleveland) is the central policy-making and fund-raising agency of the Cleveland Jewish community. On the history of the Jewish Federation system in the United States, see chapter 33, note 3.

7. Daniel Jeremy Silver (1928–1989) succeeded his father, Abba Hillel Silver (1893–1963; see chapter 25, note 34, and chapter 31, note 10), a distinguished American Jewish communal and Zionist leader, as senior rabbi of Cleveland's flagship Reform congregation, the Temple-Tifereth Israel.

8. Milton A. Wolf (1924–2005), a successful Cleveland real estate developer and Jewish communal leader, served as U.S. ambassador to Austria (1977–80) under President Jimmy Carter (b. 1924).

9. The duration of the Holocaust corresponds to the rise and fall of Nazi Germany (1933–45). The creation of the State of Israel was proclaimed on May 14, 1948.

10. The exodus of the Israelites from ancient Egypt is presumed to have occurred in the thirteenth century BCE.

United Nations, two-thirds of which have been created since 1948. We can no longer count on those transforming events to ensure Jewish continuity.

As we wrestle with this challenge, we are reminded of the situation facing Moses as his life drew to a close. He knew that he had to establish structures to support continuity as the Jewish people became more distant from the Exodus from Egypt and the revelation at Sinai.[11] That is why, on his last day, he involved his community in a commemorative event using drama, song, poetry, and teaching. His closing exhortation was "Take to heart all the words which I have warned you this day. Enjoin them upon your children, that they may observe faithfully all the terms of this Torah. For it is not a trifling thing for you: It is your very life; through it you shall long endure . . ." [Deut. 32:44–47].

So our challenge today, similar to that faced by Moses, is to bring to life for a new generation the lessons and inspirations of our past and a fervent hope for our future. The challenge is not an easy one. Our children and grandchildren do not have many of the reinforcements that supported the building of our own Jewish identities—neighborhoods with the sights, sounds, and smells of an enriched Jewish lifestyle; an older generation with first-hand memories of European Jewish culture before the Holocaust;[12] or the thrill of the creation of the State of Israel. The Jewish community turned to Jewish schools[13] to inculcate in its children what was traditionally absorbed simply by living in a Jewish household in a Jewish neighborhood. After several decades of unrealistic expectations of our schools, we now know that this approach alone cannot work. . . .

Our approach to Jewish education must change. Of course, we must bolster formal classroom learning. However, in order to survive as a people, the focus of Jewish education needs to shift from the child to the family, because our families must learn to make a Jewish home and raise a Jewish child. This challenge is all the more complex because so many singles, childless couples, and single parents have replaced traditional family units. . . . We must integrate proven "be-

---

11. According to the Hebrew Bible, the patriarch Moses, whom God did not permit to enter the Promised Land, was allowed to view it from the top of Mount Nebo before dying (Deut. 32: 48–52 and 34:4–5). The biblical narrative also relates that the Israelites camped at Mount Nebo, east of the Jordan River and opposite Jericho, during the last stage of the journey to the Land of Israel (Num. 33:47).

12. Nearly three million eastern European Jews immigrated to the United States between 1880 and 1924. Over time, this largely Yiddish-speaking generation left an indelible imprint on American Jewish life and culture and reshaped the American Jewish scene.

13. The reference is to Jewish religious schools and supplementary educational programs maintained by synagogues.

yond the classroom" education programs[14] into each child's Jewish education experience. We must enhance the ability of our day schools[15] to provide intensive Jewish educational experiences. And we must do these things now, before we raise a generation that knows neither Israel, the *Shabbat*, nor any compelling reason to be Jewish.

We had tremendous help in our task from dedicated volunteer and professional leaders.... The programs outlined in this report can have a transforming effect on the entire Jewish education system throughout Cleveland, and over time should touch virtually every family in our community.

Sincerely, Charles Ratner[16] and James Reich,[17] Co-Chairmen

MAJOR RECOMMENDATIONS

A. Cleveland Fellows: The College of Jewish Studies[18] will develop a graduate program in Jewish education for students from Cleveland and elsewhere....

B. Fellows Graduate Positions: The graduates of the Cleveland Fellows program will be hired to fill many of the new positions in new areas mandated by the Commission on Jewish Continuity.

C. In-Service Education Package: The Bureau of Jewish Education[19] and College of Jewish Studies will develop a program of individualized professional growth and in-service education to guide teachers already working throughout the community....

14. This phrase refers to experimental and experiential learning outside of a conventional classroom.

15. "Day schools" are full-time private Jewish (parochial) schools that include religious instruction.

16. Charles A. Ratner (b. 1941)—former president and CEO of Forest City Enterprises, a family-owned real estate company with properties in nineteen states and the District of Columbia—is a Cleveland business and Jewish communal leader.

17. James M. Reich (1922–2010), a Cleveland Jewish communal leader and manufacturer of household cleaning products, was active in midwestern Jewish affairs.

18. Established in 1947, the Cleveland College of Jewish Studies (formerly the Cleveland Institute of Jewish Studies) traced its origins to the Jewish Teachers Institute and the Beth Midrash L'Morim (Hebrew Teacher Training School), both of which were created in the 1920s. In 2001, the college was renamed the Laura and Alvin Siegal College of Judaic Studies. In 2012, it was absorbed into Case Western Reserve University and became the Siegal Lifelong Learning Program.

19. Such a bureau is a feature of most organized American Jewish communities. Bureaus of Jewish education typically support local Jewish religious and supplementary schools, maintain curricular resources, and provide professional development for teachers.

D. Communal Day Schools: ... the community will implement a four year plan to address ... critical salary gaps.

E. Community Teachers: The Bureau of Jewish Education will create five full-time Community Teacher positions. ...

F. Retreat Institute: This program, to be housed at the [Jewish community center],[20] will work with schools, youth groups, and others to develop retreat programs. ...

G. IISP: The Israel Incentive Savings Plan[21] attracts 100 new enrollments each year. ... The community will now approach recruitment differently. ... This should dramatically increase the number of Cleveland youth who will have an Israel experience.

H. Curriculum Renewal: ... Project Curriculum Renewal[22] should be expanded to work with each school on this critical concern.

I. Community Youth Resource Office: This program ... provides valuable communal supports to youth groups for programming, outreach strategies, and advisor training and placement. ...

J. Congregational Enrichment Fund Expansion:[23] This fund has enabled the congregations to develop important new programs in recent years in the areas of parent and family education and "beyond the classroom" education. ... An expansion of funds is now recommended to enable congregations to increase programming.

20. The local Jewish community center, a central institution in American Jewish life, celebrates Jewish arts and culture; offers classes for children, adults, and families; provides facilities for recreation, physical exercise, and summer camp; and generally serves as a nondenominational framework for Jews from all walks of life.

21. This refers to a savings program sponsored by the Jewish Federation that was created specifically to support and incentivize trips to Israel (through matching funds) for Jewish teens and young adults.

22. This refers to a project designed to support and strengthen the educational agenda of local Jewish religious and supplementary schools.

23. This refers to a pool of funds centrally managed by the Jewish Federation and awarded to synagogues in the form of special grants focused on new educational initiatives.

"THE WORLD IS NOT THE SAME SINCE AUSCHWITZ AND HIROSHIMA"

Kathy (Schwartz) Cohen's Reflections on *Tisha Beav* (1988)

◇◇◇

MINA MURAOKA

Since the end of World War II, American Jews have associated the Holocaust with the bombing of the Japanese city of Hiroshima on August 6, 1945 (the United States dropped a second atomic bomb on the southern city of Nagasaki three days later). Linked by their shared wartime context, these tragedies, albeit unique and distinct, represent the sum total of the harm that war and technology can inflict on innocent victims. In both cases, the vast majority of those killed were not military personnel but civilians. Indeed, many survivors underscored the twin relationship between Hiroshima and Auschwitz as symbols of cruel mass murders.[1] Both events, survivors argued, fundamentally changed the course of human history and raised existential questions for future generations.

Over time, the American Jewish response to Hiroshima has also, at least in part, been conflated with the religious holiday of Tisha Beav (Ninth of Av). The latter occurs in July or August according to the secular calendar and is proximate to the anniversary of the Hiroshima bombing. Thus, in addition to mourning the destruction of the First and Second Temples in Jerusalem,[2] many Ameri-

---

1. In the postwar decades, peace activists strove to accentuate the relationship between Auschwitz and Hiroshima. In 1963, for example, a group of Japanese youths marched from Hiroshima to Auschwitz and claimed that "we Japanese, as both aggressors and victims of the war, should have a special duty in calling for world peace" ("Hiroshima-Auschwitz Heiwa Koshin," *Newsletter No.1*, Hiroshima Peace Memorial Museum Archive, Kawamoto Collection, box 38, folder 1, No. 911, quoted in Ran Zwigenberg, "The Hiroshima-Auschwitz Peace March and the Globalization of the 'Moral Witness,'" *Dapim* 27, no. 3 [2013], 196). Similarly, the German-born Jewish journalist and political activist Robert Jungk (1913–1994) published several books about the atomic bomb, including *Children of the Ashes: The Story of Rebirth* (New York: Harcourt, Brace and World, 1961).

2. On the Temple in ancient Jerusalem, see chapter 6, note 6.

can Jews have come to associate the traditional themes of destruction, burning, and desecration with the tragedy of Hiroshima. Some synagogues and Jewish communities commemorate the dropping of the atomic bomb on Hiroshima in their annual Tisha Beav observances.

American Jews were not always empathetic about Japan's fate in World War II. Like other Americans in the immediate postwar years, Jews celebrated the U.S. victory and were proud of their contribution to the war effort.[3] Isidor Kaufman's two-volume *American Jews in World War II* (1947), for example, sought to provide a comprehensive list of all American Jews who fought in the U.S. military during the war. And the American Jewish press went to great lengths to highlight the contributions of Jewish scientists to the development of the atomic bomb and celebrated the Jewish war veterans who had participated in the Hiroshima bombing.[4]

The 1988 document reprinted here illustrates the trajectory of American Jewish interest in the legacy of Hiroshima and the extent to which the lessons of this tragic event became incorporated into the contemporary American Jewish understanding of world affairs. Set against the backdrop of the Cold War; the 1986 disaster at the nuclear plant in Chernobyl, Ukraine; and the 1988 presidential contest between Republican George H. W. Bush (1924–2018) and Democrat Michael Dukakis (b. 1933), the document highlights the place of anti-nuclear and pacifist sentiment in the Jewish public arena. It also demonstrates how American rabbis framed the memorialization of the Holocaust and Hiroshima in relation to Jewish theology and practice.[5] In a word, the document highlights a variety of complex issues, including the tensions between the former Soviet Union and the United States, the debate over arms control and national security issues, and the nexus between religious values and the organized American Jewish community's political agenda.

◇◇

3. "Invented Device for Bomb Test: Harry Gewertz Proud of His Contribution to Atomic Bomb," *Jewish Exponent*, August 10, 1945, 10.

4. See Meron Medzini, "Jewish Scientists, Jewish Ethics, and the Making of the Atomic Bomb," in *War and Militarism in Modern Japan: Issues of History and Identity*, ed. Guy Podoler (Folkestone, UK: Global Oriental, 2009), 120–28.

5. See, for example, "Ohabei Shalom Observes Tisha B'Av and Hiroshima," *Jewish Advocate*, July 26, 1984, 5; Robert Israel, "Linking Hiroshima, Holocaust Survivors," *Jewish Advocate*, August 13, 1987, 5; "At Hiroshima Day Commemoration," *Jewish Exponent*, August 16, 1985, 5; Mark N. Goldman, "Thoughts from the Rabbi," *American Israelite*, August 17, 1995, A2.

Kathy (Schwartz) Cohen, "Thoughts from the Rabbi," *American Israelite,* August 4, 1988

Source: Kathy Schwartz, "Thoughts from the Rabbi," *American Israelite*, August 4, 1988, 2. Reprinted by permission of Kathy (Schwartz) Cohen.

Our prayer book instructs: "The world is not the same since Auschwitz and Hiroshima. The decisions we make, the values we teach, must be pondered not only in the halls of learning, but also before the inmates of extermination camps, and in the sight of the mushroom of a nuclear explosion."[6]

Last week, on Tisha Beav, we commemorated the destruction of the First and Second Temples, the fall of Bar Kochba's last post[,] Betar,[7] the edict expelling all Jews from England in 1290[8] and the same in Spain in 1492.[9] Our long historical memory obligates us to recall the grief and despair which has befallen our people as well as the joy and exultation that we have known from time to time. During these weeks we reflect not only on the crucible of suffering through which much of our national personality has been forged, but also on the terror and fear that the world has come to know since that fateful August 6, 1945[,] in Hiroshima, Japan.

The mind is boggled by our own achievements in the field of self-destruction. Each year the military powers of the world sink billions of dollars into refining and perfecting this terribly modern science. We have raised a generation of children who are acutely aware that tomorrow may never be. Our experts tell us that we have the capacity to destroy the Soviet Union thirty times over; they [the Soviets,] of course, are capable of inflicting equivalent destruction on us. There comes a time, (and if not now, on the 43rd anniversary of the Hiroshima bomb, when?) when we must ask ourselves, "Have we gone mad?" Are we incapable of

6. See *Gates of Prayer: The New Union Prayerbook*, ed. Chaim Stern (New York: Central Conference of American Rabbis Press, 1975), 251. Stern (1930–2001), raised in an Orthodox Jewish household, gravitated to liberalism after the Holocaust and was ordained in 1958 by the Hebrew Union College–Jewish Institute of Religion.

7. In 132–35 CE, Simon ben Kosevah (Bar Kokhba) led the Jewish revolt in ancient Palestine against the Roman empire. He was martyred in the fall of Betar, the last Jewish fortress to be vanquished by the imperial Roman campaign.

8. King Edward I (1239–1307) banished the Jews from England in 1290. The expulsion decree remained in effect until 1657, when the Lord Protector Oliver Cromwell (1599–1658) permitted Jews to return.

9. The Alhambra Decree (1492) of the Spanish monarchs Isabella I of Castile (1451–1504) and Ferdinand II of Aragon (1452–1516) resulted in the conversion of some 200,000 Jews to Catholicism who sought to avoid persecution, as well as the expulsion of as many as 100,000 Jews from the Spanish kingdom.

bridling our own destructive forces? While our politicians negotiate, we awake each morning to the possibility that this day the human race will obliterate itself. A nuclear freeze will not save us nor will a slow reduction in arms guarantee our children a future. It is time that we elect leaders who are dedicated to ending this insanity of four decades. If we care about the sun rising over us tomorrow, we cannot be apathetic to the burning issue of today.

No, the world is not the same since Auschwitz and Hiroshima. With the observance of Tisha Beav fresh in our minds and the anniversary (this Sabbath)— of the bomb falling on Hiroshima, we say "*yitgadal veyitkadash shmei rabah*" (May God's great name be sanctified and exalted).[10] Let us learn how to sanctify and exalt God's name by preserving God's creation for all future generations.

10. This Aramaic phrase is drawn from the mourner's kaddish, a prayer recited in memory of the dead that is a central element of traditional Jewish liturgy.

49

"TO COMBAT HOMOPHOBIA"

Jewish Activist Gays and Lesbians
(1994)

◇◇◇

JONATHAN B. KRASNER

Few American social movements have been as successful as the modern gay rights movement in achieving a rapid change in public perceptions. According to the Pew Research Center, support for same-sex marriage jumped twenty-six percentage points (from 35 percent to 61 percent) between 2001 and 2019. A similar transformation is demonstrable in Americans' attitudes toward the acceptance of homosexuality. American Jews are even more accepting of homosexuality and same-sex marriage than the U.S. population as a whole, which is consistent with findings that American Jews as a group are more liberal on political and social issues than the general American public. Since 2012, only Orthodox Jews have refused to ordain openly gay or lesbian rabbis and sanctify same-sex religious marriages.

In the early 1990s, however, the situation on the ground was significantly different. Homosexuality was depathologized by the American Psychiatric Association in 1973, and gay men and lesbians became more visible in U.S. society in the 1980s as a result of the AIDS crisis. But most Americans continued to stigmatize homosexuality as a deviant lifestyle rather than an orientation. Gay men were accused of "recruiting" children and having a proclivity for pedophilia by right-wing religious activists, most notoriously in the late 1970s Save Our Children campaign of the singer Anita Bryant (b. 1940). Discrimination was widespread, and the U.S. Supreme Court upheld the constitutionality of state antisodomy laws in *Bowers v. Hardwick* (1986)—a ruling that was overturned in 2003. Many lesbian, gay, bisexual, transgender, and queer (LGBTQ) people felt alienated from their religious communities, although some sought religious fellowship and spiritual refuge in a small number of welcoming congregations—including those affiliated with the Metropolitan Community Church (MCC), which had an outreach effort aimed at the gay community and gender-nonconforming people. The first synagogue founded for and by lesbian and gay Jews, Beth Chayim Chadashim, in Los Angeles, emerged in 1972 from the MCC, when its founding reverend, Troy Perry, encouraged a group of Jewish church members to found their own temple. By the 1980s, there were similar congregations in other North American Jewish population centers, including in New York (established in 1973), Miami (1974), Philadelphia (1975), Chicago (1976), Boston (1976), San Francisco (1977), and Toronto (1978). In addition, in 1976 an International Conference of Gay and Lesbian Jews was held.

By the early 1990s, an increasing number of liberal Jewish congregations without a specific mission to serve the gay community were changing their policies and becoming open to and welcoming of lesbian and gay congregants. Nevertheless, when the Reform movement's Central Conference of American Rabbis voted to ordain openly gay and lesbian clergy in 1990—five years after the Reconstructionist Rabbinical College ordained its first openly homosexual student—the largest Jewish movement joined a very small group of liberal religious denominations that ordained gays and lesbians, including the United Church of Christ (starting in 1970), the MCC (1972), and the Unitarian Universalist Association (1979). At that time, none of the major religious denominations officially endorsed their clergy's solemnizing same-sex marriages. Indeed, the Conservative movement's Committee on Jewish Law and Standards voted overwhelmingly in 1992 to reject gay ordination and reaffirm traditional Jewish law's proscription of homosexual behavior.[1] One responsum, by Rabbi Joel Roth (b. 1940), which was approved by a vote of fourteen votes in favor, seven against, and three abstentions, counseled celibacy for the homosexual who could not change their sexual orientation through psychotherapy. A year later, the United States as a whole was embroiled in a debate about lesbians and gay men serving in the U.S. military, which culminated in the promulgation of the "don't ask, don't tell" Defense Department directive that barred military service by openly gay and lesbian people—while directing military personnel not to harass or discriminate against closeted homosexuals.

These events provided the backdrop and context for the emergence of Jewish Activist Gays and Lesbians (JAGL), one of the earliest organizations to advocate for the acceptance of gays, lesbians, and bisexuals within the Jewish community. (The inclusion of transgender rights under a wider queer liberation umbrella would come only in the 2000s.) JAGL emerged from a *Tikkun Magazine* youth conference in January 1993 but largely cohered a few months later, when activists organized a street protest at New York City's annual Salute to Israel Parade.[2] Under pressure from Orthodox Jewish organizations and schools, the American

1. See note 11.
2. See note 6.

Zionist Youth Foundation (which organized the parade) barred the participation of Congregation Beit Simchat Torah, the city's gay and lesbian synagogue.[3] There was a generational divide between JAGL protesters and the synagogue members, who chose to hold an Israel-themed celebration at a different venue. The university students and other young adults who were attracted to JAGL gravitated to confrontational tactics honed by AIDS activists in the 1980s — most prominently the members of the AIDS Coalition to Unleash Power (ACT UP), founded in 1987. Yet because they still craved recognition and acceptance from the larger Jewish population, they wanted to march in the parade — the largest annual Jewish communal celebration in the New York metropolitan area. Many of these young people were products of Jewish camps, day schools, and youth groups and rejected the proposition that their sexual orientation and religious identities were irreconcilably opposed. Marching under a gay banner at the parade or protesting its antigay exclusionary policy from the sidelines was a highly public performance of their gay Jewish identities and, for many, a form of coming out.

After the parade protest, JAGL went on to advocate for and provide education about lesbian, gay, and bisexual acceptance at synagogues; camps; and the Conservative movement's Jewish Theological Seminary, where students were reeling in the wake of the 1992 Committee on Jewish Law and Standards vote. The following document, an early funding request that JAGL leaders submitted to the Shefa Fund,[4] discusses the group's formation and aspirations. Although JAGL eventually disintegrated, it influenced the establishment of enduring Jewish LGBTQ groups, including Keshet, a grassroots and advocacy organization, as well as Eshel, the Gay and Lesbian Yeshiva Day School Alumni Association, and Jewish Queer Youth — all of which support LGBTQ individuals and families from Orthodox and traditional backgrounds.

◇◇◇

Description and Budget of Jewish Activist Gays and Lesbians, April 6, 1994

Source: Letter from Jonathan Springer to Betsy Tessler, including a description of Jewish Activist Gays and Lesbians (April 6, 1994), Jewish Activist Gays and Lesbians, SC-17375, the Jacob Rader Marcus Center of the American Jewish Archives, Cincinnati.

Jewish Activist Gays and Lesbians (JAGL) seeks to combat homophobia in American Jewish communities — whether institutional or individual — through

3. See note 8.
4. See note 18.

political, educational, and social activity. Our founders met at a *Tikkun Magazine*-sponsored[5] youth conference in early 1993, and we have grown in numbers ever since. Our membership consists of gay/lesbian/bisexual New York Jews in our twenties and thirties who are college students, graduate students, and working people.

Our first major activity was a demonstration at the 1993 New York City Israel Day Parade,[6] protesting exclusion of Congregation Beit Simchat Torah (CBST), New York's gay/lesbian synagogue.[7] CBST decided to hold its own celebration rather than insist upon incorporation in the parade.[8] While this may have been appropriate for CBST, we felt the larger gay/lesbian community could not allow the parade organizers' bigotry to go unprotested. We therefore organized a protest along the parade route with "Gay, Jewish, and Proud" banners. The large numbers of people who joined our protest proved to us that we were filling a much needed role by organizing a demonstration against homophobia in Jewish organizations. And the large amount of media coverage we re-

5. Founded in 1986 by Michael Lerner (b. 1943) and Nan Fink Gefen (b. 1940), *Tikkun* is a progressive Jewish magazine that features articles and reviews about politics, culture, religion, and history, as well as poetry and short fiction.

6. The Salute to Israel Parade (renamed the Celebrate Israel Parade in 2011), an annual public event in support of the State of Israel, is held in the late spring in proximity to Israel Independence Day. Created in 1965 by Haim Zohar (1944–2004), the Israeli consul in New York, in conjunction with the American Zionist Youth Foundation and the Jewish Education Committee of Greater New York, the parade stretches from midtown Manhattan to the Upper East Side. It regularly attracts tens of thousands of participants and spectators.

7. CBST, the second oldest gay and lesbian synagogue in the United States, emerged in 1973 out of a community Passover seder organized by Jacob Gubbay (d. 2018), an East Indian Jewish immigrant. By 1975, the congregation's weekly Friday night services were attracting over a hundred people, and the following year it moved to Greenwich Village. In 1992, amid the AIDS crisis, the congregation hired its first full-time rabbi, Sharon Kleinbaum (b. 1959). By the mid-1990s, CBST was attracting over two thousand worshippers to its High Holiday services. In 2016, the synagogue moved into a new building in Manhattan's Chelsea district.

8. In 1993, CBST applied to participate in the Salute to Israel Parade. Boycott threats from New York's substantial Orthodox community led to protracted negotiations between CBST and the American Zionist Youth Foundation, resulting in a compromise that allowed CBST to march with the Association of Reform Zionists of America as long as its banner did not identify the group as gay and lesbian. However, the invitation to CBST was rescinded on the eve of the parade, after news of the compromise was published in the *New York Times*. See Alex Witchel, "At Work with Sharon Kleinbaum: 'Luckiest Rabbi in America' Holds Faith Amidst the Hate," *New York Times*, May 5, 1993, C1; Alan Finder, "Another Parade Furor: Salute to Israel Uninvites Gay Group," *New York Times*, May 8, 1993, A23. In response, the synagogue's leaders decided to hold an alternative Israel-themed celebration, with Reform movement cosponsorship, at the Central Synagogue in Manhattan.

ceived helped to ensure that the parade planners will no longer risk the negative publicity that arises from exclusion of gays/lesbians from the parade. (In 1994, CBST is allowed to march.[9])

We have also sought to counteract homophobia through educational programs for high school youth. We have conducted two workshops for a total of over 250 members of the North American Federation of Temple Youth, the youth arm of the Reform movement.[10] These workshops consisted of panel discussions on "coming out" and small group discussions on stereotyping. They have been well received, judging from written feedback and from the fact that we have been asked back for more.

In the past few months, we have expanded the focus of our educational activity to include adults. Recently we have begun to target the Conservative movement because we believe it sets an intolerant tone for a large portion of the organized Jewish community.[11] We therefore collaborated with several rabbinic students at the movement's Jewish Theological Seminary (JTS) who helped us to conduct a workshop for the first two years of rabbinic students during class time, under the sponsorship of the student government.[12] The purpose of the workshop was to take the discussion of sexual orientation out of the realm of the halakhic [and] into the realm of the personal by introducing future rabbis to gay and lesbian individuals and asking them to consider our needs as congregants. This seminar was well received . . . and another one was soon held upon request of students in the fifth-year rabbinical class.

9. In fact, after 1993, CBST members were allowed to march in the Salute to Israel Parade only as part of a larger contingent and without an identifying banner. The first identifiably LGBT group to march in the parade was Jewish Queer Youth, an organization of Orthodox LGBT youth, in 2012.

10. The North American Federation of Temple Youth (originally the National Federation of Temple Youth), the Reform movement's youth organization, was founded in 1939.

11. On March 25, 1992, the Rabbinical Assembly's Committee on Jewish Law and Standards, the Conservative movement's advisory body on Jewish legal issues, voted (with nineteen in favor, three against, and one abstention) not to perform same-sex marriages or union ceremonies and not to admit openly gay or lesbian individuals to the movement's rabbinical seminaries. The committee also authorized local rabbis to decide whether gays and lesbians could serve as lay leaders or youth leaders and receive synagogue honors. At the same time, it affirmed that gays and lesbians are welcome in Conservative movement institutions, such as synagogues, camps, youth groups, and schools. On Conservative Judaism, see chapter 43, note 31.

12. Lesbian and gay students at JTS formed an underground organization known as the Incognito Club. A larger group of student allies, who called themselves the Friends of the Incognito Club, organized educational activities for the community—some in cooperation with JAGL—and tried to pressure Conservative leaders to reverse the movement's opposition to gay ordination and same-sex union ceremonies by galvanizing public opinion.

In the future, we would like to expand our activity to reach a larger audience, and to actively involve more gays and lesbians. Our priorities for the future are educational, political, and social, as follows:

* Educational: We plan to build upon the success of our seminars at JTS to influence the Conservative movement as a whole. Our first step will be to conduct a seminar at the upcoming national convention of the Rabbinical Assembly (RA), the union of Conservative rabbis.[13] To be held in the Catskills on May 3, 1994, the workshop will consist of a panel featuring gays/lesbians, as well as a parent (who happens to be a member of the RA). The panel—the first time gays and lesbians will speak openly at an RA function—will address the experiences of gays/lesbians in the Conservative movement and our practical needs as synagogue members. We also seek to operate a booth that will provide information on gay/lesbian issues to RA members. Although we have raised funds to pay for this booth, RA leadership has thus far refused to allow our participation, claiming that "advocacy" booths are not allowed. We are currently in the midst of negotiations with the RA, and have enlisted gay/lesbian-friendly RA members for help in this regard. Through the workshop and booth, we seek to create a visible gay/lesbian presence at the convention. It is our hope that this presence—like the presence of lay women at similar conventions in the last decade which ultimately led to the ordination of women—will similarly pave the way toward the eventual ordination of gays and lesbians.

   During the coming year we will also expand our educational work with youth both because this activity has been seen to have a great impact on participants and because it is an effective means of attracting new members to JAGL. We will conduct seminars at youth group events during the school year and at camps during the summer. Whereas in the past we have been approached with requests, in the future we intend to advertise our availability in order to generate more interest and create further demand for our programs. Contacts have already been made with Young Judaea[14] camps and the Reform movement.

13. Originally created in 1901 as the Jewish Theological Seminary of America's alumni association, the RA—as it came be known in 1918—sought to attract Conservative-affiliated rabbis ordained at other seminaries. The RA's law committee, a predecessor to the current Committee on Jewish Law and Standards, was established in 1927.

14. Founded in 1909, Young Judaea is a countrywide pluralistic and nonpartisan Zionist youth

An additional component of our educational work will consist of outreach to adult leadership in Jewish organizations, both religious and secular. We will seek to create and conduct workshops for brotherhoods/ sisterhoods, Hadassah, and other such membership organizations. In these cases, our aim will be to reach individuals who are in positions to make policies and set tones that will encourage the acceptance of gays and lesbians in Jewish organizations. This will involve research of organizations, cultivation of contacts, and development of promotional material.

* Political: As in the past, our political activity will continue to be geared toward securing equal rights and treatment for gays and lesbians in the Jewish community. Much of our political activity will be project-based: it will anticipate and respond to particular events. For instance, we plan to publicize the fact that New York's gay/lesbian synagogue is being allowed to march in this year's Israel Day Parade and to generate public support from other New York synagogues. We also hope to take part as an organization in the events of Stonewall 25[15] — an international celebration of gay/lesbian rights in June 1994. Further activities will include direct action as necessary to combat homophobia. This could involve staging same-sex "kiss-in's"[16] or Israeli dancing at institutions that are unwelcoming of gays/lesbians, or launching a coordinated letter-writing campaign in response to homophobia in the Jewish media.

* Social: Social events have been an important component of JAGL activity during the past year. We have held Purim[17] and Hanukkah parties, and have taught Israeli dancing at a Columbia University gay/ lesbian carnival. We intend to increase our social activities in the future, possibly adding outdoor picnics and/or outings during the summer. We feel such events are important not only to attract new members, but also

---

group. From 1967 to 2012, it was sponsored by the Hadassah Women's Zionist Organization, the largest Jewish volunteer organization in North America (see chapter 31, note 19).

15. Stonewall 25 was a march and rally in New York City on June 26, 1994, to commemorate the twenty-fifth anniversary of the 1969 Stonewall uprising and riots, the catalyst for the North American and international gay rights movement.

16. The "kiss-in" was a tactic that JAGL adopted from ACT UP, a grassroots political action organization founded in 1987 to advocate on behalf of AIDS patients.

17. The Jewish holiday of Purim (Festival of Lots) is celebrated on the fourteenth day of the Hebrew month Adar to commemorate the saving of the Jewish community of Persia from destruction, as recounted in the Book of Esther (c. fourth century BCE).

to create a true community of people who enjoy working together to realize gay/lesbian rights in the Jewish community.

Funds are requested from the Shefa Fund[18] to support JAGL's ongoing operating expenses during the upcoming year, as detailed below:

Program (includes materials for education and direct actions . . .)—$1,000
Printing & Photocopying—$1,000
Phone & Fax—$750
Postage—$750
Transportation—$1,000
Food—$500
Total: $5,000

Other funding sources:
Dobkin Family Fund,[19] for booth at RA convention—$400
Columbia University Lesbian Gay Bisexual Coalition, for materials at 1993 Israel Day Parade protest—Approx. $100

Organizational affiliations:
Alliance for Judaism and Social Justice[20]
Columbia University Lesbian Gay Bisexual Coalition

18. In 1988, the Philadelphia philanthropist Jeffrey Dekro (b. 1951) created the Shefa Fund to support progressive Jewish organizations and social causes. In 2006, it merged with the Jewish Fund for Justice. It is known today as Bend the Arc.

19. The Dobkin Family Foundation—initiated by Eric Dobkin (b. 1943), a partner at Goldman Sachs, and his wife, Barbara (b. 1943)—is a New York City–based philanthropy that supports feminist and progressive Jewish causes.

20. Active in the 1990s, the Alliance for Judaism and Social Justice was a New York City–based progressive activist network of mostly young adults.

50

"GLOBAL IDENTITY FREE OF PREJUDICES AND BOUNDARIES"

The Indian-American-Jewish Artist Siona Benjamin's
Tikkun Ha-Olam
(2000)

◇◇

An immigrant from Mumbai, India, to New York City, Siona Benjamin (b. 1960) describes herself as a "transcultural" and "Indian-American-Jewish" artist.[1] She earned an MFA in painting from Southern Illinois University Carbondale and an MFA in theater set design from the University of Illinois at Urbana-Champaign. She is the recipient of numerous awards, including two Fulbright Fellowships (in 2011 and 2016), and her work has been exhibited in the United States, Europe, and Asia and praised by art critics in the *New York Times, Chicago Tribune, Philadelphia Inquirer, Financial Times, Boston Globe, Art in America, Moment* magazine, *Times of India, Mumbai Mirror,* and other publications.

Benjamin's work and sensibility may be profitably compared to that of the iconic impressionist and cubist figures Marc Chagall (1887–1985), a Russian and French Jewish artist, and Amedeo Modigliani (1884–1920), an Italian and French Jewish painter and sculptor. Like Chagall and Modigliani before her, Benjamin employs a nonrealist mélange of colorful hues, surreal human shapes with elongated bodies, and a poetic sense of dreamy reverie to convey an elastic and capacious understanding of the modern Jewish experience. Benjamin's website includes the following statement in which she explains her cultural and religious identity as a Jewish woman of color:

> As a Bene Israel Jew from India now living in the United States, I am a Jewish artist creating cross cultural and transcultural art. My perspective bridges the traditional and the modern, and sparks discourse across cultures.
>
> My family gradually dispersed, mostly to Israel and America, but my parents remained in India. I still recall the ornate synagogues of my Bombay

---

1. Siona Benjamin, "Multicultural Art in a Multicultural World," The Art of Siona Benjamin, https://artsiona.com/.

childhood: the oil lamps, the velvet-and-silver-covered Torahs, a chair left vacant for the prophet Elijah. Having grown up in a Hindu and Muslim society, educated in Catholic and Zoroastrian schools, raised Jewish in India, and now calling America home, I have always had to reflect on cultural boundary zones.

So while I am a Jewish artist, my perspective remains transcultural and multicultural at heart. I combine the imagery of my past with the role I play in America today, making a mosaic inspired by illuminated manuscripts and multicultural mythology.

Many blue-skinned characters populate my paintings. This self-portrait of sorts takes on many roles through which I explore ancient and contemporary dilemmas. These characters enact their stories—often recycling myths from various cultures and religions—becoming symbols of a timeless global identity free of prejudices and boundaries.[2]

As demonstrated by "Exodus: I See Myself in You" (2016–18), Benjamin's art, informed by a profound self-awareness, illuminates her passion for what might be described as a uniquely poetic visual pathway to explore the human condition.[3] Her sketches and painting employ a wide array of themes and ideas, including the fluidity of identity, immigration, motherhood, the role of art in social change, "finding home," liberty and justice, and "why humans pursue and strive for perfection and paradise."[4] In a word, Benjamin's distinctive oeuvre synthesizes sacred and temporal elements, and in that synthesis she invites us to reimagine the symbolism and context of contemporary Jewish life.

Benjamin's "Tikkun Ha-Olam" (2000), reprinted here from her Finding Home series, reflects the influence of kabbalah and non-Jewish mystical themes in her art. Alluding to a cosmos filled with divine light and energy, the Hebrew phrase tikkun haolam ("repairing the world") centers on the kabbalistic notion of the world as a shattered vessel. According to Jewish mystical tradition, it is humanity's task to reconstruct the world through ethical, spiritual, intellectual, and aesthetic acts. Through the Finding Home series, Benjamin seeks to participate in the process of repairing the world.

---

2. Benjamin, "Meet Siona Benjamin," *The Art of Siona Benjamin*, https://artsiona.com/about-siona-benjamin/.

3. See Siona Benjamin, "Exodus: I See Myself in You," *The Art of Siona Benjamin*, https://artsiona.com/paintings/exodus/.

4. Quoted in Bridget Gleeson, "In Vibrant Gouache and Gold Leaf Paintings, a Jewish Indian Artists Explores Cultural Identity," *Artsy*, March 7, 2017, https://www.artsy.net/article/artsy-vibrant-gouache-gold-leaf-paintings-jewish-indian-artist-explores-cultural-identity.

Indian-American-Jewish Artist Siona Benjamin's *Tikkun Ha-Olam*, 2000. Source: Siona Benjamin, *Tikkun Ha-Olam* (2000). Reprinted by permission of Siona Benjamin.

The female figure in Benjamin's "Tikkun Ha-Olam" is a hybrid and a transcultural being with the body of a graceful Indian dancer, arms resembling a seven-branch menorah, and *hamsa* (palm-shaped amulets that offer protection) hands holding flames—a mix of Indian, Jewish, and Middle Eastern symbolism and references. The figure's blue skin signifies her hybrid nature as an ethereal being and a woman of color. Like the sky and ocean, she is seemingly limitless and borderless; she belongs everywhere and nowhere at the same time. The color blue also echoes traditional and contemporary Jewish aesthetics and attributes. For example, the Hebrew Bible requires that a blue strand be woven into the fringes of the *talit* (Num. 15:38); blue architectural adornments, decorative tile work, and interior and exterior walls are typical of Indian synagogues; and two blue horizontal stripes (reminiscent of the *talit*) and a Star of David make up the design of the Israeli flag.

The female image is literally and figuratively anchored by images of a snake (representing humanity's banishment from the Garden of Eden) and a golem-like creature that is part animal and part human, blowing a shofar (invoking the Jewish folklore of a clay figure brought to life by kabbalistic magic). While the serpent's knowledge and the golem's unbridled power hint at the perils of humanity's temporal existence and the chosen people's relationship to the divine, the central figure is perched on a lotus flower pedestal (an element typical in Asian spiritual iconography), thus centering the piece as a whole and betokening that which is immortal and divine in humanity and the concept of divine perfection.

The Marathi letters on the left side of the figure are an Indian transliteration of the Hebrew phrase tikkun haolam, and the phrase appears in Hebrew letters on the right side. Indian Jews living on India's west coast speak Marathi and are accustomed to having Hebrew prayers transliterated into Marathi. The nonbinary nature of the Marathi language, which includes masculine, feminine, and neutral forms, reinforces the multivalent nature of the artwork. Implicitly challenging Eurocentric and Ashkenazic preconceptions of Judaism and Jewish culture, the symmetry of Marathi and Hebrew testifies to the fact that Jews from non-Western ethnic backgrounds and cultures speak many languages other than Yiddish and English.

In sum, the lively mix of colors, symbols, and linguistic cues visible in Benjamin's "Tikkun Ha-Olam" draws on the many dimensions of her upbringing, identity, and cultural inheritance. Reflecting her proud identity as an Indian-American Jewish artist and a woman of color, the work serves as a vehicle to engage a broad array of viewers—Jews and non-Jews alike—and to complicate contemporary understandings of Jews and enrich our appreciation for the diversity of modern Jewish life.

—EDS.

51

"TAKING THIS PROHIBITED ACT AND USING IT TO FEEL MORE JEWISH"

American Jews and Tattoos
(2000-2020)

◇◇◇

Changing American Jewish Perceptions of Tattoos and Body Art, 2000-2020

> Source: Photograph of *zakhor* tattoo (2014) by Mark Randall, reprinted by permission of *South Florida Sun Sentinel*/TCA. Photograph of Star of David tattoo (2015) courtesy of Gail Rubin, CT.

Until recent decades, tattoos and body art were largely unheard of in mainstream American Jewish life. For traditional Jews, the matter is settled by scripture. The biblical passage proscribing men from trimming the "side-growth" of their beard, giving rise to the traditional custom of wearing earlocks, also commands: "You shall not make gashes in your flesh for the dead, or incise any marks on yourselves" (Lev. 19:27–28). Of course, for non-Orthodox, liberal, and secular Jews, no such *halakhic* requirement is binding. Today, many young American Jews, not unlike a vast portion of the wider American population, proudly display tattoos and body art.[1] Indeed, according to a self-described nonpracticing Orthodox Jew, many Jews use tattoos "to express their Judaism, or connect with God or their Jewish roots. . . . They're taking this prohibited act and using it to feel more Jewish."[2]

This new sensibility represents a subtle but significant shift in the pattern

---

1. In 2010, the Pew Research Center found that roughly 38 percent of millennials and 32 percent of Gen Xers in the United States had at least one tattoo, to 15 percent of baby boomers. The study also noted that, "when asked if their tattoos are usually visible, the vast majority (72 percent) say that they are not." In addition, 23 percent of millennials indicated that they had "a piercing in a place other than an ear lobe" (Paul Taylor and Scott Keeter, eds., *Millennials: A Portrait of Generation Next* [Washington: Pew Research Center, 2010], 58, https://www.pewresearch.org/wp-content/uploads/sites/3/2010/10/millennials-confident-connected-open-to-change.pdf).

2. Quoted in Kate Torgovnick, "For Some Jews, It Only Sounds Like 'Taboo,'" *New York Times*, July 17, 2008, https://www.nytimes.com/2008/07/17/fashion/17SKIN.html.

407

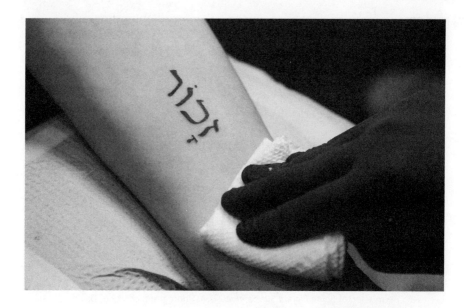

of American Jewish identity and culture since the mid-twentieth century. In the decades after World War II, consonant with the sizable wave of Holocaust survivors and other victims of the Nazi regime who immigrated to the United States, American Jews generally considered tattoos to be at odds with their sense of Jewishness. A dark reminder of Nazi persecution, tattoos were an indelible remnant of the dehumanizing treatment suffered by Jewish prisoners in Nazi death camps and concentration camps.

In the best-selling novel *The Human Stain* (2000), set in the 1990s, the celebrated American Jewish writer Philip Roth (1933–2018) deploys the symbol of a tattoo to throw light on the fraught and shifting landscape of American Jewish life in the late twentieth century. Coleman Silk, an academic at a fictional liberal arts college in New England, is discovered to be a light-skinned black who has been passing as a white Jew since his wartime service in the U.S. Navy. Roth's famous protagonist Nathan Zuckerman observes: "Also previously concealed was the small, Popeye-ish blue tattoo situated at the top of his right arm, just at the shoulder joining—the words 'U.S. Navy' inscribed between hooklike arms of a shadowy little anchor and running along the hypotenuse of the deltoid muscle. A tiny symbol, if one were needed, of all the million circumstances of the other fellow's life...."[3]

Roth's artful description, including the encoded tension between the "little anchor" and the "million circumstances of the other fellow's life," implicitly

3. Philip Roth, *The Human Stain* (New York: Vintage, 2000), 21–22.

underscores the nexus between Coleman's American, black, and Jewish identities.[4] Adrift in a "blizzard of details" and "the confusion of a human biography," Coleman's tattoo is a striking indicator of the multifaceted and fluid dimensions of human identity.[5] "Our understanding of people," Zuckerman (Roth) insists, "must always at best be slightly wrong."[6] To this end, *The Human Stain* helps us understand the tattoo as a matter of affirmation and, at the same time, something of a ruse. It may be concealed or visible. It may be a sign of compulsion or volition. It contravenes traditional Jewish norms, and it affirms the life experience of those who survived the horrors of the war.

The images reprinted here bring the discussion of tattoos and body art into the early decades of the twenty-first century. Though not definitive by themselves, they illustrate the extent to which the practice of tattooing has become normative and meaningful for a growing segment of the American Jewish population. Consider, for example, Gail Rubin's image of a colorful tattoo on a woman's hand and wrist, photographed at Congregation Nahalat Shalom, a Reconstructionist synagogue in Albuquerque, New Mexico.[7] Nahalat Shalom identifies

4. Ibid., 22.

5. Ibid.

6. Ibid.

7. In 1922, the Conservative rabbinic scholar Mordecai M. Kaplan (1881–1983) created the Society for the Advancement of Judaism (SAJ) in New York City. The first institutional mani-

itself as "a spiritual and cultural center for Jewish Renewal in the Southwest" and promotes the bringing of "creativity, relevance, joy, and an all embracing awareness to spiritual practice, as a path to healing our hearts and finding balance and wholeness—*tikuun halev*" [Hebrew for "repair of the heart"].[8] To be sure, the tattoo's arresting symbolism—a Star of David imprinted with the Hebrew word *chai* (meaning "life")—evokes a sense of spiritual and cultural connection recognizable even to those unfamiliar with the late twentieth-century Jewish Renewal movement's willingness to "rethink [Judaism's] most sacred doctrines" and its "syncretistic approach that readily borrow[s] from unpopular and even deviant strains inside Judaism and from spiritual resources outside Judaism."[9]

In the second instance, Mark Randall's photograph of Robin Zell Benveniste, a home health care nurse in Delray Beach, Florida, getting a tattoo of the Hebrew word *zakhor* (meaning "remember") raises intriguing ideas about the role of body art as an act of remembrance. Benveniste, whose family is active in the Reform congregation Bnai Israel in Boca Raton, Florida, explains the tattoo on her forearm as a tribute to Holocaust survivors with whom she developed close relationships: "It is critical to remember each and every story of our Holocaust survivors and to pass these stories on . . . from one generation to another. Very soon, there won't be any Holocaust survivors left and we will have to pass on their stories for them. My personal philosophy is to 'Pay It Forward' and this is my way of doing that for the survivors."[10] In recent years many young Jews seeking to memorialize their great grandparents and grandparents have tattooed their ancestors' concentration camp numbers on their arms. This practice, which has gained popularity in the United States and Israel, is lamented by critics who contend that it blurs the distinction between the Nazi perpetrators and their Jewish victims, including the victims' families. But many young people

---

festation of Reconstructionist Judaism, the new SAJ synagogue embodied Kaplan's theological conception of Judaism as an evolving religious tradition. He rejected the notion that the Torah had been divinely revealed at Mount Sinai and that *halakhah* is immutable and binding in Jewish religious life. Rather, he posited the necessity of adapting Jewish life and culture to the modern environment. These ideas were later fully developed in Kaplan's *Judaism as a Civilization* (1934). In March 1922 Kaplan conducted the first bat mitzvah in the United States for his daughter, Judith (Kaplan) Eisenstein (1909–1996).

8. Nahalat Shalom, "Welcome to Nahalat Shalom," https://www.nahalatshalom.org/about.

9. Shaul Magid, "Jewish Renewal: Toward a 'New' American Judaism," *Tikkun* 21, no. 1 (January-February 2006), 59–60.

10. Quoted in Randall P. Lieberman, "Nurse Gets Tattoo to Honor Holocaust Survivors," *South Florida Sun-Sentinel*, December 4, 2014, https://www.sun-sentinel.com/florida-jewish-jour nal/news/palm/fl-jjps-tattoo-1210-20141204-story.html.

like Benveniste counter it is a sign of Jewish pride. "A lot of survivors and a lot of people are ashamed of speaking of what happened because of the atrocities," explains Luke Shaft of Los Angeles, the grandson of a Holocaust survivor. "I don't think it should be kept a secret. I don't think it should be held back, I think it should be put out into the public. I wear it very proudly."[11]

Though the place of tattoos in contemporary Jewish life remains controversial, the practice is no longer peripheral and seems likely to continue into the foreseeable future. The fact that tattoos and body art are today visibly and proudly part of mainstream American Jewish life is a sign of the dynamic and elastic quality of the American Jewish experience.

—EDS.

11. Quoted in Itay Hod, "Holocaust Remembrance Day: Wearing Grandparents' Tattoos as Tribute," *Spectrum News* 1, January 27, 2020, https://spectrumnews1.com/ca/la-west/news/2020/01/27/holocaust-remembrance-day--wearing-grandparents--tattoos-as-tribute.

52

"LEVELING THE PLAYING FIELD"

Women and American Jewish Organizational Life (2008)

◇◇

DEBORAH SKOLNICK EINHORN

When in 2010 Elena Kagan (b. 1960) became the second Jewish woman appointed to the Supreme Court of the United States (following in the footsteps of Ruth Bader Ginsburg, 1933–2020), one observer quipped that it was easier for a Jewish woman to become an associate justice than the head of a major American Jewish Federation. Indeed, as the new millennium dawned women accounted for roughly 70 percent of American Jewry's organizations and led over half of the country's small Jewish Federations, but only one woman held the top post of a large federation.[1] This inequity prompted Barbara Dobkin (b. 1943) and other women philanthropists to create feminist Jewish organizations that sought to change the American Jewish landscape. The Dobkin Family Foundation, for example, provided seed funding for three key initiatives: Ma'yan, the Jewish Women's Archive, and Advancing Women Professionals and the Jewish Community (AWP). Each called for and worked toward women's greater inclusion in all realms of organized American Jewish life and leadership.

In 2008, AWP published *Leveling the Playing Field: Advancing Women in Jewish Organizational Life* by Shifra Bronznick (b. 1954), Didi Goldenhar (b. 1957), and Marty Linsky (b. 1940). In the tradition of the *Jewish Catalog* (1973, 1975, and 1980), edited some forty years earlier by Richard Siegel (1948–2018), Michael Strassfeld (b. 1950), and Sharon Strassfeld (b. 1950), *Leveling the Playing Field* challenged the status quo. A broadly construed guidebook, it combined an easy-to-read and visual format with qualitative and quantitative research data, and it documented the widespread gender inequality in mainstream American Jewish organizations. It pointed out that women did not rise to top positions in American Jewish life because of historical and structural biases, and it offered creative

---

1. Shifra Bronznick, Didi Goldenhar, and Marty Linsky, *Leveling the Playing Field: Advancing Women in Jewish Organizational Life* (New York: Advancing Women Professionals and the Jewish Community, 2008), 42.

strategies for women to gain proportionate representation, responsibility, access to power, and equal pay. If it were possible, the authors claimed, to better inform and empower an array of Jewish women, the net result would be not only the diversification of the Jewish professional arena but also improved outcomes across the board. The book was intended to reach a broad audience, and its synthesis of application and activism prompted interventions in the American Jewish public arena—including significant changes to the Conservative rabbinate, the restructuring of Jewish Federation leadership, and the launch of community-wide gender equity efforts such as the Men as Allies campaign, the Op-Ed Project, and the Better Work, Better Life initiative. In sum, AWP and *Leveling the Playing Field* aligned research with actionable plans that reshaped and continue to reverberate in the American Jewish public arena.

◇◇◇

Excerpts from Shifra Bronznick, Didi Goldenhar, and Marty Linsky, *Leveling the Playing Field: Advancing Women in Jewish Organizational Life*, 2008

> Source: Shifra Bronznick, Didi Goldenhar, and Marty Linsky, *Leveling the Playing Field: Advancing Women in Jewish Organizational Life* (New York: Advancing Women Professionals and the Jewish Community, 2008), 15–16 and 27–31. Reprinted by permission of Didi Goldenhar.

THE CHALLENGE: TAKING ON A GENDER EQUITY INITIATIVE
IN YOUR ORGANIZATION

This guidebook is about how to create a particular kind of organizational change in a particular kind of organization—*advancing women and creating gender equity in Jewish organizations.*[2]

If you believe that gender equity is vital to the health of Jewish communities and want to turn your beliefs into productive action, then this guidebook is for you.

The strategies and tools in this guidebook will be relevant wherever you are positioned in your organization.[3] The goals and tactics may vary depending

---

2. Advancing Women Professionals and the Jewish Community (AWP), the driving force behind much of this research, was founded in 2001 by Shifra Bronznick and ceased operations in 2015. On AWP, see its website at http://advancingwomen.org/.

3. The book notes that it is aimed at "CEO or member of the senior management team; middle manager; young professional early in your career; volunteer leader who contributes time,

on your formal and informal roles, but the opportunity for exercising leadership on gender equity is available to you whether you are sitting in the corner office or just getting started in your career....

OUR PURPOSE AND OBJECTIVES

From the beginning, our work on this guidebook has been motivated by three objectives:

* To provide a resource guide to the strategic options and tactical tools for a gender equity initiative that is right for you and for your organization;
* To share our learning from gender equity initiatives in Jewish communal organizations and other fields; and,
* To give you a deeper understanding of why leading organizational change is difficult and how you can minimize the risks and maximize your chances of success.

MAKING THE CASE: OUR THREE CORE ASSUMPTIONS

To begin, we think it's a good idea to state our core assumptions, drawn from our own research and experience.

* Gender inequity is embedded in Jewish organization life.
* Gender equity is vital to the health of Jewish communal organizations.
* Creating gender equity will improve overall workplace effectiveness....

THE ADAPTIVE CHALLENGE

Systems are what they are for a reason. It's not serendipitous. The arrangements, behaviors, and rules—written and unwritten—serve real goals and objectives or else they would have been changed.

This is as true for gender inequity in Jewish organizations as it is for income inequality in America. No one says that they favor the gap between rich and poor. But many people behave as though they want these inequities to continue. Why? Because other values, purposes, and loyalties are more important to them. If gender equity or income inequality is far down on the list of issues that you or others care about, these may as well be off the list entirely.

---

expertise, and money; or volunteer leader whose primary commitment is as a donor" (Bronznick, Goldenhar, and Linsky, *Leveling the Playing Field*, 16).

For individuals and groups within organizations, the unwillingness to choose among competing, and dearly held, values creates an immunity to change.

Here's one example of how *competing values* operate within the Jewish Federation system:

The CEOs of the twenty largest federations meet regularly as a group, including an annual retreat. It is widely understood that these CEOs exert enormous influence on the policies and programs of the entire federation system.

From the perspective of these CEOs, there is good reason to confine these meetings to the twenty largest federations. These executives raise the most money and need a forum to discuss the unique issues that derive from their size and the Jewish communities that they represent.

However, the consequences of honoring that value—limiting participation to large-city CEOs—means that only one woman professional (the executive leader of United Israel Appeal in Canada) currently occupies a seat at that very powerful table. Women's voices are virtually absent from these meetings. Is it any surprise that, for this group, the issue of gender equity is of low priority?[4]

These executives do not think of themselves as being opposed to gender equity, nor do they believe that they are doing anything wrong. From where they sit, this meeting makes sense. Why disturb a system that has elevated them to senior authority?[5]

BEHIND THE CURVE IN THE JEWISH COMMUNITY

We know that the gender gap exists in almost every line of work. The media regularly chronicles the difficulties faced by women in most professions. Even so, the Jewish community lags far behind the curve. There are fewer women at the high echelons in the Jewish communal areas than in comparable organizations in academia, philanthropy, and the secular nonprofit sector.

---

4. The authors ultimately recommend the very simple yet radical idea that such imbalances might be fixed through the inclusion of vice presidents, lay chairpeople, and so on. The simplicity of "stretch[ing] the category to promote more inclusive ideas about leadership" was one of the major takeaway lessons from this slim volume (Bronznick, Goldenhar, and Linsky, *Leveling the Playing Field*, 88).

5. This is a major theme related to social change in organizations and philanthropy. Since the status quo generally benefits people in power, the will to make any change is often quite limited. In addition to powerful men, upper-class women—who have many fewer privileges than their male partners—shy away from changes that could jeopardize their status and/or that of their families. See Susan A. Ostrander, *Women of the Upper Class* (Philadelphia: Temple University Press, 1986).

Moreover, the Jewish community is one of the few sectors that have *not* made serious efforts to advance gender equity. Strategies to address gender inequities have been pursued in law, medicine, business, politics, and academia; while women are still underrepresented at the upper ranks of these fields, they have made quantifiable gains. Jewish women certainly have distinguished themselves in every arena—from universities to foundations and from the Senate floor to the Supreme Court. By contrast, the Jewish community has invested very little to expand opportunities for women.

What particular aspects of our community might account for this difference? From our experience, there are several *cultural attitudes* that rank high in Jewish organizational life, but which also inhibit gender equity. Here's our list. As you read, think about which ones apply to your situation:

We're one big Jewish family. The family atmosphere that permeates Jewish organizational life allows gender stereotypes to flourish. Young women predominate [at] the entry level and in the middle ranks. Older men congregate at the top. This organizational design, underscored by the influences of older male lay leaders, creates a family pattern in which "good daughters" find it hard to demand positions of power.

You can't fix what you can't see. All nonprofit organizations cultivate donors and board members. In Jewish communal life, however, the unique collaboration between volunteers and staff is valued more than individual professional achievement. The complexity of this volunteer-professional relationship makes it harder to establish and recognize objective standards of performance.

This is my job and my Jewish life. Communal professionals view their work as a vehicle for pursuing their Jewish identity. Commitment to the Jewish people feels ideologically sound and personally fulfilling. However, this commitment sometimes influences women to set aside their own needs and aspirations. For many women, this translates into a willingness to live with the salary gender gap or other types of discrimination.

We are saving the world. Most Jewish organizations focus on rescue and renewal. We save others by fund-raising, social action, and fighting antisemitism. We build community and Jewish identity, here at home and around the world. With such noble and altruistic aims, the internal work of human resource development is seen as a distraction that pulls us away from our mission-driven activities.

Shush. Don't tell the donors. The Jewish fear of "airing dirty laundry in public" makes it risky to raise the issue of gender bias. Our organizations are characterized by boosterism—all our messages must be framed as successes, e.g., "The campaign is on the upswing!" Donors are shielded from internal problems, and in this environment, admitting the presence of gender bias is seen as unproductive.

What beliefs influence the way that women are treated in Jewish organizations? What are the *realities* that challenge these beliefs?

The way women are treated in Jewish organizations satisfies other competing, but highly cherished, values. Here are some examples of gender-related *beliefs* in the Jewish community and *realities* that contradict them:

The Stepping-Stone Belief. Jewish organizations are great training grounds for women. Look at how many young, talented women are going into the communal field.

Reality. Young, talented, and committed Jewish women start their careers in communal organizations, accepting low-paying jobs and doing great work. However, within several years, frustrated by the lack of career development and the reality of the glass ceiling, many of these young women take their career aspirations elsewhere. They are then replaced by other talented, committed young professionals. This revolving door sustains the status quo for those senior professionals who do not want their job security challenged.

The All-in-Good-Time Belief. We have a lot of women working in Jewish organizations. Over time, some of them will reach the top.

Reality. The belief that women's leadership will evolve naturally over time satisfies many leaders—both professionals and volunteers—who would prefer that this shift take place *after their tenure*. They fear that the feminization of the Jewish communal field will lead to a decline in its prestige and effectiveness. As a result, many leaders erect, consciously and unconsciously, many barriers against high-potential women.

The Round-the-Clock Belief. Jewish organizations require 24/7 or 24/6 commitment from CEOs and senior leaders. Women won't put their professional lives ahead of their families.

Reality. Work-life balance is becoming a primary factor in job choice and job satisfaction in the Jewish world and in the larger society. Many young people—women and men—are no longer willing to devote 24/7 to their professional lives. Smart companies and organizations are learning how to accommodate a range of career aspirations in order to gain competitive advantage in talent recruitment and retention. But many Jewish organization leaders are reluctant to consider that their own sacrifices, which they accepted as the price of leadership, will not be embraced by the next generation.

Finally, there is the persistent belief held by some male communal leaders that women lack the fund-raising clout needed in chief executive positions. We have heard this articulated in research interviews and informally in one-on-one meetings. *Let's put this myth to rest.* Throughout the communal arena, women professionals are succeeding in top fund-raising posts. Outside the Jewish world, women now lead 23 percent of universities in the United States, in positions that demand extraordinary fund-raising talent. The fact that women succeed in presidential posts, including four in the Ivy League, should make it abundantly clear: women can be highly effective fund-raisers for large nonprofit institutions.[6]

Letting go of these beliefs — seeing them as *assumptions* rather than truths — is an important step forward in the process of change.

---

6. The persistence of these trends in Jewish life and the lag behind the secular world is often anecdotally attributed to the larger context of a patriarchal religion. Even though only a small percentage of Jewish organizations referred to in this book are explicitly religious in nature, all are born out of this historically male-driven Jewish culture, and that has long-term effects on leadership norms and expectations.

53

"IT'S IMPORTANT FOR PEOPLE TO KNOW I AM WHO I AM"

Transgender American Jews
(2016)

◇◇◇

> Transkeit is a community building gathering sponsored by the Center for LGBTQ & Gender Studies in Religion. Transkeit features ritual, cultural programming, workshops, meals together and plenty of opportunities for informal schmoozing. This program is co-hosted by CLGS' Transgender Roundtable and Jewish Roundtable.
>
> Who is this gathering for? We welcome all transgender, genderqueer and gender non-conforming Jews and allies. Help continue to build a vibrant and safe Jewish trans community for all of us![1]

Despite the prominent "T" in the acronym LGBTQ, transgender Jews were until recently largely ignored by organized American Jewry and marginalized by the Jewish gay and lesbian community. Like American society as a whole, however, American Jewry has in recent years become increasingly aware of the needs of its transgender constituency. Openness to transgender Jews is evident across the institutional Jewish landscape—in synagogues, community centers, membership organizations, schools, and camps, as well as in other social, religious, cultural, and political frameworks. "The willingness of the Jewish community to have this conversation in a nonpushback way is amazing," reported Asher Gellis (b. 1980), the founder and director of JQ International, a Los Angeles–based programming and advocacy group for LGBTQ Jews. "Five years ago," Gellis noted in 2015, "I would send speakers to youth groups to tell their coming-out stories and to talk about bullying, and very often, in a very polite way, those groups were trying to push us away from the transgender conversation. Now, all they want is transgender speakers."[2]

---

1. "Transkeit: Affirming Gender Diversity for Jews and Allies," https://clgs.org/event-items/transkeit-affirming-gender-diversity-for-jews-and-allies/.

2. Quoted in Julie Gruenbaum-Fax, "Transgender Jews: Beyond the Rainbow," *Jewish Journal*, May 7, 2015, https://jewishjournal.com/community/236924/transgender-jews-beyond-rainbow/.

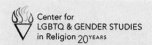

Center for
LGBTQ & GENDER STUDIES
in Religion 20ʸᴱᴬᴿˢ

A Program of Pacific School of Religion

Home About CLGS ▾ Our Work ▾ Resources ▾ News & Press ▾ Events ▾ Support ▾

TRANSKEIT
Affirming Gender Diversity for Jews and Allies

"Transkeit: Affirming Gender Diversity for Jews and Allies," Pacific School of Religion, Berkeley, CA, 2016. Source: Transkeit, Center for LGBTQ Studies in Religion, Pacific School of Religion, Berkeley, CA. Reprinted by permission of Jane Rachel Litman.

With respect to American Jewry's major synagogue movements, Gellis's assessment applies, at least in part, to the community's nontraditional sphere. The liberal wing of American Judaism—the Reconstructionist, Reform, and Conservative synagogue movements—maintain explicit policies on nondiscrimination regarding sexual orientation and gender identity. Both the Reform and Reconstructionist movements ordain transgender rabbis. Meanwhile, more conservative and Orthodox Jewish communities—with certain exceptions—are generally unwelcoming environments for LGBTQ Jews. Indeed, on the whole, Orthodox Judaism rejects nontraditional forms of Jewish expression on *halakhic* grounds.

Against this backdrop, many transgender Jewish activists seek to reshape the American Jewish communal landscape by creating new support frameworks, affinity groups, and synagogues. Moreover, as public discussion of the place of transgender Jews in American Jewish life proliferates leaders in the transgender Jewish community are vocal and forthright about the challenges and discrimination faced by transgender Jews and their aspirations. Abby Stein (b. 1991), a transgender woman from a Hasidic background and the author of *Becoming Eve: My Journey from Ultra-Orthodox Rabbi to Transgender Woman* (2019), notes: "It's important to be out there not just as openly trans, not just as openly Jewish, but as an openly Jewish trans person. . . . It's important for people to know I am who I am, and to make them comfortable with all that I am."[3] However, not all transgender Jews find the process of self-advocacy to be straightforward or uncomplicated. "It's very hard because there's a lot in Judaism that has to do with

3. Quoted in Rahel Musleah, "Abby Stein Finds Her Voice," *Hadassah*, July 2020, https://www.hadassahmagazine.org/2020/07/08/abby-stein-finds-voice/.

the body," explains Miryam Kabakov (b. 1964), executive director of Eshel, a North American advocacy organization for transgender Orthodox Jews. Especially for more traditional transgender Jews, participating in Jewish communal life is complex. "Someone in a male body has a whole other list of obligations," Kabakov notes, and when they transition "the question is, 'Do we now treat them as male or female?'"[4]

The Transkeit banner and statement reprinted here allude to the broad spectrum of American Jewry's transgender community. Transkeit, based in Berkeley, California, is sponsored by the Pacific School of Religion's Center for LGBTQ Studies in Religion. The group's playful synthesis of "trans" and "*yiddishkeit*" (Yiddish for "Jewishness") signals its proud, nonjudgmental, and welcoming Jewish stance. The group's emblem calls to mind the colors of the transgender flag (light blue, pink, and white), while its blended quality hints at the fluid spectrum of the trans community. Transkeit's explanation of its purpose and its open invitation to newcomers echoes the adaptive and capacious nature of the American Jewish scene.

—EDS.

4. Quoted in Shelby Hartman, "Jewish and Transgender," *Double Blind*, November 25, 2019, https://doubleblindmag.com/jewish-transgender-yiscah-smith/.

54

"THE *KOTEL* BELONGS TO ALL JEWS WORLDWIDE"

The American Jewish Committee and the Western Wall Controversy
(2017)

◇◇

JONATHAN GOLDEN

The year 2017 was a milestone in the history of Zionism. It included the hundredth anniversary of the Balfour Declaration,[1] the seventieth anniversary of the U.N. partition plan for Palestine,[2] and the fiftieth anniversary of the Six-Day War (June 1967).[3] A half-century earlier, the nascent Jewish state's David-like triumph over the combined military forces of Egypt, Jordan, and Syria had

---

1. In November 1917, following strenuous efforts by Chaim Weizmann (1874–1952), who was then president of the English Zionist Federation, Great Britain issued the Balfour Declaration, recognizing the "establishment in Palestine of a national home for the Jewish people" (see chapter 22, note 16). The declaration raised Jewish hopes of attaining political sovereignty in Palestine and energized the Zionist movement worldwide. While the declaration was a critical turning point in the Zionist movement's trajectory, the language used by the British was sufficiently vague as to leave the future status of the Jewish community in Palestine uncertain.

2. In May 1947, the United Nations established a Special Committee on Palestine (UNSCOP) to investigate the causes of unrest in British Mandatory Palestine. Charged with formulating a new proposal to resolve Palestine's political future, UNSCOP representatives traveled to Palestine, where they gathered testimony from both the Jewish Agency and its Arab counterpart, known as the Arab Higher Committee, as well as local Jewish and Arab groups. In September 1947, UNSCOP issued a report recommending termination of the British Mandate and the partition of Palestine into separate Jewish and Arab states.

3. In the mid-1960s, the Soviet Union encouraged Syria and Egypt to adopt a belligerent stance toward Israel and the West. Meanwhile, anti-Israel terrorism mounted, and the United Nations proved unable to curb attacks against Israel, which came largely from the newly established Al-Fatah organization in Syria and Syrian artillery. The escalating crisis in the Middle East—stoked by the Egyptian president, Gamal Abdel Nasser (1918–1970) (see chapter 38, note 10)—came to a head in May 1967 with the dispatch by Nasser of Egyptian forces into Gaza and the Sinai Peninsula and the blockade of the Straits of Tiran, followed by the sudden withdrawal of U.N. forces from the area. Israel responded with a preemptive strike against the Egyptian air force and rapidly defeated the invading Egyptian, Jordanian, and Syrian military forces in the Six-Day War (June 5–10, 1967).

been greeted by American Jews with elation and relief. This watershed event generated deeper American Jewish attachment to Israel and the resurgence of public expressions of Jewish identity. Less apparent at the time, but no less consequential in the long term, was the predicament caused by Israel's sudden conquest of the West Bank, Golan Heights, Gaza Strip, and Sinai Peninsula and the new reality's impact on the American Jewish political sensibility.

The symbolic significance of the return of Jewish sovereignty in Jerusalem, including unfettered access to the Western Wall (referred to in Hebrew as the *kotel*), ushered in a wave of Jewish pilgrimages to the site long venerated as holy due to its proximity to the Temple Mount.[4] The Kotel (the Hebrew term is commonly used in the Jewish public arena) swiftly became a destination for Jews worldwide, and the plaza in front of the wall was enlarged to 20,000 square meters to accommodate thousands of visitors at a time.[5] After 1967, American Jewish visitors, including members of organized synagogue, community, and youth group excursions, became a mainstay of Israel's tourism industry. A pathfinding development in this regard occurred in 1999 with the creation of Taglit-Birthright Israel, a heavily subsidized tour of Israel for young American Jews organized by a partnership of American Jewish Federations and Jewish philanthropic leaders. According to a Pew Research Center study, by 2013 the tour accounted for roughly 48 percent of American Jews ages 18–29 who visited Israel.[6]

In the fullness of time, however, as tensions unfolded between organized American Jewry and Israel—animated, in part, by differences over the protracted Israel-Palestine conflict—the Israeli Orthodox religious establishment's increasingly stringent control of the Kotel plaza became a focal point of conflict. When in June 2017 the Israeli government announced that it was canceling plans to allow for an egalitarian and pluralistic prayer space at the Western Wall—a compromise brokered in 2016 by a multi-denominational committee—analysts pointed to the objections of ultra-Orthodox Haredi leaders as the reason for the agreement's collapse. The timing of the announcement was symbolic: it took place a few weeks after the fiftieth anniversary of the Six-Day War and prior to a celebratory Jewish Agency for Israel gala featuring Prime Minister Benjamin Netanyahu (b. 1949). In response, the Jewish Agency board of governors canceled the gala dinner and, for the first time, passed a resolution

4. On the Temple in ancient Jerusalem, see chapter 6, note 6.

5. Simone Ricca, "Heritage, Nationalism and the Shifting Symbolism of the Wailing Wall," *Archives de sciences sociales des religions* 151, no. 3 (2010), 173–74.

6. Dov Waxman, "Young American Jews and Israel: Beyond Birthright and BDS," *Israel Studies* 22, no. 3 (Fall 2017): 193n17.

urging the Israeli cabinet to rescind its decision. Meanwhile, the nullification of the Kotel agreement coincided with new legislation (supported by the Israeli governing coalition's right-wing partners) to give the chief rabbinate exclusive control of conversions to Judaism in Israel. Underscoring the extremity of the situation, Steven Nasatir (b. 1945), the highly influential president of the Jewish United Fund/Jewish Federation of Metropolitan Chicago, declared: "The federation in Chicago will not be hosting any member of Knesset that votes for this bill. None. They will not be welcome in our community."[7]

Following the cancelation of the Kotel agreement, the venerable American Jewish Committee (AJC)[8] issued the formal statement reprinted below. The document's premise is that the failure of Israel's chief rabbinate to recognize modern Judaism's multiple streams undermines Israel's claim to represent the entire Jewish people. The AJC further asserted that the debacle threatened the decades-old U.S.-Israeli security partnership; the latter, the AJC argued, derived in no small measure from American Jewry's political support and overwhelmingly pro-Israel stance. When the AJC's annual conference was held in Jerusalem in 2018, its concluding session was at the Kotel—which visibly affirmed American Jewry's commitment to religious pluralism and the importance of the relationship between American Jews and Israel.

To this day, non-Orthodox American Jewish groups, particularly the Reconstructionist, Reform, and Conservative synagogue movements, continue to advocate for official recognition in Israel of non-Orthodox forms of Jewish expression. Moreover, Israeli Jewish public opinion largely favors the concept of religious pluralism. Yet Israel's recent governing coalitions especially under Netanyahu (1996–99, 2009–2021), have relied on right-wing and ultra-Orthodox Jewish political parties, that repeatedly block plans for a permanent space for egalitarian and pluralistic Jewish worship at the Kotel. At present, non-Orthodox Jewish worship is allowed only in a limited area known as Robinson's Arch, south of the main plaza. However, the site is regularly commandeered by ultra-Orthodox groups seeking to impede worship by egalitarian and pluralistic Jewish individuals and groups.

◇◇

7. Quoted in "Israeli Lawmakers Who Vote for Conversion Bill Not Welcome in Chicago, Jewish Federation Head Says," *Jewish Telegraphic Agency*, June 28, 2017, https://www.jta.org/2017/06/28/united-states/israeli-lawmakers-who-vote-for-conversion-bill-not-welcome-in-chicago-jewish-federation-head-says.

8. On the AJC, see chapter 35, note 24.

American Jewish Committee Statement on the Kotel Controversy, June 25, 2017

Source: "AJC Decries Israeli Government Decision to Freeze Western Wall Plan," AJC *Global Voice*, June 25, 2017, https://www.ajc.org/news/ajc-decries-israeli -government-decision-to-freeze-western-wall-plan. Reprinted by permission of American Jewish Committee Archives and Records Center, New York City.

June 25, 2017—New York, New York

[The American Jewish Committee] is deeply disappointed by today's decision of the Israeli government to withdraw from the plan to establish an egalitarian prayer space at the Western Wall (Kotel).

AJC had hailed the compromise to allow egalitarian prayer at the sacred site in Jerusalem when it was first approved by the Israeli Cabinet in January 2016.[9]

"The Kotel belongs to all Jews worldwide, not to a self-appointed segment," said AJC CEO David Harris.[10] "This decision is a setback for Jewish unity and the essential ties that bind Israel and American Jews, the two largest centers of Jewish life in the world."

In a September 2015 letter to AJC, Israeli Prime Minister [Benjamin] Netanyahu[11] stated his commitment "to strengthening the unity of the Jewish people," and pledged "to unequivocally reject any attempt to divide us or to delegitimize any Jewish community—Reform, Conservative or Orthodox."

The Conservative and Reform movements, joined by AJC and other Jewish groups, have long pressed for equal rights at the Kotel for non-Orthodox worship and religious ceremonies. The landmark compromise, adopted by the Israeli cabinet on January 31, 2016, recognized that the religious status quo at the Western Wall would continue under Orthodox authority. For egalitarian and mixed-gender Conservative and Reform prayers, however, a new space would be created at the southern wall, commonly known as Robinson's Arch. But while all streams of Judaism agreed at the time, the ultra-Orthodox representatives reneged and have steadfastly blocked its implementation.

AJC has been focusing on issues of Jewish religious pluralism in Israel for

9. On January 31, 2016, the Israeli government approved the building of an enhanced egalitarian prayer space, a single entrance to the Kotel, and a committee of non-Orthodox denominations to oversee the site.

10. David Harris (b. 1949) has served as the AJC's executive director since 1990.

11. Benjamin Netanyahu, a member of the right-wing Likud Party, served as the fourteenth (1996–99), eighteenth (2009–13), nineteenth (2013–15), twentieth (2015–19), twenty-first (2019), twenty-second (2019), and twenty-third (2020–2021) prime minister of Israel.

decades. At AJC's initiative, the effort was elevated in 2014 with the establishment of the multi-organizational Jewish Religious Equality Coalition (J-REC)
to press for recognized alternatives to [Israel's] Chief Rabbinate on procedures
relating to marriage and conversion to Judaism.[12]

12. The Jewish Religious Equality Coalition (J-REC) consists of members of the Reform,
Conservative, and modern Orthodox communities, including the leaders of major American
Jewish seminaries and synagogue organizations. J-REC seeks to create institutional alternatives
to Israel's chief rabbinate on matters of marriage, divorce, conversion, and burial.

55

"THE FULL HUMANITY AND PRECIOUS VALUE OF EVERY INDIVIDUAL BLACK LIFE"

The Haggadah Supplement of Jews for Racial and Economic Justice

(2019)

◇◇◇

American Jews can be forgiven for mistakenly believing the *Maxwell House Haggadah*[1] represents the gold standard of Passover observance. Since its appearance in 1932—as part of a corporate public relations strategy to sell coffee—some fifty million copies of the *Maxwell House Haggadah* have reputedly graced the tables of American Jewish homes. Despite the *Maxwell House Haggadah*'s ubiquity, American Jewish ritual practice has been varied and diverse since the time Jews first set foot in seventeenth-century colonial North America. Indeed, it would not be an exaggeration to suggest there have been as many *haggadot* (Hebrew plural, literally "tellings") at any period of American history as Jews seated at the seder table.

The Library of Congress contains thousands of *haggadot* from across the centuries, including many dozens, if not hundreds, that had surely found their way into American Jewish homes by the time the first cluster of Civil War–era Jewish printing houses began producing American versions of the Passover service. Among the earliest specimens in the library's holdings is L. H. Frank's *Haggadah ve-Seder shel Pesah: Form of Service for the Two First Nights of the Feast of Passover*, published in New York in 1859. Printed in Hebrew and English, with a smattering of Yiddish, the Frank haggadah includes decorative engravings.[2] Thereafter, as additional printing houses introduced further textual innovations, what might be described as a standard body of irregular Passover procedures surfaced in even the most far-flung corners of the American landscape.

---

1. The Hebrew term *haggadah* literally means "telling."

2. L. H. Frank, *Haggadah ve-Seder shel Pesah: Form of Service for the Two First Nights of the Feast of Passover* (New York: Hebrew Publishing Company, 1859), 12. See *Passover Haggadaot at the Library of Congress: A Guide to the Collections*, ed. Ann Brener (2016), entry 78, https://www.loc.gov/rr/amed/pdf/Passover%20Haggadot.pdf.

By the turn of the nineteenth and twentieth centuries, publishing Passover *haggadot* had proven to be good business, and a nascent American-based haggadah industry developed around the printing houses of Lewine and Rosenbaum, J. Fink and Son, J. Rosenbaum, Asher Lemel Germansky, the Hebrew Publishing Company, Joseph Magil, Philip Cowen, the Bloch Publishing Company, the European Hebrew Publishing Company, and countless others. The groundswell of American innovation led to the annual production of new Passover *haggadot*, each of which employed a distinctive approach to ritual observance and incorporated languages familiar to Jewish readers from different backgrounds (in addition to Hebrew). By the early twentieth century, a rich and diverse panoply of Passover *haggadot* had dotted the American Jewish landscape, including texts designed to suit Yiddish-speaking socialists, Orthodox Jews identified with competing rabbinic authorities, Sephardic Jews from different parts of the Mediterranean basin and north Africa, acculturated American Jews with little to no knowledge of Hebrew, Zionist groups, and more.

The *Black Lives Matter Haggadah Supplement* reprinted here is, in many respects, heir to the venerable tradition described above. Like thousands of other formal and informal groups, organizations, institutions, and circles of activity too numerous to catalog here, Jews for Racial and Economic Justice (JFREJ) introduced a specific text into the American Jewish orbit—in this case, a haggadah supplement—believing that it would speak to American Jews hungry to inject the Passover service with relevant and meaningful contemporary social justice content. Against the backdrop of the tragic murders of young African American men and the rise of the Black Lives Matter movement in the early twenty-first century, the JFREJ supplement stresses "the role we believe Jews must play in confronting racism and abusive policing." Opening with an evocative illustration by Ethan Heitner[3] that literally and figuratively equates "BLM" (Black Lives Matter) with the Hebrew word *haggadah* (the "telling" of the liberation of the Israelites from Egyptian bondage), the text adds a powerful contemporary racial, political, and economic dimension to the traditional Passover service.

—EDS.

◇◇

3. Ethan Heitner (b. 1983) is a New York City–based cartoonist and illustrator and JFREJ member.

Ethan Heitner

Black Lives Matter Haggadah Supplement of Jews for Racial and
Economic Justice, 2019

> Source: Jews for Racial and Economic Justice, *Living Our Commitment: Jewish Voices
> for Liberation*, 2019, https://www.reconstructingjudaism.org/sites/default/files
> /jfrej_blm_haggadah.pdf. Illustration by Ethan Heitner. Reprinted by permission
> of Jews for Racial and Economic Justice.

LIVING OUR COMMITMENT: JEWISH VOICES FOR LIBERATION

Introduction by Leo Ferguson:[4] We gather on Passover to recall a moment of resistance and liberation in the history of our people. The story of Exodus reminds
us of the transformative power that our people wield when we confront oppres-

---

4. Leo Ferguson (b. 1977), associate director of JFREJ, is founder of the organization's
Jews of Color caucus, lead organizer of the Jews of Color National Convening, and the primary
author of *Understanding Antisemitism: An Offering to Our Movement*, Jews for Racial and Economic
Justice, https://www.jfrej.org/assets/uploads/JFREJ-Understanding-Antisemitism-November
-2017-v1-3-2.pdf.

sion. This summer we witnessed the deaths of Michael Brown[5] and Eric Garner[6] at the hands of the police; in the months that followed the #BlackLivesMatter movement blossomed from that stained soil and swept the country. From Ferguson[7] to Staten Island,[8] Black people resisted the discriminatory and abusive policing targeting them. #BlackLivesMatter, a term coined by activists Alicia Garza [b. 1981], Patrice Cullors [b. 1983], and Opal Tometi [b. 1984], demands that we recognize the full humanity and precious value of every individual Black life—that we cherish and fight for all people of African heritage. In this spirit, Jews For Racial and Economic Justice collaborated with inspiring activists and leaders from around the country to produce this Haggadah supplement. In it you will find additions to the Seder rituals and Haggadah text intended to highlight the role we believe Jews must play in confronting racism and abusive policing. Each piece of the supplement may provoke discussion, reflection or even contention. We hope that this wrestling, thinking and feeling—in the great tradition of our people—will be a powerful part of your Seder and will lead to meaningful action for justice. JFREJ does not necessarily endorsed [sic] every view presented here, but we are deeply proud to help share the diversity of voices and ideas that power this movement.

5. Michael Brown (1996–2014), a black high school graduate in St. Louis, MO, was fatally shot in Ferguson, MO, by Darren Wilson, a white police officer. The incident sparked nationwide outrage. After extensive investigation, a grand jury declined to indict Wilson. The U.S. Department of Justice determined that Wilson had shot Brown in self-defense.

6. Eric Garner (1970–2014), a black father of six children, died in a Staten Island incident in which he was suffocated by a white police officer, Daniel Pantaleo (b. 1985), who wrestled him to the ground and—with assistance from other officers—pinned him down and put him in a chokehold. Garner repeatedly cried out "I can't breathe" before losing consciousness and expiring. Witnessed by passersby and caught on videotape, the incident prompted nationwide protests and gave rise to the Black Lives Matter movement. A grand jury declined to indict Pantaleo.

7. See note 5.

8. See note 6.

aliyah: Hebrew for "ascent," used to denote one who is called up to the Torah in a worship service or the act of immigrating to the Land of Israel (State of Israel).

Ashkenazic Jews: also called "Ashkenazim" (from the Hebrew name *Ashkenaz* in the Hebrew Bible [Gen. 10:3 and 1 Chr 1:6]), the term used to identify Jews of central and eastern European ancestry. Historically, the vernacular languages of Ashkenazic Jews (commonly referred to as Yiddish) derive from German and Slavic languages with elements of Hebrew and Aramaic.

Conservative Judaism: see chapter 43, note 31.

halakhah: Hebrew for "the path," used to identify the amalgam of biblical injunctions, rabbinic rulings, and customs that emerged over time to constitute Orthodox Jewish law and that historically governed public, private, and ritual Jewish life. Though seemingly fixed, the body of beliefs, rituals, and practices constituting *halakhah* has been reinterpreted and modified over time by different religious authorities in various social and cultural settings.

Hanukkah: The eight-day post-biblical Jewish holiday commemorating the Maccabean revolt (167–160 BCE) and rededication of the Temple in Jerusalem.

Hasidism: Eastern European Jewish religious movement whose followers embrace the teachings of the Polish rabbi Israel ben Eliezer (c. 1700–1760), known as the Baal Shem Tov or Besht, who opposed intellectualism and stressed emotionalism in prayer and the performance of religious rituals and ceremonies.

hazan (pl. *hazanim*): Hebrew for "cantor."

kaddish: Hebrew for "sanctification," traditional Jewish doxology recited by mourners.

kashrut: Hebrew for "lawfulness," used to denote traditional Jewish dietary laws or food that adheres to such strictures (as in "kosher food").

kibbutz: Hebrew for a cooperative rural settlement in Palestine (and later Israel).

matzah (pl. *matzot*): Hebrew for the unleavened flat bread consumed during Passover.

menorah: Hebrew for the seven-branch candelabra that has been a symbol of Judaism since the ancient period; described in the Hebrew Bible as integral to the Israelites' portable sanctuary in the wilderness (Exod. 25:31–40) and later as a feature of the ancient Temple in Jerusalem.

midrash (pl. *midrashim*): Hebrew for the body of homiletic literature created by ancient rabbinic sages that interprets and comments on the Hebrew Bible using exegesis, hermeneutics, and philology.

Mishnah: Hebrew for "to study" or "repetitive learning," referring to the written record of Jewish oral tradition redacted at the start of the third century CE by Rabbi Yehuda Hanasi. Its sixty-three tractates codifying Jewish law form the basis of the Talmud.

Orthodox Judaism: see chapter 43, note 25.

Passover: The Jewish festival of Passover derives from the Hebrew Bible (Lev. 23:5) and is intended to commemorate the liberation of the ancient Israelites from Egyptian slavery as recounted in Exodus. Observed annually, the holiday starts on the fifteenth day of the Hebrew month of Nisan and lasts for seven days (in the Land of Israel) or eight days (in the diaspora). The holiday includes unique ritual customs and dietary restrictions such as the consumption of unleavened flatbread known as *matzah* (Exod. 12:8).

pogrom: anti-Jewish riot or massacre perpetrated by the Christian population against European Jews. State-sponsored pogroms were widespread in tsarist Russia between 1881 and 1917 and Soviet Russia between 1917 and 1921. They were also common under the Nazi regime (1933–45).

rabbi: derived from *rav*, Hebrew for "master" or "teacher," the term denotes a religious authority, spiritual leader, or scholar in Judaism and Jewish communal life.

Reconstructionist Judaism: see chapter 51, note 7.

Reform Judaism: see chapter 16, note 9.

Sephardic Jews: also called "Sephardim" (from the Hebrew word *Sepharad* in the Hebrew Bible, Obad. 1:20), the term used to identify Jews of Iberian ancestry and/or Jews who trace their ancestry to the Mediterranean basin, north Africa, and the Arab lands. Historically, the vernacular languages of Sephardic Jews of Iberian ancestry (commonly referred to as Ladino) derive from Spanish and Portuguese, with elements of Hebrew and Aramaic.

Shabbat: Hebrew for "Sabbath."

talit: Hebrew for "prayer shawl."

Talmud: the term refers to either of the two works, one compiled in Babylon and the other in Palestine, that contain discussions of Jewish law. Each of these works contain the Mishnah along with the Gemara, a commentary on and a supplement to the Mishnah. While both books are authoratative documents, the Babylonian Talmud is seen as being much more important because of its greater length and historical influence over Jews and Judaism.

Tisha Beav: Hebrew for the ninth day of the month of Av. This annual fast day commemorates the destruction of the First and Second Temples in Jerusalem, which supposedly occurred on the same date. Over time, Tisha Beav also came to be regarded as a day for mourning other tragedies in Jewish history.

Torah: specifically, the Hebrew Bible or Pentateuch (Five Books of Moses). The term can also be used to refer in the abstract to the whole body of Jewish learning and literature developed over time.

yeshivah (pl. *yeshivot*): Hebrew and Yiddish for a school of advanced traditional Jewish study.

Yishuv: Hebrew term for the Jewish community in Palestine before the creation of the State of Israel in 1948. "Old Yishuv" refers to the traditional, religiously observant Jewish community established in the region prior to 1881.

Yom Kippur: Hebrew for "Day of Atonement." This Jewish holiday is a solemn day of repentance and fasting that lasts twenty-four hours on the tenth day of the month of Tishrei in the Hebrew calendar. It is a day of abstention from all manner of food, drink, work, and sexual relations. The regulations for observing Yom Kippur derive from Leviticus 16:1–34 (where it is called the "Sabbath of Sabbaths") and 23:26–32, as well as Numbers 29:7–11. According to rabbinic tradition, Yom Kippur marks the day when Moses descended from Mount Sinai with the Decalogue and announced the divine pardon of the Israelites for the sin of worshipping the golden calf.

Zionism: the political movement of modern Jewish nationalism, which emerged in the late nineteenth century and led to the establishment of the State of Israel in 1948.

SELECT BIBLIOGRAPHY OF WORKS
BY JONATHAN D. SARNA

I. BOOKS AND DISSERTATION IN REVERSE CHRONOLOGICAL ORDER

Wilburn, Cora. *Cosella Wayne: Or, Will and Destiny.* Edited. Tuscaloosa: University of Alabama Press, 2019.

Lincoln and the Jews: A History. Coauthored with Benjamin Shapell. New York: Thomas Dunne Books, 2015. [Translated into Hebrew, Dvir, 2016.]

Sisterhood: A Centennial History of Women of Reform Judaism. Coedited with Carole B. Balin, Dana Herman, and Gary P. Zola. Cincinnati: Hebrew Union College Press, 2013.

When General Grant Expelled the Jews. New York: Schocken, 2012.

Jewish Renaissance and Revival in America. Coedited with Eitan Fishbane. Waltham, MA: Brandeis University Press, 2011.

Jews and the Civil War: A Reader. Coedited with Adam D. Mendelsohn. New York: New York University Press, 2010.

New Essays in American Jewish History: Commemorating the Sixtieth Anniversary of the Founding of the American Jewish Archives, 321–27. Coedited with Pamela S. Nadell and Lance J. Sussman. Cincinnati: Jacob Rader Marcus Center of the American Jewish Archives, 2010.

A Time to Every Purpose: Letters to a Young Jew. New York: Basic Books, 2008.

The History of the Jewish People: A Story of Tradition and Change. Coauthored with Jonathan B. Krasner. 2 vols. Springfield, NJ: Behrman House, 2006–7.

Three Hundred Fifty Years: An Album of Jewish Memory. Coedited with Michael Feldberg, Karla Goldman, Scott-Martin Kosofsky, Pamela S. Nadell, and Gary P. Zola. New York: American Jewish Historical Society, 2005.

American Judaism: A History. New Haven, CT: Yale University Press, 2004. 2nd rev. ed, 2019. [Translated into Hebrew with a new introduction: *Hayahadut BeAmerika,* Jerusalem: Merkaz Zalman Shazar, 2005. Translated into Chinese in 2009].

America and Zion: Essays and Papers in Memory of Moshe Davis. Coedited with Eli Lederhendler. Detroit, MI: Wayne State University Press, 2002.

Jewish Polity and American Civil Society: Communal Agencies and Religious Movements in the American Public Square. Coedited with Alan Mittleman and Robert Licht. Lanham, MD: Rowman and Littlefield, 2002.

Jews and the American Public Square: Debating Religion and Republic. Coedited with Alan Mittleman and Robert Licht. Lanham, MD: Rowman and Littlefield, 2002.

Women and American Judaism: Historical Perspectives. Coedited with Pamela S. Nadell. Hanover, NH: University Press of New England, 2001.

435

Abba Hillel Silver and American Zionism. Coedited with Mark A. Raider and Ronald W. Zweig. London: Frank Cass, 1997.

Minority Faiths and the American Protestant Mainstream. Edited. Urbana: University of Illinois Press, 1997.

Religion and State in the American Jewish Experience. Coedited with David G. Dalin. Notre Dame, IN: University of Notre Dame Press, 1997.

The Jews of Boston. Coedited with Ellen Smith. Boston: Combined Jewish Philanthropies, of Greater Boston, 1995. [2nd ed, New Haven, CT: Yale University Press, 2005.]

Observing America's Jews by Marshall Sklare. Edited. Hanover, NH: University Press of New England, 1993.

A Double Bond: The Constitutional Documents of American Jewry. Coedited with Daniel J. Elazar and Rela Geffen Monson. Lanham, MD: University Press of America, 1992.

Ethnic Diversity and Civic Identity: Patterns of Conflict and Cohesion in Cincinnati since 1820. Coedited with Henry D. Shapiro. Urbana: University of Illinois Press, 1992.

Yehudei Artsot Ha-Berit (The Jews of America). Coedited with Lloyd Gartner. Jerusalem: Merkaz Zalman Shazar, 1992.

Yahadut Amerika—American Jewry: An Annotated Bibliography of Publications in Hebrew. Coedited with Janet Liss. Jerusalem: Hebrew University of Jerusalem Press, 1991.

The Jews of Cincinnati. Coauthored with Nancy H. Klein. Cincinnati: Center for the Study of the American Jewish Experience, Hebrew Union College–Jewish Institute of Religion, 1989.

JPS: The Americanization of Jewish Culture, 1888–1988. Philadelphia: Jewish Publication Society, 1989.

American Synagogue History: A Bibliography and State-of-the-Field Survey. Coedited with Alexandra S. Korros. New York: Markus Wiener, 1988.

The American Jewish Experience: A Reader. Edited. New York: Holmes and Meier, 1986. 2nd rev. ed., 1997.

Jews and the Founding of the Republic. Coedited with Benny Kraut and Samuel K. Joseph. New York: Markus Wiener, 1985.

People Walk on Their Heads: Moses Weinberger's Jews and Judaism in New York. Translated and edited. New York: Holmes and Meier, 1982.

Jacksonian Jew: The Two Worlds of Mordecai Noah. New York: Holmes and Meier, 1981.

"Mordecai Manuel Noah: Jacksonian Politician and American Jewish Communal Leader—A Biographical Study." PhD diss. Yale University, 1979.

Jews in New Haven. Edited. New Haven, CT: Jewish Historical Society of New Haven, 1978.

II. ARTICLES, BOOK CHAPTERS, AND ONLINE ITEMS
IN REVERSE CHRONOLOGICAL ORDER

2020

"Introduction: Rabbi Menachem Mendel Schneerson's Letter to the Jewish Community of Teaneck (November 1981)." In *The New Jewish Canon*, ed. Yehuda Kurtzer and Claire E. Sufrin, 321–25. Boston: Academic Studies Press.

"Roundtable on Antisemitism in the Gilded Age and Progressive Era." Coauthored with David S. Koffman, Hasia Diner, Eric L. Goldstein, and Beth S. Wenger. In *Journal of the Gilded Age and Progressive Era* 19, no. 3, 473–505.

"Isidor Kalisch's Pioneering Translation of Sepher Yetsirah (1877) and its Rosicrucian Legacy." In *Kabbalah in America: Ancient Lore in the New World*, ed. Brian Ogren, 138–44. Leiden, the Netherlands: Brill.

"Woodrow Wilson Was A Hero to Jews: What Should We Do with His Racism?" *Forward* (July 2).

"Enough Doom and Gloom: History Shows American Judaism Is Much More Resilient Than You Think." *Forward* (May 18).

"What If Jewish Journalism Disappears?" *Forward* (April 8).

"On the Trail of Cora Wilburn." *Jewish Book Council Blog* (January 20), https://www.jewish bookcouncil.org/pb-daily/on-the-trail-of-cora-wilburn.

"What Is Bar Mitzvah?" *Conversation* (January 17), https://theconversation.com/what-is -a-bar-mitzvah-129745.

"Antisemitism Is a Symptom." *Times of Israel* (January 1).

2019

Foreword. In Ronald Rubin, *Strangers and Natives: A Newspaper Narrative of Early Jewish America 1734–1869*, 9. New York: Urim.

"When the Wolves of Hate Are Loosed." *Brandeis Magazine* (Spring–Summer), 38–39.

"Steven M. Cohen's Prophecy in Historical Perspective." *American Jewish Year Book* 118, 81–83.

2018

"The Future of the Pittsburgh Synagogue Massacre." *Tablet* (November 5), https://www .tabletmag.com/sections/news/articles/future-pittsburgh-synagogue-massacre. [Expanded Hebrew version: "*Hayu Devarim Me'olam*," *Makor Rishon* (November 9).]

"Orthodox Jewish Lawyer-Leaders in Nineteenth-Century America." In *Ennoble and Enable: Essays in Honor of Richard M. Joel*, ed. Zev Eleff and Jacob J. Schacter, 361–70. New Milford, CT: Maggid Books.

"My Life in American Jewish History." In *Conversations with Colleagues: On Becoming an American Jewish Historian*, ed. Jeffrey S. Gurock, 161–87. Boston: Academic Studies Press.

"The Forgetting of Cora Wilburn." *Studies in American Jewish Literature* 37, no. 1, 73–87.

"Jewish Women without Money: The Case of Cora Wilburn (1824–1906). *Nashim* 32, 23–37.

"Leonard Bernstein and the Music of Boston's Congregation Mishkan Tefila." In *Brandeis University's State of the Arts* (Winter–Spring), 22–23. Brandeis University.

"What Really Happened at the Original Trefa Banquet?" *Jewish Telegraphic Agency*, January 16, https://www.jta.org/2018/01/16/news-opinion/opinion/what-really-happened-at -the-original-trefa-banquet.

2017

"The Immigration Clause That Transformed Orthodox Judaism in the United States." Coauthored with Zev Eleff. *American Jewish History* 101, no. 3 (July), 357–76.

"The Bible and Judaism in America." In *The Oxford Handbook of the Bible in America*, ed. Paul C. Gutjahr, 505–16. New York: Oxford University Press.

"'The Last Years Were the Most Difficult': A First-Person Account of a Mission to the Soviet Union in March 1986." In *Black Fire on White Fire: Essays in Honor of Rabbi Avi Weiss*, ed. Daniel R. Goodman, 131–40. New York: Yeshivat Chovevei Torah Rabbinical School.

"From Periphery to Center: American Jewry, Zion, and Jewish History after the Holocaust." In *American Jewry: Transcending the European Experience*, ed. Christian Wiese and Cornelia Wilhelm, 307–15. London: Bloomsbury.

"Louis H. Feldman (1926–2017)." *Biblical Archaeology Review* 43 (July–August), 11.

"Louisa B. Hart: An Orthodox Jewish Woman's Voice from the Civil War Era." In *You Arose a Mother in Israel: A Festschrift in Honor of Blu Greenberg*, ed. Devorah Zlochower, 95–102. New York: Jewish Orthodox Feminist Alliance.

"Praying for Governments We Dislike?" *Lehrhaus* (January 5), http://www.thelehrhaus .com/commentary-short-articles/2017/1/2/praying-for-governments-we-dislike.

2016

American Jews and the Flag of Israel. Waltham, MA: Brandeis University.

Foreword. In Wyatt Gallery, *Jewish Treasures of the Caribbean*, 6–7. Atglenn, PA: Schiffer.

Foreword. In *Kehillath Israel: The First 100 Years*, ed. Debra Block, iv–vii. Brookline, MA: Kehillath Israel.

"The Value of Canadian Jewish History to the American Jewish Historian, and Vice Versa: Another Look." In *Neither in Dark Speeches Nor in Similitudes: Reflections and Refractions between Canadian and American Jews*, ed. Barry L. Stiefel and Hernan Tesler-Mabe, 1–7. Waterloo, ON: Wilfrid Laurier University Press.

"That Other Time Jews Were Hated in America and 3 Lessons to Learn from It Now." *Forward* (November 15).

"The American Jews Who've Exchanged Their Utopian Myths about Israel for Demonic Ones." *Haaretz* (August 2).

Lechaim to Life: Celebrating 100 Years of Jewish Life at Princeton [Haggadah Supplement]; https:// www.academia.edu/35975329/Jonathan_D_Sarna_Haggadah_Supplement_Lechaim _to_Life_Celebrating_100_Years_of_Jewish_Life_at_Princeton.

"Family History Curriculum." *Chabad-Lubavitch News* (April 20), http://www2.lubavitch .com/news/article/2057407/And-You-Shall-Tell-Your-Child.html&p=2.

"Subversive Jews and American Culture: Notes on the Leonard Milberg Collection of
Early American Judaica." In *By Dawn's Early Light: Jewish Contributions to American Culture
from the Nation's Founding to the Civil War*, ed. Adam D. Mendelsohn, 189–204. Princeton,
NJ: Princeton University Library. [Reprinted without accompanying notes in *Tablet*
(February 18), http://www.tabletmag.com/jewish-arts-and-culture/books/197758
/subversive-jews-american-culture.]

"*Avraham Avinu Ve'am Ha'ivrim Be-Artso* (Abraham Lincoln and his attitude toward the
Jews)." *Et-Mol* 244 (February), 7–9.

"100 Years Later, Has Brandeis's Supreme Court Nomination Changed Everything—
or Nothing?" *Forward* (January 29).

2015

"American Orthodox Responses to Intermarriage." In *Conversion, Intermarriage and Jewish
Identity: The Orthodox Forum*, ed. Robert S. Hirt, Adam Mintz, and Marc D. Stern, 409–
26. New York: Yeshiva University Press.

"Investing in the Jewish Studies Ph.D. Talent Pool." Coauthored with Steven. M. Cohen
and Rona Sheramy. *E-Jewish Philanthropy* (December 6), https://ejewishphilanthropy
.com/investing-in-the-jewish-studies-ph-d-talent-pool/.

"Lincoln's Surprising Jewish Connections." *Beacon: The National Museum of American Jewish
History* (Summer), 6–7.

"Letter from Boston: A Friend Indeed—and in Deed." *Hadassah Magazine* 97, no. 1
(August–September), 40–41.

"America's Most Memorable Zionist Leaders." In *The Individual in History: Essays in Honor
of Jehuda Reinharz*, ed. ChaeRan Y. Freeze, Sylvia Fuks Fried, and Eugene R. Sheppard,
129–42. Waltham, MA: Brandeis University Press.

"George Washington's Correspondence with the Jews of Newport." In *Washington's Rebuke
to Bigotry: Reflections on Our First President's Famous 1790 Letter to the Hebrew Congregation
in Newport, Rhode Island*, ed. Dan Eshet, Michael Feldberg, and Adam Strom, 73–82.
Boston: Facing History and Ourselves.

2014

"The Touro Monument Controversy: Aniconism vs. Anti-Idolatry in a Mid-Nineteenth
Century American Jewish Religious Dispute." In *Between Jewish Tradition and Modernity,
Rethinking an Old Opposition: Essays in Honor of David Ellenson*, ed. Michael A. Meyer and
David N. Myers, 80–95. Detroit, MI: Wayne State University Press.

"*Hayahadut HaReformit Bat-Zmanenu: Nituah Histori*" (Contemporary Reform Judaism:
A historical analysis). In *Reform Judaism: Thought, Culture and Sociology*, ed. Avinoam
Rosenak, 499–508. Jerusalem: Van Leer Institute.

"Marking Time: Notes from the Arnold and Deanne Kaplan Collection of Early American
Judaica on How Nineteenth-Century American Jews Lived Their Religion." In
Constellations of Atlantic Jewish History 1555–1890, ed. Arthur Kiron, 49–62. Philadelphia:
University of Pennsylvania Libraries.

"Reform Jewish 'Missionaries' for Judaism: Barbara S. Goodman and the Committee on Religion of the National Federation of Temple Sisterhoods (1913–1933)." In *Why Jewish Women's History Matters: An Archive of Stories in Honor of Gail Reimer*, ed. Joyce Antler, 24–26. Boston: Jewish Women's Archive.

"From World-Wide People to First-World People: The Consolidation of World Jewry." In *Reconsidering Israel-Diaspora Relations*, ed. Eliezer Ben-Rafael, Judit Bokser Liwerant, and Yosef Gorny, 60–65. Leiden, the Netherlands: Brill.

"Why Study American Jewish History." *HaYidion: The RAVSAK Journal* (Spring), 26–27 and 52.

"United States Jewry." Coauthored with Zev Eleff. *Oxford Jewish Studies Bibliographies*, https://www.oxfordbibliographies.com/view/document/obo-9780199840731 /obo-9780199840731-0060.xml.

"Judaism." Coauthored with Jonathan Golden. In *World Book 2014 Year Book*, World Book.

2013

"America's Russian-Speaking Jews Come of Age." In *Toward a Comprehensive Policy Planning for Russian-Speaking Jews in North America*, 1–27. Jerusalem: Jewish People Policy Institute.

"'To Quicken the Religious Consciousness of Israel': The NFTS National Committee on Religion, 1913–1933." In *Sisterhood: A Centennial History of Women of Reform Judaism*, 49–71. Coedited with Carole B. Balin, Dana Herman, and Gary P. Zola. Cincinnati: Hebrew Union College Press.

"Jews and the Civil War." In *Passages through the Fire: Jews and the Civil War*, ed. Jeffrey Edelstein, 9–29. American Jewish Historical Society and Yeshiva University Museum.

"Lewis Feuer and the Study of American Jewish History." *Society* 50, 352–55.

"Letter from Boston: People of the Silver Linings Playbook." *Hadassah Magazine* 95, no. 3 (December 2013–January 2014), 10–12.

"History: Barbara Goodman, Unheralded Hero." *Reform Judaism* 42 (Winter), 14–18.

"At Battle of Gettysburg Jewish Heroes Fought for Both North and South." *Forward* (July 1).

"Judaism." Coauthored with Jonathan Golden. In *World Book 2013 Year Book*, World Book.

"Why America Has No Chief Rabbi." *Jewish Ideas Daily* (January 23).

"The Jewish Translation That Rewrote the Bible." *Forward* (January 25).

2012

"The American Jewish Press." In *Oxford Handbook of Religion and the American News Media*, ed. Diane Winston, 537–50. New York: Oxford University Press.

"American Jewish History: Backwards and Forwards." In *From Sinai to China: Essays in Commemoration of the 20th Anniversary of the Glazer Institute of Jewish Studies at Nanjing University*, ed. Xu Xin and Lihong Song, 229–38. Nanjing, China: SDX Joint Publishing Company.

"George Washington's Correspondence with the Jews of Newport." In *To Bigotry No Sanction: George Washington and Religious Freedom*, ed. Josh Perelman, 17–24. Philadelphia: National Museum of American Jewish History.

"How Matzah Became Square: Manischewitz and the Development of Machine-Made Matzah in the United States." In *Chosen Capital: The Jewish Encounter with American*

Capitalism, ed. Rebecca Kobrin, 272–88. New Brunswick, NJ: Rutgers University Press. [Revised from "How Matzah Became Square: Manischewitz and the Development of Machine-Made Matzah in the United States," Victor J. Selmanowitz Lecture, Touro College, New York City, 2005.]

"General Grant's Infamous Order." *New York Times Opinionator—Disunion Blog* (December 19), [Reprinted in *Disunion: 106 Articles from the New York Times Opinionator*, ed. Ted Widmer, 427–34. New York: Black Dog and Leventhal, 2013.]

Foreword. In Joshua Eli Plaut, *A Kosher Christmas*, xi–xii. New Brunswick, NJ: Rutgers University Press.

"The Discontinuity of Continuity: An Interview with Jonathan D. Sarna." *Reform Judaism* 41 (Winter), 24–26.

"Colonial Judaism." In *The Cambridge History of Religions in America*, vol. 1: *Pre-Columbian Times to 1790*, ed. Stephen J. Stein, 392–409. New York: Cambridge University Press.

"President Grant and the Chabadnik." *Jewish Review of Books* 3 (Spring), 10–13.

Introduction. In *Jews in America: From New Amsterdam to the Yiddish Stage*, ed. Stephen D. Corrsin, Amanda Seigel, and Kenneth Benson, 9–15. New York: New York Public Library.

"The Jewish Vote in Presidential Elections." *Sh'ma* 42, no. 686 (January), 3.

"'God Loves an Infant's Praise': Cultural Borrowing and Cultural Resistance in Two Nineteenth-Century American Jewish Sunday-School Texts." In *Interreligious Dialogue and Cultural Change*, ed. Catherine Cornille and Stephanie Corigliano, 59–77. Eugene, OR: Cascade Books. [Published in *Jewish History* 27 (2013), 73–89.]

"When General Grant Expelled the Jews." *Slate* (March 13), http://www.slate.com/articles/news_and_politics/history/2012/03/ulysses_s_grant_and_general_orders_no_11_how_the_infamous_order_changed_the_lives_of_jews_in_america_.html.

"The Redemption of Ulysses S. Grant." *Reform Judaism* 40 (Spring), 22–26 and 59–62.

"General Grant's Uncivil War against the Jews." *Jewish Week* (February 28).

"Judaism." Coauthored with Jonathan Golden. In *World Book 2012 Year Book*, World Book.

"Forward Forum: Every Four Years, Rabbis and Politics Mix." *Forward* (September 21).

"Constitutional Dilemma on Birth Control." *Forward* (March 16).

2011

"Christians and Non-Christians in the Marketplace of American Religion." In *American Christianities: A History of Dominance and Diversity*, ed. Catherine Brekus and W. Clark Gilpin, 119–32. Chapel Hill: University of North Carolina Press.

"A Writ of Release from Levirate Marriage (*Shtar Halitzah*) in 1807 Charleston." Coauthored with Dvorah E. Weisberg. *American Jewish Archives* 63, no. 1, 38–55.

"Civil War," "Columbus, Christopher," "Jewish Publication Society." In *Cambridge Dictionary of Judaism and Jewish Culture*, ed. Judith R. Baskin, 108, 323, and 623–24. Cambridge: Cambridge University Press.

Foreword. In Benny Kraut, *The Greening of American Orthodox Judaism: Yavneh in the Nineteen Sixties*, xi–xviii. Cincinnati: Hebrew Union College Press.

"Ethnicity and Beyond." In *Studies in Contemporary Jewry* 25 (Theme: "Ethnicity and Beyond: Theories and Dilemmas of Jewish Group Demarcation"), ed. Eli Lederhendler, 108–12. Oxford: Oxford University Press.

"American Jewish History: Retrospect and Prospect" [in Chinese]. In *The Jews in America: Development and Influence of a Successful Community*, ed. Pan Guang, Wang Shuming, and Luo Ailing, 3–14. Beijing: Shishi Publishing House.

"Freedom." In *Dreams of Freedom–National Museum of American Jewish History Catalog*, xiii–xix. Philadelphia: National Museum of American Jewish History.

"Man Oh Manischewitz." *Forward* (July 22).

"What the Civil War Meant to American Jews." *Forward* (March 1).

"Returning to Moscow." *Forward* (January 25).

"Judaism." Coauthored with Jonathan Golden. In *World Book 2011 Year Book*, World Book.

2010

"The Democratization of American Judaism." In *New Essays in American Jewish History: Commemorating the Sixtieth Anniversary of the Founding of the American Jewish Archives*, ed. Pamela S. Nadell, Jonathan D. Sarna, and Lance J. Sussman, 95–108. Cincinnati: Jacob Rader Marcus Center of the American Jewish Archives.

"The Relationship of Orthodox Jews with Believing Jews of Other Religious Ideologies and Non-Believing Jews: The American Situation in Historical Perspective." In *The Relationship of Orthodox Jews with Believing Jews of Other Religious Ideologies and Non-Believing Jews*, ed. Adam Mintz, 1–26. New York: Yeshiva University Press.

"Chabad-Lubavitch" and "Torah." In *Encyclopedia of Religion in America*, ed. Charles H. Lippy and Peter W. Williams, Washington, D.C.: CQ Press, 1:419–24 and 4:2194–97.

Foreword. In Fradle Freidenreich, *Passionate Pioneers: The Story of Yiddish Secular Education in North America, 1910–1960*, xi–xii. New York: Holmes and Meier.

Introduction. In Elie Kaunfer, *Empowered Judaism: What Independent Minyanim Can Teach Us about Building Vibrant Jewish Communities*, ix–xiii. Woodstock, VT: Jewish Lights.

"Judaism." Coauthored with Jonathan Golden. In *World Book 2010 Year Book*, World Book.

"New Museum on Independence Mall Is a Sign That Jews Have Arrived." *Forward* (November 26).

"When Shuls Were Banned in America." *Forward* (August 20).

"Rabbi Yoffie's Legacy: Old Ideas for Reform Judaism." *Forward* (June 25).

"Good Bye Wissenschaft, Hello Relevance." *Forward* (June 4).

"Rabbi Raphall Goes to Washington." *Forward* (February 26).

"American Jewry in Second Place." *Forward* (January 1).

Afterword. In Mark I. Rosen, *Mission, Meaning and Money: How the Joint Distribution Committee Became a Fundraising Innovator*, 151–56. Bloomington, IN: Cohen Center/iuniverse.

2009

"Two Ambitious Goals: Jewish Publishing in the United States." In *A History of the Book in America*, vol. 4: *Print in Motion: The Expansion of Publishing and Reading in the United States*

1880–1940, ed. Carl F. Kaestle and Janice A. Radway, 376–91. Chapel Hill: University of North Carolina Press.

"The Halakha According to B'nai B'rith." In *Rav Chesed: Essays in Honor of Rabbi Dr. Haskel Lookstein*, ed. Rafael Medoff, II: 165–82. Jersey City, NJ: KTAV Publishing House.

"The Economic Downturn and the Future of Jewish Communities." JPR Policy Debate Paper. London: Institute for Jewish Policy Research.

"Proskauer, Joseph Mayer." In *Yale Biographical Dictionary of American Law*, ed. Roger K. Newman, 439. New Haven, CT: Yale University Press.

"Leonard Bernstein and the Boston Jewish Community of His Youth: The Influence of Solomon Braslavsky, Herman Rubenovitz, and Congregation Mishkan Tefila." *Journal of the Society for American Music* 3, no. 1, 35–46.

"America As It Ought to Be: The Conflict between Jewish Rhetoric and American Realities." In *Ideology and Rhetoric: Constructing America*, ed. Bozenna Chylinska, 231–40. Cambridge: Cambridge Scholars Publishing.

"What's in a Name—A Response to Barry Chiswick." *Contemporary Jewry* 29, no. 1, 85–90.

"Lessons of Depression May Be Relevant Today." *Jewish Journal* (March 4).

"The American Jewish Community in Crisis and Transformation." *Contact* (Summer).

"Judaism." Coauthored with Jonathan Golden. In *World Book 2009 Year Book*, World Book.

"How Hanukkah Came to the White House." *Forward* (December 11).

"After Utopia, Loving Israel." *Forward* (October 9).

"The Long Shadow of Scandal." *Forward* (August 14).

"Saying Kaddish Too Soon? A Response to Norman Lamm." *Forward* (June 5).

"Op-Ed: At 85 Hillel Mission Remains Vital." *Jewish Telegraphic Agency* (May 27).

2008

"Two Jewish Lawyers Named Louis." *American Jewish History* 94, nos. 1–2 (March–June), 1–19.

"The Mystical World of Colonial American Jews." In *Mediating Modernity: Essays in Honor of Michael A. Meyer*, ed. Lauren B. Strauss and Michael Brenner, 185–94. Detroit. MI: Wayne State University Press.

Introduction. Laura Manischewitz Alpern, *Manischewitz: The Matzo Family*, ix–xiv. Jersey City, NJ: KTAV Publishing House.

"Judaism." Coauthored with Jonathan Golden. In *World Book 2008 Year Book*, World Book.

2007

"Intermarriage in America: The Jewish Experience in Historical Context." In *Ambivalent Jew: Charles Liebman in Memoriam*, ed. Stuart Cohen and Bernard Susser, 125–33. New York: Jewish Theological Seminary. [Hebrew version: *De'ot* (March 2019).]

"A Long Voyage to the New World: The First Jewish Settlement in North America." *Humanities* 28 (March/April), 37–39.

Foreword. In Marianne Sanua, *Let Us Prove Strong: The American Jewish Committee, 1945–2006*, ix–xi. Waltham, MA: Brandeis University Press.

"The Rise, Fall, and Rebirth of Secular Judaism." *Contemplate* 4, 3–13.

"Judaism." Coauthored with Jonathan Golden. In *World Book 2007 Year Book*, World Book.

"Boston," "Historiography—American Jewish," and "Marcus, Jacob R." In *Encyclopedia Judaica*, ed. Fred Skolnik, 4:99–101, 9:161–63, and 13:513–14. 2nd ed. Farmington Hills, MI: Jerusalem Publishing House, 2007.

2006

"Orthodoxy Confronts America" [in Hebrew]. In *Orthodox Judaism: New Perspectives*, ed. Yosef Salmon, Aviezer Ravitzky, and Adam S. Ferziger, 523–54. Jerusalem: Hebrew University Magnes Press.

"The Crucial Decade in Jewish Camping." In *A Place of Our Own: The Rise of Reform Jewish Camping*, ed. Michael. M. Lorge and Gary P. Zola, 27–51. Tuscaloosa: University of Alabama Press.

"Jacob I. Cohen." In *Dictionary of Virginia Biography*, ed. Sara B. Bearss, John G. Deal, Donald W. Gunter, Marianne E. Julienne, John T. Kneebone, Brent Tarter, and Sanra Gioia Treadway. 3345–47. Richmond: Library of Virginia.

"Port Jews in the Atlantic: Further Thoughts." *Jewish History* 20, no. 2, 213–19.

Afterword. In *My Yeshiva College: 75 Years of Memories*, ed. Menachem Butler and Zev Nagel, 355–57. New York: Yashar Books.

"Recalling Arthur Hertzberg: Public Intellectual." *Jewish Week* (April 21).

"Judaism." Coauthored with Jonathan Golden. In *World Book 2006 Year Book*, World Book.

2005

"An Eighteenth Century Hebrew Lu'ah from Pennsylvania." *American Jewish Archives* 57, nos. 1–2, 25–27. [Actual publication: 2007.]

"The Cyclical History of Adult Jewish Learning in the United States: Peers' Law and Its Implications." In *Educational Deliberations: Studies in Education Dedicated to Shlomo (Seymour) Fox*, ed. Mordecai Nisan and Oded Schremer, 207–22. Jerusalem: Keter and Mandel Foundation-Israel.

"Jacob I. Cohen and the 350th Anniversary of American Jewish Life." *Generations* 11, no. 1 (May), 1, 3, 8, and 14.

"Afterword: The Study of American Judaism: A Look Ahead." In *The Cambridge Companion to American Judaism*, ed. Dana Evan Kaplan, 417–21. New York: Cambridge University Press.

Foreword. In Manfred Gerstenfeld, *American Jewry's Challenge: Conversations Confronting the Twenty-First Century*, 5–6. Lanham, MD: Rowman and Littlefield.

Challenge and Change: History of the Jews in America—Civil War through the Rise of Zionism, ed. Shelley Kapnek Rosenberg. Historical Consultant. 2 vols. Springfield, NJ: Behrman House.

"Judaism." Coauthored with Jonathan Golden. In *World Book 2005 Year Book*, World Book.

"Evolving American Judaism." *Heritage* (May), 20–23.

2004

"In Memoriam: Leon A. Jick (1924–2005)." *American Jewish History* 92, no. 2 (June), 225–29. [Actual publication: 2006.]

"Introduction: The Jews of Rhode Island." Coauthored with Ellen Smith. In *The Jews of Rhode Island*, ed. George M. Goodwin and Ellen Smith, 1–10. Waltham, MA: Brandeis University Press.

"American Judaism." In *From Haven to Home: 350 Years of Jewish Life in America*, ed. Michael W. Grunberger, 129–45. Washington, D.C.: Library of Congress.

"Jewish Culture Comes to America." *Jewish Studies* 42 (2003–4), 45–57.

"Concentration." *Sh'ma* 35, no. 615 (November), 2–3.

"The Battle for the Jewish Vote." *Boston Sunday Globe*, October 10, 2004.

"American Jewish History: A Chance to Reflect." *Chronicle of Higher Education* (October 1).

"Judaism." Coauthored with Jonathan Golden. In *World Book 2004 Year Book*, World Book.

"What Will American Jews Celebrate on Their 350th Anniversary? [in Hebrew]." *Gesher: Journal of Jewish Affairs* 50, no. 149 (Summer), 26–31

"The 350th Anniversary of American Jewish Life." *AJS Perspectives* (Fall–Winter), 22–24.

"The Jews Come to America." *Jewish Telegraphic Agency* (March 11). [Distributed by the Jewish Telegraphic Agency and widely published (under various titles) in American Jewish newspapers.]

"From Destruction to Rebirth: The Holocaust and Israel in American Judaism." *Aufbau* 70 (February 26), 22–23.

2003

"The Question of Music in American Judaism: Reflections at 350 Years." *American Jewish History* 91, no. 2 (July 2003), 195–203. [Actual publication: 2004.]

"American Jews in the New Millennium." In *Religion and Immigration: Christian, Jewish and Muslim Experiences in the United States*, ed. Yvonne Yazbeck Haddad, Jane I. Smith, and John L. Esposito., 117–27. Lanham, MD: AltaMira Press. [Reprinted in *The Future of Religion: Traditions in Transition*, ed. Kathleen Mulhern, 68–72. Englewood, CO: Patheos Press, 2012.]

"American Judaism in Historical Perspective." David W. Belin Lecture in American Jewish Affairs (March 8), Frankel Center for Judaic Studies, University of Michigan.

"Historical Memory and Jewish Identity: 350 Years of American Jewish History: What Do They Mean?" In *Celebrating 350 Years of American Jewish Life*, 4–9. New York: American Jewish Committee.

"The Goals and Meaning of the 350th Anniversary Commemoration of American Jewish History." In *Proceedings: Celebrate 350 Inaugural National Planning Conference*, 23–27. New York: Commission for Commemorating 350 Years of American Jewish History.

"Aharon Kotler." *Conservative Judaism* 55, no. 4 (Summer), 60–62.

"Judaism." Coauthored with Jonathan Golden. In *World Book 2003 Year Book*, World Book.

"Why Study American Jewish History?" *Torah at the Center* 7 (Fall), 2–4.

2002

"Church-State Dilemmas of American Jews." In *Jews and the American Public Square*, coedited with Alan Mittleman and Robert Licht, 47–68. Lanham, MD: Rowman and Littlefield.

"Achavah and History: Reflections on the Historical Emphases of Moshe Davis." In *America and Zion: Essays and Papers in Memory of Moshe Davis*, coedited with Eli Lederhendler, 23–31. Detroit, MI: Wayne State University Press.

"Jewish Culture Comes to America" [in Hebrew]. *Gesher: Journal of Jewish Affairs* 48, no. 145 (Summer), 52–60.

"What Will Jewish Community and Jewish Values Mean for the 21st Century?" *Proceedings of the Rabbinical Assembly* 62, 80–87. New York: Rabbinical Assembly.

"Judaism." Coauthored with Jonathan Golden. In *World Book 2002 Year Book*, World Book.

2001

"The Jews in British America." In *The Jews and the Expansion of Europe to the West 1450–1800*, eds. Paolo Bernardini & Norman Fiering, 519–31. New York: Berghahn Books.

"Colonial Judaism." In *Myer Myers: Jewish Silversmith in Colonial New York*, by David L. Barquist with essays by Jon Butler and Jonathan D. Sarna, 8–23. New Haven, CT: Yale University Art Gallery/Yale University Press.

"American Jews in the Twentieth Century" [in Hebrew]. In *Album Ha-am Hayehudi*. Jerusalem: Merkaz Zalman Shazar.

"The Future of American Orthodoxy." *Sh'ma* 31, no. 579 (February), 1–3.

"Boston: Cornerstone of History." *Reform Judaism* 30, no. 1 (Fall), 38–44 and 84.

"Comment: The American Jewish Committee Statement on Jewish Education." New York: American Jewish Committee.

"Judaism." Coauthored with Jonathan Golden. In *World Book 2001 Year Book*, World Book.

2000

"The Twentieth Century Through American Jewish Eyes: A History of the American Jewish Year Book, 1899–1999." With coauthor Jonathan Golden. In *American Jewish Year Book* 100, 3–103.

"Jewish Votes Still Matter." *Jewish Week* (November 17).

"Lieberman Candidacy May Boost Modern Orthodoxy." *Forward* (August 11), 3.

"Response: The Question of Shlilat Ha-Galut in American Zionism." In *Beyond Survival and Philanthropy: American Jewry and Israel*, eds. Allon Gal and Alfred Gottschalk, 59–63. Cincinnati: Hebrew Union College Press.

"Judaism." Coauthored with Jonathan Golden. In *World Book 2000 Year Book*, World Book.

1999

"The Cult of Synthesis in American Jewish Culture." *Jewish Social Studies* 5, nos. 1–2 (Fall 1998–Winter 1999), 52–79.

"Manischewitz Matzah and the Rabbis of the Holy Land: A Study in the Interrelationship of Business, Charity and Faith" [in Hebrew]. *Gesher: Journal of Jewish Affairs* 45, no. 140 (Winter), 41–49.

"American Jewish Political Conservatism in Historical Perspective." *American Jewish History* 87, nos. 2–3 (June-September), 113–22.

"Judaism." Coauthored with Jonathan Golden. In *World Book 1999 Year Book*, World Book.

"Mordecai M. Noah," "Max Lilienthal." In *American National Biography*, ed. John A Garraty and Mark C. Carnes, 13:653–54 and 16:466–67. New York: Oxford University Press.

"The American Jewish Experience through the Nineteenth Century: Immigration and Acculturation." With coauthor Jonathan Golden. National Humanities Center. http://www.nhc.rtp.nc.us.

"The American Jewish Experience in the Twentieth Century: Antisemitism and Assimilation." With coauthor Jonathan Golden. National Humanities Center. http://www.nhc.rtp.nc.us.

1998

"Jewish Prayers for the United States Government: A Study in the Liturgy of Politics and the Politics of Liturgy." In *Moral Problems in American History: Essays in Honor of David Brion Davis*, 200–221. Ithaca, NY: Cornell University Press. [Reprinted in slightly different form in *Liturgy in the Life of the Synagogue: Studies in the History of Jewish Prayer*, ed. Ruth Langer and Steven Fine, 205–24. Winona Lake, IN: Eisenbrauns, 2005.]

"American Jewish Education in Historical Perspective." *Journal of Jewish Education* 64, nos. 1–2 (Winter-Spring), 8–21.

"The Revolution in the American Synagogue." In *Creating American Jews*, ed. Karen S. Mittelman, 10–23. Philadelphia: National Museum of American Jewish History and University Press of New England.

"Converts to Zionism in American Reform Judaism." In *Zionism and Religion*, eds. Shmuel Almog, Jehuda Reinharz, and Anita Shapira, 188–203. Hanover, NH: University Press of New England. [Reprinted from Hebrew in *Zionut Vedaat*, ed. Shmuel Almog, Jehuda Reinharz, and Anita Shapira, 223–43. Jerusalem: Merkaz Zalman Shazar, 1994.]

"A Forgotten 19th Century Prayer for the U.S. Government: Its Meaning, Significance and Surprising Author." In *Hesed Ve-Emet: Studies in Honor of Ernest S. Frerichs*, eds. Jodi Magness and Seymour Gitin, 431–40. Athens, GA: Scholars Press.

"Judaism." Coauthored with Jonathan Golden. In *World Book 1998 Year Book*, World Book.

"The Future of Diaspora Zionism." *Proceedings of the Rabbinical Assembly 97th Annual Convention*, 69–76. New York: Rabbinical Assembly. [Reprinted in Hebrew in *Gesher: Journal of Jewish Affairs* 43, no. 136 (Winter 1997), 38–44.]

"Committed Today, Divorced Tomorrow." *JTS Magazine* 7, no. 2 (Winter), 12 and 23. [Widely reprinted in Jewish newspapers.]

"10 Ways That Israel Liberated American Jewry." *Hadassah Magazine* 79, no. 10 (June–July), 14–15.

Foreword. In Gerry Cristol, *A Light in the Prairie: Temple Emanu-El of Dallas, 1872–1997*, ix–xi. Fort Worth: Texas Christian University Press.

"The Jewish Experience in American Public and Private Education." In *Vouchers for School*

Choice: Challenge or Opportunity? ed. Marshall J. Breger and David M. Gordis, 131–36. Washington, D.C.: Wilstein Institute for Jewish Policy Studies.

1997

"Two Traditions of Seminary Scholarship." In *Tradition Renewed: A History of the Jewish Theological Seminary*, ed. Jack Wertheimer, 54–80. New York: Jewish Theological Seminary of America.

"Back to the Center: The Plain Meaning of 'A Statement on Jewish Continuity.'" New York: American Jewish Committee.

"Jacob Rader Marcus." *American Jewish Year Book* 97, 633–40.

"Martha Wolfenstein." In *Jewish Women in America: An Historical Encyclopedia*, ed. Paula Hyman and Deborah D. Moore, 2:1486–87. New York: Routledge.

"Structural Challenges to Jewish Continuity." In *American Jewry: Portrait and Prognosis*, ed. David M. Gordis and Dorit P. Gray, 404–8. Washington, D.C.: Wilstein Institute for Jewish Policy Studies. [Reprinted from Hebrew in *Gesher: Journal of Jewish Affairs* 40, no. 129 (Summer 1994), 31–35.]

Untitled contribution to *One Year Later: The Rabin Symposium*. New York: American Jewish Committee.

"If You Lend Money to My People." *Learning Torah with . . .* 3, no. 18 (February 8), 1–4.

1996

"A Projection of America As It Ought to Be: Zion in the Mind's Eye of American Jews." In *Envisioning Israel: The Changing Ideals and Images of North American Jews*, ed. Allon Gal, 41–59. Jerusalem: Hebrew University Magnes Press.

"Comment." In *The Jew Within: Self, Community and Commitment among the Variety of Moderately Affiliated*, ed. Steven M. Cohen and Arnold Eisen, 72–74. Washington, D.C.: Wilstein Institute for Jewish Policy Studies.

"Why Teach American Jewish History?" In *Moving Beyond Haym Salomon: The Teaching of American Jewish History to 20th Century Jews*, 39–44. Philadelphia: Feinstein Center for American Jewish History, Temple University.

"Judaica Americana." Coauthored with Mark A. Raider, *American Jewish History* 84, no. 2 (June), 103–25.

The American Jewish Community's Crisis of Confidence, Policy Forum No. 10. Jerusalem: World Jewish Congress.

"From Antoinette Brown Blackwell to Sally Priesand: An Historical Perspective on the Emergence of Women in the American Rabbinate." In *Women Rabbis: Exploration and Celebration*, ed. Gary P. Zola, 43–53. Cincinnati: Hebrew Union College Press.

Untitled contribution to *Rebuilding Jewish Peoplehood: Where Do We Go from Here? A Symposium in the Wake of the Rabin Assassination*, 86–87. New York: American Jewish Committee.

1995

A Great Awakening: The Transformation That Shaped Twentieth Century American Judaism and Its Implications for Today. New York: Council for Initiatives in Jewish Education. [Reprinted in slightly different form as "The Late Nineteenth-Century American Jewish Awakening," in *Religious Diversity and American Religious History: Studies in Traditions and Cultures*, ed. Walter H. Conser Jr. and Sumner B. Twiss, 1–25. Athens: University of Georgia Press, 1997.]

"The Jews of Boston in Historical Perspective." In *The Jews of Boston*, coedited with Ellen Smith, 3–19. Boston: Combined Jewish Philanthropies of Greater Boston.

"The Road to Jewish Leadership." In *Expectations, Education and Experience of Jewish Professional Leaders: Report of the Wexner Foundation Research Project on Contemporary Jewish Professional Leadership*, Cohen Center for Modern Jewish Studies Research Report No. 12, 31–60. Waltham, MA: Cohen Center for Modern Jewish Studies, Brandeis University.

"The History of the Jewish Press in North America." In *The North American Jewish Press: 1994 Alexander Brin Forum*, Waltham, MA: Cohen Center for Modern Jewish Studies, Brandeis University. [Reprinted in revised form as "The History of the Jewish Press in North America," *Metro-West Jewish News 50th Anniversary Edition* (January 24, 1997), 60–66.]

"The Evolution of the American Synagogue." In *The Americanization of the Jews*, ed. Robert M. Seltzer and Norman J. Cohen, 215–29. New York: New York University Press.

"When Jews Were Bible Experts." *Moment* (October), 54, 55, 80.

"Perched Between Continuity and Discontinuity: American Judaism at a Crossroads." In *Proceedings of the Rabbinical Assembly* 56, 74–79. New York: Rabbinical Assembly.

"Judaica Americana." *American Jewish History* 83, no. 2 (June), 287–318.

"Current Trends and Issues in American Jewish Religious Life" [in Hebrew]. *Gesher: Journal of Jewish Affairs* 41, no. 132 (Winter 1995–96), 111–17. "Structural Challenges to Jewish Continuity."

"Promised Land and Golden Land." In *American Jewish-Israeli Relations: Two Perspectives*, 7–11. New York: American Jewish Committee.

"Wise, Isaac Mayer." In *HarperCollins Dictionary of Religion*, ed. Jonathan Z. Smith, 1132. San Francisco: HarperCollins.

"What's the Use of Local Jewish History?" *Rhode Island Jewish Historical Notes* 12 (November), 77–83.

"Response [to G. Zelizer]." *Judaism* 44 (Summer), 304–9.

"Fitting American Jewish History into Modern Jewish History." *Center for American Jewish History Newsletter* 1, no. 2 (September), 1 and 4.

"Dreaming the Future of the American Jewish Community." In *At the Crossroads: Shaping Our Jewish Future*, 81–82. Boston: Combined Jewish Philanthropies of Boston and Wilstein Institute for Jewish Policy Studies.

1994

"From Synagogue-Community to Citadel of Reform: Phases in the History of K. K. Bene Israel (Rockdale Temple) in Cincinnati, Ohio." Coauthored with Karla Goldman. In *American Congregations: Portraits of Twelve Religious Communities*, ed. James P. Wind and James W. Lewis, 1:159–220. Chicago: University of Chicago Press.

"The Greatest Jew in the World Since Jesus Christ: The Jewish Legacy of Louis D. Brandeis." *American Jewish History* 81, nos. 3–4, 346–64.

"The Secret of Jewish Continuity." *Commentary* 98, no. 4 (October), 55–58.

"Nathan Kaganoff's Legacy." *American Jewish History* 81, nos. 3–4, 432–34.

"Judaica Americana." *American Jewish History* 82, nos. 1–4, 295–328.

"The Israel of American Jews." *Sh'ma* 25, no. 478 (September 30, 1994). [Reprinted from Hebrew in *Gesher: Journal of Jewish Affairs* 40, no. 130 (Winter 1994), 22–25.]

"Forum: American Civil Religion Revisited." *Religion and American Culture* 4 (Winter), 19–23.

1993

"The Making of an American Jewish Culture." In *When Philadelphia Was the Capital of Jewish America*, ed. Murray Friedman, 145–55. London: Associated University Presses.

"Recent Scholarship in American Jewish History" [in Hebrew]. *Jewish Studies: Forum of the World Union of Jewish Studies* 33, 11–32.

"Jewish Scholarship and American Jewish Continuity." In *Toward an American Jewish Culture: New Perspectives on Jewish Continuity*, 4–5. New York: National Foundation for Jewish Culture.

"Comment: What Is the Most Important Thing We Can Do to Ensure Jewish Survival in America?" *Hadassah Magazine* 74, no. 10 (June–July), 10–11.

"The Jewish Romance with Modernity: A Critical Reassessment" [in Hebrew]. *Gesher: Journal of Jewish Affairs* 38, no. 126 (Winter 1992–93), 36–38.

"Listening to Eugene Borowitz." *Sh'ma* 23, no. 455 (May 28), 115–16.

1992

"Columbus and the Jews." *Commentary* 94, no. 5 (November), 38–41. [Revised and expanded as "The Mythical Jewish Columbus and the History of America's Jews," in *Religion in the Age of Exploration*, ed. Bryan F. Le Beau and Menahem Mor, 81–95. Omaha, NE: Creighton University Press, 1996.]

"A Sort of Paradise for the Hebrews: The Lofty Vision of Cincinnati Jews." In *Ethnic Diversity and Civic Identity: Patterns of Conflict and Cohesion in Cincinnati since 1820*, coedited with Henry D. Shapiro, 131–64. Urbana: University of Illinois Press. [Preprinted in abridged form in *American Israelite* (July 7, 1988).]

"Reading Jewish Books: The American Jewish Experience." In *The Schocken Guide to Jewish Books: Where to Start Reading about Jewish History, Literature, Culture and Religion*, ed. Barry W. Holtz, 108–27. New York: Schocken Books.

"What Is American about the Constitutional Documents of American Jewry? An Historical Approach." In *A Double Bond: The Constitutional Documents of American Jewry*, coedited with Daniel J. Elazar and Rela G. Monson, 52–72. Lanham, MD: Rowman and Littlefield.

"Tribalism." *Moment* 17 (October), 18.

"Necrology: Marshall Sklare (1921–1992)." *Proceedings of the American Academy for Jewish Research* 58, ed. Nahum H. Sarna, 33–35. New York: American Academy for Jewish Research.

"Louis D. Brandeis: Zionist Leader." *Brandeis Review* 2 (Winter), 22–27.

"Preserving Our Past, Our Future Depends on It." *Rocky Mountain Chai Lites* 28 (June), 2–5.

1991

"Seating and the American Synagogue." In *Belief and Behavior: Essays in the New Religious History*, ed. Philip Vandermeer and Robert P. Swierenga, 189–206. New Brunswick, NJ: Rutgers University Press.

"Jewish Identity in the Changing World of American Religion." In *Jewish Identity in America*, ed. David M. Gordis and Yoav Ben-Horin, 91–103. Los Angeles: University of Judaism. [Reprinted from Hebrew in *Gesher: Journal of Jewish Affairs* 37, no. 124 (Winter 1990–91), 33–44.]

"The Rise of Islam in America: How Will This Change Jewish Self-Identification." *Moment* 16, no. 3 (June), 35–39.

"The American Synagogue Responds to Change." *Cincinnati Judaism Review* 2 (Spring), 89–94.

"Interreligious Marriage in America." In *The Intermarriage Crisis*, 1–6. New York: American Jewish Committee.

1990

"American Jewish History." [A Ten-Year Review of the Literature]. *Modern Judaism* 10, no. 3, 343–65.

"Is Judaism Compatible with American Civil Religion? The Problem of Christmas and the 'National Faith.'" In *Religion and the Life of the Nation*, ed. Rowland A Sherrill, 154–73. Urbana: University of Illinois Press.

"From K'tonton to the Torah." *Moment* 15, no. 5 (October), 44–47.

"From Synagogue-Community to Community of Synagogues: A Turning Point in American Jewish History." Braun Chair Inaugural Lecture, October 18, Brandeis University, Waltham, MA.

Foreword. In *Judaica Americana*, 2 vols., by Robert Singerman, 1:ix–xii. New York: Greenwood Press.

"Reform Jewish Leaders, Intermarriage and Conversion." *Journal of Reform Judaism* 37, no. 1 (Winter), 1–10.

"The Editor [Henrietta Szold]." *Hadassah Magazine* 71, no. 10 (June–July), 18–20.

1989

"In Search of 'Authentic' Anglo-Jewish Poetry: The Debate over A. M. Klein's Poems (1944)." In *From Ancient Israel to Modern Judaism: Essays in Honor of Marvin Fox*, ed. Jacob Neusner, 4:125–36. Atlanta, GA: Scholars Press.

"Jews in the Colonial and Early National Periods." In *The American Jewish Experience*, 17–21. Philadelphia: National Museum of American Jewish History.

"Cyrus Adler and the Development of American Jewish Culture: The 'Scholar-Doer' as a Jewish Communal Leader." *American Jewish History* 78, no. 3 (March), 382–94.

American Jews and Church-State Relations: The Search for "Equal Footing." New York: American Jewish Committee.

"Mordecai M. Noah" and "Jewish Publication Society." In *The Blackwell Companion to Jewish Culture: From the Eighteenth Century to the Present*, ed. Glenda Abramson, 379–80 and 557–58. New York: Basil Blackwell.

"The Future of Cincinnati Jews." In *American Judaism Present and Future: Proceedings of the Inaugural Jacob and Jennie L. Lichter Lecture Series in Judaic Studies*, ed. Benny Kraut, 48–52. Cincinnati, OH: Judaic Studies Program, University of Cincinnati.

1988

"Passover Raisin Wine, the American Temperance Movement, and Mordecai Noah: The Origins, Meaning and Wider Significance of a Nineteenth-Century American Jewish Religious Practice." *Hebrew Union College Annual* 59, ed. Sheldon H. Blank, 269–88.

"Jewish Bible Scholarship and Translations in the United States." Coauthored with Nahum M. Sarna. In *The Bible and Bibles in America*, ed. Ernest S. Frerichs, 83–116. Atlanta, GA: Scholars Press.

"The Israel of American Jews." *Commentary* 85, no. 2 (February), 64–65.

Untitled contribution to "The Greatest American Jewish Leaders." *American Jewish History* 78, no. 2 (December), 193–95.

1987

"The Debate over Mixed Seating in the American Synagogue." In *The American Synagogue: A Sanctuary Transformed*, ed. Jack Wertheimer, 363–94. New York: Cambridge University Press.

"The Impact of Nineteenth-Century Christian Missions on American Jews." In *Jewish Apostasy in the Modern World*, ed. Todd Endelman, 232–54. New York: Holmes and Meier.

"Jewish-Christian Hostility in the United States: Some Perceptions from a Jewish Point of View." In *Uncivil Religion: Interreligious Hostility in America*, ed. Robert N. Bellah and Frederick E. Greenspahn, 5–22. New York: Crossroad Press.

"Christian America or Secular America? The Church-State Dilemma of American Jews." In *Jews in Unsecular America*, ed. Richard J. Neuhaus, 47–68. Grand Rapids, MI: Eerdmans. [Reprinted both in *Jerusalem Newsletter* 21 (June 1987), and in Hebrew in *Gesher: Journal of Jewish Affairs* 33, no. 116 (Summer 1987), 96–105.]

"The Jewish Publication Society, 1888–1988." *Jewish Book Annual* 45 (1987–88), ed. Jacob Kabakoff, 42–53. New York: Jewish Book Council.

"New Light on the Pittsburgh Platform of 1885." *American Jewish History* 76, no. 3 (March), 358–68.

"Henrietta Szold." In *Encyclopedia of Religion*, ed. Mircea Eliade, 14:230. New York: Macmillan.

"Principles and Challenges in the History of American Jewry" [in Hebrew]. *Gesher: Journal of Jewish Affairs* 32, no. 115 (Winter), 16–20.

"Vive la difference." *Jerusalem Post* (May 26).

1986

"The 'Mythical Jew' and the 'Jew Next Door' in Nineteenth-Century America." In *Anti-Semitism in American History*, ed. David Gerber, 57–78. Urbana: University of Illinois Press.

"American Christian Opposition to Missions to the Jews (1816–1900)." *Journal of Ecumenical Studies* 23, no. 2 (Spring), 225–38.

"American Anti-Semitism." In *History and Hate*, ed. David Berger, 115–28. Philadelphia: Jewish Publication Society.

"Comment." In *The American Jewish Community: Social Science Research and Policy Implications*, ed. Calvin Goldscheider, 109–13. Providence, RI: Brown University.

"Comment: The Meaning of the Holy Land in American Religious Life and Thought." In *With Eyes toward Zion*, ed. Moshe Davis, 2:346–49. New York: Praeger.

"Towards a New Approach to the Teaching of American Jewish History." *Principal* 31, no. 5 (May–June), 3–6.

1984

"The Literary Contributions of Mordecai M. Noah: On the Bicentennial of His Birth." *Jewish Book Annual* 42, 189–98. New York: Jewish Book Council.

"The Jewish Way of Crime." *Commentary* 78, no. 2 (August), 53–55.

"Necrology: Arthur A. Chiel." *American Jewish History* 73, no. 3 (March), 324–26.

"What Is the Use of American Jewish Community History?" *Indiana Jewish History* 18 (June), 8–17.

1983

"Introduction: The American Rabbinate, A Centennial View." *American Jewish Archives* 35, no. 2 (November), 91–99. [Reprinted in *The American Rabbinate: A Century of Continuity and Change, 1883–1983*, ed. Jacob Rader Marcus and Abraham J. Peck, 1–9. Hoboken, NJ: KTAV Publishing House, 1985.]

"'Our Distant Brethren:' Alexander Harkavy on Montreal Jews, 1888." *Canadian Jewish Historical Society Journal* 7, no. 2 (Fall), 58–73.

"Cancel the Rabbi's Lecture!" *Brotherhood* 17, no. 3, n.p.

Guide to America-Holy Land Studies, 1620–1948: Economic Relations and Philanthropy, ed. Nathan M. Kaganoff, vol. 3 (fifteen contributions). New York: Praeger.

1982

"The Pork on the Fork: A Nineteenth Century Anti-Jewish Ditty." *Jewish Social Studies* 44, no. 2 (Spring), 169–72.

"Rabbi Adolph Moses's Dream." *Journal of Reform Judaism* 29, no. 4 (Fall), 57–63.

"The Spectrum of Jewish Leadership in Ante-Bellum America." *Journal of American Ethnic History* 1, no. 2 (Spring), 59–67. [Reprinted in *Leadership Library* 1, no. 2 (February 1999), 1–13, http://research.policyarchive.org/10099.pdf.]

"Coping with Intermarriage." *Jewish Spectator* 47 (Summer), 26–28. [Reprinted in *Jewish Standard Magazine* (Toronto Edition) (October 14, 1982).]

"Jews, the Moral Majority, and American Tradition." *Journal of Reform Judaism* 29, no. 2
  (Spring), 1–8. [Reprinted in *Jewish Digest* 28, no. 2 (October), 3–9.]
"Fighting Intellectual Anti-Semitism." *Present Tense* 9, no. 3 (Spring), 10–12.
"The Great American Jewish Awakening." *Midstream* 28, no. 8 (October), 30–34.
  [Reprinted in Hebrew in *Gesher: Journal of Jewish Affairs* 1, no. 110 (Spring 1984), 91–100.]
Guide to America-Holy Land Studies, 1620–1948: Political Relations and American Zionism, ed.
  Nathan M. Kaganoff, vol. 2 (twenty-six contributions). New York: Praeger.

1981
"The American Jewish Response to Nineteenth-Century Christian Missions." *Journal of
  American History* 68, no. 1 (June), 35–51.
"The Myth of No Return: Jewish Return Migration to Eastern Europe, 1881–1914."
  American Jewish History 71, no. 2 (December), 256–68. [Reprinted in *Labor Migration
  in the Atlantic Economies*, ed. Dirk Hoerder, 423–34. Westport, CT: Greenwood Press,
  1985.]
"Anti-Semitism and American History." *Commentary* 71, no. 3 (March), 42–47.
"The Impact of the American Revolution on the American Jew." *Modern Judaism* 1, no. 2,
  149–60. [Reprinted in French as "L'influence de la Révolution américaine sur les juifs
  d'Amérique," *Dix-Huitième Siècle* 13 (1981), 91–104.]
"Jewish Education in New York—1887." *Tradition: A Journal of Orthodox Jewish Thought* 19,
  no. 3 (Fall), 244–51.
"The Value of Canadian Jewish History to the American Jewish Historian and Vice-Versa."
  Canadian Jewish Historical Society Journal 5, no. 1 (Spring), 17–22.
"Innovation and Consolidation: Phases in the History of Temple Mishkan Israel." In *Jews
  in New Haven*, ed. Barry E. Herman and Werner S. Hirsch, 3:101–9. New Haven, CT:
  Jewish Historical Society of New Haven.
"How to Write the History of Your Community." *Present Tense* 8, no. 2 (Winter), 6–8.
"Alexander Harkavy: Chapters from My Life." Translator and editor. *American Jewish
  Archives* 33, no. 1 (April), 35–52. [Reprinted in *The East European Jewish Experience in
  America: A Century of Memories, 1882–1982*, ed. Uri D. Herscher, 52–73. Cincinnati:
  American Jewish Archives, 1983.]

1980
"The Freethinker, the Jews, and the Missionaries: George Houston and the Mystery of
  Israel Vindicated." *AJS Review* 5, 101–14.
"The Myth of the Jewish President." *Sh'ma* 10, no. 198 (October 3), 143–44. [Reprinted
  in *Jewish Digest* 26 (February 1981).]
"Hebrew Poetry in Early America." *American Jewish History* 69, no. 3 (March), 364–77.
"The Roots of Ararat." *American Jewish Archives* 32, no. 1 (April), 52–58.
"From Necessity to Virtue: The Hebrew-Christianity of Gideon R. Lederer." *Iliff Review*
  37 (Winter), 27–33.
Guide to America—Holy Land Studies: American Presence, ed. Nathan M. Kaganoff, vol. 1 (sixty-
  six contributions). New York: Arno Press.

1979

"The Canadian Connections of an American Jew: The Case of Mordecai M. Noah."
  Canadian Jewish Historical Society Journal 3, no. 2 (Fall), 115–29.

1978

"From Immigrants to Ethnics: Toward a New Theory of 'Ethnicization.'" *Ethnicity* 5, no. 4,
  370–78.

"A German Jewish Immigrant's Perception of America, 1853–54: Some Further Notes on
  Mordecai M. Noah, A Jewel Robbery, and Isaac M. Wise." *American Jewish History* 68,
  no. 2 (December), 206–12.

1976

"Jewish Immigrants to North America: The Canadian Experience (1870–1900)." *Jewish
  Journal of Sociology* 18, no. 1 (June), 31–41.

JONATHAN D. SARNA

JONATHAN D. SARNA is University Professor and the Joseph H. and Belle R. Braun Professor of American Jewish History and director of the Schusterman Center for Israel Studies at Brandeis University. He is also past president of the Association for Jewish Studies and chief historian of the National Museum of American Jewish History in Philadelphia. Dubbed by the *Forward* newspaper in 2004 as one of America's fifty most influential American Jews, he was chief historian for the 350th commemoration of the American Jewish community and is recognized as a leading commentator on American Jewish history, religion, and life. In 2009, he was elected to the American Academy of Arts and Sciences. He holds four honorary degrees.

Born in Philadelphia and raised in New York and Boston, Sarna attended Brandeis University, the Boston Hebrew College, Merkaz HaRav Kook in Jerusalem, and Yale University, where he obtained his doctorate in 1979.

From 1979 to 1990, Sarna taught at the Hebrew Union College–Jewish Institute of Religion in Cincinnati, where he rose to become professor of American Jewish history and director of the Center for the Study of the American Jewish Experience. He has also taught at Harvard and Yale Universities, the University of Cincinnati, and the Hebrew University of Jerusalem. Sarna came back to Brandeis in 1990 to teach American Jewish history in its Department of Near Eastern and Judaic Studies. He chaired that department three different times, chaired Brandeis's Hornstein Jewish Professional Leadership Program twice, and now directs the university's Schusterman Center for Israel Studies. He also chairs the Academic Advisory and Editorial Board of the Jacob Rader Marcus Center of the American Jewish Archives in Cincinnati.

Sarna is married to Professor Ruth Langer, and they live in Newton, Massachusetts. They have two married children: Aaron Y. Sarna is married to Dr. Talya Housman Sarna, and Rabbanit Leah L. Sarna is married to Professor Ethan F. Schwartz and has a son, Cyrus Sarna Schwartz.

CONTRIBUTORS

Aviva Ben-Ur, PhD '98 (Brandeis U.), is a professor in the Department of Near Eastern and Judaic Studies at the University of Massachusetts Amherst. Her publications include *Jewish Autonomy in a Slave Society: Suriname in the Atlantic World, 1651–1825* (University of Pennsylvania Press, 2020) and *Sephardic Jews in America: A Diasporic History* (New York University Press, 2009).

Michael Cohen, PhD '08 (Brandeis U.), is a professor in and the chair of the Department of Jewish Studies at Tulane University. He is the author of *Cotton Capitalists: American Jewish Entrepreneurship in the Reconstruction Era* (New York University Press, 2017) and *The Birth of Conservative Judaism: Solomon Schechter's Disciples and the Creation of an American Religious Movement* (Columbia University Press, 2012).

Phil M. Cohen earned his doctorate in 1994 at Brandeis University, where he wrote a dissertation titled "David Einhorn: Biblical Theology as Response and Reform." He is rabbi of Congregation Beth Shalom, Columbia, MO, and the author of *Nick Bones Underground* (Koehler Books, 2019).

Beth Cousens is associate vice president of Jewish education and engagement at the Jewish Federations of North America. In 2008, she completed a PhD dissertation at Brandeis University titled "Shifting Social Networks: Studying the Jewish Growth of Adults in Their Twenties and Thirties."

Deborah Skolnick Einhorn is head of school at the Milton Gottesman Jewish Day School of the Nation's Capital. She previously served as associate dean of Boston's Hebrew College. She earned her PhD in 2012 at Brandeis University, where she wrote a dissertation titled "Power of the Purse: Jewish Women's Philanthropy and Social Change."

Zev Eleff, PhD '15 (Brandeis U.), is an associate professor of Jewish history at Touro College and chief academic officer at Hebrew Theological College in Skokie, IL. His publications include *Who Rules the Synagogue? Religious Authority and the Formation of American Judaism* (Oxford University Press, 2016) and *Authentically Orthodox: A Tradition-Bound Faith in American Life* (Wayne State University Press, 2020).

Jonathan Golden is the Israel curriculum coordinator and a history teacher at Gann Academy, in Waltham, MA. A graduate of Princeton University and Hebrew College, he completed a PhD at Brandeis University in 2008 and wrote a dissertation titled "From Cooperation to Confrontation: The Rise and Fall of the Synagogue Council of America."

Karla Goldman, the Sol Drachler Professor of Social Work and a professor of Judaic studies at the University of Michigan, directs the university's Jewish Communal Leadership Program. She earned her PhD from Harvard University in 1993 and is the author of *Beyond the Synagogue Gallery: Finding a Place for Women in American Judaism* (Harvard University Press, 2000) and numerous articles.

Rachel Gordan is an assistant professor in the Department of Religion and the Center for Jewish Studies at the University of Florida. She earned her PhD at Harvard University in 2012. Her academic articles have appeared in *American Jewish History, Jewish Quarterly Review, Jewish Social Studies*, and elsewhere.

Geraldine Gudefin is a modern Jewish historian from France. She earned a BA in history from Sorbonne-Paris IV, an MA in history from Yale University, and a PhD in history in 2018 from Brandeis University. She currently holds a Lady Davis postdoctoral fellowship at the Hebrew University of Jerusalem.

Jeffrey Haus, PhD '97 (Brandeis U.), is a professor of history and religion and director of Jewish studies at Kalamazoo College. He is the author of *Challenges of Equality: Judaism, State, and Education in Nineteenth-Century France* (Wayne State University Press, 2009) and numerous articles.

Felicia Herman is executive director of Natan and directs the Aligned Grant Program of the Jewish Community Response and Impact Fund. She earned a PhD in 2002 at Brandeis University, where she wrote a dissertation titled "Views of Jews: Antisemitism, Hollywood, and American Jews, 1913–1947."

Dan Judson, PhD '15 (Brandeis U.), is dean of the Hebrew College Rabbinical School. Rabbi Judson received his doctorate in Jewish history from Brandeis University. His book *Pennies for Heaven: The History of American Synagogues and Money* (Brandeis University Press, 2018) was a finalist for the National Jewish Book Award.

David E. Kaufman, PhD '94 (Brandeis U.), is a scholar of American Jewish history. He is the author of *Shul with a Pool: The "Synagogue-Center" in American Jewish History* (Brandeis University Press, 1999) and *Jewhooing the Sixties: American Celebrity and Jewish Identity — Sandy Koufax, Lenny Bruce, Bob Dylan, and Barbra Streisand* (Brandeis University Press, 2012).

Susanna Klosko earned a PhD in 2017 from Brandeis University, where she wrote a dissertation titled "The Infirm, the Unfortunate, and the Aged: 'Likely Public Charges,' Immigration Control, and the Yishuv in Theory and Practice." She is digital humanities project designer/manager for the Institute of Advanced Technology in the Humanities, University of Virginia.

Seth Korelitz earned a PhD in 2000 from Brandeis University and an MA in educational leadership, K–12 administration, in 2015 from Eastern Michigan University. His primary work has been in Jewish day schools, and he currently learns with students at Hillel Day School of Metropolitan Detroit.

Jonathan B. Krasner, PhD '02 (Brandeis U.), is the Jack, Joseph, and Morton Mandel Associate Professor of Jewish Education Research at Brandeis University. He is the author of *The Benderly Boys and American Jewish Education* (Brandeis University Press,

2011), which won the 2011 National Jewish Book Award. His articles have appeared in *American Jewish History, Contemporary Jewry, Jewish Social Studies,* and elsewhere.

Adam D. Mendelsohn, PhD '08 (Brandeis U.), is an associate professor of history at the University of Cape Town and director of the university's Kaplan Centre for Jewish Studies. He is the author of *The Rag Race: How Jews Sewed Their Way to Success in America and the British Empire* (New York University Press, 2014); coeditor, with Jonathan D. Sarna, of *Jews and the Civil War: A Reader* (New York University Press, 2010); and coeditor, with Ava Kahn, of *Transnational Traditions: New Perspectives on American Jewish History* (Wayne State University Press, 2014).

Lincoln Mullen, PhD '14 (Brandeis U.), is an associate professor in the Department of History and Art History at George Mason University and director of computational history at the Roy Rosenzweig Center for History and New Media. He is the author of *The Chance of Salvation: A History of Conversion in America* (Harvard University Press, 2017), winner of the American Academy of Religion's Best First Book in the History of Religions prize.

Mina Muraoka is an assistant professor in the College of Intercultural Studies at Kanto Gakuin University, in Japan. She earned a PhD in 2014 from Brandeis University and is the author of "American Jews at the Time of the Russo-Japanese War," *Japan Consortium for Area Studies Review* (2014).

Kerry M. Olitzky earned his DHL in Jewish education in 1985 at the Hebrew Union College-Jewish Institute of Religion. He formerly served as executive director of Big Tent Judaism; vice president of the Wexner Heritage Foundation; and rabbi at Congregation Beth Israel, in West Hartford, CT. His recent publications include *Welcome to the Seder: A Passover Haggadah for Everyone* (Behrman House, 2018).

Jason M. Olson earned a PhD from Brandeis University in 2016. He is a Navy foreign area officer and previously served as a Navy chaplain. He is the author of *America's Road to Jerusalem: The Impact of the Six-Day War on Protestant Politics* (Lexington Books, 2018).

Amaryah Orenstein earned a BA at McGill University, an MA at Ohio University, and a PhD in 2014 at Brandeis University, where she wrote a doctoral dissertation titled "'Let My People Go!' The Struggle for Soviet Jewry and the Rise of American Jewish Identity Politics." She now runs a literary agency in New York City.

Shari Rabin is an assistant professor of Jewish studies and religion at Oberlin College. She is the author of *Jews on the Frontier: Religion and Mobility in Nineteenth-Century America* (New York University Press, 2017), which won the National Jewish Book Award. She earned a PhD at Yale University in 2015.

Mark A. Raider, PhD '96 (Brandeis U.), is professor of modern Jewish history in the Department of History at the University of Cincinnati and director of the university's Center for Studies in Jewish Education and Culture. He is also a visiting professor of American Jewish history at Hebrew Union College–Jewish Institute of Religion. He recently published *The Essential Hayim Greenberg: Essays and Addresses on Jewish Culture, Socialism, and Zionism* (University of Alabama Press, 2017).

Rona Sheramy is executive director of the Jewish Foundation for Education of Women.

She previously served as executive director of the Association for Jewish Studies. She earned her PhD in 2001 at Brandeis University and is the author of numerous articles on American Jews, the Holocaust, and Jewish education.

Ofer Shiff, PhD '94 (Brandeis U.), is a professor of Jewish history at Ben-Gurion University. He is author of *The Downfall of Abba Hillel Silver* (Syracuse University Press, 2014) and coeditor, with Avner Ben-Amos, of *Profiles of Ourselves: Researching Israel, Writing Our Stories* (Ben-Gurion University Press, 2020).

Emily Sigalow, PhD '15 (Brandeis U.), is executive director of the Impact and Performance Assessment Department at the UJA-Federation of New York. She is the author of *American Jewbu: Jews, Buddhists and Religious Change* (Princeton University Press, 2019).

Holly Snyder, PhD '00 (Brandeis U.), is North American History Librarian at the Brown University Library. She is author of the forthcoming *Geographical Destinies: Jewish Identity and Social Place in the British Atlantic World, 1654–1831* as well as articles in the *William and Mary Quarterly*, *Jewish History*, and elsewhere.

Lance J. Sussman is senior rabbi of Reform Congregation Keneseth Israel, in Elkins Park, PA, and a professor of Jewish history at Gratz College. He earned his PhD in American Jewish history in 1987 at Hebrew Union College–Jewish Institute of Religion. He is the author of *Isaac Leeser and the Making of American Judaism* (Wayne State University Press, 1995) and is completing a casebook on Jews and American law.

Amber Taylor is a historian and writer of women's history for the Church of Jesus Christ of Latter-day Saints. She earned her PhD in 2019 at Brandeis University, where she wrote a doctoral dissertation titled "Contest and Controversy in the Creation of the Brigham Young University Jerusalem Center, 1984–1987."

Gary Phillip Zola, PhD '91 (Hebrew Union College–Jewish Institute of Religion), is the Edward M. Ackerman Family Distinguished Professor of the American Jewish Experience and Reform Jewish History at Hebrew Union College–Jewish Institute of Religion, executive director of the Jacob Rader Marcus Center of the American Jewish Archives (Cincinnati, OH), and editor of the *American Jewish Archives Journal*. His recent books include *We Called Him Rabbi Abraham: Lincoln and American Jewry* (Southern Illinois University Press, 2014) and *American Jewish History: A Primary Source Reader*, edited with Marc Dollinger (Brandeis University Press, 2014).

Joellyn Wallen Zollman earned her PhD at Brandeis University in 2001. She curated the 2018 exhibit *Celebrate San Diego! The History and Heritage of San Diego's Jewish Community* and edited its catalog. She is also associate producer of the documentary film *To the Ends of the Earth: A Portrait of Jewish San Diego* (San Diego History Center and Cinewest Productions, 2018).

INDEX

Page numbers in *italics* indicate illustrations.

American Museum of Immigration, 364n22

American Palestine Committee, 235

American Revolution, apocalyptic connotations for, 25n5

American Zionist Committee for Public Affairs (AZCPA), 301–12. *See also* American Israel Public Affairs Committee (AIPAC)

American Zionist Council, 305n19. *See also* American Israel Public Affairs Committee (AIPAC)

American Zionist Emergency Council (formerly ECZA), 235

American Zionist Youth Foundation, 396–97, 398n8

Andrus, Alpheus N., 115n12

Anti-Defamation League of Bnai Brith, 270n23, 300n5

anti-nuclear sentiment among Jews, 392–94

Antiochus IV Epiphanes, 35n16

antisemitism: and anti-German sentiment during WWI, 155n13; by blacks, 369; campaigning against European, 68–71; and Civil War chaplaincy controversy, 56–59; connection to blacks' experience of prejudice, 368; crucifixion of Jesus as impetus for, 44n26; and crusade to free Soviet Jewry, 316–25; Grant's ban on Jews in his command, 56; Mormon opposition to, 40n10, 43n19; and need for Jewish legal aid societies, 160–61; in Ottoman Empire, 44nn24–25; student outspokenness against during interwar period, 225–33; and Tree of Life synagogue killing, 61

anti-Zionists vs. non-Zionists, 239n22

apostasy. *See* conversion

Arab-Jewish Conflict (1948), 270–71n25, 312n45

Arab League, 270n25, 302n11, 306–7n27, 308nn34–35, 353n77

Ark of the Covenant, 277n14

arranged marriages, 78n17

Ash, Abraham Joseph, 77n11

Ashkenazic Jews, 137, 255n4, 289n21, 309n38, 431. *See also* eastern European Jews

assimilation: and continuity in 21st century, 9–10; and intermarriage, 199–202; Jewish education to combat, 48–51, 385–90; Mendelsohn's praise of Schiff for avoiding, 167; vs. need to speak out against Nazi persecution, 225; Orthodox angst over, 85–88; and Reform split on Sabbath services day, 203–14; tensions of, 17

Aswan Dam, 297–98n22

AWP (Advancing Women Professionals and the Jewish Community), 412, 413n2

AZCPA (American Zionist Committee for Public Affairs), 301–12. *See also* American Israel Public Affairs Committee (AIPAC)

Babylonian empire and exile of Jews from Israel, 276n10, 276nn7–8

Bakke, Allan, 375n24

Balfour Declaration (1917), 142, 171n16, 234, 241n29, 422n1

Baltimore Sun, 57, 59

Bamberger, Simon, 149–58

bareheaded prayer, and history of Reform, 32–33

Bar Kokhba rebellion, 87n18, 393n7

Basic Judaism (Steinberg), 274

Becoming Eve: My Journey from Ultra-Orthodox Rabbi to Transgender Woman (Stein), 420

Bellman (literary magazine), 143n4

Benderly, Samson, 187, 190n10, 253

chaplains, Jewish, 56–59

Chapman, Elizabeth (Binche), 18–19n3

charity, religious education as, 50n6. *See also* philanthropy

Chipkin, Israel S., 194n23, 253–57

Chorin, Aaron, 32

chosenness, as shared sensibility for America and Jews, 7

Christian Council on Palestine, 235

Christianity: Bernstein's use of to explain Judaism to *Life* readers, 274; conversion from Judaism to, 98–104; discrimination against Jews in America, 223–24; Jewish critiques of missionary, 91–92, 101–4; Mormons, 37–45, 149–58; and salvation by faith alone, 275n5; Unitarian, 83, 99n24

Church of Jesus Christ of Latter-day Saints, 37–45, 149–58

Cincinnati, Ohio, as center of Reform Judaism, 192n16

Cincinnati Teachers Association, 126n11

circumcision, 84

citizenship, 25n3, 25n7, 27n19, 28n25, 254

civics education, 253–57

civil liberties, dedication to protection of, 65–71. *See also* civil rights movement

civil religion, Jewish philanthropy as part of, 281

civil rights movement, 263–72, 317, 340n42, 366–68

Civil War, 10–13, 56–59

CJE (Commission on Jewish Education), 186, 187–88

Cleveland College of Jewish Studies, 389n18

Cleveland Commission on Jewish Continuity, 385–90

Cohen, Esdaile P., 32, 36n26

Cohen, Kathy Schwartz, 391–94

Cohn, Jacob, 125n5

Cold War: Ford's continuation of détente, 334; Middle East's role in, 331; Soviet Jewry, crusade to free, 316–25

collective responsibility ethic, 281–82

Columbus Platform (1937), 188

comic book stories, 356–58

Commission on Jewish Continuity, 385–86

Commission on Jewish Education (CJE), 186, 187–88

"Committee of Ten," 239n20

communal relations and institutions: American Jewish changes in attitude toward Israel, 300–312; and Board of Delegates' political influence, 67; composition of mid-20th-century institutions, 255n4; decentralized organization, 74n3, 77n12; democratization of the synagogue, 180–85; farming (1939–42), 248–52; during increased 19th-century immigration, 60–64, 167; legal aid societies, 159–65; New York City's impact, 141–48; periodicals, 137–40; Reform's impact, 52–55; in the South (1970s to 1980s), 359–65; United Synagogue of America's founding, 123–29; unity through religious education, 47–51; Western Wall controversy, 422–26; women's roles, 173–179, 412–18. *See also* education; philanthropy

companionate marriage ideal, and intermarriage increase, 201

Conference of Presidents of Major Jewish Organizations, 317, 336n15, 371

Congregation Adath Israel (Louisville), 203–14

Congregation Adath Yeshurun (NYC), 53

Congregation Beit Simchat Torah (NYC), 397, 398nn7–8, 399n9

Congregation Beth Israel (Chicago), 166

Dickinson, Charles M., 109–10

dietary laws, 84n9

dispensationalism, 37, 37n2

displaced persons (DP) camps, post-WWII, 288n19

divorce (*get*), 74–75n4; in 18th century America, 18–22; American law versus Jewish law, 75nn5–6; American press's fascination with, 72–80

Dobkin, Barbara, 402n19, 412

Dobkin, Eric, 402n19

Dobkin Family Foundation, 402n19, 412

Domestic Council (later Domestic Policy Council), 341n47

Dorsey, George W. and Mae Murray, 266n11

Doyle Dane Bernbach (DDB) advertising campaign, 313–15

DP (displaced persons) camps, post-WWII, 288n19

Dreamers of the Ghetto (Zangwill), 299

Dreyfus Affair, 146n15

Duke, David, 380n33

Dünner, Joseph Hirsch, 88n21

Dushkin, Alexander, 187, 189–92, 253

eastern European Jews: American press interest in divorce among, 73–80; as demographic group in American Jewry, 255n4; heder schools, 256n6; impact on American life and culture, 388n12; legal aid societies and, 159–65; matchmaking system, 78n17; and NYC, 141; post-WWII refugees from Communist rule, 288; Soviet Jewry, crusade to free, 316–25

economic crimes, persecution of Soviet Jews for, 322n15

Edgar, William C., 143n4

education, Jewish: on American civics, 253–57; challenge of in 19th century, 46–51; day schools, 189n5, 256n5, 389n15, 397, 421; and debate on Sunday services, 210; as explained to Christian America in *Life*, 278; heder schools, 256n6; late 20th-century shift in, 385–90; Reform's shift to support for Zionism, 186–98; Schiff's contribution to, 170; as tool to combat assimilation, 48–51, 385–90

Educational Alliance, 159–60, 162, 163, 165

Edward I, King of England, banishment of Jews, 393n8

EEC (European Economic Community), 347n65

Egypt, relationship to Jews and State of Israel, 286–87n16, 295n10, 296n14, 310, 343–44nn54–56, 345n59

Egyptian Jewish refugees, 286–87, 291

Egypt-Israel Separation of Forces Agreement (1974), 342n50

Einhorn, David, 52–55

Einstein, Albert, 215, 215–22, 280

Eisendrath, Maurice, 381n38

Eisenhower, Dwight D., 291, 295n11, 298, 302, 311n44

emergency campaigns for refugee support, 285–86n13

Emergency Committee for Zionist Affairs (ECZA), 234–47

Emergency Rescue Fund (ERF), 285–86

Enelow, Hyman G., 191n15

Eshel (Gay and Lesbian Yeshiva Day School Alumni Association), 397, 421

European Economic Community (EEC), 347n65

European Jewish refugees, 248–52, 255n4, 259–60, 283

Evans, Eli N., 360–65

"Exodus: I See Myself in You" (S. Benjamin), 404

Holocaust: Emergency Committee for
Zionist Affairs, 234–47; and Hiroshima, 391–94; loss of influence on
Jewish identity preservation over time,
387–88; support for refugees of, 283,
318; and tattoos, 408, 410

Holzer, Harold, 11

Homestead strike, 261–62

homophobia, activism to combat, 395–
402

Hull, Cordell, 246n41

human rights/humanitarianism: Board of
Delegates of American Israelites, 66;
global identity free of prejudice and
boundary, 403–6; missionary Christianity as hindrance to, 104; Soviet
Jewry, crusade to free, 316–25. *See also*
social justice activism

The Human Stain (Roth), 408–9

Hungary, Jewish refugees from, 287–88,
291, 296n15

Hyde, Orson, 37–45

identities: declension (separate identity),
9; intergenerational struggles with, 17;
intermarriage issue, 199–202; navigat-
ing, 5; striving for synthesis of, 6–8,
403–6; for transgender American Jews,
419–21. *See also* assimilation; Jewish
identity

identity politics, 370–71

immigration: Arab and Soviet bloc visa
denials for Jews, 308n31; concentration in NYC, 141n3; and ECZA's efforts
to rescue Jews during WWII, 235, 242–
43n32; expulsion of Jews from Arab
countries, 308n36; family desertion by
husbands/fathers after, 160; increased
American immigration, 60–64, 67, 83,
167; legal aid societies and, 159–65;
and National Farm School, 248–52;
to State of Israel, 297, 309n38. *See also*

eastern European Jews; Jewish refugees; Palestine

Incognito Club, Jewish Theological Seminary, 399n12

The Incredible Hulk and Sabra, 356–58

Independent Order of Bnai Brith, 270n23,
300n5, 336n18

Industrial Removal Office (IRO), 131–32

intergenerational struggles with identities,
17

intermarriage, 84, 199–202

International Synod, Mendes's call for, 81–
89

interwar period, college student identities,
223–33

Irish Home Rule movement, 293–94

IRO (Industrial Removal Office), 131–32

Isaacs, Abram S., 1–4, 5, 17

Isaacs, Myer S., 69n7

Isaacs, Samuel Myer, 61

Ishmaelite, 146n14

ISJL (Goldring/Woldenberg Institute of
Southern Jewish Life), 361

Israel, State of: *aliyah* focus of, 290, 303,
431; American Jewry's evolving relationship to, 239n22, 290–99, 300–
312; challenge for Middle Eastern
Jews, 286n15; economic growth post-
independence, 307n29, 308n33, 309;
funding for trips to, 390n21; Golda
Meir's role in promoting, 326–30;
Kaplan's role in, 244n36; loss of power
to ensure Jewish continuity, 387–88;
occupied territories, 344–45n57;
political adjustments (1960s), 309n38;
proposal to establish, 422n2; as refuge
for Jews, 288–89, 297, 309n38; relationship to Jewish Agency, 240n24;
and rise of Zionism in America, 236;
Suez Crisis period and aftermath,
300–302; Szyk's artistic influence on
support for, 258–60; tensions among

Jewish denominations in, 424–26; U.S. defense support for, 307n30, 310n42, 331–55; Yom Kippur War's impact on, 341–42n49. *See also* Ben-Gurion, David

Israel-Arab conflict, 356; Arab League boycott of American ships from Israeli ports, 308nn34–35; Bernadotte's attempt to mediate, 270–71n25; as conundrum for U.S., 331–32, 334; Six-Day War, 316, 422n3; Suez Crisis (1956) (Sinai War), 291–92, 295n9, 297n20, 302; and U.S. geopolitical priorities, 343n53; War of Independence, 270–71n25, 312n45; and Western Wall controversy, 423; Yom Kippur War, 326, 330, 333–34, 341–42n49

Israel Baal Shem Tov, 259

Israelites, 48n2

Jabotinsky, Vladimir, 238n13

Jackson, Henry "Scoop," 334

Jackson, Jesse, 372, 380–84

Jacobs, Harold M., 337n24, 353

Jacobson, Charlotte, 337n26, 352

JAGL (Jewish Activist Gays and Lesbians), 396–97

Jamaica, Jewish divorce in 18th-century, 18–22

James, William, 92

Jampel, Morton, 227–28, 231–33

Jason, high priest in Jerusalem, 35–36nn22–23

JDC (Joint Distribution Committee), 288n20

Jefferson, Thomas, 7, 28n22

Jeffries, Leonard, 381n36

Jesus as Jew, 91

Jewish Activist Gays and Lesbians (JAGL), 396–97

Jewish Agency, 234, 235, 240n24, 334, 423–24

Jewish community. *See* communal relations and institutions

Jewish community centers, 390n20

Jewish Converts, Perverts, and Dissenters (Krauskopf), 90

Jewish Council for Public Affairs, 301

Jewish culture and history, renewed focus on, 359–65, 370

Jewish Federation system: Cleveland's educational initiatives, 385–90; gender equity crusade for, 412–18; golden age of giving in 20th century, 283; historical development, 254–55n3; and women in philanthropy, 173, 174, 176–77

Jewish Forum, 195n28

Jewish identity: complexities of early 20th-century, 166–67; Conservative movement's location in fluid identity, 123–24; continuity challenge, 9–10, 385–90; education support for, 385–90; expressing in tattoos and body art, 407–11; intergenerational struggles with, 17; interwar period college students, 223–33; Judaism as hallmark of, 147–48; New York Jews, 142–43, 146–48; Reform vs. Orthodox viewpoints (19th century), 81–89; reinforcement through communal institutions, 281–82

Jewish Labor Committee (JLC), 339–40n38

Jewish National Fund, 245n38

Jewish politics. *See* politics

Jewish Publication Society of America (JPS), 1, 4–5, 90

Jewish Queer Youth, 397

Jewish refugees: as demographic group in American Jewry, 255n4; Egyptian, 286–87, 291; and golden age of giving in 20th century, 283; from Holocaust,

Mormons, 37–45, 149–58
Morrill Act (1862), 76
Morris, Charles W., 208n12
Morris, Nephi L., 150, 152n8
Mortara, Edgardo, 65
Mortara Affair, 65
Moses, Adolph, 203, 206n8
"Moses Presents the Ten Commandments to the Children of Israel" (Pissis), 118–22
Museum of the Jewish People, 363n10
Museum of the Southern Jewish Experience, 360–61
Myers, Gustavus, 363n18

Nasatir, Steven, 424
Nasser, Gamal Abdel, 286–87n16, 295n10, 296n14, 310
Nathan, Ernesto, 146n16
National Desertion Bureau, 160
National Farm School (Bucks County, PA), 90, 248–52
National Jewish Community Relations Advisory Council, 301
National Security Council (NSC), 335–36n12
National Yiddish Book Center, 359
Nation of Islam, 369–70
Nazism in Germany: efforts to rescue Jews during WWII, 235, 242–43n32, 246n39; and interwar American Jewish identity, 223; rise of Zionism in response to, 234
Nebuchadnezzar II, 276n7
Neiman, Abraham Lincoln, 363n13
Neiman, Carrie Marcus, 363n13
Nelson, Lemrick, 382n39
Netanyahu, Benjamin, 423, 425
New Amsterdam, Jews as early settlers in, 9, 141, 145n13
"The New Jerusalem" (Went), 141–48
newspapers and journals. See media

New York City, Jews in, 131–32, 138n3, 141–48
New-York Tribune, on chaplaincy controversy, 57–59
Nieto, Jacob, 120, 121–22
Nixon, Richard M., 328
Noah, Mordecai M., 6, 47
non-Zionists vs. anti-Zionists, 239n22
North American Federation of Temple Youth, 399n10
NSC (National Security Council), 335–36n12
Nuremberg Laws, 287n17
nusakh Sefard, 79n18

Oakley, Robert B., 335n11
Obama, Barack, 301
Occident and American Jewish Advocate, 46–47
occupied territories, Israel, 344–45n57
Ocean Hill–Brownsville school districts, black-Jewish tensions at, 374n22
Ochs, Adolph S., 170n13
oil imports, and U.S. response to Sinai War, 298
Olat Tamid (Einhorn), 52
Onias III, high priest in Jerusalem, 35n22
oral law, relationship to written law, 279
Orthodox Judaism: Cyrus Adler on, 127–28; Henry Pereira Mendes on, 125–26; Israeli Chief Rabbinate's control of Kotel, 423–26; Israel Miller, 339n34; and Jewish community expansion in U.S., 60–64; Modern Jewish Orthodoxy, 126; opposition to homosexuality, 396–97; rabbinical court for divorce proceeding, 75n5; vs. Reform, 53, 81–89, 191–92; and transgender persons, 420; Union of Orthodox Jewish Congregations, 337n25
Orthodox Union, 81
Ottoman Empire: an immigrant's journey to America, 130–36; antisemitism in,

Pittsburgh, 60–64; San Francisco, 118–22; Sephardic Jews in NYC, 131–32, 138n3; students at University of Michigan, 223–24; Utah's political demographics, 151n3

Positive-Historical Judaism, 81

"Power in the Promised Land" (comic book story), 356–58

prayer books, origins of Reform, 53–54

press. See media

priestly class, 76n10, 276n11

Prinz, Joachim, 301, 304n16

Progressive era and principles, 142, 150, 154n10, 170, 174

Prohibition, 154n10

proselytism, Krauskopf on, 95–98

Protas, Judy, 313

proto-Zionism, 38–39

Purim, 401n17

Rabbinical Assembly (RA), 400n13

rabbinical seminaries: Cleveland College of Jewish Studies, 389n18; Hebrew Union College, 62, 128n16; Jewish Theological Seminary, 81, 123, 124, 128nn14–15, 399n12; origin of American, 48n3

rabbis, 432; rarity of in early American Jewish history, 19; role of vs. priests, 276–77

Rabin, Yitzhak, 334, 342n51, 343n52

Rabinowitz, Isaac, 229–30

racial equality. See social justice activism

Radical Reform Judaism, 83n5, 126

radio technology, in fund-raising campaigns, 284–85n11

Randall, Mark, 410

Raphall, Morris Jacob, 53

rational religion, Judaism as, 275n6

Ratner, Charles A., 389n16

Rauch, Joseph, 210n14

Rawidowicz, Simon, 10

Reagan, Ronald, 379n30, 383n42

Reaganomics, 382n40

Reconstructionist Judaism, 186, 338n31, 409–10n7, 420

Reformed Society of Israelites (RSI), 30–36

Reform Judaism: Cincinnati as center of, 192n16; early 20th-century split in, 204; education debates, 186–98, 256n5; Einhorn's influence on, 52–55; German origin of, 52; Henry Pereira Mendes on, 126; institutional development, 126n9, 128–29n16; Krauskopf on Christian missions to the Jews, 90–104; Mendelsohn on Schiff, 166, 170; ordaining of gay and lesbian clergy, 396; vs. Orthodoxy, 53, 81–89, 191–92; Radical Reform, 83n5, 126; religious practices debates, 30–36, 61, 90, 203–14; shift to support for Zionism, 186–98; and transgender persons, 420. See also Pittsburgh Platform

refugees. See Jewish refugees

Rehnquist, William H., 377n29

Reich, James M., 389n17

Reines, Isaac Jacob, 240n25

religious faith: alienation of LGBTQ people from, 395; guarantee of freedom in, 12, 23–29, 83, 156nn15–16; Krauskopf's hereditary and social origin of, 93–94. See also Christianity; Judaism

reserved seats in synagogues, 180–81

Revisionist Zionist Party, 238n13

Rhode Island, 23–24

Rice, Abraham, 60

rights vs. toleration in U.S. religious freedom, 28nn22–23

Rischin, Moses, 4

Ritter, Bernhard Loebel, 88n22

ritual practices: circumcision, 84; communicating Judaism to gentiles, 273–80; democratization of the synagogue, 180–85; diversity of American Jewish, 427–30; Einhorn's influence on Reform, 52–55; *halakhah*, 52, 431; Hanukkah, 35n16, 431; head coverings during prayer, 30–36; *kaddish*, 394n10, 431; *kashrut*, 52, 84n9, 431; marriage and divorce, 18–22, 72–80, 84, 199–202; *nusakh Sefard*, 79n18; Orthodox anxiety over Reform movement, 81–89; Passover, 427–30, 432; Purim, 401n17; Sephardic rite, 79n18; Simhat Torah, 278n18; Sunday services, 90; *talit katan*, 279n20, 432; tattoo and body art taboo, 407–11; Western Wall controversy, 422–26. *See also* Sabbath practices

Roberts, Brigham Henry, 149, 151–58
Robeson, Paul, 373n20
Romania, persecution of Jews in, 69–70nn9–12
Roosevelt, Franklin D., 235, 242n31
Roosevelt, Theodore, 201
Rosenbaum, Yankel, 381–82n39
Roth, Joel, 396
Roth, Philip, 408–9
Rothschild, Baron Nathaniel Mayer de, 147n17
Rothschild, Jacob M., 261–72
Rothschild, Jerome J., 222n16
Rountree, William M., 306n25
RSI (Reformed Society of Israelites), 30–36
Rubin, Gail, 409
Russian Jews: migration to Palestine, 109, 110, 113; Schiff's support for, 169–70; Zionism among, 2. *See also* Soviet Jewry, crusade to free
Russo-Japanese War, 169n11

Rustin, Bayard, 381n34
Ryan, William Fitts, 319n9

Sabbath practices: Orthodox angst over modernity and Reform challenges, 82, 84, 85–86; Reform split on, 90, 203–14; special Sabbaths for community support, 54–55
Sabbath school (Hebrew Sunday School), 189n5, 256n5
Sabra (comic book heroine), 356–58
Sadat, Anwar, 343–44nn54–55, 345n59
Sadducees, 147–48n18
SAJ (Society for the Advancement of Judaism), 409–10n7
Salm, Peter, 248–52
Salonika, 137
SALT (Strategic Arms Limitation Talks), 347–48n67
Salute to Israel Parade, 396, 398n6, 399n9
salvation by faith alone vs. works, 278–79
same-sex marriage, 395, 396
Sanders, Edward, 339n35
San Francisco, as Jewish population center, 118–22
Sarna, Jonathan D.: on Civil War and Grant's expulsion of Jews, 10–11, 56; cult of synthesis, 167; on Lincoln's relationship to Jews, 11–13; pushing against criticism, 17; summary of contribution, 4–14
Schechter, Solomon, 123, 125n4
Schiff, Jacob H., 67, 166–72, 196n30
Schindler, Alexander M., 336n14, 347–48, 371–84
Scholem, Gershom, 283
Schoolman, Bertha, 237n9
Schulman, Samuel, 192–94
Schwerner, Michael, 367

Strategic Arms Limitation Talks (SALT), 347–48n67

Straus, Oscar Solomon, 3n11, 110–17, 111n3

Strauss, Charles Theodore, 105–8

Student Non-Violent Coordinating Committee (SNCC), 374n21

Student Struggle for Soviet Jewry (SSSJ, or Triple-SJ), 318–19, 323–25

Stuyvesant, Peter, 282

Stuyvesant Promise (1655), 282

Suez Crisis (1956) (Sinai War), 291–92, 295n9, 297n20, 302

Sulzberger, Arthur Hays, 363n16

Sunday school (day school for Reform), 189n5, 256n5

Sunday services (Reform), 90, 203–14

synagogues: art and architecture of, 119–22; Commission on Jewish Continuity, 386; democratization of, 180–85; founded by lesbians and gays, 395–96; origins of, 275–76. See also *entries beginning with* Congregation *and other synagogues by name*

Szold, Robert, 237n11

Szyk, Arthur, 258–60

Tabernacle, 276n9, 276n11

Taft, William H., 180

Taglit-Birthright Israel, 423

talit katan (prayer shawl), 279n20, 432

Talmadge, Eugene, 267–68n20

Talmadge, Herman, 268n20

Talmud, 53, 87n17, 279n22, 432

tattoos and body art, 407–11

Teachers College, 189–90n9

Teachers Institute of Hebrew Union College, 196n30

technological innovations, Orthodox angst over Sabbath observance amid, 82, 85–86

Temple in Jerusalem, as center of community, 55n6

Temples (synagogues). *See* synagogues

Thalheimer, William, 363n12

Thessaloniki (Salonika), Greece, 130, 144n11

This Is My God (Wouk), 274

tikkun ha-olam. *See* social justice activism

"Tikkun Ha-Olam" (Benjamin), 403–6, 405

Tikkun magazine, 398n5

Tisha Beav, 391–94, 432

Tobit's Letters to Levi (Frey), 92

Tocqueville, Alexis de, 282

toleration issue vs. rights in U.S. religious freedom, 28nn22–23

Torah, 277–78, 432

Torczyner, James, 325n22

Touro, Judah, 363n14

Touro Synagogue, Newport, RI, 24

Trajan, 143n6

transgender American Jews, 396, 419–21

Transkeit, 419, 420, 421

Trinity, 94n11, 280

Truman, Harry S., 266n11

Tu Bishvat (Hamisha Asar Bishvat), 197n36

"Turks" (Ottoman Jews), 109–17, 131–36

Tweed, Thomas, 106

Union Hymnal, 196n31

Union of American Hebrew Congregations (UAHC), 128n16, 187–88, 371

Union of Orthodox Jewish Congregations, 337n25

Unitarian Christianity, 83, 99n24

United Hebrew Charities, 160

United Jewish Appeal (UJA), 243n33, 281–89, 333, 338n29

United Jewish Communities, 284n10

United Kingdom. *See* Great Britain

BRANDEIS SERIES IN AMERICAN JEWISH HISTORY, CULTURE, AND LIFE

Jonathan D. Sarna, Editor

Sylvia Barack Fishman, Associate Editor

This series encompasses all areas of American Jewish civilization, including history, religion, thought, politics, economics, sociology, anthropology, literature, and the arts. The series emphasizes contemporary and interdisciplinary studies, and volumes that tie together divergent aspects of the American Jewish experience.

For a complete list of books that are available in the series, visit brandeisuniversitypress.com